FINANCIAL ACCOUNTING

BASIC CONCEPTS

THE WILLARD J. GRAHAM SERIES IN ACCOUNTING

CONSULTING EDITOR   ROBERT N. ANTHONY   *Harvard University*

FINANCIAL ACCOUNTING

BASIC CONCEPTS

EARL A. SPILLER, Jr., Ph.D., C.P.A.

Professor of Accounting, Washington University

Revised Edition

1971   RICHARD D. IRWIN, INC.

Homewood, Illinois   60430
Irwin-Dorsey International, London, England   WC2H 9NJ
Irwin-Dorsey Limited, Georgetown, Ontario   L7G 4B3

REVISED EDITION

First Printing, July, 1971
Second Printing, June, 1972
Third Printing, September, 1972
Fourth Printing, April, 1973
Fifth Printing, October, 1973
Sixth Printing, February, 1974
Seventh Printing, May, 1974
Eighth Printing, September, 1974
Ninth Printing, January, 1975
Tenth Printing, June, 1975

Library of Congress Catalog Card No. 70–149893

PRINTED IN THE UNITED STATES OF AMERICA

PREFACE

THIS BOOK is intended for a one-semester course in financial accounting offered for graduate students at the MBA level or advanced undergraduate students.

The text is written to introduce, with some degree of depth and critical analysis, the concepts of financial accounting. The major objective is to develop the reader's ability to understand, interpret, and analyze financial statements. To do this requires a familiarity with the accounting process and terminology; a knowledge of financial accounting principles and their impact on the financial statements; and the development of a conceptual framework, both extant and prospective, to serve as a benchmark for evaluation.

As accounting problems become more complex, the reader's knowledge has to become more sophisticated if these goals are to be reached. A number of changes have been made to this end. All chapters have been rewritten to improve clarity and to incorporate the latest accounting thought, including relevant opinions of the Accounting Principles Board. Four completely new chapters—leases and pensions, tax allocation, alternative concepts of income, and accounting systems and control—have been added to cover subjects of increased importance since publication of the first edition. More extensive treatment in Chapter Six has been given to the theory and alternative practices employed in the area of revenue recognition. Likewise, a discussion and illustration of purchase and pooling of interests has been included in Chapter Fourteen. Chapter Sixteen on statement interpretation has been significantly revised. The material on statement presentation has been reduced and incorporated in other chapters; new sections have been added on financial and operating leverage and on earnings per share. Greater emphasis on the use of statement analysis pervades the entire chapter.

The 20 chapters contained in the second edition probably include more material than most instructors will wish to cover in a single course. Chapter Seventeen makes a logical ending point for those concerned exclusively with the financial statements. The last three chapters attempt to form a bridge between financial and managerial accounting; some users may want to reduce coverage of some of the more advanced financial accounting topics in favor of this transition to managerial accounting. The three chapters on cost accounting in the first edition have been condensed into two chapters to facilitate this use.

Two other changes have been made to improve ease and flexibility in using the second edition. First, five appendixes are included which present subject matter of a specialized nature—manual data processing, long-term construction contracts, mechanics of lower of cost or market, group depreciation procedures, and present value concepts. Instructors may use or skip these depending on the objectives of their courses and the time available. Second, the accounting cycle has been condensed from six into five chapters by integrating the discussion of revenue and expense accounts with that of the balance sheet accounts.

The book is organized in five sections. Section I, the first five chapters, establishes the fundamental concepts and procedures, including the accounting cycle. Sections II and III discuss in depth selected areas of asset and equities measurement respectively. The reader will find the discussion quite intensive in these chapters. The language level, pace, and conceptual orientation of the material are designed to challenge without confusing, to explain without spoon-feeding, and to instill a critical perspective in the mature, highly motivated student audience to whom the book is directed. The fourth section concerns financial statement interpretation. Section V contains the three chapters which bridge financial and managerial accounting.

The number of discussion questions and problems contained in this edition has been increased to over 340. More importantly, the tenor of the problems has been modified even more toward the application of concepts and the development of analytical skills. Thirty-four problems have been adapted from the Uniform C.P.A. Examination, and over 50 problems have been developed from the annual reports of actual companies. Many of these place the student in the role of decision maker or evaluator of decisions.

Acknowledgments

When the first edition of this book was published, very few textbooks were written explicitly for a one-semester, introductory, graduate-level course in financial accounting. Since then, the market has expanded greatly, and almost a dozen texts now available profess this orientation. Consequently, any claim to uniqueness has disappeared. Hopefully, this edition offers instead a better organized, more clearly written exposition of more relevant and modern subject matter than the first edition. The extent to which these improvements have occurred reflects benefits derived from comments and suggestions of users of the first edition. Although too numerous to mention individually, they have my heartfelt thanks.

The contribution of a few individuals, however, merits special mention. Professor Norbert C. Terre of the University of Missouri at St. Louis was instrumental in the development and evaluation of the ideas on revenue recognition. Professor Robert N. Anthony of Harvard University read the entire manuscript. His critical insights and constructive comments were extremely valuable. Professors Phillip T. May and Robert L. Virgil of Washington University also furnished detailed commentary on each chapter. In addition, they provided helpful editorial assistance, excellent (albeit sometimes painful) critiques of my ideas, and a valuable supply of problem material. Only when one is on the receiving end of their type of assistance can he truly appreciate the real significance of the term "colleague." The extent to which the objectives and improvements outlined above have not occurred reflects my own pertinacity and inability to profit from the suggestions of all of these men.

Dean Karl A. Hill provided continuous support and encouragement throughout this revision. He secured funds for summer research and for the ancillary tasks necessary to prepare the manuscript in final form.

I wish to express my appreciation to Mrs. Craig B. Warren for her very talented efforts in editing the manuscript and improving its readability; and to Mrs. A. W. Scheetz for her willingness and ability to transform my cacography into a neatly arranged, typed manuscript. Miss Linda Spiller assisted in the preparation of the index. Mr. Donald Paterson provided valuable assistance in many different capacities.

The American Institute of Certified Public Accountants and the American Accounting Association were generous in granting permission to quote from their various publications. Also, the AICPA allowed liberal use of problem material from the Uniform Examination.

Finally, I acknowledge an everlasting debt to my family—Elinor, Linda, and Barbara—whose typing, proofreading, and other supporting activities made my efforts possible; and whose understanding, reassurance, and approval make all my efforts worthwhile.

June, 1971   EARL A. SPILLER, JR.

CONTENTS

collectible Accounts. Sales Returns. Sales Discounts. Appendix
6–A: Accounting for Long-Term Construction Contracts.

SECTION III
FURTHER ASPECTS OF FINANCIAL
MEASUREMENT—EQUITIES

SECTION V
ACCOUNTING CONTROL

SECTION I

FUNDAMENTAL CONCEPTS AND PROCEDURES

CHAPTER ONE

FRAMEWORK OF ACCOUNTING

THROUGHOUT all aspects of human activity, one important key to rational conduct is the availability of information. Each day is filled with all kinds of decisions made on the basis of information communicated to the decision maker. The soundness of these judgments, whether personal, political, social, or economic in nature, depends largely on the quality, quantity, and timeliness of that information. It provides the guide to both action and belief.

The study of accounting involves an examination of one part of the numerous processes of communicating economic information. The purpose of this chapter is to define accounting and its role as an information supplier. Also we attempt to place accounting in its context and to establish a conceptual framework upon which to build in future chapters.

INTRODUCTION TO ACCOUNTING

Accounting can be described as the systematic process of collecting and communicating data about economic events in terms of money. Its ultimate task is to provide financial information to various individuals and groups interested in the affairs of the accounting organization.

The collection function involves the selection and accumulation of financial information. It can be subdivided into three phases—identification, measurement, and recording. First, the accounting system must select from among myriad economic events those transactions with which it will deal. Even the most ambitious accounting system cannot encompass all financial data. Having identified the appropriate events, accounting then

3

must choose how these events are to be measured. Measurement is the expression of economic activities in terms of dollar values, and a number of different valuation bases can be employed. Recording involves analyzing the character of a transaction and providing a systematic procedure for keeping track of it. A simplified bookkeeping procedure for recording is described in Chapter 3.

The second major function, communication, also has three phases—classification, summarization, and interpretation. Classifying means fitting the financial data into a logical, useful framework. Huge masses of figures have little significance unless some relationships exist among them. The asset-equity framework, the subject of the next chapter, provides the basic foundation for classifying accounting data. Then the collected and classified financial information periodically must be summarized in financial statements and reports. These become the media for communication in accounting. In addition, an explanation of the accounting process—its meaning, uses, and limitations—to the users of these reports and statements is a most necessary final phase of communication. Understanding the process enables one to interpret the results of accounting, and this is really the crucial goal of its study.

In brief, then, the accounting functions consist of identifying, measuring, recording, classifying, summarizing, and interpreting. In the following pages emphasis is placed upon the communication function and the conceptual and analytical aspects of the collection function, for these constitute the major difference between bookkeeping and accounting. Bookkeeping provides the system for recording and classifying data. As such, it is concerned only with procedures—the "how to." The field of accounting, while encompassing bookkeeping, goes beyond these techniques into the rationale, interpretation, and usefulness of applying these procedures—the "why and what for."

Users of Accounting Information

Accounting is often called the "language of business." As a language, it must be concerned with both the information to be communicated and the persons or groups to whom the information is directed. The audiences of accounting information include:

1. Owners—present and prospective investors and their representatives (e.g., professional security analysts and investment advisors).
2. Managers.
3. Creditors and lenders.
4. Employees and labor organizations.
5. Regulatory agencies—the Securities and Exchange Commission, stock exchanges, various governmental commissions, and courts.

6. Taxation authorities.
7. General public.

These different audiences do not necessarily want the same information. The owner may be interested in the status of his investment as well as information he can use to forecast the future success of the business. The creditor, on the other hand, may be more interested in current financial solvency, the taxation authorities in determining legally how much tax the business has to pay, and the labor union in deciding the ability of the firm to meet higher wage demands.

But in a broader sense the information needs of all audiences share a common thread—a desire for information about the use of the economic resources controlled by the organizational unit for which the accounting is being made. Such information, according to one research study, is used for the following four broad purposes:[1]

1. Making decisions concerning the use of limited resources, including the identification of crucial decision areas, and determination of objectives and goals.
2. Effectively directing and controlling an organization's human and material resources.
3. Maintaining and reporting on the custodianship of resources.
4. Facilitating social functions and control.

The first purpose includes the decisions of investors to increase, retain, or withdraw their investments; of bankers and other lenders to judge credit worthiness; and of boards of directors and management to select from among major alternative courses of action. The second purpose specifically relates to the detailed information that internal management requires in planning and controlling the day-to-day operations. Custodianship or stewardship relates to the fact that control over resources often rests with individuals or groups acting on behalf of the owners, suppliers, or beneficiaries of the resources. Users of resources contributed by others have an obligation to give an "accounting" concerning their handling of them. The informational interfaces between organizations and certain functions of society comprise the last purpose. Data provided for use in taxation, management-labor negotiations, price or rate regulation, formulation of governmental economic policies, and accumulation of economic statistics fall into this area.

The objective of accounting is to provide financial information to meet all of these objectives. It is important to account for economic resources and to report on their use to interested parties regardless of the purposes for which the resources are employed. This is true of both a profit-making

---

[1] *A Statement of Basic Accounting Theory* (Evanston, Ill.: American Accounting Association, 1966), p. 4.

business venture, where resources are devoted to the generation of additional resources, and a not-for-profit organization such as a university, where resources must be gathered and channeled into various and often competing employments. Although the profit-seeking organization is the focal point throughout the rest of this book, the needs for financial information and, hence, the importance of accounting extend to many types of organizations. At the same time, it is equally important to remember that although accounting is a primary source of information for users, it does not and cannot supply all the information needed by all interested parties for all possible purposes. It is only one source of business information and only one of many different ways of communicating.

NATURE OF FINANCIAL ACCOUNTING

Notwithstanding the differences among recipients of financial data, one type of accounting seems central to the entire accounting process. This type is known as financial accounting. It is concerned primarily with providing information to investors and other groups not directly involved in operating the business or empowered to dictate the presentation and content of the reports prepared for them. Although specifically oriented to these external audiences, the reports of financial accounting are of interest to practically all the different users mentioned earlier. Because of its general usefulness, financial accounting represents an ideal starting point for a discussion of accounting, especially since the fundamental concepts of financial accounting provide a basic analytical structure for the recording process.

The characteristics and purposes of the financial accounting audience exert a directing influence on the type of information recorded and the manner in which the information is reported. It is the purpose of this section to examine more closely *who* the audience for financial accounting is assumed to be, *what* information is provided in financial accounting statements, and *how* that information is to be determined.

Audience

In general, the "who" of financial accounting consists of external users —present and prospective investors, creditors, security analysts, employees, etc. Of these, stockholders and creditors are dominant; other external parties are assumed to share, more or less, the informational needs of stockholders and creditors. Of course, stockholders and other investors include many different types of decision makers with varying investment objectives. Consequently, financial accounting must build upon certain assumptions about their general characteristics and informational objectives.

Purposes. The overall objective of investors in using financial information is to determine the attractiveness of a firm as an investment outlet. Stockholders must decide whether to buy, sell, or retain their ownership interests in a business entity; lenders must decide whether to make loans, and in what amounts and on what terms. In order to make intelligent investment decisions, investors need information to enable them to evaluate (1) the future earnings potential of the firm, (2) the present and future financial strength (debt-paying ability), and (3) the effectiveness of management in administering the business.

Financial accounting assumes that the most feasible inputs for these judgments (especially judgments of the third type) consist of historical information on how well the firm has performed and regular reports about the existing financial position of the firm. Business management is viewed as the steward of the firm's resources. Investors commit funds and other properties to the business with a goal of deriving an income from their investment. In turn, management has a stewardship responsibility to protect this financial commitment and to use the resources in such a manner as to increase their total. Moreover, investors expect to receive reports on the manner in which managers have exercised their stewardship of invested funds. Financial accounting attempts to fulfill this reporting obligation by providing historical information. Such information can be used in an appraisal of how productively management has used the resources entrusted to it by investors as well as the current status of the financial commitment. Moreover, this same historical reporting serves as a factual basis on which the individual may attempt to project future earnings and profitability.

Characteristics. The major characteristics of the investor audience assumed by conventional financial reporting fall into five areas: (1) technical proficiency, (2) decision-making horizon, (3) comparative analysis, (4) authority, and (5) interpretive preference. The first three are almost self-explanatory. The users of financial accounting are deemed to possess sufficient intelligence and experience to be able to understand financial data communicated to them. Moreover, investors presumably make continuing investment decisions; they perform their analytical procedures on a regular basis over a relatively short time horizon. Third, they wish to compare one business entity with another, one management team with another, and the results of one time period with another.

The characteristics of authority and interpretive preference perhaps require additional explanation. "Authority" refers to the ability of the user to dictate the presentation and content of the financial reports. Management, because of its position, has knowledge of or can directly obtain detailed information necessary for internal operating decisions. Regulatory authorities also are in a position to dictate exactly what information they desire and how it is to be arranged. Stockholders, on the other hand, must rely on reports prepared for them by management. They usually are separate from the actual operations of the firm and therefore lack intimate knowledge of events as they happen. They also lack the authority to demand specific financial information or to check directly on its reliability.

Interpretation of financial information ultimately rests with the user of the information. The characteristic of interpretive preference concerns the extent to which the user is willing to have the preparer inject his judgments or interpretations of future events into the financial statements. For the most part, financial accounting as conventionally practiced assumes that its audience wishes to retain the bulk of the interpretive task. Financial accounting's task then becomes to report what has happened, not what will happen. At the same time, this distinction is not clear-cut; as we shall see, at several points in the process of reporting the past, judgments about the future must be made. Nevertheless, the import of this assumption about investors' interpretive preference is to minimize the influence of management's expectations on the financial reports and to emphasize objective, historical events.

Financial Accounting Information

In light of the foregoing assumed purposes and characteristics of the investor audience, financial accounting attempts to provide information in two specific, basic areas—income measurement and financial condition. Financial accounting assumes that investors and creditors desire historical information on how well the firm has performed during past periods in terms of earning an income. In addition, periodic reports about the existing financial position of the firm are a necessary adjunct to the income reports.

It is not surprising, therefore, that the summarization of financial accounting is found principally in two financial statements, one directed toward each of these two information areas. The position statement, or balance sheet, presents the financial condition of the business as of a specific moment in time. It is akin to the photographer's snapshot. It portrays in terms of money the resources held by a business and the claims on and interests in those resources as of a particular date. The income statement, on the other hand, summarizes the major changes in the resources of the busi-

FIGURE 1–1

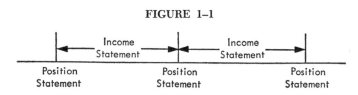

ness as a result of management's efforts to generate a return for the investors. It attempts to report on the performance of the business entity during a particular period.

Diagrammatically, these two statements are interrelated in time perspective as shown in Figure 1–1.

Objectivity, Reliability, and Relevance

Implicit in the preceding discussions on the audience served and the information presented by financial accounting have been suggestions as to how financial accounting information is to be determined. The guidelines for judging when events are recorded in the accounting system and what dollar values are used to measure them are found in three somewhat overlapping standards—objectivity, reliability, and relevance. Together they exert a pervasive influence on the measurement process in financial accounting practice and on the formulation of the basic assumptions underlying financial accounting theory. Probably, however, objectivity plays the most important role in conventional accounting.

The desire for objectivity derives from the investors' characteristics of authority (or lack thereof) and interpretive preference. Financial accounting statements must be based on actual, verifiable events and should be reported in an unbiased manner. Objective data is capable of independent verification by another competent accountant. This is one reason why accountants place great importance on transactions arising out of "arm's-length" negotiations between independent parties, in contrast to future dreams, plans, or expectations. When sound judgments are needed to make the statements useful, those judgments should be free from personal bias, self-interest, or subjective opinions. These two conditions—verifiability and impartiality—make up what accountants call "objectivity." It is, of course, a relative concept, implemented in specific situations in varying degrees. Nonetheless, its general influence is strong. Authoritative statements by all of the major accounting bodies reflect a desire for relative objectivity.

Reliability, on the other hand, relates to the confidence or trust users have in the accounting data and reports. For accounting statements to be reliable, some assurance must exist that the statements do represent, in fact, what they purport to represent. Consequently, accuracy and disclosure become important characteristics of financial accounting. Furthermore, as we shall learn shortly, the development of "generally accepted accounting principles" and the practice of auditing stem from reliability.

The aspect of relevance is somewhat more tenuous. For information to be relevant, it must be responsive to the audience's information needs. But accountants have only begun to scratch the surface here. For example, a steel wholesaler has 10 tons of steel in his warehouse. The steel cost the wholesaler $50 per ton three months ago. Because of a slowdown in the economy, similar steel can be acquired from the mills at $47 per ton. Deliveries from the warehouse to retail customers have been made recently at a selling price of $54 per ton. However, recent sales activity has been sluggish, and retail price cuts or extensive sales promotional activity is being considered by management. The question is what dollar value— $500, $470, $540, or some other figure—the accountant should assign to this steel in reporting to investors and creditors. Which of these figures is relevant to the audience? As we shall see, conventional financial accounting resolves this dilemma in favor of the $500 purchase cost on the grounds of objectivity, an *assumption* about investor's interpretive preference, and an *assumption* that historical cost is relevant to the investor's needs.

In summary, then, this section identifies the external investor as the primary audience of financial accounting and sets forth certain assumptions as to his purposes and characteristics. Likewise, the position statement and income statement are singled out as the primary subject matter for financial accounting, and objectivity, reliability, and relevance are suggested as desirable guidelines for the development of financial accounting.

FRAMEWORK OF FINANCIAL ACCOUNTING

The impact on financial accounting of the audience composed of investors and creditors is evident in the preceding discussion. This impact is manifested in the historical, stewardship perspective taken in financial accounting and in the desire for objectivity, reliability, and relevance in reports. One important step in achieving these objectives is the establishment of a set of basic concepts to guide the preparation and interpretation of financial accounting reports. With the rise of the large corporation in which absentee owners place operating control with professional managers, investors and creditors must have financial information that adheres to some general standards that are consistently applied and understood. Otherwise, the financial information—content, format, and basis—may vary drastically from one situation to another, from one time period to another, and from one management source to another.

Therefore, financial accounting must be built upon some framework of principles or concepts in order that it can be interpreted properly. The elements in this framework collectively are called "generally accepted accounting principles" (GAAP). They exist to assist the flow of understandable information from the preparer of the financial statements to the user. They add reliability to the information. Moreover, GAAP help provide the uniformity of principle needed for comparative analysis of one company with another, a major activity of investors.

Some confusion exists among accountants as to the meaning of "gener-

ally accepted accounting principles." Some see them as encompassing detailed procedures or instructions. For most accountants, though, they are
broader guidelines derived from some fundamental assumptions and implemented through particular procedures that might differ from one business to another because of differences in the underlying facts of each
case. As one observer put it,

Ideally, accounting principles should be clear and definite enough so that
intelligent, well-informed professionals, when given a description of the facts
about a given transaction and the environment in which it occurs, will agree,
reasonably closely with one another, as to how transactions should be recorded.[2]

Development of Accounting Principles

Throughout financial accounting theory and practice, a recurring
theme deals with the search to identify, establish, explain, and understand
the generally accepted accounting principles that underlie the financial
statements. This endeavor we begin in the remainder of this chapter.

Financial accounting has arisen from two rather distinct and often independent sources—the theoretical and the practical. While accounting
was developing as a practical art of collecting and reporting certain facts
and events relating to business operations, it was also evolving as a body
of theoretical knowledge founded on assumptions and containing logically
derived and internally consistent (although not necessarily practicable)
conclusions. The practical development can be traced back 500 years; the
theoretical evolution is more recent.

Figure 1–2 represents diagrammatically the development of accounting
theory (on the left) and accounting practice (on the right). Any classification of developments, approaches, ideas, organizations, and people as
being either theoretical or practical is always an oversimplification. Nevertheless, sufficiently clear-cut distinctions have existed throughout the development of accounting to aid in our general understanding. Both accounting theory and accounting practice are interested in developing
some general principles for dealing with the same real world of business
transactions and events. However, the approaches are quite different.

Development of Practice. The development of accounting practice,
the right half of the diagram, employs a problem-solving approach. As
particular problems arise in connection with individual business events,
practicing accountants design separate procedures to solve these specific
problems. The history of accounting practice consists of a problem-pro-
cedure evolution—the development of new, or modification of old, procedures as different problems occur.

---

[2] Robert N. Anthony, "Showdown on Accounting Principles," *Harvard Business
Review*, Vol. 41, No. 3 (May–June 1963), p. 101.

The search for general concepts stemming from a detailed analysis of accounting practice involves generalizing from these individual procedures. Through induction—the derivation of a broad pattern or conclusion from a number of specific instances—generalizations can be developed concerning accounting practice. In other words, the approach taken here can be described in the statement, "Accounting is what accountants do." The generalizations derived from a study of existing accounting procedures and practices are considered sound because they are accepted and used.

FIGURE 1–2

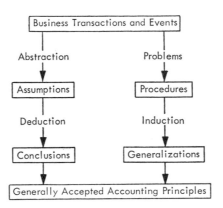

To a certain extent, this approach of defining accounting principles through a process of generalizing the existing accounting practices can be seen in the pronouncements of the American Institute of Certified Public Accountants (AICPA). The bulletins from this group of highly qualified practitioners have been, in many cases, a summary of current accounting practice containing a number of often inconsistent yet equally acceptable alternatives. Recently, this body has striven to become more deductive in its approach.

Development of Accounting Theory.   The first step in the development of accounting theory is to abstract from the existing real world of business events. By rising above the myriad of specific events, the accounting theorist attempts to set forth some basic assumptions about business activities. From these assumptions, then, conclusions can be developed concerning accounting activities through the use of deductive logic. These conclusions present the theoretical answer to the query, "What should accountants do?"

This process is identified as model building, quite similar to that employed in mathematics and economics. The degree of abstraction has not been carried to as high a level in accounting as in these other disciplines, however. Actually, there can be a number of accounting models, depending on the nature of the initial assumptions and the objectives those assumptions are trying to achieve. Our concern centers on what might be called "conventional theory," the logical system that appears to underlie present-day financial accounting. This attention does not necessarily imply that the existing theoretical framework is the best one; we explore some alternatives in Chapter Seventeen.

The publications of the American Accounting Association, another important accounting group (espousing primarily the view of educators), reflect this conceptual approach. Also, some research studies prepared under the auspices of the AICPA have employed the same approach.[3] In addition, numerous individual efforts have attempted to develop varying sets of postulates or standards for financial accounting deductively.

Interaction between Theory and Practice.   Ideally, the conclusions developed from accounting theory should be the same as the generalizations developed from a study of accounting practice. Unfortunately, the ideal world does not exist; differences between theory and practice are encountered in financial accounting statements. If the deductive theory is at variance with observable practice, then either the basic postulates are not descriptive of the real world, the logic used in deriving principles (conclusions) from the assumptions is not sound, or other influences in the accounting environment operate to counteract the reason and logic of the theoretical model.

When accounting practices are not firmly rooted in a logical foundation, generalizations in one problem area appear inconsistent with recommended treatments in other areas. When the *same* items are treated differently by different accountants with equal acceptability, either the generalizations arising from accounting practice are not sound generalizations, or the deductive process has been extended to detailed procedures so that differences in fact which might justify alternative procedures are assumed away. The result of any of these situations is likely to be a lack of comparability among the statements of different companies.

Actually, theory and practice can complement one another and provide a check-and-balance procedure in the development of accounting principles. Theory is important to the development of accounting because, to be meaningful, practice must make sense logically. Accounting theory should provide the guidelines for the future development of accounting practice and the criteria to evaluate its internal consistency. At the same time, the assumptions underlying accounting theory must be based on common

---

[3] E.g., Maurice Moonitz, *The Basic Postulates of Accounting*, Accounting Research Study No. 1 (New York: American Institute of Certified Public Accountants, 1961); and Robert T. Sprouse and Maurice Moonitz, *A Tentative Set of Broad Accounting Principles for Business Enterprises*, Accounting Research Study No. 3 (New York: AICPA, 1962).

sense and relate to the existing business world. Their validity must be continually checked empirically. Indeed, some of the assumptions themselves may result from observations of practice. In addition, any errors in logic must be weeded out. A critical examination of differences between theory and practice may aid in this process. Out of this continual interaction between the two should emerge the set of concepts which comprise what we know as generally accepted accounting principles.

Authoritative Bodies Influencing Accounting Thought

In the evolutionary process which generates the generally accepted accounting principles, the pronouncements and publications of major accounting organizations have played key roles. The American Institute of Certified Public Accountants and the American Accounting Association have been mentioned in the preceding section. Currently, probably the two most influential bodies are the Securities and Exchange Commission, a governmental organization, and the Accounting Principles Board, a separate group within the AICPA. They are the principal determinants of accounting as practiced currently.

Securities and Exchange Commission. Under the securities laws of 1933 and 1934, Congress established this agency in an attempt to assure that the investor in securities had adequate information on which to base his decisions. Congress empowered the SEC to establish the accounting principles to be followed by companies issuing new securities directly to the general public or having their securities traded on the organized exchanges. Over 7,000 firms, including practically all of the large, dominant corporations in the United States, fall under SEC jurisdiction and must comply with its regulations. Although possessing statutory power to regulate accounting procedures for these companies, the SEC has concentrated its attention more on the full and fair reporting of information than on the development of any single set of deductive principles.

Regulation S–X deals with the form and content of financial statements required by the SEC. It standardizes the format and definitions of the required statements. First issued in 1940, it remains the SEC's principal accounting regulation. Additionally, since 1937 over 100 *Accounting Series Releases* have been issued, stating the Commission's policy on numerous accounting questions. Through them the Commission has encouraged minimum standards and comparability in accounting practice more than it has developed new accounting theory. The principles which have been promulgated by the SEC have been either a reflection of existing ones set forth by the accounting profession (the AICPA and, more recently, the Accounting Principles Board) or have been worked out in close conjunction with those groups. Nevertheless, the impact of the SEC is great because of the authority vested in it, and its pronouncements are not taken lightly.

The Accounting Principles Board of the AICPA. In *Accounting Series Release No. 4*, issued in 1938, the SEC formally stated that accounting principles underlying the financial statements filed with it must have "substantial authoritative support." The SEC traditionally has looked to professional public accountants for this authoritative support. As a result the AICPA is probably the foremost speaker in the area of standards for financial accounting reports. The organization represents over 70,000 professionally trained accountants responsible for issuing opinions on the financial statements prepared by management. Each member has met certain minimum requirements as to education and experience and has passed a national examination to earn the designation "certified public accountant."

Between 1939 and 1960 the AICPA issued over 50 *Accounting Research Bulletins* and *Accounting Terminology Bulletins* recommending how specific accounting situations could be handled. Their purpose was to "narrow areas of difference and inconsistency in accounting practices, and to further the development and recognition of generally accepted accounting principles. . . ."[4] Often these bulletins more closely resembled codifications of existing accounting practice rather than conclusions drawn from underlying assumptions. They carried little formal weight other than that attributable to the general reputation and reasoning of the persons on the Committee on Accounting Procedure at the particular time a bulletin was formulated. However, because of the prestige of the AICPA they became the major source of accounting principles over the years.

In 1960 the Institute created an Accounting Principles Board (APB) as a more permanent body to issue authoritative "opinions" on GAAP. Its charge also is to narrow areas of difference and to determine appropriate practice. Currently, the Board has 18 members—15 from public accounting firms and 3 from education and industry—elected to three-year terms by the Council governing the AICPA.

Before issuing an *Opinion*, the Board discusses and debates the issues. Very frequently, a research study has been prepared under the auspices of the AICPA. The research studies analyze the problem, explore alternatives, and make recommendations. Although not binding on the Board, the research studies provide extremely valuable background for its deliberations. After consideration of all views, the Board may authorize the publication of an "exposure draft" of its opinion. This draft is widely circulated among public accountants, educators, businessmen, and financial analysts; comments and reactions are encouraged. After reviewing the feedback from the exposure draft, the Board makes any changes it feels are warranted and issues its final *Opinion*. A favorable vote of two thirds of the Board members is required for an *Opinion* to be issued.

---

[4] *Accounting Research and Terminology Bulletins, Final Edition* (New York: AICPA, 1961), p. 8.

At first the APB opinions rested on their general acceptability. However, in October 1964, the Council of the Institute took formal action to increase the importance of the Board opinions. The Council stated that (1) generally accepted accounting principles are those having substantial authoritative support, (2) *Opinions* of the APB constitute substantial authoritative support, and (3) although substantial authoritative support can exist for other accounting principles, any departures from APB *Opinions* must be disclosed in footnotes to the financial statements or in the auditor's report.

The Accounting Principles Board to date has issued 17 *Opinions*. These include a reaffirmation, with minor changes, of the pronouncements of the predecessor Committee on Accounting Procedure. Some of the earlier APB opinions retained the codifying nature of former bulletins, dealt with procedural details, or made revisions to other opinions. More recently, the Board has turned its attention to some very challenging and controversial areas. References to these opinions are scattered through the remaining chapters.

American Accounting Association.   This group, while exerting a less direct influence on accounting practice, has contributed substantially to the theoretical literature. Representing primarily the views of accounting educators, the AAA has periodically issued statements on standards or concepts which should underlie financial statements. Its latest is called *A Statement of Basic Accounting Theory* and was published in 1966. In addition, the Association has sponsored individual research projects by outstanding scholars, which have resulted in a series of monographs. The third monograph, entitled *An Introduction to Corporate Accounting Standards*, by W .A. Paton and A. C. Littleton, was published in 1940 but still remains one of the theoretical landmarks in the development of accounting thought. Both the research monographs and the statements of standards tend to take a more deductive approach than those of the other organizations. They deal with general guidelines for what financial accounting and reporting should be. Of lesser concern has been the solution of particular accounting problems. As a result, the AAA's impact on the development of accounting principles has been more subtle and continual than that of the SEC and APB.

ASSUMPTIONS OF FINANCIAL ACCOUNTING

The primary concern of this section is to examine some of the assumptions which form the theoretical framework for the conventional financial accounting model. From these assumptions we can hope to develop some general principles, which lead in turn to particular methods and procedures. In light of the many influences on the development of generally accepted accounting principles, one would be foolhardy to expect that all accountants and accounting organizations would agree entirely with the list developed below. Nevertheless, these assumptions appear in the accounting literature with sufficient frequency to form an interrelated structure upon which we can build in subsequent chapters. The words "assumption" and "concept" are used interchangeably, regardless of their minor etymological differences.

First Assumption: Matching Costs and Revenues

The general nature of business affairs lies in an acquisition-consumption-recovery cycle. Stripped of embellishments, the conduct of any business enterprise involves acquiring various types of productive resources such as raw materials, labor, equipment, etc. The resources are called *costs* or *assets* and are acquired in anticipation of using them to produce a product or a service. When the latter is sold, a resource inflow, usually in the form of cash or receivables (claims to cash), results. The accounting concept of net income involves matching the total amount of resource inflow (which we call *revenues*) received from the period's operations against the cost of resources that were consumed (which we call *expenses*) in producing the inflow. In other words, part of the revenue stream represents a recovery of the costs used up.

Thus the first and central assumption of financial accounting is that net income is best measured by matching costs against the revenues to which the costs have given rise. In this way, we are matching total resources used up in operations against total resources received from operations. It follows, therefore, that resources or costs available during a period can be divided into two groups—those applicable to the production of revenues in the current period (expenses) and those applicable to the production of revenues in future periods (assets). Costs, in theory, should be allocated between the present and the future wholly on the basis of when they benefit the process of revenue generation. In practice, uncertainty of the period of usefulness and difficulty in assigning costs cause departures from this theory. Nevertheless, the general concept is that a cost becomes an expense when the resource (asset) is consumed in the production of revenues. And by matching the two flows of revenue and expense, we can obtain a meaningful measure of performance (net income).

This matching concept is, of course, only one possible assumption. There are other approaches to income measurement. For example, the business could be valued at the end of selected periods of time, and net income could be defined as the increase or decrease in value. Or we could employ some subjective approach to determine the present value of expected future net receipts, as the theoretical economist does. Nevertheless, reasons exist for using this particular assumption. The basic rationale lies in an attempt to match effort and accomplishment. In a broad sense, revenues provide a monetary measure of the accomplishment of a firm in satisfying the wants and desires of consumers. Likewise, expenses can be viewed as a monetary expression of the effort, in the sense of resources used in satisfying consumer desires.

In addition, the matching assumption is selected because it incorporates greater objectivity and historical perspective than do other alternatives. For instance, periodic revaluation of all business assets would involve a series of appraisals that might rely heavily on subjective judgment and expectations. Although not completely free from judgmental factors, the basic information used in the matching concept—revenues and expenses —is based on actual market transactions at the time of recording. To the extent that financial accounting does not consider changes in value or future expectations, its usefulness may be limited. Whether more is gained from a greater degree of objective measurement than is lost through a historical perspective will be debated among accounting theorists for many years to come. Suffice it to say at this point that financial accounting currently centers around this fundamental assumption.

Second Assumption: Entity Concept

This second assumption asserts that accounting statements and records represent activities of the business entity rather than of the people or groups concerned with it. In our measurement of net income, we must have some perspective. This concept establishes that the accounting data relate to an organization which is a separate, distinct entity apart from its owners.

The accounting entity does not necessarily have to correspond to any specific legal or taxable organization. For example, accounting records can be maintained for a one-owner business (single proprietorship) which is not recognized as a separate entity for the levying of taxes or for most legal purposes. The entity concept indicates that the accounting records should reflect only the activities of the business and should not be mixed with the personal affairs of the owners. For example, the business records would not deal with the personal consumption expenditures of the proprietor.

The large modern corporation is recognized by law and the taxation authorities as a separate organization. Here, the accounting entity and the legal entity are the same. Because of its importance, the private business organized legally as a corporation for purposes of making a profit is primarily the accounting entity referred to in the remainder of this book. Thus we focus on events in which the corporation is an actual participant. In Chapter Fourteen we modify this single-corporation definition of the entity and explore some of the difficulties involved in trying to select an appropriate entity.

Third Assumption: Going-Concern Concept

This third assumption describes more fully the accounting entity. The going-concern or continuity concept states that in the absence of evidence to the contrary, the entity is assumed to remain in operation sufficiently long to carry out its objectives and plans. Thus the accountant can focus his attention on the matching process rather than on the liquidation values at any particular date. Future benefits can be recorded as assets and future outlays as claims. Without this assumption, allocation of the cost of long-life assets over their useful life would not be possible. Allocation implies that the concern will be in existence at least as long as the useful lives of its various assets.

Again, this is only an assumption. Not all businesses remain in existence indefinitely. If there is evidence that an entity's existence will terminate, then a different assumption should be selected and different accounting procedures developed. For instance, special accounting procedures apply to concerns in liquidation or bankruptcy. Financial accounting, however, is interested in those firms that are expected to remain in operation.

Fourth Assumption: Concept of the Accounting Period

This assumption recognizes the utilitarian nature of accounting. To fulfill its communication function, accounting must operate in a time framework. This concept states that for accounting purposes it is necessary to divide business operations into arbitrary time periods. Business actually operates on a continuum of activity. The complexity of the modern business environment, however, requires periodic measurements of operations. Users of financial reports must rely on timely data and cannot wait until the entity's life has ended to ascertain net income.

As a result of this assumption, the accountant prepares reports of net income and financial condition for time periods which are to some extent artificial, considering the continuous nature of the enterprise. Therefore, these periodic reports serve only as indices of the stream of economic activity of the entity. The results of operations (matching costs against revenues) for any short period of time are tentative. Many allocations are only uncertain estimates, but accountants make them in order to supply needed information for current decision making. Many estimating procedures, expedients, and conventions that accountants find necessary to work with have their origin in this concept.

In the application of this concept, a balance must be achieved between certainty and timeliness. The accounting period must be long enough to provide reasonably accurate results yet short enough to supply currently usable information. For reporting to investors, a yearly accounting period is commonly used. Management, however, usually requires more frequent accounting reports; monthly and quarterly accounting periods are employed. The period concept reflects the needs of those who use accounting reports.

Fifth Assumption: Monetary Concept

The monetary concept deals with the unit of account to be used in accounting. Two basic ideas are contained in this assumption. The first states that money is the best common denominator in which to express business transactions. No other means of expression is so universal, simple, and adaptable. However, this part of the postulate carries with it the result that business events which cannot be expressed in money are not recorded in the accounting framework. Such events, like a heart attack suffered by the company president, may be of great significance; nevertheless, they are not communicated through the accounting system.

The second part of this assumption states that fluctuations in the value of the dollar can be ignored without any impairment of the usefulness or validity of the financial statements. The monetary unit serves as the accountant's unit of measurement. Whenever the quantity of goods and services that people will exchange for it fluctuates significantly over time, its value or purchasing power changes. It becomes a measuring standard of varying size. The monetary concept assumes that any distortions caused by price-level changes (changes in the value of the monetary unit) will not be material enough to undermine the reliability of the financial statements. Although soundly criticized and attacked as invalid in the last 20 years, this assumption has not yet been replaced by any concept equally accepted in accounting circles. It remains, however, a point of contention in accounting theory.

Sixth Assumption: Revenue Recognition

If costs (expenses) are to be matched against the revenues to which they give rise, there is a need for a sixth basic assumption as to when the revenues themselves should be recognized. Two tests are established in this concept. Revenue should not be recognized until it has been earned and can be measured with a reasonable degree of certainty and objectivity. Revenues are effectively earned when substantially all of the activities necessary for and associated with the production of revenues have been completed. More is needed than just a knowledge that the revenues have been earned, however; they must be measurable. Because objectivity and certainty in measurement are sometimes lacking, revenues are not always recognized as they are economically earned. Rather, the accountant waits until he has some verifiable evidence, such as a legal sale plus the acquisition of some liquid asset. With few exceptions, the accountant finds this evidence when transactions with outside customers are completed. In most cases, the point of sale has become the most generally accepted time for revenue recognition. Usually, both criteria are met there. We explore some ramifications of this postulate in greater depth in Chapter Six.

OTHER ASPECTS OF THE ACCOUNTING ENVIRONMENT

In addition to these six assumptions, we cannot realistically study accounting without recognizing still other factors and conditions which influence its practice. Some writers classify them among the major concepts of accounting. However, they seem to differ from the integral package of basic assumptions, more closely resembling expedients, doctrines, or conventions rather than major concepts. A knowledge of them is mandatory, nevertheless, for a fuller understanding of accounting. These conventions can be classified into three categories—arbitrary procedural techniques, normative standards, and the environmental conditions in which businesses operate.

Procedural Techniques

Certain procedural techniques in accounting have been arbitrarily established by common acceptance. Although they could be changed without altering the fundamental character of financial accounting, they have acquired accepted meanings and customary uses. For example, the debit and credit framework discussed in Chapter Three could just as easily be reversed, with no adverse effect on the general interpretation of the accounting system. Yet certain rules currently prevail for entering data in the accounting records. Also, many of the record-keeping forms we mention spring from accepted conventions. The advent of computerized data processing already has caused changes in these forms without destroying the basic nature of accounting. Perhaps, to a lesser extent, traditional financial statement formats and account classifications also reflect a great deal of custom and habit. For instance, terms such as "current assets" and "current liabilities" (Chapter 2) have a readily accepted meaning among users of financial statements, although they could be redefined and the items classified differently.

Standards

Conventional accounting practice is also characterized by certain normative ideas of what "good" practice ought to be. These doctrines relate to desirable attitudes or states of mind on the part of accountants or to the characteristics of properly reported information. Three of the very important ones—objectivity, reliability, and relevance—have already been discussed. Other influential standards are discussed in this section. Among them are conservatism, consistency, materiality, and disclosure.

Conservatism. This standard is an outgrowth of the uncertain environment and the tentative measurements of accounting. Historically, it has been viewed, and sometimes applied, as a rule requiring understatement of income and assets. In modern accounting it finds its place as a state of mind calling for due caution and a careful assessment of risks and uncertainties. Given a situation calling for judgment, where the decision is not clear, accountants tend to select those procedures which do not overstate resources or income.

Consistency. Accounting procedures, like any reporting mechanism, should be consistently applied from one report to another to promote comparability. Because accountants deal with judgments, approximate measurements, and alternative principles, it is imperative that whatever choices are made are the same from period to period for the same accounting entity. One of the primary uses of financial statements is in comparative analyses over time to determine trends and changing relationships. Consistency does not bar a change to a more accurate or correct procedure. But in the absence of evidence that a change has been made, the reader should be able to infer that the same concepts and procedures underlie each period's statements. And when a change has been made, consistency requires that sufficient information be presented to make the reports comparable in the year of change.

Perhaps the greatest controversy over consistency concerns its extension to interfirm comparisons. Uniformity among firms in their financial reporting is thought by some to be a desirable objective. Certainly investors' analyses encompass comparisons among firms, and such analyses may be frustrated by different accounting practices. However, whether uniformity should be limited only to general concepts or should apply to detailed procedures, measurement techniques, and report formats is as yet an unresolved issue.

Materiality. This doctrine has little bearing on a theoretical framework of accounting. It does, however, help to explain differences in the handling of items between accounting theory and accounting practice and to set a guideline for reporting. Any amount or transaction that has a significant (material) effect on the statements should be recorded correctly and reported. When the difference between the theoretical treatment of an item and a more practical treatment of it is immaterial in amount or significance, the item is recorded the easiest way, since there is little difference in the end result. And minor items (immaterial ones) do not need to be reported in detail. What is material or immaterial varies from situation to situation and often requires the accountant's careful judgment based on extensive experience.

Disclosure. One of the strongest standards in accounting is that accounting reports should disclose fully and fairly the information they purport to represent. The term "full and fair disclosure" and many of its implications arose from the securities laws of 1933 and 1934 which created the SEC. The SEC, the AICPA, and the American Accounting Association have all attempted to implement this concept through their bulletins and pamphlets setting forth general guides as to how information should be reported. The phrases used by each group have varied, but the general concepts and standards are similar. In brief, the goal is the presentation of unbiased information in sufficient detail to enable the user of the statements to make sound judgments.

Full disclosure basically means that all material accounting data that might be of significance to a reasonably intelligent user should be disclosed. There should be no unnecessary summarization. Moreover, any information necessary for accurate interpretation of the statements should be available to the reader. Included in this category would be identification of accounting policies followed, departures from or changes in generally accepted accounting principles, and other supplementary information. Such interpretive data are to be displayed on the statements themselves or presented in footnotes.

Not only must complete information be given, but it must be undistorted by the value judgments and particular outlook of the person preparing it. The term "fair disclosure" covers these ideas and, hence, includes many of the aspects of financial reporting we have already discussed. Objectivity, conformity to generally accepted accounting principles, and consistency are aspects of fair disclosure. In addition, it is concerned with clarity of presentation. Reasonable condensation is desirable; statements should not be cluttered with a mass of unnecessary detail. Thus, ample use of supporting schedules should be made. In this way the detailed information is available for the interested reader but does not distract or confuse the user attempting to obtain a more general picture of financial operations. Statement titles and footnote terminology should be understandable to the reader of the statements.

Environmental Conditions

The economic and social environment of accounting may cause accounting practice to depart from the basic theory derived from the underlying assumptions. For example, business entities exist in a legal environment having certain precedents and procedures. In addition, practically all firms are regulated in varying degrees by governmental bodies. These legal and governmental influences often affect the accounting procedures used in business. At the extreme is the situation in which accounting procedures are virtually dictated by governmental bodies, as in the case of railroads and public utilities.

Another environmental factor, income tax regulations, currently plays an exceedingly important role in accounting practice. Tax laws and regulations are designed to achieve a multiplicity of political and economic purposes. Financial accounting procedures, on the other hand, attempt to achieve the proper matching of costs and revenues to measure business income. Where the two sets of concepts are not the same (and this divergence seems to be growing), the business entity is faced with a dilemma. Either separate records must be maintained for tax accounting and for financial accounting, with the attendant inconvenience and expense, or procedures designed to implement particular goals of taxation end up being used to measure periodic business income. All too frequently, the latter situation prevails, and the development of accounting practice is unduly influenced by income tax regulations.

One additional environmental factor should be mentioned briefly. Various industry practices have arisen over the years. Most firms in a particular industry, through force of habit, conform to them, even though these historical practices may depart from sound accounting concepts. We do not investigate varying industry practices in this text. Be careful, however, to remember that this factor is at work when you analyze accounting information.

OTHER ACCOUNTING ACTIVITIES

Before completing this introduction to accounting, the student should be aware of some other important aspects of accounting activity. A need exists for other kinds of detailed information besides income statements and position statements. Moreover, accountants perform other functions than the preparation of those statements.

Managerial Accounting

This area of activity involves the preparation of detailed information for management's use in planning and controlling operations and in decision making. Financial accounting reports primarily on "what is"; internal management needs to know "what should have been" and "what will be." To interpret properly and to make the fullest use of accounting information, managers must grasp the basic concepts of financial accounting. However, to act on these reports and to fulfill other functions, management needs more detailed information than does an external audience. Managerial accounting consists of the additional procedures and techniques designed to supply the particulars.

Section V of this text attempts to form a bridge between financial and managerial accounting. Most of the subjects included there (particularly Chapters Nineteen and Twenty on cost accounting) are relevant both to statement preparation and to management use. However, there is much in managerial accounting that cannot be covered in this text and has been left to other courses.

Data Processing and Systems Design

This area of accounting endeavor concerns the design of rapid and accurate means of gathering and recording business transactions at a reasonable cost. Except for Appendix 4A, which presents a brief introduction to some common data collection methods, and Chapter Eighteen, which pertains to general concepts of accounting systems and control, we are concerned only with the simplest of recording techniques. These are sufficient for our purpose of using accounting as a language of communication and a tool of analysis. However, the importance of a sound accounting system cannot be stressed too much. Without a set of orderly procedures, augmented by mechanical or electrical devices, to handle the myriad detailed information flowing into a modern business, accounting would quickly lose its usefulness. Data processing and systems design increase in importance with every increase in the complexity and magnitude of business operations.

Auditing

Financial accounting reports are prepared by management and presented to groups who are not connected intimately with the daily operations of the firm. Consequently, the party preparing them—management—is the same party being judged by them. Inherent in this situation is a potential conflict of interest that only an independent attestation can resolve. The function of verifying and appraising the accuracy, integrity, and authenticity of the financial statements is called auditing.

Auditing is a major present-day accounting activity. Professional independent accountants, called certified public accountants (CPAs), are licensed by each state and charged with the responsibility of passing expert judgment on financial statements. Many firms are required by law to submit audited financial statements to the Securities and Exchange Commission. In addition, most published financial statements for stockholders and creditors are accompanied by an auditor's report, affirming that the statements are a fair representation and have been prepared on a consistent basis in accordance with generally accepted accounting principles. The standards and procedures used in making these judgments form the subject matter of separate accounting courses and books.

Income Tax Accounting

Tax accounting is concerned with the preparation of records and reports necessary for filing tax returns. Often different from the concepts underlying financial accounting, tax regulations are a complex set of ever-changing laws and rules. Many accountants spend a majority of their time keeping up to date on tax regulations and their implications for accounting and for business planning and decision making. In terms of accounting effort expended, this specialized area ranks high on the list. However, because of their different audience, their complexity, and their changeability, detailed income tax procedures do not play an important role in this book. Nevertheless, we will be alert to some possible distortions caused by the application of tax concepts to the measurement of business income.

Regulatory Accounting

Accounting is constantly called on to prepare a variety of special-purpose reports for various federal and state regulatory agencies. These commissions usually are in a legal position to dictate the form and content of such reports. The informational needs of these groups determine the varied specialized procedures which are referred to collectively as regulatory accounting. To a large extent, the reports filed with the Securities and Exchange Commission are coincident with those prepared under financial accounting. Reports filed with other regulatory agencies are much less so. Differences in purpose and in other audience characteristics cause various types of regulatory accounting to be viewed as something apart from financial accounting.

The above pursuits probably do not exhaust all the activities found in accounting. Certainly the many detailed subphases of each of these areas have not been explored. Indeed, one could develop a separate set of concepts, procedures, and reports for each class of user of accounting information. However, even the brief discussion above emphasizes that financial accounting is only one of a number of activities that fall under the label of accounting.

SUMMARY

The purpose of this chapter is to open the door to the subject of accounting. From this brief exploration of its environmental and theoretical setting, we can reach some general observations:

1.   Accounting is a communication system designed to accumulate and report financial information.
2.   Financial accounting is only one aspect, albeit an important one, of this many-faceted area. Financial accounting has the task of providing historical information about the performance and financial condition of the business entity.

3. The income and position statements generated by financial accounting are directed primarily toward the external audience of owners and creditors.
4. Financial accounting rests on a network of underlying assumptions. It is interlaced, however, with many practical influences, environmental conditions, and traditional conventions which have a bearing on the totality we call accounting.

In subsequent chapters our primary emphasis is on the theory of financial accounting. Procedures are studied when they lend understanding or provide useful analytical tools. A sound understanding of basic concepts may help the reader to avoid the ambiguity and mystery that so often accompany the study of accounting. Nevertheless, we must recognize our limitations. Financial accounting lacks a truly consistent set of objectives and purposes on which basic postulates can be based. Accountants know so little about the impact of information on people's decision processes. Consequently, our conventional framework consists only of a thin web of interrelated assumptions about what investors want and how they behave. Then, to make matters worse, we often lack the measurement techniques to implement fully the theoretical framework we do possess.

As a result, financial reporting probably will remain for some time both an art and a science. In the sense that it attempts to develop a theoretical body of knowledge employing axioms and deductive logic, it could be called a science. And this aspect is stressed in the following pages. However, to the extent that these concepts are not fixed by laws of nature (or human behavior) but must be applied through the use of judgment, often somewhat arbitrarily, to specific circumstances, accounting is more an art. The statement is all too true that "the significance of periodic accounting profit is . . . the algebraic sum of the separate significances of the various conventions, doctrines, rules, and practices which at any particular time constitute the common law of accounting."[5]

SUGGESTIONS FOR FURTHER READING

Anthony, Robert N. "Showdown on Accounting Principles," *Harvard Business Review*, Vol. 41, No. 3 (May–June 1963), pp. 99–106.
"Basic Concepts and Accounting Principles Underlying Financial Statements of Business Enterprises," *Statement of the Accounting Principles Board No. 4*. New York: AICPA, October 1970.
Moonitz, Maurice. *The Basic Postulates of Accounting*, Accounting Research Study No. 1. New York: AICPA, 1961.

[5] Stephen Gilman, *Accounting Concepts of Profit* (New York: Ronald Press Co., 1939), p. 605.

Moonitz, Maurice. "Why Do We Need Postulates and Principles?" *Journal of Accountancy*, Vol. 116 (December 1963), pp. 42–46.
A Statement of Basic Accounting Theory. Evanston, Ill.: American Accounting Association, 1966.
Vatter, William J. "Postulates and Principles," *Journal of Accounting Research*, Vol. 1 (Autumn 1963), pp. 179–97.

QUESTIONS AND PROBLEMS

1–1.   Accounting provides information about economic resources. Explain how accounting in general and financial accounting in particular can affect decisions involving resources.

1–2.   Interested persons both within and outside of the accounting profession have advocated that authoritative principles and procedures be established by a legal commission or court.

    a)   How are generally accepted accounting principles established currently?

    b)   What advantages and disadvantages do you see in the above recommendation?

    c)   How do you think principles and procedures *should be* established? Does the distinction between principle and procedure have significance in the formulation of your answer?

1–3.   The accounting department of a privately owned electric company might be called upon to prepare accounting reports for (*a*) the stockholders, (*b*) the board of directors, (*c*) the Internal Revenue Service, and (*d*) the state public utility commission, among others.

    Describe how each of these groups might wish to use accounting reports and how the reports presented to them might differ.

1–4.   Financial accounting is formulated around generally accepted accounting principles.

    a)   What is meant by the term principles?

    b)   Why are they necessary?

    c)   Why are the principles described as "generally accepted" rather than as "correct," "fair," or "sound"?

1–5.   The following comment was made by a local proprietor operating a small family business: "I don't have to get all tangled up in revenue postulates, matching concepts, or subjective guesses. In my business, we record revenue when we get cash and expenses when we pay cash. My accounting records are simpler to keep, easier to understand, and accurate besides." Analyze and comment on this viewpoint.

1–6.   For some time the need for the study and formulation of basic postulates and principles of accounting has been recognized.

    a)   Discuss (1) the purpose of developing basic postulates and principles of accounting and (2) the benefits to be derived from their development.

    b)   Frequently advanced as a basic postulate is a general proposition dealing with "objectivity." Under what conditions, in general, is information arising from a financial transaction considered to be objective in nature?

c) Accountants acknowledge that financial statements reporting the results of operations for relatively short periods of time, say one year, are tentative whenever allocations between past, present, and future periods are required. On the other hand, the "objectivity" postulate leads to the logical deduction that changes should not be given formal recognition in the accounts earlier than the point of time at which they can be measured in objective terms. Is there a conflict between these two concepts? Can it be resolved? *

1–7.   Objectivity, reliability, and relevance are presented as related standards for evaluating accounting information.

a) In your opinion, which of these three should be most important? Why?

b) Discuss their relationship to each other and to the six assumptions presented in the chapter.

c) A company has a piece of machinery which cost $50,000. It would cost $60,000 to replace, and it is estimated that the net value (sales less all other additional costs) of the goods produced on it is $70,000. If the company were liquidated, it could be sold as a used piece of equipment for $50,000. Discuss the relative objectivity, reliability, and relevance of each of these measures of the equipment.

1–8.   Accounting is described as a communication process and is frequently called the "language of business."

a) What are the characteristics of a good language? Does financial accounting possess these traits?

b) What effect do the characteristics of its audience have on accounting's communication function?

1–9.   The following quotation is attributed to one of the early leaders in the development of accounting practice: "The allocation of income to periods of time would be indefensible if it were not indispensable."

a) What accounting concept(s) is he referring to?

b) Explain his use of the terms "indefensible" and "indispensable."

1–10.   The following comment was overheard in a discussion between two students: "The rapid advance being made in computer technology and electronic data processing equipment will make accountants as obsolete as the dodo bird. A computer can do in minutes what it would take a department of accountants a month to do—and do it more accurately."

Based on your knowledge of accounting functions, purposes, and activities, comment on this statement.

---

* Adapted from AICPA May 1963 examination.

CHAPTER TWO

ASSETS AND EQUITIES

In conducting its affairs, a business enterprise normally engages in two basic types of activities. First, it acquires various financial and productive resources. Then it operates by using these resources to produce an inflow of additional property in hopes of augmenting the original stock of resources. The cost of the resources used (expenses), when matched against the total resources received from selling a product or a service (revenues), provides a measure of net income under our first assumption.

Therefore, fundamental to the study of financial accounting is an understanding of these resources—what they are, where they come from, and how they are recorded. In the technical terminology of accounting, the resources with which a business operates are called its assets. The acquisition of assets gives rise to corresponding financial interests on the part of various groups. A financial interest may be a legal claim, as when a business borrows money from a bank. Or the source of assets may be a residual beneficial interest such as that of the owner of a share of stock. Accountants use the term "equities" to describe the general financial interests (sources of assets) in the business entity. Then the terms "liabilities" and "owners' equity" are used as subdivisions to indicate the financial interests of outside parties (creditors) and the financial interest of the owners, respectively.

The financial condition of the business entity consists of its assets and related equities. As we noted in the first chapter, one major reporting task of financial accounting is periodically to inform investors and creditors of the financial position of the firm. For this purpose, a financial statement called a position statement or balance sheet is prepared as of particular moments in time.

30

BASIC EQUATION OF THE POSITION STATEMENT

The information which appears on a position statement (balance sheet) can be arranged in the following basic equations:

$$\text{Assets} = \text{Equities}^{1}$$
$$\text{Assets} = \text{Liabilities} + \text{Owners' Equity}$$

In this manner, the statement portrays the dual analysis of business capital. It denotes the resources that the business will use in the conduct of its activities and also the financial claims or interests created by the commitment of capital to the business enterprise. It is clear that assets and equities are two sides of the same coin. They have to be equal; every asset comes from somewhere. For every resource a business entity possesses, there is a financial interest, legal or beneficial, represented as well.

Since the assets of the firm represent the wherewithal for operating and the equities portray the financial commitments or interest in the entity, the position statement serves as a beginning for our discussion of financial accounting. In this chapter our attention centers on a description and classification of the items—assets and equities—on that financial report. In addition, we tie the concept of revenues and expenses, which are incorporated in the matching assumption, to changes in the accounting equation.

ASSETS

As the term is used in financial accounting, assets are defined as property and service rights, measurable in terms of money, which are acquired in transactions made by the business entity in the expectation that these rights will have future economic benefit or value. Assets, therefore, can be looked upon as the form taken by the financial capital which is invested in the entity. This definition of assets stresses four considerations:

1. Assets may consist of *property rights* such as land, machinery, or equipment. Also, however, they may include the *right to receive certain services*. For example, a company may purchase a three-year insurance policy. This entitles the company to transfer the risk of loss to the insurance company. The right is in the form of a service to be received over the three-year period; hence, prepaid insurance qualifies as an accounting asset.

2. Assets must be capable of being *expressed in terms of money*. Some valuable rights do not arise from a *measurable dollar outlay*. For this reason, advantages such as being located in a city with a large pool of

---

[1] Occasionally one will see a position statement employing the term "liabilities" in a generic sense to describe all financial interests. Nevertheless, it is more precise and better terminology to restrict "liabilities" to creditors' equity and to use the single term "equities" as the general description of asset sources.

skilled labor or with good fire and police protection would not qualify as accounting assets. Likewise, a series of expenditures on employee training for a number of years may lead eventually to the existence of a valuable future service potential. Yet, in most cases, the dollar expression of this item would be extremely difficult to measure, and the item normally would not appear among the assets on the position statement.

3. Assets are *acquired as a result of a specific event, called a transaction, in which the business entity participates.* The transaction may result in legal ownership, as in the case of a purchase of merchandise, or only in a right to use property, as in the case of a payment of rent in advance. In both cases, however, the transaction culminates a process of negotiation over some right between the business entity and some independent party. Contrast this with employee labor services to be received in future years. Even though these services probably will be used productively in the future, no asset has been acquired as of the present time. Similarly, items such as public streets which are not assignable to the specific accounting entity are not accounting assets.

4. Finally, we are concerned only with those *rights which hold future economic benefit.* The capacity to provide future service causes resources to have value. Rights, the value of which has been used up or has expired, no longer appear as assets. Indeed, our matching concept is formulated with the idea of relating the consumption of assets to the benefits received during each accounting period.

Two General Types of Economic Value

The fourth point states that assets must possess future economic value. Actually, there are generally two kinds of potential values which assets may possess—exchange value (purchasing power) and use value. Consequently, we might classify assets into two broad groups, according to the type of potential benefit inherent in them. One group may be called monetary assets and the other unexpired costs.

Monetary Assets. Included in this division are cash, short-term security investments being held as a temporary backlog for cash, and short-term accounts and notes receivable. These assets have value to the entity because of their inherent purchasing power. Cash can be exchanged at any time to acquire other productive resources. Marketable securities represent rights which can be converted into cash practically at a moment's notice. For most purposes, the business entity views them as the equivalent of cash. Receivables represent legal claims to cash. If collection is anticipated in a reasonably short time, they are only one step removed from being cash. The right they represent is a right to receive a certain amount of current purchasing power.

Unexpired Costs. Probably the largest portion of a firm's assets consists of items which the entity has acquired to help produce revenues in future periods. In Chapter One we call these items costs, and the terms "costs" and "assets" are used interchangeably in subsequent chapters. These assets have value to the business entity because they represent stored-up services to be used over a period of time to generate additional assets. Hopefully, these costs will be recovered through the production of revenues as their related service potentials are consumed. At any moment in time, certain of these costs have not expired. They represent future economic benefits in the form of use value.

Unexpired cost outlays can be subdivided into short-term items—e.g., inventories, prepaid rent, prepaid insurance—and long-term outlays such as land, buildings, and equipment. Differing only in the length of time for which they supply service, these two groups of resources perform the same basic economic function.

Classification of Assets

When assets are presented on a balance sheet, a reasonable classification of the individual items enhances the value of the information being communicated. Based on the preceding discussion, a logical arrangement might be a threefold breakdown—monetary assets, short-term unexpired costs, and long-term unexpired costs. Over the years, however, alternative arrangements have evolved and have received sanction through use in financial and accounting circles and through formal pronouncements of the Accounting Principles Board. Normally, all of these divide assets initially into two categories—current and noncurrent.

Current Assets. Current assets are those resources that will be converted into cash or used in the normal operations of the business within a relatively short period of time. They consist of monetary assets and short-term unexpired costs. Cash, marketable securities, short-term receivables, various kinds of inventories, and prepayments make up the capital that is continually being "turned over" during the operating cycle of a firm. When presented on the position statement, these current assets are usually listed in the foregoing order of decreasing liquidity.

The operating cycle of the business is often described as the time needed to acquire (purchase or make) the product or service, sell it, and collect the receivables. Pictorially, the operating cycle of a business looks as follows:

$$\text{Cash} \rightarrow \text{Inventory} \rightarrow \text{Receivables} \rightarrow \text{Cash}$$

Of course, for each type of business, the operating cycle may be of a different length, anywhere from a few weeks to several years. Therefore the American Institute of Certified Public Accountants has recommended the use of a one-year period *or* the operating cycle, whichever is longer

This definition of current assets prevails in accounting practice; as a result, current assets may include inventories and prepayments applicable to time periods as long as three years. Hence the general definition given earlier of a "relatively short period of time" comes closest to describing the classification of current assets.

Noncurrent Assets. This category includes long-term costs plus any long-term receivables and investments. A reasonable subdivision of noncurrent assets might include the following three groupings:

1. Investments and funds—long-term investments in other companies, cash segregated for special purposes, and long-term receivables.
2. Property and plant—land, buildings, machinery, equipment, and furniture and fixtures.
3. Intangibles—patents, long-term prepayments, copyrights, and organization costs.

As the reader will discover, there is no precise, uniformly applied method of asset classification for position statements. Except for the category of current assets, arrangements and terminology vary a great deal. The caption "noncurrent assets" often does not appear. The term "fixed assets" frequently is used synonymously for "property and plant," and intangible assets often are lumped in a category labeled "other assets." Statement form is primarily a matter of convention. All that can be asked is that the classification of assets be reasonable and understandable to the reader of the statement.

Recording of Assets

Except in rare instances, nonmonetary assets are recorded at their acquisition cost. This amount is measured by the cash paid or promised or, if acquisition is not a direct cash purchase, by the cash equivalent exchanged. For instance, if the firm purchases merchandise inventory, paying $3,000 in cash immediately and promising to pay (incurring a liability of) $6,000 within 30 days, the proper amount of asset cost is $9,000. Or if a partner invests equipment having a current market value of $15,000 in the business enterprise, the asset should be entered at that amount in the financial accounting records. In each of these cases the cash-equivalent figure measures the exchange of values or the price inherent in the transaction between the business entity and another party.

Although acquisition cost and fair market value of an asset are assumed to be identical at the date of acquisition, no attempt normally is made in the accounting records to reflect subsequent fluctuations in the market value of assets. Any further transactions relating to the eventual consumption or disposition of these assets are based on original acquisition costs. The presumed purpose of financial accounting is to furnish information about transactions involving the actual cost investment made by the firm.

This "cost principle" follows as a corollary to the first basic assumption of measuring income by matching dollar acquisition costs against revenues. Presumably, management decides that the estimated value in future use or sale of a particular asset to the business is *at least* equal to its cost. Since acquisition costs are assumed to be a monetary measure of effort, they are the proper figure to be recorded when assets or resources are acquired. Then the user of the statements can base his own judgments about management's performance on the matching of these costs with their related revenues as reported on the income statement. In brief, recording assets at cost is assumed to meet the audience's needs for *objective* information about the *stewardship* of financial resources.

Despite a firm acceptance in accounting practice and theory, occasional exceptions are made to the cost principle in practice, when adhering to it would result in the omission of essential data or in the presentation of misleading information. Such might be the case when the asset is a natural resource like a timber tract, which increases physically through natural growth. Some attempt may be made periodically to augment the amount recorded for that asset, particularly if the increase can be objectively measured. Another exception may arise when current values are grossly different from the original acquisition cost. For example, a firm might have purchased land for $20,000 and later discovered oil conservatively estimated to be worth $600,000. To keep this asset recorded at $20,000 in the face of such a drastic disparity between cost and current market value would be to mislead rather than to inform, even though GAAP would sanction use of the $20,000 figure.

Over the years accounting literature has contained numerous suggestions that financial accounting depart from the original transaction-price concept. Some contributors advocate that cost be restated in terms of current dollars to recognize changes in the value of money caused by general inflation. Others recommend that attention be given to the recognition of real market-value changes in the accounting records. Advocates claim that these valuations are more relevant to the decision processes of investors than original dollar cost valuations and can be measured with sufficient reliability and objectivity. To date, these suggestions have not met with general acceptance among accounting practitioners nor even with general agreement among accounting theorists. In Chapter Seven some of these alternatives are described briefly, along with a more detailed discussion of the problem of cost determination. Then, in Chapter Seventeen, we consider more formally how alternative concepts of income and asset valuation could be implemented in financial-accounting records and statements. Suffice it to say at this point that assets are normally recorded initially at acquisition cost.

EQUITIES

The equities of a firm represent the sources of assets. They measure the financial investment in or claim on the business by particular groups or individuals. Equities are subdivided into two main groups—liabilities and owners' equity. Liabilities indicate the financial interest of creditors (those from whom the entity has borrowed) and usually reflect some type of legal obligation. Owners' equity, on the other hand, reflects the financial investment of the owners of the entity. Let us take a closer look at each of these types of equities and at some of the common items we find classified there.

Liabilities

Liabilities represent the debts and other amounts owed by the business entity. The accounting concept of liability, while encompassing legal debts, includes all obligations to disburse cash or convey other assets in the future, providing that these obligations have arisen from transactions in past or current periods and are subject to reasonably accurate monetary measurement. For example, a firm has a pension plan under which employees will receive benefits in proportion to their years of employment, but employees working less than 10 years will receive no benefits. Legally, no claim against assets arises until 10 years have passed. Nevertheless, accounting still recognizes the gradual buildup of a liability during the first 10 years as the labor services are used. The amount must be based on an estimate of the number of employees who will work longer than the 10-year period.

Most liabilities, however, represent definite amounts owed to specific groups or individuals. Such is the case with accounts payable, bank loans, bonds payable, mortgages payable, etc. These liabilities arise out of a transaction between the business entity and a creditor, and they are recorded at that time.

Accrued Liabilities. Certain liabilities gradually build up in amount until a payment date is reached, at which time the debt is liquidated. For example, employees normally are paid after they have performed services. The liability "wages payable" increases each day that employees work. Then, on pay day, the liability is satisfied. This type of liability is called an accrued liability and is illustrated by Figure 2–1.

Interest payable is another good example. Interest is the charge for the use of borrowed money. The interest owed increases as time passes, until periodic cash payments are made for the total interest related to the elapsed time. Often it may not be convenient to record the daily increase in the liability. However, if a balance sheet is to be prepared before the date of payment, we must be sure to recognize all of these accrued liabilities to the extent that they have accumulated. In Chapter Four we explore the accounting procedures whereby the accrued claims are brought up to date and formally recognized on position statement dates.

FIGURE 2-1

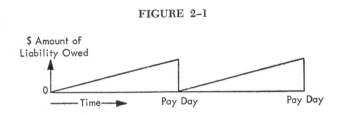

Estimated Liabilities. Sometimes a definite obligation or claim exists, but the amount owed is not known precisely. For example, if a company operates profitably for a year, it will consequently have to pay income tax. The exact amount, however, may be established only at a later date, perhaps after extended discussion with tax authorities. Nevertheless, the accountant should show that a liability for taxes exists as of the end of the year by making a reasonable estimate of the amount due. Similarly, a company that guarantees its product for a specified time period has a definite obligation to repair or replace a certain number of the units that it has sold. The identity of the claimant or the amount of repair cost will be known with certainty only as the units are returned in future periods under the guarantee. Nevertheless the obligation exists, because sales have been made in the current and prior periods. If the amount can be reasonably estimated, it should be recorded.

The estimated liability must be distinguished from *potential* and *contingent* liabilities, which are *not* recognized on the position statement. Potential liabilities are claims that will arise as a result of future events (i.e., future purchases of merchandise on credit). No debt actually exists now. Contingent liabilities represent claims that could materialize pending the outcome of a future event, such as an unsettled lawsuit. Until the lawsuit is lost, no actual claim, estimated or otherwise, exists. No formal listing of contingent liabilities is made, although they frequently are mentioned as supplementary information in notes to the position statement. The factor that distinguishes the estimated liability is that a future cash outlay, which can be reasonably estimated, has to be made because some event *has already occurred.*

Advances. Most liabilities represent claims to be settled by a cash payment. Occasionally, however, a claim against the business arises that is to be satisfied by the delivery of some product or performance of some service in the future. For example, magazine subscriptions normally are paid in advance. The publisher is under an obligation to provide the magazine during the entirety of the subscription period. The claim, though not for cash, is real and should be shown on the position statement. The source of the asset Cash is the liability Subscriptions Received in Advance. The liability is gradually decreased as the magazine is delivered. Such liabilities fall under the general label of advances, although each one usually carries a separate account title—Rent Received in Advance, Advances by Customers, Partial Payments on Uncompleted Contracts, etc.

Classification of Liabilities. The arrangement of liabilities closely parallels that of the assets. Liabilities are normally divided into two categories—current and long-term. The former represent those debts or obligations that will be paid within one year of the date of the statement or within the operating cycle of the firm when that is longer than one year. The presumption is that current liabilities will be satisfied through the use of current assets. Long-term liabilities, on the other hand, represent those debts that fall due after one year from the date of the position statement.

Owners' Equity

The other major source is owners' equity, the financial investment by the owners. Sometimes the owners' equity is called net worth, proprietorship, or simply capital. "Net worth" has fallen into disfavor because of its connotation that the amount shown somehow represents current market values. "Proprietorship" or "proprietor's equity" is satisfactory for businesses owned by a single individual but too restrictive to apply to businesses organized as partnerships or as corporations. The term "capital," although sufficiently broad, may generate confusion because it often describes assets as well as equities. In the remainder of this text, we use the term "owners' equity" as the general description. When appropriate, we can restrict our reference to particular types of business organizations through the use of the terms "proprietor's equity," "partners' equity," or "stockholders' equity." Indeed, the major differences in the accounting records of single proprietorships, partnerships, and corporations lie in the owners' equity section. Since corporations are the dominant form of business organization in this country, we set our discussion in this and subsequent chapters in a corporate framework. Most of it, however, is equally applicable to other forms of business organization.

Two prominent sources of owners' equity exist—direct investment of capital, and retention in the business of additional resources generated from the operations of the firm. The first subdivision of owners' equity denotes the financial interest arising from the voluntary commitment of capital to the business enterprise by its owners in an explicit transaction between these parties. In a corporation, shares of stock are issued to the owners as tangible evidence of their direct investment. Consequently, the caption "capital stock" is used to reflect this particular equity. Any subsequent sales or exchanges of those shares among individual shareholders are irrelevant in measuring owners' equity, because they do not involve the corporate entity as one of the parties to the transaction.

Owners' equity can also increase as a result of activities undertaken by the business entity. For instance, a firm that operates profitably experiences a net increase in assets. Asset increases, usually in the form of cash and accounts receivable, from the sale of goods and services exceed the asset decreases from the consumption of various productive resources. If the board of directors, representing the stockholders, decides not to distribute this net asset increment to the owners, then their total financial interest in the business rises. Retained Earnings is the account used to reflect the additional owners' equity arising from the retention of earned assets in the business. In this sense, retained earnings are a residual, beneficial, and indirect interest, as opposed to the direct capital stock investment. Alternative terms for retained earnings are "earnings reinvested in the business" or "earned surplus," although the latter has lost popularity because of the erroneous impression that the term "surplus" may give.

Similar sources of owners' equity exist in individual proprietorships and in partnerships. The titles used may vary in noncorporate businesses, but the concepts are the same. The owner's equity section of the position statement for Jones Drug Store might be composed of two elements: Jones, Capital, and Jones, Retained Income. These correspond roughly to capital stock and retained earnings in a corporation. However, in partnerships and proprietorships, they often are combined into a single capital account representing the total owner's equity of a particular individual. In Chapter Thirteen we discuss some of the legal and conceptual reasons for maintaining the distinction in corporate businesses.

RELATION OF INCOME MEASUREMENT
TO ASSETS AND EQUITIES

The preceding discussion emphasizes the fact that assets are secured from two activity sources—capital raising and operations. Income measurement deals only with the latter. Our first basic assumption of financial accounting states that net income is best measured by matching expenses against revenues. Revenues represent the total inflow of resources received by the entity as compensation for goods and services rendered to customers during the period. Expenses measure the acquisition cost of the assets consumed or transferred out in providing the goods and services. Net income becomes the net increase in assets.

When we consider inflows and outflows of assets from revenues and expenses in light of the basic accounting equation, an additional aspect of income transactions becomes apparent. Revenues and expenses must cause changes in owners' equity as well. For example, assume a firm sells some merchandise it has in inventory for $500 cash. The merchandise originally cost $350. The asset inflow or revenue from this event obviously is $500; the asset outflow or expense is $350. The firm's total assets increase by the net amount of $150.

However, it is not possible to increase just one side of the accounting equation. Since these asset increases and decreases are unaccompanied by changes in any other assets or liabilities, there has to be a corresponding change in owners' equity. This can be seen in the diagram below:

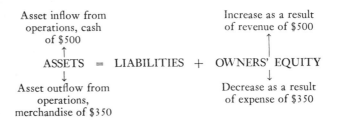

The net increase in assets of $150 is counterbalanced by a net increase in owners' equity of $150, which would appear as retained earnings if a position statement were prepared immediately after this event.

Many individual revenues and expenses cannot be related uniquely to one another as in this example. Rather, the expenses *for the period* are matched against the revenues *for the period*. Nevertheless, we can see that every revenue causes owners' equity to increase temporarily; every expense causes owners' equity to decrease temporarily. For this reason, the owners' financial interest in the business which arises out of income-generating operations is the residual element in the accounting equation. Changes in assets (and liabilities) which are not offset by equal changes in other assets or liabilities effect a change in owners' equity. Consequently, throughout much of this text, we focus on the measurement of assets and liabilities, knowing full well that as long as the accounting equation remains intact, proper measurement of total owners' equity will arise as a by-product.

POSITION STATEMENT OR BALANCE SHEET

We have now discussed in some detail the kinds of items that appear on the position statement. The basic equality of assets and equities is the reason the position statement often is called a "balance sheet." Its purpose, however, is to present financial information, not just to balance. We use the terms "position statement" and "balance sheet" interchangeably.

Illustration of Balance Sheet and Income Statement

Tables 2–1 and 2–2 present the Ampex Corporation's financial statements, taken from the company's actual annual report to shareholders for 1969 with some minor condensation of the detailed information. When the position statement is prepared with the assets on the left side and the equities on the right, it is presented in what is called the *account form*.

TABLE 2–1

AMPEX CORPORATION AND SUBSIDIARIES
Consolidated Balance Sheet
May 3, 1969 and April 27, 1968
(in thousands)

ASSETS

	1969	1968
Current Assets:		
Cash	$ 4,738	$ 4,700
Notes and contracts receivable	10,203	9,052
Accounts receivable	88,766	60,724
Other receivables and claims	1,770	1,409
Inventories:		
Finished goods	29,020	20,738
Work in process	35,934	30,365
Raw materials and parts	33,687	27,343
Prepaid expenses	11,175	9,547
Total Current Assets	$215,293	$163,878
Investments and other assets:		
Investments	$ 17,392	$ 13,626
Noncurrent receivables and other assets	20,381	15,623
Property, plant, and equipment:		
Land and buildings	$ 17,392	$ 14,724
Machinery and equipment	77,140	64,189
	$ 94,532	$ 78,913
Less accumulated depreciation	41,596	36,491
	$ 52,936	$ 42,422
Patents	$ 1,592	$ 1,944
Total Assets	$307,594	$237,493
LIABILITIES AND SHAREHOLDERS' EQUITY		
Current Liabilities:		
Notes payable to banks and commercial paper	$ 25,008	$ 24,600
Accounts payable	25,204	20,536
Accrued liabilities	19,510	13,307
Profit-sharing contribution	3,643	....
Federal and foreign income taxes	14,655	12,839
Current installments on long-term debt	3,235	1,692
Total Current Liabilities	$ 91,255	$ 72,974
Long-term debt	$ 81,454	$ 73,551
Shareowners' Equity:		
Common stock, $1 par value	$ 10,776	$ 9,629
Capital surplus	52,134	23,066
Retained earnings	71,975	58,273
Total Shareowners' Equity	$134,885	$ 90,968
Total Liabilities and Shareholders' Equity	$307,594	$237,493

TABLE 2–2

AMPEX CORPORATION AND SUBSIDIARIES

Consolidated Statement of Net Earnings
Years Ended May 3, 1969 and April 27, 1968
(in thousands)

	1969	1968
Revenue:		
Net sales and operating revenues........	$296,319	$233,433
Equity in net earnings of 50% owned companies.............................	3,959	3,651
	$300,278	$237,084
Costs and expenses:		
Cost of sales and operating expenses................................	$219,750	$180,021
Selling and administrative expenses.....	44,532	37,423
Interest expense.......................	6,689	6,079
Pension and profit-sharing retirement plans...........................	4,191	677
	$275,162	$224,200
Earnings before taxes on income...........	$ 25,116	$ 12,884
Federal and foreign taxes on income.......	11,414	5,219
Net Earnings for the Year................	$ 13,702	$ 7,665

Often, it is more convenient and easier to show detailed classifications if the equities appear below the assets. This arrangement, called the *report form*, has been used for the Ampex balance sheet.

The heading of the balance sheet contains the name of the company, the name of the statement, and the date. Remember that the position statement is like a snapshot; it displays the assets as of a particular date. In this case the annual accounting period does not coincide with the calendar year. Ampex uses a *natural* business year, which corresponds more closely to the natural ebb and flow of its operations. Nevertheless, the balance sheets still are prepared as of the last day of each accounting period.

A few comments about these financial statements are in order. The balance sheet (Table 2–1) is usually issued in comparative form, covering two years, so that the reader can see trends developing or major changes that have taken place in the capital structure (equity sources) and in the deployment of capital in various assets. The term "consolidated" means that the entity for which the statements are prepared is a combination of Ampex Corporation and all the other corporations it owns or controls (subsidiaries).

Observe the equality of assets and equities on the balance sheet. The classification of assets and liabilities conforms quite closely to the traditional arrangements described earlier. Since Ampex Corporation is a manufacturing concern, it has three types of inventory accounts; more is said about these in Chapter Seven. Similarly, the meaning and use of some of the special accounts appearing on the balance sheet, such as Accumulated Depreciation and Capital Surplus, are explained in subsequent chapters.

Table 2–2, the Ampex Corporation's statement of earnings (income statement) summarizes the operating activity during the year. Notice that it consists of revenues and expenses. The net earnings for the year of $13,-702,000 is the amount by which retained earnings increased ($71,975,000 in 1969 less $58,273,000 in 1968). Because net assets increased by this amount during the year *as a result of operations,* owners' equity representing the beneficial interest in these additional resources also increased. Inasmuch as no assets were distributed to the owners (stockholders) in the form of dividends, retained earnings reflect the entire net increase in assets from income-producing activities.

Limitations of the Position Statement

Before moving into a discussion of how to record the assets and equities, let us consider two major limitations of the position statement. An informed reader of financial statements must be aware of what a statement does *not* show as well as what it does.

First, the balance sheet does not indicate the current *value* of the firm's assets or of the firm itself. The amount listed for any individual asset does not necessarily correspond to the market value of that asset. Rather, for many assets the position statement simply shows the unexpired cost of the investment the business entity has made in them. Likewise, the amounts on the equity side, particularly owners' equity, do not reflect values either. This fact is illustrated quite dramatically in the case of Ampex Corporation. The total shareholders' equity shown on the May 3, 1969 balance sheet is $134,885,000. Since there were 10,776,359 shares of stock outstanding, the *book value per share* is about $12.52. The market value of a share of common stock on the New York Stock Exchange on that date was $44.75, almost four times as large!

In addition to the absence of market-value information for the recorded assets, it is also true that many elements of value to a business may never even appear on the position statement. A brand name that has through the years attracted customer loyalty or an industry reputation gained from always providing a quality product would rarely show explicitly as an asset. Yet, if one were attempting to place a value on the entity as an economic unit, these factors certainly would have to be considered. Financial accounting attempts to record only those resources representing a measurable commitment of capital arising out of a definite event or transaction.

The second limitation of the position statement is that it represents just one moment in time. A single position statement may be influenced by seasonal factors or unusual circumstances on a particular day. Although the statement may be accurate, it may not be representative of the typical assets and equities of the firm. In addition, very often we are more interested in changes that have occurred in balance sheet items. Even when presented in comparative form (showing the beginning and end of the year or the end of each of a series of years), position statements do not provide much detail about *why* changes occurred, particularly in the area of operations.

Uses of the Position Statement

The above factors, although limiting the balance sheet, do not destroy its usefulness. It still serves as a statement of financial position as represented by the investments in particular assets and by the financial claims or interests in the entity. Useful knowledge about the past stewardship of invested capital by management and about the solvency of the business can be gleaned from a study of the position statement. By examining the current assets and current liabilities, analysts can reach judgments concerning the entity's short-run ability to meet its financial obligations. A review of the equities reveals the nature of the financial commitments the entity has made and the relative interests of the owners and creditors. Such information may have a bearing on conclusions about the long-run safety of the firm.

By comparing earnings (net income) with the investment shown on the position statement, we can measure the past profitability of the business entity. This relationship of income to investment is called the *rate of return on investment*. It is one of the central measures of the earning power of the firm. For Ampex Corporation, it would be 5 percent for 1969—the net earnings of $13,702,000 divided by the *average* total assets of $272,-543,500. If the value of the business as a unit is in fact much greater than the sum of its assets, this should show up as excess earning power, a higher degree of profitability than other businesses. The balance sheet itself, however, usually does not reflect that total economic value.

SUMMARY

In this chapter we establish the analytical framework for financial accounting. This framework consists of the assets and equities of the business. Different assets represent the varying forms or agents for future service potentials acquired by the firm. Equities denote the sources of service potential and therefore the financial interest of various parties in the business enterprise.

Periodically, the assets and equities (liabilities and owners' equity) are formally presented on a financial statement called a position statement, balance sheet, or statement of financial condition. The arrangement illustrated in this chapter stresses the fundamental relationship

$$Assets = Liabilities + Owners' Equity$$

Classification of items on the position statement is heavily influenced by accounting convention and expediency. The same is true of the format in which the items are presented. However, reasonable subdivisions of asset, liability, and owners' equity items arranged in a clear manner can enhance the usefulness and understandability of the report. Revenues and expenses represent the changes in assets and owners' equity arising from the operating activities of the firm. The income statement summarizes these changes and, in so doing, helps to explain the net increase or decrease in retained earnings that appears on a comparative balance sheet.

Not only does the equality of assets and equities form the basic structure for the position statement, but it also provides the foundation for the recording processes employed in accounting. Each new topic to be discussed in future chapters can be accommodated in the asset-equity classification system. The recording process of double-entry bookkeeping is built on that framework and is the subject of the next chapter.

SUGGESTIONS FOR FURTHER READING

Glickman, Richard, and Stahl, Richard. "The Case of the Misleading Balance Sheet," *Journal of Accountancy,* Vol. 126 (December 1968), pp. 66–72.

Littleton, A. C. "Significance of Invested Cost," *Accounting Review,* Vol. 27 (April 1952), pp. 167–73.

Mauriello, Joseph A. "The Working Capital Concept—A Restatement," *Accounting Review,* Vol. 37 (January 1962), pp. 39–43.

Nelson, Edward G. "The Relation between the Balance Sheet and the Profit-and-Loss Statement," *Accounting Review,* Vol. 17 (April 1942), pp. 132–41.

Zeff, Stephen A. "The Balance Sheet and Income Statement—Analytically Coordinate," *NAA Bulletin,* Vol. 45 (February 1964), pp. 27–31.

QUESTIONS AND PROBLEMS

2–1. Nathan Dimlight has operated his small business for a year. At the end of the year, he presents the following information:

Assets................	$59,000
Liabilities.............	23,000
Capital invested........	40,000

He tells you: "Assets may equal liabilities plus owners' equity for some businesses, but it's not true for mine, unless I fudge the facts."

Explain to Mr. Dimlight why assets do not equal equities for the figures he presents.

2–2. Assets are commonly defined by nonaccountants as "things of value."

a) Explain why this definition is not sufficiently restrictive or practicable for use in accounting. Are there "things of value" that are not classified as accounting assets?

b) How are asset *values* defined in financial accounting? What other definitions could be employed?

2–3. The following items are obtained from the accounting department of the American Corporation as of December 31, 1972:

Accounts receivable.......	$ 3,000	Cash....................	$ 5,000
Land...................	10,000	Merchandise..............	4,000
Wages payable..........	1,000	Accounts payable.........	8,000
Capital stock............	25,000	Building................	40,000
Prepaid insurance........	1,000	Marketable securities......	500
Patents.................	10,000	Equipment..............	8,200
Mortgage bonds payable....	30,000	Retained earnings........ ...	?

a) From the above information, prepare a position statement in acceptable form and determine the proper amount to be shown as retained earnings.

b) Although the position statement balances, it still reflects numerous estimates and fails to reflect the true value of the firm. Explain what items on the statement are subject to estimation and why the statement does not reflect true value.

c) A philosophical professor comments, "All assets should be classified as intangible assets." Explain why, in a sense, he is correct.

2–4. Indicate which of the following items would be classified as assets on an accounting position statement. Give reasons for your answers.

a) Cost of developing and registering a patent.

b) Accounts owed to the firm by customers.

c) Cost of relocating machinery as part of a plant modernization program.

d) Investment in the securities (stocks and bonds) of another firm.

e) Interest earned on a bank account but not yet received in cash.

f) Cost incurred in grading a piece of land to make it suitable for use.

g) Cost of a three-year fire insurance policy.

h) Cash surrender value of a life insurance policy on the president's life. The policy is owned by the corporation, which is the beneficiary.

i) The cost of an old machine in good physical condition but no longer used because of technical obsolescence. It would cost as much to remove it as it could be sold for.

j) Amounts owing to employees for services rendered.

k) The expressway which is located directly in front of the firm's manufacturing plant, thus facilitating shipment of its products by truck.

2–5. For each of the following events, indicate the effect (+, increase; −, decrease; or 0, no change) on assets, liabilities, and owners' equity. Use the following format:

Event	Assets	Liabilities	Owners' Equity
(*a*)	+100,000		+100,000

a) In the formation of a corporation, the owners contribute a building worth $30,000 and cash of $70,000.

b) Office equipment costing $8,000 is purchased. A down payment of $3,000 cash is made, with the balance due in 90 days.

c) Advertising supplies are purchased for $500 on account. Half of them are used in the year of purchase.

d) Merchandise costing $50,000 is purchased on account.

e) Merchandise costing $25,000 is sold on account for $38,000.

f) Sales salaries of $1,500 are paid in cash.

g) Remodeling costs of $5,000 are incurred on the building. The bill must be paid within 90 days.

h) Marketable securities are purchased for $20,000 cash.

i) A $1,000 note is received from a customer to apply against his account receivable.

j) New types of equipment for possible future purchase are investigated.

k) One stockholder who originally invested $3,000 wishes to withdraw from the business. The corporation writes a check for $3,000 and retires (cancels) the stock certificate.

l) Marketable securities originally costing $10,000 are sold for $15,-000 cash.

m) Creditors' accounts in the amount of $30,000 are paid by check.

n) Interest of $800 has built up (accrued) during the period on the remaining marketable securities.

2–6. You have been employed by Mr. John Bath to help organize the financial affairs of the Bubbles Company, a wholesale distributor of children's toys, which he inherited from his Uncle Soapy, who kept very few formal records.

You uncover the following facts. The bank statement shows a balance of $3,800 as of August 31, 1971. No checks have been written since July, when Uncle Soapy died. Consequently, you are reasonably sure that all checks from earlier months have cleared the bank. The cash register contains $80 in currency plus two checks from customers. One check for $800 is dated June 28 and represents payment of an account by a major and excellent customer, Acme Toys. The other check, for $250, is dated January 13, 1965 and is from a customer who died penniless in 1968.

Uncle Soapy kept a list on a large piece of cardboard of people who owed him money. When cash was received, he would cross off the customer's name; new debts would be added at the bottom of the card. As of August 31, the total amount on the card is $8,330 (the $800 account of Acme Toys has not been crossed off because its check has not been cashed yet). The entire $8,330 represents customers' accounts except for a $300 advance to an employee and a $600 note representing a loan to a toy manufacturer. Also attached to the cardboard is a memo stating that two customers are planning to place orders totaling $8,000 in September.

A stack of supplier invoices is kept on a spindle. An analysis of these reveals that $5,200 is owed to suppliers for merchandise and supplies, and $3,000 for store equipment. The equipment had been purchased only recently and remains in the storeroom awaiting unpacking. Also on the spindle is a memo that $5,000 of toys should be ordered from one of the suppliers.

A careful survey of the store indicates merchandise of $43,000 and store supplies of $1,000 on hand. Store equipment currently in use is estimated to be $6,300. Also, advertising displays in the store are found to have been leased for one year beginning on January 1, 1971. The rental fee of $1,800 was paid in January by Uncle Soapy. The store building itself is also rented at a yearly cost of $12,000, payable semiannually. One of the last checks written was for $6,000 on June 28 to cover the second six-month period.

A cigar box full of miscellaneous documents discloses that the Bubbles Company owes the bank $5,000 on a short-term note. This fact is verified by the bank, which indicates that $200 in interest has accrued on the note through August 31. Also in the box are architects' plans for remodeling the store; Mr. Bath estimates that it would cost $2,500 to do the remodeling, but that operating costs would be reduced $3,000 a year as a result. At the bottom of the box are the legal titles to a delivery truck valued at $2,300 and used in the business, and to Uncle Soapy's car, valued at $1,650. The latter, John Bath plans to use as his personal automobile.

a) Prepare a position statement for the Bubbles Company as of August 31, 1971.

b) For any of the items excluded from the statement, explain why.

2–7. Holesale Donuts, Inc. borrowed a substantial amount of money from a local bank. As part of the five-year loan agreement, the company agreed that ". . . current assets as determined by generally accepted accounting principles will exceed current liabilities by $25,000 or the face amount of the loan can be declared payable immediately." The quarterly report to the bank showed current assets of $193,000 and current liabilities of $147,000 on the position statement for Holesale Donut.

The loan auditor at the bank has questioned the inclusion among current assets of the six items listed below. He states that if these items were reclassified, current assets would be only $163,000 and Holesale would be in violation of the agreement.

a) $10,000 of cash and securities which have been set aside as a fund for plant expansion.

b) $2,400 of prepaid insurance representing a three-year fire and theft policy.

c) $4,800 of inventory of spare parts used in the maintenance of the manufacturing equipment.

d) $3,000 noninterest-bearing note receivable from the company's president.

e) $5,600 book value of some old equipment which the company expects to sell for $1,200 next quarter. The equipment was removed from active use in a plant modernization program.

f) $4,200 cash surrender value of a life insurance policy on the president's life. Holesale Donut pays all premiums on the policy and is the beneficiary.

Do you believe the firm is in violation of the agreement? Discuss carefully the proper classification of each of the six items, giving reasons for including or excluding it from the current asset classification.

2–8. On December 31, 1971, the annual report of Brown Company showed its position statement as follows:

Assets		Equities	
Cash...............	$ 7,000	Accounts payable...	$ 5,000
Inventory.........	5,000	Wages payable......	1,000
Investments.......	3,000	Capital stock......	25,000
Land.............	10,000	Retained earnings..	9,000
Equipment.........	15,000		
	$40,000		$40,000

During January, 1972, the following changes took place:

1. Rent on the store building for the months of January and February was paid in cash, $2,000.
2. Interest earned on the investments was received in cash, $100.
3. Merchandise costing $2,500 was sold, $1,500 for cash and $3,000 on account.
4. The company paid the wages owed on December 31 and $1,500 more for labor services used up in January.
5. One half of the land was sold for $5,500. The buyer gave a note receivable to Brown Company.
6. The cost of the equipment used up (depreciation) during January was $1,000.
7. Accounts receivable totaling $1,200 were collected in cash.
8. Accounts payable amounting to $3,000 were paid.

a) Prepare a position statement as of January 31, 1972, in acceptable form, taking into consideration the above changes.

b) Prepare a schedule showing the determination of net income for January. (Note: The net income total should agree with the change in retained earnings).

2–9. In a footnote to its balance sheet as of March 31, 1966, McKesson & Robbins (now Foremost-McKesson, Inc.) explained its classification of wine and liquor inventory and related payables.

Inventories included under the caption ''Current Assets'' are stated at the lower of cost or market and classified as follows:

	1966	1965
Drugs, sundries, laboratory and hospital supplies.....	$ 97,888,269	$ 87,505,261
Wines and liquors..........	45,410,809	43,145,920
Chemicals.................	9,047,650	8,318,360
	$152,346,728	$138,969,541

```
The above inventories of ''wines and liquors'' include
whiskey aging in storage, amounting to approximately
$6,741,000 as at March 31, 1966.
     Included in ''Other Assets'' is liquor inventory, repre-
senting in-bond whiskey aggregating $7,082,242 as at March
31, 1966, which it is anticipated will be bottled subse-
quent to March 31, 1967. The balance of the in-bond
purchase price, shown as ''Liquor Accounts Payable,'' is
payable at time of bottling. (NOTE: These payables were
excluded from current liabilities).
     Inventories in bonded warehouses are exclusive of duty
and/or excise taxes which must be paid to obtain the re-
lease thereof.
```

a) Why do you think the company presented these accounts in this manner? Do you believe it is a reasonable presentation?

b) Relate the "operating cycle" concept to this presentation.

c) What relationship does the going-concern assumption have to the classification of assets and liabilities as current or noncurrent?

2–10. Hardy Lee Able, upon graduation from college, decided to establish a coffee house near his alma mater. He took a small inheritance of $15,-000 and opened a bank account for the business. On July 1, he made the following cash payments: six months' rent on a building, $6,000; kitchen supplies, $2,000; and an inventory of various blends of exotic coffees, $800. Also on that date he purchased $8,000 worth of furniture (tables, chairs, rugs, bamboo mats for the customers to sit on, etc.). He paid $2,000 in cash and gave a $6,000 note to the supplier for the balance.

During July, Hardy operated the coffee house but kept no formal accounting records. All sales and wages were received and paid in cash. During the month, he invested an additional $3,000 of his own funds. At the end of July, the bank balance stood at $4,300. All but $1,000 of the note payable had been paid off during the month. His inventories of coffees and kitchen supplies amounted to $400 and $1,400, respectively. He owed $200 for coffee purchases during the month which were not paid in cash, $100 to the college newspaper for advertisements run during July, and $300 to an electric sign company for a neon sign purchased and installed on July 31. As a promotional scheme, books of coupons that could be redeemed for various types of coffee were sold. Hardy estimated that $150 of these coupon books were still outstanding. He felt that $100 was a proper estimate of the monthly charge for the use of the furniture.

a) Prepare a position statement on July 1, taking into account the above data.

b) Prepare a second position statement as of July 31.

c) How successful was the venture during the month? How do you know?

2–11. The following items represent a complete list of assets and equities of Listless Enterprises, Inc. as of June 30, 1972:

Claims of suppliers for amounts due them for merchandise..... $ 96,000
Plant location site....................................   24,000
Promissory notes owed to insurance company (due on
    July 1, 1975)...   13,000
Warehouse lease payment (for six months)...............   9,000
Bank loan payable in 60 days...........................   16,000
Investment in U.S. government 90-day securities...........   1,800
Interest accrued on loans and notes......................   1,200
Checking account in bank.............................   3,700
Claims on customers for products sold...................   52,000
Unexpired insurance premiums.........................   2,000
Finished products awaiting sale........................   40,000
Estimated amount owed to federal government for income
    taxes...   24,000
Capital contributed by stockholders......................   130,000
Buildings..   101,000
Cash set aside for construction of building addition..........   40,000
Unused supplies......................................   1,400
Commissions owed to salesmen on products already sold.....   900
Increase in owners' equity from periodic operations.........   ?
Equipment...   28,000
Amount spent to acquire patent rights...................   9,000
Deposits received from customers to cover future servicing
    of products sold....................................   6,000

Using the above data, prepare a position statement in a form suitable for formal reporting, employing proper account titles.

CHAPTER THREE

COLLECTING FINANCIAL INFORMATION

IN THE preceding chapter the analytical framework for financial accounting is organized around the basic equation

$$\text{Assets} = \text{Liabilities} + \text{Owners' Equity}$$

This identity, when presented in statement form, results in the position statement as of a particular moment in time. Of course, business activity is not static. Assets and equities are continually changing as the result of various events affecting the entity. The position statement prepared yesterday becomes inaccurate with the first transaction of today. It would be highly impractical to prepare a new position statement each time an asset or equity changes. Consequently, we now need to develop some procedures for recording in a systematic way the changes in these items.

Two general types of information about business transactions and events are desirable. First, we want to keep a separate record of each event that transpires. In this manner, we have a chronological history of the transactions that affect the business enterprise. Secondly, we want to record the changes that take place in individual assets and equities as the result of the various transactions. To provide this dual information, two basic recording media are used in accounting—journals and ledgers. Journals report the transactions as they occur. Ledgers are used to accumulate the effects of various transactions on individual asset, liability, and owners' equity items. In a journal the transaction itself is the focal point of the recording function; in a ledger the individual assets and equities become the center of attention.

52

Although journals and ledgers constitute the bookkeeping instruments in accounting, our primary interest in them is not as recording devices per se but rather as tools of analysis and communication. Therefore, elaborate journal and ledger forms are not set forth here. Nonetheless, a study of the purposes and operation of the journal and ledger can provide an orderly method for analyzing accounting information and a concise means of communicating the results of that analysis.

LEDGER ACCOUNTS

Let us first look at the ledger. A separate ledger account is established for each asset, each liability, and each element of owners' equity. These ledger accounts represent the heart of the recording system. Ultimately, all accounting changes are entered in these accounts. The whole group of individual ledger accounts is called the general ledger. In a manual accounting system the general ledger usually consists of a loose-leaf binder, with each ledger account comprising a separate page.

Within the general ledger the individual accounts are identified by both title and number. Numbered accounts can be classified into various subgroupings and arranged in logical sequence. Moreover, a numbering system facilitates the recording process, particularly with machine accounting methods.

FIGURE 3–1

Account Title   Account No.

Date	Explanation	PR	Amount	Date	Explanation	PR	Amount

Ledger accounts usually are divided into two sides. The left half of the account is called the debit side; the right half is called the credit side. To debit (or to charge) an account means to make an entry on the left side of the ledger account; crediting the account means the opposite— making a right-hand entry. A formal ledger account in a simple accounting system might look like Figure 3–1. Notice that the details of the debit and credit sides of the account are the same, each containing a place for the date, room for any explanatory material, and a money column. The small column labeled PR (posting reference) indicates the source of the information entered in the account. Its use is explained more fully later in the chapter.

For analytical and communicative purposes, we do not have to be concerned with the precise format of a ledger account. For our purpose the essential element of a ledger account is the two sides, one for entering increases and the other for decreases. Consequently, in subsequent chapters we use an abbreviated facsimile of the ledger account, called a T account. It is illustrated below.

Title

Debit (Dr.)	Credit (Cr.)

Rules for Entering Transactions

We now are ready to establish a procedure for recording in ledger accounts the changes in assets, liabilities, and owners' equity. The following rules are used in entering transactions in the ledger accounts:

Asset accounts:
1. Increases are recorded by making left-hand or debit entries.
2. Decreases are recorded by making right-hand or credit entries.

Equity accounts (liabilities and owners' equity):
1. Increases are recorded by making right-hand or credit entries.
2. Decreases are recorded by making left-hand or debit entries.

Although these rules are arbitrary, in the sense that they could be changed without impairment to the theoretical framework of accounting, following them provides a very simple, effective recording system with built-in checks and balances. The short time necessary to memorize these rules will more than pay for itself in added ability to understand, analyze, and communicate accounting data. Expressed in a slightly different way, the rules are:[1]

Debit	*Credit*
1. Records increases in assets.	1. Records decreases in assets.
2. Records decreases in liabilities.	2. Records increases in liabilities.
3. Records decreases in owners' equity.	3. Records increases in owners' equity.

---

[1] It is clear from the above rules that the terms "debit" and "credit," when used in accounting, refer only to left and right, respectively. They do not consistently indicate either increase or decrease, because how they affect an account varies with the type of account. Nor should any favorable or unfavorable connotations be ascribed to the terms.

Illustration of Ledger Entries

By following the effect of various transactions on a few individual accounts, we can see how the system operates. Two different types of assets and a liability account serve as our examples.

Inventory Account. Assume that the following four transactions affect this asset during the period:

1. Inventory costing $500 is purchased on open account.
2. Inventory with a cost of $50 is found to be unsatisfactory and is returned to the supplier.
3. Additional inventory worth $700 is purchased for cash.
4. Inventory costing $400 is sold to customers.

These transactions would be entered in the ledger account as follows:[2]

Inventory

(1)	500	(2)	50
(3)	700	(4)	400

The first and third transactions cause the asset to increase and therefore are recorded on the left or debit side. The second and fourth transactions are credited to the account, since, according to the rules, decreases in assets are recorded on the right-hand side of the ledger. Of course, other accounts besides Inventory are also affected by such transactions. For example, the first one involves an increase in a liability account, Accounts Payable (credit entry). The Cash account is credited also, as a result of transaction 3, since that asset decreases when the inventory goes up. The purpose of an individual asset or equity ledger account, however, is to record the changes to that account caused by a number of transactions.

At the end of the period, the remaining inventory should appear as an asset on the position statement. The amount is determined by calculating the balance in the account. A comparison of the debit and credit entries reveals that the Inventory account has a debit balance of $750 ($1,200 − $450). This is to be expected. If any asset remains on hand at the end of the period, the increases (debits) must have exceeded the decreases (credits). For the same reason, liability and owners' equity accounts normally have credit balances.

Usually once a year the ledger accounts are formally balanced and ruled. The balance is entered on the opposite side of the account, and the two sides are totaled. Then, after the account is ruled, the balance is

---

[2] The identifying numbers in parentheses are used for illustrative purposes only and would not actually appear in practice. With T accounts, the use of key numbers and letters enables us to identify individual transactions. In a sense, they take the place of dates and other information recorded in a formal ledger account.

brought down on the correct side as the opening balance for the following period. This procedure is illustrated below for the Inventory account. A check mark (√) indicates that no new transaction is being recorded.

Inventory

(1)	500	(2)	50
(3)	700	(4)	400
		√Balance	750
	1,200		1,200
√Balance	750		

Balancing and ruling an account, of course, are mechanical processes and are often done by machine. They serve a useful purpose in an actual bookkeeping system by differentiating in the ledger accounts the entries of different accounting periods. The only *analytical* purpose served by these procedures is formally to emphasize an algebraic truism—the beginning balance plus the additions to an account equal the deductions from the account plus the ending balance $(0 + \$1,200 = \$450 + \$750)$. Often, we have occasion to use this equality to reconstruct various accounts when necessary to determine information that otherwise would not be directly available.

Equipment Account. Increases (debits) and decreases (credits) to an asset account may represent physical changes, as in the inventory example, or may reflect less apparent changes in economic usefulness. The asset account Equipment is an example. The types of items normally debited and credited to that account are indicated in the ledger account below.

Equipment

Invoice price	Depreciation
Freight charges	
Installation cost	

The total cost of an asset consists of the sum of all costs incurred to acquire the service potential of the asset. Although the freight charges and installation costs may cause little physical change in the asset, they do increase the use value of the equipment. Consequently, they are properly charged to the left side of the Equipment account. Likewise, as the equipment is used, a portion of that service potential expires. The total cost of the equipment should be allocated to the various accounting periods in which it is consumed. In each period a portion of the cost should be removed from the asset account to reflect this use. Such a periodic allocation of cost is called *depreciation*. The depreciation charge is credited to the asset account in each accounting period, for, even though the asset may not change a great deal physically, economically part of its service potential has been utilized.[3]

Accounts Payable Account. One more example, an equity account, should suffice to illustrate basic ledger entries. At the beginning of the period the company owes $5,000 to its suppliers from purchases in preceding periods. During the current period the following events occur:

1. Supplies costing $3,000 are purchased on account.
2. Checks are written in payment of invoices totaling $5,800.
3. A note payable of $400 is given to one supplier to substitute for an existing account payable.

The entries necessary to record the effect of these events on the liability account Accounts Payable are shown in the following ledger account. The first entry is a credit, because the liability account is increasing. The other two cause decreases in the liability and therefore are entered on the left-hand (debit) side. The account has a credit balance of $1,800 at the end of the period.

Accounts Payable

(2)	5,800	√Balance	5,000
(3)	400	(1)	3,000
√Balance	1,800		
	8,000		8,000
		√Balance	1,800

ACCOUNTING TRANSACTIONS

We now have both a conceptual and a procedural framework in which to record business events. The conceptual framework consists of the Assets = Equity identity; the procedural framework includes the system of ledger accounts and the rules for making entries in them.

Accounting transactions comprise those events involving the business entity which cause a measurable change in asset or equity accounts. For example, offers to buy and sell (purchase orders and sales orders) normally do not constitute accounting transactions. A customer may indicate that he plans to buy a large quantity of merchandise. However, only the payment of cash in advance, the delivery of the merchandise, or the creation of a legal claim for payment (accounts receivable) would trigger the making of an entry in the accounting records. The fact that no ac-

---

[3] In Chapter Four, we modify this procedure of crediting the asset account directly for the depreciation charge. The modification, however, is made for practical reasons and does not change the concept of depreciation as the using up of a noncurrent asset.

counting entry is made does not mean that the event is unimportant. A backlog of sales orders may be a significant factor in a particular business. It is one, however, that does not fit immediately into the information-reporting system of financial accounting.

Accounting transactions normally are of two types—external and internal. The former consist of express dealings between the business entity and some external party. Purchasing merchandise, borrowing money from a bank, incurring a liability for labor services received, etc., are examples of external transactions. Usually they are readily apparent. Internal transactions are changes in assets and equities which do not involve an outside party. Depreciation (using up the service potential of noncurrent assets) and the gradual expiration of prepaid insurance are examples. In this chapter most of the accounting transactions are of the external variety. In Chapter Four we record numerous internal transactions. Both types, however, must meet a fundamental criterion: a measurable change in assets or equities must have occurred.

Nine Basic Types of Transactions

Every business transaction entered in the accounting records must retain the basic equality of assets and equities. Inasmuch as every property right has a corresponding source or claim, no transaction can arise which will invalidate the equality of the two sides of the accounting equation. Given this identity, with the three different types of accounts—assets, liabilities, and owners' equity—only nine possible basic transactions can occur and still keep the position statement equation inviolate. Some of these nine occur only infrequently. However, in order to convey a complete picture and to further the understanding of ledger-account analysis, let us illustrate each of these possibilities with an actual entry.

Table 3–1 gives a complete picture of the nine possible combinations of increases and decreases. Notice in each case that the two sides of the equation balance. A transaction involves either changes in the same direction affecting opposite sides of the equation, or changes in opposite

TABLE 3–1

Summary of Basic Transactions

	Assets	=	Liabilities	+	Owners' Equity
1.	+				+
2.	+		+		
3.	(+)(−)				
4.	−				−
5.	−		−		
6.			(+)(−)		
7.			+		−
8.			−		+
9					(+)(−)

directions affecting the same side of the equation. An example is given below for each type of transaction. Notice that the increases and decreases in the ledger-account examples have been recorded in conformity with the rules given on page 54.

1. Asset Increase, Owners' Equity Increase. A corporation receives cash of $50,000 from a group of investors and issues shares of stock as evidence of the ownership interest.

Cash			Capital Stock
50,000			50,000

2. Asset Increase, Liability Increase. The corporation buys a new piece of machinery costing $13,000 but does not pay for it immediately.

Machinery			Accounts Payable
13,000			13,000

3. Asset Increase, Asset Decrease. In this type of entry one asset is replaced by another asset. No change occurs on the equity side. The purchase of $3,000 of merchandise for cash is an example. (The xxx indicates that a balance is assumed to be in existence already.)

Merchandise		Cash	
3,000		√xxx	3,000

4. Asset Decrease, Owners' Equity Decrease. If the owners withdraw assets from the business, their financial interest is correspondingly reduced. Although it is not impossible for the owners to withdraw their original capital contributions, in most cases the assumption is made that the assets withdrawn have arisen from profitable operations. Consequently, the owners' equity account reduced is usually Retained Earnings. In a corporation, withdrawal of assets (usually cash) is accomplished by the payment of dividends to stockholders. Assume that cash dividends of $7,000 are paid out.

Cash		Retained Earnings	
√xxx	7,000	7,000	√xxx

5. *Asset Decrease, Liability Decrease.* The company pays its outstanding accounts of $1,600.

Cash		Accounts Payable	
√xxx	1,600	1,600	√xxx

6. *Liability Increase, Liability Decrease.* This relatively rare type of transaction arises when one liability, say a note payable, is substituted for another liability, perhaps an account payable. If a $2,000 note were given to cancel an open account of the same amount, the entry would be:

Notes Payable		Accounts Payable	
	2,000	2,000	√xxx

7. *Liability Increase, Owners' Equity Decrease.* In large corporations, dividends are usually declared some time prior to their actual distribution in cash. At the time of declaration a legal liability is created. A portion of owners' equity is transformed into creditors' equity. Assume that the $7,000 of dividends mentioned in item 4 is declared but made payable at some later date.

Dividends Payable		Retained Earnings	
	7,000	7,000	√xxx

Then, when the cash payment is actually made, the entry is of the type illustrated in item 5—asset decrease, liability decrease.

8. *Owners' Equity Increase, Liability Decrease.* Again, this transaction is rare, arising only when some element of creditors' equity is replaced by an ownership interest. Occasionally, bonds payable (liability) are issued which can be exchanged for (converted into) stock at the investors' option. If and *when* any of the bonds are converted, the liability ceases, and shares of capital stock are issued. The entry to record such a conversion of $30,000 of bonds is:

Capital Stock		Bonds Payable	
	√ xxx 30,000	30,000	√xxx

9. Owners' Equity Increase, Owners' Equity Decrease. This rare transaction involves a reclassification of some portion of owners' equity from one account to another. The main instance of it is the "stock dividend," when additional shares of stock are given to the stockholders without any additional capital contribution on their part. More is said about this phenomenon in Chapter Thirteen. For the time being, let us simply illustrate the entry. Assume that the amount is $10,000.

Capital Stock		Retained Earnings	
	√ xxx	10,000	√xxx
	10,000		

Equality of Debits and Credits

These nine types of entries are the only possible basic transactions that can occur and still retain the equality of assets and equities. Of course, complex transactions may occur involving a number of asset, liability, and owners' equity accounts. Nevertheless, even the most complicated accounting events can be broken down into a combination of two or more of these nine basic types.

A quick review of these transactions reveals one trait in common: each recording involves equal debits and credits. Although the rules for increasing and decreasing accounts seem arbitrary, they ensure that the left-hand entries always equal the right-hand entries. For all nine of the basic types of transactions, every debit has a corresponding credit. Since all transactions consist of one or a combination of the basic types, the total dollar value of the debits must agree with the total dollar value of the credits for any given transaction, regardless of the number of individual accounts involved. And since each transaction involves equal debits and credits, it follows that the total of all debit balances in accounts at the end of the period will equal the total of all accounts with credit balances.

This particular method of recording is known as *double-entry bookkeeping*, since every transaction has at least two aspects—a debit and a credit. Contrast this system with a single-entry one, which most of us practice when we keep the stubs on our checkbooks. On the stub we maintain a running record of the increases and decreases in the asset Cash in Bank. However, for each change in the cash account, there exists a corresponding change in some other asset, liability, or owners' equity which normally goes unrecorded. The double-entry system provides a powerful tool for insuring that a complete analysis of each transaction is made and for checking the numerical accuracy of the analysis. Most bookkeeping systems used by businesses of some size and complexity are based on the double-entry principle.

TRANSACTIONS INVOLVING REVENUE AND EXPENSE

In the framework provided through double-entry bookkeeping, we can record any accounting transaction, including those associated with profitable or unprofitable operations. The main objective of a business entity is to increase the total stock of resources by receiving more in assets through the sale of a product or service than is used up in providing the product or service to the customer. Let us see how this kind of activity can be analyzed with the tools developed to this point.

It is clear from discussions in earlier chapters that the conceptual approach to income measurement in accounting is one of relating particular asset inflows (revenues) and asset outflows (expenses). From the standpoint of income measurement, our concern is with those asset changes during the period broadly connected with operating activities. However, asset accounts are used to record *all* changes during the period. While revenues represent a source of assets, not all inflows of cash or other assets necessarily represent revenues. Similarly, while expenses represent a use of assets, not all outflows of cash or other assets necessarily represent expenses. Effectively to measure net income only through asset accounts would require an analysis of each one to determine which of the asset inflows and outflows are relevant.

Direct Reflection in Retained Earnings

In Chapter Two we observe that asset increases and decreases from revenue and expense transactions cause corresponding increases and decreases in owners' equity. So whenever assets come into the firm from the sale of products or services, an equal increase in owners' equity could be recorded by a credit to Retained Earnings. The converse is true with expenses. As an asset is consumed in the generation of revenues, the asset could be credited, and Retained Earnings could be debited to reflect the equal decrease in owners' equity.

Illustration. Assume that during the month of March the following transactions take place:

1. Quality Products Company is organized. Stockholders invest $10,000 in cash and receive shares of stock.
2. The company leases a building, paying $1,000 in cash for a month's rent.
3. Merchandise costing $12,000 is purchased on account.
4. Two salesmen are hired at a cost of $1,500 each for the month, paid in cash.
5. The firm sells half of the merchandise, receiving $5,000 in cash and $7,000 of accounts receivable.

The first four transactions are relatively easy to analyze and require little explanation. Each one involves increasing some asset, with either an accompanying increase in owners' equity (item 1), an increase in a liability (item 3), or a decrease in another asset (items 2 and 4).

Transaction 5 relates to the profit-making endeavors of the firm during the month. As a result of the period's activities, certain assets flow into the business. These are cash and accounts receivable. At the same time, other resources—merchandise, prepaid rent, and salesmen's services—are being consumed or given up in making the sales. One way of recording these events is to debit and credit Retained Earnings directly, to reflect the changes in owners' equity corresponding to the individual asset outflows and inflows relating to operations. For example, the cash sale of product could be recorded as a debit to Cash and a credit to Retained Earnings. Likewise, the credit sale could be recorded separately by debiting Accounts Receivable and crediting Retained Earnings. These transactions are of the "asset increase, owners' equity increase" type. Likewise, whenever assets are consumed, Retained Earnings could be debited and the respective asset credited (asset decrease, owners' equity decrease). Table 3-2 shows the results of recording these transactions in ledger ac-

TABLE 3-2

Cash				Merchandise				Accounts Payable		
(1)	10,000	(2)	1,000	(3)	12,000	(5d)	6,000	√	12,000	(3)	12,000
(5a)	5,000	(4)	3,000			√	6,000			√	12,000
		√	11,000		12,000		17,000				
	15,000		15,000	√	6,000						
√	11,000										

Accounts Receivable				Prepaid Rent				Capital Stock		
(5b)	7,000	√	7,000	(2)	1,000	(5e)	1,000	√	10,000	(1)	10,000
√	7,000									√	10,000

Salesmen's Services				Retained Earnings		
(4)	3,000	(5c)	3,000	(5c)	3,000	(5a)	5,000
				(5d)	6,000	(5b)	7,000
				(5e)	1,000		
				√	2,000		
					12,000		12,000
						√	2,000

counts. The ending balance of $2,000 in Retained Earnings reflects the result of matching revenue and expense transactions for the month. The excess of assets gained ($12,000) over assets used ($10,000) causes owners' equity to increase.

If the firm operates unprofitably, the opposite situation occurs. Asset decreases exceed asset increases. Accordingly, the corresponding decreases in owners' equity, which are recorded on the left side of Retained Earnings, would exceed the increases recorded on the credit or right-hand side. On the position statement the negative balance in Retained Earnings is subtracted from Capital Stock and is termed a *deficit*.

Uses of Revenue and Expense Accounts

It is clear from the foregoing discussion that in the actual bookkeeping and accounting system, the income-measurement concept is implemented by a matching of increases and decreases in owners' equity which mirror those particular increases and decreases in assets from operating transactions. Although entering these owners' equity changes directly in Retained Earnings is conceptually sound, it is not the actual procedure employed in financial accounting because of the excessive number of entries made in this one account. Instead, new temporary accounts, called revenue and expense accounts, are introduced in the accounting system to aid in the recording of income-producing transactions.

As assets from the sale of products and services flow in, the asset accounts are debited, with the corresponding credit going to a separate revenue account. When asset outflows relating to the production of revenues are recorded, the assets are credited, and a special expense account is debited. Revenue accounts measure the relevant asset inflows, thereby reflecting the accomplishment of the firm. Expense accounts reflect the applicable asset consumptions, measuring the effort of the entity. Therefore, revenue and expense accounts represent the tools for implementing the matching concept stated in the first assumption. Although the theory is based on asset changes, the accomplishment occurs through owners' equity changes.

Reasons for Revenue and Expense Accounts. The primary reason for the use of revenue and expense accounts in lieu of direct entries to Retained Earnings is to provide additional, more detailed, and better classified information about the conduct of the periodic operating affairs of the firm. Owners, creditors, managers, and others need knowledge about the nature of the changes between position statement dates, not just the end results. Recording directly in Retained Earnings conceals the individual asset changes. How much of the asset increase has resulted from the sale of products, from interest earned on investments, from rental income, etc.? How does the cost of the merchandise sold compare with the selling price? What is the relationship between the selling expenses and the dollar amount of sales in the current period? What other assets have been consumed during the period, and in what amounts? These and similar questions cannot be answered easily when all operating activities are commingled in Retained Earnings. The detailed information necessary to evaluate performance is not readily available. When separate ledger accounts are maintained for each type of revenue and expense, asset flows can be properly classified and summarized.

Revenue and expense accounts also enable us to record asset changes separately, without having to match revenues and expenses on each individual sale. Even when some of the costs applicable to each sale could be determined, as is the case with merchandise, it may be extremely inconvenient to record the asset outflow at the time of sale. Consider the situation of a large supermarket. A credit to the Merchandise account is normally made only at the end of the accounting period rather than as each customer passes the check-out clerk.[4] The latter procedure would be too difficult and time-consuming. Revenue and expense accounts provide a procedure within the double-entry framework to record each asset inflow and outflow relating to operations at the time it occurs or whenever it is convenient. The asset changes can be entered independently of one another. Then net income is measured by the excess of revenues over expenses for any given *period of time*.

Illustration. In Table 3–2 we used only position statement accounts to register the transactions for Quality Products Company during the month of March. In Table 3–3 we use revenue and expense accounts to record the *same* transactions. The fifth transaction, summarizing the operating activities of the period, has been broken down into its separate components. Notice that, as assets are received from operations (items 5a and 5b), a revenue account is credited. And as each asset is used up during the period (items 5c, 5d, and 5e), a separate expense account is debited. In

TABLE 3–3

Cash				Accounts Payable				Sales Revenue			
(1)	10,000	(2)	1,000			(3)	12,000			(5a)	5,000
(5a)	5,000	(4)	3,000							(5b)	7,000

Accounts Receivable				Capital Stock				Cost of Goods Sold			
(5b)	7,000					(1)	10,000	(5d)	6,000		

[4] The cost of merchandise sold for the period is determined by counting the merchandise left at the end of the period (taking a physical inventory) and subtracting its cost from the total cost of merchandise available for sale.

TABLE 3–3 (continued)

Merchandise		Salesmen's Services		Selling Expense	
(3) 12,000	(5d) 6,000	(4) 3,000	(5c) 3,000	(5c) 3,000	

Prepaid Rent				Rent Expense	
(2) 1,000	(5e) 1,000			(5e) 1,000	

this manner we can accumulate in these special retained earnings accounts additional information about the nature of the period's activities.

Relationship to Owners' Equity. It is clear from the foregoing discussion and illustration that these new accounts are merely temporary owners' equity accounts. Specifically, they are temporary retained earnings accounts, reflecting particular types of periodic changes in owners' equity. Revenue accounts record tentative increases in owners' equity, because assets—usually cash or some type of receivable—are received from the sale of a product or service. Expense accounts, on the other hand, record the tentative decreases in owners' equity because assets are consumed, used up, or given up in operations.

Being owners' equity accounts, revenues and expenses follow the rules for increasing and decreasing equities. Revenue accounts are normally credited, inasmuch as they are positive items of owners' equity; and expense accounts, reflecting negative changes in owners' equity, are normally debited.

With the introduction of revenue and expense accounts, the accounting equation is expanded:

$$\text{Assets} = \text{Liabilities} + \text{Owners' Equity} \begin{cases} \text{Capital Stock} \\ \quad \text{plus} \\ \text{Retained Earnings} \begin{cases} \text{Revenues} \\ \text{less} \\ \text{Expenses} \end{cases} \end{cases}$$

Revenue accounts temporarily substitute for the credit side of Retained Earnings and expense accounts for the debit side.

The revenue and expense accounts by nature are single-period accounts. Their function is to collect information applicable to the operations of one period. At the end of the period their balances are summarized, and the net result is recorded in Retained Earnings.[5] For this reason, they are often called *nominal* owners' equity accounts, as contrasted with

---

[5] The procedure to accomplish this is called closing the books and is described in the next chapter.

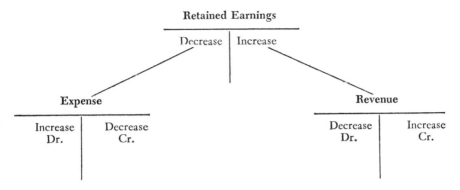

Capital Stock and Retained Earnings. Referring to the distinction made in Chapter One between status reports (position statements) and change reports (income statements), we can say that, with respect to owners' equity, Capital Stock and Retained Earnings are the status accounts, and the revenues and expenses are the change accounts.

The Income Statement

We have been discussing procedures for analyzing and recording those periodic activities of the business directed toward the generation of net income. Chapter One indicates that the income statement is the financial report used to show the amount and kind of revenues and expenses and the difference between them, which we call net income or net loss. A simplified format for the income statement is given in Table 3–4. The figures are based on Table 3–3.

TABLE 3–4

QUALITY PRODUCTS COMPANY

Income Statement for the Month of March

Revenue:		
Sales of product......................		$12,000
Expenses:		
Cost of goods sold...................	$6,000	
Selling expense.......................	3,000	
Rent expense.........................	1,000	10,000
Net Income (retained in the business) ..		$ 2,000

The heading of the income statement contains the name of the business entity and the period covered by the statement. The latter point is particularly important. A $2,000 net income for the month of March is quite different from a $2,000 net income for the year. Every figure on the income statement, under the concept of the accounting period, relates to a particular, ascertainable time span. The length of the period may vary with the needs of the business and the desires of the audience.

Recent years have seen a trend toward greater emphasis on the income statement. Because it provides the major source of information about periodic operating activities, it tends to become the focal point. In practice, the amounts on the balance sheet often becomes residuals, resulting from income determination decisions. Nevertheless, the two statements are very closely related. For the owners' equity section of the position statement, the association is direct. The income statement is a summarized analysis of changes in retained earnings due to the current period's operations. The income statement ties together the retained earnings amounts shown on the beginning-of-the-period and end-of-the-period statements (if there have been no distributions to the owners).

Costs and Expenses

One special problem in interpreting expense accounts is clearly understanding the relationship between costs and expenses. A lack of insight into this important relationship may not only cause conceptual difficulties but can lead to terminology confusion as well.

Sometimes the terms are used interchangeably in financial statements. Nevertheless, "cost" is the broader term and can be used as a synonym for the term "asset." Cost is the amount of cash or cash equivalent given up to acquire property or service rights. It is the monetary sacrifice arising out of an *expenditure* decision. Expenses then refer to those costs (assets) which are consumed during the period in the production of revenues. Expenses can be viewed as *expired costs* or expired assets. In this sense, expense is a subcategory of cost—that portion which will be matched against the revenues of the particular accounting period. An expenditure, on the other hand, refers to the acquisition of a productive resource, regardless of when consumed.

In tracing the life of a cost, it is first necessary to record the acquisition of the asset (incurrence of cost). After acquisition, several things can happen to an asset—nothing, conversion into another asset, use to liquidate a liability, or consumption in an attempt to generate revenue. Only in the last instance is there an expense. From the standpoint of eventual periodic income measurement, then, we are concerned with two stages in the life of most assets—acquisition and consumption (expiration). When an asset is acquired, a debit entry is made to the asset account, with a corresponding credit, usually to cash or some liability account. When the asset is *consumed in the production of revenue,* a credit entry is made to the asset and a debit entry to an expense account.

In the case of some costs, the period in which they are consumed in the production of revenues is the same as the period of incurrence. For example, the salary cost of a deliveryman for the month of August is applicable to the revenues during that month. We cannot store these services for later consumption. They will be consumed, thus becoming an August expense. Similarly, the monthly rental payment on a building applies only to the particular month for which it is made. In these cases the cost incurred during the period is the same as the cost consumed during the period. The bookkeeping is simplified, with no practical objections, by recording the expense at the time the asset is acquired. If we know that an asset will in all probability become an expense during the period in which it is acquired, we often debit it directly to an expense account.

This shortcut can be employed in the case of salesmen's services in the example in Table 3–3. When the cash is paid out, a single entry can be made:

Cash		Selling Expense	
$\sqrt{}$xxx	3,000	3,000	

An expense can be recognized at the time of use because use is related to the current period's revenues. Theoretically, a more accurate portrayal of what happens is reflected in the *two* entries in Table 3–3. An asset or productive resource is acquired; then it is consumed in the generation of revenue. The single entry, however, eliminates the formal recording of the asset acquisition. Similar examples include other types of periodic services which very probably will become expenses entirely in the period of incurrence—rent, insurance, and maybe even supplies.

Obviously, this shortcut generally would not apply to assets which are used in more than one accounting period (those that appear on the position statement). The cost of buildings, equipment, merchandise, and prepayments extends over more than one accounting period. Therefore, these assets are normally handled in at least two steps—acquisition and expiration. Nor should this bookkeeping shortcut be allowed to confuse the fundamental relationship between cost (asset) and expense. Neither the payment of cash nor the incurrence of a liability necessarily gives rise to the expense, although the recording procedures used may leave that impression. Expenditure and expense are synonymous only when the asset expires in the same period in which it is acquired. When that occurs, an expense account may be debited directly to facilitate the recording and classifying functions.

JOURNALS

Let us now turn to the other recording medium used in accounting, the journal. In the preceding section transactions are entered directly in the ledger accounts. In a more realistic situation, with hundreds of different ledger accounts, this procedure becomes unwieldy. In making entries directly in the individual ledger accounts, we lose the identity of the individual transaction. A particular ledger account contains only one part of a transaction. Consequently, relating individual debits and credits in various ledger accounts to one another in order to reconstruct the separate events of the period becomes almost an impossibility.

Therefore, to maintain a record of each transaction intact, we first record them in a journal. Each recording of an accounting event in the journal is called a journal entry. The use of a journal in addition to the ledger provides three advantages. First, the journal furnishes a chronological history of the period's activities. Second, a complete record is available concerning the entirety of each transaction. And finally, room usually exists in the journal to include explanatory information about the entry.

General Journal

Because transactions are first recorded in journals, the latter are often called books of original entry. Then, by a process called *posting*, the debits and credits indicated in the journal entries are entered in the respective ledger accounts. The simplest journal is the two-column general journal shown in Table 3–5. We shall use the example in the preceding section to illustrate the journalizing and posting process.

When journal entries are made, the accounts to be debited are normally listed first, with the credits following and indented. When more than one account is being debited or credited, the entry is called a compound journal entry. The dollar amounts are entered in the respective money columns. The use of the *PR* column is explained shortly. Under each entry is an explanation giving detailed information about it. Usually the explanations are much more specific and therefore more meaningful than the ones illustrated in Table 3–5.

Posting

Posting involves taking the component parts of the journal entries and transcribing them to the individual ledger accounts. To post the debit to Cash, for example, in the first entry, the bookkeeper selects the ledger page or card for the Cash account and enters $10,000 on the debit side. Also, in the *PR* (posting reference) column of the ledger account, the journal page number (and the particular journal if more than one journal is used) is entered to indicate the source of the ledger entry. Then, in the *PR* column (also sometimes labeled *LF* for ledger folio) of the journal, the account number of the Cash account is entered. This provides a convenient cross-reference between ledger and journal and indicates which items in the latter are yet to be posted. To illustrate this procedure, a formal ledger account for Cash (see Table 3–6) is shown, and the *portions*

TABLE 3–5

General Journal

Page 3

Date	Accounts	PR	Debit	Credit
1971				
Mar. 1	Cash......................	4	10,000	
	Capital Stock.........			10,000
	Issuance of shares to original investors.			
Mar. 1	Prepaid Rent.............		1,000	
	Cash.................	4		1,000
	One month's lease on store building on Elm Street.			
Mar. 2	Merchandise..............		12,000	
	Accounts Payable......			12,000
	Invoice No. 8079 received from Acme Wholesale Suppliers.			
Mar. 2	Selling Expense...........		3,000	
	Cash.................	4		3,000
	Two salesmen hired at a monthly salary of $1,500 each.			
Mar. 10	Cash......................	4	5,000	
	Sales Revenue.........			5,000
	Cash sales for the month.			
Mar. 18	Accounts Receivable.......		7,000	
	Sales Revenue.........			7,000
	Sales made on open account.			
Mar. 31	Cost of Goods Sold........		6,000	
	Merchandise...........			6,000
	Cost of the merchandise sold during March.			
Mar. 31	Rent Expense.............		1,000	
	Prepaid Rent..........			1,000
	To record expiration of lease payment.			

TABLE 3–6

Cash

Account No. 4

Date	Explanation	PR	Amount	Date	Explanation	PR	Amount
......		J–3	10,000	......		J–3	1,000
......		J–3	5,000	......		J–3	3,000
			15,000				4,000
				Mar. 31	Balance	√	11,000
			15,000				15,000
Apr. 1	Balance	√	11,000				

of the entries recorded in the journal affecting Cash have been posted. Similar procedures would apply to the other accounts.

SUMMARY

Journals and ledger accounts are the two technical devices used in the recording process. The former are used to record the analysis of specific business transactions. The result is a chronological description of the transactions of the period recorded intact and accompanied by explanatory information. When transactions are first recorded in the journal, it is easier to discover and locate errors. Through the posting process, the debit and credit elements of the journal entries are reflected in the ledger accounts.

The ledger is used to record the effect of various business transactions on individual asset and equity accounts. These ledger accounts, one for each asset, liability, and owners' equity element, comprise the underlying fabric of the entire accounting system. The use of special-purpose owners' equity accounts, called revenues and expenses, to measure relevent asset changes supplies us with additional useful information. Summarized on the income statement, these accounts not only show what the net income is but give a reasonably detailed picture of how the income has been earned.

In actual business practice the exact form the journals and ledgers assume varies tremendously. Only in a relatively simple, manual accounting system might they appear as illustrated in this chapter. Ledgers may consist of trays of punched cards, with each card representing a specific account; computer printout sheets in a binder; or a group of memory locations within a large computer. Similarly, a journal may consist of a bound volume of printed forms of varying types, a stack of punched cards (each card representing a journal entry), or a reel of magnetic tape. Nevertheless, the important aspect to remember is not the format of these devices, but the particular purpose or function that each performs.

In subsequent chapters we use both journal and ledger entries. Both require the ability to break a business event into its component parts. The sequence in analyzing and recording a transaction is

1. Determine how assets, liabilities, or owners' equities are affected by the transaction, remembering that the equality of assets and equities cannot be overturned.
2. Determine what particular accounts are to be increased or decreased, keeping in mind that the effects on owners' equity from operating transactions are recorded in revenue and expense accounts.
3. Translate these increases and decreases into left-hand (debit) and right-hand (credit) entries, employing the rules on page 54.
4. Record the debits and credits in journal or ledger form, as the case may be.

5. Determine that debits equal credits as a check on the completeness of the analysis and on numerical accuracy.

In future chapters additional ledger accounts are introduced. But these, of necessity, must represent embellishments of the existing asset-equity system. There are only three basic types of accounts—assets, liabilities, and owners' equities. Each new account will either be a subdivision or a modification of one of these. Consequently, the procedural rules for recording increases and decreases can be applied to every account, once the nature of the account is determined. A good knowledge of these debit and credit rules, along with the concept of the asset-equity framework, will facilitate greater understanding as we expand our discussion. New terms, accounts, procedures, and concepts should be related to the underlying foundation established in Chapters Two and Three.

SUGGESTIONS FOR FURTHER READING

Hatfield, Henry Rand. "An Historical Defense of Bookkeeping," *Journal of Accountancy*, Vol. 37 (April 1924), pp. 241–53.

QUESTIONS AND PROBLEMS

3–1. The General Electron company is organized on July 15, 1971. Following is a summary of its dealings prior to the commencement of operating activities on August 1:

1. Shares of stock are issued to various individuals who invest $75,-000 in cash.
2. Land and a building are purchased for $37,000, of which $9,000 is deemed applicable to the land. Of the total purchase price, $17,000 is paid in cash, and a 10-year mortgage is given for the remainder.
3. A local contractor remodels the building at a cost of $7,500, to be paid in 30 days.
4. Office equipment is purchased on account for $800.
5. A secondhand delivery truck is purchased for cash in the amount of $3,000.
6. The truck is completely overhauled and repainted at a cost of $300, which is paid in cash.
7. Inventory is purchased for $18,000; cash of $3,000 is paid, and a six-month, 6 percent note for the difference is given to the supplier.
8. Insurance premiums of $700 are paid by check.
9. A check for $750 is received from Oliver Lameduck to apply against purchases he expects to make in August.
10. Izzy Everslow is hired as a salesman at a monthly salary of $400,

payable on the last day of each month. He is to begin work on August 1.

11. Unsatisfactory inventory costing $400 is returned to a supplier.

a) Prepare general journal entries to record the above results.

b) Set up a ledger (T) account for Cash and post the relevant portions of the journal entries to it. At what amount would cash appear on the July 31 position statement?

3–2. Shown below is the position statement of the Neverready Delivery Service, Inc., as of March 31, 1972:

NEVEREADY DELIVERY SERVICE

Statement of Financial Position, March 31, 1972

Assets		Equities	
Cash..............	$ 200	Accounts payable....	$ 300
Supplies...........	400	Wages payable.......	100
Prepaid rent.......	1,000	Capital stock.......	5,000
Equipment.........	8,000	Retained earnings...	4,200
	$9,600		$9,600

1. On April 1 the stockholders invested another $4,000 in the business in exchange for shares of stock.
2. The officers of the firm contacted the local bank on April 2 and arranged a line of credit whereby the business could borrow up to $5,000 as needed.
3. The business purchased on account new equipment costing $2,500 on April 3.
4. The wages payable were paid in cash.
5. On April 15 the garage and office building, which heretofore had been rented, was purchased for $4,500. The rent that had been prepaid as of March 31 was to apply against the purchase price, with the remainder paid in cash.
6. Two new employees were hired. Their salaries, beginning on May 1, were to be $400 a month each. However, to be sure of their availability, each was advanced $100 on April 20.
7. On April 21, $200 of supplies were ordered.
8. On April 30 a $5,000 loan was taken out at the bank under the previously arranged line of credit.
9. The equipment purchased on April 3 was paid for.
10. The supplies ordered on April 21 were delivered on April 30, along with the invoice for $200.

a) Prepare journal entries for the above events.

b) Set up ledger (T) accounts, enter the opening balances, and post the journal entries.

c) Prepare a position statement as of April 30, 1972.

3–3. "Double-entry bookkeeping is too much trouble. The information recorded in the journals is simply duplicated again in the ledgers. And half of that information isn't really necessary. In my business, where most transactions are for cash, an accurate recording on my checkbook stubs is all that is necessary."

Evaluate and comment on the above viewpoint. What are the advantages of double-entry bookkeeping, with journals and ledgers, for a business having predominantly cash transactions?

3–4.   The following account balances existed on January 1, 1972:

Cash	$ 28,000	Accounts payable	$ 15,000
Accounts receivable	11,500	Notes payable	1,000
Merchandise inventory	10,000	Wages payable	300
Supplies inventory	600	Interest payable	50
Prepaid insurance	1,500	Capital stock	50,000
Store equipment	20,000	Retained earnings	33,650
Office furniture	10,400		
Buildings	18,000		
	$100,000		$100,000

During the first quarter of 1972 the following changes took place:

1. Purchases on account amounted to $40,000 for merchandise and $500 for supplies.
2. Sales of merchandise on account were as follows: sales price, $60,000; cost of merchandise sold, $28,300.
3. Cash receipts:
    a) Issuance of more capital stock, $5,000.
    b) Collected from customers, $35,900.
    c) Sale of excess store equipment, $2,500 (this was $500 more than its book amount of $2,000).
4. Cash disbursements:
    a) To merchandise and supplies vendors, $29,400.
    b) To bank for note and interest accrued in 1971, $1,050.
    c) To employees for services rendered last year *and* in 1972, $3,600.
    d) For supplies, $500.
    e) For heat, light, and other utilities, $1,600.
    f) To local newspaper for advertisements during the first quarter of 1972, $400.
5. Other changes:
    a) Supplies used, $900.
    b) Insurance expired, $300.
    c) Store equipment depreciation, $700.
    d) Office furniture depreciation, $400.
    e) Building depreciation, $250.
    f) Employee services used in 1972 but not paid for, $750.

a) Set up ledger (T) accounts for each of the accounts listed and enter the opening balances.
b) Record the changes occuring during the three months. Record all income transactions directly in retained earnings (do not use revenue and expense accounts).
c) Prepare a position statement as of March 31, 1972.
d) Did the firm operate profitably during this period? How do you know? How much income or loss did it make?

    e) What advantages would the use of revenue and expense accounts have provided?

3–5. During the month of June the following transactions took place concerning the Bugs Drive-In Restaurant:

June 1–5:
1. The business was formed as a partnership by two brothers. One brother, I. M. Dense, contributed a restaurant stand valued at $30,-000; the other brother, U. R. Dense, invested $30,000 in cash.
2. Food supplies costing $20,000 were purchased, $10,000 for cash and $10,000 on open account.
3. Restaurant equipment worth $15,000 was acquired in exchange for a note payable.
4. A check for $5,000 was given to a local "music" group called the "Bugs," for permission to use their name on the drive-in signs and in other advertising. There was no time limit on this agreement.
5. The brothers offered to buy for $3,000 an adjacent piece of land for a parking lot. No reply was received.

June 6–29:
6. Cash received in connection with food served to customers was $18,500.
7. Salaries and wage costs amounting to $5,200 were incurred; $5,000 of this was paid in cash.
8. Other miscellaneous services (utilities, etc.) acquired and used during the month were $600, paid in cash.
9. Some of the food supplies purchased on credit were found to be spoiled. Supplies in the amount of $200 were returned to the supplier.
10. A counteroffer from the owner of the adjacent land (see item 5) was received, to sell the land for $4,000 cash. The brothers Dense accepted the offer, and title to the land passed to the business.
11. Accounts payable in the amount of $2,500 were paid in cash.

June 30:
12. Entries were made to record depreciation (cost of asset services consumed) during June of $500 on the restaurant stand and $250 on the restaurant equipment.
13. Food supplies remaining on hand amounted to $8,300.

    a) Prepare journal entries for the above events.
    b) Post the journal entries for the above events.
    c) Prepare an income statement for the month of June and a position statement as of June 30.

3–6. Using ledger (T) accounts as an analytical tool, determine the item of missing information in each of the five situations below:
    a) The position statements on December 31, 1971 and December 31, 1972 showed $210 and $150 respectively for delivery supplies. The income statement for 1972 shows delivery supplies expense

of $325. What quantity of delivery supplies was purchased in 1972?

b) The income statement shows a net income of $4,900. Retained earnings at the beginning and at the end of the year are $9,800 and $13,500, respectively. How much was declared in dividends during the year?

c) If the accounts receivable balance on December 31, 1972 is $12,-500, an increase of $4,200 since the beginning of the year, and $35,000 cash is collected from credit customers during 1972, what were the total credit sales in 1972?

d) Merchandise inventory appears at $15,000 on the position statement at the beginning of the year and at $16,500 at the end of the year. If purchases were $25,000, what expense appears on the income statement for cost of goods sold?

e) Accounts payable owed are $12,500 and $9,000 at the beginning and end of the year respectively. If only the purchases of merchandise in (d) were acquired on open account, how much cash was paid out during the year to suppliers of merchandise?

3–7. One of your more mathematically inclined colleagues has summarized financial accounting in the following sets of formulas (Δ indicates "change in"):

(1)
$$A = L + OE$$
$$A - L = OE$$
$$(A - L) + \Delta(A - L) = OE + \Delta OE$$
$$\Delta(A - L) = \Delta OE$$

(2)
$$R = +\Delta OE$$
$$E = -\Delta OE$$
$$R - E = \Delta OE$$
$$R - E - NI$$
$$NI - \Delta OE$$

(3)   Substituting item 2 in item 1: $\Delta(A - L) = NI$

From this, he concludes that the only accounts necessary in a bookkeeping system are assets and liabilities. Keeping track of the changes in these will produce the net income figure.

a) Is he correct? Why, or why not?

b) Are there other reasons for the use of revenue and expense accounts which he has failed to understand?

✓ 3–8. Prepare an income statement from the following account balances selected from the ledger accounts of Mason Enterprises at the end of the first quarter of the year:

Accounts receivable........	$ 450	Salaries and wages.........	$1,200
Mortgage payable..........	900	Utilities..................	90
Sales of product...........	2,500	Accounts payable..........	375
Wages payable............	75	Inventories...............	590
Retained earnings.........	1,325	Depreciation on equipment...	80
Prepaid rent..............	60	Interest received..........	130
Cash....................	150	Supplies used.............	25
Cost of sales..............	1,050	Maintenance expense.......	15
Equipment................	900	Expired rent..............	20
Advertising..............	120	Commission revenue.......	255
Annual license fees........	150	Charitable contributions.....	15

3–9. In April 1971, Mr. Carl Marvin opened an automobile parts distributorship. In summary form below are the transactions for his first six months of operations:

1. Invested $12,500 in cash.
2. Paid $6,000 rent in advance to cover 12 months.
3. Purchased parts for the stockroom in the amount of $10,000 on account.
4. Received an order of $3,800 for parts to be delivered in three months.
5. Sold parts for cash, $3,300, and on account, $4,700. The parts cost $6,000.
6. Paid in cash $650 for wages, $280 for advertising, and $480 for other expenses.
7. Purchased new equipment for $330 cash.
8. Delivered the parts mentioned in item 4. Their cost was $2,500.
9. Collected $1,200 from his charge customers.
10. Paid $4,100 of his accounts payable and gave a $2,000 note payable in payment of another account.
11. Received a $30 refund for advertising circulars that were faultily printed.
12. Recognized additional unpaid liabilities at the end of the period of $90 for wages and $30 for other expenses.
13. Recognized rent applicable to the current accounting period.

a) Make journal entries to record these transactions, employing revenue and expense accounts wherever necessary.

b) Prepare an income statement for the six-month period ended September 30, 1971.

c) What implicit assumption did you make with respect to the advertising and wages in item 6?

3–10. At the close of business on December 31, 1971 the accounts of the Prince Toy Company had the following balances:

Cash............................	$ 6,000	
Accounts receivable................	14,000	
Inventory........................	33,000	
Supplies.........................	500	
Unexpired insurance...............	400	
Store equipment...................	4,000	
Delivery equipment................	6,000	
Accounts payable..................		$ 5,000
Wages payable....................		2,000
Rent payable.....................		3,000
Capital stock....................		50,000
Retained earnings................		3,900
	$63,900	$63,900

The following transactions, in summary form, occurred in the calendar year 1972:

1. Purchased inventory on account, $150,000.

2. Purchased supplies on account, $1,200.
3. Insurance premiums paid, $400.
4. Delivery equipment purchased on account, $500.
5. Wages paid in cash during year, $23,000; wages payable on December 31, 1972, $6,000.
6. Miscellaneous services paid for in cash, $1,800.
7. Dividends declared and paid, $2,500.
8. Payments on account, $140,000.
9. Rent paid during the year, $5,000; rent payable on December 31, 1972, $4,000.
10. Sales of toys on account, $220,000.
11. Cost of inventory sold during the year, $180,000.
12. Unused supplies, $700.
13. Insurance expired during the year, $600.
14. Equipment services used up: store, $400; delivery, $1,200.
15. Cash collected from customers, $230,000.

a) Set up ledger (T) accounts for the above accounts and enter the opening balances for 1972.
b) Make ledger entries to record the transactions for 1972, using revenue and expense accounts.
c) Prepare in good form an income statement for 1972 and a position statement as of December 31, 1972.

3–11. Lief E. Maple and his wife, Sugar, decided to open a candy store on August 1, 1971. The following were the transactions for August:

1. On August 2, they deposited their savings of $3,000 in a bank account for the new firm.
2. On August 3, Leif purchased new equipment for $2,200, paying $200 down and promising to pay the rest in 60 days.
3. Utilities were hooked up. The firm had to pay a $120 deposit which could be subtracted from its monthly utility bills in equal amounts over the next year.
4. Leif had alterations and improvements made to the inside of the store building which cost $1,500, paid in cash.
5. Candy was ordered and delivered to the store by a wholesaler. The cost was $880, payable in 30 days.
6. Candy sales for cash amounted to $300 during the first 15 days of August.
7. Candy which cost $50 was returned to the wholesaler because of spoilage. The anticipated selling price of that candy was $75.
8. Employee salaries of $200 were paid for the month.
9. Additional purchases of candy during the month were $380, unpaid as of the end of the month.
10. Supplies costing $120 were purchased for cash. Of these, approximately two thirds were used during the month.
11. Sales in the last half of the month were $700. This included $400 of credit sales, of which $350 had been collected by the end of the month.

12. It was estimated that the cost of candy on hand on August 31 was $430.
13. The unexpired cost of equipment on August 31 was $2,150. Leif estimated that $25 of the cost of improvements should be allocated to operations in August.
14. The utility bill for $80 was received. This amount less the allocated deposit is payable on September 10.
15. Rent for the month of August was $300 and was due on September 1.

a) Enter the above transactions in ledger accounts.
b) Close the revenue and expense accounts.
c) Prepare an income statement for August and a position statement as of August 31.
d) From these statements, do you foresee any difficulties for the Maples?

3–12. A. Nut and U. Bolt establish a hardware store on July 1, 1971. The transactions for the month, in summary form, are:

1. Nut and Bolt each invest $50,000 in cash in exchange for shares of stock.
2. Merchandise of $30,000 is purchased on account.
3. Rent of $3,000 on a store building is paid for July.
4. Display cases costing $25,000 are purchased on account. These are expected to last five years.
5. A supply of 100 buckets is purchased for $5 each and given away to the first 100 customers as a promotional scheme.
6. Sales are made to charge account customers in the amount of $18,000.
7. Salesmen's wages amounting to $16,000 are paid.
8. Utility bills for the month of July amounting to $3,500 are paid in cash.
9. Payment of accounts payable amount to $22,000.
10. Cash sales during July are $8,000.
11. Wages and salaries earned during July but not yet paid are $2,500.
12. Government bonds are purchased for $30,000 as a temporary investment.
13. Merchandise purchased for cash amounts to $6,000.
14. Interest of $100 is earned during July but has not yet been received in cash.
15. Cost of merchandise remaining on hand on July 31 is $12,700.
16. Depreciation on the display cases is recorded for the month.

Prepare journal entries to record the above transactions, employing revenue and expense accounts where needed.

3–13. The terms "cost" and "expense" are frequently used interchangeably in accounting practice. The following items were selected from a number of annual reports:

Position Statement Items:

Prepaid expenses (current asset)
Costs and expenses recoverable under construction contract (receivable)
Deferred research and development expense (noncurrent asset)
Accrued expenses (current liability)
Start-up costs deferred (other asset)
Relocation expenses applicable to future periods (other asset)

Income Statement Items:

Cost of goods sold
Distribution costs
Cost of dry holes
Employment costs

For each of the above items, indicate whether the terminology conforms to the conceptual distinction between the two terms. Briefly describe the nature of the item and indicate whether its classification is proper.

3–14. The T accounts below show the transactions of Harlan Company during the month of April, 1972:

Cash				Accounts Payable			
(1)	40,000	(2)	4,400	(8)	19,300	(3)	20,500
(9)	5,200	(5)	8,200	(13)	300		
(11)	22,500	(6)	1,700				
		(7)	1,200				
		(8)	19,300				

Sales				Depreciation			
		(4)	27,300	(10)	100		
		(9)	5,200				

Accounts Receivable				Cost of Goods Sold			
(4)	27,300	(11)	22,500	(12)	17,700		

Equipment				Furniture & Fixtures			
(2)	3,600	(10)	80	(2)	800	(10)	20

Inventory				Salaries & Wages			
(3)	20,500	(12)	17,700	(5)	8,200		
		(13)	300	(14)	400		

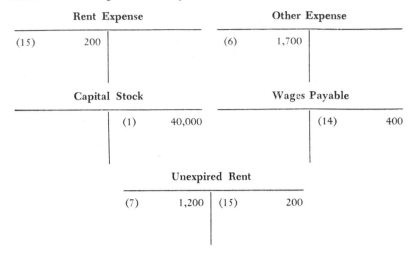

Rent Expense		Other Expense	
(15) 200		(6) 1,700	

Capital Stock		Wages Payable	
	(1) 40,000		(14) 400

Unexpired Rent	
(7) 1,200	(15) 200

a) For each of the above entries (1) to (15) explain the nature of the underlying event. Be as specific as possible.

b) Prepare an income statement and position statement.

3–15. On January 1, 1972 the account balances of the Charcoal Gray Clothing Store were as follows:

Cash	$ 3,000	
Accounts receivable	32,200	
Merchandise	45,800	
Supplies	1,200	
Prepaid insurance	1,400	
Land	22,500	
Buildings	45,000	
Equipment	15,000	
Accounts payable		$ 37,500
Salaries payable		1,500
Capital stock		100,000
Retained earnings		27,100
	$166,100	$166,100

During the year the transactions summarized below took place:

Purchases on account:	
Merchandise	$270,000
Supplies	2,000
Cash receipts:	
Sales of merchandise	75,000
Collections of customers' accounts	300,000
Cash disbursements:	
Supplies	1,200
Delivery charges on outgoing merchandise	2,200
Insurance premium	800
Payments on account	285,000
Salesmen's salaries	18,900
Utility services	2,100
Sales of product on account	310,000

Other information:

Depreciation for year on building..............	1,200
Depreciation for year on equipment............	1,500
Insurance expired during year.................	1,200
Inventory of supplies on December 31..........	900
Merchandise on hand on December 31	65,000
Unpaid salesmen's salaries...................	1,000

a) Prepare general journal entries to record the transactions for the year.

b) Open ledger (T) accounts, enter the beginning balances, and post the journal entries from part (a).

c) Prepare an income statement for the year and a position statement as of the end of the year.

CHAPTER FOUR

ELEMENTS OF THE ACCOUNTING CYCLE

FINANCIAL accounting is called upon to perform the functions of collecting and communicating financial data. Chapter Three discusses two important elements of the collection process—journals and ledgers. These media are used to accumulate and classify the results of transactions affecting the business entity. Each serves a unique recording purpose and is cross-referenced to the other in the posting process. The financial statements, adequately explained, are vehicles for the major goal of the second phase, that of communication. They signify the culmination of the accounting efforts.

In a sense, then, the journals and ledgers stand at the beginning of the accounting process and the financial statements at the end. The purpose of this chapter is to expand our knowledge concerning other accounting functions performed in between and then to place the bookkeeping and accounting procedures in their proper relationship. Specifically, the first half of the chapter discusses one additional aspect of the recording process —adjusting entries. These not only are essential to an understanding of the accounting system but also increase our ability to use accounting as an analytical tool. The second half of the chapter concludes the discussion of accounting techniques with an attempt to interrelate the various steps and to place them in a systematic sequence, called the accounting cycle.

ADJUSTING ENTRIES

Accounting transactions are classified as external and internal in Chapter Three. The former consist of explicit dealings with parties outside of

84

the business entity. In most cases the external transaction is signaled by some discrete event—the receipt of an invoice, the writing of a check, the signing of a note payable at the bank, etc. Normally, an entry is made to record these transactions at the time they occur. And unless there is some error in the recording, the accounts are usually accurate and up to date with respect to these events.

Internal transactions, on the other hand, tend to be of a more continuous nature. They reflect changes in assets and equities that are taking place gradually as time passes. A portion of the prepaid rent expires each day. Inventories of supplies are being consumed throughout the entire period. Services are being rendered continuously over the period. Labor costs, for example, are incurred each day, and a liability gradually is building. Or if the entity performs a service for someone else, such as the lending of money, interest revenue is being earned throughout the entire period in which the money is used. An asset, interest receivable, gradually accrues with the passage of time.

It would be tremendously time-consuming and expensive to record these internal changes in the ledger accounts each day. In some cases it is easier to enter them as cumulative totals only periodically. Often, this is done as part of an express, external transaction. For instance, recognition of the labor costs is deferred until pay day, when an entry is made for the entire period's cost. A similar situation may exist with interest. The interest revenue may be accumulating each day, but its recording may be deferred until the total amount is received in cash. In other words, it is not always convenient or necessary to keep all asset, liability, revenue, and expense accounts up to date at all times.

Adjusting Entries Defined

However, this prevalent clerical shortcut may conflict with accounting's purpose of furnishing audiences with accurate and timely financial statements. Obviously, before financial statements are prepared, all external and internal transactions of the period should be collected in the accounts, and account balances should be correct. Otherwise, the resultant financial statements may be incomplete, inaccurate, and hence misleading to their audience. Unless all asset and equity events have been recorded, the position statement will not portray financial condition as of the end of the accounting period. Likewise, the income statement cannot present a realistic picture of the period's operations unless all revenues and expenses of the period are taken into consideration.

Accuracy and timeliness in the accounts are achieved prior to the preparation of financial statements through the use of adjusting entries. Adjusting entries are those made at the end of the accounting period to record transactions that have taken place but have not yet been recorded and to revise entries that were made incorrectly. The recording of adjusting entries is a logical adjunct of *accrual accounting*. Revenues and expenses and their related effects upon financial position are collected and reported in the period when they occur and hence for the operations to which they relate. The point of cash receipt or disbursement may be used sometimes for recording convenience, but it does not govern which accounting events shall be presented on the financial statements.

Although adjustments may arise in a variety of situations, certain fairly common transactions are recorded as adjusting entries. Let us study some of these usual types first. Most adjusting entries for continuous transactions involve either the apportionment between accounting periods of some element already recorded on the books or the accruing of some unrecorded element that has been changing during the period. These processes of apportionment or accrual can apply to either revenues or expenses; thus there are in total four general types:

1. Apportioning the cost of assets already acquired to reflect the expense applicable to the current period.
2. Accruing the cost of expired assets (expenses) which have not yet been recorded.
3. Apportioning the amount received in advance for products or services to reflect the revenue applicable to the delivery of the product or the performance of the service in the current period.
4. Accruing the amount of unrecorded asset increases (revenues) resulting from operations during the current period.

Type 1: Cost Apportionments

Numerous examples exist of this first type of adjustment. Almost all of the assets which we labeled "unexpired costs" in Chapter Two fall into this category. They represent expenditures which will benefit more than one accounting period. As a portion of the asset's services is used up in each period, part of the cost has to be allocated as an expense of that period.

Suppose that on December 31 a ledger account for Prepaid Insurance has a debit balance of $3,300, representing the beginning balance plus the premiums paid on new insurance policies acquired during the year. Although all of the insurance policies have been expiring gradually throughout the year, no entries have yet been made. A careful analysis of the insurance policies on December 31 reveals that the unexpired cost of policies still in force amounts to $1,400. The following adjusting entry is needed:

```
Insurance Expense.......................... 1,900
     Prepaid Insurance ($3,300 − $1,400)....        1,900
```

Assume that a firm orders substantial quantities of heating oil for a store building. The purchases total $5,000 and are debited to an asset account. During the period, most of the oil is consumed; however, at the end of the period oil estimated at $200 is left in the tanks. An expense account should reflect the cost of the oil used ($4,800), and only the remaining $200 should appear as an asset on the position statement. The adjustment, shown in ledger form, to apportion the cost of the oil used would be:

Heating Expense		Heating Oil Inventory		
(1)	4,800		5,000	(1)	4,800

Similar adjustments would be required for such assets as prepaid rent, supplies, merchandise inventory, and depreciable long-lived resources.

Assets Initially Recorded as Expenses. Sometimes the acquisition cost of certain assets is debited directly to expense accounts. This procedure is used when a high probability exists that the asset will be consumed in its entirety in the production of revenues during the period. In some cases part of the asset may remain unused at the end of the period. If so, then expenses are overstated, and assets are understated. An adjusting entry similar to the one above is needed, except that in this case the cost apportionment is from the expense account back to the asset rather than the other way around.

For instance, assume that the firm in the preceding example debited the $5,000 purchase of heating oil directly to Heating Expense on the assumption that practically all of the heating oil would be consumed during the period. In this case the adjusting entry would apportion to the asset account the unused part of the cost.

Heating Expense			Heating Oil Inventory	
5,000	(1)	200	(1)	200	

Although expense accounts normally are not credited, in this case the entry is proper, for we are correcting an overstated expense.

In accounting practice both procedures are used. Similar alternatives are sometimes applied to rent, to other prepayments, and occasionally to supplies. However the initial entry is made, the end results have to be the same. All that must be determined is how much of the cost *eventually* should end up in the expense and asset accounts, respectively, by the end of the period.

Depreciation Expense. This expense represents an estimate of the cost of the services of a long-lived asset used during the period in the generation of revenues. Although the firm utilizes its buildings, equipment, furniture and fixtures, etc., continuously, a daily recording of depreciation is unnecessary and probably would be subject to significant error. Rather, the firm waits and makes an adjusting entry at the end of the period. For example, a company acquires store equipment at a cost of $25,000. The equipment is expected to last five years. At the end of each year an entry would be necessary to reflect the consumption of a year's service potential of the equipment:

```
Depreciation Expense.......................  5,000
    Store Equipment ($25,000 ÷ 5 years)....           5,000
```

In accounting practice, however, the credit entry is almost universally made to a separate account called Accumulated Depreciation or Allowance for Depreciation:

```
Depreciation Expense.......................  5,000
    Accumulated Depreciation--
      Store Equipment.....................            5,000
```

The Accumulated Depreciation account is called a contra-asset account.[1] It becomes an integral part of the asset and appears as a deduction from the asset on the position statement. For example, at the end of the year this equipment would be reported as follows:

```
Store equipment.........................  $25,000
Less accumulated depreciation...........    5,000    $20,000
```

Conceptually, making direct credits to the asset account would be a perfectly sound procedure. Although the asset may not have changed physically, economically a portion of its services has expired. By using the indirect procedure of a contra account, however, we are able to report more information—the original cost of the assets still in use, the estimate of the portion used, and the unexpired cost applicable to future periods.

---

[1] This is our first contact with a group of special accounts called *valuation* accounts. Their purpose is to modify the amounts entered in some other account to which they apply. Valuation accounts are of two general types—contra accounts and adjunct accounts. The former we use to record downward modifications to the main ledger account; the latter record upward modifications. Contra and adjunct accounts, therefore, can apply to any kind of account where a need is felt to segregate particular kinds of increases or decreases. What this amounts to, then, is that the complete record of the particular item actually may be divided between at least two places. Part of it is in the main ledger account per se, while the rest has been isolated in a contra account (in the case of offsets) or adjunct account (in the case of additions).

The general rule in the treatment of valuation accounts is that the contra or adjunct account goes wherever the main account goes. If the main account is closed out at the end of the period, as would be the case with a revenue or an expense, then any valuation account attached to it is also closed. On the other hand, if the main account appears on the position statement at the end of the period, the valuation account usually appears also.

Since depreciation is at best an estimate, its placement in a separate contra account allows the reader roughly to judge the adequacy of the provision for depreciation and to form a general idea of the age of the asset. This would not be possible if the asset were reported simply at $20,000.

Type 2: Expense Accrual

This type of adjustment is necessary whenever an asset (usually some type of service) is used during the period but is not recorded at the time of use. Rather, the entries are deferred for clerical convenience until the service is actually paid for in cash. Wages and salaries are a good case in point. Assume that salesmen's salaries are $2,000 per month, payable on the 10th of the following month. On December 31 the December salaries have not been recorded, even though the cost has been incurred. In addition, an unrecorded liability for these salaries exists on December 31. The adjusting entry to bring the accounts up to date is

```
Salesmen's Salary Expense.................. 2,000
     Salaries Payable².......................         2,000
```

For another illustration, assume that the company leases a piece of copying equipment for the office. The total rental is based on the number of copies made, at a rate of three cents per copy. Payments are remitted approximately every other month, calculated from a metered count of copies prepared. Since the last payment in November, the meter shows 2,800 copies completed up to December 31. The adjusting entry is:

```
Office Expense..................................... 84
     Equipment Rentals Payable....................         84
```

Type 3: Revenue Apportionment

Mention is made in Chapter Two of liabilities which represent customer claims to receive goods and services in future periods. These customer advances arise when cash is obtained prior to the rendering of the service or delivery of the product by the firm. For instance, a company leases a portion of its warehouse for 18 months beginning on July 1 at a monthly rental of $100. The customer pays the entire $1,800 on July 1. The $1,800 represents revenue to be apportioned one third to the current accounting period and two thirds to the following one. On July 1 the entry to record the customer advance would be:

```
Cash........................................ 1,800
     Rent Received in Advance...............         1,800
```

---

² Sometimes this account is called Accrued Salaries Payable. The term "accrued" is unnecessary, however. When it does appear, it usually signifies an account arising from an adjusting entry.

Then, on December 31 the *adjusting* entry would be:

```
Rent Received in Advance....................... 600
      Rent Revenue.............................        600
```

Some companies use an alternative recording procedure which initially credits the entire cash receipt to a revenue account. For example, a firm sells specialty products such as napkins, coasters, and playing cards to be used for advertising and other special purposes. Each item is printed with the client's name, advertising slogan, etc. Orders take about two weeks to process and must be accompanied by cash payment. During the year $87,400 cash is received on such orders and credited to revenue:

```
Cash....................................... 87,400
      Sales of Specialty Items.............        87,400
```

An analysis of unprocessed orders at the end of the year reveals that items selling for $5,920 have not been printed or delivered to customers. Consequently, that part of the revenue has not been earned this period. An adjusting entry should be made to recognize the unearned (deferred) revenue as a liability:

```
Sales of Specialty Items................... 5,920
      Customer Advances.......................        5,920
```

Whether the apportionment is from a liability account to a revenue account, as in the first example, or from a revenue account to a liability account, the purpose and end result are the same. The underlying analysis involves a determination of the amount applicable to products and services rendered this period and that applicable to future periods.

Type 4: Revenue Accrual

This fourth common type of adjustment is similar to the second. When revenue is earned during one period but the recording of it has been deferred until the cash is collected in the next period, an adjustment may be necessary to reflect the revenue and related asset claim. For instance, interest is earned with the passage of time, but it is not recorded every day. If a finance company lends $10,000 at 6 percent interest to a manufacturer for six months beginning on December 1, one month's interest revenue of $50 ($10,000 $\times$ 0.06 $\times$ $\frac{1}{12}$) is applicable to the current accounting period. On December 31 the finance company's claim has grown from $10,000 to $10,050. The adjusting entry shown below would be made to correct the concomitant understatement of assets and revenues:

```
Interest Receivable............................ 50
      Interest Revenue...........................        50
```

Any revenue-producing activity which is performed during the period but for which payment will be coming later may be subject to the same type of adjustment. For instance, a furnace-repair firm might receive a 10 percent commission from a manufacturer on all new furnaces sold to customers. If, during December, new furnaces having a retail price of $13,000 are sold, the furnace-repair firm should make the following adjusting entry, even though the cash may not be received until some time in January:

```
Commissions Receivable......................  1,300
      Furnace Commission Revenue.............         1,300
```

Adjusting Entries to Record Corrections

The foregoing adjustments represent some of the more conventional ones which the accountant makes at the end of each accounting period, almost as a matter of routine. A more difficult type of adjusting entry may be called for to revise transactions that have been made incorrectly. There are, of course, no general types of entries involved here. Each correction entry requires a careful analysis of the situation. The basic approach is to determine what the proper account balances should be and to compare them with the present balances. The adjusting entry, then, is whatever is required to get from the present balances to the desired ones.

Take, for instance, the following situation. During the period the bookkeeper erroneously records a purchase of office supplies on account as follows:

```
Accounts Payable................................  500
      Office Expense.............................        500
```

This error is discovered at the end of the period, when a physical inventory count is made. It is also determined at that time that half of the supplies have been used during the period. An analysis of the events reveals that the liability for $500 still exists on December 31. Half of the cost of the supplies should appear as an asset and half as office expense. In other words, the correct account balances should be:

Office Supplies	Office Expense	Accounts Payable
250	250	500

A comparison of where we are with where we want to be gives rise to the following adjusting entry:

```
Office Supplies................................  250
Office Expense................................  750
      Accounts Payable.........................        1,000
```

Summary of Adjusting Entries

The foregoing discussion does not exhaust the subject of adjusting entries. Only some of the more common types have been illustrated. Innumerable other examples could be cited. Throughout the remaining chapters, we encounter other kinds of adjusting entries as well as new examples of the basic ones discussed here. Practically any entry could be subject to later adjustment under a given set of circumstances. Fundamentally, adjusting entries encompass all those entries necessary at the end of the accounting period to render the asset, liability, revenue, and expense accounts as accurate as possible.

THE ACCOUNTING CYCLE

We have been exposed at this point to a number of accounting processes and functions—statement preparation, ledger entries, journalizing, and adjusting. These procedures in an accounting system are not just random happenings. Rather, they are interrelated and are performed in an established order called the accounting cycle.

Elements in the Accounting Cycle

Presented in the sequence in which they normally are performed, the elements of the accounting cycle are

1. Recording transactions in a journal.
2. Posting journal entries to ledger accounts.
3. Preparing a trial balance.
4. Journalizing and posting adjusting entries.
5. Preparing an adjusted trial balance.
6. Preparing the financial statements.
7. Journalizing and posting closing entries.

The first two of these comprise most of the bookkeeping activity during the period. The other five steps are performed at the end of the accounting period. Together, they summarize the accounting process from the initial recording function to the final reporting function. The remainder of this chapter is devoted to an elaboration of some of these elements and a discussion of their relationship to one another and to the basic functions of accounting.

Recording Transactions in a Journal

This element, of course, begins the basic recording function in accounting. It involves the analysis of a transaction into its component parts (asset and equity changes) and recording that analysis in the systematic debit and credit framework discussed in Chapter Three. The journal entry provides the original record, usually in chronological order, of the events of the period. Following the entity concept, we record only those transactions involving the business enterprise as a separate entity.

Source Documents.   Before a transaction can be entered formally in any type of journal, there must be some method of indicating to the accounting department that the transaction has occurred. Each journal entry rests on some underlying document. Some business form must flow to the accounting area to trigger the analysis and recording process necessary for journalizing. Source documents include invoices, bills of sale, requisition slips of various types, legal documents, receiving reports, etc. What forms are used, who initiates them, and how they are routed to the accounting department must be considered in designing the particular accounting and data processing system used by a company. Often the source documents are indexed or referred to in the explanation accompanying the formal journal entry. They are filed systematically to serve as the support for the making of the entry. One task that an auditor performs is to determine, on a test-check basis, whether the entries recorded are supported by proper underlying documents.

Posting Journal Entries to Ledger Accounts

Posting is the process of transferring to the ledger accounts the individual changes recorded in the books of original entry. The process of posting in a manual accounting system is explained and illustrated in Chapter Three. Whether done manually, by a bookkeeping machine, or automatically, as in many electronic data processing systems, posting to the ledger accounts is the beginning of the classifying function. It involves fitting the recorded data into a logical, useful framework of assets and equities.

Chart of Accounts.   The ledger accounts used by a particular company are arranged by type of account in a list called the chart of accounts. Often the chart of accounts is expanded to include not only the accounts making up the system but the policies to be followed for entries in each account. The resulting accounting manual provides the basic guideline for posting to the ledger accounts.

To facilitate the organization and classification of the accounts, a coded number is assigned to each account. For example, the first digit might indicate the general classification—e.g., 1 for current asset, 2 for noncurrent asset, 3 for current liability, etc. Subsequent digits in the account numbers signify various subclassifications, functions, locations, etc. A carefully worked-out coding system provides a ready identification and an orderly arrangement by statement grouping for the ledger accounts. Moreover, the account numbering system lends itself well to the adoption of mechanical means of posting and of machine accounting systems.

Subsidiary Ledgers.   Our discussion has been limited to the main asset and equity accounts combined in the general ledger. When a large amount of detailed information about a particular general ledger account must be kept, often a separate set of accounts, called subsidiary ledger accounts, is used for the purpose. For example, when a group of individual persons is involved, as is the case with accounts receivable and accounts payable, a separate record can be maintained of each person's account in a subsidiary ledger. Similarly, when a general ledger account such as an equipment account contains many different items, subsidiary ledgers can be employed to handle the detailed information applicable to each particular machine. The general ledger account shows in summary form what the subsidiary records show in detail. The general ledger account is called a *control* account. Control accounts make total balances easier to obtain; it is not necessary to sum all the individual accounts every time the total is desired.

Specialized forms and data processing equipment can be developed to facilitate the handling of the detailed information in the subsidiary ledger. For instance, each subsidiary ledger form for accounts receivable could be maintained in duplicate, with a copy sent to the customer each month as his bill. Or the subsidiary ledger for an office equipment control account might consist of a stack of punched cards, each card corresponding to a particular machine. On each card would be punched the cost of the particular machine, its location, and the depreciation rate or its useful life. A run through a computer program would automatically accomplish the computation and summing of the total depreciation expense for that period. In some instances a file of the original business forms themselves serves as the subsidiary ledger. A file of unpaid invoices arranged by number or name of supplier might be the subsidiary ledger for accounts payable. Other subsidiary ledgers might consist of insurance policies or actual notes receivable or payable.

Subsidiary ledgers provide numerous advantages. Operationally they allow for a distribution and specialization of the clerical tasks involved in bookkeeping. The general ledger is more compact and can be maintained by one person (or machine). A number of subsidiary ledgers containing the bulk of the detailed information can be employed, with different individuals responsible for each one. Perhaps the major contribution of subsidiary ledgers is their aid in error location. By recording the detail in the subsidiary ledger and the same information in summary form in the general ledger control account, we can maintain a check on the accuracy of the records, especially since the posting to the subsidiary ledger often is done directly from the source documents. Consequently, any errors made in the journals or in posting from the journals to the general ledger accounts are not repeated in the detailed records. Periodic comparisons between the subsidiary ledger and general ledger control account reveal the existence of such errors. This comparison is called *proving the subsidiary ledgers*.

Subsidiary Ledger Example. To illustrate the general concept and use of a subsidiary ledger, let us take the following brief and highly simplified example of accounts receivable. Assume that a subsidiary ledger is maintained for three individual customers, A, B, and C.[3]

1. During a particular day credit sales total $10,000. A summary entry would be made in the journal, debiting Accounts Receivable and crediting Sales. This would be posted later to the general ledger accounts. Duplicate copies of the sales slips would be sent to the accounts receivable clerk for sorting and posting to the individual accounts. Assume that the sales slips indicate sales to A of $5,000, to B of $3,000, and to C of $2,000.
2. On another day the total credit sales amount to $6,000. The entry would be handled the same way. The entire $6,000 would be recorded in the general ledger, with the sales slips sorted according to customer and entered in the respective subsidiary ledger accounts. Assume $3,000 of sales to B and $3,000 to C.
3. On a later date checks are received in the amounts of $4,000, $3,000, and $2,000 to apply on the accounts of A, B, and C, respectively. A list of the customers' names and amounts paid (or perhaps portions of the bill which the customers return) is sent to the accounts receivable department for entry in the subsidiary ledger. Another copy is totaled and serves as the underlying document for an entry debiting Cash and crediting Accounts Receivable for $9,000.

The ledger accounts shown in Table 4–1 reflect these transactions. Notice that there are no offsetting debits or credits to the amounts entered in the subsidiary ledger accounts. This is because the subsidiary ledger simply reflects in detail what is already recorded in summary form in the general ledger accounts. The equality of debits and credits is required only for general ledger entries.

At the end of the accounting period, we would prove the subsidiary ledger for accounts receivable. A schedule (see Table 4–2) would be prepared showing each customer's account balance according to the subsidiary records. We would then compare the total with the balance in the control account to check on the accuracy of the records.

Preparing a Trial Balance

The trial balance is the first step of the accounting cycle to be taken at the end of the period and represents the beginning of the summariza-

---

[3] If a firm had only three customers, a subsidiary ledger would be unnecessary. Three separate accounts receivable in the general ledger could be maintained just as easily. Multiply the three accounts by several hundred thousand, and you get a practical picture of the recording problems of a typical large department store.

TABLE 4–1

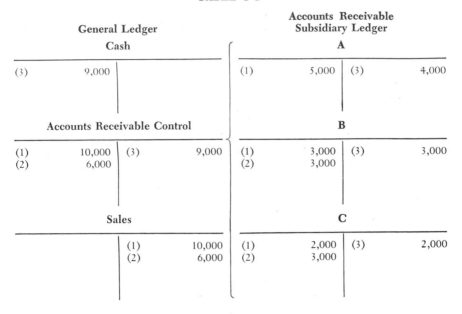

TABLE 4–2

Schedule of Accounts Receivable
(per subsidiary ledger)

A.	$1,000
B.	3,000
C.	3,000
Total (per control account).	$7,000

tion function. It consists of a list of ledger accounts and their balances, appropriately classified as debit or credit. It provides a summary of accounts for use in making adjustments and in preparing statements. The trial balance also serves as a test check on the numerical accuracy of the journalizing and posting processes.

The actual preparation of the trial balance is a routine task. Often, preprinted forms already containing the names of all accounts are used, and the calculating and transcribing of balances may be performed by accounting machines or computerized equipment. A highly condensed trial balance of the Hypothetical Company appears in Table 4–3.

The trial balance should "balance" (have equal debits and credits). Also, the control accounts in the trial balance should agree with the schedules of their subsidiary ledgers. Usually, proving the subsidiary ledgers is an ancillary activity associated with preparing the trial balance. If the trial balance does not balance, some recording error must have

TABLE 4–3

HYPOTHETICAL COMPANY
Trial Balance
December 31, 197

Account	Dr.	Cr.
Cash..	$ 3,000	
Accounts receivable.........................	10,000	
Inventory...................................	15,000	
Accounts payable............................		$13,200
Capital stock...............................		10,000
Retained earnings...........................		3,900
Sales revenue...............................		18,300
Commission revenue..........................		700
Cost of goods sold..........................	9,250	
Salary expense..............................	4,700	
Rent expense................................	1,000	
Supplies expense............................	280	
Delivery expense............................	2,870	
	$46,100	$46,100

been made. On the other hand, the converse is not necessarily true. A trial balance simply portrays the existing balances of the accounts and indicates that the entries that were made had equal debits and credits. The existing balances still may be in error or out of date with respect to what they should be. The task of correcting wrong account balances and bringing them up to date falls to the adjusting entries, the next step in the accounting cycle.

Journalizing and Posting Adjusting Entries

Determining what adjustments are necessary to the accounts listed in the trial balance is one of the primary duties of the accountant, as contrasted with the bookkeeper. Entries to adjust the accounts at the end of the period normally require the analytical abilities of an accountant familiar with the operation of the system, the types of accounts used, and the interrelationships among them. Once determined, the adjusting entries are handled like any other entry. They are first journalized and then posted to the appropriate ledger accounts.

The need for adjusting entries arises from the periodicity and matching concepts. However, there are no underlying documents that automatically signal that an adjusting entry must be made. The accountant has to generate the necessary information for the adjusting entries from his study of the trial balance, his review of the accounting system, and his analysis of information sources outside the accounting records themselves. He looks, for example, for depreciable noncurrent assets, prepayments, revenues received in advance, etc., in the trial balance, for these items normally require adjustment. He may analyze files of notes receivable and notes payable to determine interest adjustments. Insurance policies are studied to determine the portion of prepaid insurance that has expired and that is still in force. The accountant may supervise or review physical counts of inventories so as to be able to make the adjusting entries for cost of goods sold or supplies expense.

Preparing an Adjusted Trial Balance

The adjusting-entry step in the accounting cycle is followed by the preparation of another trial balance, called the adjusted trial balance. When prepared, it presents a complete listing of all ledger accounts, with accurate and current balances. The primary use of the adjusted trial balance is in statement preparation. From this listing the accountant can arrange the ledger names and balances in the proper formats for the income and position statements. Also, the adjusted trial balance may serve as a test check on accuracy in handling the adjusting entries, particularly where the latter are fairly complex.

Preparing the Financial Statements

The next step in the accounting cycle is reporting the accumulated accounting information to the various audiences through the financial statements. This stage represents the fulfillment of the summarization function and the commencement of the interpretive function. Formats of these two statements have been illustrated previously. The asset, liability, and permanent owners' equity accounts (capital stock and retained earnings) appear on the position statement. The nominal owners' equity (revenue and expense) accounts are exhibited on the income statement.

Journalizing and Posting Closing Entries

Recall from Chapter Three that the function of revenue and expense accounts is to accumulate information about operating activities during a *single* time period. Once the income statement has been prepared, revenue and expense accounts ought to be cleared to zero so that they are ready to function next period, and in the process retained earnings ought to be updated for the income earned this period. The entries necessary to do this are called closing entries.

Closing the books is a technical process of transferring and summarizing balances. Whenever an entry has been made which causes a zero balance in an account, that account is said to have been closed. The closing process necessitates making such entries in all nominal accounts and balancing and ruling the real asset, liability, and owners' equity accounts. We close each temporary account by making an entry equal in amount to the balance of the account but on the opposite side. Because revenues and expenses are temporary retained earnings accounts, one might expect that the corresponding part of the journal entry to close these accounts would be to Retained Earnings. Ultimately this is the case. Often, however, we use a temporary summary account, called the Income Summary account (or Expense and Revenue, Profit and Loss, or Operating Summary), to accumulate during the closing process information dispersed throughout the ledger in individual accounts.

The closing process for the accounts listed in the trial balance in Table 4–3 is illustrated in ledger form in Table 4–4 (we are assuming that the trial balance is an adjusted trial balance). Entries (a) through (g) transfer balances to Income Summary, thereby closing the revenue and expense accounts. The Income Summary account credit balance of $900 reflects the net result of matching revenues and expenses—the net change in

TABLE 4–4

Sales Revenue				Supplies Expense			
(a)	18,300		18,300		280	(f)	280

Commission Revenue				Delivery Expense			
(b)	700		700		2,870	(g)	2,870

Cost of Goods Sold				Income Summary			
	9,250	(c)	9,250	(c)	9,250	(a)	18,300
				(d)	4,700	(b)	700
				(e)	1,000		
				(f)	280		
Salary Expense				(g)	2,870		
				(h)	900		
	4,700	(d)	4,700		19,000		19,000

Rent Expense				Retained Earnings			
	1,000	(e)	1,000				3,900
						(h)	900

owners' equity from operating activities during the month. Entry (h) transfers this net increase to Retained Earnings, the owners' equity account established for that purpose.

After closing, the revenue and expense accounts show no balances. Neither does the Income Summary account at the end of the period. However, we have summarized in this account information concerning the period's activities. If techniques exist for summarizing information elsewhere, the nominal accounts can be closed directly without the aid of any summary account.[4] From a mechanical standpoint, a single entry could close the books by debiting all revenue accounts, crediting all expense accounts, and debiting (net loss) or crediting (net income) the difference to Retained Earnings.

Of much greater importance than scrutinizing the mechanical process, though, is learning what accounts are closed and understanding why closing entries are made. All temporary owners' equity accounts are closed. The rationale for closing entries can be traced directly to the concept of the accounting period. This concept requires that regular summaries of the period's activities be made. The activities of each single period must be segregated in the ledger accounts. The closing process is merely the last logical step in a process dictated by the periodicity concept.

SUMMARY

This chapter concludes a preliminary discussion of the procedural aspects of accounting. In it we expand further our knowledge of the basic accounting process. Included is an explanation of the adjusting process and its relationship to the accounting period. Then the discussion of the accounting cycle attempts to establish a relationship among the different procedural techniques. This normal progression of accounting functions is:

1. Journalizing.
2. Posting.
3. Trial balance.
4. Adjusting.
5. Adjusted trial balance.
6. Financial statements.
7. Closing.

A basic knowledge of how the parts of an accounting system are interrelated to generate financial information will contribute to a better

---

[4] Appendix 4–A describes the work sheet which the accountant employs to summarize and organize information. With a work sheet, summary accounts may be unnecessary.

understanding of the end result—the financial reports—and enable the student to *use* accounting as an analytical tool as well.

APPENDIX 4–A
PROCESSING DATA IN A MANUAL SYSTEM

Throughout this text we use very elementary methods for the journalizing and posting processes. The simple journal entry and the T account ledger form are our standard tools. No attempt is made to employ more advanced or complex data processing techniques, for they add little to the basic understanding of the concepts and functions of financial accounting.

Nonetheless, keep in mind that they are not an accurate representation of the *actual* recording process. No business of any consequence could maintain an effective accounting system employing only a two-column journal and a group of T accounts. Methods must be introduced to streamline data accumulation, classification, and summarization. The purpose of this appendix is to disclose two accounting procedures that have been devised to handle the processing of financial data accurately, rapidly, and relatively inexpensively. Quite naturally, we shall be dealing primarily with the first two steps of the accounting cycle, for here is where the basic recording and classifying of information take place. Our discussion begins with special multicolumn journals used in practically all manual bookkeeping systems and then proceeds to an illustration of the work sheet used to process information from the trial balance to the end of the accounting cycle.

SPECIAL JOURNALS

The only journal form introduced so far has been the general journal, containing single debit and credit columns. In this journal the account titles involved in the transactions have to be written out each time the particular account is used. Moreover, each journal entry has to be posted individually. There is absolutely no summarization in posting from the journal to the ledger accounts. The extra clerical effort involved in journalizing and posting under this arrangement makes it unsuitable for handling a large volume of transactions. Moreover, only one person can handle the general journal, and in an organization of any size a bottleneck would result.

Modifications of the Journal

To speed up the journalizing and posting processes and to allow for a division of accounting labor, most companies make two modifications to the simple journal system. First, a number of separate journals corresponding to major types of transactions are introduced. The bulk of a firm's transactions fall into four categories: (1) cash payments, (2) cash receipts, (3) sales on account, and (4) purchases on account. Separate books of original entry, called special journals or registers, can be set up for each of these types. Most firms then have at least five different journals rather than just one:

1. Cash disbursements journal.
2. Cash receipts journal.
3. Sales journal.
4. Purchase journal.
5. General journal (for entries not fitting into the special journals).

The second modification involves the introduction of special debit and credit columns in the special journals for accounts frequently used. These extra columns are specifically identified (e.g., Cash—Debit, Accounts Receivable—Credit, etc.). We can thus record repeated debits and credits to particular accounts by simply entering the dollar amount in the special column; the need to write out the name of the account with each entry is eliminated. Posting is facilitated also, because we can total the special columns and post the total rather than the individual entries.

How many special columns are employed and what accounts have special columns in each of the journals can be answered on pragmatic grounds. The number of actively used accounts determines the number of special columns. Each journal, however, contains a "key column," which identifies the essential type of transaction recorded in that journal. For example, the key column in the cash receipts book would be a Cash—Debit column. All entries recorded in the cash receipts journal of necessity involve a debit to Cash. Similarly, the key columns in the cash disbursements, sales, and purchase journals are Cash—Credit, Sales—Credit, and Accounts Payable—Credit, respectively.

Cash Disbursements Journal

Figure 4–A–1 shows a multicolumn cash disbursements book. Here we assume that Accounts Payable, Wages Payable, and Utility Expense are accounts frequently debited when Cash is credited. Of course, other special columns could be included for particular business situations. Notice, however, that in addition to the special columns, a set of Miscellaneous columns also appears. These aid in the recording of relatively complex or rare transactions involving cash disbursements.

As each check is written, the name of the payee is entered as well as the check number. For those transactions involving special columns, journalizing consists simply of entering the amounts in the appropriate

FIGURE 4-A-1

Cash Disbursements Journal

Date	Payee	Check Number	Cash Cr.	Accounts Payable Dr.	Wages Payable Dr.	Utility Expense Dr.	Miscellaneous			
							Account	PR	Dr.	Cr.
1971 July										
1	A. Bass........	181	5,000	5,000						
1	Motors, Inc........	182	4,000				Truck / Notes Payable	10 / 30	7,000	3,000
5	Wages	183	2,000		2,000					
10	B. Carp........	184	3,900	3,900						
10	C. Dane........	185	150	150						
10	City Power Co........	186	400			400				
10	Wages........	187	2,000		2,000					
13		188	15				Sales Returns	51	15	
15	Wages........	189	2,000		2,000					
20	ZT&T, Inc........	190	290			290				
20	Wages........	191	2,000		2,000					
22	C. Dane........	192	900	900						
31	Motors, Inc........	215	20				Interest	91	20	
31	Mass Gas Co........	216	580			580				
			41,890	24,425	12,000	1,430			7,035	3,000
			(1)	(27)	(28)	(5)			(√)	(√)

columns. In essence, the journal entry is recorded horizontally on one line. Bookkeeping machines frequently are employed to enter the amounts in the appropriate columns of the journal form automatically.

This simplified procedure applies to most of the entries—all but three during the month of July. For those three transactions—on July 1, July 13, and July 31—the Miscellaneous columns are used. The account titles have to be entered individually, but these situations occur only infrequently.

At the end of the month the journal columns are totaled and crossfooted as a check on numerical accuracy. As entries are made to the ledger accounts, all special columns are posted by column total. Since the individual entries are recorded in the journal, summarized information can be entered in the ledger accounts. The total credit of $41,890 for the month is made as a single entry to the Cash account. The account number of Cash (1) is placed below the column total to indicate that the posting has been done. Similar treatment is given to the other column totals for Accounts Payable, Wages Payable, and Utility Expense. Only four items, those entered in the Miscellaneous (or Sundry) columns, require individual posting. These are handled in the conventional manner described in Chapter Three. In addition, entries would be made in the subsidiary ledger for accounts payable. These could be made directly from the underlying documents or from the cash disbursements journal.

Other Special Journals

The three other commonly used special journals are for cash receipts, sales, and purchases. Let us forgo a detailed description of each of these in favor of a brief illustration of the column headings that might appear in each (see Figure 4–A–2). The mechanical process is the same as that for the cash disbursements book.

These illustrations are somewhat condensed in terms of the number of special columns employed. Also, the special columns indicated in the examples are only some of the more typical ones. In practice the journals would be tailored to the specific needs of each particular business. Moreover, although these four special journals constitute the normal books of original entry, others are sometimes used. Firms may employ a separate journal for sales returns, payroll transactions, or other specialized types of events peculiar to their businesses.

Advantages of Journal Modifications

The benefits from using separate, multicolumn journals are obvious. The increased speed and ease in processing data are enormous. These advantages lie in two areas: (1) savings in clerical time, and (2) division of recording responsibilities.

FIGURE 4-A-2

Cash Receipts Journal

Date	Explanation	Cash Dr.	Sales Discount Dr.	Accounts Receivable Cr.	Sales Cr.	Miscellaneous		
						Account	PR	Dr.	Cr.

Sales Journal

Date	Explanation	Invoice No.	Accounts Receivable Dr.	Sales Cr.	Sales Tax Payable Cr.	Miscellaneous		
						Account	PR	Dr.	Cr.

Purchases Journal

Date	Name	Accounts Payable Cr.	Merchandise Dr.	Supplies Dr.	Miscellaneous		
					Account	PR	Dr.	Cr.

Time is saved in three ways. First, several bookkeepers are able to make journal entries concurrently, working in the separate special journals. Secondly, within a journal, recording time is minimized through the elimination of writing account titles for most of the transactions. And finally, the major saving comes during posting, through the use of column totals rather than separate debits and credits.

Since the recording function is divided among a number of different individuals, efficiency is improved. The accounting system can take advantage of any specialization of labor which results from bookkeepers concentrating their attention on one particular type of transaction. Specialization has led to the development of unique forms and bookkeeping machines designed to handle particular kinds of transactions, such as sales or cash receipts. As a consequence, errors are minimized, and those that do occur are more readily detected. Moreover, having the data segregated in separate journals allows management to analyze the detailed information faster and more easily.

WORK SHEETS

A work sheet can be described as any columnar device employed as a convenient and orderly way of organizing information to be used in the preparation of adjustments and financial statements. The work sheet itself is not a financial statement or part of the formal accounting system. Rather, it serves as the accountant's scratch paper (although much neater, better organized, and more formal). It provides a way of arranging information to aid in those steps of the accounting cycle which follow the preparation of a trial balance.

Illustration

There are many forms and types of work sheets, depending on the complexity of the accounting system and the personal preferences of the individual accountant. The example in Figure 4–A–3 is one common format, consisting of five sets of debit and credit columns. The first set of columns is used for the trial balance. Instead of being reported on a separate sheet, the trial balance is listed on the work sheet. In some cases work sheet forms containing the names of all accounts are preprinted. Or a computer can be programmed to print out those accounts having balances. If additional accounts are needed, they can be added at the bottom of the work sheet. This latter arrangement is shown in the example in Figure 4–A–3.

The adjusting entries are then entered in the second set of columns. Often, making adjustments may require a great deal of analysis. Rather than journalizing the adjustments directly, the accountant uses the work

FIGURE 4–A–3

CENTRAL SALES COMPANY
Work Sheet, December 31, 1971

Accounts	Trial Balance Dr.	Trial Balance Cr.	Adjustments Dr.	Adjustments Cr.	Adjusted Trial Balance Dr.	Adjusted Trial Balance Cr.	Income Statement Dr.	Income Statement Cr.	Position Statement Dr.	Position Statement Cr.
Cash	7,700				7,700				7,700	
Accounts receivable	17,700				17,700				17,700	
Inventory	116,700			(a) 85,800	30,900				30,900	
Prepaid insurance	4,200			(b) 2,000	2,200				2,200	
Building	40,000				40,000				40,000	
Accumulated depreciation—building		18,000		(c) 2,000		20,000				20,000
Delivery equipment	9,000				9,000				9,000	
Accumulated depreciation—equipment		3,200		(d) 800		4,000				4,000
Accounts payable		8,200				8,200				8,200
Notes payable		10,000				10,000				10,000
Customers' advances		1,600	(e) 1,600							
Common stock		40,000				40,000				40,000
Retained earnings		10,600				10,600				10,600
Sales		130,000		(e) 1,600		131,600		131,600		
Administrative expenses	8,500		(c) 1,000		9,500		9,500			
Delivery expense	3,000		(b) 2,000 (d) 800		5,800		5,800			
Selling expense	14,500		(c) 1,000		15,500		15,500			
Interest expense	300		(f) 300		600		600			
Cost of goods sold			(a) 85,800		85,800		85,800			
Interest payable				(f) 300		300				300
	221,600	221,600	92,500	92,500	224,700	224,700	117,200	131,600	107,500	93,100
Increase in retained earnings							14,400			14,400
							131,600	131,600	107,500	107,500

sheet. Omissions are more likely to be detected, and errors can be corrected before they are entered in the formal accounting records. Usually. somewhere on the work sheet itself or attached to it will be an explanation of the adjustments, related to the entries by the use of a key letter or number. Notice how accounts are added to the trial balance listing whenever necessary for the completion of an adjustment. The example has been deliberately simplified, since our purpose is to illustrate the work sheet.

Explanation of Adjustments

a)   Ending inventory, as established by physical count, of $30,900.
b)   Expired insurance applicable to delivery equipment.
c)   Depreciation on building at an annual rate of 5 percent of original cost, allocated equally between selling and administration.
d)   Depreciation on delivery equipment of $800.
e)   Revenue on merchandise delivered for which payment has been received earlier.
f)   Accrual of six month's interest on bank note ($10,000 $\times$ 0.06 $\times$ ½).

We determine the third set of columns, labeled Adjusted Trial Balance, by adding horizontally the amounts in the Trial Balance and Adjustments columns for each account. When the adjustments are few and relatively simple, many accountants eliminate these columns and use only an eight-column work sheet.

Columns to accumulate information for the financial statements comprise the remainder of the work sheet. The amount listed in the adjusted trial balance for each account is placed in the appropriate debit or credit column under the name of the statement on which the particular account appears. The last two sets of columns initially will not balance. The Income Statement columns act like the Income Summary account. The temporary increases in retained earnings from the period's activities are recorded as credits; the decreases in retained earnings corresponding to expenses are listed on the debit side. The Position Statement columns do not balance, since the net increase in retained earnings for the period is not recorded thereon. The amount necessary to balance the Income Statement columns represents the net increase in retained earnings. This amount, when entered as a credit, will also balance the Position Statement columns and thus provides a check on the numerical accuracy of the work sheet manipulations.

Use of the Work Sheet

From the information on the work sheet, the accounting cycle can be completed formally as a matter of routine. A bookkeeper using the work sheet as a source document can easily journalize and post the adjusting entries. The accounts listed in the Income Statement columns contain all the temporary accounts to be closed. Simply by debiting Sales and by crediting the expenses and Retained Earnings ($14,400), a bookkeeper can mechanically close the books with a single entry. Since the information for the statement itself is already accumulated on the work sheet, no real need exists for an Income Summary account. Finally, to prepare financial statements the bookkeeper need only rearrange in proper form the accounts in the respective work sheet columns. The work sheet permits the accountant to review the information before the adjusting and closing entries are recorded and the statements are prepared formally.

In addition, the work sheet provides a way to obtain financial statements without formally closing the books. Interim statements on a monthly basis may be desirable for managerial purposes. Yet to close the temporary accounts each month may not be necessary or even desirable. The work sheet allows us to bypass the formal journalizing and posting of adjusting and closing entries.

QUESTIONS AND PROBLEMS

4–1. Adjusting entries commonly involve the following groupings of accounts:

 a) A liability is debited, and a revenue is credited.
 b) An expense is debited, and an asset is credited.
 c) An expense is debited, and a liability is credited.
 d) An asset is debited, and a revenue is credited.

Describe a specific situation (other than the ones illustrated in the chapter) that would be appropriate for each of the above types of adjustments. Make the proper adjusting journal entry for your situation.

4–2. The following information was made available. Prepare the journal entry to adjust the accounts as of December 31, 1972.

 a) On January 1, 1972 the company lent $5,000 to a supplier, receiving a two-year, 6 percent note. The interest for the year 1972 has not been received or recorded.
 b) Prepaid rent on January 1, 1972 was $400. On May 1 an additional $1,200 was paid to cover the rent through April 30, 1973.
 c) The Supplies on Hand account had a balance of $500 on January 1, 1972. During the year the company purchased $300 of supplies which was debited to the Supplies Expense account. On December 31, 1972 the inventory of supplies was $200.
 d) Accrued wages as of December 31, 1972 amounted to $3,000.
 e) Merchandise inventory of $8,000 purchased on account was erroneously charged to Office Equipment. Only half of this merchandise remained unsold by the end of the year.

f) Utility bills were received at the end of December. These included charges for electric service, $130, and for telephone service, $80. The bills have not been recorded.

g) Cash of $480 received from customers on goods to be delivered in 1973 was credited to Sales Revenue.

h) The Office Equipment account was $17,000 on January 1, 1972. The ending balance was $28,000 including the erroneously charged inventory (see (*e*)). Office equipment is depreciated at a rate of 10 percent of the beginning balance, and all additions during the year are charged at a rate of 5 percent.

4–3. The Webster Woods Civic Theatre group puts on dramas and concerts. One attraction is featured each month over the nine-month season, which begins in September. The following data relate to the first month of operation in the 1971–72 season:

1. Rented the Gaity Theatre. Rent of $1,000 per month must be paid for three months in advance. The rental agreement also calls for 10 percent of the gross revenues from each program to be remitted to the owners of the theatre building at the end of each three-month period. A check for the first three months' rent is written.

2. Sent out direct mail announcements and placed newspaper advertisements telling of the entire season's programs. The cost of $9,000 was paid in cash.

3. Contracted with Simon Simpleton Concessionaires to operate the refreshment stand. The Civic Theatre group is to receive 15 percent of all gross sales of refreshments. The amount is to be remitted on the 10th of the month for sales during the preceding month.

4. Purchased a specially designed insurance policy for $6,000 cash. The policy provides fire, theft, and public liability coverage during the nine months the group is active.

5. Received cash of $27,000 for season tickets to all nine attractions.

6. Sold individual tickets for $3,400 for September's programs.

7. Incurred monthly salary and wage costs of $7,000, payable the fifth of the following month.

8. Printed program notes for the September performances at a cost of $1,900, paid in cash.

9. Received a report from Simon Simpleton that September's refreshment sales were $3,600.

a) Assume that the group prepares monthly financial statements. Prepare journal entries to record the above transactions as well as any necessary adjusting entries on September 30, 1971.

b) Justify your treatment of the advertisements mentioned in item 2.

4–4. The following account balances were taken from the trial balance and adjusted trial balance.

	Trial Balance	Adjusted T. B.
Advances from customers	$1,800 cr.	$ 330 cr.
Accumulated depreciation	700 cr.	1,000 cr.
Interest revenue	280 cr.	540 cr.
Supplies expense	1,360 dr.	460 dr.
Unexpired insurance	0	800 dr.
Rent revenue	4,200 cr.	4,900 cr.
Office salaries	7,500 dr.	7,980 dr.
Commissions payable	0	1,430 cr.

Reconstruct the journal entries that probably were responsible for each of these account changes.

4–5. The following trial balance is prepared from the accounts of Rancid Restaurant, Inc., on December 31, 1971, the end of the first year of operation.

	Dr.	Cr.
Cash on hand	$ 200	
Cash in bank	6,000	
Inventory of food	10,000	
Operating supplies	1,400	
Wage expense	7,000	
Rent	5,400	
Heat, light, and power	1,200	
Miscellaneous expense	1,500	
Customer receipts		$25,600
Accounts payable		5,100
Equipment	8,000	
Capital stock		10,000
	$40,700	$40,700

You discover the following additional pieces of information:

1. Inventories of food and operating supplies are $600 and $200, respectively, on December 31, 1971.
2. Customer receipts include $150 received from the sale of dinner tickets in December. These tickets can be exchanged for meals during 1972.
3. Unrecorded wage expense for the latter part of December is $220.
4. Utility bills received for December services are $180. These have not been paid or recorded as yet.
5. Rental expense is $300 a month, payable six months in advance on June 30 and December 31.
6. On July 1 a new piece of equipment costing $200, to be used over a five-year period, was erroneously debited to Miscellaneous Expense.
7. Depreciation on the *other* equipment for the year amounts to $800.
8. There are two insurance policies on hand on December 31: a one-year policy purchased on September 1 for $300 and a two-year policy purchased on August 1 for $720. All premiums were charged to Miscellaneous Expense.

a) Set up ledger (T) accounts for each account in the trial balance.

b) Make all necessary adjusting entries to the ledger accounts. Set up additional accounts where needed.

c) Make all closing entries.

d) Prepare an income statement for the year and a position statement as of December 31.

4-6. The following situations are independent of each other. Prepare the journal entries necessary to adjust the accounts at the end of the period.

a) Accrued interest of $500 on notes receivable had not been recorded at the end of the period.

b) Equipment was rented at a cost of $5 per day, payable early in the month following use. The company used the equipment during the month of January and closed its books on January 31.

c) Fire insurance premiums of $300 applicable to future periods were debited to Insurance Expense.

d) Employees were paid weekly on Tuesday for work done through the preceding Saturday. Normally, no entries were made until the cash was paid. The weekly wages were $1,200. The accounting period ended on a Monday.

e) The president of the firm withdrew $2,000 in cash from the firm to meet personal expenses. The bookkeeper charged the amount to Miscellaneous Expense.

f) The entry to record cost of goods sold has already been made when it is discovered that merchandise inventory of $5,000 in a seldom used warehouse has been overlooked in taking the physical inventory count.

g) Normal maintenance expense of $500 on office equipment is erroneously debited to the Office Equipment account. Depreciation expense equal to 10 percent of the asset account is recorded.

h) Store equipment costing $2,000 is purchased at the beginning of the year. The amount is incorrectly debited to Supplies Expense. Store equipment has a useful life of five years.

4-7. The Canary Clothing Company begins business on July 1, 1972. The following data summarize the transactions for the first month of operations:

1. Stockholders invest $65,000 in cash.
2. Furniture and fixtures are acquired and installed at a cost of $24,000, paid in cash.
3. Merchandise is acquired on account at a cost of $30,000.
4. Store supplies acquired for cash are $1,800.
5. Rental payments in cash amount to $6,000.
6. Sales for the month are $35,000 on account and $5,000 for cash.
7. Wages paid in cash are $4,500.
8. Collections of accounts receivable amount to $10,900.
9. Cash payments to suppliers total $23,500.
10. Delivery charges on goods shipped to customers, paid in cash, are $2,400.

11. Advertising expenditures are $1,300.
12. Insurance premiums paid are $1,200.
13. Marketable securities costing $10,000 are purchased as a temporary investment.

Additional information is available:

14. Interest of $50 has been earned on the marketable securities.
15. Insurance expense for the month is $100.
16. Advertising supplies costing $200, purchased in item 11, remain unused on July 31.
17. Sales commissions equal to 5 percent of July sales are to be paid in early August.
18. On July 1 the rent is paid for a 12-month period.
19. Store supplies on hand on July 31 are $250.
20. Merchandise inventory on July 31 is $8,000.
21. Furniture and fixtures are estimated to have a life of 10 years.

a) Make journal entries to record the transactions in July.
b) Post the entries to ledger accounts.
c) Journalize and post adjusting entries in the light of the additional information given.
d) Journalize and post closing entries.
e) Prepare an income statement for July and a position statement as of July 31, 1972.

4–8. Your client, Bartholomew Faintheart, does his own bookkeeping. At the end of the year, he prepares a trial balance and, from this, an income statement which shows net income of $40,000 and a balance sheet which shows total assets of $118,000, total liabilities of $73,000 and owner's equity of $45,000. Before closing the books, he calls you in to review what he has done. In checking over his work, you discover the following:

1. Cash collections of accounts receivable in the amount of $800 have been debited to Cash and credited to Sales.
2. Included in the cash on hand is an I.O.U. for $300 signed by one of his employees.
3. The entire cost of an insurance policy of $2,400 has been charged to Insurance Expense, even though it is for a three-year period.
4. Interest accrued of $150 on a short-term note receivable has not been recorded.
5. No depreciation has been taken on a $3,000 truck used during the year. The depreciation rate is 25 percent.
6. In determining the amount of unused office supplies, Bartholomew has failed to count $300 of supplies on the top shelf of one of the cabinets.
7. A check for $2,500 has been received near the end of the year for merchandise to be delivered in the following year. The amount is included in Sales.
8. A sale for $580 of merchandise which cost $360 was recorded as

a debit to Accounts Receivable and a credit to Inventory of $580.
9. Wages of $320 were erroneously debited to repair expense instead of to wage expense.

a) Make general journal entries to record the necessary adjustments.
b) Set up a schedule that will allow you to determine the correct amount of net income and the correct totals for assets, liabilities, and owner's equity.

4–9. Stu Born decided to enter business for himself. He incorporated his firm under the name Adamant TV Repair Service on December 28, 1971. He invested $30,000 in cash in exchange for all the company's shares of stock. On the same day he purchased testing equipment for $10,000 cash, and parts inventory of $8,000 on account.

Because he did not wish to be bothered with details such as accounting, Stu turned over his record keeping to Mati and Hari Bookkeeping Service. The bookkeeping service kept a record of all cash receipts and disbursements during the calendar year 1972. Shortly after the end of the year, Mati and Hari presented the following "income" statement:

ADAMANT TV REPAIR SERVICE
Statement of Income on a Cash Basis for the Year 1972

Receipts from customers................		$63,500
Expenditures:		
Parts..............................	$16,700	
Wages..............................	24,400	
Rent...............................	2,400	
Utilities.........................	1,150	
Delivery truck.....................	4,500	
Gasoline for delivery truck.........	480	
Repair and maintenance..............	320	
Miscellaneous items.................	1,800	51,750
Net Cash Income.....................		$11,750

When Stu presented this statement to the bank to support a request for a loan to replenish his inventory of parts, the loan officer advised him that the statements did not adequately reflect proper "accrual" accounting principles. Also, the bank would like a properly prepared balance sheet.

You are called in to help and uncover the following additional facts:

1. Customers at the end of the year owe $4,200 for services rendered during 1972.
2. The parts inventory on hand on December 31, 1972 was $1,200.
3. A list of outstanding balances at year-end owed to suppliers of parts totaled $3,800.
4. Stu had signed a two-year lease at a monthly rent of $100, and paid the entire amount.

5. The testing equipment had a useful life of five years and the delivery truck, three years.

6. In addition to the unpaid balances due on supplies, accrued wages and miscellaneous items were $3,450 and $350, respectively.

a) Prepare a revised income statement for the year 1972, following proper accrual accounting procedures. Show how you calculated each item.

b) Prepare a balance sheet as of December 31, 1972.

4–10. The trial balance of the Cowart Corporation as of December 31, 1972, was as follows:

	Dr.	Cr.
Cash..................................	$ 2,000	
Merchandise inventory....................	48,000	
Accounts receivable......................	27,000	
Unexpired insurance......................	1,000	
Supplies................................	5,000	
Notes receivable (due 1975)..............	50,000	
Buildings...............................	55,000	
Accumulated depreciation—buildings........		$ 3,000
Sales revenue............................		72,000
Service fee revenue...........		8,000
Interest revenue.........................		1,000
Salaries expense....	12,000	
Insurance expense.......................	3,000	
Expenses applicable to service fees..........	5,000	
Capital stock............................		100,000
Retained earnings........................		24,000
	$208,000	$208,000

The accountant of the Cowart Corporation also made available the following information:

1. The inventory of supplies on hand on December 31, 1972 amounted to $4,000.

2. There was only one insurance policy still in force on December 31, 1972. This one-year policy, commencing July 1, 1972, cost $3,000. The bookkeeper debited Insurance Expense when the policy was purchased.

3. The buildings were acquired on January 1, 1971.

4. A physical count of merchandise inventory disclosed that there was $30,000 of merchandise on hand at the end of the year.

5. An additional $2,000 of salaries was earned by the employees and was owed to them by the company.

6. The annual interest rate was 3 percent on the notes receivable. Interest was normally collected three times a year on January 1, May 1, and September 1.

7. Royalty payments on merchandise sold for the year were estimated to be $3,000. They were due on February 1, 1973.

8. Service fees paid in advance were credited to Service Fee Revenue. As of December 31, 1972, $2,000 of these had not been earned.

a) Set up ledger (T) accounts for all the accounts in the trial balance, and record the existing balances.

b) Record any necessary adjustments to the ledger accounts. Use additional T accounts if necessary.

c) Record the closing entries for the period.

d) Prepare an income statement for the year and a position statement as of December 31.

4–11. The Lacklustre Corporation began operations on October 1, 1971. The following transactions took place in October:

Oct. 1 Issued capital stock for cash, $15,000.
1 Paid three months' rent, $1,200.
1 Purchased equipment with a useful life of 10 years for cash, $3,600.
2 Purchased merchandise from Lincoln Brothers, Inc., for $200 on account.
3 Sold merchandise on account, $450 ($300 to J. Young and $150 to Virgil Roberts).
4 Cash sales, $600.
6 Purchased supplies on account, $650 ($350 from Brand Corporation and $300 from Lincoln Brothers, Inc.).
8 Paid freight bill on goods shipped to customers, $50.
9 Purchased merchandise from Lincoln Brothers, Inc., $1,700 on account.
10 Virgil Roberts paid his account.
12 J. Young returned merchandise for credit, $100.
14 Purchased merchandise from Lincoln Brothers, Inc., $3,000 on account.
15 Paid $200 to Lincoln Brothers, Inc.
16 Sold goods to Nunn Company on account, $600.
16 Paid salaries of $500 in cash for the first half month.
16 Bought a delivery truck with a useful life of five years from Stall Motors, Inc., for $3,000 cash.
20 J. Young paid for the goods he purchased on October 3, less returns.
24 Sold merchandise to Nunn Company on account, $500.
29 Paid Lincoln Brothers, Inc., for the shipment of October 9.

Additional information:

1. On October 31, there were $100 of supplies on hand and $3,600 of merchandise on hand.

2. Salaries for the period October 16–31 were to be paid on November 1.

a) Journalize the above transactions in a general journal. (Include a date and posting reference column in the journal form.)

b) Post from the journal to the ledger accounts, both general and subsidiary. (Assign account numbers to your general ledger accounts and use these in the posting process.)

c) Take a trial balance and prepare schedules of subsidiary account balances for accounts receivable and accounts payable to see that they agree with the control accounts.

d) Journalize and post all adjusting entries.

e) Prepare an adjusted trial balance.

f) Prepare an income statement and a position statement.

g) Journalize and post closing entries.

4–A–1. Hot and Cold Air is a small sales and service business operated by Dewey Blow. The business sells and services air conditioners in the summer and furnaces in the winter.

Revenues arise from the sale of new air conditioners, commissions on sales of new furnaces, repair service charges on air conditioners, installation charges on furnaces, and repair service charges on furnaces. All sales of new air-conditioning units are on account. Dewey keeps a regular inventory of air conditioners. On furnace sales, Dewey acts only as an agent, receiving a sales commission from the furnace manufacturer and an installation charge from the customer. The customer pays the manufacturer directly for the furnace, and Dewey maintains no inventory of furnaces. Most repair work on both furnaces and air conditioners is done on a cash basis except for 12 major customers who are billed on account for all repair work.

In addition to himself, Dewey has three employees. Two of them are repairmen who do the maintenance work on the furnaces and air conditioners and install the furnaces. The other employee is a bookkeeper-clerk-receptionist who handles various administrative chores. Dewey does all the selling himself. The repairmen are paid in cash weekly; the bookkeeper is paid once a month. Dewey also draws a salary monthly.

Operating costs consist of supplies and parts used in repair work. Inventories of both supplies and spare parts are maintained. Also included in operating costs are rent (paid in cash at the beginning of each month), utility services (paid in cash monthly), and depreciation and running costs of a truck.

Purchases of air conditioners and spare parts are made quite frequently for cash. Supplies are purchased on account. Because he must buy his air-conditioner inventory for cash, Dewey frequently borrows from the local bank on notes, particularly during the summer months.

a) Set up a chart of accounts for Hot and Cold Air in *sufficient detail* to provide the foundation for a useful accounting system.

b) Prepare journal forms for a cash receipts book *and* a cash disbursements book which would be suitable for this company.

c) Explain in detail how the cash receipts book you set up would be posted.

4–A–2. On June 30, 1972, the end of the fiscal year, the unadjusted trial balance of Brownell Bowling Alley, Inc., shows the following accounts and balances:

	Dr.	Cr.
Cash	$ 18,000	
Supplies and accessories	50,000	
Prepaid insurance	12,000	
Prepaid rent	24,000	
Alleys	100,000	
Alleys—accumulated depreciation		$ 12,000
Furniture and fixtures	5,000	
Furniture and fixtures—accumulated depreciation		1,000
Accounts payable		32,000
Term loan payable—due in 1975		40,000
Capital stock		50,000
Retained earnings		15,000
Bowling games paid		100,000
Sales of accessories		17,000
Wage expense	40,000	
Utilities	18,000	
	$267,000	$267,000

Additional information:

1. Prepaid insurance represents a three-year policy taken out on July 1, 1971.
2. The company leases the pinsetting machines at a cost of $0.10 per game. Meters on the machines indicate that 225,000 games have been bowled during the year.
3. Rent expense is $18,000.
4. Depreciation on the alleys is $10,000 per year and on furniture and fixtures, $1,000.
5. Accrued wages on June 30 amount to $1,300.
6. An inventory of supplies and accessories amounts to $38,000.
7. The interest rate on the term loan is 5 percent.

a) Prepare a work sheet, following the format illustrated in Appendix 4–A.
b) Prepare an income statement for the year ended June 30, 1972 and a position statement as of June 30, 1972, in good form.

4–A–3. The Neverchange Auto Supply Corporation operates a manual accounting system containing a multicolumn sales journal. The company sells to about 50 different customers, each purchasing on the average of twice a month. A subsidiary ledger for accounts receivable is maintained. All sales are on account. Separate sales accounts are maintained for each of the major product lines—tires, batteries, accessories, and repair parts. The company adds to the invoice price 4 percent for sales tax, which it is required to collect from the customer and periodically remit to the appropriate governmental unit. Also, on accessory sales, there is a 5 percent "luxury" tax for which the customer is billed.

The following are selected sales transactions during May:

1. Customer: Stall Motors
   Invoice: No. 538, dated May 2
   Items sold:
   Tires... $ 300
   Batteries..   50
   Repair parts.......................................   400

2. Customer: Rip-M-Up Body Shop
   Invoice: No. 555, dated May 10
   Items sold:
   Accessories....................................... $ 400
   Repair parts....................................... 2,500

3. Customer: Car Service Center, Inc.
   Invoice: No. 563, dated May 19
   Items sold:
   Tires... $ 200
   Batteries..   100
   Accessories..   700

4. Customer: Rambling Wreck Repair Shop
   Invoice: No. 590, dated May 25
   Items sold:
   Accessories....................................... $ 100
   Repair parts....................................... 1,350

a) Set up a multicolumn sales journal with column headings suitable for *this* company, and enter these four transactions.

b) Total the journal and describe the posting procedure that would be employed.

4–A–4. The trial balance of Lotta Noise Sound Equipment Corporation as of December 31, 1972, appears below:

Debits

Cash... $ 4,000
Accounts receivable.............................   14,000
Inventories.....................................   86,000
Leasehold improvements..........................   5,000
Equipment.......................................   30,000
Retained earnings...............................   10,700
Selling expense.................................   18,800
Delivery expense................................   2,500
Administrative expense..........................   4,600
Rent expense....................................   2,400
                                                  $178,000

Credits

Allowance for amortization—leasehold
  improvements.................................. $ 2,400
Accumulated depreciation—equipment..............   5,000
Accounts payable................................   31,900
Capital stock...................................   40,000
Sales...   87,000
Revenue from consulting assignments.............   4,900
Repair revenue..................................   6,800
                                                  $178,000

In the course of reviewing the records, the accountant discovers the following facts:

1. The cost of the ending inventory is $36,200.
2. Sales include a down payment of $2,000 on a customized hi-fi system to be delivered in 1973.
3. Amortization of leasehold improvements is provided for in the amount of $600 per year.
4. Depreciation on equipment totals $3,000 for the year, chargeable 10 percent to selling, 60 percent to delivery, and 30 percent to administration.
5. Administrative expense includes the $360 cost of a one-year insurance policy purchased on October 1, 1972.
6. The board of directors declares $1,000 in dividends, payable on January 15, 1973.

a) Set up a work sheet and use it to record the adjusting entries and to organize the information for the preparation of the income statement and the balance sheet. Add accounts at the bottom of the work sheet if necessary.

b) Prepare the financial statements from the work sheet columns.

c) Prepare a single compound journal entry to close the books at the end of the period. (You may assume that the adjusting entries have already been journalized and posted.)

4–A–5. A firm uses the following journals as its books of original entry: a cash receipts book, a cash disbursements book, a sales journal, an invoice payable register, and a general journal. Direct posting from source documents to subsidiary ledger accounts is practiced. The following transactions are selected from those occurring during the month:

1. Sales on account for a day.
2. Insurance expired during the month.
3. Payment of monthly rent.
4. Purchase of office equipment.
5. Purchase of merchandise on account.
6. Cash received from customers.
7. Shares of stock issued to the president of the company for cash.
8. Employees' bimonthly wages are paid.
9. A freight bill covering costs of goods shipped to customers is received.
10. A supplier's invoice is paid.
11. Cash sales.
12. Supplies are purchased on account.
13. A 90-day note is received from a customer in settlement of an open account.
14. Wages are accrued at the end of the month.
15. The company borrows from the bank, giving a six-month note payable.

For *each* of the above transactions, indicate:

a) What journal it would be recorded in.
b) The account(s) that would be debited and credited.
c) Describe the underlying source document that the accountant would probably use to support the making of the transaction.
d) Whether the account(s) listed in part (*b*) would be posted individually or as part of a column total.

4–A–6. Bailey Beetle was assistant chief accountant of the Showme Company. He had just completed the work sheet for the year 1972 and left it on his desk at home. Unfortunately his son Ringo was playing at the desk with some ink eradicator. Ringo managed to apply the eradicator fairly liberally to many of the figures on the work sheet, as evidenced by the resulting form, reproduced as Exhibit 1.

Copy and complete the work sheet.

4–A–7. Two recent business school graduates decided to form a corporation to operate a wholesale distributing business. They set up a chart of accounts for the accounts they thought would be used (given below). In addition, four specialized journals (cash receipts, cash disbursements, purchases, and sales) plus a general journal were to be used, along with appropriate subsidiary ledgers.

No.	Title	No.	Title
100	Cash	800	Sales
120	Accounts Receivable	900	Cost of Goods Sold
125	Notes Receivable	910	Supplies Expense
200	Inventory—Merchandise	920	Wages Expense
210	Inventory—Supplies	930	Miscellaneous Selling Expense
230	Prepaid Insurance	932	Advertising Expense
320	Equipment	940	Miscellaneous General Expense
321	Accumulated Depreciation	942	Insurance Expense
510	Accounts Payable	943	Utilities Expense
520	Notes Payable	944	Rent Expense
700	Capital Stock		
710	Retained Earnings		

The following transactions occurred during November, the first month of operations:

Nov. 1 Issued capital stock for cash in the amount of $100,000.
   1 Signed a lease on a combination office and warehouse. **Paid** the monthly rent of $2,000.
   1 Purchased equipment costing $50,000 on account.
   2 Purchased merchandise from A on account, $30,000.
   2 Purchased supplies from C on account, $10,000.
   3 Sold merchandise to W for $4,000.
   5 Sold merchandise to Z for $3,000.
   6 Purchased merchandise from B on account, $20,000
   7 Sold merchandise to W for $2,000.
   7 Paid weekly wages of $2,000.
   8 Merchandise returned by W, $1,000.

EXHIBIT 1

SHOWME COMPANY
Work Sheet, 1972

	Trial Balance Dr.	Trial Balance Cr.	Adjustments Dr.	Adjustments Cr.	Adjusted Trial Balance Dr.	Adjusted Trial Balance Cr.	Income Statement Dr.	Income Statement Cr.	Position Statement Dr.	Position Statement Cr.
Cash	21,900								47,400	
Accounts receivable	207,100									
Accrued interest receivable									3,800	
Merchandise	30,500				42,300					
Supplies	18,700		2,500		2,500					
Prepaid rent				6,000	6,000					
Investments									30,500	
Equipment										
Accumulated depreciation		5,000				15,800				6,000
Accounts payable		40,000								
Notes payable				1,000						1,000
Interest payable						1,200				1,200
Salaries payable										
Common stock		50,000								
Retained earnings, January 1, 1972		41,200		3,800						41,200
Sales								254,000		
Interest revenue										
Delivery expense	4,500									
Salaries expense			1,200				48,000			
Rent expense	16,100									
Supplies expense										
Depreciation expense	1,000				2,000					
Interest expense										
	406,000	406,000	—	—	413,000	413,000	—	—	—	—
Cost of goods sold										
Net income										

9   Paid freight charges on merchandise delivered to customers, $50.

10   Purchased supplies from D on account, $1,500.

13   Cash was received from W for the November 3 sale, less the returns on November 8.

14   Paid weekly wages (see entry on November 7 for amounts).

15   Sold merchandise to Y for $8,000.

15   Paid $30,000 to A for November 2 purchase.

16   Purchased merchandise from A on account, $20,000.

16   Paid newspaper for running an advertisement twice a week during the month, $300.

16   Paid $10,000 toward the bill from purchase of equipment on November 1 and gave a $40,000, 6 percent, 60-day note for the balance.

17   Cash was received from W for the November 7 sale and from Z for the November 5 sale.

18   Sold merchandise to Z for $12,000.

19   Paid freight bill of $1,500 for delivery of products sold to customers.

20   Purchased merchandise from B on account, $7,000.

20   Returned merchandise costing $2,000 to A.

21   Paid utility bills for the month of $30.

21   Made payments on accounts, $10,000 to A and $10,000 to B.

21   Paid weekly wages.

28   Received a note for $8,000 from Y in settlement of his account.

28   Sold merchandise to Z for $3,000.

28   Paid weekly wages.

29   Purchased merchandise from A on account, $13,000.

30   Paid additional utility bills applicable to November, $80.

31   Purchased a delivery truck for cash, $5,000.

a) Identify those accounts in the ledger that are control accounts necessitating a subsidiary ledger.

b) After a careful review of the above transactions, set up the journal forms for this company. Employ whatever special columns you believe are appropriate.

c) Enter the transactions that relate to the *cash disbursements* journal. If you find it necessary to open any new accounts not listed in the chart of accounts, assign a number to them consistent with the coding system being used.

d) Indicate how the cash disbursements journal would be posted by placing ledger account numbers in the appropriate places.

CHAPTER FIVE

ACCOUNTING NET INCOME

THE PRECEDING chapters develop the conceptual framework and some of the bookkeeping tools necessary to measure accounting net income. Our basic assumption states that net income is best measured by matching costs (specifically, expired costs or expenses) against their related revenues. In this chapter we discuss some expansions and elaborations of this concept of accounting income as well as some of the problems involved with it. Before doing so, however, let us tie together some of the threads of thought relating to income measurement developed in the earlier chapters.

REVIEW OF THE MATCHING CONCEPT

The foundation for the accounting concept of income rests on the relationship between assets received and assets consumed in the periodic operating activities of the business. The asset inflows, usually consisting of cash or accounts receivable, from the sales of goods or services provide a monetary measure of the accomplishment of the firm in satisfying consumer needs. Similarly, the various assets consumed in this process afford a monetary expression of the effort expended. Matching the inflow and outflow of assets for particular time intervals gives us periodic readings about the performance of the business entity.

In double-entry bookkeeping we find it more practical to implement the matching concept through the use of temporary owners' equity accounts. Beginning with an equality of assets and equities on the position statement, we observe that any change in assets associated with operating activities causes similar changes in owners' equity. Revenue accounts are introduced to record the increases in owners' equity as assets flow into the business from operations. They represent sources of assets. Various expense accounts are set up to record the decreases in owners' equity as assets are consumed in the production of revenues. They represent uses of assets. The actual periodic measurement of income involves finding the expense transactions that match the revenue transactions. Nevertheless, the revenue-expense flows merely reflect the relevant asset changes. The heart of the accounting concept of net income still rests in a matching of asset inflows and outflows.

A number of practical problems arise in the implementation of this income-measurement model. Two in particular serve as the center of discussion in this chapter. The first involves difficulties in the determination of exactly which revenues a particular cost should be matched against. Out of this discussion comes the concept of the period expense. The second limitation of the theoretical revenue-expense model is its failure clearly to encompass other equity changes broadly related to period operations. In other words, we may wish to report on other aspects of performance in conducting periodic business activities. Our income concept must therefore be expanded to include transactions other than just revenues and expenses.

PERIOD EXPENSES

When costs can be closely associated with the sale of a product, they are relatively easy to match against the revenue they help to produce. For instance, the costs of merchandise purchased for resale are attached to specific units of product. These costs may include both the direct purchase price and indirect items, such as freight charges and the costs of operating the purchasing department (handling costs). By being related to units of product, they become part of the expense "cost of goods sold" when the product is sold. In this way, they are fairly accurately matched against the proper revenue inflow. Another example is sales commissions. Here again, the relationship between effort and accomplishment is direct; sales commission expense arises at the time a sale is made and is matched against the revenue produced from the sale.

Ideally, we should like to be able to relate all costs to the revenues of various accounting periods with equal accuracy. The use of some assets, however, cannot be closely identified with particular revenues. Rather than being associated with a specific unit of product or with an identifiable revenue transaction, their use is related to activities which occur during a *time period* in which the revenues are produced. Examples include administrative salaries, training costs, expenditures on new product development or methods improvement, operating costs of the firm's computer system, etc. They do represent the use of productive resources; the question is one of determining the accounting period or periods in which their benefit is received. These types of cost seem to relate more to the passage of a period of time and have only an indirect association with the particular revenues of the period. They are often referred to as *period costs*.

Many of these period costs actually benefit more than one accounting period. For example, the cost of conducting an institutional advertising campaign certainly is expected to help produce revenues in future periods as well as the period in which the costs are incurred. However, the problem is to determine what portion of the cost is applicable to future periods, which future periods receive benefit, and to what extent each period benefits. These questions must be answered before a precise matching of costs and related revenues can occur. Unfortunately, with present means of measurement this goal simply cannot be reached for certain types of costs.

As a consequence, most period costs are treated as expenses of the period in which they are incurred. For example, the salary cost of the president of the firm is treated as an administrative expense in each period. A theoretical argument could be made that a portion of the salary cost should be deferred and matched against revenues of future periods to the extent that some of the services received in the current period benefit the operations in future accounting periods. The amount and length of any future benefit would be practically impossible to measure, however. Other examples of period costs which pertain to several accounting periods but which are nevertheless expensed upon incurrence are costs of market surveys, normal advertising expenditures, public relations costs, and legal and accounting services.

Although the treatment of certain costs as period expenses may be admittedly inaccurate to some extent, the practice is justified on two points. First, often no feasible alternative is open. Asset values, it is argued, should be carried forward only when there is a clearly demonstrable and reasonably measurable future period of benefit. For many period costs, the relationship between cost incurrence in this period and revenue generation in future periods is so tenuous that accountants cannot sanction deferring any asset cost beyond the current period. To do so would violate established norms of objective and conservative measurement.

The second justification for period expenses is that, with recurring types of costs, any deviations in net income from the ideal matching probably are not material The actual cost incurred in each period probably does not differ materially from the cost that would be assigned to the period on the basis of a theoretical allocation of each period's expenditures to the revenues they help produce (even if this were practically possible) because of a compensating lag effect. The portion of the president's salary for this period that would be allocated to future periods is counterbalanced approximately by portions of the salary which were incurred in past periods but are applicable to the current period. Notice, though, that for this argument to be valid, the period cost should be similar in amount each period, have the same useful life, and follow the same pattern of use over that life.

The concept of the period expense and the rationalizations on which it rests should not be used as an excuse for failure to make a reasonably intelligent analysis of the benefit received from particular costs. There would be little justification, for instance, for treating unused advertising supplies as an expense simply because advertising costs are normally handled as period expenses. The reader of financial statements should be alert to possible distortions from an inappropriate use of the period expense idea.

Research and Development Costs

The distinction between asset cost and period expense has become tremendously important in the treatment of research and development costs. Careful and continuing analysis is necessary here if accounting is not to suffer from too facile use of the period expense concept to solve assignment problems. Research and development costs include salaries of scientists, engineers, technicians, and administrators as well as supplies, tools, perishable equipment, and other indirect costs. Often great uncertainty surrounds the interconnection between R&D expenditures and future revenue inflows. As a result, accounting difficulties arise at two points—in determining whether an asset has been created by the expenditures and, if so, in determining how many future periods will benefit. Three alternative treatments can be found for dealing with these difficulties: (1) setting up R&D costs as assets by individual project, (2) writing off R&D costs as an expense in each period, and (3) handling R&D costs as an intangible asset to be spread out as expense over an arbitrary time period.

Some firms are able to gather these costs for each individual research project. Costs applicable to a project are accumulated in separate asset accounts until the project is complete. Then, if a patentable item results, the costs of that project are transferred to the Patent account and written off over the life of the patent. If, instead of a patent, some other determinable future benefit results (e.g., a government contract), the costs can be allocated over the estimated life of the future benefit. If no lasting benefit results from the project, the costs are expensed. Completion of some projects may take place many years later. Care must be taken that unproductive expenditures on projects are not allowed to build up as assets simply because the projects are not yet completed.

Most firms treat research and development costs as period expenses, on the grounds that these costs are too difficult to segregate and that their period of benefit is unknown. Such a treatment might be justified for the cost of pure research activities, where the uncertainty of future benefit may be very great, or for *general* research carried on continuously to improve existing products and processes, which can be viewed as an on-going activity not unlike institutional advertising, necessary for success in the long run. Presumably, much of the benefit is realized very shortly, and no valid basis exists for measuring the portion which may benefit future sales. Consequently, writing off each year's costs as an expense is probably just as accurate as attempting to allocate costs to different periods. Disadvantages arise when this approach is applied too broadly to R&D expenditures that are irregular in size and timing and do actually give rise to future benefits. Then period expense treatment creates distortion. Moreover, period expense treatment may allow management to manipulate periodic net income reported to stockholders by fluctuating R&D expenditures.

A few companies take a middle position, charging all research and development costs to an intangible asset to be amortized over an arbitrary time period, such as 5 or 10 years. The basis for this procedure rests on a recognition that these costs benefit more than one accounting period. The assumption is that although the exact period of usefulness is not known, less distortion in net income is involved if they are amortized over a reasonable time interval than if they are all written off when incurred. An example might be research on new products or processes. Here future benefits often do arise, although identification with specific projects may not be feasible. Perhaps a write-off over an average period based on past experience would be appropriate.

It is clear that part of the diversity in treatment of R&D costs stems from differences in the nature and purpose of the costs and in the particular situation faced by a firm. Pure research costs probably should be handled differently from project-oriented development costs. Similarly, in a large firm new product costs may be of a recurring nature, while in a smaller firm they may fluctuate substantially from year to year. In the former case, the period expense expedient may be justified; in the latter case, perhaps not. The point is that under given sets of circumstances each of the procedures described above can be justified. Unfortunately, generally accepted accounting principles permit any of these alternatives under practically *any* circumstances.

Research and development would seem to be an area where a careful segregation and analysis of different types of costs would yield a more accurate matching with related revenues. Unfortunately, in many companies this detailed classification is not made, and all R&D costs are lumped together and handled exactly the same way on the financial statements. More often than not, immediate write-off of all such costs is the result. This treatment receives support from income tax regulations, which allow most R&D costs to be treated as deductions for tax purposes in the year incurred. However, for the large and growing expenditures being made in this area, treatment on the financial statements simply as period expenses may be increasingly difficult to justify.

OTHER PERIODIC ACTIVITIES

Period costs represent only one problem encountered when the matching concept is applied to real-world transactions. The matching concept, narrowly conceived, assumes a normal pattern and causal relationship between revenue and expense occurrence. However, certain other events, aside from capital stock transactions, may affect owners' equity during the reporting period. In many cases these events relate broadly to the use of assets and the conduct of business operations. Yet, they do not fit exactly into the scope of the activities we have introduced so far.

Consequently, there is a need for additional temporary accounts in which to record these other changes. It may also be necessary to modify and expand our existing concept of net income to encompass some of these events. In this section we discuss certain of these special accounts—gains, losses, taxes, interest charges, and dividends.

Gains

A special type of increase in owners' equity may arise if noncurrent assets are disposed of for more assets than are given up. Assume that a parcel of land which originally cost $5,000 is sold for $6,000 in cash. This transaction would be recorded by the following entry:

```
Cash.......................................  6,000
     Land......................................           5,000
     Gain on Sale of Land....................            1,000
```

The Gain on Sale of Land account reflects an addition to retained earnings because net assets have increased other than through owners' investments or revenues.

Gains represent events favorable from the stockholders' perspective and not connected with the normal operations of the firm. Disposition of non-inventory assets, advantageous settlement of liabilities, or other nonrepetitive events (e.g., damages collected on a lawsuit) all may give rise to gains. Gain accounts are closed to Income Summary and appear on the income statement.

Losses

Losses occur when assets disappear and no contribution to the ordinary or normal operations of the business is received. They represent costs which, when acquired, were intended to be utilized in the production of revenues but which for some reason have been eliminated instead. Some common examples of losses are the cost of merchandise destroyed by fire, the undepreciated cost of equipment that has to be scrapped, cash embezzled by an employee, etc.

To record these kinds of transactions, we use loss accounts, which are debited when the assets which have disappeared are credited. For instance, the three losses mentioned above would be recorded as follows:

```
Loss from Fire Damage.......................... xxx
     Merchandise Inventory...................... xxx          xxx

Loss on Retirement of Equipment................ xxx
     Equipment.................................. xxx          xxx

Embezzlement Loss.............................. xxx
     Cash...................................... xxx          xxx
```

Or, if the land in the preceding gain example were sold for only $3,500, the *net* decrease in assets and owners' equity would be recorded in a loss account as follows:

```
Cash.......................................... 3,500
Loss on Sale of Land.......................... 1,500
     Land..................................... 5,000
```

Theoretically, a distinction exists between an expense and a loss. In actual business practice it is often difficult to determine where one concept ends and the other begins. For example, is spoiled merchandise a loss or simply a necessary cost of producing revenue and hence an expense? In practice, losses, like gains, generally arise from nonrecurring, relatively unusual transactions.

The term "loss" also has a second meaning. It is used to signify the excess of total revenue deductions over revenues. In this sense "net loss" becomes a counterpart to "net income." It indicates the net decrease in owners' equity when asset outflow or consumption exceeds asset inflow from business activities during the period.

Taxes

Taxes are a claim on business assets by various governmental authorities. Some types of taxes require special treatment in the accounting records. However, instead of discussing these specialized taxes in detail here, let us concern ourselves with the more common types, such as property taxes and the corporate income tax. The latter is perhaps the most important and serves as our example.

As the tax liability accrues, there is a concomitant decrease in owners' equity. This decrease is recorded in a special temporary account. The entry to record income taxes is:

```
Income Taxes.................................. xxx
     Estimated Liability for Income Taxes........     xxx
```

Income taxes in many ways are similar to an expense. In a broad sense they can be viewed as a payment for government services which are used up during the period or as a necessary period expense for the privilege of conducting business as a corporation. On the other hand, the amount of assets that is eventually distributed to governmental bodies often bears at best only an indirect and varying relationship to the amount of service received by the business entity. Some, therefore, liken taxes more to an outright distribution of a portion of the assets than to an expense in the sense of the cost of assets used up in the production of revenues. Probably there are elements of both concepts in the income tax charge. Nevertheless, there can be no net increase in retained earnings from the activities of the period until the claims represented by taxes are provided for.

Interest Charges and Dividends

Another major aspect of performance during a period involves the financing of the firm's activities. When assets are paid or promised to various creditors as payment for the use of borrowed money, this fact should be included on the report of the activities for the period. If assets are acquired through the incurrence of interest-bearing liabilities, then as time passes an interest liability, a legal claim on assets, accrues. This increase in a liability and corresponding decrease in owners' equity is recorded as follows:

```
Interest Charges............................... xxx
    Interest Payable...........................        xxx
```

Then, when cash is actually distributed to the bondholders or other creditors, the liability is liquidated. Interest Charges (Interest Expense) is the special-purpose retained earnings account used to accumulate the total compensation for the use of funds supplied by creditors during that period. Interest payable represents the unpaid portion of that claim as of any particular date.

Much as interest represents the eventual distribution of assets to creditors, the Dividends account is used to record the decline in owners' equity when assets are withdrawn by the owners of the business entity or are promised to them. In a corporation the owners are the stockholders, and withdrawal of assets from the entity is accomplished normally by declaration of a dividend. If the dividend is declared and paid immediately, the entry is:

```
Dividends...................................... xxx
    Cash.......................................        xxx
```

More commonly, the dividend is declared, and payment occurs later. Unlike interest, dividends do not accrue merely with the passage of time. When declared, however, the dividend represents a decrease in retained earnings and a corresponding increase in a liability. For informational reasons, a separate temporary account is often used instead of a direct debit to Retained Earnings. The entry is:

```
Dividends...................................... xxx
        Dividends Payable........................        xxx
```

The actual distribution of assets simply liquidates the claim previously recognized.

Summary

The special-purpose accounts studied so far are presented below:

Increases in owners' equity:
Revenues.
Gains.
Decreases in owners' equity:
Expenses.
Losses.
Taxes.
Interest charges.
Dividends.

They all have one trait in common; they reflect temporary changes, upward or downward, in retained earnings. The reason for the change is different for each one. Each represents a particular aspect of periodic performance; together, they show the net change in retained earnings arising from noncapital-raising activities.

AN EXPANDED CONCEPT OF ACCOUNTING INCOME

Prior to this chapter our concept of income encompassed only revenue and expense changes. Having introduced additional owners' equity changes, we must now choose those which we wish to include in our income concept. There probably is no single answer. Several relevant subtotals from among the array of owners' equity changes could be singled out for emphasis as "income" calculations. How broadly or narrowly should periodic business "operations" be defined? Do they include "unusual" nonrecurring items such as gains and losses? Does *net* income exist before or after income taxes? Is the latter an expense or a distribution of a portion of the business income to the government? Should the net income figure encompass financial charges, such as interest and dividends? These are only a few of many questions that reflect varying views of net income. Conceivably, we may have a whole series of different income figures, depending on the point of view and the purpose of the user of the income statement.

Without attempting to resolve all of these questions (if indeed there is a resolution), this section considers three major topics—net income to owners, reporting of extraordinary items, and format variations of the income statement.

Net Income to the Owners

We say in Chapter One that an objective reporting on past activities of the firm provides the owners of the firm with a measure by which they can evaluate the stewardship of their investment and help to project the future. Owners comprise the major audience assumed under financial accounting theory. They represent the ultimate risk takers in the business endeavor. Consistently with the purpose of financial accounting to serve its audience, the perspective of the stockholders should dominate the income calculation.

From the stockholders' viewpoint, all legal (taxes) and financial (interest) claims must be deducted before the owners' interest in the firm's assets can be said to have increased. Net income, therefore, is the net asset amount available to the owners. Thus, revenues, expenses, gains, losses, taxes, and interest are all *determinants* of net income. The net effect of these periodic events is the increase in owners' equity. Dividends, on the other hand, are viewed as a *distribution* of a portion of the income to the owners. Because of the importance of the stockholder audience, net income is most often interpreted in accounting practice as the net increase in the stockholders' interest in the business. This is the sense in which the term is used in the remaining chapters. Only dividends are treated as a deduction *from* net income. (i.e., dividend = part of net income)

Earnings of the Entity. Many theorists and financial analysts contend that another subtotal should be emphasized, although it usually does not appear separately on published income statements. This is the earnings applicable to all suppliers of financial capital. In accordance with the entity concept, an income figure which portrays the overall use of assets by the entity, regardless of their original source, is a meaningful complement to the income figure calculated from the perspective of a particular class of investors, such as stockholders.

Interest and dividends represent charges for the use of investor capital by the business entity. All financial capital suppliers have a similar type of interest in the business. They have committed their funds to the entity for a time period in anticipation of earning a return thereon. Only the degree of risk and the nature of the commitment differ. Under this interpretation both interest charges and dividends are treated as divisions or distributions, rather than determinants, of income. While varying in their legal refinements, interest charges and dividends both relate to the manner in which resources are acquired. They differ somewhat from other expenses and losses, which relate to the use of the resources.

The earnings of the entity, defined as net income before interest but after taxes, represent the increase arising from the use of assets, regardless of where the financial capital to acquire those assets happens to be obtained. This figure is useful to readers of the statement, for it gives an idea of the effectiveness with which all assets have been utilized, no matter how they are financed. We use this figure in the analysis of financial statements in Chapter Fifteen. In most instances, however, this figure has to be calculated by the analyst himself, as it is not explicitly shown on the income statement.

Statement of Retained Earnings. Dividends can be deducted directly from net income on the income statement. In this case the last figure on the income statement is the increase (or decrease) in retained earnings for the period. To reconcile the period's change in retained earnings more completely with the balances on the comparative position statements, however, many firms introduce a separate statement of retained earnings. The statement starts with the balance of retained earnings at the beginning of the year and includes any other changes in retained earnings not shown on the income statement. The major one, of course, is dividends, but occasionally other direct debits and credits to retained earnings are recorded. An example of such a statement is shown for Monsanto Company in Table 5–2. A compromise approach also frequently encountered is a single statement combining the information that otherwise would be reported on separate statements of income and retained earnings (see Table 5–3).

Reporting of Extraordinary Items

One extremely perplexing problem area related to income statement preparation is the reporting of unusual items. Unusual items include the gains and losses discussed earlier as well as any corrections of prior period errors or other adjustments to retained earnings. Until the Accounting Principles Board acted in 1966, viewpoints of accountants seemed to gravitate toward one or the other of two concepts of reporting.

All-Inclusive versus Current Operating Concepts. Our discussion of gains and losses implies that the income statement of the current period should reflect all transactions, normal or extraordinary, affecting owners' equity during the period—except, of course, transactions in capital stock and dividends. In this way a series of income statements gives a complete picture of the history of the retained earnings account. This approach to reporting is known as the *all-inclusive* income statement concept.

The contrasting view asserts that only the "normal" changes in retained earnings should be reported on the income statement. All unusual items should be debited or credited directly to Retained Earnings and should appear on the separate statement of retained earnings. In this way the net income figure reflects only the *current operating performance* during the period. This view is founded on the belief that the primary use of the income statement is to forecast future earnings and to compare with other companies and periods. Thus, any nonrecurring gains, losses, or adjustments from prior periods would distort the net income figure for these purposes by giving an inaccurate reading as to the normal stream of the firm's operations.

APB Opinion No. 9.   This controversy again illustrates the basic dilemma of financial accounting in trying to serve a number of different audiences. No one really knows exactly by whom the statements will be used, for what purposes they will be used, and whether the user is qualified to evaluate the contents of the report. Although not answering the underlying questions, the Accounting Principles Board attempted to resolve the reporting problem in its *Opinion No. 9.*[1]

The basic recommendation is that net income should reflect all items of profit and loss recognized during the period, except for prior period adjustments. Extraordinary items, however, should be shown separately as an element of net income for the period. In short, then, the APB established two guidelines for reporting. First, unusual events should be divided into two categories—extraordinary items and prior period adjustments. The former should appear on the income statement; the latter should involve an adjustment to the beginning balance on the separate statement of retained earnings. Secondly, on the income statement, the results of extraordinary transactions should be segregated from the results of ordinary, recurring operating transactions. The income statement form would highlight the following elements:

```
Income before extraordinary items........... $xxx
    Extraordinary items......................  xxx
Net Income.................................. $xxx
```

In its opinion the APB also set forth criteria for distinguishing between the two categories of unusual events. Extraordinary items include material gains and losses of the nature described earlier. These are events which are significantly different from the customary activities of the firm and which are not expected to recur as part of the ordinary operating processes. Prior period adjustments are also nonrecurring but are much rarer. Four criteria were established for an unusual item to qualify as a prior period adjustment: (1) it can be specifically identified with activities of particular accounting periods, (2) it is not attributable to economic events occurring since the prior period, (3) it must depend primarily on determinations by persons other than management, and (4) it must not have

---

[1] *Reporting the Results of Operations, Opinion of the Accounting Principles Board No. 9* (New York: AICPA, December 1966).

been susceptible to reasonable estimation at the time it occurred.[2] For example, the settlement in 1971 of an income tax case relating to 1966 income, or the final judgment in 1971 of a patent infringement lawsuit from 1967, would be prior period adjustments not reported on the income statement.[3]

Income Statement Format

A condensed income statement and statement of retained earnings for Monsanto Company for 1969 are presented in Tables 5–1 and 5–2. These particular formats encompass the various ideas mentioned earlier.

TABLE 5–1

MONSANTO COMPANY
Statement of Consolidated Income
For the Year Ended December 31, 1969
(in thousands)

Net sales............................		$1,938,838
Cost of goods sold.............		1,425,355
Gross profit.....................		$ 513,483
Less:		
Selling and administrative expenses....................	$221,105	
Research, development, patent, and engineering expenses..................	101,479	322,584
Operating profit................		$ 190,899
Other income charges, net.....		8,060
Income before income taxes......		$ 182,839
Provision for income taxes....		73,473
Income before extraordinary credits.......................		$ 109,366
Extraordinary credits.........		6,741
Net income.....................		$ 116,107

Single- versus Multiple-Step Statements. The particular format for Monsanto's income statement is, of course, only one way of presenting the revenue and expense information. It illustrates one position in a controversy revolving around how many subtotals should be shown before the final arrival at a net income figure. The multiple-step approach used by Monsanto follows from the view that since the income statement's purpose is to communicate information for a number of purposes, data should

---

[2] *Ibid.,* p. 115.

[3] One area left open by this Opinion is the proper reporting of changes in accounting methods, changes in estimates, and corrections of accounting errors. Under a strict interpretation of the criteria for prior period adjustments, these items would not qualify. At the time of this writing, the APB is formulating a new Opinion to deal with these matters.

TABLE 5–2

MONSANTO COMPANY
Statement of Consolidated Retained Earnings
For the Year Ended December 31, 1969
(in thousands)

```
Balance at beginning of year:
  As previously reported...............  $480,482
  Adjustments..........................    18,854
  As restated..........................  $499,336
Addition—net income for the year.......   116,107
                                         $615,443
Deductions:
  Dividends............................  $ 63,114
  Other................................     2,273
                                         $550,056
```

be arranged in such a manner as to highlight significant subtotals on the statement. Notice the various "income" subtotals in Table 5–1—"gross profit," "operating profit," and "income before taxes" (nonoperating revenues and expenses have been offset in the "other income charges, net" deduction)—as well as the required "income before extraordinary credits" and "net income" figures.

Two minor criticisms can be made to this approach. A theoretical objection arises from the implied preferential recovery of costs. The facts are, of course, that all costs rank the same in being matched against revenues. None is recovered before others. Secondly, there really is no net income until all costs have been recovered. Cluttering up the statement with numerous "income" subtotals may detract from, rather than add to, clarity of presentation. The opponents of the format in Table 5–1 prefer a single-step statement, in which only one net income figure appears. The Minnesota Mining and Manufacturing statement in Table 5–3 is an example. All revenues are grouped together, as are the revenue deductions. The only subtotals that appear are for the accumulations of various types of deductions. No sequential subtractions appear on the statement. While other subtotals besides the final net income figure may be helpful for some purposes, advocates of the single-step form reason that the reader of the statement is sufficiently intelligent to use the figures presented in whatever ways are appropriate for *his* purposes. Most published financial statements actually follow a format somewhere between these two extremes, and it simply is impossible to say which is optimal.

A REFLECTION ON ACCOUNTING INCOME

The foregoing discussion should emphasize the tentative nature of income measurement. It is clear from the problems that are encountered in the implementation of the matching concept and the uncertainty as to

TABLE 5–3

MINNESOTA MINING AND MANUFACTURING COMPANY
Statement of Income and Net Income Retained
for Use in the Business
for the Year Ended December 31, 1969
(in thousands)

Sales and other income:	
Net sales and other operating revenue.......	$1,612,563
Investment, royalty, and other income.......	18,703
Total.....................................	$1,631,266
Cost of goods sold and other expenses:	
Cost of goods sold.........................	$ 869,033
Selling, general, and administrative expenses..................................	388,986
Other expense..............................	7,837
Provision for income taxes.................	186,000
Total.....................................	$1,451,856
Net income for the year......................	$ 179,410
Net income retained for use at beginning of year....................................	754,848
Total.....................................	$ 934,258
Dividends...................................	87,182
Net Income Retained for Use at End of Year....	$ 847,076

exactly which figure really can be called "net income" that any amount so labeled must be carefully examined by the reader of the statement. These amounts are no more accurate than the concepts on which they are founded and the solutions to the problems encountered when the concepts are put to use. Inasmuch as this chapter completes this first section on Fundamental Concepts and Procedures, a brief review of the relationship between the basic concepts and the financial statements is in order.

Influence of the Matching Concept

The matching concept provides the major foundation for the income statement. In the main, it asserts that resources consumed during the period which have a direct (e.g., merchandise) or an indirect (e.g., office salaries) association with the revenue of the period should be related to those revenues in the calculation of periodic net income. As a consequence, of course, any unexpired resources appear as residuals (assets) on the position statement.

In Chapter One mention is made that the matching concept is only one possible approach to income measurement. It is appropriate to restate this idea here, as we conclude the basic explanation of matching. Perhaps the income concept most frequently mentioned as an alternative is that of "economic income," which is based on *expectations* concerning *future* inflows and outflows of resources. Conventional accounting rejects concepts of economic income as being too uncertain and subjective, even though there is little doubt that such future events are relevant to current decision making. Rather, the matching concept presumes that the basic subject matter of financial accounting is actual transactions, usually with outside parties. Therefore, it has primarily a *historical* perspective and is concerned with preparing reports on stewardship. Because of their objective tone, accounting reports may also have predictive value, but these income projections are left to the judgment of the individual user. Economic concepts of income go much further and explicitly attempt to measure current values by projecting future changes in income.

In addition, the matching concept underlying conventional financial accounting (matching of *acquisition* cost and revenue) is only one of a number of *possible matching approaches* to income measurement. Under it, assets are not revalued before being matched against the revenue they produce. Thus, our "cost principle" for asset valuation derives directly from this conventional notion of matching. Other matching concepts could be used to calculate income. These would employ opportunity costs (the value of the asset in its next best alternative use) or various other types of current values in measuring assets matched against revenue. In Chapter Seventeen we explore some of these other concepts of income measurement.

One other point concerning the matching concept should be kept in mind. Although perhaps overall it is more certain and less subjective than alternative income systems, it is still a concept, not a precise measurement. A potential hazard to the unwary reader of an income statement is that different methods can be used for matching particular costs against revenues. Many of these are discussed further in later chapters, but already we have encountered examples in connection with research and development costs and other period expenses. Faced with inconclusive evidence as to the exact relationships between costs and revenues and with uncertainty as to how the end result is used, accountants have adopted a number of reasonable, yet arbitrary, procedures to implement the matching concept. Consequently, if there is no generally accepted "right way" for handling a particular item, there can hardly be any single resultant figure that represents *the correct* net income.

Influence of Other Basic Concepts

The periodicity concept is second to the matching concept in terms of direct impact on the financial statements. By establishing a time framework within which matching occurs, the concept of the accounting period determines that the income statement is always prepared for a specified time period. In a sense the classifications of current and noncurrent assets on the position statement also spring from this concept.

The concept of the accounting period causes numerous problems that limit the precision and reliability of accounting net income. Although our basic data—revenues and expenses—result from objective market transactions, subjective judgments are needed to fit them into an arbitrary time framework. The adjusting entries for accruals and prepayments and the period cost concept are two examples. In future chapters some additional estimating procedures and assumptions are introduced, primarily for the purpose of helping to match costs and revenues within a specified time period. Although making an estimate may be more accurate, more useful, and even more objective than doing nothing, it nevertheless increases the tentativeness of the income calculation. At best, the income figure serves only as an *index* of a continuing stream of economic and financial activity.

The monetary postulate obviously supports the use of dollar amounts in the communication process. It also asserts that the dollars of different vintages are addable. Only by assuming that fluctuations in the value of the dollar can be ignored are we able to sum the cash in the bank, the cost of the merchandise bought in December of last year, and the amount spent on constructing a building 10 years ago into a single amount called total assets. While the monetary postulate aids the meaningful presentation of information, it may impair interpretation in times of monetary instability. If there is an increase in general price levels, causing the size of the measuring unit to decline, the asset items above really are not addable. The yardstick with which the accountant measures dollar amounts changes over time. The ignoring of price-level changes in conventional accounting statements may become increasingly limiting in future years. This subject also is covered in greater depth in Chapter Seventeen.

In the area of revenue recognition, the subject matter of Chapter Six, financial accounting usually insists on a market transaction in which the firm supplies some good or service to a consuming unit outside the entity before recognition is given to value changes in the assets. But in economic terms, increases and decreases in the value of assets do not suddenly come into being as the firm acquires various input factors and uses them to produce a salable output. By insisting that revenue be earned and measured with a reasonable degree of certainty and objectivity before being recognized, financial accounting may exaggerate the importance of the sales transaction and may tend to delay the recognition of accretion in values beyond their occurrences in an economic sense. Also, since revenue recognition is the initiating event in the matching process, the timing of income may vary under different revenue-recognition expedients.

The entity and going-concern concepts help set the stage for financial statements. Their initial impact is obvious. The separate-entity concept determines the organizational unit covered by the statements and, hence, which items are included in assets, liabilities, etc., and which transactions get recorded. The going-concern postulate supports the rationale behind the matching concept. Specifically, it focuses attention away from periodic liquidation values for assets and allows for the allocation of costs, such as depreciation, over the useful lives of the noncurrent assets.

A Final Note

So all of the basic assumptions of financial accounting may serve simultaneously to enhance and to limit the usefulness of the statements. They are not immutable decrees; neither are they random assertions. Hopefully, they lead to some reasonable and useful, albeit tentative, results about the nature and management of a firm's resources. They certainly do not produce precise figures or even "correct" figures according to other standards. To view the financial statements apart from the assumptions on which they rest or to use accounting measurements without being aware of their limitations is foolhardy.

The purpose of this chapter and of this first section is to provide an insight into the items that appear on conventional financial accounting statements, particularly the income statement. With an understanding of the meaning and implications of these terms and concepts and given sufficient information through explanation or disclosure, the reader should be able to ascertain the elements comprising a particular net income figure, evaluate its usefulness, and maybe modify it for a specific purpose.

In the next section we talk in greater detail about specific problem areas in the process of measuring accounting income. There the reader has occasion to employ many of the accounts and concepts discussed in this chapter and section.

SUGGESTIONS FOR FURTHER READING

Bedford, Norton M. "A Critical Analysis of Accounting Concepts of Income," *Accounting Review*, Vol. 26 (October 1951), pp. 526–37.

Hawkins, David F. "The Case of the Dubious Deferral," *Harvard Business Review*, Vol. 41 (May–June 1963), pp. 163 ff.

Powell, Weldon. "Extraordinary Items," *Journal of Accountancy*, Vol. 121 (January 1966), pp. 31–37.

Sprouse, Robert T. "The Significance of the Concept of the Corporation in Accounting Analyses," *Accounting Review*, Vol. 32 (July 1957), pp. 369–78.

QUESTIONS AND PROBLEMS

5–1. The Linda Jane Shoe Store was organized on July 31. The activities listed below took place during August. Prepare journal entries to record the transactions for the month.

1. Issuance of capital stock in exchange for cash, $50,000.
2. Purchase of store building, $10,000 cash and a $40,000 mortgage bearing interest at the rate of 6 percent per year.
3. Cash paid for legal services, incorporation fee, printing of stock certificates, and other costs of organizing the corporation, $1,000.
4. Furniture and fixtures bought for cash, $10,000.
5. Purchase of merchandise on account, $30,000.
6. Payment of administrative salaries, $500.
7. In unloading the furniture and fixtures, the employees of the store dropped a display case costing $200, completely ruining it.
8. Sales of shoes on account, $13,000; for cash, $18,000.
9. Payment of selling commissions, $4,500.
10. Bought U.S. government bonds for $10,000.
11. Purchase of delivery truck on account, $3,000.
12. Paid monthly merchant's tax to the city, $500.
13. Collected $6,000 from accounts receivable.
14. Paid suppliers $19,000.
15. Received an advance order from an orphan's home for 500 pairs of shoes at $10 a pair. The shoes were to be delivered over a three-month period beginning in September. The order was accompanied by a cash deposit of $2,000.
16. The government bonds were sold for $10,350 plus accrued interest of $50.
17. Paid other administrative costs in cash, $1,500.
18. The delivery truck hit a tree and required $300 of repairs, paid in cash.
19. Interest for the month accrued on the mortgage, $200.
20. Depreciation for the month on building, $400; on furniture and fixtures, $150; on delivery truck, $50.
21. Cost of the ending inventory of shoes, $9,000.
22. Dividends declared, $1,000.
23. Income taxes applicable to August, $500.
24. Received an offer to sell the entire business for $60,000.

5–2. In its 1968 balance sheet, Flying Tiger Corporation showed the following item among its noncurrent assets:

Unamortized training and preoperating costs relative to aircraft fleet
  acquisitions. $5,152,366

A similar item with varying amounts had appeared for a number of years. In 1969, however, this asset no longer appeared; it had been written off as an adjustment to retained earnings. The company explained in a footnote:

Financial statements for 1969 reflect a change in accounting treatment for initial training and preoperating costs relative to aircraft fleet acquisitions to charge off such costs when incurred. Previously initial training and preoperating costs had been deferred and amortized over a five-year period.

a) Explain why this item appeared as an asset prior to 1969. As a stockholder, what additional information would you want to know about it?

b) Why do you think the company changed its policy? Do you agree?

c) Discuss the treatment of the adjustment as a direct correction of retained earnings rather than as an extraordinary loss.

5–3. Prepare an income statement and a statement of retained earnings from the accounts given below, taken from the adjusted trial balance of the Titus Canbe Company at the end of its fiscal year on July 31, 1972. Follow the requirements of *Opinion No. 9* of the Accounting Principles Board.

Sales......................................	$490,000
Selling expenses............................	62,000
Dividends received..........................	15,000
Dividends declared..........................	7,500
Cost of goods sold..........................	312,500
Administrative expense.......................	44,000
Interest revenue............................	6,200
Income taxes...............................	41,000
Write-off of inventories determined to be obsolete and unusable...............................	6,500
Gain on sale of investment securities..............	10,000
Tax adjustment—additional tax assessment for 1970..	5,000
Loss on sale of equipment......................	60,000
Retained earnings, July 31, 1971................	132,000

5–4. Classify each of the following items as (a) an element to be included in the determination of net income before extraordinary items, (b) an extraordinary item to be shown in a separate section of the income statement, or (c) a prior-period adjustment to retained earnings. Justify your treatment of each item on the 1972 financial statements and assume that all amounts are material.

1. Royalties received in 1972 from patented items licensed to others. The patents were granted in 1965.
2. Gain on sale of investments. The investments were purchased in 1968.
3. Loss on lawsuit for antitrust violations in the period 1968–70.
4. Extra depreciation charged in 1972 to correct for underdepreciation of special-purpose machinery in past years.
5. Proceeds from a life insurance policy on an officer who died during 1972.
6. Federal income taxes for 1972.
7. A payment of $50,000 in 1972 to a visitor who was injured during a plant tour. Damages of $300,000 were originally assessed by a lower court in 1970. Upon appeal, the state supreme court reduced the amount of damages to only $50,000. A loss and estimated liability for $300,000 had been recognized originally in 1970.
8. Christmas bonus paid to employees for their extra efforts in making 1972 an extremely profitable year.
9. Uninsured fire loss.
10. The loss resulting from a very large customer going bankrupt

and being unable to pay his account receivable. The bankruptcy was completely unexpected and unpredictable.

11.   Tax refund due to settlement of litigation over company's 1969 tax return.

5–5.   You are requested to personally deliver your auditor's report to the board of directors of Sebal Corporation and answer questions posed about the financial statements. While reading the statements, one director asked, "What are the precise meanings of the terms cost, expense, and loss? These terms sometimes seem to identify similar items and other times seem to identify dissimilar items."

  a) Explain the meanings of the terms cost, expense, and loss as used for financial reporting purposes. In your explanation discuss the distinguishing characteristics of the terms and their similarities and interrelationships.

  b) Classify each of the following items as a cost, expense, loss, or other category and explain how the classification of each item may change:
  1. Cost of goods sold.
  2. Cost of drilling dry holes (oil company).
  3. Depreciation cost.
  4. Organization costs.
  5. Cost of spoiled goods.

  c) The terms "period cost" and "product cost" are sometimes used to describe certain items in financial statements. Define these terms and distinguish between them.

  d) What is the theoretical justification given by some who contend that interest should be treated differently from expenses, losses, and taxes? *

5–6.   In its annual report for 1969, Xerox Corporation listed as an asset on its balance sheet $22,563,000 of deferred research and development. The corresponding amount as of December 31, 1968 was $18,938,000. In the statement of income for 1969, $11,157,000 was deducted as an expense to charge these deferred R&D costs against revenue. Net income was $161,368,000 for 1969.

The Deferred Research and Development account first appeared in the 1967 report, where the company explained it as follows:

Prior to 1967, a portion of research and engineering expenditures was added to the capitalized value of rental equipment and depreciated as part of the cost over the life of the equipment. Beginning in 1967, the Company changed its method of accounting for these expenditures by charging the deferred portion to a separate account and amortizing this portion on a straight-line basis over three years. This change had no material effect on net income.

The 1969 report contains the statements: "The percentage of our total research and development expenditures capitalized was further reduced

---

* Adapted from AICPA May 1969 examination.

in 1969. Eventually we intend to expense all such expenditures as incurred."

a) What would net income for 1969 have been if Xerox had been following the policy of expensing all R&D expenditures as incurred?

b) Do you agree with their existing policy? Why or why not?

c) What factors might be responsible for the movement toward the policy of expensing as incurred, as implied in the last quotation?

d) Why did the change in policy in *1967* have no material effect on net income?

5–7. You are in charge of the audit of the financial statements of United Soap and Tar Corporation for 1971. The audit work on each account balance has been completed, and you are satisfied that the accounts have been kept in conformity with "generally accepted accounting principles." The only major part of the audit remaining, then, is to review the form of the financial statements that management proposes to use.

Presented below is the income statement that management proposes for 1971:

Statement of Income

Revenues:	
Sales of product	$745,200
Income from investments	28,000
Gain on sale of power plant	92,100
Adjustment in retained earnings (Note A)	15,400
	$880,700
Expenses:	
Cost of goods sold	$445,100
Selling, general, administrative	139,800
Interest	75,800
	$660,700
Net income before depreciation	$220,000
Depreciation	10,400
Net income before taxes	$209,600
Income taxes for 1971	51,000
Refund of overpayment of taxes in 1968	(20,000)
Net Income	$178,600

Note A: The company changed its method of accounting for the income from certain investments. The new procedure is more in keeping with generally accepted accounting principles and has been approved by our auditors. The change caused an increase of $15,400 in retained earnings as of the beginning of 1971, representing the unrecognized income from prior years.

Management also proposed to present a statement of retained earnings to show the changes taking place in retained earnings in 1971. The proposed statement follows:

```
                    Statement of Retained Earnings
Retained earnings, beginning of the year...... $ 304,100
Increases during the year:
  Net income (see income statement)...........    178,600
                                               $ 482,700
Decreases during the year:
  Dividends declared........................    (100,000)
  Expenses and losses incurred in connection
    with the discontinuance of certain
    division operations.....................    (290,000)
Retained Earnings, End of Year...............  $   92,700
```

As noted, you are satisfied with the amounts in these accounts. However, you are concerned with the way the company intends to report the amounts.

a) Redraft the statements of income and retained earnings in good form in accordance with *Opinion No. 9* of the Accounting Principles Board.

b) The president of the company complains to you:

"Frankly, I don't understand why the accounting profession spends so much time on a matter such as reporting extraordinary items. So long as disclosure is adequate, it doesn't matter how the item is reported. If the reader does not agree with the company's way of reporting, well, he simply can modify statements to fit his needs."

Comment on this position.

5–8. The Boomorbust Bomb Shelter Distributing Company was incorporated on July 1, 1971. Prepare general journal entries to record the following transactions, which summarize the activities of the company for the fiscal year ended June 30, 1972.

1. Capital stock was issued for $150,000 cash.
2. The following assets were purchased for cash: land, $13,500; building, $40,000; equipment, $33,000.
3. Insurance expense for the year paid in cash, $1,500.
4. Merchandise and supplies acquired on account, $330,000.
5. General office and administrative work was done during the year at a cost of $24,000, paid in cash.
6. Selling commissions were $13,000, of which $4,500 was unpaid at the end of the year.
7. Promotional and entertainment costs were $19,300, paid in cash.
8. All sales of the product were made to a single foreign government, Middle Iamurpalia. A check for $30,000 was received early in the year to apply as a deposit against future deliveries.
9. Deliveries of products during the year totaled $650,000.
10. Boomorbust sold some vacant land (acquired in item 2 for $2,500) for $3,300 cash.
11. Some equipment exploded while being tested. The cost of the equipment was $8,000. The loss was partially covered by insurance

and the company collected cash equal to half of the loss from the insurance company.

12. Additional equipment costing $10,000 was purchased. A cash payment of $2,000 was made; and a 5 percent, $8,000 note payable was given to the supplier.

13. Collections of cash from Middle Iamurpalia amounted to $510,000.

14. The cost of merchandise sold was $310,000.

15. Depreciation amounted to $2,800 on equipment and $1,600 on the building.

16. Property taxes paid in cash, $16,000.

17. Estimated income taxes applicable to the fiscal year, $98,500.

18. Payments to suppliers were $315,000.

19. On June 30, 1972, the board of directors declared a dividend of $100,000, payable on July 15, 1972.

20. Accrued interest on the note in item 12 was $200.

5–9. The following three notes were taken from the actual financial reports of the indicated companies.

Celanese Corporation, 1968 Report: Prior to 1968, it was the policy of the Forest Products group to defer preoperating costs associated with the construction of new facilities and to amortize these expenditures over a five-year period starting at the time the new facilities become fully operational. In 1968, this policy was changed so that preoperating costs are charged to expense as incurred.

Hoffman Electronics Corporation, 1968 Report: The Company had in prior years deferred $1,900,000 of research and development costs, of which $435,200 has been amortized as a charge to current operations. Amortization of these costs is based upon units produced and shipped under contract. As of December 31, 1968 the Company had not received contracts for quantities sufficient to fully amortize $980,000 of these costs on the above basis.

National Cash Register Company, 1969 Report: The company charges current operations with all research, engineering, product development, sales and service training and software development expenses. With respect to NCR Century series computer systems, the company defers that portion of the marketing costs represented by advance compensation paid certain domestic field employees, since this expense relates to future rental income. . . .

a) For each of the situations, discuss the alternative reporting procedures available to the company. Which of the companies' policies most closely conforms to the matching concept?

b) Give examples of some "preoperating costs" to which Celanese refers. What arguments could be advanced to support the original policy of deferral? What factors might be responsible for the change?

c) Explain the meaning of the last sentence of the Hoffman Electronics note. What potential danger does this suggest in a policy of deferral?

d) Why does National Cash Register differentiate in policy between the advance compensation and other period charges? Give the journal entries (without numbers) that the company probably makes with respect to the deferred marketing costs.

5–10.   Using the following incomplete data, prepare a balance sheet as of December 31, 1971 and an income statement for the calendar year 1971.

The Hardware and Furniture Company (a sole proprietorship) did not have complete records on a double-entry basis. However, from your investigation of its records, you established the information shown below:

1.   The assets and equities as of December 31, 1970 were:

	Dr.	Cr.
Cash.................................	$ 5,175	
Accounts receivable....................	9,816	
Fixtures...............................	2,020	
Prepaid insurance.......................	158	
Prepaid supplies........................	79	
Accounts payable.......................		$ 4,244
Accrued miscellaneous expenses...........		206
Accrued taxes..........................		202
Merchandise inventory..................	19,243	
Notes payable..........................		5,000
Roberts, capital........................		26,839
	$36,491	$36,491

2.   A summary of the transactions for 1971, as recorded in the checkbook, showed:

Deposits for the year........................	$82,883
Checks drawn during the year................	84,070
Bank service charges........................	22

3.   The following information was available as to accounts payable:

Purchases on account during year..............	$57,789
Returns of merchandise allowed as credits against accounts by vendors.......................	1,418
Payments of account by check...............	55,461

4.   Information as to accounts receivable showed the following:

Accounts collected...........................	$43,083
Balance of accounts on December 31, 1971......	11,221

5   Checks drawn during the year included checks for the following items:

Salaries....................................	$10,988
Rent.......................................	3,600
Heat, light, and telephone...................	394
Supplies....................................	280
Insurance..................................	341
Taxes and licenses..........................	1,017
Withdrawals by owner.......................	6,140
Miscellaneous expense.......................	769
Merchandise purchases.......................	2,080
Notes payable.............................	3,000
	$28,609

6. Merchandise inventory on December 31, 1971, was $17,807. Prepaid insurance amounted to $122 and supplies on hand to $105 as of December 31, 1971. Accrued taxes were $216, and miscellaneous accrued expenses were $73 at the year-end.
7. Cash sales for the year were assumed to account for all cash received other than that collected on accounts. Fixtures were to be depreciated $313 per year.*

* Adapted from AICPA November 1951 examination.

SECTION II

FURTHER ASPECTS OF FINANCIAL MEASUREMENT– ASSETS

CHAPTER SIX

ACCOUNTING FOR REVENUES AND RECEIVABLES

IN A SENSE, revenue recognition controls the determination of periodic income. Revenues first have to be assigned to periods. Then the costs incurred to produce the assigned revenue can be measured, with appropriate accrual or deferral where necessary, and matched against it. Apart from income measurement, the revenue figure also is frequently used as a significant measure of the current volume of business activity and of the relative size and growth of business entities.

Up to this point we have recorded revenue from products whenever a sale is made. When the sale does not involve the immediate receipt of cash, a debit is made to a current asset, Accounts Receivable, and the credit goes to a temporary retained earnings account, Sales Revenue. Similar entries are made for such revenues as interest and rent, which have no "point of sale" as such. These revenues are recognized at various times, usually upon receipt of cash or by year-end accrual. In any case, the debit records the inflow of assets to the business; the credit in the revenue account represents the source of assets.

In a realistic business setting, complexities arise. Revenue can be recognized at times other than the point of sale. Amounts billed to customers may include other items, such as sales taxes, in addition to the charge for products or services. Cash eventually collected from accounts receivable may be less than the amount billed because of returned merchandise, failure on the part of the customer to pay, or discounts offered for prompt payment. All of these possibilities suggest that our existing procedures and accounts have to be clarified and expanded.

153

This chapter looks at the problems and procedures in determining when to recognize revenue and how much revenue to recognize. Separate sections of the chapter present (1) a closer examination of the concept of revenue, (2) a more detailed explanation of the meaning and implications of the revenue postulate, (3) a study of its applications to situations other than the point of sale, and (4) a description of procedures used to record modifications to revenue for events subsequent to the point of sale.

THE CONCEPT OF REVENUE

In earlier chapters, revenue is defined as the inflow of assets from the provision of goods and services by the business entity. The business engages in various activities designed to deliver products or to render services. Revenue is the reward to the enterprise for performing these activities. Whether the revenue derives from a major activity (such as the sale of a product) or from a lesser, nonoperating service (such as lending money) one factor is common to all revenue flows. The firm is being compensated for efforts expended during the period in satisfying consumer wants. This factor distinguishes revenues from other inflows of assets—capital contributions, gifts, gains on noncurrent asset sales, and tax refunds.

Revenue and Cash Receipts

If revenue is the reward to a business for efforts expended during the period, it then becomes necessary to define how the reward (asset inflow) is to be valued. The following observations may be helpful. The total revenue over the life of the business cannot exceed the amount of cash collected from customers. Merchandise that is never delivered to customers and receivables that are never collected provide no compensation to the firm. The receivable arising from a revenue transaction has no intrinsic value per se. Its value, as we have seen in Chapter Two, derives from its convertibility into cash.

These impressions suggest that revenue should be defined in terms of *ultimate cash receipts*. Revenue for a period is the cash received, cash to be received, or cash needs satisfied as a result of the firm's performance during the period.[1] Until it is turned into cash, revenue is just an estimate. It may be represented by an inflow of assets other than cash, but the *value* of that inflow is determined by the amount of cash the firm expects to collect.

A word of caution is necessary. Defining revenue in terms of cash

---

[1] "Cash needs satisfied" refers to those rare situations when the reward for efforts expended takes the form of a cancellation of a liability or a receipt of a tangible asset that can be used directly in the business. Here the revenue is measured by the amount of cash that otherwise would have been paid out—i.e., the cash needs fulfilled.

receipts does not imply that cash collections during a period equal the revenues of that period. Revenue is the compensation for *performance during the period*. Cash receipts may be prior to the expenditure of effort, concurrent with it, or subsequent to it. The timing of revenue is determined by when the efforts necessary to provide goods and services are expended, not when the cash is actually collected.[2] But the existence and amount of the eventual cash receipt determine how much total revenue can be recognized.

Adjustments for Nonrevenue Receipts

This more precise concept of revenue is helpful in later sections, where we explore the revenue recognition postulate and some of the measurement problems involved in it. Even now, however, it should be clear that revenue results only from amounts which are or are to be received from customers and which reflect the supplying of goods or services. Amounts billed or collected for sales taxes, customer deposits on containers, or some transportation costs are not rewards for the firm's efforts, even though a cash receipt results. They should not be recorded in the revenue accounts.

For example, a firm delivers merchandise having a sales price of $1,000. A state sales tax of 4 percent must be collected from the customer as well. The proper entry is

```
Accounts Receivable.......... ................. 1,040
    Sales Revenue................................        1,000
    Liability for Unremitted Sales Tax......           40
```

When the $40 is remitted to the state tax authorities, the liability will be debited. The sales tax represents neither a revenue nor an expense to the business entity, which serves only as a collection medium for the government.

Transportation costs can represent a more complex area. If delivery of the product is a necessary and vital part of the package of services being sold, the cost of performing this service is a business expense, and the compensation received is revenue. On the other hand, if the seller contacts and pays the carrier merely as a convenience to the customer (e.g., the goods are shipped f.o.b. shipping point so that the freight charge is the obligation of the buyer), the reimbursement from the customer is not revenue. The seller simply serves as an agent for the customer in paying the carrier.

---

[2] If a material time period exists before cash is collected, the eventual cash receipts probably include compensation for waiting (interest) as well as for the current period's efforts. The interest element is the reward for waiting and should be allocated to the waiting period. In this situation the revenue for the current period is actually the present value of cash to be received. Present-value concepts and procedures are explained further in Chapter Ten and Appendix 10–A.

CRITERIA FOR REVENUE RECOGNITION

The criteria that we have laid down for recognizing revenue are two-fold. One aspect concerns the economics of earning revenue and the other the practical problem of measuring it. Consequently, our sixth assumption states that revenue should not be recognized until it has been earned and can be measured with a reasonable degree of objectivity and certainty. The first criterion is implied by the definition of revenue. Since revenue is the reward for productive efforts expended, it cannot exist and therefore should not be recognized until it has been earned through performance. However, during an accounting period many efforts are exerted for which the rewards will be received in subsequent periods. Only if these future rewards are known can the revenue be recognized and reported. Thus, recognized revenue is that revenue which is subject to measurement.

This dual approach attempts to achieve a balance between certainty and timeliness. The earning criterion tries to relate the revenue to the period in which the economic functions are performed, so as to provide timely monetary measures of the results of the period's efforts. The criterion of measurability confirms that a degree of objective certainty in the figures is also desirable for accounting to communicate useful information, particularly to external audiences. It attempts to minimize the reporting of inaccurate revenue.

Earning Criterion

Each cash receipt from a particular sale or event represents the reward for a combination of efforts—organizing, purchasing, producing, selling, delivering, collecting, and others. Because these functions may be carried out over a period of time, the revenue also may be a joint item with respect to accounting periods. Only that portion of the ultimate cash receipt which is compensation for efforts exerted during the accounting period should be reported as revenue for the period. So one of the accounting tasks necessary in the recognition of periodic revenue involves allocating the total estimated cash receipt to the periods in which the efforts are exerted, if all are not performed in the same accounting period.

What criterion should the accountant use for these allocations? Theoretically, the ultimate cash receipt (revenue) should be allocated on the basis of the relative importance of each function to the total efforts required to earn revenue. Accountants traditionally consider cost to be a measure of effort since our matching concept implies that costs are incurred to generate revenue. So, as a general rule we can say that cost incurrence is a measure of functions performed. If a large portion of cost has not been incurred, signifying that some function associated with the production of particular revenues is unperformed, a portion of the revenue has not been earned. Of course, sometimes cost may not be a good measure of relative importance, in which case we must revert to some noncost measure. But the general principle stands. Revenues can be recognized only to the extent that efforts have been completed.

Measurability Criterion

The second part of the dual standard for revenue recognition is that a change has to take place with enough certainty and objectivity to justify recognizing the revenue in the accounts. When some or all of the efforts of the firm are exerted in periods prior to the actual cash receipt, a measurement of the revenue earned for these periods requires a prediction of the amount of the cash receipt. The measurability criterion states that this estimate should be made objectively and reliably.

In Chapter One objectivity is described generally as verifiability and impartiality. Applied to revenue recognition, it means that intentional or unintentional bias should be kept to a minimum. The estimate should be free from distortion and subject to independent verification. It should follow the earning process as closely as possible. Artificially delaying or advancing the time of revenue recognition introduces a bias. Likewise, personal biases of management, whether optimistic or pessimistic, could affect the revenue estimate. Consequently, accountants traditionally have accorded great weight to market transactions and arm's-length negotiations with outside parties. These provide demonstrable evidence (although not the only evidence) that the revenue estimates are objectively determined.

Certainty or reliability refers to the probability that the revenue estimates will approximate the actual value. The measurement of revenue from a product manufactured and sold during the period might be completely objective inasmuch as the amount conforms to the earning process and can be verified by other investigators examining the transaction. Yet later events may prove this figure unreliable if the customer in fact never pays his account. Of course, absolute certainty would have to wait upon the final receipt of cash from the customer. What is referred to here is that the accountant must have a sufficient degree of assurance that the amount of revenue being predicted is reasonably reliable. Again, accountants have often found such assurance in market transactions and the receipt of liquid assets from customers.

Realization

The foregoing discussion focuses on criteria for revenue *recognition*. In accounting literature and practice, the term "realization" is most commonly associated with revenue. Some, for example, state the revenue postulate as: revenues should not be recognized until they are realized. But this declaration signifies little, for realization can be interpreted in many different ways.

Historically the realization concept seems to have been used first to describe the conversion of assets into cash. It arose in response to income tax and dividend laws, which stressed ability to pay and possession of assets in distributable form. However, its use soon broadened to include other ideas as well—liquidity (conversion of assets into monetary assets), measurability (predictability of ultimate cash to be received), and severability (separation of the asset from the business via a transaction with an external party). A combination of all of these ideas led to its most frequent use in accounting—conversion through a legal sale or similar process.

The net result, unfortunately, has been that although most accountants use the term and subscribe to a realization criterion, the concept lacks a precise or common meaning. For some it means earning, for others it implies measurability, and for still others it signifies a sale. A few writers use the term to cover the entire criteria for revenue recognition, and a few still use it in its more narrow sense of cash conversion. Care must be taken to interpret it correctly in context.

APPLICATION OF THE REVENUE POSTULATE

Our earning criterion asserts that the ultimate cash receipt is a joint product of manifold activities and that revenue is earned in relation to the importance and completion of these activities. But, as a practical matter it is extremely difficult or impossible to determine precisely how much revenue is attributable to any single activity. Therefore, accountants have adopted the expedient of normally visualizing revenues as arising at a particular moment of time after certain events have occurred. In a sense this meshes with the measurability criterion. The longer the point of measurement is postponed, the more certain it will be. The risk of recognizing unearned revenue or of recording revenue inaccurately is minimized. However, the postponement of recognition also increases the likelihood of leaving earned revenue unrecognized.

Two conclusions seem to follow. First, the selection of a single point at which to recognize revenue is a useful expedient only if it does not magnify unduly either of these measurement errors. If it does, then either an alternative method which recognizes revenue in stages should be adopted, or subsequent adjustments should be made to the initial recording. Secondly, the optimum point of measurement would seem to be that which minimizes the total effects of the offsetting errors—recognition of unearned or inaccurate revenue and failure to recognize earned revenue.

According to the criteria discussed in the preceding section, if revenue is to be recognized at one point, then the *earliest* point of revenue recognition is when (1) the major revenue-producing activity[3] has been performed *and* (2) the ultimate cash receipt can be estimated objectively within a small margin of error. In most cases this is the point of sale, when goods are delivered or services performed. However, there are some differences from point-of-sale timing that should be discussed. These variations can be explained through the use of the revenue postulate.

Point-of-Sale Recognition

Recognition at the point of sale is common because for many businesses, selling is the principal activity in the earning process. Once the sale is made the probability of recognizing unearned revenue is substantially reduced. Practically all the costs associated with producing the revenue have been incurred; any additional costs necessary are either negligible or can be estimated, and adjustments can be made for unearned portions. Also the probability of accurately measuring the revenue is substantially increased. We have a reasonably certain and objective measure of the amount, because the customer has either paid cash or pledged via an account receivable that he will pay cash within a short period of time. Minor adjustments for uncollectibles, returns, and discounts can usually be estimated with a sufficient degree of assurance to satisfy the measurement criteria. These adjustments and the procedures for recording them comprise the last section in this chapter.

Customer Advances. The importance of the first criterion of earning in point-of-sale recognition can be seen in the case of the customer advance. The normal order in recognizing sales revenue is to delay until it can be measured with a reasonable degree of certainty and objectivity. Even though the earning of revenue has taken place throughout the ordering, production, and selling phases, recognition is usually delayed until the point of sale.

However, if customers pay in cash first, the opposite situation arises. We have an objective, certain measure of the revenue in the cash receipt but have not yet earned it. Therefore, we should not recognize the revenue at that time. Rather, an entry should be made:

```
Cash....................................... xxx
     Customer Advances......................      xxx
```

Then, when the product is manufactured and delivered, the revenue has been earned and can be recognized:

```
Customer Advances........................... xxx
     Sales.................................      xxx
```

---

[3] Some authors use the term "critical event" or "limiting factor" to describe this activity.

Until product delivery or service performance occurs, the customer has a claim against the assets of the firm. The Customer Advances account represents a liability. It is one that probably will be satisfied by the delivery of goods or the performance of a service, but it is nonetheless a liability. If the goods are not supplied or the service is not performed, the customer usually can claim a cash refund.

Similar situations exist with the sale of custom-made equipment, bus tokens, magazine subscriptions, etc. In these cases the advances from customers may be given special account names. Nevertheless, the cash collected represents, not revenue, but simply an advance payment for services or goods to be received in the future. A liability account—Customers' Paid Orders, Tokens Outstanding, Unexpired Subscriptions, etc.—should be credited.

Adjustments for Cash Receipts Not Earned.   In the above case of the advance, none of the cash receipt is recognized until the major earning functions are completed. Similar results sometimes can be accomplished more expeditiously by recognizing all potential cash receipts as revenue initially. Then any unearned portion at the end of the period can be determined and deducted from revenue. This type of adjustment is required when additional efforts on the part of the firm are necessary after the point of sale, indicating that part of the cash to be received has not been earned. These efforts might include costs of completing (installation), storage, collection, or servicing.

For example, an appliance dealer sells household appliances under an arrangement where the firm will provide "free" repair and maintenance service on the appliances for two years following the date of sale. Other customers can purchase such service agreements separately for $50 a year. If the total price of an appliance sold on January 1 is $600, the initial entry would be:

```
Cash or Accounts Receivable.................... 600
    Sales.......................................        500
    Liability under Service Contracts..........        100
```

The service function has not been performed; therefore, the portion of the ultimate cash receipt attributable to that function has not been earned. In this case the unearned amount is $100 (two years at $50), as measured by the price of separate maintenance contracts. At the end of each year, an entry would be made:

```
Liability under Service Contract.................. 50
    Service Contract Revenue.....................        50
```

If the actual costs of servicing are $30, this amount would be recorded as expense.

The measurement problem often is not so clear-cut. The portion of total revenue to be deferred to future periods may be unknown. Nevertheless, it would seem that at least the *cost* expected to be incurred in performing under the service contract should be recognized as a liability. This represents the minimum amount of the contract price to be deferred. Assuming $30 per year is a reasonable cost estimate, the entry then would be:

```
Cash (or Accounts Receivable)................... 600
     Sales.......................................        540
     Liability under Service Contracts...........         60
```

This procedure may overstate sales revenue of the current period by any profit element attributable to the servicing function. But it is more accurate than treating the entire $600 as revenue.[4] Of course, from a practical standpoint, unless the future service costs are fairly large, the revenue measurement would not be materially affected by the failure to estimate them.

Completed Production

Recognition of sales revenue before products are sold normally cannot be justified because the revenue is not substantially earned and is not susceptible to objective, reliable measurement. However, in some cases these conditions can be met at the time production is completed but prior to actual delivery and sale. The completed production basis has its primary applications where a ready market with a quoted price exists to absorb the completed production. No additional selling effort is required, and the amount of revenue can be determined as soon as the major function of production is completed. Examples include the extraction of precious metals or the harvesting of grains and certain other agricultural products.

The amount of revenue recognized is the market price for the completed units less any marketing costs yet to be incurred. This amount is called "net realizable value." Thus, a gold-mining company values its mine output at selling price, $35 per ounce, because the United States Government stands ready to purchase all completed production at that price. Likewise, the farmer may value wheat, corn, or other staple crops at net selling price. A ready-made market at a nearly fixed price exists in which he can dispose of his entire output with little additional effort. Income is recognized in the period of production, not in the period of sale or delivery.

In these restricted circumstances our dual criteria are met. When it is

---

[4] The procedure normally used for material items treats the entire $600 as revenue but sets up an estimated expense through the following entry:

```
Estimated Service Expense........................... 60
     Liability under Service Contract..................     60
```

Although this treatment achieves the same net income effect as showing sales as $540, treating the $60 as a deduction from sales (i.e., as unearned revenue) would be more in keeping with the earning criterion of the revenue postulate.

unnecessary to locate a buyer and convince him to purchase at a negotiated price, revenue is substantially earned when production is completed. Any material costs of additional functions which have to be performed, such as delivery of the product to market, can be estimated, and the revenue figure appropriately adjusted to net realizable value. Likewise, the cash reward from the production efforts can be predicted objectively and accurately at the point of completed production. Objectivity is found, not in a specific transaction with a particular buyer, but in the existence of an independent market which will be relatively unaffected in terms of quantity or price by the production offered by any particular seller. Reliability of the estimate is found in the fixed price currently existing in the market.[5]

Completed production also might be appropriate for companies which produce special orders under a binding contract. Sometimes there are no substantial costs of selling, and delivery is a formality, often at the convenience of the buyer. The selling price is a certainty and any additional costs of storage, servicing, collection, etc., are immaterial or estimative.

Percentage of Completion

A modification of the method which relates revenue recognition to production is the percentage-of-completion expedient. It shares the same feature of recognizing revenue before the point of *final* sale but provides for the recording of revenue as work progresses rather than when production is completed. Percentage of completion generally is employed for individual projects involving substantial amounts of revenue and considerable amounts of time from inception of the project to its completion. Typical examples include manufacture of airplanes and ships and the construction of roads and bridges.

When the work span covers numerous accounting periods, reporting all of the revenue in the period the work is completed may be misleading as a measure of business activity and performance. Further, waiting until the point of final sale is not necessary for measurability. Unlike conventional sales orders, which may be modified or canceled, a long-term construction contract represents a firm commitment based on an external valuation by an outside purchaser. The amount of revenue is either established in the contract or related directly to the cost incurred, as in a cost-plus contract. Interim cash collections of portions of the sales price fre-

---

[5] If the seller can sell the harvested product in the current market with practically no additional effort and chooses *not* to do so, he really is speculating on possible future price changes. Any gain or loss attributable to speculation properly belongs to the period between the point of completed production and point of final sale. But the revenue earned through *raising the product* is reliably measured by the current market price at the time production is complete.

quently are made as the project is worked on. Consequently, there is sufficient objectivity and certainty concerning the total revenue measurement.

Under this recognition expedient, the amount of revenue earned each period is based on the percentage of completion during that period. Often the percentage of completion (work done) is measured by the ratio of the costs of the current period to the total estimated contract cost, or through some physical measure such as miles of highway laid, number of floors erected, or engineering estimates.

Illustration.   A construction company entered into a long-term contract for a total price of $1 million. Estimated costs of the contract amounted to $900,000. During the first year, $270,000 of construction costs were incurred; in the second year $540,000 of such costs were incurred. The remaining work was completed in the third year at a cost of $90,000. Table 6–1 summarizes the revenue and gross margin results from using percentage of completion.

TABLE 6–1

	Year	*Year 2*	*Year 3*	*Total*
Percentage of completion (work done).............	$30\% \left(\dfrac{270}{900}\right)$	$60\% \left(\dfrac{540}{900}\right)$	$10\% \left(\dfrac{90}{900}\right)$	100%
Revenue to be recognized ($1,000,000 $\times$ %)........	$300,000	$600,000	$100,000	$1,000,000
Construction costs incurred...	270,000	540,000	90,000	900,000
Gross margin.............	$ 30,000	$ 60,000	$ 10,000	$ 100,000

If no revenue and income were recognized until final sale (delivery) in the third year, the first two years would show no income, while the third year would show all $100,000. Percentage of completion spreads the revenue recognition over the period of construction activity in a reasonable manner.[6] In this example, actual costs agreed exactly with the estimate. Realistically, adjustments and corrections of prior revenue accruals have to be made with most contracts, but these adjustments are minor compared to the distortion of the earning process that would result from delaying recognition until the end of the contract. However, if reasonable estimates of work done or costs to complete the project are practically impossible to make, revenue estimates under this method could be so uncertain as to be meaningless and perhaps misleading. Then postponement of revenue recognition until the contract is completed is required.

---

[6] The accounting for construction contracts actually can be quite complicated. Appendix 6–A discusses in greater detail the recording problems and illustrates the accounts and actual journal entries that could be employed.

Installment Method

The last exception to point-of-sale recognition of revenue to be discussed is the installment sale. Here, recognition of revenue is postponed until *after* the point of sale. Revenue is recognized in proportion to the cash received each period. The emphasis rests on the collection of receivables instead of their acquisition. The method finds its major use in retail businesses specializing in sales transactions requiring only a nominal down payment, with the balance to be paid in monthly installments.

The fact that this method is available for tax purposes often leads to its overuse in the financial records. Nevertheless, two possible theoretical justifications could apply in some situations. The collection costs may be quite large and the waiting period long, or the risk of uncollectibility may be high. In the former case collecting and financing become a major part of the earning process. Therefore, revenue is substantially *unearned* at the point of sale and should not be recognized. In the latter case there may be insufficient certainty in measurement to recognize revenue at the point of sale because of the high, unpredictable risk involved in estimating the ultimate cash receipt.

Illustration. An automobile dealership occasionally sells large trucks and delivery equipment on installment contracts. On July 1, 1971 the firm sold three large trucks, each having a cost of $7,500, to a customer for a total of $30,000. The customer made a $6,000 downpayment. The balance of $24,000 will be paid at the rate of $6,000 at the end of each of the next four 12-month periods plus interest of 8 percent per year on the unpaid balance. The following entries would be made in 1971:

```
July 1, 1971
  Cash.......................................  6,000
  Installment Receivables................... 24,000
      Truck Inventory......................              22,500
      Deferred Gross Margin on Installment
         Sales[7] ............................               7,500

December 31, 1971
  Interest Receivable ($24,000 × 0.08 × ½)...   960
      Interest Revenue from Installment
         Contracts.........................                 960

  Deferred Gross Margin on Installment
     Sales................................. 1,500
      Recognized Gross Margin on Installment
         Sales.............................               1,500
```

Since one fifth of the total expected cash collections ($6,000/$30,000) is received in 1971, one fifth of the gross margin is recognized in 1971. Another way of arriving at the same result is to apply the gross margin

---

[7] **Firms** having a lot of installment sales establish Installment Sales and Installment Cost of Sales accounts, which are then offset at the end of the year to establish the Deferred Gross Margin on Installment Sales account.

percentage ($7,500 ÷ $30,000 = 25%) to the cash collection (25% × $6,000 = $1,500).[8] Interest has been recognized as it accrues ($24,000 × 0.08 × ½), although to be consistent with the philosophy of the installment basis, one might argue that it too should be deferred until cash is actually collected. In 1972 the following entries would be made:

```
July 1, 1972
  Cash........................................ 7,920
        Installment Receivable..................        6,000
        Interest Receivable.....................          960
        Interest Revenue........................          960

December 31, 1972
  Interest Receivable ($18,000 × 0.08 × ½).... 720
        Interest Revenue from Installment
          Contracts.............................          720

  Deferred Gross Margin on Installment
    Sales..................................... 1,500
        Recognized Gross Margin on Installment
          Sales................................        1,500
```

Similar entries would be required in 1973, 1974, and 1975. Only interest would differ.

The Recognized Gross Margin account appears on the income statement as a type of net revenue, along with interest revenue. Installment Receivables and Accrued Interest Receivable are included in current assets on the position statement. Deferred Gross Margin on Installment Sales has a credit balance. It also should be shown on the balance sheet, preferably as a contra account to Installment Receivables (the reasoning behind this suggestion will be discussed shortly).

Evaluation.   Three criticisms of the installment method should be analyzed. First, the practice of deferring only the gross margin is undesirable. Since sales and cost of sales are netted into the gross margin, the reader of the statement is deprived of information relating to the total volume of revenue being recognized and one of the major expenses applicable to that revenue. Moreover, if revenue recognition is delayed, proper matching would suggest that all related expenses, selling and administrative costs as well as cost of goods sold, be deferred.

Secondly, more often than not the Deferred Gross Margin account appears as a liability on the balance sheet. This treatment cannot be justified; the customer has no claim against the firm. The product has already been delivered. The account represents the unearned or unrecognized gross margin element from the installment sale, for only as cash is collected

---

[8] If many sales are involved, the gross profit percentage is an average based on all installment sales for 1971. This average is applied to all cash collections of 1971 receivables regardless of when the cash is received. Cash receipts in some future year, say 1973, may include collections of receivables created in 1971, 1972, and 1973. In this case the cash receipts have to be identified by year so that the appropriate gross margin percentage can be applied.

is income assumed to be generated. This is tantamount to saying that no increased asset value has been recognized, for income measurement and asset valuation go hand in hand. Consequently, classification as a contra receivable appears reasonable. Offsetting the Deferred Gross Margin reduces the balance of receivables to an amount equal to the unrecovered cost of the items sold. This is precisely the only asset value that can exist and still be consistent with nonrecognition of gross margin at the time of sale.

That many companies object to classification of Deferred Gross Margin as a contra asset, claiming that the face amount of the receivables does represent a valid asset, is evidence of the third and more fundamental defect in the installment method. Except in very unusual situations, it postpones revenue needlessly. The reasons for postponement suggested at the outset of this section usually are not applicable. A separate interest charge accompanies many installment sales. This charge, not the gross margin, represents the compensation for the financing and collecting functions which are not yet performed. The second justification normally given for revenue postponement with the installment sale is the greater risk of uncollectibility. However, the amount of uncollectibles is not the relevant matter; the *ability to predict* the ultimate cash receipts is. As long as reasonable estimates of uncollectible accounts can be made, deferral of the gross margin is not proper.

> Collection of receivables is not necessarily less predictable because collections are scheduled in installments. . . . Any uncertainty as to collectibility should be expressed by a separately calculated and separately disclosed estimate of uncollectibles rather than by a postponement of the recognition of revenue.[9]

If reasonable estimates cannot be made except with great uncertainty and subjectivity, a deferral of the *entire* amount owed on the account, not just the gross margin, would seem to be appropriate.

In summary, the installment method should not be used except in very restricted circumstances, and in those cases probably not in the manner most commonly found. The restricted circumstances would be (1) when financing and collecting are the major function and no separable estimate of interest and collection costs can be made, and (2) when there is no reasonable basis for estimating the degree of collectibility. This conclusion concurs with that of the Accounting Principles Board, which found the installment method of recognizing revenue to be unacceptable except in the circumstances mentioned in (2).[10]

---

[9] Robert T. Sprouse and Maurice Moonitz, *A Tentative Set of Broad Accounting Principles for Business Enterprises*, Accounting Research Study No. 3 (New York: AICPA, December 1966), p. 48.

[10] *Omnibus Opinion—1966, Opinion of the Accounting Principles Board No. 10* (New York: AICPA, December 1966), p. 149.

MEASUREMENT ADJUSTMENTS UNDER
THE SALES METHOD

Even a strict following of the recognition postulate in its most common application at the point of sale does not lead automatically to a single dollar amount of revenue to be recorded. Indeed, the postulate acknowledges that exact accuracy is not necessary for the initial revenue entry. The original debit to Accounts Receivable and credit to Sales Revenue are at best tentative figures subject to later modification. Subsequent events may alter the amount of cash eventually to be received. The remainder of this chapter deals with the accounting procedures necessary to handle three specific modifications—uncollectible accounts, returns, and discounts. Often these modifications are of sufficient importance to be given special attention in the accounting records by means of contra revenue and contra receivable accounts. These special accounts are used to segregate decreases in revenues and receivables in the three areas mentioned.

Uncollectible Accounts

Some of a firm's credit sales may result in accounts receivable which are never collected. To the extent that this happens, both the sales revenue for the period and the accounts receivable at the end of the period are incorrect. Uncollectible accounts do not represent a valid claim to cash. Likewise, the sale which was originally recorded at the selling price turns out actually to have been made for nothing. Unfortunately, a firm cannot specifically identify the uncollectible accounts at the time of sale. Only after time has elapsed and repeated efforts at collection have failed is a firm willing and able to classify a particular account receivable as uncollectible. Therefore, the actual determination of a specific bad debt account often takes place in an accounting period later than the one in which the sale was originally reported on the income statement.

On the other hand, to wait is contrary to both the revenue concept and the periodicity concept. It is the revenues of the period in which the sale was made that are overstated because of the bad debt, not the revenues of the period in which the bad debt was discovered. If the uncollectible sales are adjustments of revenue, they should be so treated in the period the sales were made. Moreover, to ignore bad debts until they can be identified specifically would lead to an incorrect position statement because of the overstatement of accounts receivable until then.

Fortunately, there is an answer to this dilemma. Many businesses can estimate with a reasonable degree of accuracy the amount of uncollectible accounts generated in total from a period's sales. The estimate is based on the past experience of the firm itself or, in the case of new firms, on the experience of similar companies in that particular line of business. By estimating doubtful accounts, the firm can adjust sales and accounts receivable without having to wait until individual accounts are judged to be uncollectible.

Since any adjustment will involve both the revenue and the receivable, the estimate can be expressed as a percentage of credit sales for the period *or* can be based on a detailed analysis of outstanding accounts receivable at the end of the period. The estimate based on sales emphasizes the income statement, while the estimate derived from an analysis of accounts receivable takes a balance sheet approach. Let us illustrate how each of these estimating methods is used.

Adjustment Based on Credit Sales. Assume that a company has credit sales of $100,000 during 1971; collections during the year amount to $90,000, leaving an outstanding balance of $10,000 in accounts receivable. Assume also that past experience indicates that one half of 1 percent of credit sales turn out to be uncollectible. The estimate of bad debts would be $500 (0.5% × $100,000). An adjusting entry has to be made at the end of the period for both sales and accounts receivable.

```
December 31, 1971
  Sales Uncollectibles.......................... 500
      Allowance for Uncollectibles...............      500
```

The $500 decrease in sales revenue could just as easily have been debited to the Sales account. However, for the purpose of more complete reporting of financial information, it is segregated in a special *contra revenue* account. Similarly, in the case of accounts receivable we are reducing our assets by $500. Nevertheless, rather than reduce the asset directly, we choose to record the credit in a separate *contra asset* account. The reason in this case is a practical one. Accounts Receivable is a general ledger account controlling numerous individual receivables in a subsidiary ledger. If we credit Accounts Receivable directly, we should also credit some subsidiary ledger accounts to maintain accuracy between the subsidiary ledger and the control account. However, at this point we are unable to identify the specific individuals who will not pay. All that can be said now is that of the $10,000 owed to us, we do not expect to collect $500. This is exactly the meaning of the balance in the contra asset account.

Sales and Sales Uncollectibles, being temporary accounts, are closed at the end of the period and appear on the income statement. Allowance for Uncollectibles appears on the position statement as a subtraction from Accounts Receivable. An alternative reporting treatment would be to show only the net amount of receivables on the statement, with the amount of the contra account given in parentheses.

Let us pursue our example one more year. In 1972 the firm has credit sales of $150,000 and cash collections of $135,000, leaving an ending balance in Accounts Receivable of $25,000. The adjustment at the end of the year is still one half of 1 percent of the credit sales for the period of $150,000, or $750, if we assume that our experience is unchanged.

```
December 31, 1972
  Sales Uncollectibles........................... 750
    Allowance for Uncollectibles................      750
```

The year-end treatment of the accounts is the same as before. Sales and Sales Uncollectibles are closed; Allowance for Uncollectibles remains with a credit balance to be deducted from Accounts Receivable on the position statement. It simply says that of the $25,000 owed to us, we do not expect to collect $1,250 but are unable specifically to identify any portion of the $1,250 of anticipated bad debts. In practice, it would be rare if after two years no individual subsidiary accounts had been judged to be bad. We shall deal shortly with the entries to be made when specific accounts are discovered.

Under this method of adjustment the estimate is based directly on the income statement figure of credit sales. The asset is adjusted as the counterpart to the adjustment of revenue. The balance in Accounts Receivable is not directly involved in the calculation. One potential defect of this approach is that over a number of periods the balance in the contra asset account might become too small or too large relative to the outstanding receivables, which would indicate that the estimate being used is inaccurate.

Adjustment Based on Accounts Receivable. The alternative estimating procedure concentrates on an accurate determination of accounts receivable, with the adjustment of sales as the by-product. Taking the preceding example, assume that past experience indicates that of the outstanding receivables existing at the *end* of any given year, 5 percent is never collected. Instead of applying a percentage to total credit sales, we determine our adjustment for doubtful accounts by valuing the accounts receivable. Of the $10,000 of receivables outstanding at the end of the first year, 5 percent, or $500, is expected never to be collected. Therefore, $500 is the balance we desire to have in the Allowance for Uncollectibles to show the proper amount of assets. The adjusting entry is the same as that shown above for the end of 1971. At the end of the second year, the balance in Accounts Receivable is $25,000, suggesting that $1,250 (5 percent) is uncollectible. Since a balance of $500 already is in the allowance account, we would make an adjustment in year two for $750. The entry is the same as that shown above for the end of 1972.

The accounts receivable approach is widely used. In fact, to achieve a higher degree of accuracy, the individual accounts receivable often are aged. *Aging* involves a detailed analysis of all accounts, classifying them according to the length of time they have been outstanding, e.g., 0–30 days, 31–60 days, 61–90 days, over 91 days, etc. Then, instead of an average uncollectible percentage like the 5 percent used above, a different percentage is applied to each age group. Experience might show that accounts less than 30 days old may have only one chance out of a hundred of becoming bad debts, while accounts more than a year old might be 90 percent bad debts. Aging not only provides a more accurate method of estimating uncollectibles but also can present information to be used by management to evaluate credit-granting policies and collection efforts.

Identifying Specific Uncollectibles. Let us go back to the entry made at the end of the first year. Regardless of the estimating method employed, both sales and accounts receivable have been reduced by $500 through the indirect means of contra accounts. It is reasonable to expect that during the following accounting period individual accounts receivable will be specifically identified as bad debts. The entry to write off these uncollectible accounts will be:

```
Allowance for Uncollectibles................... xxx
    Accounts Receivable (also subsidiary
    account)..................................        xxx
```

The only reason for the contra asset account is the initial inability to pinpoint particular subsidiary accounts as uncollectible. Therefore the reduction in receivables is recorded by a credit to the contra account rather than to the control account. However, in later periods when the subsidiary accounts can be pinpointed, the need for the contra account disappears. The effect of the above entry is simply to remove the credit from the contra account and to enter it in the main account. Corresponding credits are entered in the subsidiary ledger accounts also. The entry *causes no net change in assets or in owners' equity*. They were reduced by the original estimating entry.

To perceive the effect of this entry, assume that $400 of specific accounts receivable are discovered to be bad and are written off. The accounts receivable and contra before and after the write-off appear below:

	Before	*After*
Accounts receivable........................	$10,000	$9,600
Less: Allowance for bad debts..............	500	100
Realizable value of accounts receivable........	$ 9,500	$9,500

Recovery of Bad Debts. What happens when an account that has previously been written off as a specific bad debt is collected? Two possible treatments exist. One possibility is to interpret the write-off as a mistake. On the basis of later events the account really never should have been deemed uncollectible. Suppose that the $400 of accounts written off during the year includes one receivable of $25 which ends up being collected in December. Under this alternative the write-off entry should be reversed, and the cash treated as an ordinary collection of a receivable:

```
Accounts Receivable (also subsidiary account)..... 25
    Allowance for Uncollectibles.................            25

Cash............................................... 25
    Accounts Receivable (also subsidiary
      account)....................................            25
```

A complete record of the eventual collection of the account appears in the subsidiary ledger account.

The second approach is to treat the cash collected as a fortuitous circumstance giving rise to a special item of revenue in the period. The entry to reflect this would be:

```
Cash............................................... 25
    Bad Debts Recovered (Revenue)................            25
```

The first procedure seems to have more logic behind it. Particularly, it applies when arbitrary policies are followed to declare an account uncollectible. For example, a firm as a matter of policy might write off all accounts with balances over one year old. This policy may result in some accounts being erroneously charged off as uncollectible. Logic again would suggest the first procedure, when an account is recovered in the same year in which it is written off. On the other hand, if an account when written off is turned over to a special agency for additional intensive collection efforts, Bad Debts Recovered might provide a measure of the benefits from the additional collection costs.

Income Statement Classification.   The foregoing analysis begins with the assumption that the original entries to record charge sales are subject to future adjustment for uncollectible accounts. Revenue is equal to the amount of cash ultimately to be collected from the receivables. The uncollectible accounts have a net realizable value of zero. Revenue from these sales does not exist. Hence the estimate of uncollectibles is deducted from gross sales to obtain the net revenue figure.

Some accountants believe that the uncollectible accounts should be viewed as expenses to be *deducted from* revenue. In practice, a Bad Debt Expense account is employed. The argument is made that a certain amount of uncollectibles is a financial expense inevitable in doing business on credit. This view is not entirely without merit, particularly from a managerial standpoint. Nevertheless, it views the original debits to Accounts Receivable as reliable measures of value. This interpretation of the original entry does not seem to fit most situations. The value of a claim to cash reasonably should not be divorced from the amount of cash expected to be received. At the time of sale we have only a reasonable degree of certainty in our measurement; we leave the door open for later modifications. Uncollectibles are not like other expenses in the sense of resources used up to produce revenues. They represent revenue never received rather than costs incurred.

Whether the estimate of uncollectibles is treated as a contra revenue or as an expense causes no practical difference in the calculation of net income. Either treatment results in a decrease in income. Also, either way, the amount is segregated in a special account for informational purposes; the statement classification does not alter that usefulness.

Evaluation of Bad Debt Procedures.   Under the procedures described above, the contra asset account is increased periodically by the estimated adjustment for doubtful accounts. At the same time, as individual uncollectible accounts are identified, entries are made debiting the Allowance for Uncollectibles. Consequently, if the original estimate remains accurate, the balance in the contra account should bear a fairly close relationship to the balance in the asset account. When using an estimate based on sales be aware of the possibility of the Allowance for Uncollectibles growing too large or too small relative to the end-of-period receivables. If the estimate is faulty, the resultant over- or understatement of receivables could go undetected.

Applying the estimate to accounts receivable avoids the possibility of a disproportionate relationship developing between the asset and the contra account. At the end of each accounting period the contra account is adjusted by *whatever amount* is necessary to make it conform to the uncollectibility percentage (based on receivables) being used. The defect of this method is emphasized by the italicized words. The income statement adjustment is not calculated directly but arises as a by-product of the adjustment to receivables. Consequently, any errors made in handling receivables—prior periods' misestimates or errors in identifying specific bad debt accounts—are automatically compensated for in the current period's estimate, with the result that both the past and the current periods' income calculations are in error.

In our example the percentages are selected to give identical results under either method. In practice the two methods would not give the same figure, although they should be close if the estimates are accurate. Normally, only one method is used regularly, the other being used periodically as a check. Theoretically, the sales approach is preferred from the standpoint of income measurement to obtain a basic estimate proportionate to sales volume. Then, as a check using aging of the accounts receivable balance, the adequacy of the resultant allowance balance can be appraised in relation to the ending receivables balance and in light of any changes in business conditions. Further adjustment may be necessary; but if so, analysis should be undertaken to determine why.

If the periodic estimate being used turns out to be inaccurate, then the Allowance for Uncollectibles should be adjusted. If the estimate is too high, for example, the contra asset will be overstated. Net income in the past will have been understated. Consequently, a special extraordinary gain account must be credited. The correcting entry is:

```
Allowance for Uncollectibles................... xxx
    Extraordinary Gain—Adjustment of Prior
    Years' Estimates of Uncollectibles........         xxx
```

The possibility of having to make a subsequent correcting entry may raise a basic question of whether the use of an estimate opens the door to subjectivity and inaccuracy. Many small businesses do not estimate, but wait until specific bad debts are identified. In most instances, however, more accurate (and perhaps even more objective) periodic financial statements result if estimates are used than if the situation is ignored. Keep in mind that there is no automatic way of determining exactly when an account is uncollectible. Under the estimate procedure the specific write-off of an account does not affect income. Thus the estimate procedure removes a possibility of distortion in income measurement arising from the purposeful speeding up or postponement of the identification of specific uncollectible accounts.

Sales Returns

In addition to nonpayment of an account, the possibility exists that some customers will return the merchandise they have purchased on account. If the returned goods are accepted by the seller, the result is the opposite of the original transaction. When the merchandise is returned, the sale is in effect canceled and the account receivable claim disappears. The entry to record this is:

```
Sales Returns.................................... xxx
    Accounts Receivable (also subsidiary
    account)....................................         xxx
```

In the form of a contra account, as opposed to a direct debit to Sales, this particular decrease or modification in revenue is segregated and highlighted for management's attention and analysis. Because we know the exact customers who are returning the merchandise, we do not need a contra asset account.

Credit Balances in Accounts Receivable. Occasionally a customer returns merchandise for which he has already paid. An entry is made in the usual manner, debiting Sales Returns and crediting Accounts Receivable. Because the merchandise already has been paid for, the customer in essence has overpaid his account; he has a claim against the firm. But this liability of the firm currently is recorded as a credit balance in a subsidiary asset account. In most cases this situation is temporary. The customer normally purchases additional merchandise, and the credit balance is short-lived. If, however, at the end of the period any subsidiary accounts receivable exist with credit balances, they should not be offset against other receivables. They should be shown as liabilities, with the full amount owed by other customers shown as accounts receivable.

Estimating Sales Returns. The Sales Returns account is clearly a contra revenue and generally is treated as such in practice. However, what about sales made at the end of the current accounting period that will be returned in the next accounting period? If we debit the contra revenue when the return actually takes place, we shall be matching cancellations of the present period's sales against the next period's sales. The theoretical alternative would be to estimate the amount of sales at the end of the current period which normally would be canceled by returns taking place in the next period. Then an adjusting entry could be made similar to the adjustment for bad debts, with the credit being made to a contra asset, Accounts Receivable—Allowance for Returns. When specific returns actually take place, they will be handled much like the identification of a specific bad debt—that is, written off against the contra asset.

The adjustment for estimated returns, however, differs from the adjustment for bad debts. The amount is small, relatively constant from year to year, and often more difficult to determine than uncollectibles. Moreover, the adjustment for returns, unlike that for bad debts, also entails a judgment concerning the *cost* of merchandise that is estimated to be returned. The end results may not be any more accurate and useful than if the theoretical violation were ignored. For these reasons an adjustment for estimated returns is very rare in accounting practice.

Sales Discounts

One additional recording problem may arise in purchase-sale transactions between certain businesses. This is the problem of the discount offered for prompt payment of accounts. Particularly in the wholesale trade, the seller often allows a discount from the billed amount if payment is made within a certain time. What amount of revenue is to be recorded at the time of the initial sale? The invoice price is referred to as the *gross price*. The price after deduction of the discount for prompt payment (often called the "cash discount") is termed the *net price*.

Sales are recorded more commonly at gross prices than at net prices. Nevertheless, logic favors the net method. The truth of the matter is that the "cash discount" is actually a penalty charged to those customers who do not pay on time. The revenue expected from the sale of the merchandise is the "cash" price or net price. In effect there are two separate potential sources of revenue—the price charged for the product and the additional amount charged for deferred payment—and the net method clearly distinguishes between these revenue sources. Under the net method, Sales is credited only with the pure price of the product. A separate revenue account is credited whenever additional cash is collected because the customer pays late. Under the gross method both of these revenues are combined together in the Sales account.[11]

Despite the theoretical advantages of recording sales at net prices initially, both methods are used in practice, and both usually require later adjustments. If sales are entered at gross prices, then modifications are necessary whenever customers take the discount. On the other hand, if sales are initially recorded at net prices, then adjustments are necessary during the period for all discounts lost by customers.

Example. A simple example illustrates both methods. Suppose two sales of $10,000 each (gross price) are made on September 1. One account is paid on September 9; the other is paid on September 30. Further, let us assume that the firm sells on terms which allow a 2 percent discount if the customer pays his account within 10 days of the invoice date. Otherwise, the full gross price is due within 30 days.

The journal entries in Table 6–2 show how these transactions are han-

TABLE 6–2

Gross Price Recording

Sept.	1	Accounts Receivable.............	20,000	
		Sales.......................		20,000
Sept.	9	Cash..........................	9,800	
		Sales Discounts................	200	
		Accounts Receivable.........		10,000
Sept.	30	Cash..........................	10,000	
		Accounts Receivable.........		10,000

Net Price Recording

Sept.	1	Accounts Receivable.............	19,600	
		Sales ($20,000 less 2%).....		19,600
Sept.	9	Cash..........................	9,800	
		Accounts Receivable.........		9,800
Sept.	30	Cash..........................	10,000	
		Accounts Receivable.........		9,800
		Sales Discount Revenue......		200

dled under both the gross and the net methods. Obviously an individual firm would employ one or the other, not both. However, a comparative study highlights the differences between the two. Under the gross method payment within the discount period necessitates an adjustment to revenue by means of a debit to the contra account, Sales Discounts. When payment is made after the discount period in the gross amount, no adjustment is necessary, as gross is the basis for the original entry. Basically, the

---

[11] The recent "truth-in-lending" law requires many merchants to disclose to the customer the effective interest rate that is hidden by the use of a higher gross (delayed payment) price and then allowing a deduction for prompt payment.

opposite occurs under the net method. No adjustment of revenue is necessary on September 9; the sale has been recorded under the assumption that the customer would take the discount, and he has done so. Gross payments after the discount period has expired, however, involve recognizing an additional $200 of revenue from those customers who elected the deferred-payment privilege.

End-of-Period Adjustments. As in the case of returns, some outstanding accounts receivable at the end of the period will represent sales from the last few weeks of the accounting period and, because of sales discounts to be taken, will not reflect accurately the amount of cash to be received. Theoretically, revenue and receivables should be adjusted. If original sales are recorded gross, then an adjustment should be made at year-end for discounts to be taken next year on outstanding receivables. The entry would be:

```
Sales Discounts.............................. xxx
     Accounts Receivable—Allowance for
        Discounts.............................       xxx
     To adjust for discounts available on out-
     standing receivables.
```

Under the net method for any outstanding accounts on which the discount period has already expired, adjustment is theoretically necessary to increase both assets and revenue to reflect the unrecorded fact that the customer owes additionally for his failure to pay within the discount period. The entry would be:

```
Accounts Receivable.......................... xxx
     Sales Discount Revenue.....................       xxx
```

In accounting practice few companies make these end-of-period adjustments. Sales Discounts or Sales Discount Revenue are normally recorded in the period the accounts are paid. This practical expedient is justified on two grounds. The amounts involved often are too immaterial to worry about. Also, the adjustments omitted at the end of the period are counterbalanced by amounts from previous years included at the beginning of the period.

SUMMARY

This chapter attempts to focus attention on three issues concerning revenues. They are (1) what constitutes revenue, (2) when to recognize revenue, and (3) how much revenue to recognize.

The first question is answered by defining revenue to be the cash received, cash to be received, or cash needs satisfied as a result of the firm's activity during a period associated with supplying goods and services to customers. This definition has four elements: (1) revenue is a period concept, (2) it measures productive activity during the period, (3) the measurement is in terms of the reward resulting from the activity, and (4) the reward is expressed in terms of ultimate cash receipts or equivalent.

The definition of revenue provides a guideline for what is to be recognized and the total amount that can be recognized. However, it does not answer the second question concerning the timing of revenue recognition. This question is satisfied in concept by the revenue postulate, which assumes that two conditions have to be met before revenue is recorded in financial accounting; it must have been earned, and it must be measurable with a reasonable degree of certainty and objectivity. We illustrate how this concept attempts to balance two desirable but conflicting goals —certainty and timeliness. We also explore the application of this postulate to revenue recognition at times other than the point of sale.

The final question of how much revenue to recognize is answered in part by the definition of revenue and the revenue postulate. However, instances are identified wherein the originally recorded revenue measurement has to be adjusted. These adjustments fall into three categories. First, the cash receipt may not represent a reward for activities associated with the supplying of goods and services to customers and, hence, not be revenue—sales and excise taxes, container deposits, and freight reimbursements. Secondly, the cash received or to be received may not yet have been earned because additional efforts are required on the part of the firm subsequent to the initial entry—production, storage, financing, and servicing. Finally, events subsequent to the initial entry may alter the amount of cash eventually to be received—uncollectibles, returns, and discounts.

The theory behind each of these types of adjustments is discussed, and illustrative entries are presented. In the case of uncollectibles, returns, and discounts, contra revenue accounts are used to segregate the particular decreases in revenues for informational purposes. In some cases contra asset accounts also are used to reduce overstated accounts receivable. Many firms in presenting their income statements to external audiences condense the sales and contra revenue accounts. As a consequence, the vast majority of income statements begin with the caption "net sales," the returns and discounts already having been subtracted.

APPENDIX 6–A
ACCOUNTING FOR LONG-TERM CONSTRUCTION CONTRACTS

Long-term construction contracts—such as contracts for buildings, ships, highways, and other major projects which extend over more than one accounting period—present some special accounting problems. Chapter Six mentions the problems of when and how to recognize revenue. One method suggested there is called *percentage of completion*. It recog-

nizes revenue (and matches expense) periodically as the work progresses. Income is accrued over the life of the contract in proportion to
the amount earned each period. A second accepted method, called *completed contract*, conforms more closely to the traditional sales basis by
recognizing income only when the constructed asset is "delivered" to
the customer. During construction the costs incurred each period are accumulated in an inventory account, to be matched against revenue only
in the period when the contract is completed.

Long-term construction contracts contain other features that require
careful treatment in the accounts. Under the terms of most contracts, the
contractor may bill the customer periodically for partial payment. These
progress billings may or may not conform to the amount of work completed. Of the amounts billed, it is common for the customer to withhold
a specified percentage until final completion as a guarantee of performance. In addition, some contracts virtually guarantee some income; others
may result in either income or loss.

TYPES OF CONTRACTS

Three general types of contracts are employed on long-term construction projects. The most common type of contract is for a fixed
total amount of revenue. The other two types provide for revenue equal
to the costs incurred plus a fee representing the gross margin under the
contract. One, called cost-plus-fixed-fee, specifies the fee as a fixed *dollar*
amount. The other, known as cost-plus-a-percentage, calculates the fee
as a fixed *percentage* of cost. Both cost-plus contracts guarantee a positive
gross margin and are found most often in government contract work.
The gross margin on the cost-plus-fixed-fee contract does not require an
estimate; however, its allocation to different accounting periods does.
With cost-plus-a-percentage-of-cost contracts, the amount of gross margin applicable to any particular accounting period is known with certainty, since it is a constant percentage of the cost incurred that period.

On a fixed-price contract, on the other hand, the ultimate gross margin may be positive or negative, depending on the amount of costs. Prior
to completion of the job, the gross margin can be calculated only by *estimating* the total costs for the job and deducting them from the fixed contract price. To spread this gross margin over a number of accounting
periods, as in percentage of completion, requires an additional judgment
as to the proportion earned each period. It would seem, then, that under
percentage of completion, fixed-price contracts pose more difficult problems than do cost-plus contracts. And, since they comprise the majority
of long-term contracts, we use a fixed-price contract in the following
illustrations.

To contrast the recording procedures under completed contract and percentage of completion and to serve as a common point of departure for a discussion of problems, a single numerical example is helpful. Assume that a builder contracts to construct a two-story apartment dwelling. The total contract price is $1.5 million. The estimated total cost of construction over the two and a half years' expected completion time is $1 million. The contract calls for three equal periodic billings—when the basement and foundation are completed, when the first story is completed, and when the entire project is completed. Each billing is collectible within 90 days, except for a 10 percent retainer to be paid upon final acceptance by the purchaser. Table 6–A–1 summarizes pertinent data during the construction period.

TABLE 6–A–1

(in thousands)

	Year 1	Year 2	Year 3
Construction costs incurred	$400	$300	$325
Estimated costs to complete	600	350	...
Progress billings	500	500	500
Collections on progress billings	...	450	900
Collection of retainer	...	...	150
Administrative expense (period charge)	25	25	25

COMPLETED CONTRACT

The entries to be made during each of the three years appear in Table 6–A–2 in condensed form. Only those entries unique to long-term construction contracts are illustrated.

Financial Statement Presentation

During Years 1 and 2, the income statement will show only $25,000 administrative expense and, consequently, a $25,000 net loss (assuming no other contracts or revenue). In Year 3, net income will be $450,000 ($475,000 gross margin from the contract less $25,000 administrative expense). On the position statement, Construction Receivables Billed[12] and Construction Contract in Progress would be disclosed in the current asset section. The former would appear among the receivables, the latter as a specially identified item of inventory.

The most troublesome account to classify is Advances from Partial Billings. The preferred treatment is to show it as a current liability. Since

---

[12] A separate receivable account could be set up for the 10 percent retainer.

TABLE 6–A–2

Entries under Completed Contract
(in thousands)

	Year 1		Year 2		Year 3	
1. To record incurrence of construction costs:						
Construction Contract in Progress.............	400		300		325	
Cash, Materials, Payables, etc.............		400		300		325
2. To record administrative expenses:						
Administrative Expense.........	25		25		25	
Cash, Payables, etc.........		25		25		25
3. To record progress billings:						
Construction Receivables Billed.................	500		500		500	
Advances from Partial Billings.................		500		500		500
4. To record collections of billings:						
Cash......................			450		900	
Construction Receivables Billed..............				450		900
5. To record collection of retainer:						
Cash......................					150	
Construction Receivables Billed..............						150
6. To recognize revenue and expense:*						
Advances from Partial Billings.................					1,500	
Construction Revenue.......						1,500
Cost of Construction Contract Completed.......					1,025	
Construction Contract in Progress..........						1,025

* In practice, the revenue and expense normally are not recognized separately. Only the difference between them, or gross margin, appears in the accounts. A single journal entry is made upon completion of the job (in thousands):

Advances from Partial Billings...............................	1,500	
Construction Contract in Progress.........................		1,025
Gross Margin on Construction Contracts...................		475

revenue is being recognized only at the completion of the contract, amounts collected from customers must represent advances (i.e., claims against assets that will be satisfied by subsequent delivery of the product). In practice most companies treat the credit arising from progress billings as an offset to Construction Contract in Progress. This procedure was recommended by the AICPA's Committee on Accounting Procedure in 1955 and was subsequently endorsed by the Accounting Principles Board. The net differences between construction costs and progress billings is to be shown as a current asset (costs of uncompleted contracts in excess of related billings) or as a current liability (billings on uncompleted contracts in excess of related costs). For example, at December 31 of Year 1, the current portion of the balance sheet would show:

Current Assets	*Current Liabilities*
Construction receivables billed. $500,000	Billings on uncompleted contracts in excess of related costs of $400,000. . . . . $100,000

The reasoning behind this offsetting of assets and liabilities is obscure. Ostensibly, offsetting is accepted in practice because of the close relationship between the two accounts and because, in a sense, the project has been "sold" although no profit has been recognized. However, this offsetting confuses the issue, particularly when a net credit balance results, as in our example. The contractor does not owe the net amount. Either he owes the gross amount (the entire advance is a liability), or the net amount is a gross-margin element properly includable in income and retained earnings. The latter view, of course, negates the assumption underlying completed-contract. Consequently, separation of the asset and liability accounts makes more sense.[13] The position statement treatment (offsetting) records the inventory as if it were being sold piecemeal, while the income statement reports as if it were not being sold.

Use of Completed Contract

The inconsistency mentioned in the preceding paragraph is symptomatic of the basic limitation of the completed-contract method for many contracts. The method does not reflect current productive activity, even though other conditions which warrant recognition of revenue and asset changes in the accounts are present. Therefore, its use should be restricted to situations in which these other conditions are not present.

---

[13] A possible exception might be a government contract, where progress billings are treated as an offset to inventory on the ground that any portion completed and billed legally becomes the property of the government. Despite its superficial appeal, this treatment still suffers from the same internal inconsistency.

Only when a lack of dependable estimates prevents accurate forecasts or when no signed contract exists would completed-contract be appropriate. It would be inappropriate for most cost-plus contracts.

When it is used, an attempt should be made to defer attributable selling and administrative costs as well as construction costs in order to achieve a better matching when revenue is recognized. Costs of preparing bids, commissions on specific contracts, drawings, and perhaps other selling and administrative costs can be directly identified with and allocated to specific contracts. Care must be exercised to avoid arbitrary allocations of these administrative costs, but generally more accurate income measurement results. If a firm is engaged in numerous contracts, however, direct treatment as period expenses probably will not distort income materially.

PERCENTAGE OF COMPLETION

There are two methods of recording which may be employed under percentage of completion. The more common method uses the same framework of accounts as completed-contract except for a periodic revaluation of inventory to reflect the earned profit element. The other approach uses slightly different accounts to record full sales and expense information. Under the first approach, entries 1 through 5 in Table 6–A–2 are the same as those under completed contract. Entry 6 differs as shown below (in thousands):

	Year 1	Year 2	Year 3
6. To recognize income:			
Construction Contract in Progress	200	100	175
Gross Margin on Construction Contracts	200	100	175
Advances from Partial Billings		1,500	
Construction Contract in Progress			1,500

The gross margin earned each year is found from the calculations shown in Table 6–A–3.

Financial Statement Presentation

The Gross Margin on Construction Contracts account will be closed to Income Summary each year and will appear among the revenues on

TABLE 6–A–3

(dollars in thousands)

	Year 1	Year 2	Year 3
Contract price......................	$1,500	$1,500	$1,500
Less:			
Actual cost incurred to date........	$ 400	$ 700	$1,025
Estimated cost to complete.........	600	350	...
	$1,000	$1,050	$1,025
Total estimated gross margin..........	$ 500	$ 450	$ 475
Percentage of gross margin earned to date.	$\frac{\$\ 400}{\$1,000} = 40\%$	$\frac{\$\ 700}{\$1,050} = 66\tfrac{2}{3}\%$	100%
Total gross margin earned to date........	$ 200	$ 300	$ 475
Gross margin recognized in prior periods.	...	200	300
Gross margin to be recognized.........	$ 200	$ 100	$ 175

the income statement. It is a net revenue, in that cost of goods sold has already been subtracted. Thus it fails to provide complete information concerning the volume of construction activity during the period, as measured by the contract prices, or the amount of construction costs incurred to earn that revenue. However, the net income figures, Gross Margin less Administrative Expense ($175,000 in Year 1, $75,000 in Year 2, and $150,000 in Year 3) clearly present a more rational picture of business activity over the period than that which resulted under completed-contract.

The treatment of items on the position statement is the same as under completed-contract, with one exception. The asset Construction Contract in Progress is revalued upward each period by the amount of gross margin recognized during the year. So instead of being at cost, it is valued at cost plus the income element recognized. The credit balance in Advances from Partial Billings is still offset against the inventory account, and only the net asset is shown. The balance sheet at December 31 of Year 1 would show:

Current Assets	*Current Liabilities*
Construction receivables	
billed..................... $500,000	
Cost of uncompleted contracts	
in excess of related billings	
of $500,000.............. 100,000	

Alternative Procedure

A different set of entries is illustrated in Table 6–A–4. The effect on income is the same, but this procedure shows full revenue and expense accounts, and the unbilled portion of the gross margin appears on the position statement as a receivable. Table 6–A–4 shows the two entries that are different.

TABLE 6–A–4
(in thousands)

	Year 1		Year 2		Year 3	
3. To record progress billings:						
Construction Receivables						
Billed...............	500		500		500	
Construction Receiva-						
bles Unbilled.......		500		500		500
6. To recognize revenue and						
expense:						
Construction Receivables						
Unbilled...........	600		400		500	
Construction						
Revenue...........		600		400		500
Cost of Construction						
Completed.........	400		300		325	
Construction Contract						
in Progress*.......		400		300		325

* In Years 1 and 2 a contra asset account might be credited instead, so that Construction Contract in Progress could act as a control account for managerial purposes.

The total contract price of $1.5 million is allocated over the three-year period in the same manner as the gross profit in the preceding illustration (see Table 6–A–3). The percentage of completion is applied to revenue rather than just to gross margin (e.g., in Year 2, the calculation is $66\frac{2}{3}\%$ × $1,500,000 = $1,000,000 earned to date; $1,000,000 − $600,000 = $400,-000 to be recognized.)

Measurement Problems

A comparison of the results under percentage of completion with those under completed-contract clearly reveals the superiority of the former as to the *earning* criterion. The only factor that might prevent its use in *all* long-term construction contracts is *measurability*. Problems can occur in four areas: (1) objective and certain determination of total revenue, (2) uncertainty regarding collection, (3) measurement of percentage of completion, and (4) cost estimation.

As mentioned in Chapter Six, sufficient objectivity and certainty of total revenue normally can be found in the contractual relationship between buyer and seller. The existence of an outside purchaser provides the objectivity. The total price is known in advance in a fixed-fee contract or is determinable with certainty by the terms of the contract in cost-plus arrangements. Therefore, a contract and a committed customer are essential requisites for use of percentage of completion. Ordinarily, major projects are not undertaken unless a customer has agreed to purchase the completed project. Nevertheless, occasionally speculative building (say, of houses) is undertaken without definite contracts, specified prices, or customers. Percentage of completion would not be appropriate under those circumstances.

Reliable measurement also requires that we can predict with reasonable accuracy that ultimate cash receipts equal to the total amount of revenue will be collected. Normally, the likelihood of not being able to collect from the purchaser is small. A construction project requires sizable long-term risks on the part of the contractor. These are not undertaken without a thorough review of the credit standing, reputation, financial position, etc., of the customer. Large, financially established firms and governmental bodies tend to be the ones which qualify. The risk is further reduced by progress billings. Nevertheless, instances could arise—threat of renegotiation or cancellation of a government contract—where this aspect of measurement would not be reliable. Even in these cases the uncertainty is usually not sufficient to cause postponement of revenue recognition.

A third aspect of reliable measurement concerns how accurately the earned portion of total revenue may be measured. This measurement, of course, is absolutely certain on contracts covering cost plus a percentage of cost. But for fixed-price and cost-plus-fixed-fee contracts, some estimate of the portion earned is necessary. With fixed-price contracts the estimate of percentage earned is used to allocate the full amount of revenue. With cost-plus-fixed-fee contracts it is used only to allocate the fixed fee.

The examples in Chapter Six and in this appendix use cost incurred as a percentage of total cost to measure the portion earned. This assumes that every dollar of cost earns an equal amount of revenue. Such an assumption may not be appropriate if one of two conditions is present. First, if the construction consists of identical or very similar segments and varying costs are incurred on different segments, it may be more reasonable to assume that each segment produces equal revenue. For example, a contract may call for the construction of three similar lakeshore cottages at a total price of $75,000. If the foundation on the second cottage has to be repoured because of shifting sand, the portion of revenue attributable to the period in which the second cottage is worked on probably should not be increased because of that fact.

The second reservation about the use of cost arises if substantial material costs or subcontracting costs are involved. Material stockpiled at a construction site does not adequately measure work done. Likewise, if revenue is to represent the reward for the contractor's efforts, large and irregular costs of subcontractors' work may distort the measurement of the prime contractor's contribution. To take a somewhat extreme case, assume that a contractor is to construct an apartment building, including the laying of expensive wall-to-wall carpeting throughout. The latter function is subcontracted to a rug company at a cost of $20,000. Other building costs total $80,000. The carpets are laid during the last week, after all other work is complete. If cost is used as a measure of earning, only 80 percent of the revenue (and profit) is assumed to be earned by putting up the apartment building, perhaps over a two-year period. Then, in the last week the other 20 percent is assumed to be earned simply by contacting the subcontractor and having him lay the carpets.

To avoid these potential limitations on cost as a measure of the portion earned, the AICPA has approved other methods of estimating. These include engineering estimates of the percentage of work completed or physical measures of completion. Progress billings usually are not a satisfactory measure of work done, because they tend to be dictated by financial rather than production considerations. Therefore, they lead or lag behind actual performance under the contract. Nevertheless, under some government contracts the job can be broken down into a number of homogeneous physical units, which are billed as the completed units are delivered. Here, the amounts billed may be an appropriate measure of partial performance.

If cost incurred as a percentage of total cost is used to estimate the percentage of completion, a fourth measurement problem arises. The accuracy of the percentage of completion depends directly on the predictability of the total cost of the project. This prediction may be uncertain or inaccurate and thereby cause error in computing the percentage of work done. This occurs in the illustration shown in Table 6–A–3. The original estimate of total cost was $1 million. After the first year it was revised to $1,050,000 and finally turned out to be $1,025,000.

The particular procedure used in the illustration to determine each period's allocation of revenue contains an automatic error-correction mechanism. By estimating *total revenue earned to date* and then subtracting the portion previously recognized, we include in any particular year the portion earned that year plus any corrections of prior periods, all based on the most recent cost estimates. But even the most recent cost estimates may not turn out to be accurate. Table 6–A–5 compares the amounts actually recognized, the amounts earned each period as determined by the most recent cost estimates without error correction, and the amount that would have been recognized if perfect foresight had been available. Comparison of the first two columns gives the magnitude of the error correction. Comparisons of either the first or second column with the third in-

TABLE 6–A–5

	Amounts Based On		
	Actually Recognized	Best Estimate Available	Perfect Foresight
Year 1	$ 600,000	$600,000 $\left(\dfrac{400}{1,000}\right)$	$ 585,366 $\left(\dfrac{400}{1,025}\right)$
Year 2	400,000	428,571 $\left(\dfrac{300}{1,050}\right)$	439,024 $\left(\dfrac{300}{1,025}\right)$
Year 3	500,000	475,610 $\left(\dfrac{325}{1,025}\right)$	475,610 $\left(\dfrac{325}{1,025}\right)$
	$1,500,000		$1,500,000

dicates the range of inaccuracy in the revenue estimate. The percentage deviation in gross margin, of course, would be even greater.

This degree of inaccuracy is caused by cost estimates that are less than 5 percent in error. Undoubtedly, the reliability of cost estimates varies considerably by industry and project. In those cases where cost estimates are subject to large errors, the percentage-of-completion method may not provide sufficiently reliable measurements, particularly for fixed-price contracts. Keep in mind, however, that the alternative may be completed-contract, wherein no revenue is recognized until completion. The accountant must decide which error is more important—failure to recognize the reward for efforts expended (completed-contract) or inaccurate and perhaps misleading measurement of periodic revenue (percentage of completion when cost estimates are not dependable).

ESTIMATED LOSSES ON LONG-TERM CONTRACTS

What should be done if the estimate of cost to complete a project indicates that the total costs will exceed the total revenue? A negative gross margin on a long-term contract can occur only, of course, with a fixed-price contract. Weather conditions, labor disputes, shortages of crucial construction materials, and price changes are just some of the factors which could cause a contract that initially appeared worthwhile to be completed at a loss.

One approach might be to deal with the problem as a normal event. Whatever revenue-recognition procedure is being followed would be applied consistently regardless of whether profit or a loss resulted. If revenue were being recognized under completed-contract, the total revenue would be recognized in the year of completion along with the total costs (expenses). No loss would be recognized until the last year, just as no profit would be recognized until completion. If percentage of completion were being employed, the loss would be spread over the period of construction in the same manner as a positive gross margin is recognized. Revenue would be measured in the normal manner. However, the costs to be matched each period would exceed the periodic revenue; the result would be a negative gross margin on that contract each period. In both cases the fact that an additional loss is anticipated could be communicated to the reader of the income statement via a footnote.

Although the procedure described in the preceding paragraph applies revenue-recognition criteria consistently, it is not generally accepted. The AICPA in *Accounting Research Bulletin No. 45* states, "When the current estimate of total contract costs indicates a loss, in most circumstances provision should be made for loss on the entire contract."[14] This provision is accomplished by a debit to a loss account and a credit to the inventory account Construction Contract in Progress for the *full* amount of the anticipated loss.[15]

Assume that for our example, at the end of Year 2 it is clear that total costs will amount to $1,550,000 rather than the $1 million originally estimated. The revised total estimated costs will exceed by $50,000 the total revenues of $1.5 million. The entire anticipated loss of $50,000 is recognized in Year 2 under completed-contract by the following entry:

```
Anticipated Loss on Construction
    Contract............................ 50,000
    Construction Contract in Progress........        50,000
```

Under percentage of completion, the write-down (loss) would be $250,-000—the anticipated total loss of $50,000 plus the positive gross margin of $200,000 already recognized in Year 1.

The rationale for this write-down is twofold. First, on grounds of conservatism, many accountants believe that all known losses—past, present, and future—should be recognized immediately but that profits should not be recognized until earned. Second, some accountants feel that assets should never be valued at more than their net realizable value, the net amount for which they can be sold. If a portion of the cost of the asset cannot be recovered through sale, then that portion represents a cost that has no future value. Charging the entire anticipated loss against the Construction Contract in Progress account ensures that its value will never exceed net realizable value, provided the new cost estimates are accurate. More is said about this concept in Chapter Eight, in the section dealing with lower-of-cost-or-market valuation of inventories.

---

[14] "Long-Term Construction-Type Contracts," *Accounting Research Bulletin No. 45* (New York: AICPA, 1955), p. 5.

[15] Under the alternative procedure for percentage of completion, no balance remains in the Construction Contract in Progress account. The credit would have to be made to Construction Receivables Unbilled.

SUGGESTIONS FOR FURTHER READING

American Accounting Association, Concepts and Standards Research Committee—The Realization Concept. "The Realization Concept," *Accounting Review*, Vol. 40 (April 1965), pp. 312–22.

Arnett, Harold E. "Recognition as a Function of Measurement in the Realization Concept," *Accounting Review*, Vol. 38 (October 1963), pp. 733–41.

Horngren, Charles T. "How Should We Interpret the Realization Concept?" *Accounting Review*, Vol. 40 (April 1965), pp. 323–33.

Myers, John H. "Critical Event and Recognition of Net Profit," *Accounting Review*, Vol. 34 (October 1954), pp. 528–32.

Paton, William A. " 'Deferred Income'—A Misnomer," *Journal of Accountancy*, Vol. 112 (September 1961), pp. 38–40.

———. "Premature Revenue Recognition," *Journal of Accountancy*, Vol. 95 (October 1953), pp. 432–37.

QUESTIONS AND PROBLEMS

6–1.   An advertising agency in 1971 made a number of one-minute spot advertisements for a local radio station. The latter planned to use the advertisements to promote its own programs. The cost of development and recording to the advertising agency was $50,000. In exchange for the advertisements, the agency received a specified number of minutes of "free" air time. There was a ready market for air time, and the agency normally would have paid $80,000 for this amount of time. In 1972, the agency used the air time in advertising campaigns for other clients. It billed the clients $80,000 for the time plus a 15 percent commission.

    a)   How much revenue should be recognized by the advertising agency in 1971? 1972?

    b)   Justify your answer to (*a*) using the concept of revenue and the revenue recognition criteria.

    c)   Record the journal entries to be made in both 1971 and in 1972.*

6–2.   Happy Jack's Funfair Amusement Park is open from April 1 through September 30 of each year. The company sells books of admission tickets to customers at $10 per book. The book contains 10 tickets good for admission any time from April through September. The regular admission price is $1.25. The following statements are prepared for April, May, and June:

	April	*May*	*June*
Sales	$3,250	$6,500	$8,750
Expenses	1,890	2,900	3,280
Net Income	$1,360	$3,600	$5,470

---

* This problem has been adapted from one cited in *The Texas CPA*, November 1958, p. 87, and noted in Sidney Davidson, "The Realization Concept" in Morton Backer (ed.), *Modern Accounting Theory* (Englewood Cliffs, N.J.: Prentice-Hall, Inc., 1966), p. 103.

Sales include the cash received from the sale of coupon books during each month. The number of books sold were 100 in April, 350 in May, and 500 in June. An analysis of admissions reveals that 630; 2,310; and 4,870 admission-book tickets have been presented in the three months, respectively. No entries have been made for these tickets in the accounts.

a) Prepare corrected income statements for each of the three months. Also, determine the liability for tickets outstanding at the end of each month.

b) What would you do with any balance remaining in the liability account on September 30 when the park closes down?

6–3. The Chaos Corporation has recently been turned down for a loan because of the "poor quality" of its accounts receivable. Hy Price, the president, has called you in as a consultant. The following report, dealing with the firm's credit sales, accounts receivable, etc., since the firm's founding in 1970, has been prepared for you:

	1970	1971	1972
Sales on account...................	$220,000	$330,000	$210,000
Cash collections:			
From 1970 sales.................	180,000	35,000	3,300
From 1971 sales.................	...	280,000	46,000
From 1972 sales.................	...	...	180,000
Estimate of bad debts..............	3,300	4,950	3,150
Specific accounts written off:			
From 1970 sales.................	100	1,500	100
From 1971 sales.................	...	500	1,800
From 1972 sales.................	...	...	100

a) Set up ledger accounts for Sales, Accounts Receivable, Cash, Sales Uncollectibles and Allowance for Doubtful Accounts. Record the entries over the three-year period.

b) How would the accounts receivable be shown on a position statement at the end of 1972?

c) How has the company been determining its estimate of bad debts? Comment on the adequacy of this rate.

d) An aging schedule of accounts receivable at the end of 1972 shows the following:

Age	Amount
Current..................................	$16,000
0–60 days past-due........................	8,000
60 days–six months past-due................	4,000
6 months–one year past-due.................	1,900
Over one year past-due....................	1,700
	$31,600

You determine from experience with similar firms in the industry that the following uncollectibility percentages are reasonable for each category: 1 percent for current accounts; 5 percent for 0–60 days; 10 percent for 60 days–six months; 25 percent for six months–one year; and 50 percent for over one year.

Does this confirm or disagree with your conclusion in part (c)? Prepare the necessary adjusting entry based on the information in this part.

6–4. Downtime Computer Sales Corporation sells time-sharing computer terminals with a three-year warranty at $1,500 each. Under the warranty contract, the corporation agrees to provide at no cost to the customer all necessary repairs, both labor and replacement parts, arising from other than misuse of the equipment. From its past experience, the company estimates that labor costs under the warranty agreement will be $300 per unit and replacement parts will be $120 per unit.

During 1971 Downtime sold 100 terminals evenly throughout the year. Repair costs for warranty work in 1971 amounted to $5,300 for labor and $1900 for replacement parts.

a) Prepare the journal entries necessary to record the transactions for 1971. Set up an estimated liability for warranty work.

b) Indicate where the accounts employed in (a) would appear on the financial statements for 1971 and explain why they are so classified.

c) By how much would net income have been changed if the company treated warranty costs simply as a period expense? Which method better measures net income?

d) How might one argue that the method in (a) overstates revenues and hence net income?

6–5. Rippling Road Construction Company entered into a contract for a 20-mile circumferential highway around town. The firm was to be responsible for grading, pouring cement, and finishing the shoulders and median strip. The contract price was $300,000 ($15,000 a mile) and the estimated cost was $240,000 ($12,000 a mile). Payments under the contract are received according to the following schedule: 50 percent of the per-mile price after the concrete is poured, an additional 40 percent when a mile is completely finished, and the remaining 10 percent when the entire highway is completed and approved.

Data relative to the contract are summarized below:

	1971	1972	1973
Total costs incurred...................	$60,000	$120,000	$60,000
Number of miles completely finished.....	3	12	5
Additional miles of cement poured........	5	2	...

a) Determine the amount of revenue and gross margin to be recognized in each year under the percentage of completion method.

b) Determine the amount of cash payment received by the company each year under the contract.

c) The president of Rippling Road Construction Company suggests that revenue be recognized as cash is received, as in part (b).

"Nothing is surer than cash," he says. Explain why percentage of completion provides a better measure of revenue recognition.

d)   The controller suggests a third alternative—recognize revenue as each mile is completed. He suggests that this method does not delay recognition until cash is received, but at the same time avoids the problem of making estimates that is inherent under percentage of completion. What would revenue be each year under his plan? What are its advantages and disadvantages relative to percentage of completion?

6–6.   The A Company, the B Company, the C Company, and the D Company allow their customers a discount of 2 percent of sales when accounts are paid within 10 days of the invoice date.

In its accounts the A Company debits its customers with 98 percent of the gross amount billed them. If payment is made after the 10-day period, the customer's account is credited for 98 percent of the amount paid, the remaining 2 percent being credited to Sales Discounts Not Taken and shown on the income statement as an item of other revenue.

The B Company debits its customers' accounts with the full amount billed them (gross). When payment is made within the 10-day period (gross amount less 2 percent), the customer is credited for the full amount billed, the 2 percent not remitted being charged to Discounts on Sales and shown on the income statement as a deduction from sales.

The bookkeeping procedure of the C Company is the same as that of the B Company; but on the income statement, discounts on sales are treated as an administrative expense.

Company D debits the customers' accounts at the billed amount (gross), but credits Sales for only 98 percent, the remaining 2 percent being credited to Sales Discounts Available. Then, whenever a customer pays within the 10-day period, Accounts Receivable is credited at the billed amount (gross), and the 2 percent not remitted is charged to Sales Discounts Available.

a)   Discuss the theory underlying each of the above treatments; state which method you prefer, and why.

b)   Illustrate each method with journal entries, using a $1,000 gross account, assuming that collection is made within the 10-day period and collection is made after the 10-day period.*

6–7.   U.S. government Series E bonds are purchased at a discount from face value, e.g., a $100 bond costs $75 initially. Then, as time passes, the bond increases in value as interest builds up. If the bond is held to maturity (seven years), the investor will have earned 4.25 percent annual return. At any time during the period the bond can be redeemed according to a schedule of values. This schedule, however, does not build up at a constant 4.25 percent rate. The redemption value increases slowly in the early years and more rapidly in the last few years.

Assume that a purchaser buys a $1,000 Series E government bond

---

* Adapted from AICPA May 1948 examination.

for $750. The question arises concerning how to recognize the interest revenue each year. Three suggestions have been made:

1. Recognize revenue in each period in an amount equal to the increase in redemption value during that period, according to the redemption table.
2. Recognize revenue in each period at a rate equal to 4.25 percent of the current value of the bond.
3. Do not recognize interest revenue until redemption or maturity. Then recognize the entire increment in value as revenue during that year.

a) Evaluate each of these alternatives from a theoretical standpoint. Which do you prefer? Why?

b) Only items 1 and 3 are acceptable for income tax purposes. Can you suggest why this is the case?

6–8. The Ampere Electric Company determines its estimate of uncollectibles in each period from an analysis of outstanding accounts receivable. The Allowance for Uncollectible Accounts shows a current balance of $2,724. At the end of the year the following aging schedule is prepared:

Age	Amount
0–30 days	$425,422
30–60 days	78,165
60–90 days	18,828
Over 90 days	1,290
	$523,705

According to past experience, accounts over 90 days old are 90 percent uncollectible; those 60–90 days old, 5 percent uncollectible; those 30–60 days old, 1 percent uncollectible; and those 0–30 days old, half of 1 percent uncollectible.

a) Prepare the adjusting entry at the end of the fiscal year.

b) What advantages does this method have over the basing of uncollectible estimates on credit sales? Disadvantages?

c) Mr. Claus Trophobia, the chief accountant, objects to this procedure, saying: "Accounting should record objective facts based on realized transactions, not guesses; recording a loss for accounts that we expect to go bad in the future is not sound accounting." Evaluate and reply to his argument.

6–9. Hot Shot Appliance Company purchased 100 refrigerators at a cost of $200 each on January 15, 1971. On March 31, 1971 it sold 50 of these to a single construction firm for $300 each. An installment contract was signed calling for a $3,000 down payment plus five installment payments of $2,583 each, to be paid quarterly on May 31, August 31, December 31, March 31, 1972 and May 31, 1972. The installment payments include an interest factor of 10 percent on the unpaid balance.

a) Prepare journal entries for the 1971 transactions, assuming Hot Shot Appliance uses the installment method of recognizing revenue.

b) How would the accounts you employed in (*a*) be classified on the financial statements for 1971?

c) Compare the net income (ignoring other expenses) for 1971 under the installment method with the amount that would be shown under the conventional sales approach? Which best reflects the firm's activities?

d) How would you handle a 20 percent sales commission that was paid on April 1, 1971 to the salesman obtaining the order?

6–10. The financial statements for the first 11 months of the year for National Merchants Company show the following balances among the accounts.

	Dr.	Cr.
Sales.....................................		$800,000
Sales returns.............................	$ 15,000	
Sales discounts..........................	7,300	
Provision for doubtful accounts.............	16,000	
Accounts receivable......................	215,000	
Allowance for doubtful accounts............		38,000
Bad debts recovered......................		1,800

The company sells on terms of 1 percent cash discount allowed for all accounts paid within 15 days from the invoice date. The company's past experience indicates that 2 percent of sales on account normally are not collected, and a monthly adjusting entry is made to reflect this. All recoveries on uncollectible accounts are credited directly to a special revenue account.

During December, the following transactions occur:

1. Sales of $180,000, of which $30,000 are cash sales.
2. Gross amounts of accounts collected, $260,000, of which $230,000 represents gross accounts collected within the discount period.
3. Gross amounts of returns, $3,500.
4. Accounts charged off as uncollectible, $19,500.
5. Recoveries made of accounts previously written off, $200.
6. The adjusting entry for doubtful accounts is made.

a) Journalize the December transactions.

b) A detailed study of the outstanding accounts receivable at year-end indicates that 10 percent of them will eventually prove uncollectible. Assuming this information is correct, comment on the accuracy of the estimate being used for uncollectible accounts.

c) Assume that December sales were spread evenly over the month and that most customers do not pay until the 15th day. What theoretical adjustment could be made on December 31 with respect to sales discounts? Would you make it? Explain.

d) What alternative treatment could have been employed concerning the recovery of uncollectible accounts? What would be its effect on total assets? Net income? Which do you prefer?

6–11. The Consolidated Bus Company puts into effect a new fare schedule on June 1. The charge for a one-way trip down Main Street is $0.25.

The company also offers patrons the opportunity of buying bus tokens at a price of five for $1. Each token can be used for a one-way ride. During the month of June the following transactions occur: bus tokens sold, 5,000; drivers' reports show cash fares were 4,300, token fares 3,600.

a) Prepare journal entries to record these transactions. The company would like the accounting system to indicate in some manner the amount of discount on the tokens.

b) Can you foresee any other adjustments that might be made in future periods in connection with the tokens?

6–12. Highly Distinct Industries sells testing equipment. The units are quite sensitive and require extensive adjustment and maintenance. Although the adjustments can be made by anyone skilled in the area, many purchasers prefer to have the technicians at Highly Distinct Industries do the work. Consequently, the firm normally sells on a two-price basis —$2,000 per unit if purchaser does his own adjustment and maintenance, or $2,150 per unit if Highly Distinct is to do the work for one year after date of purchase. Adjustment and maintenance agreements can be purchased separately for subsequent years at a cost of $150 per year. The adjustment and maintenance work costs Highly Distinct about $110 a year and is done by a separate department within the firm.

On October 1, 1971, the company sold the following: 10 units without the adjustment provision (price $2,000 each); 6 units with the adjustment provision (price $2,150); and 4 units to the state government under special terms. These terms called for a 10 percent price allowance to be granted (selling price therefore was $1,800 per unit) and for the adjustment and maintenance work to be done free for one year.

The department doing the adjustment work incurred costs applicable to the units sold on October 1 of $180 in 1971 and $885 in 1972.

a) Prepare journal entries for the sale of these machines in 1971 and their adjusting in 1971 and 1972. Explain your reasoning for each entry.

b) What was the average adjustment cost per unit compared to the estimate of $110? How would you handle the difference?

6–13. In 1969 Chic Kenhouse decided to devote his entire efforts to his hobby of making miniature automobiles. Chic had been an antique car buff for years. During his spare time, in his basement, he constructed working models of many of the famous old cars. These models were one-half actual size. They were so authentic and well-built that Chic began to receive requests to make models for others. Consequently, he retired from his full-time job and launched his own private business on January 1, 1970.

Three models of automobiles were initially offered. They all cost approximately $4,800 to make (parts and a reasonable charge for Chic's labor). By pricing them at $6,000 each, Chic figured that he could cover his other costs and earn a reasonable net profit.

The models were built only upon receipt of a firm order accompanied by a $1,000 cash deposit. Another $3,000 was payable at time of delivery and the remaining $2,000 had to be paid six months after delivery. Each model car took from four to eight months to make, depending on the availability of parts and on the number of orders he was working on at one time.

The following events took place during 1970, 1971, and 1972.

Order Number	Date of Order and Deposit	Date Delivered	Costs Incurred		
			1970	1971	1972
01........	1–1–70	5–1–70	$5,000	...	...
02........	1–1–70	9–1–70	4,700	...	...
03........	3–1–70	10–1–70	4,700	...	...
04........	8–1–70	2–1–71	3,600	$1,200	...
05........	4–1–71	9–1–71	...	4,400	...
06........	7–1–71	1–10–72	...	4,000	$1,000
07........	2–1–72	7–1–72	...	...	4,600
08........	3–1–72	9–1–72	...	...	4,800
09........	5–1–72	Unfinished	...	...	4,000
10........	10–1–72	Unfinished	...	...	2,400

a) Compute the gross profit (sales less cost of goods sold) that would have been shown for each of the three years under each of the following assumptions:
   1. Revenue is recognized at the time of delivery.
   2. Revenue is recognized on an installment basis—two thirds ($4,000/$6,000) at the time of delivery and one third ($2,000/$6,000) six months later.
   3. Percentage of completion (use $4,800 as total estimated cost in measuring percentage of completion).

b) Which of these three bases of revenue recognition is most suitable for this company? Justify your choice by comparing its advantages and disadvantages with those of the other methods.

c) Which method best matches costs and revenues? Explain.

6–14. Sagging Suspension Bridge Corporation erects large spans over superhighways. Most projects require 15 to 22 months to complete. During the period 1970–72, the firm worked on four major projects. Relevant data applicable to each one is presented below (in thousands of dollars):

Project Number	Contract Price	Total Estimated Cost	Cost Incurred		
			1970	1971	1972
362433........	$375	$350	$350	...	...
362434........	600	480	120	$300	$ 60
362435........	450	400	...	200	200
362436........	540	500	...	100	250

a) Determine the amount of gross margin to be recognized in each year if percentage of completion is used to recognize revenue.

b) What would you do if the total of the actual costs incurred under the contract differed from the estimated cost?

c) The bookkeeper of Sagging Suspension drew up the following schedule of gross margin under "conventional" accounting (in thousands):

	1970	1971	1972
Sales......................	$375	$ 0	$1,050
Construction costs...........	470	600	510
Gross margin..............	($ 95)	($600)	$ 540

Do you agree that this is the result from conventional accounting? Explain. Revise the figures to show the margins under a proper interpretation of the conventional sales basis of accounting.

d) Explain why your revised figures in (*c*) are still an unsatisfactory measure of the firm's activity.

6–15. A portion of the footnote describing inventories from the 1969 Annual Report of American Smelting and Refining Company reads, "Inventories of smelters, refineries and secondary metals plants include . . . $45,977,000 at sales prices for metals sold under firm contracts for future delivery."

a) *Assume* the cost of these metals is $40 million. Prepare the journal entries the company probably made in 1969 in connection with these inventories.

b) Has revenue been properly recognized in this case? Explain.

c) What entry will the company make upon delivery of these metals in future years?

d) Why is the amount of $45,977,000 shown as inventory rather than as a receivable?

6–16. The Jones Manufacturing Company of No-Account, Nevada (population, 47), sells office supplies in small orders to approximately 1,000 business firms on terms of 1/10, *n*/30. Orders are usually taken one to three weeks before production begins. The production time for an order is from three days to one week, at the end of which the goods are shipped and the invoice is sent. Collection records show that 80 percent of the customers pay within the discount period, the other 20 percent usually paying within the 30 days allowed.

The problem of when to recognize revenue of the Jones Manufacturing Company has been raised at a committee meeting. Among the major contentions are:

1. Credit and collection manager: "We shouldn't recognize any revenue until the *entire* transaction has been completed—after the customer has paid."

2. Sales manager: "I disagree. Revenue should be recognized as soon as the *order* is taken by the salesman."

3. Production manager: "You're both wrong. Revenue is earned throughout the entire manufacturing-selling-collection process. It should be recognized, therefore, as the work progresses. I would recommend that we recognize one third of it at the end of each of these three major stages."

You are called in, as the only accountant within 300 miles, to resolve the company's problem. As to *each* of the above positions, tell whether you agree or disagree, and why. What recommendation would you make? Give reasons.

6–17. Hot Ice Diamond Jewelers, Inc. commonly sells merchandise on the installment plan to college students. Because of the unpredictability of their payment habits, the company feels the installment method of revenue recognition is to be preferred. The summarized statistics for 1970, 1971, and 1972 are given below:

	1970	1971	1972
Installment sales	$35,000	$45,000	$40,000
Cost of sales	21,000	30,000	28,000
Selling expenses	4,800	7,000	8,800
Administrative expenses	900	1,300	1,800
Collection of:			
1970 installment receivables	14,000	14,000	3,500
1971 installment receivables	. . .	22,500	17,000
1972 installment receivables	. . .	. . .	23,000

a) Prepare income statements for each of the three years under the installment method.

b) Prepare, in journal form, the entries required in 1972.

c) What is the balance in the Deferred Gross Margin account as of December 31, 1972? How should this amount be presented in the balance sheet as of that date?

6–18. The president of the D'Anna Company, a manufacturer, is concerned about the auditor's proposed objection relating to material investments in marketable securities presented on its financial statements at the closing prices traded on the New York and American Stock Exchanges at December 31, 1971. The closing prices were substantially in excess of acquisition cost.

He stated, ". . . the thousands of transactions in shares of open-end investment trusts at prices reflecting current market values of their portfolios are evidence that most people view these value changes as equivalent to realization. Indeed, the cost of the investment is an incredibly low figure to present."

a) What should be considered in selecting the method of revenue recognition that is most appropriate for a particular situation?

b) Discuss the appropriateness of D'Anna Company's proposal to recognize as revenue the excess of closing prices on the stock exchange over the cost of the investment.*

6-A-1. Dru P. Cable Building Company signed a contract to construct an office building at a fixed price of $1 million. Estimated costs are $900,000. The financial agreement specified that the contractor was to receive $100,000 immediately. Progress billings were to be made at various times as specified in the contract based on approved work to date. However, 20 percent of each progress billing was to be retained until final approval of the building; 80 percent was due within 10 days of the billing date. The 20 percent retainer less the $100,000 initial advance was payable 30 days after final inspection.

Yearly data relating to this contract are summarized below (in thousands):

Year	Costs Incurred	Estimated Cost to Complete	Progress Billings	Cash Collections
1	$200	$710	$150	$220*
2	450	300	500	400
3	320	...	350	380

* Includes $100,000 initial advance.

a) Prepare journal entries for each year, assuming that the completed contract method was used. Indicate where and in what amounts each account (other than cash) would appear on the financial statements for each of the three years.

b) Repeat part (a), assuming the company uses percentage of completion.

6-A-2. The Metro Construction Company commenced doing business in January 1972. Construction activities for the year 1972 are summarized below (in thousands):

Project	Total Contract Price	Contract Expenditures to Dec. 31	Estimated Costs to Complete	Cash Collections to Dec. 31	Billings to Dec. 31
A	$ 310	$187.5	$ 12.5	$155	$155
B	415	195.0	255.0	210	249
C	350	320.0	...	300	350
D	300	16.5	183.5	...	4
	$1,375	$719.0	$451.0	$665	$758

The company is your client. The president has asked you to compute the amounts of revenue for the year ended December 31, 1972 that would be reported under the completed contract method and the

* Adapted from AICPA November 1967 examination.

percentage of completion method of accounting for long-term contracts. The following information is available:

1. All contracts are with different customers.
2. Any work remaining to be done on the contracts is expected to be completed in 1973.
3. The company's accounts have been maintained on the completed contract method.

a) Prepare a schedule computing the amount of revenue by project for the year ended December 31, 1972 that would be reported under:
   1. The completed contract method.
   2. The percentage of completion method.

b) Prepare a schedule under the completed contract method computing the amounts that would appear in the company's balance sheet at December 31, 1972 for (1) costs in excess of billings, and (2) billings in excess of costs.

c) Prepare a schedule under the percentage of completion method that would appear in the company's balance sheet at December 31, 1972 for (1) costs and estimated earnings in excess of billings, and (2) billings in excess of costs and estimated earnings.*

6–A–3. Excerpts have been taken from the 1969 annual reports of Martin Marietta:

Inventories of $157,958,000 included costs on contracts in progress in the amount of $64,818,000 and were net of progress payments of $56,397,000 on contracts under which title with respect to related inventories of approximately $98,975,000 had passed to the United States Government. Fixed-price type contracts are carried in inventories on the bases of accumulated costs, less costs applicable to deliveries . . . and inventories include unbilled costs on cost-type contracts.

Amounts reported as sales under cost-type contracts are based on incurred costs as approved plus an estimate of the fee earned. Sales under fixed-price type contracts are recorded when deliveries are made.

a) Does Martin Marietta employ percentage of completion or completed contract? Explain carefully its revenue recognition procedures.

b) Why does the company treat cost contracts differently from fixed-price types?

c) If legal title on some contracts has passed to the government, why are these units still included in the inventory of Martin Marietta?

d) Alternatively, how might the company show progress payments? Discuss.

6–A–4. Fantastic Flying Machine Corporation enters into a contract with the government to produce three models of a new aircraft that can fly backward as well as forward. Because of the extreme uncertainty

---

* Adapted from AICPA November 1966 examination.

surrounding the venture, the company insisted on a cost-plus-fixed-fee contract. The contract is to run no longer than four years, with delivery of the models to be made as soon as they are completed. Under the terms of the contract, the government is to pay all allowable costs plus a $1.2 million fee to cover general administrative costs and profit. The company's original proposal estimated the costs at $6 million. An initial payment of $1 million is received upon signing of the contract on January 1, 1970. Within 60 days after the close of each year, the government will pay 80 percent of the costs incurred in the preceding year. In addition, the government will pay $400,000 upon receipt of each aircraft model. The balance due under the contract will be paid at the close of the contract.

Relevant data with respect to the contract is given below (in thousands):

	Year			
	1	2	3	4
Costs incurred................	$1,500	$3,000	$1,500	$2,000
Estimated cost to complete.....	4,500	3,000	2,000	...
General administrative costs....	180	205	208	220

The first model was delivered at the end of year 2; the second in year 3; and the third in year 4.

a) Prepare a schedule to determine the amount of *cash* received each year under the contract.

b) Prepare an abbreviated income statement for each year, under the assumption that the company uses percentage of completion to estimate the portion of the fee earned.

c) Indicate the accounts that would appear on each year-end position statement along with their amounts and classification.

d) Compare the revenue estimates in (b) with an after-the-fact allocation of revenue based on the final total cost rather than the annual cost estimates. How inaccurate is the revenue estimate in (b) compared to this "perfect-knowledge" calculation?

e) Calculate the amount of revenue to be recognized each year if delivery of the models is used to determine the portion of the fee earned. Is this a more satisfactory method than percentage of completion? Explain.

f) Calculate the amount of revenue to be recognized each year under percentage of completion if the contract contains an incentive provision whereby the fee is increased or reduced $10,000 for every $100,000 of cost under or over $6 million.

6–A–5. Firms employing the percentage of completion method for long-term contracts treat the Excess of Cost over Partial Billings as a receivable, as an inventory, or as a separate current asset.

a) Which of these treatments do you prefer? Explain.

b) How does this item appear under the alternative procedure for recording percentage of completion discussed on page 184? Why?

c) Why is it *theoretically* appropriate to offset the Advances from Partial Billings account against Construction Cost in Progress under percentage of completion, but not under completed contract?

CHAPTER SEVEN

COST DETERMINATION

IN CHAPTER ONE, the concept of measuring net income by matching, on a historical basis, resources used against total resources received from revenue-producing operations provides the fundamental direction to financial accounting. From the matching concept, we derive the principle that assets should be recorded initially at cost. The acquisition cost of an asset includes all costs necessary to acquire the services of that asset: the cost to acquire the asset per se, the costs of getting the asset to the place of business, and any other costs incurred to render it available for its intended use. On occasion, certain costs may be incurred unnecessarily in the acquisition of an asset. Examples might include rehandling costs, lost discounts, and demurrage charges for the detention of ships or railroad cars beyond the time allowed for unloading. These abnormal costs should not be treated as part of the cost of the asset; they are period expenses or losses. *Necessary* expenditures include all outlays which may reasonably be said to increase the use value of the asset for revenue production.

This chapter explores the application of this general concept of cost determination to four particular types of assets—labor services, purchased inventory, manufactured inventory, and noncurrent assets. After examining the currently accepted cost concepts and the manner in which they are handled in the accounting records, we take a brief look at some alternative approaches to cost determination that have been recommended.

COST OF LABOR SERVICES

Labor services are just as much a productive resource as are the various tangible properties a business uses. Yet this resource rarely appears on a position statement, because it normally is transformed into some other resource or used in revenue production during the period. In fact, when we know that the labor services will be consumed in the production of revenue during the accounting period, we debit an expense account directly when the services are acquired. Nevertheless, the amount of the entry is determined by the cost of the asset, labor services. There are two important factors to remember in determining the total cost of labor services:

1. The amount of wage cost actually incurred by the company is usually more than the amount paid in cash to employees.
2. Total labor costs include more than just the wage and salary cost.

The first point arises out of the fact that the company acts as a collecting agent for other groups by withholding amounts from the employees' pay checks. For instance, the employer is required by law to retain a portion of the earnings for employees' income taxes and social security taxes. Other withholdings may be sanctioned by the worker for such purposes as contributory insurance programs, purchases of government bonds, payment of union dues, etc. Nevertheless, the *wage and salary cost* is the amount actually *earned* by the employees. The amounts withheld must be recognized as liabilities, to be remitted periodically on behalf of the employees to the various governmental and other groups concerned. From the company's point of view, the total wages and salaries earned are eventually paid out.

The second general point recognizes the cost of various fringe benefits as part of the total cost involved in maintaining a labor force. For example, an employer must contribute an additional amount for social security. He must pay for unemployment compensation insurance and may spend additional sums for various employee welfare programs as a result of union contracts or company personnel policies. Often these fringe benefit costs are recorded for information purposes in separate cost accounts. Conceptually, however, they are costs incurred to acquire labor services.

Numerical Example

Keeping in mind these two major points, let us assume that a company, in preparing the payroll for the week, encounters the following situation:

1. Total salaries earned amount to $10,000—$7,000 by salesmen and $3,000 by office employees.
2. The company is required to withhold 18 percent of employee earnings for income taxes and 5 percent for social security taxes.[1]

---

[1] The withholding rates used for these items are only approximations for illustrative purposes. The exact rates vary with the particular circumstances of each employee and with changes in legislation.

3. In addition, certain employees have authorized the company to deduct from their salaries their contributions to the United Fund. These amount to $200. Also, each employee contributes 1 percent of his salary to the group life insurance program.
4. The company is required to match the employees' contributions for social security and must contribute 3 percent of payroll for the unemployment compensation insurance program.
5. The company contributes an additional 2 percent to the employee group life insurance program and 10 percent of gross salaries earned for a retirement program.

The following entry would be made to recognize the salary cost of labor services and the liability to employees and other agencies for the salaries earned:

```
Sales Salaries Expense.......................  7,000
Office Salaries Expense......................  3,000
    Employee Income Tax Withheld.............          1,800
    Social Security Taxes Payable²...........            500
    United Fund Contribution Withheld.......            200
    Employee Insurance Premiums Payable.....            100
    Wages Payable...........................          7,400
```

Obviously, the manner of recording the debits would vary with the type of employee and the degree of detail desired in expense classification. A single debit to Wage Expense might suffice for a small business.

Remembering our second point that total labor cost includes the cost of various fringe benefit programs, we must also record the accruing of these costs and their related liabilities. The entries to accomplish this follow:[3]

```
Social Security Taxes.......................   500
    Social Security Taxes Payable...........            500

Unemployment Insurance Taxes...............   300
    Unemployment Taxes Payable.............            300

Employee Insurance Cost....................   200
    Employee Insurance Premiums Payable....            200

Pension Fund Cost..........................  1,000
    Liability for Employee Pensions........          1,000
```

These debits all represent costs over and above the salary cost incurred for the purpose of maintaining a labor force. They have been recorded in separate accounts to supply additional information about the total labor cost. The credits in the foregoing entries show the liabilities or additional amounts owed to various groups. In most cases they are current liabilities, with the possible exception of the liability for employee pensions.

---

[2] This liability is often called FICA Taxes Payable (Federal Insurance Contributions Act) or OASI Taxes Payable (Old Age and Survivors Insurance).

[3] Sometimes Social Security Taxes and Unemployment Insurance Taxes are grouped together under a single title, Payroll Taxes.

COST OF PURCHASED INVENTORY

The costs necessary to acquire inventory and render it available for use include the net invoice price, sales and excise taxes, freight charges into the business, and any handling costs incurred in unloading and storage. Each of these expenditures is properly chargeable to the asset amount. Each adds to the usefulness of the asset in supplying its intended service. Together with the beginning inventory, they make up a total pool of merchandise cost, eventually to be divided between the goods sold (expense) and the goods remaining on hand at the end of the period (asset).

Recording the Elements of Inventory Cost

Assume that a firm begins the accounting period with a merchandise inventory of $5,000. During the period the following *summary* transactions occur:

1. Merchandise is purchased for $15,000 at net invoice prices.
2. Freight charges of $1,500 are incurred on the incoming merchandise.
3. The firm incurs $500 of wage costs in unloading, unpacking, inspecting, and stocking the incoming merchandise.
4. In the receiving department, merchandise costing $3,000 is discovered to be of the wrong size and is returned.

According to our cost concept, the first three items properly could be debited to the Merchandise Inventory account. Similarly, the returned merchandise signifies a reduction in the asset and could be credited to the asset account.

On the other hand, if all of these elements of inventory cost are lumped together in one account, some desirable managerial information may be hidden. For instance, the firm may wish to have the purchases recorded separately to facilitate analysis. Comparisons between total purchases and total freight charges may be desirable in the evaluation of the purchasing department's activities. For purposes of cost control, a knowledge of freight charges and handling costs on incoming merchandise would be helpful. Similarly, extensive purchase returns may indicate defects in the ordering procedures or inefficiencies on the part of the suppliers.

Many businesses, therefore, record each element of inventory cost in a separate account, as illustrated on page 207. This procedure provides ledger accounts with the additional information needed for cost control and analysis. The Purchases, Freight-In, and Handling Costs accounts are asset *adjunct* accounts to Merchandise—segregated increases in the asset. Purchase Returns is a *contra* asset account.

Merchandise		Purchases		Purchase Returns	
Beg. Bal. √5,000		(1) 15,000			(4) 3,000

Freight-In		Handling Costs	
(2) 1,500		(3) 500	

Together with the beginning inventory, all these account balances make up the total cost of goods available for sale. In this example the total would be $19,000 ($5,000 + $15,000 − $3,000 + $1,500 + $500). At the end of the accounting period the contra and adjunct accounts, having served their purpose, can be closed out. Assume, for example, that the ending inventory is counted and a cost of $6,500 (including applicable freight and handling cost) is determined for it. The adjusting entry to record cost of goods sold of $12,500 ($19,000 − $6,500) and the ending inventory would be:

```
Merchandise..............................    6,500
Cost of Goods Sold.......................   12,500
Purchase Returns.........................    3,000
    Merchandise..........................              5,000
    Purchases............................             15,000
    Freight-In...........................              1,500
    Handling Cost........................                500
```

In theory the cost of goods sold and the cost of the ending inventory should include all charges incurred directly or indirectly in bringing the merchandise into its existing location and condition. In practice the difficulty in tracing certain costs may lead to their being treated as period expenses rather than as part of the inventoriable costs. Costs of ordering and warehousing are common examples. Even indirect costs which are recorded in accordance with sound theory may be allocated somewhat arbitrarily. For instance, freight charges and handling costs may be divided between items sold and items on hand in proportion to the respective dollar amounts, number of units, weight, or some other variable. Indeed, some firms do not allocate any of the freight and handling cost to the ending inventory. All of it becomes part of cost of goods sold because the increased accuracy is considered not worth the work involved. When cost of goods sold is very large compared to the inventory and the latter is fairly constant, this departure from theoretical soundness probably causes no material difference in income.

Purchase Discounts

A company purchasing from suppliers who allow a discount for prompt payment is faced with the choice of recording purchases at gross prices initially and then adjusting for discounts taken, or using net prices to begin with and adjusting subsequently for any discounts lost. The net method seems to have all-around superiority over the gross method in terms of theoretical soundness, practical recording, and managerial usefulness.

Theoretically, we must realize that the net price is the real price of the inventory. The purchasing company can acquire the physical asset for this amount, the so-called "cash price." Any amount above this is related to how the acquisition of the asset is financed. If the gross price is eventually paid, the extra amount represents the penalty for late payment—a type of financial or administrative charge—not the cost of an increase in the asset's usefulness. Recording gross prices would initially overstate the asset, necessitating downward adjustment later for the amount of the discount.

Moreover, from a practical, bookkeeping viewpoint, the net method is to be preferred. Most companies take their "cash discounts," because failure to do so is expensive[4] and adversely reflects upon the company's credit-worthiness. Under the net price procedures, we have to account only for the discounts that are lost. Since these normally are few, the bookkeeping procedure is simplified. No adjustments or special entries are needed when the bills are paid. A purchase of $5,000 gross, subject to a discount of 3 percent if paid within 15 days and paid within the discount period, simply would be recorded as follows:

```
Merchandise................................. 4,850
    Accounts Payable.......................        4,850
    To record purchase.

Accounts Payable........................... 4,850
    Cash...................................        4,850
    To record payment within discount period.
```

Still a third advantage of the net method exists whenever the discount is not taken. Assume that the account in the preceding example is not paid within the 15-day period. The entry under the net method would be:

```
Accounts Payable........................... 4,850
Loss on Discounts Not Taken...............   150
    Cash...................................        5,000
```

It is highly desirable for management to know when resources have been wasted because of negligent delay on the part of the cashier's office in paying bills or because of insufficient cash being available for prompt payment of liabilities. Under the net price procedure, any amount in excess

---

[4] When it loses the discount, the firm buying on terms calling for a 2 percent discount if paid within 10 days or the full amount payable in 30 days has to pay 2 percent for the privilege of waiting an additional 20 days to pay its bill. This is approximately equivalent to an annual simple interest charge of 36 percent.

of the net invoice price is automatically isolated in a separate account, Loss on Discounts Not Taken, as a natural part of the bookkeeping entry.

Recording at Gross. It is possible, of course, to accomplish the same end results with the gross method. The entries for the above example would be:

```
Merchandise................................ 5,000
     Accounts Payable.......................        5,000
     To record purchases.

Accounts Payable........................... 5,000
     Cash.......................................        4,850
     Purchase Discounts.....................          150
     To record payment within the discount
     period.

Accounts Payable........................... 5,000
     Cash.......................................        5,000

Loss on Discounts Not Taken...............   150
     Purchase Discounts.....................          150
     To record payment after the discount
     period.
```

To reduce the asset to its true net cost, a contra asset, Purchase Discounts, is credited when the amount is paid. This special entry is necessary for all discounts available, whether or not they are taken. As a contra account to Purchases, Purchase Discounts would be closed as part of the summary entry segregating the cost of goods sold and the cost of the ending inventory (see entry on page 207).

In the case of lost discounts, a tendency exists in practice to make only the entry paying off the gross liability. The result is that the inefficient use of resources is never highlighted for management's attention, for the loss remains buried in a permanently overstated asset. The net method automatically prevents the risk of this potential error. Also, when the gross method is used in practice, the contra asset account Purchase Discounts sometimes finds its way onto the income statement as a revenue because it has a credit balance. The fallacy of this practice is clear. Revenue measures the inflow of assets from the sale of the product; it does not arise from purchases and prompt payments. A company taking all available discounts will have a higher net income than otherwise, but the result comes about, not from an increase in the inflow of assets, but from a decrease in the use (or wasting) of assets.

COST OF MANUFACTURED INVENTORY

Our illustrations so far involve merchandising or trading concerns, where most of the assets used up—merchandise, labor services, equipment, etc.—are consumed in an attempt to generate the current period's revenue. Consequently, we have focused our attention on two major stages in the life of an asset—acquisition (cost incurrence) and consumption (cost expiration). In a manufacturing concern an additional aspect is introduced —transformation or conversion. Some assets are utilized during the period, not to produce revenue immediately, but to produce another asset, the manufactured product. The costs of these assets are not recorded in expense accounts at the time of utilization. Instead, they become the cost of the new asset (product) being manufactured. In the accounting system a clear separation of these three stages—acquisition, transformation, and finally consumption in the generation of revenues—is necessary.

Our purpose in this section is to set up the conceptual framework and introduce some new accounts and procedures applicable to a manufacturing company. Specifically, we try to see how the cost-determination concept is implemented when the product is made rather than purchased.

Nature of Manufacturing

Manufacturing involves physically converting raw material, labor, and other resources into a finished product ready for sale. Cost accounting systems for manufacturing companies reflect this process. They attempt to record the flow of costs out of the accounts representing the assets being converted and into new accounts corresponding to the new asset forms which result from the manufacturing activity. In other words, the manufactured cost of the product is developed through a careful tracing of the cost of assets utilized in production to the products being manufactured. As Paton and Littleton state in their oft-quoted monograph,

When production activity effects a change in the form of raw materials by the consumption of human labor and machinepower, accounting keeps step by classifying and summarizing appropriate portions of material costs, labor cost, and machine cost so that together they become product-costs. In other words, it is a basic concept of accounting that costs can be marshalled into new groups that possess real significance. It is as if costs had a power of cohesion when properly brought into contact.[5]

The cost of raw materials, labor services, and other assets used in manufacturing affect net income (become expenses) only in the period when the products containing these costs are sold. Consequently, the accounting system in manufacturing must be relatively detailed, to allow for the accumulation of the various costs of making the product and the "storing" of these costs in inventory until the product is sold. We are concerned only with those assets associated with the production process. Costs incurred in selling or in general administration, of course, should be matched against the current period's revenues. They are handled the

---

[5] W. A. Paton and A. C. Littleton, *An Introduction to Corporate Accounting Standards* (Columbus, Ohio: American Accounting Association, 1940), p. 13.

same in a manufacturing firm as in a merchandising firm. A clear distinction must be made, however, between the incurrence, conversion, and expiration of costs involved in the *manufacture* of the product. These costs, often referred to as product costs, are generally classified into three main categories—raw materials, direct labor, and factory overhead (burden).

Raw material cost includes the cost of all material entering into the actual production of the physical units and becoming part of the specific product being manufactured. Iron ore for a steel company, lumber for a furniture firm, and steel for an automobile manufacturer are all examples of raw materials. Direct labor includes the cost of labor service directly identified with specific products—the cost of laborers who actually manufacture or assemble the product or operate the machines that do so.

Factory overhead, on the other hand, is a diverse category used to describe all manufacturing costs *except* raw materials and direct labor. It includes the indirect production costs not readily identified with any specific units but necessary to facilitate the manufacturing process. Among the costs to be included in factory overhead are the following:

1. Indirect labor—factory supervisors, foremen, maintenance employees, production engineers.
2. Factory supplies—oil, coal, maintenance supplies.
3. Utility services for the manufacturing portion of the business—heat, light, power, water.
4. Depreciation on factory buildings and equipment.
5. Repair and maintenance of factory equipment.

Flow of Costs in Manufacturing

A typical cost accounting system for a manufacturing firm is depicted by the sequence of ledger accounts shown in Table 7–1. Separate accounts are used to keep a record of the utilization of the raw materials, direct labor, and factory overhead and to accumulate the cost of the products being manufactured.

Raw materials, direct labor, and factory overhead all represent assets that will be used in production and costs that will eventually become part of the cost of the manufactured product. The latter two are temporary assets, in that they normally are utilized during the period. Factory Overhead serves as a summary account. Individual elements of factory burden may be recorded first in separate cost accounts—e.g., Indirect Labor, Factory Supplies Used, Depreciation of Factory Equipment, Factory Utility Costs, etc. Eventually, these separate cost elements are transferred to one or more Factory Overhead accounts. An alternative approach often employed is to treat Factory Overhead as a control account and to record the individual, detailed cost elements in subsidiary ledger accounts.

TABLE 7–1

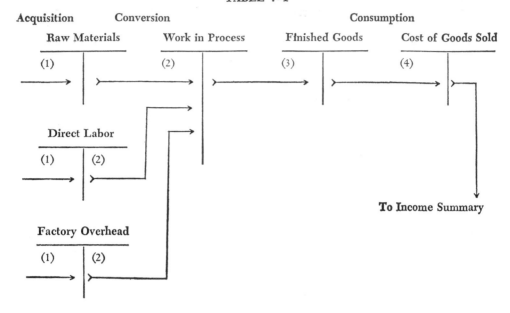

Explanation of the Flow:

1. Recording the incurrence of costs for raw material, direct labor, and factory overhead reflects asset acquisition. Corresponding credits are to various other asset or liability accounts.
2. These entries record the conversion of the basic cost elements into a manufactured product. The cost of making the product is accumulated by a transfer to Work in Process of the cost of raw materials, direct labor, and factory overhead utilized during the period.
3. As units are completed in the manufacturing process, the costs assigned to them are transferred to Finished Goods Inventory.
4. As units in finished goods are sold, their manufacturing cost is transferred to Cost of Goods Sold.
5. When the books are closed, Cost of Goods Sold is closed to the summary account as one of the expenses.

Raw Materials is a more permanent account and commonly shows a balance at the end of the period. This ending inventory represents the cost of raw materials acquired but not used during the period. Work in Process and Finished Goods are also inventory accounts; their ending balances represent the manufacturing costs attached to the partially completed goods and to the finished but unsold units of product, respectively. Finished Goods corresponds to the Merchandise Inventory account in a merchandising firm.

Cost of Goods Sold is the only *expense* account in this flow of costs. Part of the amount in this account may represent costs which have been incurred in production in some prior accounting period. These costs have been stored as part of work in process and finished goods until the product is sold. Then, as part of the total cost of the product, they are matched against the revenue produced this period by the product's sale. Likewise, the raw materials, direct labor, and factory overhead costs acquired and utilized during the *present* accounting period may not all flow through to cost of goods sold in this period. Part may remain in the inventories (Raw Materials, Work in Process, or Finished Goods) at the end of the period and will affect cost of goods sold in future periods.

Numerical Illustration

Let us follow these concepts in the example in Table 7–2. The following journal entries are necessary during or at the end of the month to record the incurrence, transformation, and expiration of the costs.

TABLE 7–2

		June 1		*June 30*
1.	Inventories:			
	Raw materials	$14,400		$21,300
	Work in process	15,750		11,850
	Finished goods	32,400		34,800
			Transactions during June	
2.	Raw material purchases		$136,800	
3.	Wage and salary costs:			
	Direct factory labor		93,000	
	Indirect factory labor		18,750	
	Sales salaries		13,000	
	Executive salaries		50,000	
4.	Other factory costs incurred:			
	Depreciation on factory building		3,300	
	Depreciation on factory equipment		4,050	
	Factory supplies used		10,050	
	Heat, light, and power (80% applicable to production operations)		8,000	

```
1.  Raw Materials...................... 136,800
        Accounts Payable...............             136,800
        To record the acquisition of ad-
        ditional raw materials.

2.  Direct Labor....................... 93,000
    Factory Overhead...................  18,750
    Selling Expense....................  13,000
    Administrative Expense.............  50,000
        Wages and Salaries Payable......            174,750
        To record the incurrence of labor
        costs for the month and to
        classify them by type.

3.  Factory Overhead................... 17,400
        Accumulated Depreciation—Fac-
            tory Building...............              3,300
        Accumulated Depreciation—Fac-
            tory Equipment..............              4,050
        Factory Supplies Inventory......             10,050
        To record other indirect factory
        costs in Factory Overhead.
```

```
4.  Factory Overhead...................    6,400
    Administrative Expense.............    1,600
        Accounts Payable...............               8,000
        To allocate heat, light, and power
        costs for the month between manu-
        facturing cost and general ex-
        pense.

5.  Work in Process.................... 129,900
        Raw Materials.................               129,900
        To record the cost of raw ma-
        terials put into production dur-
        ing the month ($14,400 + $136,-
        800 − $21,300).

6.  Work in Process.................... 135,550
        Direct Labor...................                93,000
        Factory Overhead...............                42,550
        To transfer the direct labor and
        total factory overhead costs to
        Work in Process to record the
        utilization of these assets in the
        manufacturing process.

7.  Finished Goods..................... 269,350
        Work in Process...............               269,350
        To transfer the total manufactur-
        ing cost attached to the units of
        product completed during the month
        ($15,750 + $129,900 + $135,550 −
        $11,850).

8.  Cost of Goods Sold................. 266,950
        Finished Goods................               266,950
        To record the total manufactur-
        ing cost of the units of product
        sold during the month ($32,400 +
        $269,350 − $34,800).
```

Statement of Cost of Goods Manufactured and Sold

Frequently, a separate financial report summarizes the manufacturing activity. Normally, the income statement merely shows the single expense Cost of Goods Sold. A manufacturing cost report presents to management more detailed information concerning the elements determining cost of manufacturing and cost of goods sold. Such a statement for the preceding illustration appears in Table 7–3.

The $265,450 cost of manufacturing represents the production costs incurred during June. Management focuses on this figure for monthly cost control. It is combined with the beginning inventories of Work in Process and Finished Goods to make up the total pool of manufacturing costs. This pool is divided among Cost of Goods Sold and the ending inventories of Work in Process and Finished Goods. The subtotal "cost of goods manufactured" of $269,350 represents the cost of new salable products produced during the period. It is analogous to the amount in the Purchases account discussed on page 207, except that in this case the cost is a production cost rather than a purchase cost.

TABLE 7–3

Statement of Cost of Goods Manufactured and Sold
For the Month of June, 19—

Raw material inventory, June 1	$ 14,400	
Plus: Raw material purchases	136,800	
	$151,200	
Less: Raw material inventory, June 30	21,300	
Cost of raw materials used		$129,900
Direct labor cost		93,000
Factory overhead costs:		
Indirect labor	$ 18,750	
Supplies	10,050	
Depreciation, building	3,300	
Depreciation, equipment	4,050	
Heat, light, and power	6,400	42,550
Total cost of manufacturing		$265,450
Plus: Work in process, June 1		15,750
		$281,200
Less: Work in process, June 30		11,850
Cost of goods manufactured		$269,350
Plus: Finished goods, June 1		32,400
		$301,750
Less: Finished goods, June 30		34,800
Cost of Goods Sold		$266,950

COST OF NONCURRENT ASSETS

The same cost principle that we have applied to labor services and inventory also applies to noncurrent assets. This section explores some of the problems involved in determining the cost of acquiring and rendering certain noncurrent assets available for use.

Land

The total initial acquisition cost of land consists of its purchase price (the amount of cash given up and any liabilities incurred) plus any other expenditures made for the purpose of acquiring ownership and use of the land. Such expenditures might include legal fees for title search, registration of deeds, brokerage fees, etc. There might also be a need for draining, filling, or additional surveying of the land. These costs also are debited to the Land account as charges necessary to render the property available for its intended purpose. They increase the utility of the land and, hence, benefit all the periods in which the land is used. Care must be exercised, however, to see that expenditures are not charged to the Land account beyond the point when the land is available for its intended use. For example, the cost of excavating for a new building is clearly part of the cost of the building, not of the land.

Some theoretically interesting situations may arise to tax the analytical skills of an accountant recording acquisitions of land. One gray area, where management's intention plays a key role, is the purchase of land with an existing structure on it. If the original intention is to acquire the land and the building as separate assets, the purchase price should be allocated between the two assets acquired. If, however, the original intention is simply to acquire a flat piece of land, the cost of subsequently razing the old building is added to the cost of the land. It is a necessary expenditure to render the land available for its intended use. Rational management certainly considers this additional cost in reaching its decision to acquire a particular piece of property. Presumably, it would be willing to pay a higher purchase price for the land if removal of the unwanted structure were not necessary. Again, careful judgment must be used in such situations to distinguish between the acquisition of two assets—land and building—and the acquisition of a single asset, land. Often management's original intention is not clear. Suppose the firm uses the old building one or two years and then tears it down to make a parking lot. Is the razing cost part of the cost of the asset "land" or part of the loss on destruction of the asset "building"?

One reason care must be taken in establishing the cost of land is that this asset is usually not considered as being subject to depreciation. Although the nondepreciable nature of land follows from its infinite service life, the same treatment does not apply to such land improvements as fences, pavements, sprinkler systems, etc. The cost of these items should be debited to a separate asset account, Land Improvements, and written off as expenses over their respective useful lives. Some land improvements have permanent lives. Their cost usually is combined with the land cost in a single asset account, Land. Examples include the cost of landscaping, drainage systems, and one-time levies for sewers to be owned, maintained, and replaced by a governmental agency.

An asset with a finite life can originate when we pay a fee for a limited interest in someone else's land. For instance, we might pay $10,000 for the privilege of using a road across a neighboring piece of property for a period of 20 years. This right is called an easement and really represents a long-term prepayment. Each year we use up a portion of our right, although our neighbor's land may remain unchanged. The easement has a limited life, and its cost therefore should be amortized.

Purchased Assets

The cost of equipment, machinery, furniture, and fixtures includes the net invoice price, transportation costs, and any unloading, installation, or remodeling costs. A machine delivered to the factory is more effective than one which rests on the supplier's loading dock. Likewise, a machine installed, tested, and ready for production is more useful than one sitting idle in the plant, waiting to be connected. Consequently, freight, installation, and testing charges represent additional necessary costs to put the asset into economically useful condition and are properly debited to the asset account. A similar treatment would be accorded any costs of renovating a recently purchased building to make it suitable for its new use. These costs are necessary if the business is to receive the intended benefit from the use of the building over its remaining life.

Lump-Sum Acquisitions.   It is not uncommon for a firm to purchase at one time practically all of the assets of another business. When more than one asset is acquired by means of a single payment, the result is called a "basket" or "lump-sum" purchase. The accounting problem becomes one of reasonably allocating the total purchase cost among the individual assets acquired. No single solution to this problem will suffice for all cases. The accountant must look at various sources of evidence—replacement costs, appraisal values, insurable values, valuations for tax assessments—to find a way of approximating the "net cash cost" of each asset.

Assume that a company acquires the assets of a firm going out of business. Because it is willing to buy the entire group of assets—inventory, land, warehouse, and warehouse equipment—the company is able to purchase them for a total of $170,000. The inventory consists of commonly purchased items that could be acquired on the wholesale market for $20,000. The buyer has the other assets appraised by a competent appraisal firm, whose report shows the estimated values to be: land, $60,000; warehouse, $80,000; and warehouse equipment, $40,000. The following entry might be made to record the acquisition:

```
Inventory................................  20,000
Land.....................................  50,000
Warehouse................................  66,667
Warehouse Equipment......................  33,333
     Cash................................            170,000
```

In this case the $150,000 cost of the *noncurrent* assets was allocated among them in proportion to their relative appraised values.

Financial Charges.   The particular way management chooses to finance the acquisition of an asset, whether by borrowed capital or stockholder capital or some combination, does not increase the service potential of that asset. Consequently, financing charges should be excluded from the asset's cost.[6] Interest charges relate to how a business acquires its financial capital, not to how much money must be expended to acquire a particular asset. Payments to various investor groups for the use of their

---

[6] A common exception is found in public utility companies. There a normal interest charge on all funds tied up in the construction of an asset is included as part of the asset's cost. The argument is that these funds are committed to an asset which is not yet available for use and that some mix of capital is a necessary cost of acquiring the asset.

money normally represent period charges which have to be covered by the net income of the business entity. The "cash" price is the initial cost of the asset. Often, however, the financing charge is implicit in the means by which the asset is bought. For instance, a firm can acquire a machine by paying $125,000 cash or making 12 monthly payments of $11,000 each ($132,000 total). If the latter alternative is accepted, the accountant has to go behind the scenes to pull out the $7,000 differential. This represents the financing charge for delayed payment, not part of the asset's cost.

Constructed Assets

Often a firm constructs some noncurrent asset for its own use. How do we determine the cost when there is no purchase? The answer lies in the application of some concepts discussed earlier. The cost of a product being manufactured consists of the cost of the assets consumed in its production. A similar treatment applies to a constructed noncurrent asset; its acquisition cost includes the cost of all resources, both short-term and long-term, which are utilized in constructing it.

Let us take as an example a firm which decides to construct rather than buy a building for its home office. A special asset account, Construction in Progress—Building, is established to accumulate the various costs incurred in erecting the building: the cost of materials used, the cost of labor services devoted to construction, depreciation on any other long-term assets used in construction, and any other expenditures incurred for the purpose of creating the new asset. Upon completion of the construction project, an entry is made to transfer all relevant costs to the noncurrent asset:

```
Office Building................................ xxx
      Construction in Progress—Building.......... 	      xxx
```

Ideally, we should like to be able specifically to identify each cost or asset element used in erecting the building. Practical problems of measurement often arise, however, when workers normally employed in production are temporarily assigned to construction work and some of the resources normally part of factory overhead are diverted to the making of some noncurrent asset. It may be difficult to determine what portion of these costs (indirect labor, power, supplies, etc.) should be debited to Construction in Progress rather than to Work in Process. At a minimum, any *increase* in factory overhead items caused by the construction project should be assigned as part of its cost. Some accountants would stop at this point, arguing that management's decision to incur cost includes *only* the incremental costs. In many cases this approach seems to ignore the benefits received from the use of resources which otherwise would have been employed in other capacities or wasted. Consequently, other accountants take the view that all factory overhead costs *traceable* to the construction project should be added to its cost.

Natural Resources

Natural resoures such as oil fields, mines, etc., are unique in that the additional costs over and above the initial acquisition price play a major role in cost determination. Here the original purchase price may be only a fraction of the total costs which the firm has to incur in order to develop the resources. Such subsequent expenditures as the sinking of shafts, construction of tunnels, and removal of topsoil (in the case of strip mining) are expenditures that benefit future periods. These expenditures are treated as part of the cost of the asset, for they enable the firm to use the acquired natural resources. Sometimes they are set up in asset accounts separate from the natural resource, particularly when the life of the development is different from the life of the natural resource. The services of a particular mine shaft may expire economically before the mine itself. In this case, amortization would be easier if the two were recorded separately. Nonetheless, the major point is that these developmental costs are assets and conceptually can be charged to the asset account of the natural resource.

A major difficulty in determining the cost of natural resources involves the handling of exploration and drilling expenditures when future benefit is uncertain. Many of the same considerations discussed in connection with research and development costs in Chapter Five are applicable here. Should the cost of drilling oil wells, for example, be set up as an asset or be treated as a period expense? Varying circumstances may call for different answers. If the drilling is on scattered wildcat wells, many of which will be dry holes, then it is reasonable to treat drilling costs as an operating expense except in the case of a well which is completed as a producer. On the other hand, if the drilling costs are to develop an existing field known to contain oil reserves, one could rightfully claim that all costs of drilling, whether or not they always result in a producing well, are necessary costs of preparing the asset "oil field" for its intended use. Sound judgment, consistently applied, becomes extremely important in borderline cases for accurate income measurement in later periods.

Intangible Assets

Careful cost determination is no less important with intangible assets than in the case of tangible assets, and the general principles are the same. When intangible assets are purchased, the amount paid is the initial measure of the asset's cost. Often they are acquired as part of a lump-sum purchase. The amount allocated to the intangibles usually is the excess of the total purchase price over the sum of the separate market values of the tangible assets. Unfortunately, this excess commonly is dumped into a single intangible, goodwill. Whenever possible, an attempt should be made to identify specific intangibles more precisely.

Many intangible assets are developed internally. Determining the cost of these assets is extremely difficult, in fact often impossible. Some of these problems are discussed in Chapter Five in the section on period costs. When internal development costs can be specifically identified with particular intangibles—e.g., when a patentable product emerges from a company research project—the cost of the asset includes all research and development costs traceable to it. To this amount would be added any registration fees or other costs that enhance the utility of the intangible. In the case of a patent, these would include the cost of a successful legal defense of the patent right.

ALTERNATIVE CONCEPTS OF COST

The concept of cost which we have been discussing embraces all actual dollar outlays necessary to acquire the resource. Under the conventional matching concept, this figure measures the monetary effort of the firm. Serious questions have been raised throughout the accounting profession concerning the use of historic acquisition cost as the basis for the representation of properties when prices change. Some accountants prefer the use of current cost (replacement cost) as the carrying value of the asset. Others would retain historic outlays but restate them for changes in the general level of prices.

These alternative approaches also match costs against revenues, as does conventional accounting, to provide a net income figure after consideration of the recovery of capital committed to the various assets consumed. They differ, however, in their *measurement* of the recovery of capital or cost.

Perhaps a very simple example will highlight the differences in these cost concepts. Assume that merchandise is purchased at a cost of $1,000 when an index of the general price level stands at 100. The merchandise is held until the end of the year and then sold for $1,500. At that time the general price index stands at 120, and the current acquisition cost (replacement cost) of the merchandise is $1,300. What is income? Under the conventional matching concept and monetary postulate, we would subtract the original acquisition cost of the asset consumed ($1,000) from the selling price of $1,500 and report a monetary income of $500.

Purchasing Power Approach

Those who advocate the purchasing power alternative question the monetary postulate under conditions of general inflation or deflation

The dollar is the accountant's measuring unit. When the general price level changes, the purchasing power of the monetary unit and, hence, its "size," changes also.

In our example, the $1,000 original acquisition cost and the $1,500 revenue are not comparable in their general purchasing power. Each dollar in the $1,000 represents more purchasing power than each dollar of revenue. This situation can be corrected by restatement of the cost in terms of the present general price level. The income calculation then would be as follows:

$$
\begin{array}{ll}
\text{Revenues.} \dots\dots\dots\dots\dots\dots\dots & \$1,500 \\
\text{Expenses.} \dots\dots\dots\dots\dots\dots\dots & \underline{1,200} \\
\text{Income.} \dots\dots\dots\dots\dots\dots\dots & \$\ \ 300
\end{array}
\left(\$1,000 \times \frac{120}{100} \right)
$$

Since prices in *general* have increased 20 percent, the $1,000 expended at the beginning of the year is equivalent to $1,200 of purchasing power at the end of the year. That latter amount must be recovered out of revenues for the firm to be as well off in terms of its pool of available purchasing power. Restating past costs in terms of current purchasing power, it is argued, provides a more meaningful measure of the preservation of capital. Conversely, not to restate is analogous to subtracting apples from oranges.

Replacement Cost Approach

The replacement cost approach departs from dollar acquisition cost in favor of a more current measure of the asset's worth. Supply and demand conditions affecting a productive resource may cause its specific value relative to other goods and services to increase or decrease. The monetary representation of assets should reflect these changes in exchange value. Likewise, no net income should result until the firm recovers the current value of asset services being consumed in the generation of revenues.

Under this concept the income statement might look like this:

$$
\begin{array}{ll}
\text{Revenues.} \dots\dots\dots\dots\dots\dots\dots & \$1,500 \\
\text{Expenses.} \dots\dots\dots\dots\dots\dots\dots & \underline{1,300} \\
\text{Income.} \dots\dots\dots\dots\dots\dots\dots & \$\ \ 200
\end{array}
$$

Since it would cost $1,300 currently to replace the asset used up, this figure provides a better measure of the real sacrifice (effort) involved in using it. The $1,300 represents the opportunity cost of the asset.

A modification of this approach which attempts to incorporate both original acquisition cost and current replacement cost has also been suggested. According to this idea, income consists of two parts—an operating income of $200, as previously calculated, and a price gain of $300 from holding the inventory during a time of dollar-value increase, as calculated below:

$$
\begin{array}{lr}
\text{Current replacement cost} & \$1,300 \\
\text{Original acquisition cost} & 1,000 \\
\text{Price gain from holding inventory} & \$\ \ \ 300 \\
\end{array}
$$

If recognition is also given to changes in the value of the dollar in general, the $300 holding gain could be expressed in *real* terms as follows:

$$
\begin{array}{lr}
\text{Current replacement cost} & \$1,300 \\
\text{Original acquisition cost expressed in dollars of} & \\
\text{present purchasing power } \left(\$1,000 \times \dfrac{120}{100}\right) & 1,200 \\
\text{Real increase in value from holding inventory} & \$\ \ \ 100 \\
\end{array}
$$

These brief excursions into the area of alternative cost concepts do not do justice to the many theoretical ramifications, practical complexities, recording problems, or possible uses of these alternatives. The purpose of the discussion is simply to acquaint the reader with some of the alternative concepts that might be used in financial accounting. In Chapter Eight we have occasion to refer to these concepts. Some conventional accounting practices involving inventories rest to some extent on these alternative cost concepts.

None of these alternatives, however, has been implemented in practice to any great degree. The reasons seem to be a lack of agreement on which concept should replace the existing postulates, the absence of legal or tax recognition of these ideas, and the existence of practical difficulties in measurement. The case is a strong one, nevertheless, that these alternative approaches do supply additional valuable information in the appraisal of managerial performance. A logical first step would seem to be the incorporation of one or more of these concepts into the preparation of a separate set of supplementary statements. Some suggestions as to how this might be accomplished are contained in Chapter Seventeen along with a more complete discussion of these concepts.

SUMMARY

In this chapter we attempt to establish more detailed accounting procedures for determining the cost of specific productive resources. The general theme is that cost includes not only acquisition cost but any other necessary costs which contribute to the preparation of the asset for its intended use. In the case of most noncurrent assets, these costs are combined directly with the net purchase price in a single account. With labor services and inventory, the separate cost elements are accumulated in individual ledger accounts for management's attention and analysis. In a manufacturing firm a quite elaborate recording system has to be set up to collect the production costs and assign them to units sold, units completed but not sold, and units partially completed. More detailed procedures in this area of cost accounting are presented in Chapters Nineteen and Twenty.

SUGGESTIONS FOR FURTHER READING

Hendriksen, Eldon S. "Purchasing Power and Replacement Cost Concepts —Are They Related?" *Accounting Review*, Vol. 38 (July 1963), pp. 483–91.

Paton, W. A., and Littleton, A. C. *An Introduction to Corporate Accounting Standards*, American Accounting Association Monograph No. 3 (AAA, 1940), pp. 11–18, 24–37.

Sprouse, Robert T. "Historical Costs and Current Assets—Traditional and Treacherous," *Accounting Review*, Vol. 38 (October 1963), pp. 687–95.

QUESTIONS AND PROBLEMS

7-1. The Sandy Claws Corporation manufactures and sells children's toys. Prepare a statement of cost of goods manufactured and sold for 1972 from the following costs and expenses incurred during the year.

Purchases of raw materials	$332,000
Direct labor	120,000
Indirect labor	44,000
Depreciation on factory building	25,000
Property taxes on factory building	3,000
Depreciation on factory equipment	20,000
Depreciation on office furniture and fixtures	5,200
Light, heat, and power (70% applicable to manufacturing, 10% to selling, 20% to office)	13,000
Salesmen's salaries	39,000
Maintenance costs on factory equipment	1,000
Office salaries	28,000
Advertising supplies purchased and used	3,600
Factory supplies purchased	14,000
Factory manager's salary	20,000

Relevant inventory accounts show the following balances:

	Jan. 1	*Dec. 31*
Raw materials	$22,000	$31,000
Goods in process	54,000	58,000
Finished goods	30,000	28,000
Factory supplies	3,000	4,500

7-2. The Hillandale Corporation purchases a parcel of farm land on the outskirts of town for the purpose of building a new plant. Hillandale plans to use its own resources for most of the construction work. Prepare journal entries to record the following events:

1. Farm land is purchased for $125,000, including an old farmhouse which will be razed. The value of the structure as a farmhouse is $15,000. An 8 percent mortgage of $50,000 is assumed, together with $2,000 of accrued interest. The balance is paid by check.
2. The realty firm handling the transfer submits a bill and is paid for the following:

Recording of deeds	$ 100
Appraisal fee	200
Commission	7,500

3. Labor costs incurred (credit Wages Payable):

Razing of farmhouse	$ 8,000
Construction of new plant	320,000
Repairing faulty work (see item 5)	29,000

4. Material costs incurred:

New building	$75,300
Repair of faulty work (see item 5)	4,000
Value of material recovered from farmhouse	(2,800)

5. During construction, it becomes necessary to tear out and reconstruct the foundation and wall on one side of the building. The original work was faulty due to a lack of care. The material and labor costs involved in repairing it were $33,000.
6. Other costs incurred and paid in cash:

Factory manager's salary (he spent about one half of his time supervising construction and the rest at the company's other plant)	$18,000
Subcontracting costs:	
Excavation	35,000
Plumbing and electricity	8,000
Landscaping	3,500
Liability insurance premiums on construction workers	1,500
Street and sewer assessments	3,000

7. Two cranes purchased at a cost of $2,500 each were used exclusively on this building for two years. However, cranes of this type normally had a useful life of four years, and the company anticipated that there would be future need for them on other projects.
8. Legal fees amounted to $1,000 for title search to land and $4,000 for general legal counsel for the company.
9. The company anticipated that it saved at least $13,500 by constructing the building itself.

10. A check is written for the first installment payment on the mortgage consisting of:

Interest....................... $4,000
Principal...................... 5,000
                              $9,000

7–3. The Modern Company buys merchandise from the New Company on terms of 2/10, n/30. Purchases during January, 1972, are as follows (amounts are gross price figures):

Purchase Date	Amount	Payment Date
Jan. 5.................	$4,000	Jan. 13
Jan. 9.................	3,600	Jan. 18
Jan. 15................	2,500	$1,000 returned Jan. 22; remainder paid Feb. 10
Jan. 27................	6,000	Feb. 10

a) Using the net price method, record the entries that would be made on the books of the Modern Company for the month of January and for February 10. The company prepares monthly financial statements.

b) Repeat part (*a*) using gross prices.

c) Record the entries for the same dates on the books of the New Company, using the net price procedure.

d) Repeat part (*c*) using gross prices.

7–4. On November 1 the trial balance of Greasy Kidstuff Enterprises showed the following:

	Dr.	Cr.
Cash..........................	$ 33,900	
Accounts receivable..............	16,100	
Materials and supplies...........	9,600	
Work in process.................	9,800	
Finished goods..................	17,200	
Prepayments on building lease......	12,000	
Equipment......................	30,000	
Accounts payable................		$ 20,300
Capital stock...................		90,000
Retained earnings...............		18,300
	$128,600	$128,600

The following transactions took place during November:

1. Purchased materials and supplies on account, $40,400.

2. Wage costs incurred: direct labor, $40,000; indirect labor $10,000; selling and administrative labor, $30,000. Amounts withheld by the company: 15 percent for federal income taxes and 5 percent for social security taxes.

3. Accrued the company's share of social security taxes and assigned it to respective cost areas.

4. Materials and supplies used: raw materials, $25,000; factory supplies, $4,300; office supplies, $3,600.
5. Sales on account, $147,000.
6. Collections of accounts, $141,000.
7. Cash disbursements: suppliers, $43,700; employees, $64,200; utilities, $5,500 (factory, $4,800; selling and administrative, $700); other costs and expenses, $21,900 (factory, $17,200; selling and administrative, $4,700).
8. Equipment depreciation: factory $5,300; selling and administrative, $1,100.
9. Expiration of building lease, $2,000 (factory, 70 percent; selling and administrative, 30 percent).
10. Ending inventories: work in process, $11,300; finished goods, $16,500.

a) Set up ledger (T) accounts, and enter the November 1 balances.
b) Enter the transactions for the period, including entries to determine cost of goods sold.
c) Calculate "cost of manufacturing" and "cost of goods manufactured." Explain how they differ.
d) Prepare an income statement and a position statement.

7–5. Patterson Company acquired a machine with a list price of $50,000 and debited the Machinery account for that amount. The account was paid within the 30-day discount period and the company took the 5 percent cash discount. A credit for $2,500 was made to Purchase Discounts. Transportation costs of $1,200 were paid by Patterson Company and charged to Freight Expense. Installation was done by a consulting engineer outside the company assisted by a few of Patterson's own employees. The fee of the consulting engineer of $1,000 was debited to the Machinery account; the wages of the employees, amounting to $600, were charged to Wage Expense. Supplies of $500 were used in the installation and raw materials of $300 were destroyed in testing. The former cost was debited to the Machinery account; the latter cost, to Loss on Testing.

a) Prepare a schedule showing the total cost at which the machine should be recorded.
b) Prepare any adjusting entries necessary to correct the accounts.
c) Assume Patterson Company did not pay within the 30-day discount period. How would this affect the cost of the asset and the entries made?
d) Six months later, the Patterson Company decides to move the machinery to a different wing of the plant. The cost (primarily wages) is $3,000. How would you handle this relocation cost?

7–6. The Poorland Company begins operations on October 1, 1972. The following selected transactions relate to purchases and sales of inventory during October:

1. Merchandise purchases on account amount to $400,000 at gross prices.
2. Bills are received for freight charges on incoming merchandise of $20,000.
3. Merchandise costing $16,000 is returned.
4. The accounts payable from merchandise purchases are paid; $4,500 of discounts are taken and $2,500 of discounts are lost.
5. The receiving department costs are $15,000 for the month, consisting of $12,000 of labor cost and $3,000 of supplies.
6. A bill for $500 is received for demurrage charges for failure to unload and return a railroad car within the allotted time.
7. Bills in the amount of $12,000 are received for freight charges on merchandise delivered to customers during October.
8. Ninety percent of the net merchandise purchased during October is sold on account at a price of $410,000.

Record the selected transactions relating to purchases and sales of inventory during October in general ledger (T) accounts. The company uses separate accounts for the individual cost elements. Include the necessary entries to determine cost of goods sold and the October 31 merchandise inventory.

7–7. The following diagram is a pictorial representation of the statement of cost of goods manufactured and sold shown in Table 7–3. Circle

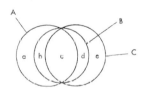

A (segments a, b, c) represents cost of manufacturing; circle B (segments b, c, d) represents cost of goods manufactured; and circle C (segments c, d, e) represents cost of goods sold.

a) Identify by segment letter (a, b, c, d, or e) the following items: beginning work-in-process inventory, ending work-in-process inventory, beginning finished goods inventory, ending finished goods inventory.
b) Explain in your own words exactly what segment c represents. (You may find it helpful to employ the conceptual distinction between "cost" and "expense.")

7–8. The Octopus Manufacturing Company is planning to expand its existing operations extensively during the coming year. Prepare journal entries to record the following events which transpire during the year. Explain the reasoning behind your treatment of each item.

1. To put the company in a financially liquid position so as to be able to take advantage of opportunities, the board of directors borrows $400,000 by issuing 7 percent, 10-year bonds.

2. The company buys the land, buildings, and machinery of another firm for a total price of $30,300. The land has an assessed valuation for property tax purposes of $3,000; an investigation reveals that property is assessed at approximately one third of its current market value. The building has never been assessed, since it was only recently completed at a cost of $5,000 to the prior owner. The machinery in its present condition could be sold for $14,000 as used equipment. The purchase agreement requires that Octopus pay half of the property taxes; the original owner had prepaid these taxes for the year in the amount of $600.

3. Octopus hires a consulting firm to help it find a plant site for later development. The consultants recommend a swamp in a small town in Florida, and the property is acquired. The following expenditures are made:

Search fee paid to consultants........................	$ 5,000
Purchase price of swamp.............................	22,000
To get clear title to the land, Octopus pays back taxes for 5 years...	2,500
Legal fees in connection with purchase.................	500
Leveling and filling of land..........................	3,200

4. Before the building acquired in item 2 can be used, the following expenditures have to be made:

Repairs and renovation..............................	$8,000
Rewiring of entire building with heavy-duty electric lines...	500
Construction of parking lot...........................	3,500
Installation of fences around property.................	5,400

5. The following expenditures are made in connection with the used equipment purchased in item 2:

Cost of concrete reinforcing in floor...................	$1,200
Cost of preliminary test runs prior to operation..........	100
Costs of manufacturer's representative who spends 2 weeks instructing employees on how to adapt machinery to existing products................................	500

6. Repair costs to the building, which has been hit by lightning, amount to $2,400. Three fourths of this will be recoverable under the company's insurance program.

7. Interest charges of $28,000 on the bond issue in item 1 are paid.

7–9. On December 31, 1971, the following account balances appeared among the liabilities of the Wilson Company:

Wages payable..................................	$6,840
Social security taxes payable......................	260
Employee income tax withheld.....................	1,100

The following selected transactions occurred during January, 1972. Prepare journal entries to record them according to management's direction:

1. The total amount of gross wages for the month was $8,000. The company was required to withhold 14 percent for employee income tax, 5 percent for social security taxes, and $150 for the employees' share of hospital insurance premiums. The $8,000 gross payroll was represented by $6,000 of direct labor wages, $1,000 of indirect labor wages, and $1,000 of administrative wages.

2. Other fringe benefit costs, not included above, were: employer's contribution to social security, 5 percent of gross payroll; employer's tax for unemployment compensation, 3 percent of gross payroll; employer's contribution to hospital insurance program, $300; and pension fund cost, $1,200. All fringe benefit costs were to be recorded first as separate cost items (debit the social security and unemployment taxes to Payroll Taxes) and then were to be divided by type of worker. The portion applicable to indirect labor would go to Factory Overhead, direct labor to Direct Labor, and administrative labor to Administrative Wages.

3. Checks drawn during the month:

Employee wage checks..........................	$12,500
For income taxes withheld and social security	
contributions................................	3,280

7-10. You are engaged to audit the books of the Brand X Manufacturing Company. Its records show the following figures at the end of the period:

Work-in-process inventory......................	$32,900
Finished goods inventory.......................	17,600
Net income....................................	28,400

In the course of the investigation, you discover the following facts:

1. A purchase of raw materials in the amount of $3,000 has never been recorded, even though they have been used in production.
2. Depreciation of factory equipment has been overstated by $1,500.
3. The bookkeeper has failed to accrue $12,000 of direct labor costs applicable to the period when making adjusting entries.
4. Selling expenses of $4,500 have been charged in error to Work in Process.
5. Rent costs of $6,000 have been charged to Factory Overhead; 25 percent of this should have been allocated to selling and 25 percent to administration.

Of the production costs incurred in the period, one third are still in process. Of the finished goods manufactured during the year, 80 percent have been sold.

a) Prepare a schedule showing the effect of these errors on the ending inventories and net income for the period, and showing the correct amounts for these items.

b) Prepare a journal entry (or entries) necessary to adjust all of the accounts, assuming the books have not been closed.

7–11. Select Products Corporation engaged in several activities during the year with respect to noncurrent assets. Several of them are described below. Briefly explain how you would have accounted for each of the following costs both initially and in future periods if relevant.

1. Paid an advertising agency $50,000, two fifths for recurring media advertising and the remainder for a consumer behavior study that was to provide a basis for marketing strategies during the next three or so years.

2. Purchased land with an abandoned frame house on it for $35,000. Incurred the following additional costs:

Razing frame house	$ 2,500
Removing tree stumps	350
Constructing a new building	200,000
Constructing sidewalks and driveways	3,000
Landscaping	2,500
Fencing	900

3. Material is recovered from razing of the frame house in item 2. A local building material and supply dealer offers to buy it for $200. However, the firm decides to donate the material to a local boy's club building project.

4. Bought office equipment and factory machinery from a firm going out of business for a total price of $13,000. The factory machinery is in very bad condition. Before it can be used, extensive overhauling estimated to cost $3,000 will be necessary. After overhauling, the factory machinery will have a current value of $12,500.

5. Donated $20,000 to Mid-Mississippi University School of Organizational Ecology to help defray the costs of a research project on computer pollution. The project is of great importance to Select Products, although the results will be published by the University Press.

6. Incurred the following costs with respect to research activities:
   a) Annual salaries of the company's two applied scientists who conducted continuing product research activities, $30,000.
   b) For contracted research work incurred to develop a new patentable process for making cigarette filters, $10,000.
   c) Paid $5,000 to Crazy Al, a local inventor, who claimed to have developed the process in part (*b*) first. Rather than risk a court fight, Select Products bought his "rights."
   d) Application fee to register patent, $300.
   e) Legal fees in a court case in which Select Products sued another firm for patent infringement, $2,500. Select Products won the suit.

    f) Legal fees in an appellate court case stemming from an appeal from the decision in (*e*), $3,000. The appellate court reversed the decision and ruled against Select Products. No further appeals are contemplated.

7. Spent $50,000 for retooling and rearranging of equipment in one department. The equipment is to be used to manufacture a special order over a three-year period.

8. Exchanged some marketable securities originally costing $89,000 for all the inventory and equipment of a small local business. The securities had a market price of $110,000 on the day of the exchange. The inventory and equipment on the books of the local company were recorded at $30,000 and $50,000 respectively. An appraiser hired by Select Products determined the replacement cost of the inventory to be $40,000 and the current value of the equipment to be $80,000.

7–12. On April 1 the inventory of Royal, Inc. at net cost, including applicable freight and handling costs, amounted to $22,000. The company records all purchases at gross prices and initially records all elements of inventory cost in separate accounts for purposes of analysis and control. During the month of April the following transactions, in summary form, took place:

1. Inventory amounting to $85,000 gross invoice price was purchased on terms allowing a 3 percent discount if paid within 10 days.

2. The company discovered that $20,000 gross amount of inventory did not meet specifications. It returned $13,000 and was granted a purchase adjustment allowance of $2,000 by the vendor on the remaining amount.

3. The company ordered and received $10,000 gross amount of additional inventory (also subject to the 3 percent discount for prompt payment). This merchandise replaced part of that which was returned in item 2.

4. Transportation costs applicable to April purchases amounted to $1,000.

5. Wage payments made to the warehouse employees during the month were $2,500. It is estimated that 80 percent of the warehouse time is spent unloading and handling incoming purchases.

6. The accounts payable were paid. All purchase discounts were taken except $500.

7. Merchandise inventory on April 30 amounted to $17,150, at net invoice prices and applicable transportation and handling costs.

a) Journalize the above transactions.
b) The chief accountant recommends that the $10,000 in item 3 be debited to Purchase Returns, since it in essence cancels part of the original return. Evaluate this suggestion.

7–13. On March 31 the following account balances existed for the Brennecke Bowling Ball Manufacturing Company.

	Dr.	Cr.
Cash....................................	$ 3,000	
Raw materials............................	10,000	
Work in process..........................	10,000	
Finished goods...........................	8,000	
Building.................................	50,000	
Accumulated depreciation on building..........		$ 5,000
Factory equipment........................	10,000	
Accumulated depreciation on equipment........		2,000
Accounts payable.........................		5,000
Capital stock.............................		50,000
Retained earnings.........................		29,000
	$91,000	$91,000

During the month of April the following transactions took place:

1. Raw materials purchased on account, $40,000.
2. Raw materials used in production, $43,000.
3. Supplies (of all types) purchased on account, $8,000.
4. Supplies used, $6,700. Of this amount, $2,800 was used in production operations, $2,300 by the selling department, and $1,600 in the general office.
5. Direct labor costs incurred were $38,000; indirect labor costs amounted to $20,000 (credit Wages Payable).
6. Salaries in the selling department and for general administration amounted to $22,000 and $18,000, respectively (credit Wages Payable).
7. Depreciation on the building, $2,000.
8. Depreciation on factory equipment, $800.
9. Power cost for the month, $300 (credit Accounts Payable).
10. Sales on account were $136,500.

Additional information:

1. The factory occupied three of the five floors in the building; the selling department occupied half of the first floor and the general office, the rest of the building.

2. Power cost was allocated on the basis of metered amounts, 80 percent to manufacturing, 5 percent to selling, and 15 percent to general administration.

3. Inventory of work in process and finished goods on April 30 amounted to $12,000 and $9,000 respectively.

a) Set up ledger (T) accounts, and enter the opening balances. Record the entries during April, including any necessary entries based on the additional information provided. Use *only* the accounts in the trial balance plus the following: Supplies, Direct Labor, Indirect Labor, Wages Payable, Factory Overhead, Administrative Expense, Selling Expense, Building Depreciation Cost, Equipment Depreciation Cost, Power Cost, Cost of Goods Sold, Accounts Receivable, and Sales.

b) Prepare a statement of cost of goods manufactured and sold and an income statement for April.

c) Discuss carefully the nature of the following accounts: Indirect Labor, Building Depreciation, and Power Cost.

7–14. Duncan owned a supermarket that he leased to a food store chain. The food chain needed more parking space, and told Duncan it would not renew the lease if Duncan could not supply additional parking. The only adjacent land was residential, and its owners knew of Duncan's problem. The owners charged Duncan $75,000 for land having a current market value of $4,000 and residences having a current market value of $33,000. Duncan promptly demolished the residences at a cost of $14,000 and built a parking lot for $3,000.

Discuss carefully how each amount should be handled on the books of Duncan to match costs and revenues properly. Indicate exactly what amounts would be involved, what accounts would be used, and how the items would be handled in future years.

7–15. Pankoff & Sons, a newly formed corporation to manufacture hockey equipment, entered numerous transactions in a single account called Property. During the course of an audit at the end of the year, you decide to set up separate noncurrent asset accounts for the various noncurrent assets and to reclassify all of the items in the Property account.

Debit Entries:

1. Contract price of $47,000 for a package purchase of land and building as a construction site for a new plant (appraised value of building is $8,000).
2. Payment to current tenant of the building to cancel a two-year lease, $3,000.
3. Legal fees relating to conveying of title, $630.
4. Cost of surveying the land, $2,000.
5. Direct costs incurred in demolition of old building, $14,600.
6. Cost of building permits and licenses, $150.
7. Cost of excavation, $12,600.
8. Invoice cost of materials and supplies used in construction and wage costs of construction labor, $220,000.
9. Net cost of temporary structures (tool sheds, construction offices, etc.) erected for use in construction activity, $6,000.
10. Accrued interest on bonds issued during the year to finance construction, $2,000.
11. Architects' fees, $10,000.
12. Employer's share of the year's social securtiy taxes for all employees who worked on the construction, $1,200.
13. Allocated portion of the salary of Rock Pile, the company engineer (allocation based on time devoted to planning and supervision of construction), $6,000.
14. Allocated overhead for the period of construction, $18,000. Normal overhead is $24,000. During construction it increased to

$36,000. Since construction labor hours and factory labor hours were approximately equal, one half of the overhead cost was allocated to construction.

15. Special municipal assessments for larger sewerage lines necessitated by the altered use of the site, $500.
16. Premiums for insurance against natural hazards during construction, $480.
17. Invoice price of new machinery purchased, $32,000. A 3% cash discount was available but not taken.
18. Delayed delivery date charges, $280. Pankoff & Sons had agreed to accept the machinery in June, but since the building was not completed until August it had to pay a penalty for having the manufacturer hold the machines.
19. Cost of installing the equipment, $600.
20. Contract cost to landscaping firm for sod, trees, and shrubs, $3,000.
21. Driveways, sidewalks, and fences, $9,100.
22. Severance pay for employees laid off because of acquisition of new machinery in item 17, $3,400.
23. Estimated profit of $22,000 on construction of new building, computed as follows: lowest contractor's bid less new building construction costs. (Corresponding credit was made to a gain account.)

Credit Entries:

1. Proceeds from sale of materials salvaged from razing of the building in item 5, $5,200.
2. Discounts earned for early payment of invoices from item 8, $2,100.

Indicate the reclassification of all items in the Property account to the proper accounts. Set up a columnar sheet similar to the one below and enter the transaction number and the amount in the appropriate column. The first one has been done for you as an example.

				Other Accounts	
Transaction	Land	Buildings	Machinery	Title	Amount
(1)	$47,000				

7–16. On July 4 a fire destroys the factory building and warehouse of Faulty Filter Fabricators, including all inventories. The insurance company has agreed to settle the claim on the following basis: 100 percent of the material inventory, 110 percent of the cost of the in-process inventory, and 120 percent of the cost of any finished goods inventory destroyed—provided a competent cost accounting expert can determine these amounts. You are asked to serve in that capacity.

Your investigation of the last position statement on June 1 reveals inventories listed as follows: materials, $7,000; work in process, $20,000; and finished goods, $36,700. Other information you obtain is as follows:

1. Purchases of materials since June 1, $40,000.
2. Materials (direct and indirect) requisitioned by factory foreman, $37,700.
3. Total factory payroll since June 1, $35,000.
4. Charges to Factory Overhead since June 1, $24,000, which includes $4,000 for indirect labor and $2,100 for indirect materials.
5. Cost of goods manufactured since June 1, $66,000.
6. Sales from June 1 to July 3, $80,000. In years past, cost of goods sold has averaged 75 percent of the selling price; the insurance company is willing to accept this estimate as being reasonably accurate.

Prepare an orderly presentation to determine the claim that should be filed with the insurance company. (You may find it helpful to set up T accounts and reconstruct the flow of costs.)

7–17. The following quotations are taken from the annual reports of American Zinc Company (1970) and the Standard Oil Company of New Jersey.

American Zinc shows an asset of $6,707,000 labeled Deferred Exploration and Mine Development Expense. In a footnote it explains its policy:

The amount shown in the consolidated balance sheet at June 30, 1970 includes

(a) $1,121,000 representing exploration expenditures relating to properties for which mineral rights have not been purchased or on which the commercial feasibility of mining has not been determined. If warranted by results of exploration or other future developments, the applicable exploration expenditures are transferred to the property accounts. . . . If exploration is deemed unsuccessful or other developments occur which negate future commercial development, the applicable expenditures are then expensed in full.

(b) $5,586,000 representing expenditures in developing new mines and major new areas in existing mines. . . . Regular recurring mine development expenditures are not deferred and are charged to production costs in the year incurred.

Standard Oil Company of New Jersey explains its policy concerning oil wells as follows:

Costs of productive wells, both tangible and intangible, as well as productive acreage are capitalized [Note: set up as an asset]. . . . Costs of that portion of undeveloped acreage likely to be unproductive, based on historical experience, are amortized over the period of exploration. Minimum work commitments are capitalized to the extent such expenditures relate to the acquisition of acreage expected to be productive. Other exploratory expenditures, including geophysical costs, dry hole costs, and annual lease rentals, are charged to income.

a) Evaluate the policy of American Zinc. Are there any differences between the two types of expenditures that could lead to *different* policies for each of them? Why is a distinction made *within* the mine development expenditure area between costs set up as assets and regular recurring expenditures? Do you agree?

b) Describe in your own words Standard Oil's asset policy. Do you think it reasonably implements the matching concept? What does the company mean by "tangible and intangible costs of productive wells"?

7–18. The following data are made available to you concerning the merchandise inventory of Grandma Crow's Discount Store:

	Cost
Inventory, January 1	$ 19,000*
Purchases	187,500
Cost of goods sold	181,000†
Inventory, December 31	25,500‡

* Wholesale cost on January 1, $22,000.
† Wholesale cost at date of sale, $217,000.
‡ Wholesale cost at December 31, $30,000.

Total sales for the year were $250,000 and selling and administrative expenses were $30,000.

a) Prepare an income statement employing conventional measures of cost.

b) Prepare a revised income statement employing a replacement cost concept and recognizing holding gains. What additional information does this statement provide?

c) The president of the company remarks that he prefers the approach in (*b*) because "it recognizes the impact of general price inflation." Comment on his view.

7–19. Many airline companies must place orders for new aircraft two or three years in advance of delivery. Since the planes are made to order, the manufacturers require substantial advance payments from the airlines to help finance construction.

Because of the large sums involved, the airlines commonly borrow substantial amounts to make these payments. The interest charges on these borrowed funds frequently are treated as part of the cost of the acquired aircraft.

For example, Pan American World Airways, Inc., showed $218 million of "advances on equipment purchase contracts" on its December 31, 1969 balance sheet. During 1969, it incurred $42.5 million of interest charges, of which $16.2 million was capitalized. A note to the statement states, "The cost of certain flight and ground property and equipment includes interest capitalized on funds invested therein prior to utilization of such equipment in revenue service."

a) Do you agree with this policy? Support your position with reasons.

b) How does this situation differ from the inclusion of interest charges as part of the cost of factory machinery when the latter is acquired in exchange for a short-term note payable?

c) Pan American operated at a net *loss* before taxes of $46,771,000 in 1969. By what percentage was the loss before taxes reduced because of this policy?

7–20. Assume that machinery is purchased at a cost of $9,000. The machinery will be depreciated over a six-year period in equal amounts ($1,500) each period. It is now the end of year 3. Information concerning the general price level and the replacement cost of the equipment is given below (assume that the figures given represent both the amount at the end of the indicated year and the average amount for the indicated year):

	General Price Index	Replacement Cost
Year:		
0....................	90	$ 9,000
1....................	100	8,000
2....................	100	10,000
3....................	120	15,000

a) At what amount would the machinery appear as of the end of year 3 on a position statement which has been adjusted for general purchasing power?

b) At what amount would it appear if the position statement reflects replacement costs?

c) What would the depreciation charge for year 3 be if general price-level changes were recognized?

d) What would the depreciation charge for year 3 be if it were based on replacement cost?

CHAPTER EIGHT

ACCOUNTING FOR INVENTORIES

THE DISCUSSION of inventory costs in the preceding chapter deals with the determination of acquisition and production costs. In this chapter our concern is with the recording of cost when the inventory is used or sold. In order to trace the pool of inventory cost to its eventual destinations, we need an understanding of some alternative procedures for determining cost of goods sold and ending inventory. These procedures involve decisions as to when inventory usage should be recorded and how inventory cost should be assigned. Conditions under which inventory costs should be charged to expense prior to the time of sale and procedures used to estimate inventory cost in retail establishments are also studied.

INVENTORY FLOW

This section deals with some elaborations and analytical techniques associated with the flow of inventory costs. Assume that a given company has a beginning inventory of $7,200. During the year its purchases, including all applicable freight and handling costs, total $51,000 and the ending inventory is assigned a cost of $15,000. The analytical procedure to reflect the accumulation and subsequent division of the pool of inventory cost can be summarized in the following convenient formula:

Beginning inventory..	$ 7,200
+ Net purchases (including freight and handling costs)........	51,000
= Cost of goods available for sale.........................	$58,200
− Ending inventory....................................	15,000
= Cost of goods sold..................................	$43,200

By determining the cost of the ending inventory, we also determine the cost of what is sold, or vice versa. Actually, the emphasis is most often placed on cost of goods sold (income measurement), and the ending inventory is given secondary consideration. The alternative procedures we discuss later in this chapter for assigning costs to the ending inventory are viewed in terms of their effects on both the income statement and the position statement.

Impact of Inventory Errors on Income Measurement

Because of its simplicity, the inventory formula can be used to analyze the effects of inventory errors or alternative inventory costing methods on the financial statements. If the ending inventory is inadvertently understated, it is clear from the formula that cost of goods sold will be overstated and net income understated by the same amount. Moreover, if the error is not detected, the opposite effect will occur during the following period. The understated ending inventory becomes the beginning inventory. If the beginning inventory is understated, cost of goods available for sale is understated. Proper determination of the ending inventory will result, therefore, in cost of goods sold being understated and net income being overstated.

The inventory formula can be used to trace the effects of many types of errors affecting inventory and cost of goods sold. Assume that a firm reports net income of $39,800 in 1971 and $75,700 in 1972. Its preliminary results for 1973 indicate a net income of $23,900. However, an audit of the records made at the end of 1973 reveals the following errors:

1. Inventory worth $5,300 on December 31, 1971 was not included in the ending inventory. This merchandise had been received and recorded as a purchase, but, because it was still in the receiving department, it was overlooked in the inventory count.
2. Goods of $18,200 received on December 30, 1972 were not recorded as a purchase until January 2, 1973. The goods were properly included in the December 31 inventory, however.
3. A clerical error in adding the ending inventory on December 31, 1972 caused the total to be overstated by $9,000.
4. An invoice for a $17,400 purchase in November, 1973 was never recorded. The error came to light when the supplier repeatedly requested payment.

Table 8–1 on the next page summarizes the effect of each of these errors on the various elements in the inventory formula and, hence, on net income. The numbers in parentheses refer to the errors numbered above, and the symbols +, −, and 0 mean that the item is overstated, under-

TABLE 8-1

Item	Effect of Errors on Inventory Elements		
	1971	. 1972	1973
Beginning inventory.......	0	→ − 5,300 (1)	→ + 9,000 (3)
Purchases...............	0	− 18,200 (2)	{ +18,200 (2) { −17,400 (4)
Goods available for sale....	0	−23,500 (1, 2)	+ 9,800 (2, 3, 4)
Ending inventory.........	−5,300 (1)⌐	+ 9,000 (3)─	0
Cost of goods sold.........	+5,300 (1)	−32,500 (1, 2, 3)	+ 9,800 (2, 3, 4)
Net Income..............	−5,300 (1)	+32,500 (1, 2, 3)	− 9,800 (2, 3, 4)

stated, and not affected, respectively. From the table we can see that the corrected net incomes are:

1971............... $45,100 ($39,800 + $ 5,300)
1972............... $43,200 ($75,700 − $32,500)
1973............... $33,700 ($23,900 + $ 9,800)

Notice that a single inventory error normally affects only two accounting periods and has opposite effects in each of them. The $9,000 overstatement of the ending inventory at the end of 1972 causes the net income for 1972 to be overstated and the net income for 1973 to be understated. Over the two accounting periods, the error "washes itself out." Regardless of how complex the situation may be, the inventory formula serves as a handy analytical tool for examining or predicting the ultimate effect on net income of errors or changes in inventory determination.

Periodic versus Perpetual Inventory

The inventory formula illustrates the procedure followed in a periodic or physical inventory system. Cost of goods sold is recorded only at the end of the period. A physical inventory count is taken, and the cost of the units on hand is determined. This amount is then subtracted from the sum of the beginning inventory and net purchases.

Although widely used, particularly among merchandising concerns, the periodic procedure suffers from two disadvantages. It automatically includes in cost of goods sold the cost of merchandise which has been wasted, stolen, or otherwise lost. Little information to aid in the control of inventory usage is available under this accounting procedure. Secondly, the time-consuming job of taking a complete physical inventory before statements can be prepared effectively limits the frequency of accurate financial reporting.

Many firms, including most manufacturing firms, record the use of merchandise or raw material on a *perpetual* basis. Cost of Goods Sold (or

Work in Process) is debited each time the inventory is decreased through sale or use, and a running, up-to-date record is kept of the number of units on hand and their cost. The perpetual inventory system provides more timely and accurate information about inventory balances and withdrawals. Control is enhanced by a periodic comparison of the perpetual inventory records with a physical inventory count. However, in this case the physical inventory can be taken at any convenient time, often on a rotating basis for different items in the inventory. Preparation of financial statements does not *require* a physical inventory count.

Because of the detailed record keeping, a perpetual inventory system is easier to use when only a few items of inventory with infrequent purchases and sales are involved. As a result, perpetual inventory procedures were once restricted to inventory items of high unit cost. However, mechanization of the detailed bookkeeping function has led to much wider usage of this technique.

INVENTORY COSTING METHODS

Whether a firm employs perpetual or periodic inventory procedures, whenever it purchases a number of units at varying prices and sells only some of them the accountant is faced with the question of which costs to assign to the units sold and which to the units in the ending inventory. In considering this question, we discuss a number of alternative methods by which costs may be divided. Because the periodic inventory formula better focuses attention on cost of goods sold and ending inventory and on the relationship between them, we use it as our general framework for discussion. However, attention is drawn to points at which perpetual inventory procedures might yield different results.

Specific Identification

Perhaps the first method of assigning inventory costs that comes to mind is that of relating a specific purchase cost to each item in the inventory. We could accomplish this by attaching to each unit, as it is received, a tag indicating its specific cost. Or we might link a separate invoice to each item by a serial number or a unique description of the item. Then, when the item is sold, its specific cost can be identified and assigned to the expense account. For those items remaining unsold at the end of the period, we can easily determine the total cost by adding the tags or relevant invoices.

For practical reasons, specific identification is suitable primarily for high-unit-value merchandise of which purchases and sales are relatively few. For instance, an automobile dealer would have a separate invoice for each automobile in his inventory. Since each car can be separately identified and its individual cost determined, assigning inventory costs to expense and ending inventory becomes a mechanical process of identifying units and cost invoices. Appliances, jewelry, and furniture are other examples of inventories often costed under specific identification.

As a method of matching resources consumed against revenues generated, specific identification commands great support because it adheres to the actual physical flow of inventory. Nevertheless, two criticisms are raised against this method. First, specific identification can not be used for completely interchangeable units, for it could lead to a biased result. If *identical* units have different costs, management, through an arbitrary selection of which units to deliver, can influence the size of the cost of goods sold and, in turn, manipulate the amount of income reported.

The second criticism is a practical one. Some goods cannot be kept separate physically or be identified specifically. Gasoline in underground tanks and items stored in bins are examples. Moreover, it is usually too costly to maintain separate records for each unit when the inventory consists of numerous small items of varying types. Even when it is feasible to maintain perpetual records of the number and cost of units received and used, it still may be difficult to identify the exact unit sold and its specific cost.

TABLE 8–2

	Number of Units	Unit Cost	Total Cost
Beginning inventory...........................	900	$ 8.00	$ 7,200
Purchased March 18...........................	1,000	9.10	9,100
Purchased August 3...........................	3,000	10.20	30,600
Purchased November 28.......................	1,000	11.30	11,300
Total goods available for sale................	5,900		$58,200
Ending Inventory.............................	1,500		

Consequently, in many practical cases some assumption has to be made as to which goods are left on hand at the end of the accounting period and which goods have been sold. Some of the more common of these assumptions about inventory flows constitute the remaining methods of inventory costing to be discussed. Let us use the data in Table 8–2 to illustrate and contrast the various methods. Our problem is to determine how much of the $58,200 should be assigned to the 1,500 units in the ending inventory and how much to the 4,400 units sold.

Average Cost

One popular assumption is that the units on hand and the units sold represent a mixture of all the units available for sale. This assumption might be particularly valid for liquids or items stored in bins. If the ending inventory consists of parts of a number of purchases, logic would suggest that they be costed at a weighted average cost. This method applied to the above example would produce the following results:

Units available for sale......................	5,900
Cost of goods available for sale..............	$58,200
Weighted average cost ($58,200/5900)........	$ 9.864
Ending inventory ($9.864 × 1,500)............	$14,796
Cost of goods sold ($58,200 − $14,796).......	$43,404

Often the average cost method is used even when the units are not mixed physically. It is argued that average costing of interchangeable units minimizes possible distortions from short-term price fluctuations. If specific identification or some other alternative is used, cost of goods sold may fluctuate unnecessarily from period to period. Misinterpretation may result. Average costing has the tendency to "normalize" the unit costs for the period. For short time periods, such a procedure may have justification.

One of the objections raised against applying a *periodic* average cost method, as in the example above, is that costs incurred early in the period may influence the cost of the ending inventory as much as or more than costs incurred near the end of the period. To this extent, periodic average cost is theoretically inaccurate. A moving average cost, as would be required if the average cost method were applied on a perpetual basis, would be better. After each purchase a new average cost would be computed for costing out units sold until the next purchase occurs. However, this procedure requires a number of arithmetic calculations, particularly when purchases are made with great frequency. Both periodic and perpetual average cost methods are used, but they do not necessarily give identical results.

First-In, First-Out

In the selection of criteria by which to judge an assumed flow of costs, one factor that often receives mention is the physical flow of goods. Under this view the best inventory assumption is the one that most closely approximates the physical movement of the inventory. In most cases this leads to the first-in, first-out (or Fifo) inventory costing method. Under this method the oldest inventory (first-in) is assumed to be sold (first-out), and the ending inventory consists of the most recently purchased items. In our example the units sold are assumed to consist of the 900 units in the beginning inventory, the 1,000 units purchased on March 18, plus 2,500 of the units from the August 3 purchase. The ending inventory consisting of the newest merchandise, then, is costed accordingly:

```
Ending inventory:
   1,000 units @ $11.30................. $11,300
     500 units @ $10.20.................   5,100
   1,500 units..........................  $16,400
Cost of goods sold ($58,200 − $16,400).... $41,800
```

In addition to its reasonableness as an approximation of the physical flow of merchandise, Fifo also provides the same results whether applied on a perpetual or on a periodic basis. As long as the oldest merchandise is considered to be sold first, cost of sales is the same whether it is recorded at the end of the period or after each individual sale. Moreover, the inventory balance shown on the position statement under Fifo approximates the replacement cost of the asset. These factors probably account for its being the costing method most commonly employed in accounting practice.

The major objection to Fifo is that price gains (or losses) from holding inventory are included as part of operating income. For example, if changes in selling price closely parallel changes in cost, the merchandise sold in December, in our illustration, was sold at prices based on the then current cost of $11.30. If selling prices are normally 150 percent of cost, the selling price was $16.95 (150% × $11.30). Yet the cost matched against it was probably only $10.20 (the purchase cost in August). Many accountants would contend that instead of having a unit gross margin of $6.75 ($16.95 − $10.20), the firm has only a unit gross margin of $5.65 ($16.95 − $11.30) and a price gain from holding inventory of $1.10 ($11.30 − $10.20).

By assuming that the oldest merchandise is sold first, Fifo may match low-cost inventory against high selling prices during periods of rising prices and high-cost inventory against low selling prices in periods of falling prices. Under Fifo, gains (losses) from holding inventories which increase (decrease) in cost are reflected in net income through a *cost of goods sold* that is lower (higher) than the *current* cost of the resources used. This "inventory profit" should be segregated for reporting purposes on the income statement, because it is of a different nature from operating income and may result from external factors beyond management's influence.

Last-In, First-Out

Last-in, first-out (Lifo) assumes that the cost of the most recently purchased merchandise should be matched against revenue as cost of goods sold. Correspondingly, the goods remaining on hand are assigned the costs of the oldest merchandise. Using the figures in Table 8–2 and applying Lifo on a periodic basis, we find the following results:

Ending inventory:
        900 units @ $8.00................. $ 7,200
        600 units @ $9.10.................   5,460
    1,500 units......................... $12,660
Cost of goods sold ($58,200 − $12,660).... $45,540

Application of the Lifo concept to the ending inventory results in an inventory consisting of a number of layers. The basic layer is the beginning inventory, and each period's net additions are added, beginning with the earliest purchases. Schematically, the ending inventory in our example would appear as follows:

| 600 units @ $9.10 | .... | Layer added this period from first purchase |
| 900 units @ $8.00 | .... | Basic Lifo layer from beginning inventory |

If the ending inventory were 2,000 units at the close of the next accounting period, we would add an additional layer of 500 units, at the cost of the first 500 units purchased in that period.[1] Conversely, since the units sold are assumed to come off the top layer, any decrease in inventory would first reduce the 600 units costed at $9.10. As long as the ending inventory for each period remains 1,500 units, its cost would be $12,660. Under Lifo, inventory is viewed as a quasi-fixed asset, with current purchases being used to meet current sales.

Lifo assumes a "flow of costs" which usually does not approximate the actual physical movement of the inventory. However, many accountants and businessmen claim that more useful income figures can be obtained by matching costs other than those approximating the historical cost of the actual physical units sold. While using historical costs, Lifo actually attempts to value cost of goods sold at replacement cost. In practice, Lifo is applied on a periodic basis, which is required for tax purposes.[2] Therefore, for practical purposes, Lifo becomes an approximation to a replacement cost method in all cases where physical inventories at the end of the period are equal to or greater than the beginning inventory. The most recently incurred costs (the cost of replacing goods)

---

[1] Under current income tax regulations the incremental layer added during a period need not be costed at the earliest purchase prices of that period. For tax purposes the Lifo concept extends only to the layers, not to the costing within a particular layer.

[2] The Internal Revenue Code also requires that companies using Lifo for tax purposes use it in their financial accounting reports as well. This is one of the very few areas where, by law, tax accounting methods and financial accounting methods must be identical.

are charged to expense; the oldest inventory costs are assumed to remain in inventory.

This aspect of Lifo often is characterized by the phrase "matching current costs against current revenues." By matching an approximation of current costs against revenues, Lifo provides more useful information for making future decisions and for projecting future net income. Particularly if prices are rising, Lifo charges the higher purchase costs against the higher selling prices and thereby more closely measures the current cost-price margin. This figure, it is claimed, is more characteristic of current operating conditions than is the historic cost-price margin. Current decisions regarding the setting of selling prices are made on the basis of current costs, not past costs.

Comparison of Lifo and Fifo. The results from using Fifo and Lifo differ significantly only when prices change. Let us look at their comparative effects on the financial statements. Table 8–3 presents some information about the sales and purchases of a basic product during a five-year period. Unit sales prices are deliberately set at 150 percent of cost so that the current gross margin *percentage* is a constant 33 ⅓ percent.

TABLE 8–3

| | Purchases | | | Sales | | |
Period	Units	Unit Cost	Total Cost	Units	Unit Price	Total Sales
Beg. Inventory.........	2,000	$5.00	$10,000			
Year 1...............	3,000	5.20	15,600	3,000	$ 7.80	$23,400
Year 2...............	3,000	6.00	18,000	3,000	9.00	27,000
Year 3...............	6,000	6.80	40,800	5,000	10.20	51,000
Year 4...............	3,000	6.60	19,800	4,000	9.90	39,600
Year 5...............	4,000	6.40	25,600	4,000	9.60	38,400

Table 8–4 displays the pertinent financial statement information under Fifo and under Lifo. First-in, first-out accentuates the fluctuations in gross margin as prices change. The historic gross margin percentage is higher than the current gross margin during times of price upswing and lower in times of price declines. The reason is, of course, the inclusion of price gains or losses on inventory in the gross margin figure. For instance, a $400 inventory price gain is included in Year 1 (2,000 units increased in cost from $5 to $5.20) and a $1,600 price gain in Year 2 (2,000 units increased in cost from $5.20 to $6). Conversely, in Years 4 and 5 there are inventory price losses of $600 and $400, respectively. The ending inventory, however, is stated at current cost each year.

As we surmised, the gross margin under Lifo closely approximates

TABLE 8–4

Fifo

Year	Sales Revenue	Cost of Goods Sold	Gross Margin	Gross Margin %	Ending Inventory
1..........	$23,400	$15,200	$ 8,200	35.0%	$10,400 (2,000 @ $5.20)
2..........	27,000	16,400	10,600	39.3	12,000 (2,000 @ $6.00)
3..........	51,000	32,400	18,600	36.5	20,400 (3,000 @ $6.80)
4..........	39,600	27,000	12,600	32.0	13,200 (2,000 @ $6.60)
5..........	38,400	26,000	12,400	32.3	12,800 (2,000 @ $6.40)

Lifo

Year	Sales Revenue	Cost of Goods Sold	Gross Margin	Gross Margin %	Ending Inventory
1..........	$23,400	$15,600	$ 7,800	33.3%	$10,000 (2,000 @ $5.00)
2..........	27,000	18,000	9,000	33.3	10,000 (2,000 @ $5.00)
3..........	51,000	34,000	17,000	33.3	16,800 {2,000 @ $5.00 / 1,000 @ $6.80}
4..........	39,600	26,600	13,000	32.8	10,000 (2,000 @ $5.00)
5..........	38,400	25,600	12,800	33.3	10,000 (2,000 @ $5.00)

the 33⅓ percent relationship between current purchase and sale prices. Net income arises only after provision has been made for the maintenance (replacement cost) of the operating assets used in its generation. (In Year 4 it is off slightly because the carry-over of 1,000 units of inventory from Year 3 which were charged as cost of sales in Year 4 resulted in the inclusion of a $200 inventory price loss [$6.60 − $6.80] in cost of goods sold.) In a period of rising prices, Lifo gives a higher cost-of-goods-sold figure and a lower net income than Fifo. The converse is true in a period of falling prices. Over a complete cycle of prices, total net income would be the same under both inventory methods.

Rationale for Lifo. Lifo "normalizes" the gains and losses associated with holding inventory when specific prices change. The increase in the cost of the same physical quantity of inventory when prices rise and the decrease in the cost of inventory when prices fall are removed from the calculation of net income. This exclusion, in a period of rising prices, is often justified on two grounds.

First, the holding gains really are not income, because the inventory sold must be replaced at higher prices. Lifo's orientation is toward an income concept of disposability after provision has been made from revenue for replenishment of resources consumed. In a period of rising prices, funds in addition to the original cost of goods sold usually must be reinvested to replace the same physical inventory. Because of the need to reinvest at a higher cost, Lifo views the gain from holding inventory as false profit. Lifo eliminates it, thus giving a better measure of *disposable* net income available for other uses. The second argument advanced is that holding gains do not represent real gains because they result from price inflation. By eliminating gains which do not represent true increases in economic value, Lifo helps to compensate for the inadequacies of the monetary postulate, which ignores changes in the value of the measuring unit.

Criticisms of Lifo.   With respect to the first contention, many critics seriously question the assertion that inventory profits are unreal, that the increased cost of replacing inventory should be included in cost of goods sold. Such a statement assumes that the income cycle is not complete until the investment is replaced. The general nature of business operations, however, is not from one investment to another investment but rather from uninvested funds back to uninvested funds available for reinvestment *or some other purpose.* Each investment is an independent management decision based on future expectations. New investment is not made automatically simply because resources have expired. Nor are the amount and type of reinvestment determined by the amount and type of past investment consumed. It is argued that Lifo, by insisting on reinvestment, confuses *income determination* with *income administration.* Income exists when the old investment is recovered. Whether that income is paid out in dividends or reinvested is a separate management decision dealing with the use or administration of the income, not with its measurement.

Much can be said for a measure of income based on a matching of current costs against current revenues. Such a measure does more accurately reflect current operating conditions. This does not mean, however, that price gains or losses should be ignored. Rather, proper reporting on the stewardship of the owners' investment would seem to require that effective purchasing—buying at a low price merchandise that later increases in value—be reflected in a periodic measure of income. Perhaps price gains or losses should be isolated as a separate part of the income calculation. However, Lifo does not isolate the effect of price fluctuations; it ignores them.

Moreover, last-in, first-out retains an ending inventory valuation at the oldest incurred costs. The inventory figure shown on the position statement may represent costs incurred many years earlier. This distortion on the position statement affects any judgments or computations involving current assets. Lifo can be justly criticized for leading to an income statement that approximates current costs at the expense of an increasing inutility in the position statement.

The second contention, that Lifo helps to compensate for inflation, arises from the fact that our economy has generally been experiencing an inflationary trend for the past 30 years, resulting in a general decline in the purchasing power of the dollar. This tendency for price inflation has focused attention on the deficiencies of the monetary postulate. However, the problem of the monetary postulate deals with changes in the *price level,* which should properly be determined by reference to some indicator of general purchasing power. Lifo, on the other hand, has to do with changes in *price structure*—the relative value of goods and services—an entirely different problem. If the two price movements are dissimilar, then Lifo offers no real solution to the problem of an unstable yardstick.

The spiral of rising prices has also emphasized the merits of Lifo more as a practical tax gimmick than as a method of income measurement. When prices are increasing, Lifo causes taxable income and income tax charges to be lower than they would be under Fifo or average cost. It is unfortunate that taxes and general inflationary conditions have clouded the basic issue underlying Lifo—its income concept. The merits and criticisms of Lifo should be centered on the basic concept rather than on ancillary implications.

The discussion above provides the conceptual criticism of Lifo. Other technical criticisms can be made. For example, costs under Lifo only approximate current replacement costs. Unless a short time elapses between purchase and sale of the product, there is no assurance that the most recently incurred costs under Lifo will be the same as current replacement costs. The longer an item is in inventory, the greater the potential disparity between the two. In addition, management might manipulate cost of goods sold and hence net income by accelerating or postponing purchases toward the end of the accounting period. And finally, unless the physical volume of inventories remains constant or increases during the period, Lifo inventory costing can lead to a gross mismatching of costs and revenues. The oldest—and during inflation, probably the lowest—cost layers represent the closing inventory. If inventory quantities are substantially depleted, these lower cost layers, which may represent costs incurred many years earlier, must then be matched against current revenues, counter to the basic purpose of Lifo.

Summary of Lifo. Lifo incorporates some features of different income concepts. It retains the use of historical costs employed in conventional financial accounting theory, while attempting to recognize and deal with the problem of changing prices. Yet it does not adequately satisfy any of these concepts. As an attempt to measure income based on current cost, Lifo is inferior to a direct replacement cost procedure, illustrated in Chapter Seven. Moreover, some replacement cost concepts do recognize the difference between original acquisition cost and replacement cost as a separate category of income (holding gains). Lifo, of course, ignores this factor entirely.

Similarly, in the conventional framework, Lifo appears illogical. In a concept of income closely tied to the historical matching of the cost of assets consumed against revenues, a method premised on a use of product clearly at odds with the flow of goods to the consumer seems unsound. Lifo violates the conventional framework too greatly, besides misrepresenting the investment cycle of the business, to be defensible within the theoretical confines postulated in Chapter One.

The Lifo controversy highlights some deficiencies in the existing accounting framework. Prices change, and these changes in many cases have economic significance. The monetary postulate ignores general price changes which affect the value of the dollar. The historical matching concept, by concealing certain specific price changes, may be less useful than a concept based on replacement cost. The significance of Lifo probably lies in the recognition of valid objectives in other cost concepts and not necessarily in the manner in which it attempts to reach those objectives.

LOWER OF COST OR MARKET

The inventory methods discussed in the preceding section attempt to determine the cost of goods on hand and the cost of goods sold. Although they differ in the assumptions made as to which goods are sold, they all use historical cost figures. An extension of these cost methods is the approach known as "lower of cost or market" (LCM). It assigns to the ending inventory either a historical cost amount *or* a current market valuation, whichever is lower. It is used in conjunction with one of the cost methods.

This method is a carry-over from earlier periods of accounting thought, when the balance sheet was of prime importance and conservatism was a prized virtue. If market valuation declined below original acquisition cost, it was assumed that a loss had occurred that should be recorded. Writing down the inventory to the lower market figure "recognized" this loss and gave a more conservative value to the inventory in case the business had to be liquidated. In more recent years, as attention has shifted to the income statement and the matching concept, the interpretation of LCM appears to be that only costs possessing future use value should be carried forward to be matched against future revenues. Costs that cannot be recovered satisfactorily are seen to have lost their usefulness:

A departure from the cost basis of pricing the inventory is required when the utility of the goods is no longer as great as its cost. Where there is evidence that the utility of goods, in their disposal in the ordinary course of business, will be less than cost, whether due to physical deterioration, obsolescense, changes in price levels, or other causes, the difference should be recognized as a loss of the current period. This is generally accomplished by stating such goods at a lower level commonly designated as market.[3]

Meaning of Market

In order to implement the idea of LCM, we first must determine how to measure utility and what is meant by the term "market." Two interpretations have been advanced through the years.

Net Realizable Value. One reasonable meaning implied by the above quotation is that utility should be measured by what the company will receive upon disposal of the inventory. This amount, called "net realizable value," equals expected selling price reduced by any anticipated costs to complete and sell the inventory item. LCM, then, implies that inventory should not be stated at a figure greater than its *recoverable* cost. The inventory write-down or "loss of the current period" should include any portion of the acquisition cost which cannot be recovered out of anticipated revenue. This interpretation of market has commonly been employed to record losses on damaged or obsolete merchandise in periods prior to their sale.

For example, a company develops and manufactures 500 pollution control units for automobiles. Because of the firm's inexperience, the actual costs are $300 per unit. Management estimates that the selling price will have to be set at $290 to be competitive with other devices on the market. A 20 percent dealer commission is normal for this type of good. Net realizable value in this case is $232 ($290 − $58). Of the $300 total cost per unit, $68 (300 − $232) will not be recovered. Consequently, that portion has no future service potential and should not be carried forward as an asset.

Replacement Cost. On the other hand, the general idea expressed in the earlier quotation led the AICPA to define market as *replacement cost,* the price currently being paid for the item in the wholesale market. Under this interpretation utility is the equivalent expenditure necessary to provide the same use value. However, subsequent discussions by the AICPA and others seem to return to the idea of *realizability.* Replacement cost is employed as evidence of realizability when there is a close association between purchase prices and selling prices. If replacement cost has fallen, the contention is that net realizable value also has declined or will decline shortly.

Despite its lack of precise meaning, lower of cost or market is widely used by many companies to determine ending inventories. For purposes of our general discussion, we assume that it means either net realizable

---

[3] *Accounting Research and Terminology Bulletins, Final Edition* (New York: AICPA, 1961), p. 30.

value or replacement cost. The reader may consult Appendix 8–A for a more detailed analysis of alternative meanings of market, the application of LCM under the AICPA guidelines, and the theoretical implications of its many facets.

How LCM Operates

To be able to appraise LCM, we must first understand its basic mechanics. Assume that a physical inventory of 50 units exists at the end of the period. The original acquisition cost assigned to these units is $80. Market at the end of the period is determined to be $65. Assume further that cost of goods available for sale (beginning inventory plus purchases) amounts to $10,000. The effects of using lower of cost or market to value the ending inventory can be seen below:

	Cost	LCM
Ending inventory	$4,000	$3,250
Cost of goods sold	6,000	6,750

Lower of cost or market increases cost of goods sold by $750. This is the amount of the decline in the market value of the inventory [50 × ($80 − $65)] since the item was initially purchased. Of course, the inventory decline is unrelated to the goods sold; it concerns the inventory still on hand. Logic would suggest that if the market decline is to be recognized, it should be segregated as a separate deduction. Rarely, however, is this method of presentation used in accounting practice.

With respect to income measurement, lower of cost or market has the effect of shifting income from one accounting period to another. Through a write-down to market in the current period, future period's earnings are relieved of charges that otherwise would be recorded then. However, the reduced ending inventory value, which causes cost of goods sold to be higher and income to be lower this period, becomes the beginning inventory of the following period. It has an opposite effect on income then.[4] With respect to the balance sheet, LCM prevents the inventory from being recorded at a figure above its future realizable value.

Criticisms of LCM

The objections to cost or market, whichever is lower, entail both theoretical and practical points. Some of the theoretical criticisms relate

---

[4] For tax purposes *Lifo* cannot be used to determine the cost element in LCM. Under Lifo, any inventory value previously written down to market would remain as long as a minimum inventory quantity was maintained rather than flow through cost of goods sold in the following period. Consequently, lower of Lifo cost or market would result in a relatively permanent inventory value at the lowest purchase price that ever existed at the end of a period.

to the varying concepts of income implied by the alternative definitions of market. These are considered in depth in Appendix 8–A. Two, however, are of general import.

First, the charge of inconsistency plagues lower of cost or market. The inventory may be at cost one year and at market the following year. This is because market prices are deemed relevant only when they are below cost. It seems inconsistent to many to recognize a decline in replacement cost or net realizable value below cost as a loss before sale, while at the same time maintaining that gains arising from market's being above cost should be deferred until sale takes place.

Second, in some circumstances LCM will cause inventory to be written down even though the acquisition cost is still expected to be recovered out of future revenues. This occurs when the original acquisition cost is greater than replacement cost but less than net realizable value. Many theorists argue that as long as the merchandise can be sold at some profit (net realizable value is above cost), no loss has occurred. The only event that has occurred is simply a reduction in potential profit margin, not a loss. The inventory write-down records a hypothetical loss for the current period, permitting a greater profit to be recorded during the following period. It is not the purpose of accounting to shift income unnecessarily from one accounting period to another.

Three other criticisms concern practical limitations. First, LCM buries a "loss" from market declines applicable to the ending inventory in cost of goods sold. This may distort income statement relationships and may make year to year comparisons difficult. Second, the market figures at the close of the firm's accounting period may be quite misleading in measuring any type of "value" of inventory. A risk always exists in using market figures at one particular moment, because they may not be representative of the future. This risk is heightened if the moment of time is the end of an accounting period, when activity (purchasing and selling) may be at a low ebb. Finally, different results are achieved with LCM depending on whether it is applied to the inventory as a whole or to each individual item.

RETAIL INVENTORY METHOD

The preparation of monthly or quarterly financial statements requires either frequent physical inventory counts of the ending inventory or maintenance of perpetual inventory records. Both are arduous tasks for firms selling large quantities of many different products. Yet the need for interim financial information exists for these firms as well as for others.

Consequently, many merchandising concerns employ a method known as the retail inventory method to estimate the *amount* when a periodic inventory cannot conveniently be taken. Retail establishments also use this procedure to find the *cost* of a physical inventory without having to go through the time-consuming job of sorting out the costs of a number of small individual items. In many retail firms, when a physical inventory is taken, it is taken at the current retail prices listed on the items. Then the retail procedure is employed to estimate the cost of the ending inventory.

Let us take the following monthly figures to illustrate:

	Cost	Retail
Beginning inventory	$10,000	$13,200
Net purchases	11,000	14,800
Goods available for sale	$21,000	$28,000

The retail method employs the relationship between cost and retail prices existing in the basic periodic inventory formula. The method requires that we keep track not only of the cost of purchases but of the selling price assigned to them as well. If we do so, we can find a relationship between the cost of goods available for sale and the retail price of goods available for sale. This relationship, expressed as a "cost ratio," is 75 percent (21,000/28,000) in our example. We can then apply this cost ratio to the retail value of the ending inventory to estimate its cost.

If sales for the month are $13,600, the retail price of the ending inventory can be determined by subtraction to be $14,400:

	Cost	Retail
Goods available for sale	$21,000	$28,000
Less: Goods sold	?	13,600
Ending inventory	$?	$14,400

Multiplication of the $14,400 by the cost ratio of 75 percent gives an estimate of the cost of the ending inventory of $10,800. The cost ratio can be applied either to an estimate of the ending inventory at retail prices, as in this case, or to an actual physical count of the ending inventory taken at retail prices.

Use of the cost ratio in the above manner approximates fairly accurately the average cost of the ending inventory *if* we can assume that the cost-retail relationship existing for goods available holds true for the goods sold and for the goods in the ending inventory. Such may not be the case if different products have quite varying cost ratios and the product mix of the goods sold is not the same as the mix comprising the ending inventory.[5]

---

[5] The use of the retail method becomes slightly more complicated when we consider that changes often occur in the initial selling prices before the goods are sold. These changes are called additional markups and markdowns. Because they modify the retail price, they can also affect the cost ratio. The coverage of the technical aspects of handling markups and markdowns is left to later courses.

SUMMARY

In this chapter we are primarily interested in how the pool of inventory cost is divided between the goods sold and the ending inventory. The inventory formula provides us with a helpful analytical tool for examining this and other inventory problems and their effects. An exploration of the inventory "valuation" problem reveals a number of procedures, conventions, or expedients among which the accountant is forced to choose. The effect of each of these choices on the income statement and position statement depends on the circumstances.

To promote the readers' understanding of the financial statements it behooves the firm to report clearly what its inventory policies are. Likewise, an intelligent user of financial information must be able to understand the meaning of inventory terminology and be able to assess the general impact of alternative procedures on the statements. This chapter tries to lay a groundwork for a rational interpretation of financial statements in the inventory area.

APPENDIX 8–A
MECHANICS OF LOWER OF COST OR MARKET

As we have seen in Chapter Eight, despite the general notion of realizability or recoverability that underlies lower of cost or market, the primary interpretation of market is replacement cost. The rationale for LCM appears to be as follows. If replacement cost has fallen, then the net selling price of the merchandise on hand has probably declined also. Therefore the firm cannot realize as much profit as it has anticipated. Hence the asset has lost part of its revenue-producing ability and has declined in value. Such a decline in value should be recognized as a loss.

Limitations on Replacement Cost

This rationale contains some key assumptions. To the extent that these assumptions are not valid, the definition of market as replacement cost may lead to unreasonable results. Consequently, the AICPA, in formulating the cost-or-market principle, modified replacement cost as the determinant of market by attaching an upper and lower limit:

As used in the phrase *lower of cost or market* the term *market* means current replacement cost (by purchase or reproduction, as the case may be) except that:
(1) Market should not exceed the net realizable value (i.e., estimated selling price in the ordinary course of business less reasonably predictable costs of completion and disposal); and

(2) Market should not be less than net realizable value reduced by an allowance for an approximately normal profit margin.[6]

Lower Limit. One potential problem arises if the decline in selling prices is negligible or less than proportionate to the decline in purchase prices. In this case, to reduce inventory to the replacement cost would be to recognize a loss in the current period, only to show an *abnormal* income in the following period when the units are sold.

To avoid this fallacy, the AICPA has specified a lower limit on the market figure—net realizable value less a normal profit margin. Only a loss equal to the difference between cost and this lower limit would be included in the cost of goods sold of the current period. Then, if the merchandise is sold in the following period as anticipated, a normal margin will be realized. The lower limit prevents recognition of purely hypothetical losses. Once an item can be sold at a normal profit, no additional loss has occurred, even if replacement cost has declined more.

Upper Limit. Another unrealistic result may occur when goods are obsolete or damaged. The cost of replacing these goods may actually be above both original cost and net realizable value. Consequently, no reduction would result under the normal interpretation of market as replacement cost. Yet, if net realizable value is below cost, a portion of the cost cannot be recovered and a loss in this period should be recorded.

In this case replacement cost does not measure the real loss in utility due to obsolescence. A loss equal to the difference between original cost and net realizable value will be incurred. Many accountants claim that since the obsolescence or damage occurred in the current period, the loss should be recognized then by a decrease in the inventory to net realizable value, even though replacement cost has risen.

Floor and Ceiling. The results of the modifications described above are sometimes likened to a room. The ceiling is net realizable value; the floor is net realizable value less a normal profit. Market means replacement cost only as long as it lies between the floor and the ceiling. If replacement cost is below net realizable value less a normal profit, the latter is used as the definition of market. Net realizable value less a normal profit presumably measures the *maximum* loss suffered by the firm. If replacement cost is above net realizable value, then the latter is substituted for it as the meaning of market. A write-down to net realizable value measures the *minimum* loss suffered by the firm.

Analysis of Lower of Cost or Market

The lower-of-cost-or-market rule as applied in accounting practice offers four different concepts of utility for inventory items:

1. Acquisition cost (AC).

---

[6] *Accounting Research and Terminology Bulletins, op. cit.,* p. 3.

2. Net realizable value (NRV).
3. Replacement cost (RC).
4. Net realizable value less normal profit (NRV − NP).

The last three represent alternative views of market depending on particular circumstances. Conceivably, all three concepts of market could be used by a single company at the same time for different types of inventory or at different times for the same inventory. Of course, the market figure, however determined, is applicable only if it is below cost.

The information in Table 8–A–1 has been gathered for five items in an

TABLE 8–A–1

Item	AC	RC	Estimated Sale Price	Estimated Cost to Sell	Normal Profit
A	$ 6.00	$ 6.50	$ 7.50	$0.70	$1.20
B	15.30	15.40	15.50	1.20	2.00
C	10.50	8.20	11.80	1.10	1.60
D	5.20	5.00	6.30	0.50	1.00
E	8.60	8.00	9.40	1.10	0.50

ending inventory. Assume that we are to determine the proper dollar amount per unit for each item in accordance with the LCM procedure, as interpreted by the AICPA. This example illustrates how the procedure works and also serves as a focal point for an analysis of each alternative.

Table 8–A–2 presents the results of the procedure used to determine lower of cost or market in each case. The relevant market figure is shown in the bold type.

TABLE 8–A–2

Item	AC	Market NRV	Market RC	Market NRV − NP	LCM
A	$ 6.00	$ 6.80	$ **6.50**	$ 5.60	$ 6.00
B	15.30	**14.30**	15.40	12.30	14.30
C	10.50	10.70	8.20	**9.10**	9.10
D	5.20	5.80	**5.00**	4.80	5.00
E	8.60	8.30	**8.00**	7.80	8.00

Item A: Cost. The ending inventory is valued at the acquisition cost of $6 per unit, since cost is below both net realizable value and replacement cost. The applicable market figure is the usual one, replacement cost, since it is between the floor and the ceiling. But it is still above cost. Consequently, no adjustment is made; LCM gives the same results as the conventional cost method. The inventory is deemed not to have suffered any decline in utility, even though the profit recognized in the next period will be only $0.80 ($6.80 NRV − $6 AC), less than the normal profit of $1.20.

Item B: Net Realizable Value. For some reason the output value of the items on hand is less than the input value for similar replacement goods. This circumstance is rather rare. Goods subject to major style or model changes and those prone to breakage or deterioration are affected chiefly. In any case, the ceiling governs the determination of market. The firm is assumed to have suffered a loss of utility at least equal to $1 per unit ($15.30 − $14.30). The only impact of LCM in this instance is that the loss is recorded in this period—by write-down of the ending inventory— instead of next period, when the goods are actually sold. If the ending inventory is valued at the $14.30 market figure, then no income or loss occurs in the next period, when the goods are actually disposed of at a net selling price of $14.30.

Of all the market alternatives under LCM, this one draws the greatest theoretical support. Some accountants, in fact, would like to see inventories valued at net realizable values whether they are *above or below* cost. But even most of those supporting the conventional cost valuation contend that losses from damage, obsolescence, and similar causes are significant, measurable, economic events of the period in which they occur. Consequently, the notion that an unrecoverable cost is not an asset draws quite wide support. But as we shall see in the next examples, LCM often goes further than merely reducing inventory to net realizable value.

Item C: Net Realizable Value less Normal Profit. Here, replacement cost evidently has declined proportionately more than selling prices. Replacement cost is below cost, but it is also below net realizable value less a normal profit. If the inventory were reduced in value to replacement cost, a loss of $2.30 ($10.50 AC − $8.20 RC) would be recorded this period, and an income of $2.50 ($10.70 NRV less the decreased value of $8.20) would be recorded next period. This profit of $2.50 per unit would be much greater than the normal profit of $1.60.

Therefore, the lower limit of net realizable value less normal profit becomes the applicable market figure. Through a reduction of the ending inventory to $9.10 and a concomitant charge to income this period of $1.40 ($10.50 AC less $9.10), a normal profit of $1.60 ($10.70 NRV less the decreased inventory value of $9.10) is recorded in a later period.

Two major objections are raised against this result. First is the charge of profit manipulation mentioned in Chapter Eight. The normal profit in the subsequent period results from a write-down of assets this period. The accounting system should not adjust the financial records in one period just to show what the anticipated, desired, or normal profit should be in the next period. Since net realizable value ($10.70) is above cost ($10.50), any "loss" recorded this period is entirely hypothetical in a conventional accounting sense.

The second objection is a practical one. What, in fact, is a normal profit? The foregoing example assumes a constant dollar amount regardless of changes in selling prices or costs. However, is this a hoped-for figure, an average figure for this particular product over a business cycle, or an average return for the business as a whole? Or is it a percentage return on sales? Grave doubts exist whether any practical quantification *could be or should be* given to a concept of "normal" in a dynamic, changing, business environment.

Items D and E: Replacement Cost. In both of these cases, replacement cost is the applicable market figure, because it is between the upper and lower limits. It is also the relevant figure for inventory valuation under LCM, because it is below the original acquisition cost. A write-down to replacement cost in these instances records a holding loss equal to the difference between original cost and current cost. Whether a loss under the conventional matching concept is involved depends on the circumstances. In the case of item D, the net realizable value of $5.80 still remains above the acquisition cost of $5.20. It is anticipated that item D will be disposed of at a profit, albeit not a normal one. Many accountants question whether the utility of the inventory has fallen merely because an anticipated profit margin has shrunk. But even if we accept the viewpoint that unless the firm can sell at a normal profit it has suffered a loss, we notice that LCM in this instance does not achieve that objective, either. After being reduced to a replacement-cost value of $5, the inventory will be sold at a net selling price of $5.80 for a profit of only $0.80 per unit rather than a normal profit of $1. Only a write-down to net realizable value less normal profit ($4.80) would insure a subsequent disposition at normal profit.

In the case of item E, the firm obviously does incur a loss upon disposition. Application of LCM results in a reduction of inventory to the replacement cost of $8. A loss of $0.60 per unit ($8.60 AC less $8 RC) is recognized in the current period, and a profit of $0.30 per unit ($8.30 NRV less the decreased inventory value of $8) will be recorded in the following period. In this case, LCM does not write the inventory down sufficiently far to allow for a normal profit, nor does it accurately reflect the actual loss in item E. The loss in total is only $0.30 per unit ($8.30 NRV less $8.60 AC). The $0.30-per-unit profit in the subsequent period is below the "normal profit" of $0.50, by virtue of the fact that the goods have been written down only to $8 rather than to the net realizable value less normal profit of $7.80.

Summary of LCM

Lower of cost or market departs from a strict matching of original acquisition cost against revenues. It records losses, often hypothetical losses (in the conventional sense), on units which have not been sold. In so doing, it employs different concepts of cost and of income from those which normally underlie financial accounting. The introduction of these concepts, of course, is not unique to LCM, nor does their use necessarily imply a poor procedure. Actually, the real difficulty with LCM is that it adheres to no consistent concept of income. No fewer than three alternative concepts of inventory value in addition to cost—replacement cost, net realizable value, and net realizable value less normal profit—find their way into this procedure, none of them consistently.[7]

The method basically uses replacement costs, which would imply a current-cost approach to income. However, replacement cost is not used if it is above cost or below net realizable value less normal profit. Thus, concepts of current cost and disposable income evidently do not provide the framework for LCM. The method also implies that part of an asset has expired if its original cost cannot be recovered. This argument, which also has some validity, would result in a write-down to recoverable value (net realizable value). However, LCM often goes further and reduces the inventory below net realizable value. Here enters the third concept. The avowed purpose for a write-down below net realizable value is to allow for disposition at a normal profit later. This procedure introduces a concept of loss that falls outside of either conventional accounting or economics. Moreover, LCM may not uniformly achieve that objective either, for whenever replacement cost is above net realizable value less normal profit the former is used.

Despite its inconsistencies and imprecision, lower of cost or market continues to be the most commonly used basis of valuation for inventories. It may be that in many cases where LCM is used, the inventory still is recorded at cost, because it is normally lower than the applicable market figure. Unfortunately, the external reader usually does not know the extent of the write-downs, if any. By burying any inventory loss that does exist in cost of goods sold, most firms provide little or no help to the reader in interpreting what impact LCM has had on the financial statements.

SUGGESTIONS FOR FURTHER READING

American Accounting Association, Committee on Concepts and Standards—Inventory Measurement. "A Discussion of Various Approaches to Inventory Measurement," Supplementary Statement No. 2, *Accounting Review*, Vol. 39 (July 1964), pp. 700–714.

Johnson, Charles E. "Inventory Valuation: The Accountant's Achilles Heel," *Accounting Review*, Vol. 29 (January 1954), pp. 15–26.

---

[7] The empirical evidence that exists suggests tha_ when market figures are applicable, replacement cost and net realizable value are employed with almost equal frequency.

McAnly, H. T. "The Case for Lifo: It Realistically States Income and Is Applicable to Any Industry," *Journal of Accountancy*, Vol. 95 (June 1953), pp. 691–700.

Moonitz, Maurice. "The Case Against Lifo as an Inventory-Pricing Formula," *Journal of Accountancy*, Vol. 95 (June 1953), pp. 682–90.

Staubus, George J. "Testing Inventory Accounting," *Accounting Review*, Vol. 43 (July 1968), pp. 413–24.

QUESTIONS AND PROBLEMS

8–1.   The M. I. Stake Company discovered the following errors in the costing of its merchandise inventory:

Dec. 31, 1968...................... $2,600 overstatement
Dec. 31, 1969...................... 3,800 understatement
Dec. 31, 1970...................... 4,100 understatement
Dec. 31, 1971...................... 2,400 overstatement

The reported net income for 1969, 1970 and 1971 was $8,900, $10,700 and $12,300, respectively. Each error was independent of the others, and none was detected or corrected (although they may be self-correcting).

a)   Prepare a schedule showing the determination of corrected net income for 1969, 1970, and 1971.

b)   Assume that adjusting entries have already been made on December 31, 1971, but that the books have not been closed. Prepare the journal entry to correct the books, based on your analysis in part (*a*).

8–2.   The Cardinal Company's purchases and sales of one of its products for the month of January are shown in the following tabulation. All sales were made at a price of $30 per unit:

	Purchases		
Date	Tag Number	Cost per Unit	Units Sold
Jan. 1..............	530	$21	
4..............	589	22	
5..............	598	23	
7..............			No. 589
9..............	609, 610	25	
12..............			Nos. 598,610
13..............	618	26	
14..............	625	25	
17..............			Nos. 609, 625
19..............	631, 632	24	
22..............	643	25	
26..............	657	26	
27..............	660	28	
30..............			Nos. 632, 643, 657

In order to evaluate the effect of alternative inventory costing methods, management asked April Showers, the bookkeeper, to prepare a summary schedule of gross margins under various alternatives. Unfortunately April neglected to label her results.

	(1)	(2)	(3)	(4)	(5)
Sales...............	$240	$240	$240	$240	$240
Cost of sales..........	203	195	196	191	193
Gross margin.........	$ 37	$ 45	$ 44	$ 49	$ 47

Identify the method of inventory costing—specific identification, fifo, average cost on a perpetual basis, average cost on a periodic basis, and lifo cost on a periodic basis—used for each of the above calculations.

8–3. The following information is made available to you concerning product GBA:

Units sold during 1971..............................	50
Units on hand, Dec. 31, 1971.......................	10
Unit cost in 1971....................................	$30
Unit selling price in 1971............................	$50
Direct unit selling cost in 1971......................	$10
Unit replacement cost, Dec. 31, 1971.................	$27
Expected unit selling price in 1972..................	$45
Expected direct unit selling cost in 1972..............	$12
Gross income margin as a percentage of sales..........	20%

a) Compare the cost of the ending inventory on December 31, 1971 with its market value as determined by (1) net realizable value and (2) replacement cost. Discuss the reasoning that underlies the use of each of these alternative concepts of market.

b) Prepare partial income statements for 1971 and 1972 showing gross income (sales less direct expenses and cost of goods sold), assuming that the ending inventory on hand on December 31, 1971 is valued at the lower of cost or market (replacement cost), and is sold during 1972 under the conditions anticipated.

c) What effect does the use of LCM have in the two years? Can you think of a better way to disclose the effect in 1971?

8–4. The president of the Willing-to-Change Corporation has asked you to assist in making a decision concerning inventory policy. Specifically, he is considering whether to use Lifo or Fifo. In order to evaluate the impact of each on income determination and inventory valuation, he asks you to prepare a schedule showing a comparison of the two methods. He provides you with the following historical information for the company for each quarter during the last three years.

Period	Purchases			Sales		
	Units	$/Unit	Total	Units	Price	Total
Year 1:						
Q–I	3,000	5.10	$15,300	1,000	$6.80	$ 6,800
Q–II	2,000	5.40	10,800	2,000	7.20	14,400
Q–III	1,000	6.00	6,000	2,000	8.00	16,000
Q–IV	2,000	6.30	12,600	1,000	8.40	8,400
Year 2:						
Q–I	4,000	6.60	26,400	2,000	8.80	17,600
Q–II	2,000	7.05	14,100	3,000	9.40	28,200
Q–III	1,000	7.20	7,200	2,000	9.60	19,200
Q–IV	2,000	6.90	13,800	3,000	9.20	27,600
Year 3:						
Q–I	2,000	6.30	12,600	3,000	8.40	25,200
Q–II	3,000	6.00	18,000	1,000	8.00	8,000
Q–III	1,000	5.40	5,400	1,000	7.20	7,200
Q–IV	1,000	5.10	5,100	2,000	6.80	13,600

a) Prepare two schedules following the general format used in Table 8–4 in the chapter. In the first, assume that the company uses a Fifo periodic method to cost its inventory at the end of each of the three years. In the second, assume that the company employs Lifo periodic.

b) Interpret your results for the president concerning the relative impact of the alternative methods. Particularly note the differences in years 1 and 3. Discuss the degree of fluctuation in income and the reasons therefor. Evaluate the accuracy and usefulness of the resulting figures.

8–5. The following selected paragraphs are reprinted by special permission from an article entitled "Worrisome Windfall for Steel" in the November 14, 1959 issue of *Business Week:*

Inventory depletion during strike means—by reverse twist of LIFO accounting—bookkeeping profits and a painful income tax bite for some companies, notably warehousers.

. . . .

These outfits have been caught in the backfire of a special mechanism for figuring up inventory costs on tax returns. It's known to accountants as LIFO, or last in, first out. Ironically, it's designed to slice the corporate tax bill in a time of rising prices.

Going into Reverse. To make the tax saving, you must have inventory left over at the yearend. The system, in fact, is based on the assumption that a company carries over from year to year a certain base stock. But when—as in the case of this year's steel strike—a strike lasts much longer than anyone expects and eats up inventories, there's a boomerang effect.

Steel warehousers, with nothing left on their shelves, are forced to dip into the LIFO stocks they've been building up for years on their balance sheets. This means deducting from gross revenue inventory costs based on purchases ten or fifteen years ago. In some cases this will result in profits double or triple what would have been expected without LIFO.

"If we have to pay taxes on these profits," says one warehouser, "it will be close to catastrophic. Our working capital will be wiped out when we need it most to rebuild inventory."

What to Do? It's against this background that companies are casting around for a way out of their fix. According to the big accounting firm of Arthur Andersen & Co., which has been studying the problem, there are three ways steel companies could avoid these taxes:

Switch their tax year to end in September, when steel inventories were still fairly high. There are several hitches, however. Internal Revenue Service must be notified within two-and-a-half months after the proposed closing date—that means a November 15 deadline for switching back to September 1. A company can make such a switch only once in ten years. And if it's done obviously to avoid taxes, IRS may say "No."

Buy up inventory like mad in the next month-and-a-half—or merge with a company using LIFO that still has inventory on hand.

Get Congress to exempt from taxation the windfall profits resulting from involuntary liquidation of LIFO inventories. There's considerable precedent for this in special relief passed during World War II and Korea. Rep. Noah Mason (R., Ill.) has introduced a bill that would give steel warehousers the help they want, but Treasury officials say they haven't yet formed an opinion about it.

. . . .

a) Prepare a short numerical example to illustrate the problem being discussed in this article.

b) Can you design a method of reporting this situation on the general financial statements which will make clear to the reader what has happened?

c) Some accountants have advocated that the liquidation of inventory quantities be priced at current replacement costs with a credit to a type of liability account for the excess cost of replacing the liquidated inventory. Evaluate this suggested modification to Lifo from the standpoint of financial accounting.

d) Comment on the suggestions made in the article for coping with this problem.

e) Based on your general knowledge of Lifo and the situation presented in the article, when and under what conditions would you recommend that a company adopt Lifo?

8–6.   The following information is taken from the accounts and other records of the Slowdrain Department Store, Inc.:

	Cost	Retail
Beginning inventory	$ 12,000	$ 20,000
Purchases	105,000	175,000
Freight-in	6,000	
Purchase returns	3,000	5,000
Sales		173,000
Sales returns		8,000

a) Use the retail inventory method to compute an ending inventory figure which approximates cost.

b) Discuss carefully the assumptions inherent in your calculation in part (*a*) and their validity.

8–7. Koehring Company presented its inventories as follows in its 1969 annual report (in thousands):

	1969	1968
Inventories:		
At current cost (approximates first-in, first-out method)	$101,270	$ 87,222
Less allowance to reduce domestic inventories to cost (last-in, first-out method)	(19,029	(15,377)
	$ 82,241	$ 71,845

Net earnings reported for the year ended December 31, 1969 were $8,120,000. An extensive note explains the company's inventory policy:

As of December 1, 1956, the Company changed from the first-in, first-out (Fifo) method to the last-in, first-out (Lifo) method for determining the cost of domestic inventories for income tax and financial reporting purposes. The effect of this change to the Lifo method has been to charge higher costs to cost of products sold while deferring relatively lower costs in inventories, thereby reducing earnings and inventories both for financial reporting and income tax purposes. Therefore, had the Lifo method not been adopted:

1. The reported net earnings for 1969 . . . would have been higher by $1,680,000 . . .
2. Inventories as of November 30, 1969 would have been $19,029,000 greater;
3. Earnings retained in business at November 30, 1969 would have been increased by approximately $9,380,000; and
4. Additional federal income taxes of approximately $9,650,000 would have been paid or accrued from 1957–1969, inclusive.

a) What type of account is the "allowance to reduce domestic inventories to cost?" What account was debited when the allowance was credited in 1969?

b) Why does the company claim that current cost approximates the first-in, first-out method? What conditions must exist for this statement to be true?

c) Assume that the income tax rate for 1969 was 54 percent. Demonstrate how Koehring arrived at the conclusion that reported net earnings would have been higher by $1,680,000 if Lifo had not been used.

d) Why is not the increase in retained earnings that would occur equal to the increase in inventory value that would occur?

e) Evaluate the usefulness of this reporting procedure.

8–8.   O. B. Solete Corporation values its inventory at average cost. It reported a $10,000 net income for 1971 and a $12,000 net *loss* for 1972. Inventory data at average cost and at replacement cost as of the end of selected years are as follows:

	Cost	Market
1969	$30,000	$28,000
1970	44,000	41,000
1971	38,000	21,000
1972	20,000	22,000

Recompute the net income (or net loss) for 1971 and 1972, assuming that cost or market, whichever is lower, had been used to value the company's inventory at the end of each of the four listed years.

8–9.   "The last-in, first-out procedure for determining inventory cost may be said to represent a technique for coping with the impact of changing prices and inflation on the financial statements without departing from the strict original dollar cost basis."

a) Explain the basis for this quotation.

b) Does Lifo cope equally well with changing prices *and* inflation?

c) In what ways does Lifo *fail* to cope with the problem of changing prices? With the problem of inflation?

8–10.   The books of the Talent Corporation are closed monthly. The purchases and sales for the months of January and February are given below:

Date	Purchases Units	Purchases Cost	Unit Sales
Jan. 1	5,000	$ 7	
7			2,000
10			1,000
15	7,000	8	
20			5,000
30	3,000	8	
31			4,000
Feb. 10	2,000	9	
11			4,000
15	1,000	9	
25			1,500
27	500	10	

The replacement costs are $6 and $10.50 on January 31 and February 28, respectively.

a) Compute inventory as of *January 31*, using the following inventory costing procedures: (1) Fifo periodic, (2) Lifo periodic, (3) Fifo perpetual, (4) Lifo perpetual, and (5) average cost periodic.

b) Assuming that the same method is used during both months, compute cost of goods sold for the month of February, using (1) Fifo periodic and (2) Lifo periodic. In light of the price trends during February, do you see any apparent inconsistency in the results of items 1 and 2? Explain.

c) Compute the inventory as of January 31 and as of February 28, using the lower of Fifo cost or market.

8-11. The annual report for Gimbel Brothers, Inc., contained the following Statement of Consolidated Earned Surplus and explanatory note:

Comparative Consolidated Earned Surplus

	Fiscal year Ended January 31	
	1969	1968
Balance at beginning of year:		
As previously reported.............	$112,450,087	$119,600,923
Adjustments (Note 1)...............	6,225,776	5,316,350
As restated....................	$118,675,863	$124,917,273
Net profit.........................	23,817,128	23,493,344
	$142,492,991	$148,410,617
Deduct dividends declared on common stock—$1 per share................	$ 8,495,644	$ 8,495,644
Deduct amount transferred to common stock in connection with two-for one stock split.........................	....	21,239,110
	$ 8,495,644	$ 29,734,754
Balance at end of year............	$133,997,347	$118,675,863

Notes to Financial Statements, Year Ended January 31, 1969:
Note 1: Merchandise inventories are generally stated at FIFO (first-in, first-out) cost as determined under the retail inventory method.
As explained in the report for the year ended January 31, 1948, the LIFO (last-in, first-out) cost method was claimed by Gimbel Brothers, Inc. and its subsidiaries for all years commencing with the fiscal year ended January 31, 1942 and financial statements since that date had been prepared on the basis of stating merchandise inventories at LIFO cost as determined under the retail inventory method. As a result of an unfavorable decision in December 1968 in the court case concerning the Company's assertion of its right to use the LIFO method for the year ended January 31, 1943 and subsequent years (for tax purposes), the Company has decided to retroactively adopt the FIFO method for financial reporting purposes.
Accordingly, the financial statements at January 31, 1968 and for the year then ended have been restated as follows (000's omitted):

	Originally Reported	Increased (Decreased)	Restated
Balance Sheet:			
Merchandise inventories....	$ 76,767	$14,912	$ 91,679
Overpayment of Federal taxes claimed.................	5,960	(5,960)	—0—

```
Federal income taxes—
  deferred and prior
  years...................    12,550      2,726     15,276
Earned surplus.............   112,450      6,226    118,676
Profit Statement:
  Cost of goods sold.........  547,519     (1,816)   545,703
  Profit before provision for
    income taxes.............   45,639      1,816     47,455
  Income taxes...............   23,055        907     23,962
  Net profit.................   22,584        909     23,493
```

a) Explain why the change from Lifo to Fifo caused Merchandise inventories, Earned Surplus, and Cost of Goods Sold to change as they did.

b) In the schedule contained in Note 1, earned surplus is increased $6,226,000 in 1968. Yet the statement of comparative consolidated earned surplus for 1968 shows only a $5,316,350 adjustment. How do you account for this difference?

c) Should the adjustment have been handled as a prior-period adjustment or as an extraordinary item on the income statement? Discuss.

d) Comment on the company's reasons for the change. What does it suggest about Gimbel's original reasons for adopting Lifo?

8–12. Mammoth Market was a retail establishment selling a variety of products. On March 18, 1972, a fire occurred which destroyed two thirds of its inventory and damaged the rest. Since the firm took a periodic inventory only once a year, it had no perpetual inventory records to determine the amount of the loss.

The company's inventory on January 1, 1972, cost $18,000 and was priced to sell at $22,000. From January to the date of the fire, the firm had purchased goods costing $40,000, returned goods costing $2,000, and paid freight and handling costs of $4,000. The retail price set on the purchased merchandise (net of returns) was $50,000. Sales from January 1 to March 18 were $27,500 on account and $20,000 for cash; sales returns amounted to $2,500.

The one third of the inventory that was only damaged by the fire had an estimated net realizable value of $3,000 and was held for a special sale.

a) Estimate the amount of the inventory loss from the fire.

b) How would you show the inventory on a position statement prepared after the fire?

8–13. Hot Ice Jewelry Wholesalers reported net income before taxes as follows: for the year 1970, $68,600; for the year 1971, $73,400; and for the year 1972, $74,800. In making an audit for the first time, the CPA detects the following errors in his review of these three years:

1. Merchandise costing $5,700 was sold in December, 1970. However, the customer asked the company to temporarily hold the merchandise for him. The company did not segregate the merchandise;

hence, it was incorrectly included in the physical inventory on December 31, 1970.

2. In counting the December 31, 1970 inventory, one lot costing $3,600 was included twice.

3. Merchandise costing $5,100 was received late in 1970 and was properly included in the ending inventory. However, the supplier did not send an invoice until January, 1971. Hence, it was recorded as a purchase in 1971.

4. The inventory taken on December 31, 1971 was understated by $4,200, the amount of some merchandise that inadvertently was omitted from the physical count.

5. During 1971 some merchandise costing $6,000 was shipped on approval to a customer. It was not included in the 1971 ending inventory. The customer did not definitely agree to keep it until February, 1972, at which time it was properly recorded as a sale.

6. In taking the ending inventory on December 31, 1972, the inventory clerk erroneously listed merchandise at $4,100. It had actually cost only $1,400.

  a) Prepare an orderly determination of the correct net income before taxes for each year.

  b) What accounts in the position statement at the end of each year were misstated? By how much?

  c) Prepare the journal entry to correct the accounts as of December 31, 1972. Assume that none of the errors had been discovered previously and that the accounts for 1972 have not yet been formally closed.

8–14. Payless Company is considering the adoption of the Lifo inventory method as a way of cutting taxes. Below are the purchases and sales by quarter for 1970 and 1971.

	Purchases		Units
Period	Units	Cost/Unit	Sold
Beginning inventory, 1–1–70	3,000	$2.00	
1970: I	2,000	2.20	3,000
II	3,000	2.30	3,000
III	1,000	2.40	1,000
IV	2,000	2.50	1,000
1971: I	2,000	2.70	2,000
II	3,000	2.70	2,000
III	2,000	2.80	3,000
IV	3,000	3.00	4,000

  a) Determine cost of goods sold and ending inventory for the years 1970 and 1971 assuming the company uses (1) Fifo periodic inventory and (2) Lifo periodic inventory.

b) If the corporate income tax rate is 40 percent, how much tax "savings" did the firm receive from Lifo?

c) Compute cost of goods sold for 1970 and for 1971 at current cost (defined as the current purchase price during the quarter the items were sold). How much price gain or loss (holding gain or loss) is included in income each year under each of the other methods (Fifo and Lifo)?

d) Verify in detail the price (holding) gain for Fifo in 1970 that you calculated in (c). Did Lifo completely eliminate the price gain in 1970? Why not?

e) "The real test of the popularity of Lifo will come when and if we experience an extended period of declining prices." Describe the general effects on the financial statements from using Lifo during a period of declining prices. Why would these effects provide a real test for Lifo?

8–A–1. You are the chief accountant for Quam Corporation. Your assistant has gathered information about items in the ending inventory. You are to determine the proper dollar amount for each item and the total ending inventory in accordance with the lower-of-cost-or-market procedure, as interpreted by the American Institute of Certified Public Accountants.

Item	Units	Original Cost	Replacement Cost	Estimated Selling Price	Estimated Cost to Sell	Normal Profit
A	200	$ 6.00	$ 5.00	$ 7.00	$0.70	$1.20
B	500	13.80	13.00	18.00	1.40	2.70
C	1,000	3.50	2.40	3.60	0.40	0.70
D	30	3.90	3.50	5.00	0.40	0.75
E	90	10.00	10.00	12.50	1.00	2.00
F	150	0.90	1.00	1.30	0.10	0.20
G	400	8.60	8.50	10.50	0.85	1.70

8–A–2. Poorland Company uses the average cost method to assign dollar amounts to cost of goods sold and to ending inventory. Its income statement for 1972 appears below.

```
Sales (100,000 units @ $0.90)................          $90,000
Cost of goods sold:
  Beginning inventory.......................  $12,800
  Purchases.................................   72,400
  Goods available for sale
    (120,000 @ $0.71).......................  $85,200
  Ending inventory (20,000 @ $0.71)..........   14,200
    Cost of goods sold (100,000 @ $0.71).....           71,000
Gross margin................................          $19,000
Selling expenses (100,000 @ $0.10)..........           10,000
Net income (10% of sales revenue)...........          $ 9,000
```

For each of the three situations described below, analyze the effect of lower of cost or market. Include in your analysis a calculation of the dollar impact on net income this period and next period if market is defined as replacement cost or if market is defined as net realizable value. Discuss the reasonableness of using each of these definitions in the particular situation. Indicate how the AICPA rule would apply to each situation and why.

a) On December 31, 1972, the replacement cost of a unit of inventory is $0.67 and the selling price is only $0.78. Selling expenses will increase to $0.13 per unit.

b) On December 31, 1972, the replacement cost of a unit of inventory is $0.55 and the selling price is only $0.78. Selling expense remains at $0.10 per unit.

c) On December 31, 1972, the replacement cost of a unit of inventory is $0.65 and the selling price is expected to be only $0.85. Selling expense will increase to $0.13 per unit.

CHAPTER NINE

ACCOUNTING FOR NONCURRENT ASSETS

CHAPTER SEVEN sets forth the basic determinants of the cost of various long-lived assets. This chapter shows how these costs are treated during the accounting periods following their incurrence. In so doing, we focus on two areas: (1) methods of allocating the cost among various accounting periods to reflect the use of the long-lived asset, and (2) entries made upon disposition of a noncurrent asset. Also analyzed is the treatment of expenditures subsequent to the asset's acquisition associated with repairing, partially replacing, or improving plant assets; these subjects are discussed under the heading "Other Asset Modifications."

DEPRECIATION, DEPLETION, AND AMORTIZATION

Depreciation, depletion, and amortization in many respects can be discussed together, for they relate to the same accounting process. Each term refers to the estimation of the consumed cost of a long-lived asset, corresponding to the cost of the services of that asset used during the period. Every productive resource acquired represents a bundle of services or service capacity to be used over time. Some are consumed rapidly; others last a long time. But for most the service life is limited. Consequently, it becomes necessary to allocate the cost of an asset to the accounting periods in which it is used. "Depreciation" is the name given to the process of allocating the cost of plant assets over their useful service lives. "Depletion" and "amortization" are the names given to the cost allocation process applied to natural resources (wasting assets) and intangibles, respectively.

Of course, only those noncurrent assets which in fact have a limited service life are subject to these processes. Land, for example, is usually not considered to be depreciable; its use value is assumed to remain indefinitely. Certain intangible assets—such as organization costs, stock issue costs, and trademarks—also have a perpetual service life. In this chapter we concentrate our attention only on those noncurrent assets with finite service lives.

Depreciation is a process of cost allocation reflecting the expiration of asset services, *not* a measure of the decline in market value of the asset. Nor is it a process of generating funds to replace a particular asset. By matching depreciation expense against revenues, we attempt to recover the original monetary investments in noncurrent assets made in the past. If revenues are sufficient to cover all expenses, dollar capital will be recovered. Nonetheless, revenues, not depreciation, are the source of the asset inflow. Furthermore, the depreciation process is not contingent on whether past investment is recovered or whether any of the recovered capital is used for replacement.

Depreciation Base

The depreciation base (depletion base, amortization base) is the asset cost to be allocated to the various periods in which the asset provides service. In most cases, it is defined as follows:

Depreciation base = Acquisition cost   − Net salvage value
Cost of using asset = Original investment   Portion of cost recovered at
                      to be recovered   end of asset's useful life

Net salvage value is the estimated disposal value at the end of the asset's useful life, less estimated costs of removal. For natural resources, such as oil wells or mines, the net salvage value consists of the estimated value of the residual land. For some assets, such as trucks or certain types of equipment, a substantial amount is recovered when the asset is retired. In other cases the assumption is frequently made that scrap value will be offset by the removal costs, so that estimated net salvage value is zero; the acquisition cost then becomes the depreciation base.[1]

Major Problems in Determining Depreciation

In establishing a procedure for allocating the cost of noncurrent assets, accountants encounter two problems. One involves estimating the useful service life of the asset; the second, determining a proper way to spread the depreciation base over this service life.

---

[1] Under current regulations, salvage value up to 10 percent of the cost of an asset may be ignored in computing the depreciation base for income tax purposes.

The useful life of the asset is its period of service to the particular business entity, not necessarily its total conceivable life. Our entity concept restricts the determination of useful life to that period of service relevant to the business entity. Even here, however, two factors affecting an asset's useful life have to be considered:

1. Physical limitations on life:
   a) Intensity of use.
   b) Action of elements.
   c) Adequacy of maintenance.
   d) Simple passing of time, as with legal rights protected by law for a limited period.
2. Economic limitations on life:
   a) Technological development or shifts in demand for the product rendering the asset obsolete.
   b) Business growth or expansion for which the asset is inadequate.

The useful life of a particular asset is governed by the shortest life derived from a consideration of these factors. Each asset may be affected differently. For a natural resource, useful life is probably most often determined by physical considerations—namely, intensity of use. At the same time, however, situations calling for alternative treatment can readily be imagined. For example, the useful life of the mine may be determined by obsolescence (it becomes uneconomical to continue operations) rather than by physical exhaustion. On the other hand, the life of a building is primarily determined by action of the elements, although in some cases obsolescence or inadequacy may be relevant. The legal life of a patent is 17 years, although economically its service potential may be exhausted much earlier because of technological change.

The point of this discussion is that a determination of useful life requires a careful consideration of a number of factors. Even with a careful appraisal of all these factors, establishing an accurate useful life is still a difficult task. Consequently, many firms employ the "guideline lives" established by the Internal Revenue Service for tax purposes as reasonable approximations of the lives of various plant assets for financial accounting purposes also.

The second problem then arises. How should the cost of using the asset be allocated to the accounting periods contained in its useful life? Should each accounting period receive the same dollar charge, or should depreciation, depletion, or amortization cost be greater in some periods than in others? The overriding consideration in selecting a depreciation method for financial accounting purposes is that it should result in a pattern of cost allocation that reasonably reflects the expiration pattern of the related services. Cost should be allocated among the periods of use in ratio to the net service values consumed in the various periods. Although this ratio may be difficult to determine precisely, a definite policy should be established and followed consistently over the life of the asset. The next section discusses some systematic allocation methods commonly encountered.

Depreciation Methods

The term "depreciation methods" is used here in a very general sense, inasmuch as the methods described may be applicable to various noncurrent assets. They are most often mentioned in connection with plant assets, but our discussion applies to wasting assets and intangibles as well.

There are four major methods of spreading the depreciation base. These methods account for almost all of the depreciation policies used in accounting practice and can be classified in terms of the type of periodic charge that results from their use:

1. Uniform charge per period—straight-line method.
2. Decreasing charge per period:
   a) Sum-of-the-years'-digits method.
   b) Double-declining-balance method.
3. Varying charge per period—activity method.

Let us use the following situation to illustrate and compare the various depreciation methods. Assume that a machine has a total acquisition cost of $10,000 and an expected net salvage value of $1,000 at the end of a useful life of five years.

Straight Line Method. This method is the simplest and easiest to understand and compute. The depreciation base is spread evenly over the number of accounting periods in the asset's useful life. Each accounting period receives the same dollar charge for asset services consumed. For our example the annual depreciation charge would be determined by the formula:

$$\frac{\text{Cost} - \text{net salvage}}{\text{Useful life}} = \frac{\$10,000 - \$1,000}{5} = \$1,800$$

Table 9–1 summarizes the changes in the account.

TABLE 9–1

Year	Annual Depreciation Cost	Balance in Accumulated Depreciation Account	Undepreciated Cost
0	...	...	$10,000
1	$1,800	$1,800	8,200
2	1,800	3,600	6,400
3	1,800	5,400	4,600
4	1,800	7,200	2,800
5	1,800	9,000	1,000

The undepreciated cost at the end of each year is determined by subtraction of the Accumulated Depreciation account from the original cost recorded in the Machinery account and is commonly called *book value*. It represents the cost of that portion of the asset's services which has not been used and charged to operations. At the end of the fifth year the asset's book value appears at $1,000, its expected net salvage value.

The straight-line method is widely used because of its simplicity in concept and calculation. As a method of approximating the cost of using an asset's services, however, it implies a number of limiting assumptions. It presupposes that the services of the asset are consumed uniformly over its useful life. In addition, there should be no impairment in the efficiency or quality of the service received from the asset as it becomes older—i.e., its contribution to revenue should not lessen over time. These assumptions may not be true for many types of machinery and equipment. Conceptually, the straight-line method would seem to be most accurate when mere passage of time is the most important element governing the expiration of the asset's service. It could be used when the asset supplies a service capacity for a limited period of time and the availability of the service is more important than the actual use of the service.

Decreasing-Charge Methods.   Until 1954, the straight-line method was used almost universally, because it was the only technique commonly allowed for tax purposes. In the Internal Revenue Code of 1954, two additional methods, both resulting in a decreasing depreciation charge over the life of an asset, were approved for general taxpayer use. One method —sum-of-the-years'-digits (SYD)—achieves a decreasing charge by applying a decreasing rate to a constant depreciation base. The other method —double-declining-balance (DDB)—applies a constant depreciation rate to a decreasing depreciation base. These two mathematical procedures have little justification in and of themselves, except that they are accepted, systematic ways of obtaining a decreasing charge.

The general rationale for a decreasing-charge depreciation method stems from the fact that many assets contribute more service in the earlier years of their life than in the later years. Often an asset becomes less actively used, so that the quantity of service received from it each period declines. Or the asset may become increasingly obsolete or inefficient, so that the quality of services each period is less. An increasing risk of obsolescence also may reduce the probability that future services will even reach fruition; hence, their value is less. Still another reason given for the use of accelerated depreciation methods is the fact that repairs, maintenance, and other operating costs tend to rise over the life of a plant asset. The *total cost* of an asset's service is viewed as consisting of all costs of the asset—the depreciation base, repairs, maintenance, reconditioning, etc. If the amount of service received each period is the same, the total cost should be relatively constant, but the depreciation portion should decline as the repair and maintenance portion rises. In summary, the effect of any or a combination of these factors is that the overall contribution to operations and ultimately to the production of revenues lessens as many assets grow older. Inasmuch as depreciation attempts to measure the consumption of asset services, in these cases we ought to charge more depreciation in the earlier years of life.

Sum-of-the-Years'-Digits. This method starts by summing the digits in the expected useful life of the asset.[2] If the expected service life is six years, the sum is 21 $(6 + 5 + 4 + 3 + 2 + 1)$. The depreciation base of the asset is viewed as representing a number of service units adding up to this sum. These service units are assumed to expire in an order determined by the fractions N/SYD, $(N - 1)/SYD$, $(N - 2)/SYD$, . . . $1/SYD$. Applying this method to our example gives the results summarized in Table 9–2. The depreciation base still is $9,000 (cost less salvage). Since the useful life is assumed to be five years, the sum of the years' digits equals 15.

The total depreciation charge of $9,000 over the asset's life is the same as with the straight-line method. However, through a decreasing depreciation rate each year, more cost has been allocated to the earlier years of life in a systematic manner.

TABLE 9–2

Year	Depreciation Rate	Annual Depreciation Cost	Balance in Accumulated Depreciation	Book Value
0	. . .	. . .	. . .	$10,000
1	5/15	$3,000	$3,000	7,000
2	4/15	2,400	5,400	4,600
3	3/15	1,800	7,200	2,800
4	2/15	1,200	8,400	1,600
5	1/15	600	9,000	1,000

Double-Declining-Balance. With this method we apply a constant depreciation rate each year to a decreasing base. We determine the constant rate by doubling the straight-line rate. For our example, the straight-line rate is 20 percent (five-year life); double-declining-balance would use a rate of 40 percent for this asset. The depreciation base under this expedient is *book value* (cost less accumulated depreciation). The double-declining-balance method gives a larger first-year depreciation charge and is used in practice a little more frequently than the sum-of-the-years'-

---

[2] A general shortcut in computing this sum for any asset is expressed by the formula:

$$SYD = N(N + 1)/2$$

digits. It gives the results shown in Table 9–3 (amounts are rounded to the nearest dollar).

Two facts concerning double-declining-balance should be noted. First, the depreciation base ignores any consideration of salvage value. Logically, it would not seem appropriate for assets having a large expected net salvage value. Secondly, the method does not reduce the net asset to expected salvage.[3] For instance, in Table 9–3, we have actually depreciated the machine below its net salvage. Assuming that the net salvage figure is accurate, depreciation in the last year should be adjusted to only $296, the amount necessary to reduce the net asset to $1,000. For tax purposes, a firm may switch from the double-declining-balance method to the straight-line procedure at any time. Often this is done in accounting practice as well, to eliminate a need for adjustment in the last year of life.

TABLE 9–3

Year	Depreciation Base or Book Value	Depreciation Rate	Annual Depreciation Cost	Balance in Accumulated Depreciation
1	$10,000	40%	$4,000	$4,000
2	6,000	40	2,400	6,400
3	3,600	40	1,440	7,840
4	2,160	40	864	8,704
5	1,296	40	518	9,222

Activity Method. This particular expedient takes a somewhat different approach. Instead of viewing depreciation initially as an allocation of cost to *time* periods, the activity method relates the cost first directly to some unit of asset service and then to periods of time. The asset's useful life is expressed in terms of service units, and the depreciation rate is expressed in dollars per service unit. Then the depreciation charge *per period* fluctuates with the amount of activity of the asset.

Service units can be expressed in any number of ways—hours, units of production, units of output, or practically any other convenient and relevant measure of activity. Hence, this method also is labeled the working-hours method, the production method, the output method, etc. These terms all relate to the general objective of allocating cost in relation to asset activity.

---

[3] A formula is available which will give a declining-balance depreciation rate which takes salvage into consideration and reduces the asset to salvage at the end of its life. The formula for the rate, R, is:

$$R = 1 - \sqrt[N]{S/C}$$

where N is useful life, C is acquisition cost, and S is net salvage. This method is rarely used in practice; the rate used in most cases is twice the straight-line rate.

Take the machine which costs $10,000. Assume that during its useful life it is expected to run 30,000 hours. The depreciation rate would be

$$\frac{\text{Cost less salvage}}{\text{Expected activity}} = \frac{\$10,000 - \$1,000}{30,000 \text{ hours}} = \$0.30 \text{ per hour}$$

Here the useful life is viewed as 30,000 service hours rather than five years. If over the next five years the pattern of activity shown in Table 9–4 transpires, the relevant depreciation charge in each period will be as indicated in that table.

TABLE 9–4

Year	Hours Worked	Depreciation Rate	Annual Depreciation Cost	Balance in Accumulated Depreciation
1	7,700	$0.30/hr.	$2,310	$2,310
2	5,700	0.30/hr.	1,710	4,020
3	6,600	0.30/hr.	1,980	6,000
4	5,300	0.30/hr.	1,590	7,590
5	4,700	0.30/hr.	1,410	9,000
	30,000		$9,000	

Although not used as widely as the other methods, this procedure seems particularly appropriate when physical use is the most important determinant of the expiration of asset services. For example, airplane engines are commonly depreciated on a flying-hour basis. The cost of automobiles, trucks, or taxicabs can be allocated in relation to miles traveled during each period. Certain types of machinery where intensity of use is a major factor also lend themselves quite readily to this expedient. The method probably has wider applicability than is currently recognized.

The major problems associated with it tend to be practical ones—difficulty in estimating life in service units and the extra effort involved in keeping track of the actual activity in each period. Also, the activity method does not take into consideration declines in physical efficiency (loss of precision or production speed), although theoretically, they could be compensated for through a declining rate per service unit. In addition, if exclusive reliance is placed on the activity method in setting useful life, the economic factors of inadequacy and obsolescence may be ignored, even though they may limit an asset's life before its estimated life in *service units* has expired. However, if these other economic factors are used to establish the total life, then the activity method seems to give a very reasonable allocation of the depreciation base to the various accounting periods within the total life.

Depletion

The activity method is most widely used in the recording of depletion costs of natural resources. The cost allocation of a wasting asset bears a definite relationship to its exhaustion in physical terms. To illustrate its application here, assume that the total cost of acquiring and developing (exploration, drilling, etc.) a natural gas well is $3.8 million. Geologists estimate that the well contains 100 million cubic feet of natural gas. The residual value of the land is expected to be $300,000. The depletion rate would be $0.035 per cubic foot:

$$\frac{\text{Cost less residual value}}{\text{Estimated production}} = \frac{\$3,800,000 - \$300,000}{100,000,000 \text{ cubic feet}} = \$0.035 \text{ per cu. ft.}$$

Each year the depletion cost would vary with the amount of gas pumped. If during the first year, for instance, two million cubic feet were pumped out, the entry to record depletion would be:[4]

```
Depletion Cost.......................... 70,000
    Accumulated Depletion—Gas Well
    (2,000,000 × $0.035)................          70,000
```

Two questions can be raised concerning this practice. First, the implication that each unit of output should have the same depletion cost may not be realistic where differing qualities of output may be recovered— e.g., high-grade and low-grade ore—or where some units are easier and less costly to mine—e.g., ore in veins close to the surface. The second difficulty is the practical one of estimating the recoverable units contained in a natural resource. The original estimates are subject to great geological uncertainties, and the quantity of economically feasible production is a function of both future market conditions and technological changes. As a result, revisions in future estimated production ("recoverable reserves") and thus in the depletion rate are made periodically as additional knowledge becomes available.

Amortization of Intangibles

There are many types of intangible assets. Some appear to have an unlimited term of existence and life—e.g., trade names, subscription lists, perpetual franchises, and organization costs. Other intangibles provide service benefits only during a term of existence limited by law, regulation, agreement, or by their general nature. Examples include patents, copyrights, and limited franchises.

Estimating useful life for these assets is often a very difficult task. Few,

---

[4] For *tax* purposes, depletion is either (*a*) determined by the quantity of gas actually sold, as above, or (*b*) stated as a specified percentage of the gross income from the property, whichever amount is larger. The latter, of course, bears no relation to cost or to matching for financial accounting purposes.

if any, last forever. Yet neither does a specifically limited finite life apply to many of them. Legal and contractual factors may govern in such cases as licenses, franchise fees, or patents. But even here the factor of obsolescence may cut short the useful life well before the legal or contractual period expires. With other types of intangible costs, the estimate becomes even more perplexing. In fact, the lives of many intangibles are simply indeterminate.

The Accounting Principles Board proposed the establishment of somewhat arbitrary guidelines. Reasoning that the service potential of all intangible assets eventually disappears, the Board ruled that the cost of *all* intangible assets should be amortized over some estimate of useful life. The estimate might vary with the type of intangible, but in no case can the period be longer than 40 years.[5]

Straight-line amortization is almost universally employed with intangible assets. In fact, the APB requires it unless a company can demonstrate that some other method is more appropriate. Some intangibles may have a high degree of uncertainty surrounding their future service potential that might imply a decreasing charge for amortization. Or the amount of revenue directly attributable to the asset—e.g., royalties derived from a patent—may not be constant from period to period. Unfortunately, the accounting profession has not defined in more precise terms exactly what is meant by the future service potential of an asset. Does a patent contribute equal service each period because it provides the same legal protection, or does it contribute decreasing service each period because the sales of the patentable item decline over time? Until more definite guidelines are established, straight-line amortization probably will prevail, particularly since this is the only tax method allowed currently for intangibles.

Goodwill. One particularly thorny intangible is "purchased goodwill." Frequently in merger or acquisition transactions the price paid by the acquiring business for the total net assets (or outstanding stock) of the acquired firm exceeds the fair market value of the individual assets less the liabilities assumed. This excess is usually debited to an intangible asset called "excess cost applicable to acquired companies" (or some similar title) or simply "goodwill."

The account which receives the charge for "purchased goodwill" has been aptly described as a "master valuation" account. Theoretically, it should measure the value of the excess earning power of a firm over that of a "normal" business. Practically, it is the difference between the total value of a business entity, taken as a whole, and the sum of the fair market value of its tangible and its identifiable intangible assets. It is the combined value placed on the sources of future earning power which cannot

[5] *Intangible Assets, Opinion of the Accounting Principles Board No. 17* (New York: AICPA, August 1970), pp. 338–41.

be separately traced. It may include the value of a particular organization structure, past research and development efforts, trade names, secret processes, strategic locations, or simply a favorable attitude toward the firm on the part of employees, customers, or regulatory authorities. In any case, the acquiring firm invests in it in order to possess the income-producing power of the acquired firm.

Historically, little enthusiasm existed for periodic amortization of the goodwill amount. Amortization of goodwill is not deductible for tax purposes, on the ground that it is a permanent asset. This same line of reasoning carried over to financial accounting. If future earnings do not decline, it has been argued, goodwill must still exist. A variation of this view is that future expenditures on research and development, training, employee benefits, advertising, etc., will maintain the purchased goodwill. Since these charges normally will be treated as period expenses, double counting would be involved if companies also write off the original purchased goodwill to expense.

More recently, cogent arguments have been advanced in favor of periodic amortization. Viewed from the buyer's perspective, purchased goodwill represents a type of start-up cost. The businessman pays for certain economic factors which provide a transferable momentum to the new business. Payment for purchased momentum is an alternative to incurring costs necessary to have the tangible assets in place and in an environment already capable of producing normal or above-normal earnings. The payment for goodwill is the value of the excess earnings accruing to the new owner as a result of the momentum built up in a going concern. As these future earnings arise, for the new owner they are a *recovery of investment*, not income. Amortization of the purchased goodwill reflects the fact that the momentum which produced these earnings will not persist indefinitely. Logically the new owner would not pay more for this momentum than what he otherwise would have to give up in the way of promotional expenditures and lost profits to build the business from a fresh start. Consequently, the cost of the purchased momentum should be matched against the revenues it produces by means of periodic amortization over a relatively short period of time. Under APB *Opinion No. 17*, purchased goodwill must be amortized over a period not longer than 40 years.

Revision of Depreciation Accruals

The purpose in establishing a depreciation (depletion, amortization) policy is to allocate systematically the cost of using an asset over its service life. The alternatives of charging the asset to expense either in the year it is acquired or in the year it is retired are not as accurate or useful as a systematic allocation. Nevertheless, the periodic cost resulting from allocation policies is still an estimate based on certain judgments, not a precise measurement. These judgments involve three areas: (1) determining the useful life, (2) projecting the net salvage value, and (3) selecting the proper depreciation expedient. What happens if one or more of these estimates is found to be in error?

A policy, once adopted, should not be perpetuated if the basis for that policy is no longer valid. If the useful life has been overstated, the estimated salvage value overstated, or the straight-line method used when a decreasing-charge method should have been used, annual depreciation charges will be too low, and the Accumulated Depreciation account will have too small a credit balance. The understated depreciation expenses eventually are closed to Retained Earnings. Consequently, it will be overstated. On the other hand, if depreciation has been too high in the past, then Accumulated Depreciation will be overstated and Retained Earnings understated. In either case a correcting entry should be made for the difference between the depreciation actually charged and the revised amount based on the new estimates.

Numerical Example. Assume that a piece of equipment costing $90,000 is expected to have zero salvage at the end of a useful life of 15 years and that straight-line depreciation is appropriate. During the fifth year, before entries are made to record depreciation, the firm realizes that the equipment will last only 5 years more, for a total life of only 10 years rather than 15.

During the first four years annual depreciation of $6,000 is charged, and the balance in the Accumulated Depreciation account currently stands at $24,000. Based on the revised estimate of useful life, the depreciation cost should have been $9,000 each year, and the balance in Accumulated Depreciation should be $36,000 rather than $24,000. Retained Earnings is correspondingly overstated. Under APB *Opinion No. 9*, direct debits or credits should not be made to Retained Earnings for depreciation adjustments. Instead a special income statement account is set up. The following entries would be made at the end of the fifth year:

```
Extraordinary Charge: Correction of
    Depreciation.......................... 12,000
    Accumulated Depreciation.............          12,000
    To correct the accounts for inaccurate
    depreciation in prior years.

Depreciation Cost......................... 9,000
    Accumulated Depreciation.............           9,000
    To record depreciation for the fifth
    year based on revised estimates.
```

After these entries are posted, the Accumulated Depreciation account appears as follows:

Accumulated Depreciation

	6,000
	6,000
	6,000
	6,000
	12,000
	9,000

Its balance of $45,000 indicates that one half of the depreciation base has been charged to operations, which is the correct situation at the end of the fifth year. The Extraordinary Charge account appears as a special deduction on the current period's income statement.

The above approach to the problem of inaccurate depreciation estimates is to correct the accounts that are inaccurately stated and then record depreciation in future periods based on the revised information. Obviously, we are concerned only with material adjustments in the depreciation charge. Continuous revision for minor amounts would be unnecessarily time-consuming and would run the risk of destroying the concept of a systematic depreciation policy.

Compensating-Error Approach. An alternative procedure commonly used in accounting practice is to revise future depreciation rates to adjust for past errors. In the above example the book value or undepreciated cost is $66,000 ($90,000 − $24,000) at the end of the fourth year. Since there are six years of useful life remaining, the depreciation cost is revised to charge off the remaining amount over that time ($66,000 unrecovered depreciation base ÷ 6-year remaining useful life = $11,000 per year). By charging $11,000 of annual depreciation in the next six years, we shall fully depreciate the asset by the end of the revised useful life.

This approach, although commonly employed, seems unsound. The purpose of accounting reports is to communicate financial information as accurately as possible. This goal is not achieved by an excess depreciation charge in future years to compensate for a deficiency charged in the past, or vice versa. Under this procedure, none of the periodic income statements reflects an accurate depreciation charge. The ultimate example of this approach is a firm which continues to use fully depreciated assets for substantial periods of time. Because depreciation has been overstated in the past, no depreciation is charged in current periods, even though the asset continues to render service. This is contrary to the matching concept and to the concept of depreciation. The support for this compensating-error approach is found in its simplicity and in the fact that it is required for income-tax purposes. Nevertheless, in terms of a logical development of financial accounting, there is little justification for either continuing past errors or compensating for them in future accounting periods.

DISPOSITION OF NONCURRENT ASSETS

The second major problem to be discussed in this chapter involves the entries made when the business entity disposes of a noncurrent asset. Disposition may occur at or before the end of the asset's original useful life. The retirement may be made with or without the acquisition of a replacement. In all cases the basic elements of the retirement entry should be handled in the same way. The old asset is being disposed of, and this is the event on which we want to focus first. When the asset is retired, both the main account and the Accumulated Depreciation account must be closed. The asset, in essence, is reflected in two accounts; balances in both the asset and the contra asset must be removed.

Entries to Record Asset Retirement

The basic retirement process involves isolating the undepreciated cost of the asset plus other factors involved in determining the total gain or loss on retirement. For example, any costs of removing or dismantling the asset increase the potential loss on retirement. Conversely, the amount of any scrap, reusable material, salvage value, or insurance proceeds (in the case of a casualty loss) represents gain. The difference in all of these factors determines the net gain or loss.

Let us take the example in Table 9–2. Assume that at the end of the fourth year the machinery is retired. First, we must make sure that depreciation is recorded up to the date of retirement, that all charges for the *use* of the asset have been entered. If so, according to the depreciation schedule in Table 9–2, under sum-of-the-years'-digits, $8,400 has been allocated to the four years in which the machine has been used. The entry to isolate the book value of $1,600 would be:

```
Loss on Retirement of Machinery............  1,600
Accumulated Depreciation...................  8,400
    Machinery...............................           10,000
```

In addition, assume that the firm incurs $300 of wage cost for removal and sells the dismantled machinery for $800 cash. The following entries would be made:

```
Loss on Retirement of Machinery.................  300
    Wages Payable...............................        300

Cash............................................  800
    Loss on Retirement of Machinery.............        800
```

The loss account now has a balance of $1,100, which represents the net decrease in owners' equity associated with the disposition of the asset. If all information about the retirement is known at the same time, a single journal entry could be made.

The loss on retirement (or gain when salvage value exceeds book value plus removal costs) is reported in the period in which it is recognized. However, it may be caused either by an event in that period or by errors in prior periods. For instance, if the machine in our example is retired because of gradual obsolescence, then the original five-year estimate of life, as well as the estimated net salvage, is inaccurate. One could argue that the loss in the period of retirement results from inaccurate past depreciation which has never been revised. To this extent, the loss account is akin to a correction of retained earnings. However, since it does not qualify as a prior period adjustment under APB *Opinion No. 9*, we would report it on the income statement.

If the asset retirement is accompanied by a replacement purchase, we must be careful not to interpret the loss as part of the cost of the new asset. Two distinct transactions are occurring. The fact that the old asset has been retired to make way for the new one does not increase the service potential of the replacement asset. The loss, whether it be large or small, still is a measure of an asset that has disappeared without the firm's receiving full benefit from it. It should not be deferred as an expense of future periods by being buried in the acquisition cost of the new asset.

Exchange and Trade-Ins

An area where the separation of asset retirement from asset acquisition is difficult is the exchange or trade-in. Here, two explicit events are telescoped into one. There exist a simultaneous sale of an old asset and the purchase of a new one between the business entity and the same outside party. Under these circumstances, it is sometimes difficult to determine the real substance of the individual transactions.

Assume that on January 1, 1971 a delivery truck is purchased for $2,000. The truck is to be depreciated by the straight-line method over a useful life of four years, with no expected net salvage value. On June 30, 1972 the company decides to trade in the truck toward the purchase of a new one having a list price of $4,400. The dealer will allow an amount of $1,400 for the old truck; the company has to pay the $3,000 difference in cash. The old truck has a current market value of $1,000.

With this set of facts, three alternative entries actually might be made. However, first we would record a half year's depreciation for the six months' use in 1972:

```
Depreciation Expense..............................  250
    Accumulated Depreciation......................        250
```

Together with the $500 depreciation recorded for the year 1971, this entry brings the balance in the Accumulated Depreciation account to $750 and the book value of the truck to $1,250 ($2,000 − $750). The three

TABLE 9-5

	Alternatives					
	No. 1		No. 2		No. 3	
	Dr.	Cr.	Dr.	Cr.	Dr.	Cr.
Delivery Truck....	4,000		4,250		4,400	
Accumulated Depreciation....	750		750		750	
Loss on Retirement (Gain)....	250					150
Delivery Truck......		2,000		2,000		2,000
Cash.........		3,000		3,000		3,000

entries shown in Table 9-5 reflect alternative amounts assigned to the disposal value of the old asset and to the acquisition cost of the new one.

The first alternative is to be preferred. It recognizes the economic substance of the transactions—both in the disposition of the old truck and in the acquisition of the new. This method employs the current market price of the old truck as the best estimate of its value at the time of disposition. An estimate of current market value may be determined from activities in a secondhand market or from a study of independent opportunities to sell the old asset. If the old truck had been sold in a separate transaction, $1,000 would have been received and a loss of $250 (book value of $1,250 less $1,000) recorded. The simultaneous acquisition of another truck should not be allowed to becloud the basic transactions. Furthermore, the real cost of the new truck consists of the current values exchanged for it. In this case the company gives up $3,000 in cash plus an old truck currently worth $1,000. Cash plus fair market value of the trade-in would seem to be a better indicator of acquisition cost than list price. Indeed, in this type of situation the company probably could have purchased the new truck outright for cash at a figure very close to $4,000.

The second alternative recognizes no gain or loss on the disposition of the old truck, and the cost of the new truck is cash plus the *book value* of the trade-in. This approach fails to distinguish between the two separate transactions making up the exchange. Any errors in recording past depreciation, which normally would result in a gain or loss on disposition, become buried in the cost of the new truck. Clearly, this approach is unacceptable except as a last alternative, when there is *no* way of determining either the real cost of the new asset or the current value of the old. However, this method is required for tax purposes and unfortunately is frequently used on the books as well, as a matter of convenience.

The third alternative assumes that the trade-in allowance represents the current value of the old truck and that the list price indicates the acquisition cost of the new truck. In cases where this assumption is valid, the results are the same as those under the first alternative. On the other hand, adjustments to the initial list price are not uncommon in business. And when a simultaneous purchase and sale are tied together, as they are in an exchange, the trade-in allowance is often overstated to disguise a modified sales price. In our example there is valid evidence that this has occurred. The $150 "gain" on retirement actually has resulted from an overstatement of the new truck cost. A trade-in allowance should be accepted only when there is objective evidence that it approximates the value of the old asset.

OTHER ASSET MODIFICATIONS

Often an asset is modified as the result of expenditures made during its lifetime. These expenditures frequently involve an addition to the asset or partial replacement of it. Major overhauls are made, with old parts or components being replaced by new ones. These modifications represent expenditures that benefit future periods and therefore should be treated as assets. Yet they may not represent the acquisition of any new physical item. At the same time, portions of the old asset may be retired, although there may not be a complete replacement of one asset by another, as we have seen in previous examples.

Different terms describe these events—additions, improvements, betterments, renewals, and replacements. "Additions" normally refer to modifications that increase the physical size or capacity of the asset, such as an extension on a building or the installation of central air conditioning. "Improvements" and "betterments" apply to major modifications that increase the service to be received from the asset. For instance, a major overhaul may extend the useful life of a delivery truck or increase the speed or efficiency of a machine. Or the betterment may take the form of a new attachment which allows the equipment to perform a variety of tasks rather than only a single job. In each case the use value of the asset has changed, even though the physical change in the asset may not be great. Finally, the terms "renewals" and "replacements" generally are used to describe more minor modifications, often of a more or less recurring nature. The periodic replacement of tires on a truck, relining the inside of a chemical tank every three years, and the intermittent renewal of special filters in pumping equipment are examples. In accounting practice these terms are often employed interchangeably. They appear to differ primarily in the magnitude of the amounts involved and the importance of the modification, either in economic or in physical terms.

The accounting treatment accorded these modifications may vary a great deal among firms. The theoretical objectives and procedures are fairly clear. The extent to which these can be applied in practice, however, depends on two important practical factors: (1) the degree of detail used in recording noncurrent assets, and (2) the policy with respect to capitalization of subsequent expenditures.

Noncurrent Asset Records

As a general goal, accounting records for plant assets should be kept in as great detail as is feasible. Detailed asset records will facilitate more accurate estimates of depreciation. Assume, for example, that a firm acquires a large and complex piece of machinery and a group of attachments. The economic life of the machine is 12 years, while the attachments have to be replaced at the end of 3 years. Recording the expenditure in two separate asset accounts would allow the cost of the machine itself to be allocated over a 12-year period and the cost of the attachments over a 3-year period. On the other hand, combining the machinery and attachments as one asset would result in under depreciation of the attachments.

A second advantage, directly germane to our discussion of asset modifications, is that the use of detailed asset records helps in separating true maintenance cost from partial or entire replacement of an asset. Theoretically, maintenance means simply keeping the asset in good working condition but in no better condition than when it was purchased. It is the recurring cost to maintain the service initially expected from the asset. Therefore, what costs are classified as maintenance or repairs depend on how we classify assets. In the case above, if the attachments are part of the total cost of the machinery, then replacement of the attachments could be treated as repairs—costs necessary to maintain the asset service. Yet the benefit from this expenditure will certainly be received over more than one accounting period. If the degree of detail involved in asset records provides for the attachments to be set up as a separate asset, their replacement every three years is not a maintenance charge at all. It represents a retirement of one asset and the acquisition of a replacement.

Capital Expenditures versus Expense

A second practical consideration, closely related to the matter of records detail, is the distinction a firm makes between capital expenditures and expenses. The term capital expenditures refers to costs that are to be treated as assets, in contrast to work such as maintenance to be charged against operations for the period. In theory any expenditure which benefits future accounting periods should be capitalized. In practice there are limitations. Each nut or bolt or minor part cannot be set up as a separate asset. At some point, expenditures for repairs and replacements have to be treated as period costs. This point is determined by company policy.

Many firms differentiate capital expenditures from expenses in terms of physical units, called units of property. A depreciation unit is selected, and any subsequent modification short of the depreciation unit is handled as a periodic charge to operations. For example, trucking companies frequently classify truck chassis, tires, and engines as separate asset units. Telephone poles are an asset group for utility companies, as are the crossbars. The glass insulators attached to the crossbars are not. The replacement of a crossbar is a capital expenditure (asset replacement); costs of replacing the insulators are handled as repairs. Wastepaper baskets and pencils, although they might last more than one accounting period, are usually charged to expense, since for practical purposes they are not defined as property units. Typewriters, on the other hand, frequently are a property unit, and expenditures for them are capitalized.

Instead of establishing physical classifications, another way of making the distinction is in terms of dollar amount. Any expenditure over a pre-established amount, say $500, will be capitalized. Expenditures less than that are treated as period expenses. Or if the expenditure on an existing asset is greater than a certain percentage of the original cost, it will be treated as an asset replacement; otherwise, it is handled as a repair cost. What is feasible depends on the practical difficulties of record keeping and on the materiality of the amounts involved.

At the same time we should recognize that the policy regarding capital expenditures can have a significant influence on income measurement. Sound policies must be formulated and consistently followed to achieve an equitable allocation of the *total* cost of services of noncurrent assets. Repairs, replacements, etc., are an integral part of this total cost. Care must be taken to see that these costs are not unreasonably charged against the revenues of a single period to distort income, or treated as expenses one year but capitalized the next to manipulate income. Unless the expenditure is small or its future benefit is insignificant or unmeasurable, the presumption should be towards capitalizing the amount rather than expensing it.

Recording Major Modifications

Many additions and practically all improvements and betterments require some change in the old asset. The installation of a new air-conditioning system may require the removal of the old ducts. The enlargement of windows in the factory may necessitate the complete removal of the old windows and casements. Even most periodic replacements—rebricking the inside of a blast furnace, for example—involve the removal of part of the old asset.

Ideally, if the old asset is partially removed, that part should be retired and replaced with the new one. This involves removing the cost of the part of the old asset from the asset account, removing the accumulated depreciation on the portion displaced from the contra asset account, recognizing a loss or gain on retirement if necessary, and debiting the cost of the new portion to the asset account. In this way, future periods are not burdened by depreciation charges on costs no longer in existence but are charged only with those expenditures that benefit operations in the future.

Assume that a building having a useful life of 20 years is constructed at a total cost of $20,000. After 10 years the wood-shingle roof is replaced with a slate roof costing $3,000. A study of the original construction records reveals that $2,000 is an accurate estimate of the original cost of the wood-shingle roof. It would be erroneous simply to charge the $3,000 to the Building account without recognizing the underdepreciation on the old roof. The entries to record the partial replacement are:

```
Accumulated Depreciation....................  1,000
Loss on Retirement..........................  1,000
    Building................................          2,000
    To remove the shingle roof and its re-
    lated depreciation.

Building....................................  3,000
    Cash (or Accounts Payable).............          3,000
    To record replacement with new slate roof.
```

When these entries are posted, the Building account and its related contra will appear as follows:

Building		Accumulated Depreciation	
√20,000	2,000	1,000	√10,000
3,000			

The book value of the asset has increased to $12,000 ($21,000 − $9,000). This represents the cost which should be depreciated over the next 10 years (assuming the new roof does not increase the useful life of the building). Depreciation rates and amounts, of course, would be revised as a result of this major modification in the asset.

Perhaps a more accurate procedure initially would have been to record the various structural elements—roof, foundation, heating system, etc.—of the building as separate assets, with the roof being depreciated over 10 years rather than 20. If this had been done, the treatment of the new roof as a simple asset replacement would be obvious. The fact that this was not done, however, does not relieve the accountant of his responsibility to reflect as accurately as possible the exhaustion of the service potential of the old roof.

Minor renewals and replacements theoretically should be, and sometimes are, handled in exactly the same way as major ones. However, from a practical standpoint it may become extremely difficult and probably unnecessary to record each substitution of a minor part of an asset as a replacement. Consequently, in accounting practice minor modifications are often charged as repairs or maintenance cost. The dividing line between capitalizable costs and repair costs is largely dependent on the materiality of the amount and the detail in the asset records.

Charging Accumulated Depreciation

A hybrid treatment of replacements, improvements, and "extraordinary repairs" commonly found in accounting practice and sanctioned by income tax regulations is to debit the cost of the modification to the Accumulated Depreciation account. This approach recognizes that the particular expenditure should not be treated as a cost of the current period only. At the same time, it does not directly identify in the asset account the cost of the old asset (or portion thereof) removed from service and the cost of the new one added. If the cost of the new roof in our previous example had been handled this way, the entry would have been:

```
Accumulated Depreciation...................  3,000
    Accounts Payable.......................          3,000
```

This causes the book value of the asset to increase by $3,000, although the asset account itself remains unchanged. This procedure will leave net assets overstated by $1,000, the amount of the loss not recognized on retirement. Any gain or loss on the old component remains buried in the asset account, to be charged to a future period. In addition, this method ignores any difference between the cost of replacement and that of the original part. Consequently, the asset account does not reflect the original cost of the plant *actually in service*, nor does the Accumulated Depreciation account provide an indication of the portion of that original cost which has been charged to operations.

Costs which benefit future periods should be treated directly as assets rather than being brought in through the back door as in this procedure. In theory a clear-cut distinction between the retirement of a portion of the asset cost, with attendant entries to Accumulated Depreciation and Loss on Retirement, and the acquisition cost of a new service benefit is desirable, particularly for major modifications. Practically it often is difficult, if not impossible, to determine the amount of original cost to be written off against the Accumulated Depreciation account. When significant losses and gains are not involved, the impact of this expedient on book value is the same as that of the theoretical approach.

SUMMARY

This chapter concentrates on three major topics involving noncurrent assets—periodic use, disposition, and modifications due to subsequent expenditures. Each topic includes an exploration of major concepts, a presentation and analysis of alternative procedures, and a discussion of practical influences relevant to them. The interaction between the theoretical concepts and practical necessities of record keeping requires that accounting entities adopt policies to deal with each of the major problems:

1. Capitalization versus expensing at acquisition.
2. Estimates of useful life and salvage.
3. Choice of depreciation methods.
4. Distinction between repairs and replacements.
5. Treatment of trade-ins.

The accounting procedures and methods following from these policies have no effect on *total* noncurrent asset charges. Their important impact is on the *timing* of these charges and the form they take—depreciation, repairs, or losses (gains) on retirement.

The relative lack of precision in these policy areas does not mean, however, that "any old way" will suffice. Sound policy must be formulated, consistently followed until major evidence is accumulated to indicate that it needs modification, and adequately disclosed if the ultimate communication purpose of the financial statements is to be fulfilled. In recognition of the significant effects on financial position and income measurement from variations in these policies, the Accounting Principles Board stated that the following information should be disclosed in the financial statements or in the notes accompanying them:

1. Depreciation expense for the period.
2. Balances of major classes of depreciable assets at the balance sheet date.
3. Accumulated depreciation, either by major classes of depreciable assets or in total, at the balance sheet date.
4. A general description of the method or methods used in computing depreciation with respect to major classes of depreciable assets.[6]

APPENDIX 9-A
GROUP DEPRECIATION PROCEDURES

The depreciation methods described in Chapter Nine rest on the presumption that the cost of each asset is assigned individually to the accounting periods in which it is used. An estimate is made of each asset's expected useful life, and its individual cost (less salvage) is allocated in some reasonable manner over that period. If the asset is retired prior to the end of its useful life, an extraordinary gain or loss is recorded, equal to the difference between the remaining book value (as shown in a separate subsidiary

[6] *Omnibus Opinion—1967, Opinion of the Accounting Principles Board No. 12* (New York: AICPA, December 1967).

ledger account) and the amount received upon retirement. For many large, individual assets such a *unit* depreciation procedure is reasonable.

However, a firm's depreciable assets include numerous smaller items, often acquired in groups. Examples are the telephone poles of a utility company, the typewriters in a large office, tires acquired by a trucking company, and small tools used in a manufacturing concern. These expenditures benefit more than one accounting period and should be capitalized as assets subject to periodic depreciation. Yet treating each telephone pole, tire, typewriter, or tool as a separate asset causes two potential problems. The first is the almost insurmountable clerical chore involved in maintaining separate records for each individual item. Secondly, unit depreciation based on the *average* life of units in the group may distort periodic charges against revenues. With a large number of units one would expect a mortality dispersion within the group around the average life. Unit depreciation fails to reflect this typical and often predictable dispersion. Unit depreciation indicates gains and losses on units retired before the avearge life, even though some were expected to be retired. Likewise, it records no depreciation on units lasting longer than the average life, although, again, this is an expected occurrence.

Description of Group Depreciation

To overcome these two difficulties, many large firms employ group depreciation procedures. Although the method itself had been used for many years, income tax regulations passed in 1962 provided an increased impetus to the use of the group method. The tax procedures encouraged firms to classify their assets by fairly broad guideline classes. Calculating depreciation on some of these multiple-asset accounts involved a natural extension of group depreciation procedures. The chief characteristics of the group depreciation method are given below:

1. All units in a group are treated as a single asset, with the individual costs being combined in a summary account and with only a single contra asset or Accumulated Depreciation account applicable to the entire group.
2. A depreciation rate is based on the expected *average* life of the units in the group. The depreciation rate is applied to the asset balance each period to determine the depreciation charge.
3. No gain or loss is recognized upon retirement of an individual unit from the group. This is the key procedural difference from unit depreciation.

Illustration. A typing service company purchases 50 electric typewriters, each costing $300. They are to be depreciated as a group over an average useful life of four years, with an expected salvage value of $30 per unit. Table 9–A–1 shows the actual experience with the asset group.

TABLE 9–A–1

Year	Retirements at End of Year	Salvage per Typewriter
1.....................	4	$60
2.....................	8	50
3.....................	8	30
4.....................	11	30
5.....................	9	30
6.....................	5	20
7.....................	3	0
8.....................	2	0
	50	

The following journal entries illustrate the basic features of the group method.

1. To record acquistion of the asset:

```
Typewriters..........................  15,000
     Cash.................................                15,000
```

2. To record depreciation for first year:

```
Depreciation Expense—Typewriters.......  3,375
     Accumulated Depreciation—Type-
        writers.........................                 3,375
```

```
Cost......................................... $15,000
Salvage......................................   1,500
Depreciation base............................ $13,500
Annual depreciation ($13,500 ÷ 4)............ $ 3,375
Depreciation rate based on original cost ($3,375 ÷
   $15,000)..................................      22.5%
```

3. To record retirement of four units at end of first year:

```
Cash......................................... 240
Accumulated Depreciation—Typewriters..... 960
     Typewriters.........................                1,200
```

4. To record depreciation for second year:

```
Depreciation Expense—Typewriters.......  3,105
     Accumulated Depreciation—Type-
        writers.........................                 3,105
          22.5% × ($15,000 − $1,200)
```

5. To record retirement of eight units at end of second year:

```
Cash......................................... 400
Accumulated Depreciation—Typewriters... 2,000
     Typewriters.........................                2,400
```

Similar entries are made in each of the remaining six years. Depreciation expense calculated at 22.5 percent of the remaining gross asset balance each year is recorded as long as some asset units are still in service. No gain or loss is recognized on units retired; Accumulated Depreciation is debited for the difference between original cost and actual net salvage value. The reasoning behind this procedure is that under the group method these early retirements were expected. Consequently, more of the first year's depreciation expense of $3,375 applied to these units than to those units that were expected to last longer than average. Indeed, the group method assumes that sufficient depreciation has been charged applicable to each unit retired to reduce it to actual net salvage value.

Based on the information given in the problem, the ledger accounts for the asset and contra asset would appear as follows:

Typewriters				Accumulated Depreciation—Typewriters			
(1)	15,000	(1)	1,200	(1)	960	(1)	3,375
		(2)	2,400	(2)	2,000	(2)	3,105
		(3)	2,400	(3)	2,160	(3)	2,565
		(4)	3,300	(4)	2,970	(4)	2,025
		(5)	2,700	(5)	2,430	(5)	1,283
		(6)	1,500	(6)	1,400	(6)	675
		(7)	900	(7)	900	(7)	337
		(8)	600	(8)	600	(8)	135
					13,420		13,500
	15,000		15,000	Bal.	80		
					13,500		13,500
						Bal.	80

At the end of eight years the asset account shows no balance. If all estimates had been entirely accurate, the Accumulated Depreciation account would show no balance either. The $80 balance remains because the average salvage value was slightly greater than $30 per typewriter. When the last unit in the group is retired, the balance could be closed out to a gain account.

Composite Depreciation. The same procedures illustrated above for group depreciation are sometimes applied to a collection of heterogeneous assets differing as to kind and useful life. Such procedures are called *composite depreciation.* The depreciation rate is based on the weighted average life of the assets comprising the composite group. Unfortunately, the theoretical justification for the group method probably is absent from the composite method. The concept of an expected mortality dispersion around an average life applies only to groups of homogeneous units. The practical advantages of simplified record keeping, of course, are still present.

Evaluation of Group Depreciation

The advantage of the group method in saving clerical effort is obvious. Detailed asset and contra asset accounts for each unit are not necessary, and entries upon the retirement of individual units are simplified.

More Accurate Periodic Depreciation. Perhaps not so obvious is the fact that, with a truly homogeneous group of items, the group depreciation method provides a more accurate assignment of cost to periods in which the items are actually used. Table 9–A–2 compares the total charges against revenues for the above example under the unit depreciation method and under the group depreciation method. Under the unit method, depreciation expense is calculated only for four years, the average useful life. The retirement loss is the undepreciated cost of each typewriter less salvage at retirement.

TABLE 9–A–2

Comparison of Annual Charges under Group and Unit Depreciation Methods

Year	No. of Units in Use	Group Depr. Expense	Unit Depr. Method Depr. Expense	Unit Depr. Method Retirement Loss	Unit Depr. Method Total Charge
1	50	$ 3,375	$3,375	$690	$ 4,065
2	46	3,105	3,105	920	4,025
3	38	2,565	2,565	540	3,105
4	30	2,025	2,025	. . .	2,025
5	19	1,283	. . .	. . .	. . .
6	10	675	. . .	50	50
7	5	337	. . .	90	90
8	2	55*	. . .	60	60
		$13,420			$13,420

* Includes $80 gain on retirement of group.

The total charge over the eight years is the same under both methods. The group method, however, attempts to distribute this total cost in closer relation to the actual usage of the assets. The group method attempts to achieve a *uniform charge per service year* rather than a uniform write-off over the life of each individual item. With a normal dispersion of lives around the average useful life, a uniform write-off for each unit is almost impossible, except on a post-mortem basis. The significant retirement losses indicate the inability to achieve this goal. The group method views the asset group as consisting of 200 years of service. Under a straight-line assumption, each year of service carries an equal charge. But the total charge each year varies with the number of units in service that year.

Limitations of the Group Method. The group method theoretically is applicable only for groups consisting of large numbers of homogeneous units. Many of the conceptual underpinnings of the group method come from those used in insurance and actuarial calculations. The average age of an individual item is actuarially calculated just like the average life expectancy of human populations. The expected mortality distribution also is similar to that employed in life insurance computations. It is obvious, therefore, that the asset group must be sufficiently large and the units similar enough in nature so that the concepts of average life and mortality distribution have statistical validity.

The other major difficulty of the group depreciation method is that errors in average useful lives may go undetected for many years. With unit depreciation a gain or loss on retirement of an individual unit may trigger a reexamination of depreciation rates and lives of other similar assets. Under the group method no such gain or loss on retirement is recorded until the last unit in the group is retired. The depreciation expense may be too large or too small for a substantial time period before the error in the depreciation estimate becomes apparent.

SUGGESTIONS FOR FURTHER READING

Battista, George L., and Crowningshield, Gerald R. "Accounting for Depreciation and Repair Costs," *NAA Bulletin*, Vol. 45 (December 1963), pp. 21–30.

Nelson, Robert H. "The Momentum Theory of Goodwill," *Accounting Review*, Vol. 28 (October 1953), pp. 491–99.

Reynolds, Issac N. "Selecting the Proper Depreciation Method," *Accounting Review*, Vol. 36 (April 1961), pp. 239–49.

Virgil, Robert L. "The Purpose of the Buyer as a Guide in Accounting for Goodwill," *NAA Bulletin*, Vol. 44 (April 1963), pp. 33–39.

Thomas, Arthur L. "The Allocation Problem in Financial Accounting Theory," *Studies in Accounting Research No. 3*. American Accounting Association, 1969.

QUESTIONS AND PROBLEMS

9–1. A machine is purchased for $5,000. It is expected to last four years and have a scrap value of $200. It is estimated that the machine will operate 10,000 hours before being retired.

   a) Calculate the depreciation for *each* of the years, using (1) the straight-line method; (2) the declining-balance method, with a rate twice the straight-line rate; (3) the sum-of-the-years'-digits method; and (4) the production or activity method (the machine is operated 2,400 hours during the first year, 2,800 hours during the second year, 2,650 hours during the third year, and 2,100 hours during the fourth year).

b) "The choice of depreciation method is influenced by both the quantity and quality of asset services." Explain this quotation in relation to how you would decide which of the above methods was best.

9-2. The Hawkins Corporation engaged in the following transactions and events during the year. Indicate whether each of the expenditures would be accounted for as current period or as capital costs. Also discuss how the other events should be reflected in the accounting records, both initially and in future periods.

1. Incurred costs for several projects in the existing factory building, including:
   a) Replacing wood shingles with slate on the roof of one building.
   b) Installing heavier grates in the furnace.
   c) Waterproofing the walls.
   d) Replacing a window.
   e) Building a new cement foundation to replace an older wooden one that had been eaten by termites.
   f) Repainting the entire interior of the factory.
   g) Replacing a few shingles that had been blown off in a windstorm.
2. Purchased a used delivery truck from a local dealer for $5,000. Arranged with a garage to have the delivery truck fixed up and to have similar trucks already owned by the company serviced. The following expenditures were made:
   a) License and insurance on the "new" truck.
   b) Replacing spark plugs on the other trucks.
   c) Installing a new battery on the "new" truck.
   d) Replacing the motor in one of the other trucks.
   e) Repainting the "new" truck.
3. Purchased a new machine for $15,000 to replace one that originally cost $18,000. The new machine had a lower rated capacity than the old one. Removal costs of the old machine were $1,500. The cost incurred to adapt the floor of the factory building for the installation of the new machine was $3,000.
4. Accidentally discovered that an unused portion of the company's land contained a substantial copper deposit. Immediately spent $25,000 for the services of a consulting engineer to ascertain the feasibility of mining the ore for commercial purposes. The engineer eventually issued an affirmative report. Spent $500,000 to strip overburden and to develop the mine, plus another $35,000 for mining equipment.

9-3. The following schedule for property and plant assets is taken from a company's detailed asset records:

	Asset Accounts (in 000's)		
	Balance, January 1, 1972	Additions at Cost	Retirements and Sales
Oil fields..........................	$137,641	$18,937	$ 3,876
Gas fields.........................	98,760	14,780	9,344
Refining plants....................	33,700	8,556	5,689
Distribution equipment.............	19,332	3,190	1,680
Other equipment..................	1,009	581	392
Land..............................	4,300	...	108
Total........................	$294,742	$46,044	$21,089

	Contra Asset Accounts (in 000's)		
	Balance January 1, 1972	Additions during 1972	Charges for Retirements and Renewals
Oil fields..........................	$100,030	$13,808	$ 3,330
Gas fields.........................	76,050	10,110	8,609
Refining plants....................	12,310	4,375	4,273
Distribution equipment.............	5,800	2,203	1,680
Other equipment..................	600	297	334
Total........................	$194,790	$30,793	$18,226

On the basis of this information, answer the following questions:

a) What were the total capital expenditures made by the company during 1972?

b) Make the journal entry to record the depletion and depreciation costs for the year.

c) Assume cash of $82,000 was received in connection with the retirement and sale of other equipment. Make the journal entry to record the disposition.

d) Explain what the term "renewals" refers to in the heading "charges for retirements and renewals" shown in the contra asset accounts. What policy is being followed?

e) What do you think happened in connection with the disposition of distribution equipment during the year?

f) Why is there no contra account related to Land?

9–4. The general ledger of Enter-tane, Inc., a corporation engaged in the development and production of television programs for commercial sponsorship, contains the following accounts before amortization at the end of the current year:*

---

* Problem adapted from the AICPA May 1960 examination.

Account	*Balance (Dr.)*
Sealing Wax and Kings...................	$51,000
The Messenger........................	36,000
The Desperado........................	17,500
Shin Bone............................	8,000
Studio Rearrangement..................	5,000

An examination of contracts and records revealed the following information:

1. The first two accounts listed above represent the total cost of completed programs that were televised during the accounting period just ended. Under the terms of an existing contract, Sealing Wax and Kings will be rerun during the next accounting period at a fee equal to 50 percent of the fee for the first televising of the program. The contract for the first run produced $300,000 of revenue. The contract with the sponsor of The Messenger provides that he may, at his option, rerun the program during the next season at a fee of 75 percent of the fee on the first televising of the program.
2. The balance in The Desperado account is the cost of a new program which has just been completed and is being considered by several companies for commercial sponsorship.
3. The balance in the Shin Bone account represents the cost of a partially completed program for a projected series that has been abandoned.
4. The balance of the Studio Rearrangement account consists of payments to a firm of engineers which prepared a report relative to the more efficient utilization of existing studio space and equipment.

   a) State the general principle (or principles) of accounting that are applicable to the first four accounts.
   b) How would you report each of the first four accounts in the financial statements of Enter-tane, Inc.? Explain.
   c) In what way, if at all, does the Studio Rearrangement account differ from the first four? Explain.

9–5. In preparing to make the adjusting entry on December 31, 1972, you review the Machinery account and the related Accumulated Depreciation account. Machines in this particular account are depreciated based on a four-year life. The entries made in the accounts are:

Machinery				*Accumulated Depreciation—Machinery*	
Jan. 1, 1969	2,000	July 1, 1971	600	Dec. 31, 1969	500
Jan. 1, 1970	1,600	July 1, 1972	200	Dec. 31, 1970	1,050
July 1, 1970	1,200			Dec. 31, 1971	700
Jan. 1, 1972	2,000				

The first three debit entries to the Machinery account represent purchases of three machines, one on each date indicated. The entries in the Accumulated Depreciation account are the yearly provisions for depreciation that were actually made.

On July 1, 1971 machine No. 1, purchased on January 1, 1969, was sold for $600 cash. The bookkeeper debited Cash and credited Machinery for $600.

On January 1, 1972 machine No. 2, purchased on January 1, 1970, was traded in on a newer model. The purchase price of the new machine was $2,400. A trade-in allowance of $400, equal to the value of the old machine, was allowed. The remainder of $2,000 was paid in cash. The bookkeeper debited Machinery and credited Cash for the $2,000.

On July 1, 1972 machine No. 3, purchased on July 1, 1970, was so thoroughly damaged in an accident that it had to be sold for junk; the company received $100 in cash. A settlement of $200 was received from the insurance company also. The bookkeeper debited Cash for $300, credited Machinery for $200, and credited Miscellaneous Revenue for $100.

a) Prepare the correct journal entries that *should have been made* to record *any* entries that were recorded incorrectly.

b) Prepare a single compound journal entry to correct the books *and* to record depreciation for the year 1972.

9–6.   The president's letter in an annual report to stockholders made the following comments on the company's depreciation policy:

> The depreciation policy of your company has been very sound. The directors realize that it is necessary to charge depreciation in order to value assets correctly. We therefore always use the most liberal depreciation method the tax authorities will allow for both tax return and annual financial statement purposes. Stockholders, therefore, are not deceived by the accounting fraud of having two sets of books—one for the tax authorities and another for the stockholders. In addition, stockholders can be assured that the large "accumulated depreciation" account assures funds for the replacement of assets when that time arises.

List (and describe briefly) *all* the misconceptions about accounting and depreciation which are evidenced by the above quotation.

9–7.   The ABC Corporation purchased a machine on January 1, 1971 trading in an older machine of a similar type.* The old machine was acquired on January 1, 1961 at a cost of $68,000. Both old and new machines had an estimated 20-year life and no net salvage value. The terms of the purchase provided for a trade-in allowance of $30,000 (the fair market value of the used machine was $25,000) and called for an additional cash payment of $125,000 or 12 monthly payments of $11,000 each, the first payment due in one month.

ABC chose to accept the latter alternative. Other costs incurred in connection with the exchange were as follows:

* Problem adapted from the AICPA November 1955 examination.

Wage costs for:

Removal of old machine	$ 800
Repairs to factory floor	700
Installation of new machine	900

Invoices received:

Sales engineer who supervised installation	400
Hotel, meals, travel, etc., for sales engineer	200
Freight-in—new machine	1,100
Freight-out—old machine	1,000

a) Make journal entries to reflect the exchange on the books of the ABC Corporation (the old machine was being depreciated on a straight-line basis).

b) Why did you treat the $700 repairs to the factory floor in the manner that you did?

c) How would your entry in (*a*) differ if the procedure acceptable for income tax purposes were used? What impact would this difference have in future years?

d) Compute depreciation on the new machine for the years 1971 and 1972 (1) on the straight-line basis, (2) on the sum-of-the-years'-digits method, and (3) on the double-declining-balance method. Show all computations clearly labeled.

9–8. Computer Sciences Corporation listed the following three noncurrent assets among its total assets of $33,857,000 as of March 29, 1968.

Investments in proprietary programs and systems in progress	$3,242,000
Computer	2,326,000
Excess of cost of business acquired over related net assets	1,586,000

In various notes to the statements, CSC explained its policies with respect to each of these assets:

Proprietary Systems. It is the Company's policy to accumulate during the development period and thereafter to amortize the costs of each proprietary program or system including the applicable technical and marketing efforts on the basis of estimated revenues or over a period of up to five years, whichever provides the earlier amortization. An unamortized balance is expensed (1) at the time a program or system is abandoned, or (2) to the extent that projected revenues will be less than the amortization expense.

Computer. The computer is used by the Company in the performance of a contract which has a shorter term than the estimated economic life of the computer (10 years). In the opinion of management, the computer will be sold or re-leased at the end of the contract term at amounts sufficient to recover the remaining investment.

Excess Cost. The excess of cost of business acquired over related net assets is related to a subsidiary acquired in prior years and will not be amortized so long as this asset has continuing value.

Comment on the capitalization and amortization policies with respect to each of these assets, giving particular attention to the following questions.

a) Why does CSC capitalize developmental cost? Is estimated revenues a reasonable basis to use in computing amortization expenses? Why is the amortization period limited to five years even though estimated revenues may last longer? Explain the firm's policy on expensing of unamortized balances.

b) Is 10 years a reasonable life for a computer? What other information would you like to have? Do you agree with management's reasoning?

c) Explain what the "excess of cost . . ." account represents and how it arose. Do you agree with management's decision not to amortize it? Why or why not? Would such a procedure be according to generally accepted accounting principles now? Explain.

9–9.   Wild Cat Oil Corporation specializes in speculative drilling ventures. During 1971 it signed a lease with the owner of a farm, acquiring the rights to drill for oil for the next five years on the land. The terms of the lease called for (1) an immediate payment of $30,000, (2) an additional payment of $3,000 for each year in which the company actually did any drilling or pumping activity, (3) a payment of 10 cents for each barrel of oil sold during a year, and (4) a provision that Wild Cat would clean up and restore the land to its original condition for farming at the end of the five years (estimated cost to do this is $20,000).

In 1971 a successful well was drilled at a cost of $50,000. Total oil reserves in the well were estimated to be 200,000 barrels. Of these, 25,000 barrels were pumped and sold in 1971 and 40,000 barrels were pumped and sold in 1972. Operating costs were $30,000 in 1971 and $38,000 in 1972. The selling price was $2 per barrel.

a) Calculate the total receipts the lessor (owner of the farm) would receive each year.

b) Prepare an income statement for Wild Cat for 1971 and for 1972. Explain carefully the depletion and other accounting policies you adopt.

c) Indicate what accounts and amounts related to the above items would appear on the position statement as of December 31, 1972. Indicate how they would be classified.

9–10.   The following quotations describe the depreciation and other noncurrent asset policies of Jones and Laughlin Steel Corporation and Martin-Marietta. The descriptions are taken from reports filed with the Securities and Exchange Commission.

Jones and Laughlin Corporation: Prior to January 1, 1954, manufacturing properties, exclusive of blast furnace linings, were depreciated over their estimated service lives at composite rates ranging from 3% in years of low operations to 5% in years of high operations; blast furnace linings were depreciated over their productive lives; mining, railroad and other properties were depreciated over their estimated service lives. . . .

Beginning January 1, 1954, properties acquired . . . after January 1, 1954 are depreciated by declining balance method.

Beginning January 1, 1968, depreciation on assets is provided for accounting purposes on a modified straight-line basis.

Provisions for depletion of mineral properties and amortization of stripping and development expense capitalized are computed by multiplying tonnage mined by a rate determined by dividing undepleted cost by estimated mineral reserves. Stripping and development expense has been charged to income beginning January 1, 1951.

In general, properties retired are eliminated from property accounts and accrued depreciation applicable to such properties is eliminated from depreciation reserve, resulting profit or loss being credited or charged to income. In some instances, such profit or loss is credited or charged to depreciation reserve.

Martin-Marietta: For accounting purposes, the Cement and Lime, Chemical, and Rock Products divisions generally employ the straight-line method for computing depreciation for substantially all of their assets, while Aerospace operations use straight-line and declining-balance methods. . . .

Depletion of mineral deposits was computed on a unit rate of production basis applied to the cost of individual properties. . . .

Maintenance and repairs, and expenditures for renewals and betterments not calculated to extend the useful lives or materially increase the productivity of the properties affected, were charged to cost of sales and other costs and expenses as incurred. Other renewals and betterments were capitalized.

Generally at the time of sale or abandoment of equipment or building units, the applicable amounts of costs and accumulated depreciation were eliminated from the accounts and the net carrying amounts less proceeds of disposal were charged or credited to income, except for those classes of equipment or building units depreciated under the group rate method, whereby no gain or loss is recognized upon disposition.

a) Evaluate the policy of Jones and Laughlin with respect to (1) the reasons for the 3 or 5 percent varying depreciation policy prior to 1954, (2) the reasons for the changes in 1954 and again in 1968, and (3) the depletion provisions, particularly the handling of stripping and development expense.

b) Evaluate the policy of Martin-Marietta with respect to (1) the propriety of different depreciation methods being used by different divisions and (2) its policies with respect to subsequent expenditures.

c) How do the firms handle sales and retirements? Is there any difference between them?

d) In Martin Marietta, no gain or loss is recognized on disposition of assets being depreciated under the group rate. Explain why.

9–11. Mixomess Chemical Corporation stores large quantities of acids in storage tanks with specially designed linings. During the spring of 1972 the company found it necessary to drain one of the tanks and repair the lining, which was leaking. As the work progressed, it became apparent that the deterioration of the lining was much worse than had been anticipated. The decision was made to reline the entire tank at a cost of $16,000; this task was completed by June 30, 1972. The cost of removing the old lining, included in the $16,000, was $2,000.

The storage tank itself had been built 10 years earlier at a cost of $135,000. It was being depreciated on a straight-line basis over an estimated life of 50 years. The cost of the original lining was estimated at $15,000.

Because of the corrosive nature of the acids, technical advisors estimated that relining probably would be necessary every 10 years or so.

a) The company charged the $16,000 to Repair Expense. Discuss the propriety of this treatment. Prepare the *correcting* entry necessary to handle the transaction as a partial asset replacement.

b) What other recommendations would you make to the company concerning its noncurrent asset records?

c) Compute the amount of depreciation cost to be charged for the year ended December 31, 1972.

9–12. The Sweetbriar Garbage Company purchased an abandoned quarry for $120,000 for use as a dumping ground. Several other garbage-hauling companies bid on it, since the location was favorable and dumping could proceed without exhaustive preliminary preparation of the land. It was anticipated that the value of the quarry land would be considerably less after it was filled, due to the fact that no one would want to build on a garbage dump. The quarry land could be sold for only about $20,000 after it was filled. The accountant suggested that this quarry land should be depreciated as the hole was filling up with garbage. Write a brief report to management giving your opinion. In your report, you should indicate the objective of depreciation and then go on to explain how this objective is or is not achieved by recording depreciation on the land. Be as specific as possible in your recommendations.

9–13. The Luchardt Corporation purchased a machine in January, 1969 for $30,000. It was estimated that the equipment would be used for seven years, with a salvage value of $2,000 at the end of its life. The company depreciated it using the sum-of-the-years'-digits method. On January 1, 1972 Luchardt decided to trade it in for a new one with a list price of $50,000.

The Terry New and Used Equipment Company, the dealer, offered $15,000 as a trade-in allowance for the old machine. It was established, however, that the wholesale value of the old machine as a used machine was about $8,000.

a) On the books of the Luchardt Corporation, record the necessary journal entries.

b)   The following entry was made on the books of the Terry New
and Used Equipment Company:

```
Cash......................... 35,000
Used Machinery Inventory........ 15,000
     Sales...................          50,000
```

Criticize this treatment from a conceptual viewpoint. Can you
see any disadvantages from the standpoint of *management's* need
for information?

9–14.   The following quotations are taken from the formal descriptions of
accounting policies with respect to depletion and drilling costs of four
mining and oil companies.

Anaconda Company: The cost of metal mining properties is
being amortized at the rate of 2% per year on the declining-
balance method. The amount of amortization provided by this
procedure does not necessarily reflect the actual dimunition of
ore reserves nor the decline, if any, in income properties.

The cost of timberlands and phosphate and gravel deposits
is depleted generally on the unit-of-production method.

Deferred mine development costs represent expenditures relating to future operations . . . and are amortized as ore is ex-
tracted at rates based on estimates of ore bodies benefited.

Atlantic Richfield Company: Other fixed assets are written
off . . . on either a straight-line or unit method. Rates under
unit methods are based upon estimates of recoverable reserves.

Intangible development costs applicable to productive wells
are capitalized and amortized on a unit of production method,
based upon estimates of recoverable reserves.

Costs incidental to drilling of development wells are initially
capitalized but charged to expense if hole is determined to be dry.
Costs of drilling exploratory wells are charged to expense as incurred but capitalized and credited to expense if well proves to
be productive. Non-productive exploratory costs, including geological and geophysical costs, dry hole costs, and annual delay
rentals are charged to expense as incurred or when result of expenditure is determined to be non-productive.

Continental Oil Company: Intangible development costs applicable to productive oil or gas wells or to the opening of new
coal mines are capitalized and amortized on a unit of production
basis. Costs of additional mine facilities required to maintain
production after a mine reaches the production stage, generally
referred to as "receding face costs," are charged to expense as
incurred; however, costs of additional air shafts and new portals
are capitalized and amortized.

Exploratory expenses, including geological and geophysical
costs and annual delay rentals, and all dry-hole costs are charged
to income as incurred.

Tenneco Corporation: Tenneco Inc. and its subsidiaries capitalize all productive and nonproductive well drilling costs applicable to the exploration for and development of oil and gas reserves. Depreciation, depletion, and amortization of producing and undeveloped oil and gas properties is provided on a composite basis using the unit-of-production method . . . a rate is determined by dividing the total unrecovered book cost of all such properties by the total quantity of remaining reserves.

a) Compare the policies of the companies concerning treatment of intangible drilling and mine development costs. In what ways are they similar? In what ways do they differ? Which treatment is the most "conservative?"

b) How can the methods described in (*a*) all be generally accepted accounting principles? What factors inherent in these types of costs encourage a disparity in procedure? Which policy do you think is best? Why?

c) How might Tenneco justify its capitalization of both productive *and nonproductive* well drilling costs?

d) Illustrate the depletion method used by Anaconda for its metal mining properties. What message is the company trying to communicate in the second sentence of the first paragraph describing its policies?

e) What is the basis of rationale behind Continental's distinction among development costs of new mines, "receding face costs," and costs of air shafts, etc?

9–15. The O. B. Solete Corporation acquired a piece of processing equipment at a total cost of $40,000. The machine was to be depreciated over a 10-year life, using double-declining balance. During the first two years of operation, technological advances were rapid. At the beginning of the third year management realized that the equipment was becoming obsolete. It spent $3,000 on accessories which served to modernize the basic equipment. Even with these improvements, however, the management revised the depreciation policy to a total useful life of only seven years from the date of original purchase.

At the end of the fifth year the equipment was put on standby usage. The firm decided to switch to straight-line depreciation for the last two years.

At the end of the sixth year the equipment was given to a local machine shop in exchange for some spare parts with a fair market value of $800 which O. B. Solete could use to repair other machines.

a) Prepare a schedule showing the amount of depreciation that was charged in each of the six years.

b) Prepare the journal entry (or entries) during the third year to record the purchase of the accessories and the change in depreciation policy.

c) Prepare the journal entry at the end of the sixth year to record the disposition of the equipment.

9–16. Up to 1967 American St. Gobain Corporation accounted for major furnace repairs by debiting Provision for Furnace Repairs (an expense) and crediting Reserve for Furnace Repairs each year for an estimate of the average annual cost of major furnace repairs. Then, when the repairs took place, the actual costs were debited to the reserve. In its annual report for 1967 the company indicated a change in its procedure, as described in a note to the financial statements:

Note 6—Change in Accounting Method:

As a result of the examination of the Company's Federal income tax returns for the years 1965 and 1966, the Internal Revenue Service required major furnace repairs to be capitalized and depreciated over their useful life. In prior years, for tax purposes, the Company had deducted such repairs in the year in which the repairs were made. For financial statement purposes, the Company had provided for such repairs during the operating cycle of each furnace. Actual repairs were than charged against this reserve. The Company had provided for the future tax benefit relating to the difference between tax and financial accounting for this item. In order to conform financial accounting with the method required by the Internal Revenue Service, the Company has changed its method of accounting for major furnace repairs.

As a result of the change in method of accounting and Federal income tax examination, retained earnings at January 1, 1967 have been increased by $2,148,108 from the amount previously reported to reflect the following items:

Elimination of reserve for furnace repairs as of January 1, 1967 net of future tax benefits	$1,822,525
Capitalization of major furnace repairs made in 1965 and 1966, net of applicable depreciation	293,779
Other adjustments	31,804
	$2,148,108

Of this amount, a net charge of $624,315 (per share $.55) is applicable to 1966 and has been reflected in the restatement of the 1966 statement of earnings as follows:

Reversal of provision for major furnace repairs, net of tax benefit	$(547,274)
Expensing of emergency furnace repairs, net of tax benefit	252,289
Other adjustments relating to furnace repairs in 1966	(9,810)
Net increase in restated 1966 earnings resulting from change in method of accounting	$(304,795)
Elimination of special item credit for future tax benefits relating to provisions for furnace repairs and pensions prior to January 1, 1966	895,612
Other adjustments resulting from Federal income tax examination	33,498
Net charge	$ 624,315

The balance, a net credit of $2,772,423, is applicable to years prior to 1966 and has been added to retained earnings at January 1, 1966.

a) Three separate treatments of furnace repairs are mentioned in the note: (1) capitalize and depreciate (as required by IRS and now to be employed in the financial accounting records), (2) charge to expense as incurred (as used previously for tax purposes), and (3) accrue estimated repairs (as used previously for the financial statements). Which of these alternatives most appropriately matches major repair costs against revenues? Explain.

b) Under the company's former financial reporting method, how should the credit balance in the Reserve for Furnace Repairs be handled on the position statement? Why?

c) Comment on the rationale given by the company for making the change.

d) To the extent possible, explain why the change in method had the impact it did on retained earnings, as detailed in the note. What other accounts were involved in the adjusting entry for change in method?

9–17. Two enterprising geologists decide to form a corporation to carry on their exploration and mining ventures. The following transactions take place:

1971:

Oct. 2   One geologist invests $75,000 in cash; the other invests $55,000 in cash and some used pumping equipment having a fair market value of $20,000, and with an estimated life of four years. The Digdeep Drilling Corporation is formed, and stock is issued to the owners.

Nov. 8   The corporation acquires oil drilling rights on a piece of property. It agrees to pay $50,000 cash for the rights plus a royalty of 10 cents per barrel on each barrel *sold*.

Dec. 1–15   The corporation spends $70,000 in cash to sink shafts, and oil is found. It is estimated that the oil field contains 1.2 million barrels.

Dec. 15   The corporation borrows $100,000 from the bank.

Dec. 15–31   The corporation buys additional pumping equipment costing $30,000 and with an expected useful life of five years. Pumping supplies of $38,000 are purchased on account, and a crew is hired.

1972:

Jan. 1–
Dec. 31   The company starts operations on January 1. During the first year the following costs are incurred:

Pumping crew labor............. $60,000
Supplies used................... 25,000
Administrative salaries.......... 20,000
Selling commissions............ 5,000

During the year, 300,000 barrels of oil are recovered, and 200,000 barrels are sold. The selling price is 73 cents per barrel.

July 31   The used pumping equipment breaks down midway through the year, requiring extensive overhauling. Major components having an estimated original value of $10,000 have to be discarded and replaced with new parts costing $13,000. The overhauling does not extend the useful life of the equipment.

Make journal entries to record the foregoing transactions, including recognition of depletion, depreciation, and royalty costs. (Hint: set up all your drilling and pumping costs—depreciation, depletion, pumping labor, and supplies—as separate cost accounts. Then, transfer them to Oil Inventory to obtain the total cost of oil recovered during the year. From this figure, Cost of Oil Sold can be calculated.)

9–18.   Sorenson Manufacturing Corporation was incorporated on January 3, 1971. The corporation's financial statements for its first year's operations were not examined by a CPA.* You have been engaged to examine the financial statements for the year ended December 31, 1972 and your examination is substantially completed. Some relevant accounts taken from the corporation's trial balance appear below:

Machinery.................................	$ 75,000)
Accumulated depreciation.................	(10,000)
Patents..................................	85,000
Leasehold improvements..................	26,000
Organization expenses...................	29,000
Goodwill...............................	24,000
Licensing agreement No. 1...............	50,000
Licensing agreement No. 2...............	49,000

The following information relates to accounts which may yet require adjustment:

1. Patents for Sorenson's manufacturing process were acquired January 2, 1972 at a cost of $68,000. An additional $17,000 was spent in December 1972 to improve machinery covered by the patents and charged to the Patents account. Depreciation on fixed assets has been properly recorded for 1972 in accordance with Sorenson's practice, which provides a full year's depreciation for property on hand June 30 and no depreciation otherwise. Sorenson uses the straight-line method for all depreciation and amortization.

2. On January 3, 1971 Sorenson purchased two licensing agreements which were then believed to have unlimited useful lives. The balance in the Licensing Agreement No. 1 account includes its purchase price of $48,000 and expenses of $2,000 related to the acquisition. The balance in the Licensing Agreement No. 2 account includes its $48,000 purchase price and $2,000 in acquisition expenses, but it has been reduced by a credit of $1,000 for the

---

* Problem adapted from AICPA May 1968 examination.

advance collection of 1973 revenue from the agreement. In December 1971 an explosion caused a permanent 60 percent reduction in the expected revenue-producing value of licensing agreement No, 1, and in January 1973 a flood caused additional damage which rendered the agreement worthless. A study of licensing agreement No. 2, made by Sorenson in January 1972, revealed that its estimated remaining life expectancy was only 10 years as of January 1, 1972.

3. The balance in the Goodwill account includes (a) $8,000 paid December 30, 1971 for an advertising program which it is estimated will assist in increasing Sorenson's sales over a period of four years following the disbursement, and (b) legal expenses of $16,000 incurred for Sorenson's incorporation on January 3, 1971.

4. The Leasehold Improvements account includes (a) the $15,000 cost of improvements with a total estimated useful life of 12 years which Sorenson, as tenant, made to leased premises in January 1971, (b) movable assembly line equipment costing $8,500 which was installed in the leased premises in December 1972, and (c) real estate taxes of $2,500 paid by Sorenson in 1972 which under the terms of the lease should have been paid by the landlord. Sorenson paid its rent in full during 1972. A 10-year nonrenewable lease was signed January 3, 1971 for the leased building which Sorenson used in manufacturing operations.

5. The balance in the Organization Expenses account properly includes costs incurred during the organizational period. The corporation has exercised its option to amortize organization costs over a 60-month period for federal income tax purposes and wishes to amortize these costs for accounting purposes.

Prepare journal entries necessary to adjust accounts that require adjustment. A separate account should be used for the accumulation of each type of amortization and for each prior-period adjustment.

9–19. During the examination of the financial statements of the Fender Company, your assistant calls attention to significant costs incurred in the development of EDP programs (i.e., software) for major segments of the sales and production scheduling systems.*

The EDP program development costs will benefit future periods to the extent that the systems change slowly and the program instructions are compatible with new equipment acquired at three- to six-year intervals. The service value of the EDP programs is affected almost entirely by changes in the technology of systems and EDP equipment and does not decline with the number of times the program is used. Since many system changes are minor, program instructions frequently can be modified with only minor losses in program efficiency. The frequency of such changes tends to increase with the passage of time.

---

* Problem adapted from AICPA November 1966 examination.

a) Discuss the propriety of classifying the unamortized EDP program development costs as:
1. A prepaid expense.
2. An intangible fixed asset with limited life.
3. A tangible fixed asset.

b) Numerous methods are available for amortizing assets that benefit future periods. Each method (like a model) presumes that certain conditions exist and, hence, is most appropriate under those conditions. Discuss the propriety of amortizing the EDP program development costs with:
1. The straight-line method.
2. An increasing-charge method (e.g., the annuity method).
3. A decreasing-charge method (e.g., the sum-of-the-years'-digits method).
4. A variable-charge method (e.g., the units-of-production method).

9–A–1. Missingpart Manufacturing Company uses a large number of drill presses in its operations. In 1971 it purchased 20 presses at a cost of $3,000 each. The presses were to be considered together as an asset group to be depreciated on a straight-line basis over a six-year period. Anticipated salvage value was negligible. The schedule below shows the number of units and the salvage per unit for retirements in each year. Assume that all retirements take place on January 1.

	Units	Salvage		Units	Salvage
1971	0	0	1976	4	50
1972	1	$200	1977	6	0
1973	0	0	1978	3	0
1974	1	200	1979	2	0
1975	2	100	1980	1	0

a) Prepare a schedule indicating the total depreciation expense each year under the group method. Remember that retirements occur at the beginning of the year.

b) Prepare a similar schedule showing the depreciation expense and yearly gain or loss on retirement assuming these presses had been depreciated over a six-year life by the unit method. Compare the results with part (*a*) and comment.

c) Prepare the entries on January 1, 1972, 1974, and 1975 to record the retirement of the presses in those years.

d) In retrospect, how accurate was the estimate of an average six-year life? (Hint: calculate the actual average number of years of service per machine).

e) What is the gain or loss on the entire group? Why does it exist?

9–A–2. Creon Corporation owns numerous electric calculating machines. Every year new machines are added and older ones retired. Although the machines differ slightly, they all have approximately a 10-year service life and are sufficiently similar to be treated together as an open-ended asset group (i.e., new additions are added into the same group). Expected salvage value is estimated at 10 percent of original cost. On December 31, 1971, the account balances were:

Calculators (at cost)....................... $60,000
Accumulated depreciation.................. (20,000)

For depreciation purposes, all acquisitions and retirements during a year are treated as if they occurred on January 1. The following schedule sets forth pertinent data concerning subsequent activity in the account.

	Additions at Cost	Retirements	
		Cost	Salvage
1972...........	$8,000	$ 7,000	$1,000
1973...........	6,000	5,000	400
1974...........	3,000	10,000	1,300
1975...........	9,000	4,000	300
1976...........	4,000	6,000	500

a) Prepare journal entries to record the additions and retirements and to reflect the yearly depreciation charge.

b) How would the account balances appear on the December 31, 1976 balance sheet?

c) Would you expect that the depreciation figures from your entries under the group method would be more accurate than those accumulated under the unit method? Explain.

9-A-3. Horizon Corporation purchases four new machines on January 1, 1972. Although the machines are quite dissimilar, the company decides to depreciate them as a composite group. Relevant information concerning them is given below:

Machine	Estimated Life	Cost
1.......................	5 years	$15,000
2.......................	15 years	30,000
3.......................	6 years	24,000
4.......................	10 years	11,000
		$80,000

a) Prepare journal entries to record the acquisition of the machines and the depreciation expense under a composite straight-line method. Ignore salvage values (Hint: the depreciation rate is found by expressing the total annual depreciation for all machines as a percentage of their collective cost.)

b) If machine No. 1 were sold at the end of three years for $1,500, what entry would be made? What would the depreciation expense for the fourth year be?

c) Comment on the soundness of the composite method in this instance. What are the strengths and weaknesses of the composite method? Are the depreciation figures more accurate than if each machine were depreciated separately?

9–A–4.   Meatball Express Company uses the group method of depreciation for its fleet of delivery trucks. The group account is open-ended, that is new acquisitions are added to the same group.

The trucks are expected to last an average of four years, with no salvage value. Data concerning purchases and retirements for the first few years are as follows (assume acquisitions and retirements are made on January 1):

New Trucks Acquired			Trucks Retired		
Year	No.	Unit Cost	No.	Original Cost	Salvage
1.......	5	$7,000	0	0	0
2.......	5	7,600	1	$ 7,000	0
3.......	6	8,000	2	14,000	0
4.......	3	8,500	4	31,600	$2,000

a) Prepare journal entries to record purchases, retirements, and depreciation expense each year under a straight-line group depreciation method.

b) Repeat part (a) using a double-declining-balance group depreciation method.

c) Contrast the impact of a retirement on the depreciation calculation for the subsequent year under the straight-line group method and the double-declining-balance group method.

d) What effect will the existence of salvage values have on subsequent depreciation calculations under the double-declining-balance method?

SECTION III

FUTHER ASPECTS OF FINANCIAL MEASUREMENT— EQUITIES

CHAPTER TEN

NOTES AND BONDS

THIS CHAPTER marks the beginning of Section III, which is devoted to a further development of the concepts and procedures pertaining to the recording of *equities*. One area having an important impact on the financial statement presentation of equities is the treatment accorded monetary claims in the form of notes and bonds. Normally, notes and bonds are represented by a formal document having a definite maturity date. They bear interest either explicitly, in the form of a specific percentage, or implicitly, through inclusion of the interest in the face amount of the claim (e.g., the United States Government Series E bond). Notes commonly refer to relatively short-term claims involving a single creditor, whereas bonds usually arise out of long-term borrowings, often from a number of individuals.

The procedures associated with bonds are slightly different from those employed with notes, but the general concepts are the same. The major common concepts concern the element of interest and the resultant recording of monetary claims at their present value. Indeed, the impact of the present value concept is the connecting thread between the discussions of notes and bonds. Consequently, we begin the chapter with a brief explanation of present value and its relationship to the valuation of liabilities. The second section discusses the use of present value techniques and other procedures in the recording of bond liabilities. The concluding section contains the description and analysis of recording practices for short-term notes payable and receivable.

LIABILITIES AND THE PRESENT VALUE CONCEPT

In a general sense liabilities represent the debts or amounts that the business entity owes to creditors. They represent both sources of and

319

claims against the assets of the enterprise. Their incurrence brings assets into the firm. At some future time, though, an outlay of assets or services (usually cash) normally must be made in settlement of each liability. *When* the cash disbursement is made has an important bearing on the recording of liabilities. In Chapter Two liabilities are classified as current or long-term, depending on the date of payment. Even more fundamental, however, is that the date of payment may influence the valuation of the liability.

Because liabilities involve future disbursements, the force of interest is often present and should be recognized. Ask yourself the question, "Would you rather have a dollar now or a dollar a year from now?" Obviously, your answer will be, "I'd rather have a dollar now." Why? You can earn something with the dollar during the coming year by having it now. Money is worth more now than at some time in the future because of the interest factor, the earning potential of the money. Or put in another way, a promise of money at some future date is not worth that same amount of money today. Rather, its *present value* is less because the future amount includes the interest element, the charge for having to wait for payment.

Because money has this time value, the face or contractual amount of most liabilities probably includes some amount of interest. At least theoretically, the liabilities reported at any point in time should represent the total amount owed at that moment in time. If the liability involves a promise to pay a future amount, that future amount should be shown currently at its present value—that is, minus the interest element. The real claim against assets is measured by the cash equivalent that would effectively discharge the obligation as of the balance sheet date, even though payment may actually be delayed. We can ascertain this cash equivalent (present value) directly in some cases or measure it by excluding from the face amount of the future payments the amount of interest included therein. The present value of the liability arises from discounting future payments at the effective rate of interest inherent in the transaction. This discounting process is explained more fully in the next section and in Appendix 10–A.

Because the waiting period between incurrence of the liability and future payment is very short for many current liabilities, the element of interest is negligible. Usually no explicit recognition is given to it. For these obligations—trade accounts payable, taxes payable, wages payable, etc.—the face values of the liabilities are reasonable approximations of their theoretical present values. However, where the interest factor is specifically recognized in the transaction or where long time spans cause the amount of interest to be significant, liabilities should be recorded at the present value of the future payments necessary to liquidate them.

Introduction to Present Value

One of the easiest ways to grasp the concept of present value is to think first about the process of interest accumulation or compounding. A typical savings account is a good example. Suppose that on January 1, 1971 a person deposits $1,000 in a bank paying 5 percent interest compounded annually. The growth of his bank account is depicted in Figure 10–1. During

FIGURE 10–1

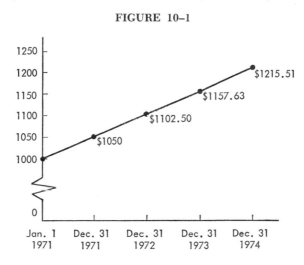

the first year, he receives $50 interest (5% × $1000). During the second year, however, he earns 5 percent not only on the $1,000 but also on the first year's interest. This gives a total increase of $52.50 (5% × $1050). This "interest-on-interest" phenomenon is called compound interest and causes his bank account to grow to $1215.51 by the end of four years.

Present value is the reverse process. It involves sliding down the compound interest curve. In other words, $1,000 is the present value of $1215.51 four years from now, discounted at 5 percent. Rather than indicating how much will accumulate in four years if $1,000 is deposited, present value shows how much has to be deposited now in order to have a specified amount four years from now. Or to state it from a slightly different perspective, the present value of some future amount is the dollar value you would be willing to accept now in lieu of the amount at a later date, or the amount you would be willing to pay now for a promise of the future amount.

Present Value of an Amount Due in _n_ Periods

There are two present-value concepts which relate to interest-bearing liabilities. The first is the one we just discussed—the present value of a promise to pay a single amount at some specific time in the future. For example, how much are you willing to accept now instead of receiving $1,000 in five years? Or how much would you pay now for a promise of $1,000 in five years?

The answers to these questions depend on what could be earned with the money now. Let us assume an earning rate of 6 percent. If the $1,000 is due in one year, we can determine its present value by dividing $1,000 by 106 percent. Similarly, if we are to receive the $1,000 two years from now, its present value would be $1,000/(1.06)^2. Thus the present value of $1,000 due in five years is $1,000/(1.06)^5. The answer of $747 is the amount which, if invested now at a 6 percent return, would accumulate to $1,000 in five years. Thus, if a person could earn 6 percent on his money, he should be indifferent to accepting $747 now or $1,000 five years from now. Similarly, he would be willing to pay $747 now in exchange for a promise of $1,000 in five years.

Fortunately, it is not necessary to compute each figure needed. This type of present-value calculation has been worked out in a table called "Present Value of One Dollar," a portion of which is contained in Appendix 10–A. This table gives the present value of $1 due in various periods of time and at various interest rates. To determine the present value of any amount, simply find the present value of $1 for the particular period and interest rate and multiply by the specified amount.

Present Value of an Amount Due Each Period for n Periods

The second present-value concept builds upon the first. It deals with the present value of a series of payments in the future. Such a series of amounts due in each period for a number of future periods is called an annuity. The question of the present value of an annuity might be phrased, How much are you willing to accept now in lieu of receiving $10 per year for the next five years? Another way of phrasing it would be, How much are you willing to pay now for a promise of $10 per year for five years?

One way of determining the answer is to calculate the present value of each $10 payment. Adding these individual present values would give us the present value of the series. For example, the present value at an earning rate of 6 percent of the first payment, which is one year away, is $10/1.06, or $9.43. The second payment, which is two years away, has a present value of $8.90 [$10/(1.06)^2]. Similar computations for the other payments are shown in Table 10–1. Each succeeding payment has a lower present value, because it is to be received further in the future.

The total of these present values, $42.12, is the current worth of the series of $10 payments. Again, fortunately, we do not actually have to make the above calculations. They are contained in a table called "Present Value of One Dollar per Period" (see Appendix 10–A). From such a table

TABLE 10–1

Present Value @ 6%	*Annual Amount to be Received in Year*				
	1	*2*	*3*	*4*	*5*
$ 9.43............	$10				
8.90............		$10			
8.40............			$10		
7.92............				$10	
7.47............					$10
$42.12					

we can read that the present value of $1 per period for five periods at 6 percent interest is $4.212. The present value of the series of five $10 payments is $10 × $4.212 or $42.12, the figure determined in Table 10–1.

These two present-value concepts are used in the next section to value the liability for bonds payable. The mathematical formulas for these concepts, as well as a more extensive explanation of their derivations and other applications, are covered in Appendix 10–A.

BONDS PAYABLE

Bonds are issued in many forms, containing varying provisions and privileges. For our purposes we are not concerned with detailed features of specific bond issues or their methods of distribution.[1] Most bonds, in essence, represent a group of contractual promises on the part of the issuing company made in exchange for the receipt of money from the purchaser of the bond. The two most important promises from an accounting standpoint are to pay a specified sum (face amount or principal) some time in the future, usually 15 or more years, and to pay interest periodically on the borrowed money. Furthermore, the bond contract or indenture usually contains other provisions, called covenants, which the company must respect and fulfill.[2] The responsibility of seeing that all promises contained in the bond indenture are kept usually lies with a trustee, who acts on behalf of the individual bondholders.

The existence of a bonds payable liability poses two accounting problems. First, how do we record the initial issuing (sale) of the bond? Second, how do we record the periodic accrual and payment of interest? To

---

[1] An interested reader can consult any textbook on business finance for a description of debenture bonds, mortgage bonds, convertible bonds, income bonds, etc., and how they are issued—through underwriters, direct placement, etc.

[2] These covenants may concern steps to be taken in case of default, restrictions on payment of dividends, provisions for sinking (retirement) funds, restrictions on issuing more bonds, maintenance requirements on any mortgaged property under the bond issue, and others. They need not concern us here.

understand the recording process better, the accountant should have some basic knowledge of the factors influencing the market valuation of bonds. Those factors include applications of present-value concepts.

Bonds and Present Value

Perhaps the connection between bonds and present value is already apparent. A bond basically consists of two promises—a promise to pay a specified sum (face value) at the end of a period of time and a promise to pay a specified sum (interest) in each period for a certain number of periods. If the reasoning in the previous section is sound, a bond should be worth an amount which represents the total of the present value of these two promises.

If the contractual or nominal rate of interest (rate stated in the bond contract) is the same as the market or effective interest rate, the bond will sell at face value (maturity value). Take, for example, a $10,000, five-year bond paying interest annually at a stated rate of 8 percent. The promises represented by this bond are to repay $10,000 in five years and to pay $800 in interest (8% × $10,000) each year for five years. If the market rate of interest is also 8 percent, the investor will be willing to pay the present value of these promises at an 8 percent earning rate:

```
Present value of $10,000 due in five years at 8%
    ($10,000 × 0.6806)...............................  $ 6,806
Present value of $800 per year for five years at 8%
    ($800 × 3.9927).................................    3,194
Total present value................................  $10,000
```

What happens if the rate required by investors in the financial markets differs from that offered in the bond contract? If the market rate is higher than the stated rate, the investor is willing to pay less than face value; the bond sells at a *discount*. This seems only logical; you would be unwilling to pay face value for a bond which gives an 8 percent return on your investment when you have alternative uses for your money which would earn, say, 10 percent. Rather, you would pay some lesser amount, so that your effective return would be 10 percent. How much less? You can determine this amount by valuing the two bond promises above at an interest rate of 10 percent:

```
Present value of $10,000 due in five years at 10%
    ($10,000 × 0.6209)...............................  $6,209
Present value of $800 per year for five years at 10%
    ($800 × 3.7908).................................    3,033
Total present value................................  $9,242
```

Having paid $9,242 for this bond, an investor would earn 10 percent each year on his investment. Part of his return would be in the form of periodic payments of $800 and part in the form of a payment at maturity date when he receives back more than he originally has lent.

In financial and accounting terminology this bond is sold at a discount of $758, because of differences between the market rate of interest and the rate promised in the bond contract. An alternative way of viewing and directly calculating the bond discount is in terms of an interest deficiency. Given the market rate of 10 percent, the issuer would have to offer $1,000 annual interest in order to sell it at face value of $10,000. However, the issuer is promising only $800 per year. Therefore, the investors attach a discount equal to the present value of the $200 annual deficiency (present value of $200 per year for five years at 10 percent equals $200 × 3.7908 or $758).

Conversely, if the market rate of interest is below the nominal rate, the bond will sell for more than face value, the excess being called a premium. An investor satisfied with only a 6 percent return on his money for a particular risk would be willing to pay more for a bond contract offering an 8 percent rate. How much more can be readily calculated:

Present value of $10,000 due in five years at 6% ($10,000 × 0.7473)	$ 7,473
Present value of $800 per year for five years at 6% ($800 × 4.2124)	3,370
Total present value	$10,843

The investor buying this bond will receive a 6 percent return every year on his investment. A portion of the $800 he receives in each period is a return of part of the principal investment he has made. The bond sells at a premium of $843 because the stated rate of interest on the bond is larger than the effective market rate of interest set by competition among borrowers and lenders. As in the case of the discount bond, the premium can be calculated directly as the present value of the "excess interest" of $200 ($800 less $600) per year (present value of $200 per year for five years at 6 percent equals $200 × 4.2124, or $843).

Notice that in both of these illustrations the contractual rate of interest determines only the dollar amount of interest payment. It does not enter into the present-value calculation. The time value of money is measured by the effective or market interest rate. An investor, however, does not even use present-value tables to determine what to pay for a bond. The two present-value concepts are combined into "bond tables." Bond tables simply indicate the price (expressed as a percentage of face value) of various bonds, depending on their stated interest rate, length of life, and the market rate of interest. For example, a bond table for five-year bonds would tell us that an 8 percent, five-year bond would sell for 92.42 percent of face value in a 10 percent market and for 108.43 percent in a 6 percent market.

Recording the Issuance of Bonds

Of primary concern to accountants is how to record the issuance of bonds after the investor has bought them. But an understanding that at the time of issuance and throughout the life of the bond, the liability account should represent the present value of the obligations (to repay principal and pay periodic interest) in the bond is helpful when we make entries on the books. We have seen that, if the market rate of interest and the contractual rate are the same, the bond will be issued at maturity value. The entry to record this case is easy:

```
Cash...................................... 10,000
     Bonds Payable........................         10,000
```

Bonds Issued at a Discount. The recording problems arise when bonds are sold at a premium or discount. A discount indicates that the investor is demanding a higher interest return than the particular bond in question promises to pay. Take, for example, the 8 percent, five-year bond, being issued at a time when the investor is demanding a return of 10 percent. The cash received by the company is $9,242, which also represents the present value of its liability. The initial liability is the amount of money committed by investors. That $10,000 is due in five years is irrelevant now. Accountants conventionally record this situation through the use of two accounts—the maturity value in one account offset by a contra liability called Bonds Payable—Discount.[3] The journal entry appears below:

```
Cash...................................... 9,242
Bonds Payable—Discount ....................   758
     Bonds Payable........................         10,000
```

The Bonds Payable—Discount account should be shown on the position statement as a deduction from bonds payable. It is not an asset. Although the liability at maturity will be $10,000, the source of assets at the date the bonds are issued is only $9,242, the amount borrowed. This is the present value of the obligations under the bond contract. The discount represents the portion of the total interest charge that will not be paid or collected until maturity date. Since the discount is a phenomenon of interest, it becomes a liability only gradually as time passes and interest is earned at the effective rate.

---

[3] It is interesting to note that, when the asset counterpart is recorded on the investor's books, the contra-account procedure normally is not used. An investor buying the bond would simply debit Investment in Bonds for $9,242 (plus any additional costs, such as brokerage fees).

Bonds Issued at a Premium. If the 8 percent, five-year bond is sold in a market where the effective return is only 6 percent, the investor would pay more than face value for it—namely, $10,843. Here again, the initial liability is the amount borrowed. This liability gradually will be reduced over time, so that at the end of five years it will be only $10,000. Nevertheless, at this moment the equity is the present value of the obligations under the bond contract, $10,843. The face amount is recorded in one liability account, and the excess or premium in a liability adjunct account, as follows:

```
Cash.......................................  10,843
     Bonds Payable........................            10,000
     Bonds Payable—Premium...............                843
```

Bonds Payable—Premium represents the portion of the liability that will be returned to the investor over the life of the bond issue via periodic "interest" payments which are larger than those required by the investor.

Bond Issue Costs. Businesses may incur additional costs in issuing bonds, which in some cases run as high as 5 percent of the principal amount being issued. Examples include fees of auditors, charges for legal services, printing of the bonds, registration and filing fees for the Securities and Exchange Commission and stock exchanges, and commissions and other distribution fees to the underwriters who actually sell the bonds to the investing public. These collectively are called bond issue costs and represent an intangible asset. They are an expenditure of funds for which benefit is received each year for the life of the bonds, *not* an expense only of the period in which the bonds are issued. At the end of each period an adjusting entry is made to amortize a portion of the bond issue costs as an expense of that period:

```
Amortization of Bond Issue Costs...............  xxx
     Bond Issue Costs..........................            xxx
```

Recording Periodic Interest Charges

Interest on bonds is paid periodically. If the bonds are issued at face value, then the stated rate of interest equals the actual rate. In other words, the total of the periodic payments represents the interest charge for the use of money. In each period an entry is made debiting Interest Charges and crediting Interest Payable (or Cash in Bank). If the accounting period ends between interest-paying dates, an adjusting entry accrues the interest charge for the elapsed period of time since the last payment date.

When bonds are issued at a discount or premium, though, the interest entries are more complicated. In these cases the effective interest rate is not the same as the contractual rate being paid each year. Indeed, the existence of a disparity between contractual and market rates of interest is the precise reason why some bonds sell for more or less than face value.

The important point to remember is that interest is the charge for using money. Therefore, the interest cost for each period is the amount of money actually used in that period multiplied by the effective market rate of interest at the time the bond is issued.

Interest on Bonds Issued at a Discount

When bonds are issued at a discount, the effective interest rate is greater than the stated rate in the bond contract. As a consequence, the actual interest charges are more than the stated interest payment; part of the interest charge in each period is deferred until the maturity date, when the borrower repays more than he originally received. For example, assume that the bond issued at a discount in the previous section is dated January 1, with interest payable once each year thereafter.[4] Although the bond bears an 8 percent coupon rate, the effective interest charge the bondholder makes for lending his funds is 10 percent. The total interest for the five years consists of the difference between total payments and the total received, or $4,758:

Total payments:		
Coupon interest ($800 × 5)...............	$ 4,000	
Repayment at maturity....................	10,000	$14,000
Total received at issuance..................		9,242
Total interest cost for five years............		$ 4,758

Knowing the effective rate of interest and the amount borrowed, the accountant can spread the total charge over the five-year period in such a manner that each period's actual interest charges are recorded.

Although the final repayment will be $10,000, during the first year the amount actually borrowed is only $9,242. Consequently, on December 31 when the company accrues interest for the year, the actual interest charges are $924 ($9,242 × 0.10). The amount of the lender's money actually invested during the year is multiplied by the market rate of interest inherent in the bond contract. However, the borrower, by contract, is only obligated to pay $800 in cash annually. The $124 difference represents interest earned by the investor but not paid to him immediately. Since it has been earned by him and is owed to him by the borrower, the latter should recognize it as an addition to the long-term liability. The entry to do this is:

---

[4] Many corporate bonds pay interest semiannually. In this case we would use half the yearly interest rate and the number of six-month periods making up the life of the bond. Interest entries would then be made every six months. To keep our example simple, we use yearly periods.

```
Dec. 31 Interest Charges......................... 924
          Interest Payable.......................        800
          Bonds Payable—Discount ................        124
```

To increase the company's liability, we credit (reduce) the contra liability account, Bonds Payable—Discount. Since the borrower's liability is always the difference between the main account and the contra liability, the net liability has increased by $124. It is now $10,000 less $634 (the new balance in Bonds Payable—Discount), or $9,366. The $124 is often called the amortization of bond discount.

On January 1 of the second year, the contractual interest would actually be paid in cash:

```
Interest Payable.............................. 800
     Cash.......................................        800
```

On December 31 of the second year another entry accruing that year's interest would be made. Again, the true interest charges are calculated as the market rate of interest times the amount of money actually borrowed. The amount of the lender's money invested during the second year, however, is larger than during the first year because of the addition to the company's liability for the interest earned but not paid to the investor in the first period ($124). The entry would be:

```
Dec. 31 Interest Charges (0.10 × $9,366)........ 937
          Interest Payable......................        800
          Bonds Payable—Discount...............        137
```

This same procedure is followed every year for the life of the bond issue.[5] As a result each period is charged for the effective interest cost. Followed consistently, this method will leave Bonds Payable—Discount with no balance at the last interest payment date. At that time the liability will be represented only by the balance of $10,000 in the Bonds Payable account. Table 10–2 shows the effective interest charge for each of the

TABLE 10–2

Year	Interest Charge (10% of Net Liability)	Interest Paid (Cash)	Discount Amortization	Balance in Bond Discount Account	Net Liability (Maturity Value less Bond Discount)
0...........	...	...	...	$758	$ 9,242
1...........	$ 924	$ 800	$124	634	9,366
2...........	937	800	137	497	9,503
3...........	950	800	150	347	9,653
4...........	965	800	165	182	9,818
5...........	982	800	182	0	10,000
	$4,758	$4,000	$758		

---

[5] If the accounting period ends within an interest period, an adjusting entry to accrue interest for the elapsed time is necessary. Accruing the interest simply involves dividing up the annual entry.

five years, along with the periodic amortization of bond discount and the resulting net liability (amounts have been rounded to the nearest dollar).

At any time during the five-year period, the difference between Bonds Payable and Bonds Payable—Discount represents the present value of the two promises remaining under the bond contract. For instance, at the end of the third year, according to Table 10–2, the position statement will show:

Bond payable......................	$10,000	
Less: Bond discount................	347	$9,653

Since the bond has a remaining life of two years, the effective liability should be:

Present value of $10,000 due in two years at 10% ($10,000 × 0.8264)..................................	$8,264
Present value of $800 per year for two years at 10% ($800 × 1.7355)......................................	1,389
Total present value......................................	$9,653

Interest on Bonds Issued at a Premium

When bonds are issued at a premium, the contractual interest rate on the bond is greater than the market rate. The so-called "interest" payment which the borrower is legally obliged to pay in every period is more than the interest charge actually transacted by the investor. The actual interest charge can be calculated as the product of the amount of funds actually borrowed from the investor during the particular period in question multiplied by the market rate of interest.

The 8 percent, five-year bond issued in a 6 percent money market serves as a good example. When the bond is issued, cash of $10,843 is received (see entry on page 327). The total interest cost for the five years can be measured by the difference between amounts paid out and received. This amount of $3,157 equals the coupon payments less the bond premium:

Total payments:		
Coupon interest ($800 × 5)...............	$ 4,000	
Repayment at maturity..................	10,000	$14,000
Total received at issuance...................		10,843
Total interest cost for five years.............		$ 3,157

On the first interest date the company writes a check for $800. However, the true interest charges are only $651 ($10,843 × 0.06). From

January 1 to December 31 the borrower has used $10,843 of the investor's funds at an effective rate of 6 percent. In this case the borrower is obligated to pay more cash than the actual interest charges. The excess payment represents a return to the lender of a portion of the initial amount borrowed. The liability is gradually reduced in each period by debiting the liability adjunct account, Bonds Payable—Premium:

```
Interest Charges................................ 651
Bonds Payable—Premium........................... 149
    Cash........................................          800
```

Table 10–3 summarizes the information which would be used in making entries over the five-year period.[6] Notice that the size of the interest

TABLE 10–3

Year	Interest Charge (6% of Net Liability)	Interest Paid (Cash)	Premium Amortization	Balance in Bond Premium Account	Net Liability (Maturity Value + Bond Premium)
0..........	...	...	...	$843	$10,843
1..........	$ 651	$ 800	$149	694	10,694
2..........	642	800	158	536	10,536
3..........	632	800	168	368	10,368
4..........	622	800	178	190	10,190
5..........	610	800	190	0	10,000
	$3,157	$4,000	$843		

charge declines each year, with a concomitant increase in the size of the bond premium repaid (amortization of bond premium). The interest charge decreases because a portion of the original amount borrowed is returned to the investor with each interest payment, and therefore the amount of money used in each succeeding year decreases. By the end of the fifth year, all of the bond premium will have been returned to the investor. The only liability remaining at the maturity date is the $10,000 balance in Bonds Payable. At any time until maturity the net liability (the total of the balances in Bonds Payable and Bonds Payable—Premium) is the present value of the remaining obligations under the contract.

Straight-Line Amortization of Premium and Discount

The above method of recording interest is called the effective interest method. It charges each period with an amount of interest directly related

---

[6] A slight complication is introduced when the accounting period ends between interest periods. First, a determination should be made as to what the total entry would be for the *interest* period. Then merely divide this basic entry to conform to the *accounting* period involved.

to the transacted rate and the actual amount of money being used. Under this method the interest charge varies in each period, although the yield rate is constant. Amortization schedules similar to Tables 10–2 and 10–3 can be calculated and printed out in a matter of minutes with an electronic computer.

In accounting practice, however, a less accurate procedure is often used. This procedure amortizes the premium or discount over the life of the bond issue on a straight-line basis. Each period receives the same interest charge, which we determine by taking the nominal interest (cash payment) plus an equal portion (straight-line amortization) of the bond discount—or minus an equal portion of the bond premium.

Bonds sold at a discount:

```
Interest Charges.........................  951.60
    Bonds Payable—Discount ($758 ÷ 5) ....            151.60
    Cash.................................            800.00
```

Bonds sold at a premium:

```
Interest Charges.........................  631.40
Bonds Payable—Premium ($843 ÷ 5) ........  168.60
    Cash.................................            800.00
```

For each of the five years an identical entry would be made. At maturity date, no premium or discount remains. Comparing the above entries with Tables 10–2 and 10–3 you will notice that this procedure approximates the true interest charge only in the third year.

Extinguishing the Bond Liability Prior to Maturity

Although bonds are usually issued for relatively long periods of time, it is not uncommon for the liability to be extinguished prior to maturity. Most bond issues contain a call provision, whereby the borrower can redeem the issue at certain set prices during its life. Usually the redemption price includes a call premium to compensate the investor for having to give up his investment prematurely. In addition to retiring bonds by call, a company also can redeem an issue by purchasing its own bonds in the open market.

Some other bonds, known as convertible bonds, contain a provision allowing the bonds to be exchanged for capital stock at the holder's option. The conversion option offers the investor an opportunity to gain if the firm is successful and the market price of the capital stock increases. Yet the bond still provides creditor protection and a preferential return in the case of average or below-average earnings. From the firm's viewpoint, the conversion feature may allow the bonds to be issued at a lower market rate of interest or to be used as an indirect way of issuing capital stock. If all or part of a bond issue is converted into capital stock, the liability disappears and owners' equity replaces it.

Our primary interest is in analyzing the basic transaction when bonds are extinguished. Whether this is accomplished by call, by open-market purchase, or through conversion, and whether the issue is retired in total or only partially, does not affect the analysis involved. Therefore, a simple example is used to illustrate redemption or conversion. Assume that the account balances relating to a bond issue are as follows on a particular date:

	Dr.	Cr.
Bonds payable............................		$100,000
Bonds payable—discount...................	$4,000	
Bond issue costs.........................	200	

The balances in the contra liability account, Bonds Payable—Discount, and the asset account, Bond Issue Costs, are not the original amounts. Each has been partially amortized during the period the bond issue has been outstanding. Our concern, however, is with the balances on the date of retirement on conversion.

Redemption. The redemption price (call price) is usually expressed as a percentage of maturity value. The excess above maturity value is referred to as the call premium and is the extra payment required of the business entity for the privilege of retiring the bonds early. If, for example, this bond issue is callable at a price of 105, the company has to pay 105 percent of face value, or $105,000. The entry to record the retirement is:

Bonds payable..........................	100,000	
Loss on Bond Redemption.................	9,200	
Bonds Payable—Discount		4,000
Bond Issue Costs....................		200
Cash................................		105,000

The loss on redemption arises from two factors: (1) we have to pay $9,000 more than the net liability shown on the books [$105,000 − (100,-000 − $4,000)], and (2) an asset of $200 suddenly expires. In many respects the Loss on Bond Redemption account is an adjustment to prior years' earnings. Since the life of the bond issue is shorter than anticipated, the interest charge and amortization of bond issue costs during past years have been too low. The loss is reported as an extraordinary item in the period.

Refunding. An additional accounting problem concerning bond retirement is introduced by refunding—issuing a new bond and using its proceeds to redeem an old one, often to take advantage of lower interest rates. An existing 10 percent bond issue may be called prior to its maturity, and a new 8 percent bond sold to take its place. The question raised is whether the call premium and the unamortized costs of the old bond issue in any way continue as assets beyond the refunding date.

In many ways this situation is analogous to an exchange of noncurrent assets. A strong argument can be made for treating the refunding as two separate transactions: (1) retiring the old bond issue, as illustrated above, and (2) recording the issuance of the new one. The old bond issue is being terminated because it has become comparatively uneconomical. The costs of ending the liability—unamortized discount, unamortized bond issue costs, and call premium—are part of the loss recognized upon elimination of the old bond.

Many accountants, however, advocate deferring these costs to future years. They argue that the unamortized discount and call premium have to be incurred to accomplish refunding. The benefit of these costs is received in future periods and should be amortized over those periods. One school of thought would spread the refunding costs over the remaining life of the old bond issue. Advocates of this view reason that the unamortized discount and call premium represent costs of achieving a more advantageous arrangement (e.g., lower interest rates) for the remaining life of the old bonds. A second school of thought would amortize these items over the remaining life of the new bond issue. This argument rests on the view that the old and new bond issues are really one continuous borrowing arrangement. Consequently, all costs should be spread over the entire borrowing period.

The Accounting Principles Board has affirmed the acceptability of both of these deferred procedures in addition to direct write-off. Upon close scrutiny, neither deferral method can be defended. Both hinge on the mistaken assumption that these costs are necessary in order that the firm may acquire new borrowed money on more favorable terms. Instead, however, the terms of any new bond issue are set by competitive conditions in the financial markets, not by adjustments related to past bond contracts. The unamortized discount reflects a correction of past years' interest charges. The call premium may be interpreted either as a correction of prior years' interest or as a penalty in the current period for the cancellation of a liability. In neither case do they provide benefit in future periods. Consequently, amortization over future periods, despite the authoritative support, does not seem as sound as a direct write-off. The old bond contract is gone, and all accounts related to it should be removed. Direct write-off, interestingly enough, is the only treatment allowed for income tax purposes.

Conversion. When bonds are converted into stock, two approaches have been suggested to record the retirement of the bond liability and the concomitant increase in contributed capital. Under one method the current *market value* of the bonds issued is assumed to represent the contributed capital. Under the second method the *book value* of the bond issue is assigned to contributed capital.

Our earlier example can be used to illustrate these two methods. Assume that the bond issue described above contains a conversion option entitling each $1,000 bond to be converted into stock at a price of $50 per share. This means that the entire bond issue, if converted, could be exchanged for 2,000 shares ($100,000 ÷ $50) of stock. If the market value of the stock rises, say, to $54 per share, the current market value of the bond would tend to reflect its conversion value (equivalent worth in stock). The bond issue should have a market value of approximately $108,000. Some accountants claim that this amount represents what would be necessary to pay off the liability and also the amount that would be received if the stock were issued for cash. Accordingly, the conversion entry should be:

```
Bonds Payable..........................  100,000
Loss on Bond Conversion.................   12,000
    Bonds Payable—Discount .............            4,000
    Capital Stock.......................          108,000
```

This method views the conversion as two distinct transactions—the retirement of bonds and the issuance of stock.

The alternative procedure increases capital stock by the amount that the bond liability decreases. The entry would be:

```
Bonds Payable...........................  100,000
    Bonds Payable—Discount .............            4,000
    Capital Stock.......................           96,000
```

Obviously, the bondholders have elected to convert because the market value of the stock has risen. However, as far as the corporate entity is concerned, no increase in assets or equities has occurred. The bond issue is canceled, and stockholders' equity takes its place. Total corporate resources and sources of capital remain constant. Adherents to this position maintain that unlike a bond refunding, a bond conversion does not consist of two independent events. The initial proceeds of the bond issue reflected the fact that the bonds could be converted into stock. Indeed, the convertible bonds may have been designed specifically to serve as an indirect way of issuing capital stock. The actual conversion simply completes what was contemplated originally. To record a "loss" upon the issuance of capital stock, as in the first method, appears inconsistent with the entity concept and with the nature of capital-raising transactions.

SHORT-TERM NOTES

Notes payable and notes receivable accounts can arise directly from a purchase transaction or indirectly by being substituted for an account payable or receivable sometime later. Or notes payable may result from a direct loan from a bank or other creditor. In any case the note represents a signed promise by the debtor or borrower to pay a certain sum on a particular date to the creditor or lender.

Notes, like bonds, are recorded at their present value. However, the implementation of this recording involves some features that differ from those employed with bond liabilities. These differences are attributable to the fact that notes usually result from short-term transactions with a single creditor, and to the influence of legal conventions.

Because of the short time period (usually one year or less), interest normally is paid at the time the principal is paid. As a result, only infrequently is there compound interest present. The charge for using money is calculated under the simple interest formula:

$$I = P \times R \times T$$
$$\text{Interest} = \text{Principal} \times \text{rate} \times \text{time}$$

Businesses employ a number of conventions related to short-term notes. First, unless stated otherwise, the interest rate is assumed to be an annual rate. Secondly, if the time period is expressed in days, then the time period begins with the day after the date of the note and runs up to and includes the maturity date. For example, a 30-day note dated December 15 is due on January 14; a one-month note dated December 15 is due on January 15. Because of differing numbers of days in various months, most notes for less than a year are expressed in terms of days rather than months. A third convention that influences interest calculations states that for interest purposes the year consists of 360 days. Thus, if we borrow money for 60 days, the time period is 60/360, or one sixth of a year.

If a note is explicitly interest-bearing, the written document indicates that fact. For instance, if one were to borrow $3,000 and give an 8 percent, one-year note in exchange, the note would promise to pay in one year $3,000 plus interest at the rate of 8 percent. The interest of $240 ($3,000 × 0.08 × 1) would be paid at maturity date.

The initial present value of this note is its face value of $3,000. This can be demonstrated by discounting the maturity amount (face value plus interest) of $3,240 at 8 percent ($3,240/1.08 = $3,000). Here there is no premium or discount, because the stated rate of interest on the note is assumed to equal the market rate of interest. The transaction is between a single lender and a single borrower. Usually no reason exists to believe that the rate of interest they agree upon does not represent the market interest rate. The present value of $3,000 will grow to $3,240 by the end of the year. Consequently, accountants would record this note initially at its face value and then accrue the contractual interest separately as time passes.

Discount Notes and Interest Calculation

If a note does not bear interest explicitly, the legal document refers only to the amount due at maturity. In most cases, however, an interest factor is present but included in the maturity value of the note. The amount of money actually borrowed, or the present value, is less. For the implicitly interest-bearing note, the charge for using money is computed by the discount procedure described below; hence the term "discount note."

Assume that we sign a promissory note to pay $3,000 one year from now and that the note is discounted at 8 percent. The 8 percent *discount* rate is applied to the *maturity* value of the note to get the amount of discount (total charge for using money). In this example, the maturity value is $3,000 and the interest charge is $240. But we would receive only $2,760 now. Included in the $3,000 we repay a year from now is the $240 interest charge. We have paid $240 for the use of only $2,760, an effective interest rate of about 8.7 percent ($240/$2,760).

An 8 percent discount rate, then, is not the equivalent of an 8 percent interest rate. We apply a discount rate to the maturity value and subtract the resulting charge to get the present value or amount actually borrowed (this is referred to as the proceeds). We apply an interest rate to the amount actually borrowed. However, both interest rates and discount rates result in an initial value that is the present value of expected future outlays. The present value of $2,760 derived under the discount procedure agrees with the present value calculated with an equivalent interest rate ($3,000/1.08696 = $2,760).

Notes Payable

Assume that a firm buys machinery on May 15 for $5,000 and gives a 10 percent, 90-day note in exchange. The note would be due on August 13. In making entries for this note payable, we must make sure to accrue the interest for the time passed in an adjusting entry whenever an accounting period ends. Since the legal document explicitly recognizes interest as a separate item, the accrued interest payable is normally recorded in a separate liability account.

If the firm's accounting period ends on June 30, the following entries would be made concerning the above note:

```
May   15   Machinery......................  5,000.00
              Notes Payable..............              5,000.00
           To record purchase of ma-
           chinery in exchange for a
           10%, 90-day note.

June 30    Interest Charges..............     63.88
              Interest Payable...........                 63.88
           To accrue interest at 10%
           for 46 days (16 days in May
           and 30 days in June).

Aug.  13   Interest Charges..............     61.12
              Interest Payable...........                 61.12
           To accrue interest at 10%
           for 44 days.
```

```
Interest Payable..............   125.00
Notes Payable.................. 5,000.00
    Cash.......................              5,125.00
    To record the payment of
    liabilities for interest and
    principal.
```

Discount Notes. Assume that a firm goes to a finance company on December 1 and borrows money, signing a noninterest-bearing 60-day note for $6,000. The finance company discounts the note at 7 percent. The firm employs a calendar-year accounting period. The amount of cash actually received is $5,930 ($6,000 maturity value less $70 discount). Included in the maturity value is the charge of $70 for the use of money. The entry would be:

```
Dec. 1   Cash................................. 5,930
             Notes Payable.....................        5,930
```

Notice that in this direct approach the liability is recorded at its present value on December 1, not at the ultimate legal liability 60 days in the future. Liabilities represent a source of assets; in this case the source is only $5,930 on December 1.

It is true, however, that the liability will increase as time passes and interest accrues. On December 31 we would make an adjusting entry to record the 30 days' interest applicable to December:

```
Dec. 31   Interest Charges.......................... 35
              Notes Payable..........................        35
```

Notice that, although we are recording interest, we do not use a separate liability account. This procedure is consistent with the legal document, which includes interest in the face amount of the note. The December 31 position statement would show notes payable of $5,965.

On the due date of January 30 the remaining interest is accrued. This brings the note up to its face value of $6,000, which is the amount owed at maturity. The entries would be:

```
Jan. 30   Interest Charges.....................   35
              Notes Payable...................          35

          Notes Payable.......................  6,000
              Cash.............................         6,000
```

Another method of recording this type of transaction, commonly found in accounting practice, involves crediting the note at its face value with an offsetting debit to a contra liability account:

```
Dec. 1   Cash................................. 5,930
             Notes Payable—Discount ..............   70
             Notes Payable.....................         6,000
```

This approach has the advantage of reflecting the ultimate legal liability in the accounts. It is also easier to use when the general ledger account is a control account for a number of individual notes recorded in a subsidiary ledger. The Notes Payable—Discount is analogous to the Bonds

Payable—Discount account. The market rate of interest, as reflected in the discount rate of 7 percent, is above the stated rate of interest, which in this case is zero. Hence, the present value of the note is less than its maturity value.

As interest accrues, we debit Interest Charges and credit the contra liability account, thereby increasing the total liability. The entries under this procedure on December 31 and January 30 are:

```
Dec. 31  Interest Charges.....................   35
             Notes Payable—Discount ..........          35

Jan. 30  Interest Charges.....................   35
             Notes Payable—Discount ..........          35

         Notes Payable........................ 6,000
             Cash................................        6,000
```

Notes Receivable

The recording of notes receivable parallels that for notes payable. If the note is explicitly interest-bearing, entries may be made periodically to record the accruing of an asset, interest receivable, and the earning of interest revenue.

Discount Notes. If the note receivable is discounted instead, the holder of the note may either record the present or discounted value directly or use a contra-account approach. The finance company in the above example could record the series of entries in either of the ways shown in Table 10–4. The contra-account procedure is more common. If this approach is used, Notes Receivable—Discount, often called Unearned Discount, is a contra asset representing the amount of interest that will be earned if the note is held to maturity. On the position statement it should be subtracted from the face amount of the note.

TABLE 10–4

			Direct Approach		Contra-Account Approach	
Dec.	1	Notes Receivable.......	5,930		6,000	
		Notes Receivable—Discount........				70
		Cash..............		5,930		5,930
Dec.	31	Notes Receivable.......	35			
		Notes Receivable—Discount............			35	
		Interest Revenue...		35		35
Jan.	30	Notes Receivable.......	35			
		Notes Receivable—Discount............			35	
		Interest Revenue...		35		35
		Cash..................	6,000		6,000	
		Notes Receivable...		6,000		6,000

Discounting Notes Receivable

A method of financing business operations frequently employed by wholesalers and retailers of durable consumer products involves the discounting of customers' notes with a finance company or bank. A dealer receives a note from a customer. Instead of holding the note until maturity, he turns it over either immediately or some time before maturity to a financial institution in exchange for cash. The bank or finance company pays what the note is currently worth, usually employing the discount procedure to compute its present value.

Take the following situation: an appliance company sells a group of appliances to a builder of apartment houses. The latter gives a 6 percent, 120-day note for $2,000, dated July 1. On July 31 the dealer discounts the note with a finance company. The discount rate is 7 percent. The finance company would compute the present value of the note as follows:

```
Maturity value ($2,000 plus $40 interest)..................  $2,040.00
Discount (charge for using money 90 days @ 7%).........        35.70
Proceeds or present value of note.......................     $2,004.30
```

The appliance company receives $2,004.30 for the note and, upon transfer of the note to the finance company, makes the following entries:

```
July 31   Cash............................. 2,004.30
                Notes Receivable...........             2,000.00
                Interest Revenue...........                 4.30
```

The interest revenue of $4.30 actually results from a netting of the interest earned on the note for 30 days ($10) and the financial or discount charge levied by the finance company ($5.70). Although the note is worth $2,010 at a 6 percent *interest* rate, its value is less to the finance company, which desires to earn a 7 percent *discount* rate (about a 7.5 percent equivalent interest rate). If a net debit results from this difference in valuations, it can be viewed as a type of financing expense.

In most cases the note is transferred "with recourse," that is, the finance company may return the note to the seller for payment if the builder should default. In this situation the appliance dealer is contingently liable on the note. If the note is not paid by the customer, the dealer has to pay the full amount due. Sometimes a type of service charge called a protest fee is added by the lending institution for its inconvenience.

Dishonored Notes Receivable

If the maker of a note defaults in paying at maturity, the note is said to have been dishonored. Exactly how the dishonored note is handled in the holder's accounting records depends on the circumstances of the particular situation. The interest that has been earned is usually brought up to date, so that the accounts for notes and interest reflect the full legal claim of the holder of the note. Then, to reflect the formal dishonoring of the note, the balances in those accounts associated with the note are removed. If there is reasonable certainty that collection will eventually take place, a special account receivable would be debited:

```
Accounts Receivable—Past-Due Notes.............. xxx
    Notes Receivable...............................      xxx
    Interest Receivable (if all interest has
    been accrued)................................      xxx
```

On the other hand, if the note will not be collected, it should be written off along with any accrued interest to a special loss account. Or, if the company's estimate of bad debts was established to cover uncollectible notes as well as accounts receivable, the contra asset Allowance for Bad Debts would be charged, as in the case of a write-off of a specific uncollectible account receivable.

SUMMARY

The impact of legal and financial conventions on the recording process is quite evident in the handling of notes and bonds. Examples include the tendency for accountants to record maturity values of discount notes and bonds in the main accounts, using contra and adjunct accounts to reflect their present value; the recording of interest receivable and payable in separate accounts except in the case of discount notes; and the use of both discount rates and interest rates in calculating the interest charge. Nevertheless, do not lose sight of the basic concepts of interest as the charge for the use of money and of present value as the valuation basis for recording notes and bonds. The amount of money actually being used, not the ultimate maturity value, determines the initial asset or equity. This amount times the effective interest rate gives the true periodic interest charge. As the interest accrues with the passage of time, the present value of the note or bond moves toward the maturity value.

APPENDIX 10–A
COMPOUND INTEREST AND PRESENT VALUE

The purpose of this appendix is twofold. First, it presents the basic elements of compound interest in a formal manner. Included are discussions of both compound interest and present-value formulas, an explanation of the use of present-value tables, and some elaboration of the basic concepts. Second, some uses of present-value techniques are outlined and illustrated in an attempt to acquaint the reader with this commonly employed analytical aid in decision making.

Compound Interest

Interest is the growth of an amount of money during a time period because a price must be paid (received) for the use of it. Thus, if $1,000 is deposited at an interest rate of 5 percent, the amount receivable at the end of the year is $1,050. This example illustrates *simple interest*—that is, interest for one time period only. The basic formula is:

$$a = p + ip = p(1 + i)$$

where a equals the amount of money accumulated, p is the principal, and i is the rate of interest per time period.

Any growth in amount during the year, if not withdrawn, becomes part of the invested sum. Therefore, in future periods the interest element from past years will also draw interest. This phenomenon is called *compound interest*. It lies at the heart of many financial decisions involving sums of money borrowed or invested for more than a single time period.

Amount of $1. The amount of $1 at compound interest refers to the future value of a sum of money.[7] To what amount would a sum of money accumulate in n periods if invested today at i rate of interest? Our knowledge of simple interest would indicate that the amount at the end of a single period would be $1 plus the interest earned on it.

$$a_1 = (1 + i)$$

If the amount is left to accumulate, the compound interest phenomenon becomes operative. During the second period, the entire sum at the end of the first period earns interest. Therefore,

$$a_2 = a_1(1 + i) = (1 + i)(1 + i) = (1 + i)^2$$

A continuation of this process would lead to a general formula:

$$a_{\overline{n}|i} = (1 + i)^n$$

where $a_{\overline{n}|i}$ is the amount to which $1 would accumulate if invested at i rate of interest for n periods.[8]

---

[7] In deriving and using formulas involving compound interest and present value, users find it easier to work in terms of a single dollar. Expressions and tables for values of $1 provide a generalized form that can be used in problems having different dollar amounts. All that is necessary is to multiply the compound interest or present value factor for $1 by the principal amount actually involved in the problem.

[8] Varying symbols and names describe this concept. Some authors use s instead of a and r instead of i. Alternative names include the sum of one, the future value of one, or the future worth of one.

To determine the amount of any quantity of money other than $1, multiply $a_{\overline{n}|i}$ by that quantity. For example, if $5,000 is invested for five years at 6 percent interest compounded annually, the accumulated amount at the end of five years can be determined as follows:

$$a_{\overline{5}|.06}\ \$5,000 = \$5,000\ (1+i)^n$$
$$= \$5,000\ (1.06)^5$$
$$= \$5,000\ (1.3382)$$
$$= \$6,691$$

If interest were compounded semiannually, we would calculate the amount for 10 six-month periods at 3 percent per period.

$$a_{\overline{10}|.03}\ \$5,000 = \$5,000\ (1.03)^{10}$$
$$= \$5,000\ (1.3439)$$
$$= \$6,719.50$$

Notice that the future amount is greater in this case because we have more opportunity to earn "interest on interest" than with annual compounding.

Amount of $1 per Period. A closely related and natural extension of the concept of the future amount of $1 is the amount of $1 per period. This concept deals with the future growth of a series of equal investments made at the end of equal time intervals. The term *annuity* is used to describe a group of periodic deposits, receipts, or payments of this type. The basic question underlying the amount of an annuity might be phrased: To what amount would a periodic deposit of money accumulate in n years if a deposit is made at the end of each of the n years and earns at i rate of interest? We will use the abbreviation $A_{\overline{n}|i}$ for the amount of an annuity.

The derivation of a generalized formula for the future amount of an annuity is not so straightforward as that for a single investment. However, the general concept is the same. For example, $1 is deposited at the end of each year for four years. The growth of each year's deposit is summarized in Table 10–A–1. Being made at the end of the first year, the first year's deposit earns compound interest only for three years. Years

TABLE 10–A–1

End-of-Year Deposit	Accumulated Value at End of Year				For n Years
	1	2	3	4	
First............ $1		$(1+i)$	$(1+i)^2$	$(1+i)^3$	$(1+i)^{n-1}$
Second...........		1	$(1+i)$	$(1+i)^2$	$(1+i)^{n-2}$
Third...........			1	$(1+i)$	$(1+i)$
Fourth				1	1

2, 3, and 4. The last year's deposit has earned no interest and adds only its original quantity to the total amount.

The amount of this annuity at the end of four years is the total of the accumulated-value column for Year 4. The generalized notation at the right indicates that the amount of any annuity of $1 for n years is:

$$A_{\overline{n}|i} = (1+i)^{n-1} + (1+i)^{n-2} + (1+i)^{n-3} + \cdots + (1+i) + 1$$

This expression is a geometric series, the sum of which is:

$$A_{\overline{n}|i} = \frac{(1+i)^n - 1}{i}$$

The formula for the amount of $1 per period can be used in any situation in which there are regular periodic payments or receipts.

Example. A firm has entered into a contract under which it receives $2,000 for its services at the end of every six months for five years. The buyer has asked the firm how much it would be willing to accept in a lump-sum amount at the end of five years instead of the periodic fees. Assume that the firm can earn 6 percent compounded semiannually.

$$A_{\overline{10}|.03}\,\$2,000 = \frac{(1.03)^{10} - 1}{0.03} \times \$2,000$$
$$= \frac{1.3439 - 1}{0.03} \times \$2,000$$
$$= \$22,928$$

Annuity Due. The preceding discussion assumed that all payments, receipts, or deposits are made at the end of the interest period. Such a series is called more precisely an *ordinary annuity* or *annuity in arrears*. If payments occur at the beginning of the periods, the series is called an *annuity due* or an *annuity in advance*. In an ordinary annuity for five years, there are only four interest periods, since payments are not made until the end of the year. Consequently, an annuity due for five years has the same number of interest periods as an ordinary annuity of six years. Of course, it would not have the payment at the end of the sixth year. Generalizing from this, we can arrive at the formula for the amount of an annuity due ($A_{D\overline{n}|i}$) in terms of an ordinary annuity:

$$A_{D\overline{n}|i} = A_{n+\overline{1}|i} - 1$$

This simple conversion allows us to deal with situations involving receipts or payments either at the beginning or the end of the period through use of the same annuity factors.

Compound Interest Tables. Tables are available for both the amount of $1 and the amount of an annuity of $1. These tables simplify the calculations by presenting the results for varying interest rates and time periods. Brief extracts from such tables are presented in Tables 10–A–4 and 10–A–5 at the end of the appendix.

Present Value

The concept of present value is the opposite of compound interest. Instead of showing how much a single payment or series of payments will increase over time, present value indicates how much you have to pay now in order to have a certain amount or series of amounts in future periods. Present value is the current cash equivalent of some designated future amount or amounts.

Present Value of $1. The formula for the present value of $1 received n periods in the future at an interest rate of i percent ($p_{\overline{n}|i}$) can be derived from the formula for the amount of $1. If we let x equal the present value of $1 n years in the future, we can solve for x as follows:

$$a_{\overline{n}|i} (x) = x (1 + i)^n = 1$$

$$x = \frac{1}{(1 + i)^n} = (1 + i)^{-n} = p_{\overline{n}|i}$$

In brief, a reciprocal relationship exists between the present value of $1 and the amount of $1.

This formula can be applied to any situation in which we desire the present value of some future amount.

Example. A customer owes you $7,500 due in six years. He approaches you about the possibility of paying off the debt early with a single payment now. What is the minimum amount you would be willing to accept now if the interest rate is 8 percent?

$$p_{\overline{6}|.08} \$7,500 = \$7,500(1.08)^{-6}$$
$$= \$7,500(0.6302)$$
$$= \$4,726$$

Present Value of $1 per Period. Commonly, business and financial problems involve a series of equal amounts spaced at approximately the same interval in the future. What single cash receipt (or payment) now is the equivalent of a series of cash receipts (or payments) to be made at the end of each of n years if the earning value of money is i? The abbreviation $P_{\overline{n}|i}$ is used for the present value of an annuity.

The present value of an annuity of $1 is closely related to the present value of $1 and to the amount of an annuity of $1. It is the sum of a series of individual calculations of the present value of $1. Likewise, the present value of an annuity is the reverse process of the amount of an annuity. Consequently, its formula can be derived from either of these other concepts.

For example, the amount of an annuity of $1 for n years at i rate of interest is $([1 + i]^n - 1)/i$. This is the single future amount which is the equivalent of the annuity. If we desire the single present amount which is the equivalent of the annuity, we must take the present value of the future amount. We can determine the present value of any future amount by multiplying it by $(1 + i)^{-n}$. Putting these facts together gives us the following:

$$P_{\overline{n}|i} = p_{\overline{n}|i}(A_{\overline{n}|i})$$
$$= [(1 + i)^{-n}]\left[\frac{(1 + i)^n - 1}{i}\right]$$
$$= \frac{1 - (1 + i)^{-n}}{i}$$

Through use of this formula we can solve for the present value of any annuity or for other variables (interest rate, periodic payment) we are interested in.

Example.   A customer owes you $1,250 at the end of each year for the next six years.[9] He approaches you about the possibility of paying off the debt early with a single payment now. What is the minimum amount you would be willing to accept now if the interest rate is 8 percent?

$$P_{\overline{6}|.08}\,\$1,250 = \$1,250\left[\frac{1 - (1 + i)^{-n}}{i}\right]$$
$$= \$1,250(4.6229)$$
$$= \$5,779$$

Present Value Tables.   Present value tables for the single amount of $1 and for an annuity of $1 are presented in Tables 10–A–6 and 10–A–7 and supply us with the factors to use in expressing any dollar figures in terms of their present values. A few observations about them may enhance their usefulness. Table 10–A–6 gives the amount one would have to invest now at various interest rates in order to have $1 at the end of various time periods in the future. Table 10–A–7 gives the amount one would have to invest now at various interest rates in order to withdraw $1 at the end of each period for various time periods.

Annuity Due.   An annuity due is defined as a series of payments (or receipts) occurring at the beginning of equal intervals of time. Therefore, an annuity due for four years would have payments at the beginning of years one, two (end of year one), three (end of year two), and four (end of year three). If we ignore the first payment, the result is identical to an ordinary annuity for three years. Since the present value

---

[9] Notice that this example is quite similar to the previous one except that in this case, the $7,500 is payable in six yearly payments rather than in one payment at the end of six years. Because the series of receipts is not as distant as the single receipt, the present value of the annuity is larger ($5,779 vs. $4,726) than that of the single receipt six years hence, even though the total number of dollars is the same.

of the first payment is the full amount, the present value of an annuity due of four years is the equivalent of the present value of an ordinary annuity of three years plus one payment or receipt. In general terms, this is expressed

$$P_{\overline{D n}|i} = P_{n-\overline{1}|i} + 1$$

Infinite Annuity. If annuity payments (receipts) continue for a large number of periods, the n in the present-value formula below would become very large.

$$P_{\overline{n}|i} = \frac{1 - (1 + i)^{-n}}{i}$$

As a result, the expression $(1 + i)^{-n}$ would become very small. In fact as n approached perpetuity, $(1 + i)^{-n}$ would approach zero and the whole formula would approach the reciprocal of the interest rate $(1/i)$. By dividing the annuity payment (receipt) by the interest rate, we can calculate its present value, assuming an indefinite time period.

Continuous Discounting. With shorter compounding intervals, the future amount of any given quantity of money becomes greater. We would expect the opposite to be true with respect to the discounting of amounts to present value. The shorter the length of the interest period, the smaller the present value. With more frequent interest accumulations, more interest is earned on prior interest accumulations. Consequently, it is necessary to invest a smaller sum now if interest is compounded monthly than if it is compounded only annually. Or, to put it another way, because amounts grow more rapidly with shorter interest periods, the "cost of waiting" for a delayed cash receipt is higher. Consequently, the current cash equivalent or present value is lower.

When the compounding period becomes infinitely short, the entire present-value formula[10] becomes $1/e^{in}$. The process giving rise to this formula is called continuous discounting. It refers to interest's being accumulated and added to principal continuously rather than only at intermittent times. Some authors rightly contend that the use of continuous discounting is more accurate when future cash receipts or payments consist of continuous flows throughout a time interval rather than of discrete quantities at specified intervals.[11]

---

[10] The mathematical constant e, which is approximately 2.718, is used frequently in mathematical computations involving natural logarithms.

[11] Continuous discounting (compounding) is more useful in mathematical operations involving calculus. Theoretically it may be more accurate for certain types of investment decisions. Nevertheless, most financial transactions—borrowing and lending—are not based on continuous discounting. Practically, it does not produce results materially different from that of annual or semiannual discounting when interest rates are not unduly high or time periods excessively long. Therefore, tables like those presented in this appendix are more widely employed and are suitable for most situations.

Applications of Present-Value Techniques

Uses of the compound interest concepts can be found wherever managerial or investor decisions require a comparison of dollar amounts at two different points in time. In these cases consideration must be given to the time-value of money. The examples in this section briefly illustrate the use of present-value techniques in some accounting and financial areas and provide an opportunity for using the compound interest tables.

Asset Valuation.   Assets are acquired to produce future economic benefits. Presumably, in deciding to acquire an asset, an investor makes a comparison between future inflows from the asset and the present outflow to acquire the asset. Ideally, the value he places on the asset should be equal to the present value of the expected future net receipts derived from it.

Bond and Loan Investments.   Present-value analysis directly underlies the valuation of bond and loan investments. An investor in bonds is willing to pay an amount equal to the present value of the expected interest receipts plus the present value of the maturity amount. From his standpoint the value of his investment asset (hence, the maximum price he would be willing to pay) is the summation of those two present values.

For another example, assume that a bank is considering the acquisition of a $50,000 face value five-year note to be issued by a nearby municipality. The note will be held to maturity as an investment. It bears no interest explicitly but is being offered to the bank at a price of $40,000. The bank can invest its funds in alternative opportunities yielding 4 percent. Compound interest techniques can be used in a number of ways to help the bank decide whether to lend money on this note. First, if the bank invests its $40,000 in other opportunities, the $40,000 would grow to only $48,668 ($a_{\overline{5}|.04}$ $40,000 = $40,000 \times 1.2167 = $48,668$), which is significantly less than the $50,000 it would receive from the municipality. Or the bank could determine the present value of the note to be $41,100 ($p_{\overline{5}|.04}$ $50,000 = $50,000 \times 0.8219 = $41,100$). If the bank wishes to earn 4 percent, it could lend up to $41,100. Since the bank has to loan only $40,000 to earn the $50,000 dollar return, the value of the asset to management ($41,100) is greater than its cost ($40,000).

Equipment.   Present-value techniques play a large role in analyses of capital expenditures on plant assets. Take the following example. A manufacturing firm, by purchasing a new piece of machinery for $30,000, could process its product one stage further. The more valuable product would command a higher selling price and cause sales to increase by $10,000 a year. The only cost outside of the machine itself would be $6,000 wages for an operator. The company believes that it can sell the machine for $5,000 at the end of its useful life of 10 years. The company will not undertake this investment unless it can earn a return of 10 percent. The maximum amount that the company should offer for the equipment is the present value of the expected returns from the equipment—the values to be received from its future use, discounted at 10 percent. The future values consist of a net return of $4,000 each year for 10 years ($10,000 additional sales less $6,000 wages) and $5,000 at the end of 10 years.

$$\text{Present value of machine} = P_{\overline{10}|.10}\,\$4,000 + p_{\overline{10}|.10}\,\$5,000$$
$$= 6.1446(\$4,000) + 0.3855(\$5,000)$$
$$= \$26,506$$

Consequently, the firm would not pay $30,000 for this asset.[12]

Liability Valuation and Financing Decisions

We have already explored the relationship between present-value concepts and bonds and notes payable. These same concepts can be extended to the valuation of other types of liabilities, such as leases, pensions, and various alternative forms of financing. Leases and pensions are discussed in Chapter Eleven. A few examples of the application of present value to installment contracts and deferred payment plans are given in this section.

Example 1: Determination of Installment Payments. A delivery service can acquire a new truck from a dealer by signing an installment note for $6,200. The note is to be liquidated over a 15-month period with interest at a rate of 1 percent per month. For financial planning, management wishes to know what the monthly installment payments will be. The face amount of the note can be viewed as the present value of a series of payments of x amount for 15 periods at 1 percent per period.

$$P_{\overline{15}|.01}\,(x) = \$6,200$$
$$x = \$6,200 \div 13.8651 = \$447.17$$

As a separate exercise the reader can verify that 15 payments of $447.17 will, in fact, repay the $6,200 debt plus interest at 1 percent per month.

Example 2: Calculation of Effective Interest Rates. A metal fabricator purchased a stamping press costing $50,000. A deferred payment plan was arranged under which the purchaser would make a $10,000 down payment and a $50,000 payment at the end of the second year. What effective rate of interest is inherent in this arrangement? The general analysis can be set forth in terms of present-value formulas as follows:

---

[12] This approach is called the *net present value* method of analysis. For simplicity, we have ignored the many difficulties involved in actually determining future returns in realistic situations, including the impact of income taxes. An alternative approach, called the *discounted or time-adjusted rate of return*, solves for the interest rate that will make the present value of future receipts exactly equal to $30,000. In this case, the rate is approximately 7 percent, substantially below the desired 10 percent return.

$$\$50,000 = \$10,000 + p_{\overline{2}|i}(\$50,000)$$
$$p_{\overline{2}|i} = 0.8000$$
$$i = 12\%$$

Example 3: Comparison of Financing Plans. A real estate developer owns a piece of land at the edge of the city. Two companies have offered to purchase it under varying financial plans, as described below:

Offer 1: $10,000 payment at the beginning of each year for five years.
Offer 2: $15,000 down payment plus a four-year note for $35,000 face amount, bearing interest at the rate of 4 percent payable annually (i.e., $1,400 per year).

If the same risk is inherent in each offer and money is worth 6 percent to the company, the best offer is that which has the greatest present value.

Offer 1: $= P_{\overline{5}|.06} \$10,000$
$\quad = P_{\overline{4}|.06} \$10,000 + \$10,000$
$\quad = (3.4651)(\$10,000) + \$10,000$
$\quad = \$44,651$

Offer 2: $= \$15,000 + P_{\overline{4}|.06} \$1,400 + p_{\overline{4}|.06} \$35,000$
$\quad = \$15,000 + (3.4651)(\$1,400) + (0.7921)(\$35,000)$
$\quad = \$47,575$

The comparisons above involve listing the various cash inflows from each of the financing plans and then determining the present value of each inflow. On this basis, Offer 2 is the more advantageous.

Depreciation Calculations

The common accounting procedures for systematically allocating the cost of depreciable assets over their useful lives result in uniform, decreasing, or varying patterns of depreciation over time. One additional possibility is an increasing depreciation charge over time. Two procedures based on present-value concepts provide such a pattern. Both approaches employ the assumption that the cost of a depreciable asset represents the present value of a series of future amounts. For example, if it were known that a piece of equipment would produce net cash inflows of $7,000 each year for the next four years and that a return of 10 percent should be earned on the investment, management would be willing to pay $22,190 for the asset ($P_{\overline{4}|.10} \$7,000$).

Annuity Method. Two features distinguish this depreciation method. First, each year depreciation expense equals the cost divided by the present value of an annuity ($\$22,190 \div P_{\overline{4}|.10}$ or $7,000).[13] This constant depreciation charge includes a portion of the cost of the asset plus an imputed interest return on the investment. Presumably it reflects the total cost of a year of asset service, including interest specifically as a cost element. The second feature is that the interest that could have been earned by not having funds tied up in the asset is recorded specifically as interest earned. The difference between the interest and the depreciation charge is credited to accumulated depreciation (see Table 10–A–2). Total net

TABLE 10–A–2

Year	Depreciation Expense (Dr.)*	Interest Revenue (Cr.)†	Accumulated Depreciation (Cr.)‡	Asset Status		
				Cost	Accum. Dep.	Book Value
0............	...	...	...	$22,190	0	$22,190
1............	$ 7,000	$2,219	$ 4,781	22,190	4,781	17,409
2............	7,000	1,740	5,260	22,190	10,041	12,149
3............	7,000	1,215	5,785	22,190	15,826	6,364
4............	7,000	636	6,364	22,190	22,190	0
	$28,000	$5,810	$22,190			

* $22,190 ÷ $P_{\overline{7}|.10}$.
† 10% of book value at beginning of year.
‡ Depreciation expense minus interest revenue.

income is unaffected by the hypothetical interest revenue, because depreciation also is higher by the amount of the interest element. But since the interest element declines each period because of the decrease in unrecovered investment, the result is an increasing net charge against income.

Capital Recovery Method. This method explicitly offsets the imputed interest revenue to obtain an increasing depreciation charge. Each periodic cash inflow of $7,000 is viewed as comprising an income return and a recovery of capital (depreciation expense). For instance, the $7,000 receipt in the first year consists of $2,219 (10% × $22,190) income and $4,781 ($7,000 − $2,219) recovery of capital. The latter is the amount debited to Depreciation Expense. In the second year the income portion declines to $1,740 (10% × $17,409), since the unrecovered investment is smaller. As a consequence, the capital recovery portion (depreciation expense) increases to $5,260 ($7,000 − $1,740).

Evaluation of Increasing Charge Methods. The net effect of these methods is the same, although the rationale in each case is slightly different. The advantage claimed for them is that they provide a constant return on investment over the life of the asset, as can be seen in the comparison in Table 10–A–3 between the interest methods and the straight-line expedient.

---

[13] The formula for annuity depreciation is (Cost − present value of salvage)/$P_{\overline{n}|i}$. In our example, salvage is assumed to be zero.

TABLE 10-A-3

	1	2	3	4
Interest Method				
Net revenues...............	$ 7,000	$ 7,000	$ 7,000	$ 7,000
Depreciation expense.........	4,781	5,260	5,785	6,364
Net income (*a*).............	$ 2,219	$ 1,740	$ 1,215	$ 636
Asset cost..................	$22,190	$22,190	$22,190	$22,190
Accumulated depreciation.....	...	4,781	10,041	15,826
Net asset investment (*b*)......	$22,190	$17,409	$12,149	$ 6,364
Return on investment (*a* ÷ *b*).................	10%	10%	10%	10%
Straight-Line Method				
Net revenues...............	$ 7,000	$ 7,000	$ 7,000	$ 7,000
Depreciation expense.........	5,548	5,547	5,548	5,547
Net income (*a*).............	$ 1,452	$ 1,453	$ 1,452	$ 1,453
Asset cost..................	$22,190	$22,190	$22,190	$22,190
Accumulated depreciation.....	...	5,548	11,095	16,643
Net asset investment (*b*)......	$22,190	$16,642	$11,095	$ 5,547
Return on investment (*a* ÷ *b*).................	6.5%	8.7%	13.1%	26.2%

For external reporting purposes, objections are raised to the complexity of these methods and to the automatic assumption of a specific, positive earning rate on the asset. Some accountants also feel that the increasing pattern of depreciation over time is contrary to the actual usage of asset services. However, that objection begs the questions of what constitutes an asset's service and how we measure the total cost of the services consumed.

Despite their rare use, the present-value approaches to depreciation do shed additional light on the nature of the investment process and the cost of asset services. In addition, for the managerial purposes of planning or internal evaluation of divisions, they actually may provide more meaningful information concerning rate of return on investment. They suggest an alternative view of what matching means—a view stressing the relation of income to investment rather than the relation of expense to revenue.

Summary

There is an old adage which states that time is money. Compound interest and present-value concepts simply put this adage into formulas and tables. The fundamental point is that differences in the timing of cash inflows and outflows must be considered when those flows are evaluated and compared. When we are concerned with determining the future amount that is equivalent to a given sum now, compound interest is involved. When the focal point is the amount now that is equivalent to a given sum in the future, present value is employed.

TABLE 10–A–4

Future Amount of One Dollar $(1 + i)^n$

Number of Periods	Rate of Interest						
	1%	3%	4%	5%	6%	8%	10%
1......	1.0100	1.0300	1.0400	1.0500	1.0600	1.0800	1.1000
2......	1.0201	1.0609	1.0816	1.1025	1.1236	1.1664	1.2100
3......	1.0303	1.0927	1.1249	1.1576	1.1910	1.2597	1.3310
4......	1.0406	1.1255	1.1699	1.2155	1.2625	1.3605	1.4641
5......	1.0510	1.1593	1.2167	1.2763	1.3382	1.4693	1.6105
6......	1.0615	1.1941	1.2653	1.3401	1.4185	1.5869	1.7716
7......	1.0721	1.2299	1.3159	1.4071	1.5036	1.7138	1.9487
8......	1.0829	1.2668	1.3686	1.4775	1.5938	1.8509	2.1436
9......	1.0937	1.3048	1.4233	1.5513	1.6895	1.9990	2.3579
10......	1.1046	1.3439	1.4802	1.6289	1.7908	2.1589	2.5937
15......	1.1610	1.5580	1.8009	2.0789	2.3966	3.1722	4.1772
20......	1.2202	1.8061	2.1911	2.6533	3.2071	4.6610	6.7275
25......	1.2824	2.0938	2.6658	3.3864	4.2919	6.8485	10.8347
30......	1.3478	2.4273	3.2434	4.3219	5.7435	10.0627	17.4494

TABLE 10–A–5

Future Amount of One Dollar per Period $\left[\dfrac{(1 + i)^n - 1}{i} \right]$

Number of Periods	Rate of Interest						
	1%	3%	4%	5%	6%	8%	10%
1.......	1.0000	1.0000	1.0000	1.0000	1.0000	1.0000	1.0000
2.......	2.0100	2.0300	2.0400	2.0500	2.0600	2.0800	2.1000
3.......	3.0301	3.0909	3.1216	3.1525	3.1836	3.2464	3.3100
4.......	4.0604	4.1836	4.2465	4.3101	4.3746	4.5061	4.6410
5.......	5.1010	5.3091	5.4163	5.5256	5.6371	5.8666	6.1051
6.......	6.1520	5.4684	6.6330	6.8019	6.9753	7.3359	7.7156
7.......	7.2135	7.6625	7.8983	8.1420	8.3938	8.9228	9.4872
8.......	8.2857	8.8923	9.2142	9.5491	9.8975	10.6366	11.4359
9.......	9.3685	10.1591	10.5828	11.0266	11.4913	12.4876	13.5795
10.......	10.4622	11.4639	12.0061	12.5779	13.1808	14.4866	15.9374
15.......	16.0969	18.5989	20.0236	21.5786	23.2760	27.1521	31.7725
20.......	22.0190	26.8704	29.7781	33.0660	36.7856	45.7620	57.2750
25.......	28.2432	36.4593	41.6459	47.7271	54.8645	73.1059	98.3471
30.......	34.7849	47.5754	56.0849	66.4388	79.0582	113.2832	164.4940

Note: For an annuity due, take one more period and subtract 1.000.

TABLE 10–A–6
Present Value of One Dollar $(1 + i)^{-n}$

Number of Periods	Rate of Interest						
	1%	3%	4%	5%	6%	8%	10%
1	.9901	.9709	.9615	.9524	.9434	.9259	.9091
2	.9803	.9426	.9246	.9070	.8900	.8573	.8264
3	.9706	.9151	.8890	.8638	.8396	.7938	.7513
4	.9610	.8885	.8548	.8227	.7921	.7350	.6830
5	.9515	.8626	.8219	.7835	.7473	.6806	.6209
6	.9420	.8375	.7903	.7462	.7050	.6302	.5645
7	.9327	.8131	.7599	.7107	.6651	.5835	.5132
8	.9235	.7894	.7307	.6768	.6274	.5403	.4665
9	.9143	.7664	.7026	.6446	.5919	.5002	.4241
10	.9053	.7441	.6756	.6139	.5584	.4632	.3855
15	.8613	.6419	.5553	.4810	.4173	.3152	.2394
20	.8195	.5537	.4564	.3769	.3118	.2145	.1486
25	.7798	.4776	.3751	.2953	.2330	.1460	.0923
30	.7419	.4120	.3083	.2314	.1741	.0994	.0573

TABLE 10–A–7
Present Value of One Dollar per Period $\dfrac{1 - (1 + i)^{-n}}{i}$

Number of Periods	Rate of Interest						
	1%	3%	4%	5%	6%	8%	10%
1	0.9901	0.9709	0.9615	0.9524	0.9434	0.9259	0.9091
2	1.9704	1.9135	1.8861	1.8594	1.8334	1.7833	1.7355
3	2.9410	2.8286	2.7751	2.7232	2.6730	2.5771	2.4869
4	3.9020	3.7171	3.6299	3.5460	3.4651	3.3121	3.1699
5	4.8534	4.5797	4.4518	4.3295	4.2124	3.9927	3.7908
6	5.7955	5.4172	5.2421	5.0757	4.9173	4.6229	4.3553
7	6.7282	6.2303	6.0021	5.7864	5.5824	5.2064	4.8684
8	7.6517	7.0197	6.7327	6.4632	6.2098	5.7466	5.3349
9	8.5660	7.7861	7.4353	7.1078	6.8017	6.2469	5.7590
10	9.4713	8.5302	8.1109	7.7217	7.3601	6.7101	6.1446
15	13.8651	11.9379	11.1184	10.3797	9.7122	8.5595	7.6061
20	18.0456	14.8775	13.5903	12.4622	11.4699	9.8181	8.5136
25	22.0232	17.4132	15.6221	14.0939	12.7834	10.6748	9.0770
30	25.8077	19.6004	17.2920	15.3725	13.7648	11.2578	9.4269

Note: For an annuity due, take one less period and add 1.000.

SUGGESTIONS FOR FURTHER READING

Anton, Hector R. "Accounting for Bond Liabilities," *Journal of Accountancy*, Vol. 98 (September 1956), pp. 53–56.

Moonitz, Maurice. "The Changing Concept of Liabilities," *Journal of Accountancy*, Vol. 113 (May 1960), pp. 41–46.

QUESTIONS AND PROBLEMS

10–1. The Nodice Corporation needs to borrow money to build a new plant. It decides to issue $2 million of 20-year bonds. The current market rate of interest for bonds of similar type and risk is 5 percent. The vice president of finance is weighing alternative nominal interest rates. He suggests two possibilities:

    1. Pay annual interest of 6 percent of the face amount, or $120,000.
    2. Pay annual interest of 4 percent of the face amount, or $80,000.

    a) Calculate the amount of money that will be received under each of these plans.

    b) Explain *why* more money is received under the first plan than the second, even though the face amount of the bonds is the same.

    c) Assuming the first plan is followed, calculate the interest charge for each of the first three years. Why does it decrease in each period?

    d) What dollar amount of annual interest would be required if the bonds were to be issued at par? Determine the present value for 20 years at 5 percent of the difference between this amount and the amount paid under the first alternative. What does your answer represent? Why?

10–2. Prepare journal entries to record the following transactions affecting the Groundown Company:

    1. One of their customers, Bridget Bardahl, owed the company $2,400 on open account. Bardahl offered to settle the account by giving the company a noninterest-bearing 90-day note with a face value of $2,445. The offer was accepted on June 21.

    2. Groundown closed its books on June 30.

    3. On July 9, Groundown discounted the note at a local finance company, with recourse, at a rate of 8 percent.

    4. Bardahl failed to pay the note at maturity, and Groundown was forced to remit the face amount of $2,445 to the finance company.

    5. The Groundown Company attempted to collect from Bardahl, but was unsuccessful when the latter claimed diplomatic immunity in France.

    6. A year later a check was received for the dishonored note with interest at 7 percent for the added year.

10–3. On July 1, 1971, the Abbott Company issued $500,000 maturity amount of 15-year, 5 percent bonds at a price to yield an effective rate of 6 percent. The bonds were dated July 1, 1971. Interest was payable *semiannually* on January 1 and July 1. The Abbott Company closed its books annually on December 31. The company also paid $10,000 cash for printing, legal, and other fees in connection with the issuance of the bonds.

a) Compute the proceeds that were received (1) by calculating the present value of the payments to be made under the bond contract and (2) by calculating the amount of bond discount directly.

b) Journalize the entries that would be made on (1) July 1, 1971; (2) December 31, 1971; (3) January 1, 1972; and (4) July 1, 1972. Assume the interest method of computing interest charges and the straight-line method of amortizing bond issue costs are employed.

c) Indicate how the accounts affected by this bond issue will appear on a position statement prepared as of July 1, 1981. Show the accounts, their classification on the statement, and their dollar amounts (calculate the latter directly; do not prepare a complete amortization schedule year by year).

10–4. The Simon Machinery Sales Corporation sold a lathe to the Garfunkle Processing Company. The Simon Corporation received a 120-day noninterest-bearing note from Garfunkle for $3,600. The note was dated July 1 and was discounted by Simon at 7 percent. The note was paid at maturity.

a) Make dated journal entries on the books of the Simon Machinery Sales Corporation relating to the above note. Assume the books are closed on July 31. Record using the direct procedure.

b) Make dated journal entries on the books of the Garfunkle Processing Company. Record using the contra account procedure.

10–5. The Whisk Corporation, maker of brooms, issued $300,000 of five-year, 6 percent convertible bonds on January 1, 1972. Interest was payable semiannually on July 1 and January 1. The bonds were issued at 98 percent of face value. Each $1,000 bond is convertible into 50 shares of common stock, which is currently selling at $15 per share on the open market.

On January 2, 1975, holders of $60,000 face value of the bonds decide to convert their bonds into common stock. The common stock has a current market value of $28 per share.

a) Prepare the journal entry to record the issuance of the bonds.

b) Prepare the necessary entries to accrue and pay the interest on July 1, 1972. Use straight-line amortization.

c) Prepare the journal entry to record the conversion of bonds into stock on January 2, 1975, (1) assuming book value of the bond issue is the measure of contributed capital, and (2) assuming market value of the stock is the measure of contributed capital.

10–6. A note has the following history:

May 21   Brutal Cutlery Shop sells goods to Adolph Caesar for $5,000 and receives an 8 percent 90-day note in exchange.

June 17 Brutal discounts the note with Anthony State Bank at a discount rate of 10 percent.

Aug. 19 The note is dishonored by Caesar, and the amount due plus a protest fee of $5 is paid by Brutal.

Aug. 20 An agreement is reached with Caesar under which Brutal receives a new 10 percent, 30-day note for the entire balance due, including the protest fee.

Sept. 19 Caesar pays the note plus interest.

Prepare dated journal entries relating to the above transactions for:

a) Caesar (fiscal year ends on August 31).
b) Brutal (fiscal year ends on June 30).
c) Anthony State Bank.

10–7. The RES Company issued $1 million face value of bonds. The bonds were dated January 1, 1972 and were due on January 1, 1982. Interest of 6 percent was payable annually on January 1. The bonds were issued on an annual yield-rate basis of 8 percent.

a) Prepare an amortization table for the entire 10-year period on an effective interest method of amortization. Use the following headings for your table.

Year	Liability, Beginning	Interest Charge	Nominal Interest	Amortiza- tion of Discount	Unamor- tized Discount	Liability, End of Period

b) Repeat part (a) assuming that a straight-line amortization method is employed.

c) How should the bond be reported on the position statement prepared as of December 31, 1973 under part (a)?

10–8. Eastinghouse, Inc. shows the following accounts on its trial balance at the end of 1972:

Bonds payable, 8% (due in 1982) . . . . $100,000 Cr.
Unamortized bond premium . . . .   2,300 Cr.
Unamortized bond issue costs . . . .   900 Dr.

The bonds are callable at 102 percent of face value. The company has an opportunity to borrow money more cheaply from an insurance company. The terms would be a 20-year, 6 percent bond for $90,000 to be purchased by the insurance company at 99 percent of face value. Accordingly, the company calls in and retires the old bond issue and issues the new one to the insurance company. The chief accountant makes the following entry:

```
Cost of Successful Refunding.....    3,000
Bonds Payable, 8%.................  100,000
Unamortized Bond Premium.........    2,300
     Unamortized Bond Issue
        Costs......................                900
     Bonds Payable, 6%............              90,000
     Cash........................              14,400
```

The credit to Cash is the difference between the $102,000 disbursed to call the old bonds and the $89,100 received from the issuance of the new bonds, plus $1,000 costs involved in calling the old bonds and $500 legal fees associated with issuing the new ones. The chief accountant describes the Cost of Successful Refunding account as an intangible asset to be amortized over the next 10 years, the remaining life of the old bond issue.

a) Prepare entries to record the refunding of the bonds in accordance with the method preferred by the text.

b) Exactly what comprises the $3,000 "cost of successful refunding?" Do you agree that it should be amortized over the next 10 years? Why, or why not? What would you do with the item?

10–9.   You are engaged in your fifth annual examination of the financial statements of Stack Corporation.* Your examination is for the year ended December 31, 1966. The client prepared the schedules of Trade Notes Receivable and Interest Receivable below for you at December 31, 1966. Prepare the adjusting journal entries you would suggest at December 31, 1966 for the following information revealed by your examination:

1. Interest is computed on a 360-day basis. In computing interest, it is the corporation's practice to exclude the first day of the note's term and to include the due date.

2. The Atkins Company's 90-day note was discounted on May 16 at 6 percent and the proceeds were credited to the Trade Notes Receivable account. The note was paid at maturity.

3. Forster Industries became bankrupt on August 31 and the corporation will recover 75 cents on the dollar. The corporation uses the direct write-off method for recording bad debt expense. All of Stack Corporation's notes receivable provide for interest at the legal rate of 6 percent on the maturity value of a dishonored note.

4. J. Stack, president of Stack Corporation, confirmed that he owed the corporation $10,000 and that he expected to pay the note within six months. You are satisfied that the note is collectible.

5. Listi Corporation's 60-day note was discounted on November 1 at 6 percent and the proceeds were credited to the Trade Notes Receivable and Interest Receivable accounts. On December 2 Stack Corporation received notice from the bank that Listi

---

* This problem adapted from AICPA May 1967 examination.

STACK CORPORATION
Trade Notes Receivable

Maker	Issue Date	Terms	Interest Rate	Balance 12-31-65	1966 Debits	1966 Credits	Balance 12-31-66
Brehm Co.	4-1-65	One year	6%	$60,000	$ 20,000	$ 60,000	
Atkins Co.	5-1-66	90 days	:%		4,000	19,750	$ 250
Forster Ind.	7-1-66	60 days	6%		10,000		4,000
J. Stack	8-3-66	Demand	6%		40,000		10,000
Listi Corp.	10-2-66	60 days	6%		40,000	40,000	40,000
Ho.shue Inc.	11-1-66	90 days	3%		42,000	35,000	7,000
Simpson Co.	11-1-66	90 days	6%		24,000		24,000
Totals				$60,000	$180,000	$154,750	$85,250

Interest Receivable

Due From	Balance 12-31-65	1966 Debits	1966 Credits	Balance 12-31-66
Brehm Co.	$2,700	$ 900	$3,600	$ 40
Forster Ind.		40		200
J. Stack		200		202
Listi Corp.		400	198	210
Holshue Inc.		210		240
Simpson Co.		240		
Totals	$2,700	$1,990	$3,798	$892

Corporation's note was not paid at maturity and that it had been charged against Stack's checking account by the bank. Upon receiving the notice from the bank, the bookkeeper recorded the note and accrued interest thereon in the Trade Notes Receivable and Interest Receivable accounts. Listi Corporation paid Stack Corporation the full amount due in January 1967.

6. The Holshue Inc. 90-day note was pledged as collateral for $35,000, 60-day, 6 percent loan from the First National Bank on December 1.

7. On November 1 the corporation received four $6,000 90-day notes from Simpson Co. On December 1 the corporation received payment from Simpson Co. for one of the $6,000 notes with accrued interest. Prepayment of the notes is allowed without penalty. The bookkeeper credited Simpson Co. Accounts receivable account for the cash received.

10–10. The Shady Sales Company, maker of aluminum awnings, originally issued $100,000 of 10-year, 6 percent bonds for $92,000 on January 1, 1969. Bond issue costs were $300.

On July 1, 1972, at the same time as the semiannual interest payment, the corporation called the bond issue and repurchased it for $101,000. The bookkeeper made the following entry to record the retirement:

```
Interest Charges................    3,000
Bonds Payable...................  100,000
Loss on Bond Retirement.........    1,000
    Cash.......................            104,000
```

Accumulation of bond discount and amortization of bond issue costs were computed on a straight-line basis through December 31, 1971.

Prepare the journal entry necessary to *correct* the books. Be sure to show all calculations clearly.

10–11. On September 1, 1971 the Crockett Company issued $1 million maturity amount of 10 percent, 10-year bonds. The bonds were issued when the market rate of interest was 8 percent, and the company received $1,135,902 for them. Interest is payable semiannually on March 1 and September 1. The Crocket Company's fiscal year ends on June 30.

a) Make journal entries for the Crocket Company as follows, using the interest method of bond amortization: (1) September 1, 1971; (2) March 1, 1972; (3) June 30, 1972; and (4) September 1, 1972.

b) Mr. M. T. Head, the treasurer, stated that the entry on September 1 should be:

```
Cash........................ 1,135,902
    Bonds Payable...........            1,000,000
    Gain on Issuance of
        Bonds...............              135,902
```

He argues, "By issuing our bonds at a premium, we were able to obtain $135,902 that we won't have to pay back to the bond-holders. Therefore, the $135,902 is part of the income for fiscal 1972, the year in which we took the action that led to the gain." Carefully evaluate his contention. Include a discussion of the nature and meaning of a bond premium.

10–12. The following transactions were selected from the Chowder Company. Make journal entries to record them.

June 3 Purchased merchandise on account from the Welsh Company, $650.

18 Discounted a 30-day noninterest-bearing note payable for $5,000 at the First National Bank; discount rate, 6 percent.

21 Sold merchandise on account to Emerson, Inc., $700.

29 Sold merchandise on account to Y. C. Lee, $1,200.

July 3 Issued a 60-day, 7 percent note for $650 to the Welsh Company in settlement of account.

18 Issued a check to the First National Bank for the amount due on the note dated June 18.

21 Received from Emerson, Inc., a 60-day, 6 percent note for $700 to apply on account.

29 Received from Y. C. Lee a one-month, 6 percent note for $1,200 to apply on account.

Aug. 10 Discounted Emerson, Inc.'s $700 note, dated July 21, at the Security National Bank; discount rate, 6 percent.

29 Received cash from Y. C. Lee of $850 and a new 7 percent, 60-day note for the balance owed on note dated July 29.

Sept. 1 Issued check to the Welsh Corpany in payment of note dated July 3.

19 Received notice from the Security National Bank that Emerson, Inc., had dishonored its note dated July 21. Issued a check to the bank in payment of the amount due plus a $5 protest fee. The Chowder Company expected to collect the total amount later from Emerson, Inc.

29 Received cash from Emerson, Inc., for the principal, interest and protest fee on its dishonored note, plus additional interest at 8 percent on the total amount from September 19.

10–13. The Lee Kefawsit Company issued $400,000 of 20-year, 6 percent bonds on June 1, 1963. The bonds were issued at 96 percent of face value, callable at 103. In June, 1972, the company was able to issue new bonds with an interest rate of 5 percent. It called in the old issue and issued $500,000 of new 15-year, 5 percent bonds at 99 percent of face value. Assume the discount on the old bond issue was amortized on a straight-line basis.

a) Prepare journal entries to record the refunding on June 1, 1972 and to record the payment of six months' interest on December 1, 1972, under the assumptions that any unamortized discounts on the old bonds and the call premium are to be (1) written off as a loss on refunding in 1972, (2) amortized over the remaining life of the old bonds, or (3) amortized over the life of the new bond issue.

b) Discuss the arguments in favor of each of these alternatives. Which do you prefer? Why?

10–14. General Host Corporation in its 1969 annual report listed under the category of "other assets" an amount of $35,482,000 labeled "unamortized bond discount" (total assets were $337,591,000). The discount related to $159,258,000 of 7 percent subordinated debenture bonds due February 1, 1994 which were issued during the year. The $159,258,000 was shown under long-term debt. In a note, the company explained, "The original issue discount relating to the 7% subordinated debentures in the amount of $35,833,000 is being amortized for accounting purposes by the interest method and the annual amortization will increase from $351,000 in 1969 to $3,482,000 in 1993."

a) Evaluate the presentation of this bond issue on the position statement.

b) Reconstruct the journal entry that was made to record interest expense for 1969. Assume the bonds were issued on February 1, 1969.

c) Estimate the effective (market) interest rate being charged on the debentures.

d) Why does the amount of discount amortization increase over time?

e) For income tax purposes, General Host plans to amortize the discount by the straight-line method. What advantages accrue to the company from using a different method for tax purposes?

10–A–1. Compute the future amount for each of the following cases. Use the tables at the end of Appendix 10–A–1.

a) $100 to be deposited at the end of each of the next 10 years. Interest is compounded annually at 8 percent for 10 years.

b) $500 to be deposited at the end of each of the next five years and $1,000 to be deposited at the end of the sixth year. No additional deposits after that. Interest is compounded annually at 6 percent for 10 years.

c) $1,000 to be deposited immediately, $2,000 at the end of the first year, and $3,000 at the end of the second year. No additional deposits after that. Interest is compounded annually at 10 percent for five years.

d) $5,000 to be deposited immediately. Interest at 4 percent is compounded quarterly for five years.

e) $1,000 to be deposited immediately. Interest at 6 percent is compounded semiannually for the first three years, and then interest at 8 percent is compounded semiannually for the next three years.

10–A–2. The following exercises concern the understanding and use of present value tables.

    a) Determine the present value of $300 under each of the following conditions:

	Year of Receipt	Interest Rate
1.	10	8%
2.	4	10%
3.	8	4%

    b) Determine the present value of an annuity of $500 payable semiannually under the following conditions (assume semiannual discounting):

	No. of Years	Interest Rate
1.	5	10%
2.	10	8%
3.	15	6%

    c) If you invest the sum specified in the first column, you will receive a single or a series of $100 payments in the year or years indicated in the second column. For each case, determine the actual annual rate of interest earned.

	Invested	Year(s) of Receipt
1.	$ 75.13	3
2.	$ 48.10	15
3.	$ 574.66	1–8
4.	$1,729.20	1 30
5.	$ 791.63	1–10

    d) In Table 10–A–6 (Present Value of One Dollar), the present values become smaller as you move either down or across the table. Explain carefully why this is true.

10–A–3. A small, family-held company wishes to build up a fund which can be used, if necessary, to repurchase and retire the stock of a major stockholder upon his demise.

    a) How much will accumulate in the fund if deposits of $5,000 at the end of each year for the first five years and $10,000 per year for the next five years are made? Interest is compounded annually at the rate of 8 percent for the first five years and 10 percent for the next five years.

    b) If a fund of $100,000 is desired in eight years, how much should be deposited at the end of each six-month period, if interest of 8 percent is compounded semiannually?

10–A–4. The Diversionary Amusement Park is contemplating the construction of a new ride called the Gyroscope. To construct the ride will cost an estimated $2,500,000. Financing will be accomplished by issuing 6 percent, 20-year bonds with interest payable annually.

The Diversionary management plans to have admission fees sufficiently large to cover interest on the bonds, annual maintenance and operating costs of $50,000, a contribution to income of $100,000, and an annual deposit in a sinking fund to retire the bonds at maturity. The sinking fund will earn 4 percent annually.

If the admission price is $1 per person, how many people annually must pay for the ride in order to meet the management's plans?

10–A–5. U. O. Memoney has an account receivable from I. M. Tight for merchandise purchased over the last couple of years. The current balance in the account is $420,000. Under threat of court action, Tight agrees to a formal plan to liquidate the debt by making 10 equal annual payments, including interest at the rate of 10 percent. The first payment must be made immediately and the remaining payments yearly thereafter.

a)   What is the amount of the annual payment?

b)   Prepare a schedule that Memoney can use to determine interest revenue and repayment of principal each year.

10–A–6. A warehousing company is negotiating for a building to use for storage. The building can be purchased for $150,000 cash or can be acquired under a 10-year lease at an annual rental of $20,000, payable at the beginning of each year. The building's estimated resale value at the end of 10 years is $10,000. Under either arrangement, the warehouse company would pay all operating costs, maintenance, and property taxes.

Which plan is better if the interest rate is assumed to be 6 percent? (Ignore income taxes.)

10–A–7. Over the last few years, A. Lumnus has borrowed quite extensively from the bank. As of December 31, 1971, he owes the following amounts:

1.   A discount note with a face value of $3,000 due on December 31, 1972.
2.   A $5,000 note due on December 31, 1973. Interest is payable annually at the rate of 6 percent.
3.   An installment loan with a current face value of $6,000, payable in three installments of $2,000 on December 31, 1972, 1973, and 1974.

Lumnus has just learned that he is the beneficiary of a large trust fund which will come into his possession in December 1974. He approaches the bank with the suggestion that all his current debts be combined into a single obligation due on December 31, 1974. He agrees to sign a new note for a single payment to be made on that date and to pledge the trust fund as collateral.

If money is worth 10 percent annually to the bank what should be the amount of the new note?

10–A–8. Ty Coon has had a very successful career as an executive. On his 55th birthday, he is hired by a new company to serve as its president until he reaches age 60. He is offered a choice of three compensation plans:

1. An annual salary of $50,000 for five years.
2. An annual salary of $40,000 for five years plus a deferred compensation plan paying $20,000 for the next five years (from age 60 to age 65).
3. An annual salary of $30,000 plus a bonus equal to 10 percent of each year's profits. The payment of the bonus is spread over the next two years, that is, the bonus based on the first year's profits would be paid half in year 2 and half in year 3. Ty estimates that profits will be $200,000, $220,000, $250,000, $250,000, and $250,000 in years 1 through 5, respectively,

   a) If money is worth 8 percent, which of these plans should he choose?
   b) Assume Ty elects the second plan. Assume further that all monies received are put into a fund to be invested at 8 percent compounded annually. How much can Ty withdraw at the end of each year for 10 years, beginning on his 66th birthday?

10–A–9.   Assume your firm wishes to earn 10 percent on all investments in new equipment. It has under consideration the following three proposals (ignore income taxes).

		Cash Receipts	
Project	Cash Outlay	Amount	Years
A...............	$ 40,000	$10,000	1–5
B...............	120,000	18,000	1–9
		25,000	10
C...............	15,000	2,000	1–5
		4,000	6–10

   a) Advise the company which of these projects it should accept and reject. Show your calculations.
   b) Would your answer be different if the desired earning rate was only 5 percent?

10–A–10.   On January 1, 1972, Constant Return Corporation purchased a machine for $41,000. The machine is expected to generate net cash inflow of $10,000 each year for five years and to have a net salvage value of $5,000 at the end of five years.

   a) Assuming the company uses straight-line depreciation, for each year calculate (1) the net income after depreciation, (2) the book value of the investment as of the beginning of the year, and (3) the return on investment, derived from dividing (1) by (2).

b) Repeat part (a) assuming the company uses the annuity method of depreciation with an implicit interest cost of 10 percent.

c) Repeat part (b) assuming an implicit interest cost of 6 percent. Do the results suggest a potential difficulty in using the annuity method for external reporting purposes?

10–A–11. Barium Deep Casket Company is considering the purchase of two new machines. It has asked for your recommendation (ignore income taxes).

a) Machine A will cost $40,000. It will last 30 years and produce an annual net cash inflow of $3,500 per year plus a net salvage value of $6,000 at the end of its life. What rate of return on its money will Barium Deep be earning if it acquires this machine?

b) Machine B is expected to produce the following net cash flows: $5,000 for years 1–5; $8,000 in years 6 and 7; $9,000 in year 8, $10,000 in year 9, and $3,000 in year 10. Assuming a desired earning rate of 6 percent applies, what is the maximum amount Barium Deep could afford to pay for this machine?

10–A–12. Loose Lease Rental Agency is considering the purchase of a new office building. It estimates that the net rental inflows from leasing space in the building will be $20,000 per year. The building should last 20 years and have a salvage value at that time of $50,000.

a) If the company wishes to earn 8 percent on its investment, what is the maximum amount which should be paid for the building?

b) Assume the building was purchased at a price of $180,000. What implicit interest cost would you advise that the company use in depreciating the building under the annuity method?

c) Prepare condensed income statements for the first three years assuming the use of (1) the annuity method of depreciation and (2) the straight-line method. Calculate also the return on beginning of the year investment for each year under each depreciation method.

CHAPTER ELEVEN

LEASES AND PENSIONS

CHAPTER TEN begins an exploration of some of the accounting problems associated with liabilities. Although notes and bonds, discussed in that chapter, represent legal claims, it is well to remember that the concept of a liability extends beyond specifically determinable legal obligations. Liabilities encompass all measurable future outlays of assets (normally cash) or services that result from past or current transactions.

Sometimes an interest factor is used to give formal recognition to the fact that a time period exists between incurrence of the liability and its ultimate payment. The total cash payments include an interest charge for the delayed payment, and the liabilities are valued at the present (discounted) value of the future payments. This amount represents the current cash equivalent to discharge the debt.

The purpose of this chapter is to discuss the accounting for leases and pensions. These liabilities constitute two relatively controversial areas in accounting. In recent years their importance has increased significantly as measured by both the dollar amounts involved and the attention given to them in the accounting literature. Moreover, they represent areas where present-value concepts are extremely useful.

ACCOUNTING FOR LEASES

A lease agreement between parties involves the conveyance of the use of property from its owner (the lessor) to a second party (the lessee) in exchange for some type of compensation, usually a periodic cash payment. The typical rental agreement for a house or apartment between a landlord and tenant is a common example. The length of time the property may be used, any restrictions on its use, the amount and timing of lease payments, and other pertinent features normally are specified in the lease contract. In the last decade or so, it has become popular for businesses to use leasing arrangements to acquire a variety of asset services. As might be expected, the length of time covered by a lease may vary from a few hours or days (renting an automobile) to the entire life of the asset (leasing a store building for 40 years). The purposes for which items are leased are equally diverse. Some leases provide for the temporary use of asset services without the lessee's having to assume any ownership rights or risks. These *operating leases* are generally for short periods of time, cancellable at will, and often part of a package of services provided by the lessor.

Other leases, commonly called *financial leases*, permit the acquisition of long-lived assets without immediate cash payments. In these long-term leases, which are usually noncancellable, the term of the lease often approximates the useful life of the asset, or the lease payments cover the entire cost of the asset. The lessor simply makes available the property for the specified lease period; the rental payments are calculated to cover amortization of the lessor's investment plus an interest return on his investment. The lessee pays all of the other normal costs of ownership—property taxes, insurance, operating costs, maintenance, etc.

Clearly, financial leases represent an alternative long-term financing instrument. For various financial, economic, and tax reasons, firms may prefer to lease property and equipment under a long-term contract rather than purchase the items outright. An outright purchase would require the use of funds acquired from other generally available long-term sources, such as bondholders or stockholders. Many accountants contend that the financial lease is a form of debt financing, not unlike a serial bond issue in its effects on the business entity.

Our concern is to examine how these long-term lease arrangements should be reflected in the accounting statements. In particular, under what circumstances should the rights to use property and the related obligations to make rental payments be given formal recognition in the position statement of the lessee? The discussion in the first half of the chapter centers primarily on three points:

1. Treatment of lease contracts that are essentially installment purchases of property.
2. Capitalization of property rights and obligations under other long-term financial leases. Capitalization of leases involves showing the right to use property as an asset and the corresponding obligation for future rental payments as a liability on the lessee's books.
3. Accounting for sale and lease-back transactions, where the business buys or constructs property, sells it to someone else, and simultaneously leases it back under a long-term noncancellable lease.

Leases That in Substance Are Purchases

An installment purchase of an asset requires a down payment plus a series of cash payments over a future period usually shorter than the life of the property. The periodic cash outlays cover principal payments and interest. Lease contracts are sometimes drawn in a very similar manner. The "rental" payments are nothing more than disguised installment-contract payments. Historically, accountants have insisted that the substance of these arrangements, rather than the legal form, should govern. This view is affirmed by the Accounting Principles Board in *Opinion No. 5*.[1] When the initial term of the lease is significantly less than the useful life of the asset and the lessee has the option to renew the lease at a nominal rental or to purchase the asset at a bargain price, interpretation of the transaction as a purchase clearly appears to be warranted. Therefore, the property right and related obligation to pay should be recorded as an asset and liability, respectively, in an amount equal to the present value of future lease payments.

Illustration. Assume that a company can acquire a machine having a useful life of 10 years under a "lease" contract calling for five "rental" payments of $2,240 each, the first payment to be made at the time of signing the lease and subsequent payments to be made at the beginning of each of the next 4 years. At the end of the five-year lease period, the company can purchase the asset for $1. If the interest rate for similar installment loans is 6 percent, the asset's cost and the present value of the liability should be recorded at $10,000, the discounted value of the future payments:[2]

$$P_{\overline{4}|.06}\,\$2,240 = (3.465)\$2,240 = \$\ 7,760$$
$$\$2,240 + \$7,760 = \$10,000$$

In some instances the cost can be determined directly, as when the company has the alternative of paying $10,000 immediately or leasing. Then the effective interest cost inherent in the lease is the rate that will equate the present value of the series of payments to $10,000 (in this case, 6 percent).

In any case, the transaction more closely resembles an installment purchase than a true rental agreement. The $10,000 machinery cost should be depreciated over the useful life of 10 years. The liability of $10,000 will be liquidated by the periodic payments, each one beyond the first consisting partially of an interest element, as indicated in Table 11 1.

---

[1] *Reporting of Leases in Financial Statements of Lessee, Opinion of the Accounting Principles Board No. 5* (New York: AICPA, September 1964).

[2] The symbol $P_{\overline{4}|.06}$ means the present value of an annuity of $1 for four years at 6 percent interest.

TABLE 11-1

Payment	Liability Balance Prior to Payment	Dr. to Interest Expense (6% × Col. 2)	Dr. to Liability	Cr. to Cash
1...................	$10,000	...	$2,240	$2,240
2...................	7,760	$466	1,774	2,240
3...................	5,986	359	1,881	2,240
4...................	4,105	247	1,993	2,240
5...................	2,112	128	2,112	2,240

Capitalization of Other Long-Term Leases

Many accountants advocate that similar procedures be applied to all long-term leases which are used as financing devices.[3] They argue that the signing of certain leases creates property rights and related obligations that should be reported on the financial statements even if ultimate purchase at the end of the lease is not contemplated or allowed. The methodology for reporting such leases is basically the same as that applied to leases that are really installment purchases. The asset cost is measured by the liability assumed in acquiring it. The liability, in turn, is recorded at the present value of the future payments.

Theory of Lease Capitalization. The important issue in lease capitalization is the problem of identifying which leases (if any) give rise to property rights and related obligations. The answer of those proposing lease capitalization can be summarized as follows:

To the extent, then, that the rental payments represent a means of financing the acquisition of property rights which the lessee has in his possession and under his control, the transaction constitutes the acquisition of an asset with a related obligation to pay for it. To the extent, however, that the rental payments are for services such as maintenance, insurance, property taxes, heat, light, and elevator service, no asset has been acquired, and none should be recorded.[4]

This answer distinguishes between payments for the *right to use* property and payment for other services yet to be performed. Delivery of the leased asset constitutes a service completely performed by the lessor. The lessee or rentor has the right to use the leased property for a specified time period. For other services requiring continuous or periodic performance by the lessor in the future, an asset does not exist. This situation is analogous to future labor services, for which the right to use exists only as the services actually are performed.

With many long-term noncancellable financial leases, the lessee has the

---

[3] Perhaps the most widely read argument for this view is found in John H. Myers, *Reporting of Leases in Financial Statements,* Accounting Research Study No. 4 (New York: AICPA, 1962).

[4] *Ibid.,* p. 5.

same rights to use as he would have under an outright purchase. It is well to keep in mind that even with direct ownership, the asset acquired really is not the physical item itself but the future service potential inherent in it. Certain leases represent assets to the lessor in the form of limited user rights, limited only in that the lessee has no residual rights in the property at the end of the lease period. The lease payments, save for the portion applicable to additional services, constitute a type of installment payment for these user rights. The lessee has an irrevocable obligation to make the installment payments (rentals), including the interest element.

Illustration. Suppose a firm can lease a building for 10 years at an annual rental of $10,000, calculated to give the owner a return of 8 percent. The tenant will pay all maintenance costs and property taxes during the life of the lease, but has no purchase or renewal options at the end of 10 years. The lease would be capitalized at $67,100, the present value of an annuity of $10,000 discounted at 8 percent (on the assumption that the annual rent is paid at the end of the year). The entire $10,000 payment each year, in this case, is for user rights and for interest. The fact that the building probably will last longer than 10 years is irrelevant to the valuation of the asset acquired by the tenant. The liability assumed under the lease, less the interest element which is removed by discounting, is equivalent to a current cash outlay of $67,100. This is the cost incurred for a certain portion of the service potential embodied in the building.

Without capitalization of the lease no asset or liability would appear on the position statement. The income statement each year would show only a $10,000 rent expense equal to the cash payment. With capitalization an asset and liability are accounted for in the following entry:

```
Rights to Leased Property................ 67,100
    Liability under Lease Contract........        67,100
```

The liability is partially extinguished and interest expense is recognized with each yearly lease payment. The asset is amortized to expense over its 10-year life. Consequently, on the income statement capitalization

. . . removes the charge for "rent" in the accounts as an occupancy cost and instead treats it simply as a payment of an obligation and interest thereon. In its place is put "amortization of property right acquired under lease" (an occupancy cost) and "interest" (a financial expense).[5]

Thus, normally, over the life of the asset the sum of the periodic charges for amortization and interest will be the same as the sum of the rentals, but the periodic timing may be different, because the interest expense and occupancy cost (amortization) are accounted for independently of one another.

Since each lease payment consists of interest and liability retirement, the first two annual payments would be recorded as follows:

---

[5] *Ibid.*, p. 6.

```
Interest Expense.......................... 5,368
Liability under Lease Contract............ 4,632
     Cash.................................            10,000
     To record first lease payment and to
     recognize interest equal to 8 percent of
     the unpaid balance (8% × $67,100 = $5,368).

Interest Expense.......................... 4,998
Liability under Lease Contract............ 5,002
     Cash.................................            10,000
     To record second lease payment and to
     recognize interest equal to 8 percent of
     unpaid balance [8% × ($67,100 - $4,632)].
```

Entries thereafter would follow the schedule given in Table 11–2. This effective interest method always gives a book value of the lease liability equal to the present value of the remaining future payments.

Since the right to use the leased property is limited to 10 years, the $67,100 cost of the asset should be spread over that period. At first glance, one might assume that the pattern of amortization should follow the liquidation of the liability, i.e., $4,632 the first year, $5,002 the second year, etc. This amortization method would be consistent with the pro-

TABLE 11–2

Payment	Interest	Liability Retirement	Payment	Interest	Liability Retirement
1...........	$5,368	$4,632	6...........	$3,194	$6,806
2...........	4,998	5,002	7...........	2,650	7,350
3...........	4,597	5,403	8...........	2,062	7,938
4...........	4,165	5,835	9...........	1,427	8,573
5...........	3,698	6,302	10...........	741	9,259

cedure used to determine initial asset value and would result, when added to the interest charge, in a total expense charge equal to the annual rental payment. Nevertheless, the asset and liability are separate economic phenomena, even though their initial valuations were the same. The amortization of lease rights should depend on service usage, which may depart significantly in some instances from the financial pattern involved in liquidating the liability.[6] Consequently, the preferred procedure would amortize the asset, using the principles and procedures introduced in Chapter Nine. If straight-line amortization were deemed most accurate, the entry each year would be:

```
Amortization of Rights to Leased Property... 6,710
     Rights to Leased Property..............            6,710
```

---

[6] Extreme examples of this difference would occur with unequal lease payments but relatively constant asset usage, or with leased property which became obsolete long before the end of the lease term. In the latter case the asset should be written off entirely, but the liability would remain.

Evaluation of Lease Capitalization

The advantages claimed for lease capitalization can be gleaned from a review of the foregoing entries. If the concepts of asset and liability encompass rights to use and obligations to pay, failure to capitalize results in an understatement of balance sheet information. The recording of resources under the control of and used by management to generate income is not complete. Consequently, attempts to accurately relate income figures or sales volume to asset investment will be frustrated. And comparisons of asset size and composition between firms which purchase their property and those which lease it will be misleading. Even more lamentable is the failure to consider the lease obligations as an alternative form of debt. Proper disclosure of all liabilities is essential in evaluating the debt position of the firm. Capitalization recognizes that lease payments constitute a claim against assets prior to that of the residual stockholders. Moreover, on the income statement it clearly segregates the financial charge for the use of this borrowed capital rather than burying it in an operating expense category (rent).

Objections to Capitalization. Numerous objections have been raised to the capitalization of leases on the balance sheet. One group of objections centers around potential unfavorable consequences that might result from disclosing leases as assets and liabilities. Examples of these arguments are:

1. Firms relying extensively on lease financing would suffer an impairment in their borrowing ability.
2. Leased assets could be subject to local property taxes.
3. The advantageous treatment of lease rentals on government contracts and on income tax returns would be in jeopardy.

Such views really are not relevant to the major issue of whether capitalization best reflects the nature of long-term financial leases and their impact on financial position and operating performance. That creditors, stockholders, and government authorities might react differently if confronted by different "facts" should not deter accountants from disclosing relevant information.

A second set of objections to capitalization raises questions about the possibility of measuring the asset and liability amounts accurately. Estimates must be made of the portion of lease rentals which are payments for property rights and the portion representing payments for other services. Similarly, the rate to be used in discounting and the frequency of discounting may not be known with precision. However, the judgments and estimates involved would seem to fall well within the tolerances existing for other areas in accounting. The discount rate, if not explicit in the lease contract, could be determined by a comparison of lease prices and purchase prices, if the latter are available, or through objective determination of the market rate of interest for leases (usually one half to one percentage points higher than what the company is currently paying on other loans). In any case, for most situations the differences in present value caused by different estimates of interest rates or compounding periods are probably immaterial.

The fundamental view that financial leases represent assets and liabilities is the point of attack of a third set of objections. Some of these objections define assets narrowly, equating them with legal ownership or, at least, eventual ownership. Others claim that lease obligations are not debt because in case of bankruptcy or reorganization, courts traditionally have treated leases differently from other liabilities. This latter idea, however, is premised on a liquidation rather than on a going-concern concept.

The most perplexing argument in this category states that leases are merely executory contracts, both sides of which are equally unperformed. Performance by the lessor is viewed as a continuous concept involving either his implicitly approving each period the use of the asset by the lessee or his replacing a faulty, destroyed, or obsolete asset. If the lessor does not continuously perform, the lessee has no obligation to pay. Therefore, leases should be recorded as are other executory contracts—e.g., long-term employment contracts or purchase commitments. An asset is recorded only if a prepayment is made; a liability is recorded only when services actually are received.

Accounting Principles Board Opinion.   The Accounting Principles Board took this latter position in *Opinion No. 5*. Other than leases which are essentially installment purchases, "the right to use property and a related obligation to pay rents over a definite future period are not considered by the Board to be assets and liabilities under present accounting concepts."[7] It ruled that only when an equity in the property is being built up by the lessee should the capitalization procedure be followed.

However, the Board did expand the criteria for determining whether an equity in the property was created by the lease. In addition to the criteria mentioned on page 369 for obvious installment purchases, the existence of one or more of the following circumstances in connection with a noncancellable lease indicates a purchase arrangement:

1. The property was designed specifically for the purpose of the lessee and would have little value to any other user.
2. The lease covers the entire useful life of the asset and requires the lessee to pay the expenses incidental to ownership.
3. The lessee has promised to pay any long-term liabilities of the lessor if the latter is unable to do so.
4. The lessee has treated the lease as a purchase for tax purposes.

---

[7] APB *Opinion No. 5, op. cit.,* p. 32.

5. The lessor is a corporation owned or controlled by the lessee and dependent on the lessee for its operations.

In addition, for leases that are not capitalized the Board recommended greater disclosure of relevant information in footnotes. This information would include the minimum annual rentals under such leases, the rental for the current year if it differs significantly from the minimum, the period over which lease payments are due, types of property leased, and the significant provisions of the lease agreement.

Sale and Lease-Back Transactions

Under a sale and lease-back transaction the owner of an asset sells it to another party and then turns around and leases it back for a period approximating its remaining useful life. The new owner, and lessor, frequently is a financial or lending institution. The lease rentals repay the financial institution for the cash paid out plus interest. The lessee continues to pay taxes, insurance, and operating costs just as if he were still the legal owner.

Clearly, the sale and lease-back are not independent events. The original owner retains use of the asset throughout its life in exchange for a series of payments basically covering principal and interest. If the sale and lease-back are recorded as a secured borrowing in the accounts, few problems arise. For example, assume a business owns a building having a book value of $50,000. It "sells" the building to an insurance company for $60,000 and signs a 30-year noncancellable lease promising to pay $5,325 rental at the end of each year ($5,325 for 30 years will completely repay $60,000 plus interest at 8 percent on the unpaid balance). The entries would be:

```
Cash...................................  60,000
     Liability Resulting from Sale and
          Leaseback..........................          60,000
     To record initial transaction.

Interest Expense.......................   4,800
Liability Resulting from Sale and
     Leaseback.............................     525
          Cash.................................           5,325
     To record first rental payment.
```

The asset remains on the original owners' books. No gain is recognized for the difference between $60,000 and $50,000, because no sale is considered to have taken place.

APB Opinion. The Accounting Principles Board, while concurring in the judgment that the sale and lease-back could not be treated as independent transactions, did not explicitly recommend the above procedure. Rather, it prescribed the same treatment for the lease-back as for other leases (i.e., capitalization only if the lease is an installment purchase or results in the creation of a material equity in the property). As to the treatment of "gains or losses" on the "sale," the Board stated:

> . . . material gains and losses resulting from the sale of properties which are the subject of sale-and-leaseback transactions . . . should be amortized over the life of the lease as an adjustment of the rental cost (or, if the leased property is capitalized, as an adjustment of depreciation).[8]

To implement this recommendation would require the following series of entries:

(1)   If the lease were not capitalized:

```
Cash...................................  60,000
     Building..............................           50,000
     Deferred Gain on Sale................           10,000
Rent Expense...........................   5,325
     Cash................................            5,325
Deferred Gain on Sale..................     333
     Rent Expense.......................              333
     To amortize 1/30 of gain.
```

(2)   If the lease were capitalized:

```
Cash...................................  60,000
Rights to Leased Building..............  60,000
     Building..............................           50,000
     Liability under Lease Contract......           60,000
     Deferred Gain on Sale..............            10,000
Interest Expense.......................   4,800
Liability under Lease Contract.........     525
     Cash................................            5,325
Amortization of Rights to Leased
     Building..............................   1,667
Deferred Gain on Sale..................     333
     Rights to Leased Building..........             2,000
     To record amortization cost
     (straight-line basis).
```

The APB's recommendation treats the transaction as neither fish nor fowl. Professor Maurice Moonitz stated in his dissent to that portion of the opinion:

> The adoption of this recommendation in practice will result in the introduction into the balance sheet of "deferred credits to income" for gains and "deferred charges to income" for losses. In a sale-and-leaseback transaction, neither of these deferred items qualifies as a liability or as an asset. Their effect is to permit a smoothing of reported net income over a number of years. This result stems from the attempt to treat the transaction as though no sale has been made, insofar as the effect on net income is concerned, while treating the property as sold, in the balance sheet. If the property has in fact been sold, it should be so reported in consistent fashion in all financial statements. If it has not, the balance sheet should not be made to report that it has.[9]

---

[8] *Ibid.*, p. 33.

[9] *Ibid.*, p. 34.

Accounting Problems of Lessors

Over a year and a half after *Opinion No. 5*, the Accounting Principles Board dealt with the lease problem from the perspective of the lessor or owner of the property. In this opinion, however, emphasis shifted from problems of balance sheet presentation to problems of proper matching of costs and revenues on the income statement. Two procedures, one for operating leases and one for financial leases, are recommended for recording leases on the lessor's books. The choice between the two methods should be based on the same factors which help distinguish which leases might be capitalized on the lessee's books.

Operating Method. This method can be applied to either short- or long-term leases. The important feature is that the lessor retains the risks of obsolescence, unprofitable operation, breakdown, and idle capacity. Similarly, he retains any rewards from profitable operations or increases in residual values. The owner of an apartment building and an automobile leasing agency are examples of firms which should employ the operating method.

Under the operating lease, gross rentals are the source of revenue. Expenses such as maintenance, taxes, insurance, utilities, operating costs, etc., are recorded in the normal fashion. Depreciation on the leased property is recorded on the lessor's books in a manner consistent with its useful life, estimated salvage value, and expected pattern of service expiration. The only change from normal accounting and reporting procedures is that the cost of the property being leased, less accumulated depreciation, is shown as a separate item, Equipment Leased to Others or Property Held for Lease, in the property section of the position statement.

Financing Method. As the name implies, only long-term financial leases should be accounted for by this method. The lease assumes the characteristics of an installment sale with interest, since the lessee undertakes most ownership costs. The excess of the aggregate lease rentals over the cost of the asset being leased represents interest revenue to be recognized over the life of the lease. Each lease payment received consists of two elements: interest revenue and a return of principal. If the lease payments are the same each year, the interest portion of each succeeding payment declines in recognition of the partial recovery of capital. The lessor (owner) has transferred his property rights to the lessee in return for a claim against the lessee for periodic rental payments. The principal assets of the lessor are a net receivable and the value of any residual property rights remaining at the end of the lease.

Let us take the following situation as an illustration. The owner of a building is willing to lease it for 15 years at an annual rental of $7,000, payable at the end of each year. The building cost $78,000 and is expected to have a salvage value of $10,000 at the end of the 15-year period. The following entry would record the initial transaction:

```
Receivable from Leased Property Contract. 105,000
Estimated Residual Value of Leased
   Building......................................  10,000
      Unearned Finance Charges.............               37,000
      Building.............................               78,000
```

The $10,000 salvage value expected to be recovered at the end of the lease period should be shown in the balance sheet as a separate classification of property, plant, and equipment. The other $68,000 of the building's cost represents the present value of a series of 15 payments of $7,000. The interest rate inherent in the lease, therefore, must be about 6 percent (P $_{\overline{15}|.06}$ $7,000 = $67,984$).[10]

The present value of the lease receivable is recorded in two accounts —the full amount of lease payments to be received ($7,000 \times 15 = $105,000$) less a contra receivable for the portion representing interest that will be earned over the life of the lease. Unearned Finance Charges should be shown as a subtraction from the main account in the balance sheet. As each payment is received, cash is debited for $7,000, interest revenue is credited for 6 percent of the unpaid balance, and the net receivable is reduced by the remainder. The entries for the first two payments are as follows:

```
Year 1   Cash................................... 7,000
            Unearned Finance Charges
               (6% × $68,000)..................... 4,080
               Receivable from Leased Property
                  Contracts......................          7,000
               Interest (Lease) Revenue..........          4,080
Year 2   Cash................................... 7,000
            Unearned Finance Charges
               (6% × $65,080)..................... 3,905
               Receivable from Leased Property
                  Contracts......................          7,000
               Interest (Lease) Revenue..........          3,905
```

Similar entries are made each year until, at the end of 15 years, the entire gross receivable of $105,000 has been collected and the unearned interest of $37,000 has been recognized as revenue.

Relationship to APB Opinion No. 5. The astute reader will detect an inconsistency between the recommendations applicable to lessors and lessees concerning financial leases. The former should capitalize long-term financial leases as a receivable; however, lessees should capitalize them as a payable only when they are in substance installment purchases of property. The Accounting Principles Board rationalized this inconsistency on the grounds that capitalization is required for lessors to achieve the proper

---

[10] In this case no gain or loss on the sale is assumed. The cost of the building equals the present value of the lease rentals. A gain or loss could be recognized if the interest rate in the lease were explicitly stated to make it clear that the present value of the lease rentals differs from the cost of the property, or if the value of the asset can be independently measured. Such is the case, for instance, when a manufacturer of a standard piece of equipment offers his customers the choice of outright purchase or rental for the entire useful life of the product.

allocation of revenue and expense to accounting periods in order to measure net income properly.

ACCOUNTING FOR PENSIONS

As Chapter Seven points out, the overall cost of acquiring labor services and rendering them available for use includes the cost of various fringe benefits. One of the most important of these fringe benefits, particularly during the last 25 years, has been retirement programs for employees. These plans commonly go by the title of "pension plans."

For purposes of subsequent discussions, pension plans are classified as *funded* or *unfunded*. Under a funded plan the employer actually sets aside cash amounts to be used for future distributions to retired employees by making periodic payments to some funding agency. Under an *insured* plan the payments go to an insurance company, which invests the funds until needed. Usually the legal obligation to pay pensions is that of the insurance company. In *trusteed* plans a bank or trust company receives the payments from the employer. The trustee has the responsibility for investing the pension fund and making disbursements to retired employees, but the ultimate legal responsibility still rests with the employer. In unfunded plans no assets are actually set aside to accumulate. The employer relies on his current cash position to make direct payments to retired employees as they come due.

The accounting for pension costs and liabilities historically has followed a multifarious pattern. At one extreme, some companies attempted to accrue all pension costs for a given group of employees in a reasonable manner over the remaining period of active service of the workers. At the other extreme, some companies adopted a "pay-as-you-go" approach, charging as expense only the amount actually paid to retired employees. No recognition was given to obligations to workers currently employed. The middle ground consisted of the majority of companies, for which the amount paid to a funding agency was the periodic expense. In some instances the funding pattern also resulted in a reasonable accrual of the pension expense. However, in other cases the amount paid each period was influenced by tax considerations, cash availability, level of net income, and other factors not directly related to theoretical concepts of expense and liability.

Determining expense by the amount of cash payment resulted in low or no expense when payments were reduced or stopped in a given accounting period. Similar variations arose if during the year a gain was realized by the trustee on the sale of pension fund assets. Some firms reduced their contributions accordingly, others ignored the gain, and still others recognized the effect of the gain through reduced contributions over a period of years. In short, accounting for pension costs and liabilities was plagued by a diversity of plans, a lack of uniformity of principles among companies having similar pension plans, and an inconsistent application of procedures from one period to the next within a single company.

Two early bulletins issued by the Committee on Accounting Procedure of the American Institute of Certified Public Accountants dealt with particular portions of the accounting problem but failed to reduce significantly the wide variations among businesses and year-to-year fluctuations within a firm. Then, in November 1966, the successor Accounting Principles Board issued an opinion after reviewing a complex research study on the subject.[11] The opinion did not attempt to resolve all points at issue. Rather, its goal was to narrow the range of practices significantly and to prevent distortion or manipulation in the accounting for pensions.

The general approach of the APB is to require that pension costs be systematically accrued by means of rational and consistently applied present-value procedures. Pension accounting should be neither discretionary nor necessarily governed by cash payments. Only rarely are pension programs terminated once they are started. Notwithstanding clauses which allow for termination or other legal limitations, pension plans continue as long as the firm continues in business. Therefore, pension costs should be accounted for on the assumption that benefits will be provided indefinitely. Pension costs are a real cost of employment associated with the present work force. In accordance with the accrual basis of accounting and under the matching concept, expense should be recorded in the periods during which the benefit of that work force is received.

Accounting for the cost of pension plans and any related liabilities is a complicated task. In the next section we discuss some technical factors which are necessary background to an understanding of accounting for pensions. Then we highlight some major aspects. These include (1) the two major components to a firm's pension cost—normal cost and past service cost, (2) an illustration of some of the basic entries, and (3) a brief exposure to the problems of actuarial gains or losses and unrealized appreciation or loss on pension assets. Recommendations and reasoning from the Accounting Principles Board opinion are integrated throughout this discussion so that the reader may have a firm grasp of generally accepted accounting principles in the pension area.

Complicating Factors

The general recommendation for accrual accounting unfortunately does not establish definitive guidelines for implementation. The basic questions of what amount of pension cost to account for, and specifically

---

[11] Ernest L. Hicks, *Accounting for the Cost of Pension Plans,* Accounting Research Study No. 8 (New York: AICPA, 1965).

how to record it, hinge on differing views of pension cost and the complexities of actuarial calculations and assumptions.

Actuarial Assumptions. Pension cost calculations involve a determination of the present value of benefits to be paid in the future to employees after they retire. Such calculations necessarily require that judgments and estimates be made concerning future events. These estimates normally demand the expertise of an actuary—a professional person trained in the science of compound interest, probability and mortality distributions, and other aspects of insurance. The assumptions that actuaries tentatively make about future uncertainties affecting the pension cost are called actuarial assumptions. Some of the more important ones relate to future levels of compensation to the extent that they influence the amount of future benefits; the proportions of the employee group who will withdraw from the plan, die, become disabled, reach retirement age, etc.; the rate of interest or earning to use in discounting future payments to the present; and the amount and timing of vested benefits (employee benefits the rights to which are no longer contingent on the employee's continuing to work for the employer). These and similar assumptions are necessary for the actuary to estimate the present value of benefits to be paid under a pension plan and, in turn, to calculate the amount of contribution necessary for funding or the amount of cost necessary for accounting purposes. To the extent that these factors are not accurate or require subsequent modifications, actuarial "gains" and "losses" result.

Actuarial Cost Methods. Actuarial assumptions influence the determination of total pension cost; actuarial cost methods determine how that cost is assigned to the various accounting periods. Specifically, an actuarial cost method is a "particular technique used by actuaries for establishing the amount and incidence of the annual actuarial cost of pension plan benefits . . . and the related actuarial liability."[12] Although developed primarily as funding plans, most of the actuarial cost methods also are appropriate for the determination of accounting cost. The Accounting Principles Board specifically endorsed five; but each makes different assumptions as to the circumstances of the pension plan and, consequently, different actuarial cost methods can cause the periodic pension cost to vary significantly.[13]

Effect of Funding. Actuarial cost methods were designed originally to calculate the amount of contribution necessary each period to provide

---

[12] *Accounting for the Cost of Pension Plans, Opinion of the Accounting Principles Board No. 8* (New York: AICPA, November 1966), p. 98.

[13] The interested reader can find detailed descriptions of these methods in Appendix A of *Opinion No. 8;* in Appendix C of Accounting Research Study No. 8; or in W. A. Dreher, "Alternatives Available under APB Opinion No. 8: An Actuary's View," *Five Articles on Accounting for the Cost of Pension Plans* (New York: AICPA, 1968).

a fund sufficiently large to pay the pension benefits. An interest element (present-value factor) is implicit in the calculations. Cash payments made to a fund accumulate at compound interest. Therefore, the periodic contributions (accounting cost) need be only the present value of the pension benefits attributable to the period.

However, in an unfunded plan cash payments are not made as pension costs accrue. As a result the total amount accrued under any of the acceptable actuarial cost methods will not be adequate to cover pension needs, because all methods assume that interest will be earned on an actual fund. Consequently, the periodic pension cost and accrual must be increased by an amount equal to the assumed interest that would be earned if the plan were funded. In fact, whenever the pattern of cash payments differs from that of the cost provision made under one of the acceptable methods, this interest equivalent must be recognized. Pension expense is increased if funding lags behind cost incurrence and is decreased if funding is faster than cost incurrence.

Pension Cost: Normal Cost Portion

Assume that a firm begins business in late 1964. It establishes a funded pension plan for all new employees effective January 1, 1965. The plan requires that the company deposit with a trustee periodic amounts necessary to establish a fund sufficiently large to pay benefits to retired employees according to a predetermined schedule. On the basis of actuarial assumptions relating to numbers of employees, turnover, retirement age, mortality distributions, etc., actuaries have determined that a contribution of $10,000 at the end of each year will be necessary to create such a fund. A 4 percent interest rate is applicable in the actuarial calculations.

The $10,000 is called the *normal* pension cost. It represents the present value of pension benefits attributable to each year after the date of the plan. The annuity of $10,000 each year will accumulate, at an earning rate of 4 percent, to an amount that will cover all payments to retired employees under the plan, provided that the actuarial assumptions are accurate. (This particular method, which gives an equal annual provision, is called "entry age normal.") Each year the company would accrue pension costs as follows:

```
Pension Expense......................... 10,000
    Accrued Liability under Pension Plan..         10,000
```

Since this plan is funded, the liability will be eliminated by a cash payment made to the trustee at the end of each year. If the plan were unfunded, the liability would appear on the company's position statement as a long-term liability. In addition, future years' pension costs would be increased by an interest equivalent of 4 percent of the unfunded amount.

Pension Cost: Past Service Portion

Let us modify the illustration by assuming that the company does not institute its pension plan until January 1, 1975, 10 years after it first began operations. In determining the amount of future pension benefits, pension plans commonly recognize years of employee service prior to the adoption of the plan. An employee who has 10 years of service before the pension plan goes into effect and who then works 10 more years before retiring normally would receive retirement benefits based on 20 years of employment, not just 10. Many actuarial cost methods assign a separate portion of the total cost of pension benefits, called *past service* cost, to these years of service prior to the adoption of the plan. Other actuarial cost methods assign all anticipated costs of the pension program to years of service after adoption of the plan as part of normal cost.

In our example, assume that the original employees are still with the company, and no new ones have been added in the 10-year interim. Therefore, if the company plans to grant pensions based on total years of service, the employees on January 1, 1975 already have 10 years of service to their credit. The entry-age-normal method assumes that level annual payments of $10,000 were made from the time employees first would have become eligible if the plan had been in existence. However, the plan was not in existence for the first 10 years. Consequently, if service from January 1, 1965 is formally recognized in the granting of pension benefits, many accountants would claim that a substantial liability for past service benefits exists upon adoption of the plan. This amount would be equivalent to the sum of an annuity of $10,000 each year for 10 years compounded at 4 percent ($A_{\overline{10}|.04}$ $10,000 = $120,061$).

The past service cost of $120,061 represents the present value of the retirement benefits the employees would have earned had the plan been in existence from the date of employee eligibility.[14] It also is the initial accrued *actuarial* liability. These interpretations suggest the two major accounting problems associated with past service cost: (1) when and how past service cost should be recognized as expense; and (2) what, if any, recognition should be given to the liability for past service on the balance sheet.

---

[14] A quite similar problem arises if the pension plan is modified in subsequent years. At that time a new actuarial valuation is made which typically recognizes service prior to the date of the modification. The term *prior service* cost applies to the portion of the revised total pension cost that the actuarial cost method identifies with periods prior to the date of the new actuarial valuation. It includes any remaining past service cost and any changes in normal cost for years prior to that date. Prior service cost is determined in basically the same way as past service cost and causes the same accounting problems. Consequently, the single term "past service cost" is used here to encompass amounts arising both upon adoption of the plan and upon amendment of the plan.

Recognition of Past Service Cost in Expense

To some extent, "past service cost" is a misnomer. Pension plans are adopted in order to realize present and future benefits. Although the calculation of pension costs is measured by past services, the portion of the cost attributable to the period of past service is not literally a past cost. The benefits derived from, and therefore the costs of, a pension plan surely cannot precede its adoption, regardless of how the costs might be calculated. Following this line of reasoning, the AICPA since its first bulletin in 1953 has consistently concluded that all pension costs—normal and past service—should be related to current and future periods.

The future period over which past service cost should be allocated, however, was a point of major issue in *Opinion No. 8*. Three basic positions were advanced—each one, to a large extent, reflecting a different view of pension plans and past service costs.

1. Past service cost should be reflected in expense over the remaining years of service of the employees covered by the plan.
2. Past service cost should be reflected in expense over some reasonable future period not necessarily limited to the service lives of existing employees.
3. Past service cost should not be recognized at all. Only an interest equivalent on the unfunded portion of past service cost should be provided, to keep the past service cost from increasing.

The first viewpoint derives from a belief that the cost of pension benefits, whether past costs or normal costs, fundamentally are related to specific individuals. Since it is they who will receive the pensions measured by past service, it is reasonable that the period of benefit to the company from granting pensions is related to the time period from the adoption of the plan to retirement of the existing employee group.[15]

The second recommendation stems from a broader view of pension plans. Proponents view the past service cost as a separate element of cost. Pension benefits based on past service are granted to older employees in order for the company to gain general future benefits, such as improved employee morale, increased efficiency resulting from older employees retiring, ability to attract and retain better employees, etc. These benefits extend beyond the remaining service lives of a particular group of employees. Pension costs, particularly the past service portion, are related to a continuing employee group and pension plan. Therefore, past service costs should be accrued over a future period somewhat longer than that under the first position discussed.

The third line of reasoning also views pensions from the broad perspec-

---

[15] Those actuarial cost methods which do not separately identify a portion of the cost as past service cost accomplish this objective directly, by treating the past service costs as part of the normal cost to be recognized in future periods over the remaining service lives of the employees.

tive, one so broad that no provision for past service costs is deemed necessary. The period of benefit from past service costs is assumed to be indefinite; past service cost is like a perpetual intangible which does not require amortization. The real support for this view is a financial one. It is not necessary to *fund* past service costs in order to maintain the plan in operation on a continuing basis. Normal cost plus interest on unfunded past service cost will provide sufficient amounts to meet all payments. However, this is true only because current contributions for all employees can be used to pay pension benefits to those who have retired. This lag in cash needs should not overshadow the fact that for a going concern *all* pension costs associated with existing employees will eventually be paid out and thus should be recognized in expense.

Under either of the first two positions, an equal annual amount (including interest) of past service cost typically is charged to expense in each of the future years. Determining the equal annual cost to be recognized involves dividing the total past service cost by the present value of an annuity. This gives the amount of expense to be charged each period so that the total past service cost plus interest will be recognized over the desired time period. In our example total past service cost was $120,061. If this amount is to be accrued over a 20-year period, pension expense should include $8,835 to cover past service costs and interest ($120,061 ÷ $P_{\overline{20}|.04}$ = $120,061 ÷ 13.590 = $8,835) in addition to the $10,000 of normal cost each year.

Accounting Principles Board Opinion. Although preferring some method which recognizes a portion of past service cost in pension expense, the Accounting Principles Board saw some merit in all the views expressed. Hence, it concluded that the disparity in recording practices would be reduced significantly if the accounting expense provision based on an acceptable actuarial method fell between a maximum and minimum amount. The maximum basically includes (1) normal cost, (2) 10 percent of past service cost until fully provided for[16] and, (3) interest equivalents on the difference between amounts charged to expense and amounts funded. The minimum basically consists of (1) normal cost, (2) interest on any unfunded past service costs, and (3) a provision to accrue the present value of vested benefits within a reasonable period of time.[17] These limits differ only as to past service cost.

---

[16] Because of the interest element included in any periodic recognition of past service cost, a period longer than 10 years would actually be necessary to charge all original past service cost to expense. For example, it would take slightly over 13 years to accrue $120,061 in equal annual amounts, including interest at 4 percent, if the equal annual amounts were limited to $12,006.

[17] Calculation of the additional charge for vested benefits is complicated and beyond the scope of this introductory discussion. Probably the most common of the ways it can be computed is as the amount necessary to bring periodic pension expense up to that which would result if past service cost were being accrued over 40 years.

Not coincidentally, the maximum is the same as that allowed under the income tax law, and the minimum is the amount that must be funded in order to claim a tax deduction. Between them there is room for considerable difference in total pension expense. It seems unfortunate that after making such an exhaustive study of the subject of pensions, the Accounting Principles Board was unable to narrow the differences in determining accounting charges to expense any further than these tax- and funding-oriented limits.

Disclosure. Because of the complexities and alternatives accompanying pension calculations, the APB also insists on full disclosure of the following significant factors in the financial statements or notes to them:[18]

1. A statement that such plans exist, identifying or describing the employee groups covered.
2. A statement of the company's accounting and funding policies.
3. The provision for pension cost for the period.
4. The excess, if any, of the actuarially computed value of vested benefits over the total of the pension fund and any balance sheet pension accruals, less any pension prepayments or deferred charges.
5. The nature and effect of significant matters affecting comparability for all periods presented, such as changes in accounting methods (actuarial cost methods, amortization of past and prior service cost, treatment of actuarial gains and losses, etc.), changes in circumstances (actuarial assumptions, etc.), or adoption or amendment of a plan.

Past Service Cost as a Liability

The second major accounting question associated with past service cost is the question of liability recognition. Some accountants contend that if retirement benefits are based on past service, an obligation arises at the inception of the pension plan. They suggest that a pension liability should be shown equal to the present value of past service costs, and an asset account should present the portion not yet charged to expense. In our example the entry would be:

```
Deferred Past Service Pension Cost...... 120,061
    Liability for Past Service Pension
    Costs..........................         120,061
```

Expense recognition would be accomplished by amortizing the asset (plus interest) over future periods; liability liquidation would occur when and if payments actually were made to fund the past service cost.

The Accounting Principles Board disagreed. Past service cost is to be recognized as a liability (and simultaneous asset) only if a specific legal obligation exists. Such might be the case if the past service benefits are

---

[18] APB *Opinion No. 8, op. cit.,* p. 84.

vested immediately or if the company had contracted with the funding agency, such as an insurance company, to pay the past service cost immediately or in installments. Except for these cases, however, unfunded past service cost should not appear on the balance sheet. The only liability or asset normally appearing would be the difference between the amounts charged as expense and the amounts funded. In short, the Board takes a strict future-accrual approach to both expense and liability recognition.

The case for recognizing a simultaneous asset and liability would appear to be strongest for those who view past service cost as an element separate from normal cost. They would argue that the company has acquired an intangible asset (employee goodwill, etc.) upon inception of the plan. The cost of the asset is equal to, and measured by, the present value of obligation already assumed. This treatment would be analogous to that accorded property rights under capitalized long-term leases. Nevertheless, the analogy is weak, because labor agreements are purely executory contracts. Except perhaps in the case of vested benefits, an employee receives a pension, not because he has worked, but because he will continue to work until retirement. The amount he receives may be conditioned by past events, but the fact that he will receive it depends on future events. If a company were to sign a labor contract under which it agreed to paid hourly wages which averaged 10 percent above the going rate, employee morale, worker efficiency, and the ability to hire and retain employees assuredly would improve. However, few would argue that the present value of the excess wages to be paid under the agreement should be recorded as an offsetting asset and liability. Is a pension plan really significantly different?

Unresolved Issues Concerning Past Service Cost

The objective of the APB in issuing *Opinion No. 8* was to narrow the range of existing accounting practices, and its suggestions concerning past service costs help to accomplish this goal. On the other hand, the fundamental nature of past service cost remains unresolved. As a consequence, certain logical inconsistencies are apparent to the careful observer:

1. If past service cost is part of the total pension expense of specific employees and is not fundamentally different from normal cost, then those actuarial cost methods which do not distinguish between past service and normal cost should be preferred. Others would be tolerated only if past service costs were accrued over individual employees' remaining service lives. In any case, no liability would exist until accrual occurred as future services were received; no asset would exist unless prepayment (immediate funding) occurred.

2. On the other hand, if past service cost is a separate element related to the plan itself and to employees in general, then actuarial cost methods

which do *not* segregate past service cost should be unacceptable. A similar conclusion applies if past service costs are deemed to give rise to a liability equal to their present value immediately upon inception of the plan. An asset and a liability equal to the unfunded past service cost are created by the pension agreement and should be shown on the statement. Then the accompanying questions about the asset must be faced forthrightly. Does it have a limited or indefinite life? If it has a limited life, how can this be measured, and what pattern of amortization best reflects the consumption of the asset?

Entries to Record Pension Costs

Let us return to our example. Past service costs amount to $120,061, and normal cost is $10,000 per year. If the firm elects to recognize past service costs (plus interest) in expense over a 20-year period, $8,835 additional expense is required. Assuming that the firm also chooses to fund all pension costs accrued, the following entry is made at the end of each year:

```
Pension Expense.......................... 18,835
    Cash..................................         18,835
```

No asset or liability appears on the year-end balance sheet, except perhaps for a current liability of $18,835 if the cash payment to the trustee is not made until the beginning of the following year.

Periodic charges to expense would differ from that above if past service costs were recognized over a period other than 20 years or if funding did not coincide with the expense accrual. Recognizing past service costs as expense over a longer or shorter period presents no new problems. If 15 years is chosen, the additional expense for past service is $10,799 ($120,061 $\div$ $P_{\overline{15}|.04}$); if 30 years is chosen, the amount is $6,943 ($120,061 $\div$ $P_{\overline{30}|.04}$). Added to the normal cost of $10,000, each of these policies would result in an expense charge between the maximum of $22,006 [$10,000 + ($120,061 $\times$ 0.10)] and minimum of $14,802 [$10,000 + ($120,061 $\times$ 0.04)].

On the other hand, a pattern of funding different from that implicit in the expense accrual gives rise to *interest equivalents* on amounts not funded and also to the recognition of prepaid or accrued pension costs. Let us assume as an example that the company funds the past service cost over a period of 30 years; however, past service cost is to be recognized in expense over a period of 20 years. Table 11–3 summarizes the pertinent information for this situation.

The journal entries should be clear from an examination of the table. Any amounts charged to expense but not paid in cash are credited to the Accrued Liability under Pension Plan account. In later years, when cash payments exceed expense, the liability will be debited.

TABLE 11–3

Financial Statement Information Based on Recognition of Past Service Costs in Expense over 20 Years and Funding of Past Service Costs over 30 Years

Year	Amount Charged to Expense				Cash Payments (e)	Balance Sheet Liability at Year-End (f)
	Normal Cost (a)	Past Service Cost (b)	Addition for Interest (c)	Total (d)		
1.........	$10,000	$8,835	...	$18,835	$16,943	$ 1,892
2.........	10,000	8,835	$ 76	18,911	16,943	3,860
3.........	10,000	8,835	154	18,989	16,943	5,906
4.........	10,000	8,835	236	19,071	16,943	8,034
5.........	10,000	8,835	321	19,156	16,943	10,247
10.........	10,000	8,835	800	19,635	16,943	22,712
15.........	10,000	8,835	1,384	20,219	16,943	37,879
20.........	10,000	8,835	2,093	20,928	16,943	56,331
25.........	10,000	...	1,456	11,456	16,943	30,927
30.........	10,000	...	267	10,267	16,943	...

Note: Column (b) is $120,061 ÷ $P_{\overline{20}|.04}$. Column (c) is 4% of (f) on the preceding line. Column (d) equals (a) + (b) + (c). Column (e) is $10,000 + ($120,061 ÷ $P_{\overline{30}|.04}$). Column (f) equals the preceding balance + (d) − (e).

The interest equivalent is an addition in this example, because funding lags behind expense recognition. The $8,835 past service expense assumes funding over a 20-year period, not over a 30-year period. Hence, the interest element included in it is too small, because only $6,943 is being funded each period for past service cost. The additional interest element on unfunded accruals included in the expense provision recognizes the additional cost associated with this factor.

Other Problem Areas

Undoubtedly, the most troublesome and controversial area in accounting for the cost of pension plans is the treatment of past service cost. However, two additional areas can cause distortion in periodic pension expense and therefore necessitated comment by the APB. They are the handling of actuarial gains and losses and the treatment of unrealized appreciation and depreciation in the value of pension investments.

Actuarial Gains and Losses. These arise either when the actuarial assumptions underlying the pension calculations are modified to meet changing conditions or when actual experience differs from that originally assumed. They can result from mortality and turnover assumptions as well as substantial gains or losses on the sale of pension investments. Immediate recognition of these actuarial gains and losses may cause significant fluctuations in the year-to-year charge for pension expense. For example, if during the year the funding agency sold securities which had greatly appreciated in value, the gain might more than offset the entire normal pension cost. If the gain is recognized immediately, the result would be no pension expense for the year.

To be sure, actuarial gains and losses do influence the total pension cost; the important question concerns the timing of their impact on expense. The Accounting Principles Board reasoned that such gains and losses should be dealt with in a manner consistent with the long-range nature of pension cost. Actuarial assumptions are only estimates of future events. Actuarial gains and losses may indicate only short-term deviations from the estimates. In fact, they are in the nature of estimates themselves, subject perhaps to further modification. Treating them as adjustments to any particular year's pension expense or even as corrections of prior years' earnings overemphasizes their short-term character. Such changes are an integral part of the framework for estimating pension expense. Consistent with this line of reasoning, the APB recommended that actuarial gains and losses should be recognized over the current and future years.

Unrealized Appreciation and Depreciation.   A similar problem concerns the effect of value increases and decreases in pension fund investments which have not been realized by sale. For example, assume that shares of stock are purchased by a pension fund at a price of $5 per share. The stock steadily increases in value each year. The shares are not sold by the pension fund, however, so technically no actuarial gain or loss exists. Should this appreciation be ignored in calculating pension cost? Should it be offset against the pension expense each year? Should it be recognized as an actuarial gain only when disposed of by the pension fund, perhaps at some later date?

Ignoring unrealized appreciation in a pension fund overlooks the fact that those gains can be realized and thereby be used to reduce the total contribution from, and hence the total cost to, the employer. Changes in the value of these assets will have an ultimate impact on pension cost. On the other hand, recognition of appreciation and depreciation each year as an adjustment of that year's pension expense is subject to the same criticism as immediate recognition of actuarial gains and losses. It could cause wide fluctuations in annual pension expense by emphasizing short-term fluctuations. Finally, to wait until the gains and losses are realized by sale makes a fetish of the turnover of pension fund investment. Moreover, it might result in failing to recognize a material reduction (or increase) in pension cost for many years.

The conclusion of the Accounting Principles Board was that unrealized appreciation and depreciation were not significantly different from actuarial gains and losses. Therefore, these value changes "should be recognized in the determination of the provision for pension cost on a rational and systematic basis that avoids giving undue weight to short-term market fluctuations."[19]

---

[19] *Ibid.,* p. 80.

SUMMARY

That the problems of accounting for leases and pensions are complex is apparent from the discussions in this chapter. Each area has its theoretical controversies, its logical inconsistencies, its practical compromises, and its baffling detail. The simplified calculations and examples focus on the application of present-value concepts in the valuation of liabilities and, to some extent, assets and expenses. Dollar amounts to be paid or received over future periods of time can be dealt with effectively only in this manner. Whether these present values are recorded as accounting liabilities (assets) may depend on other criteria and definitions, but the valuation methodology is unmistakably clear.

A fundamental understanding of the basic procedures and concepts is necessary on two counts. First, the recommendations contained in *Opinions No. 5* (lessee), *No. 7* (lessor), and *No. 8* (pensions) are currently the generally accepted accounting principles governing the reporting of pensions and leases on financial statements. To understand what the reported figures represent, to interpret what influence they have, and to evaluate their underlying concepts is the goal of the informed statement reader. As accounting problems become more complex, the reader's knowledge has to become more sophisticated if that goal is to be achieved. Second, pensions and leases are areas where only a beginning has been made. A mastery of the basic principles now will help one to understand future developments.

SUGGESTIONS FOR FURTHER READING

Cook, Donald C. "The Case Against Capitalizing Leases," *Harvard Business Review*, Vol. 41 (January–February 1963), pp. 145–62.

Dreher, William A. "Alternatives Available under *APB Opinion No. 8:* An Actuary's View," *Journal of Accountancy*, Vol. 124 (September 1967), pp. 37–51.

Graham, Willard J., and Langenderfer, Harold O. "Reporting of Leases: Comment on *APB Opinion No. 5*" *Journal of Accountancy*, Vol. 119 (March 1965), pp. 57–62.

Hall, William D. "Current Problems in Accounting for Leases," *Journal of Accountancy*, Vol. 124 (November 1967), pp. 35–42.

Hicks, Ernest L. *Accounting for the Cost of Pension Plans*, Accounting Research Study No. 8. New York: AICPA, 1965.

Myers, John H. *Reporting of Leases in Financial Statements*, Accounting Research Study No. 4. New York: AICPA, 1962.

Philips, G. Edward. "Pension Liabilities and Assets, *Accounting Review*, Vol. 43 (January 1968), pp. 10–17.

Phoenix, Julius W., Jr., and Bosse, William D. "Accounting for the Cost of Pension Plans *APB Opinion No. 8*," *Journal of Accountancy*, Vol. 124 (August 1967), pp. 27–37.

————. "Accounting for the Cost of Pension Plans—More Information on *APB Opinion No. 8*," *Journal of Accountancy*, Vol. 124 (October 1967), pp. 31–40.

Zises, Alvin. "Leases—For Full Disclosure without Capitalization," *NAA Bulletin*, Vol. 44 (March 1963), pp. 45–49.

QUESTIONS AND PROBLEMS

11–1. To meet the needs of its expanding operations, Anderson Corporation obtained a charter for a separate corporation whose purpose was to buy a land site, build and equip a new building, and lease the entire facility to Anderson Corporation for a period of 20 years. Rental to be paid by Anderson was at an amount sufficient to cover expenses of operation and debt service on the corporation's 20-year serial mortgage bonds. During the term of the lease, the lessee has the option of purchasing the facilities at a price that will retire the bonds and cover the costs of liquidation of the corporation. Alternatively, at the termination of the lease, the properties will be transferred to Anderson for a small consideration, and the lessor corporation will be dissolved.

    The lessor corporation acquired the land and built and equipped the building at a total cost of $7,500,000. Anderson signed the 20-year lease for an annual rental, payable at the end of the year, of $825,000. Of this, about $62,100 was considered to be payment for current yearly operating expenses, and the rest was to cover the interest and principal of the lessor corporation's serial bonds.

    a) Under generally accepted accounting principles, does this leased property have to be included in the balance sheet of a lessee even though legal title remains with the lessor? Explain carefully.

    b) What is the implicit interest rate inherent in the lease?

    c) If the lease were capitalized, what entry would Anderson Corporation make during the first year?*

11–2. On January 1, 1972 the Barbarajo Record Company adopted a pension program for employees. Normal pension cost is $68,000 per year; past service cost is $240,000. The applicable interest rate is 4 percent. The total amount funded at the end of each of the first two years is $75,000.

    a) Prepare the journal entry to record the payment to the pension trust and pension expense under the maximum pension cost provision for the first two years.

    b) Repeat part (*a*) under the minimum pension cost provision.

11–3. During the course of your audit of a new client, Warehouse Company, for the year ended December 31, you learned of the following

---

* Problem adapted from AICPA November 1967 examination.

transactions between Warehouse Company and another client, Investment Company:

1. Warehouse Company completed construction of a warehouse building on its own land in June 1965 at a cost of $500,000. Construction was financed by a construction loan from the Uptown Savings Bank.

2. On July 1, 1965 Investment Company bought the building from Warehouse Company for $500,000, which Warehouse Company used to discharge its construction loan.

3. On July 1, 1965 Investment Company borrowed $500,000 from Uptown Savings Bank to be repaid quarterly over four years with interest at 5 percent. A mortgage was placed on the building to secure the loan and Warehouse Company signed as a guarantor of the loan.

4. On July 1, 1965 Warehouse Company signed a noncancellable 10-year lease of the warehouse building from Investment Company. The lease specified that Warehouse Company would pay $65,000 per year for 10 years, payable in advance on each July 1, and granted an option, exercisable at the end of the 10-year period, permitting Warehouse Company to either (1) purchase the building for $140,000, or (2) renew the lease for an additional 15 years at $25,000 per year and purchase the building for $20,000 at the end of the renewal period. The lease specified that $10,650 of the annual payment would be for insurance, taxes, and maintenance for the following 12 months; if the lease should be renewed, $11,800 of each annual payment would be for insurance, taxes, and maintenance.

5. The building has a useful life of 40 years and should be depreciated under the straight-line method (assume no salvage value).

6. Warehouse Company and Investment Company negotiated the lease for a return of 6 percent. You determine that the present value of all future lease payments is approximately equal to the sale price and that the sale-and-lease-back transaction is in reality only a financing arrangement.

For balance sheet presentation by Warehouse Company at December 31, 1966, prepare schedules computing the balance for the following items:

a) Prepaid insurance, taxes, and maintenance.
b) Warehouse building, less accumulated depreciation.
c) Current liabilities arising from the lease.
d) Long-term liabilities arising from the lease.*

11–4. The 1969 annual report of Armco Steel Corporation contained the following information concerning its pension plans:

---

* Problem adapted from AICPA November 1967 examination.

Armco and its consolidated subsidiaries have in effect several pension plans covering substantially all of their employees. Pension costs (defined as normal cost plus interest on unfunded past service costs and, if required, an amount for vested benefits) are funded. Income for the year was charged with $20,-942,000 (as compared with $18,167,000 in 1966). Additional information is presented on page 18.

The additional information referred to in the above note to the financial statements stated in part;

Based on actuarial estimates, the total amount required at year end to provide fully for past service cost was $382,479,000. The adjusted value of assets held by pension funds at year-end was $264,604,000 and the unfunded past service cost was estimated at $117,875,000.

a) Is Armco following the minimum or maximum alternative for determining pension cost?

b) Differentiate "normal cost" from "past service cost." Where and when does the past service cost get charged?

c) Why is interest on the unfunded past service cost included as part of the pension cost?

d) What arguments are advanced in support of and in opposition to Armco's procedure?

e) Explain the term "unfunded past service cost." Of what use to the analyst is knowledge that this figure is $117,875,000?

11–5. Flibinite Computer Manufacturing Company makes and sells a computer model, Series 1984. The cost to Flibinite is $1,570,000. Customers can acquire the computer at a cash sales price of $1,644,-000, or they can acquire it under a 10-year lease arrangement. The lease is noncancellable and requires an immediate cash payment of $100,000 plus a cash payment of $200,000 at the end of each of the 10 years. Maintenance and service are contracted for separately under either the cash sale or lease arrangement. On January 1, 1971 Short Circuit Electric Company acquired one of the Series 1984 computers under the lease arrangement.

a) Prepare the journal entries that would be recorded on the books of Flibinite on the following dates, assuming the company uses the financing method of recording lease receivables.
  1. January 1, 1971.
  2. December 31, 1971.
  3. December 31, 1972

b) Would this lease have to be capitalized on the books of Short Circuit Electric? Explain why or why not?

11–6. Marcus Wollaby Medical Supply Corporation adopted a pension plan for its employees on January 1, 1972. According to independent actuarial calculations, the cost allocated to past services is $300,000, and the normal cost is $40,000. The interest rate used in actuarial calculations is 5 percent. The company plans to fund $60,000 a year and to accrue past service costs over a period of 20 years.

a) Prepare a schedule that will show the determination of pension expense each year for the first five years. (*Note:* Pension expense will consist of normal cost, amortization of past service cost, and interest equivalents.)

b) What account(s) and dollar amounts related to the pension plan will appear on the balance sheet at the end of each of the first five years?

11–7. Libby, McNeill & Libby in its 1968 annual report presents the following footnote information concerning its lease commitments.

Annual rentals under leases on property and equipment in effect on June 29, 1968 aggregate $4,800,000, of which $3,400,000 is applicable to leases that expire within ten years from the above date and $1,400,000 applicable to leases that expire thereafter.

Included in the aggregate amount above are net lease rentals of:

1. $210,000 applicable to citrus groves leased by the company until 1976, financed by the lessor principally by the issuance of 4¼% to 5% bonds, of which $2,697,000 are outstanding at June 29, 1968. Of these bonds, the Company owns $591,000 and has guaranteed payment of principal and interest on an additional $1,195,000. The Company has an option to purchase the groves on June 1 of any year at a price equal to the bonds then outstanding plus a premium which decreases ratably from its present 2¼% to zero in 1976.

2. $504,000 applicable to property, plant, and equipment leased by the company until 1988. The lessor acquired such property in a sale and leaseback transaction, and financing was obtained through the issuance of 4¾% to 5% 25-year secured notes. . . . The Company has an option to purchase the property on or after November 1, 1973, at a price equal to the bonds then outstanding, plus a premium which decreases ratably from 5% in 1973 to zero in 1983.

a) Why did Libby, McNeill & Libby choose to lease these assets rather than buy them outright and borrow the money directly?

b) Discuss the merits of each of these situations with respect to whether the lease should be capitalized.

c) Assuming that lease payments are made at the beginning of each year and that the relevant interest rate in 1968 was 6 percent, estimate the amount of asset and liability that would appear on June 28, 1968 if these leases were capitalized.

11–8. The notes to the financial statements of Bunker-Ramo Corporation on December 31, 1965 contained the following information concerning its pension plan.

> The Company has trusteed pension and death benefit plans for eligible employees. The costs of the plans to the Company, including a portion of past service benefit costs, amounted in 1965 to approximately $522,000. The company has elected to pay the past service benefit costs of the plans over a 30-year period from January 1, 1964. The unpaid past service benefit costs, based on a single sum payment, were actuarially estimated to be approximately $1,218,000 at December 31, 1965.

a) What is meant by a "trusteed" plan? Does the type of plan have a bearing on the calculation of pension expense?

b) Assuming the interest factor for the pension fund is 5 percent and that the company funds the pension cost accrued, what amount of the total pension cost is for amortization of past service cost? (*Note:* The present value of $1 each year for 28 years at 5 percent is $14.8981.)

c) What would be the minimum pension expense that the company would have to charge under APB *Opinion No. 8?*

d) What accounts and amounts relating to the pension plans would appear on the financial statements in 1965?

e) What impact on the financial statements would occur if Bunker-Ramo were to pay a lump-sum payment to the trustee of $1,218,000 on December 31, 1965? How would this affect the determination of pension expense in future periods?

11–9. Finagel Finance and Leasing Company shows the following accounts among its assets and liabilities:

```
Assets:
    Contracts receivable for rental equipment (due in
        installments)......................................$458,750
        Less: Allowance for possible losses..................  (1,635)
                                                             $457,115
    Rental equipment (at estimated residual values)..........  59,700
Liabilities:
    Unearned rental income (to be taken into income over
        the life of the rental agreements)...................  101,060
```

a) Is this company employing the financing or the operating method of recording leases on the lessors' books? Explain how you know. Under what circumstances is each method appropriate?

b) Explain what each of the accounts listed above are and why they appear on the position statement.

c) Do you agree that Unearned Rental Income is a liability? Explain. Will this account be taken into income in equal installments over the life of the rental agreements? Why or why not?

d) If the interest rate implicit in the lease arrangement is 8 percent, what summarized journal entry would be made next year to record collection of installments on the rental contracts of $50,000?

11–10. On January 1, 1972 the Alfred Corporation has the opportunity to acquire a piece of equipment for $49,200 cash, or it can lease the equipment for $10,000 per year under a six-year noncancellable lease. The equipment has a useful life of about six years with a very nominal salvage value. Lease payments are to be made at the end of each year. The company decides to lease the asset and to capitalize the lease rights and related obligations.

a) Demonstrate that the effective interest rate implicit in the lease is 6 percent.

b) Prepare the journal entries on January 1, 1972.

c) Prepare the journal entries to record the lease payments on December 31, 1972 and December 31, 1973.

d) Management decides to amortize the lease rights using sum-of-the-years'-digits. Record the journal entries on December 31, 1972 and December 31, 1973. Comment on the propriety of recording amortization expense under a decreasing charge method but paying off the liability under an increasing principal repayment plan (point c).

e) What amounts will appear on the December 31, 1973 balance sheet relative to this lease?

11–11. Bubbling Beverage Company first adopted a formal pension plan on January 1, 1967. At that time, the past service cost was actuarially computed to be $600,000, and normal cost was set at $50,000 annually. The company decided to accrue past service costs over a 20-year period. The applicable interest rate is 5 percent. The company funded each year the normal cost plus the amount of past service cost accrued.

Effective January 1, 1972, the pension plan was modified to increase the retirement benefits. As a result, normal cost was increased to $60,000 per year, and $300,000 was added to past service costs. The company decides to accrue all past and prior service costs over the original 20-year period. This means that the incremental past service costs will be amortized over 15 years. However, the company decides to continue *funding* the *same dollar* amount as in the preceding five years.

a) What does the statement that "past service costs were actuarially computed to be $600,000" mean? Explain exactly what the $600,000 represents. Would you show it on the balance sheet?

b) Compute the total amount of prior service cost on January 1, 1972.

c) Prepare the journal entries to record pension expense and the amount funded in 1971, 1972, and 1973. Show computations for each year's pension expense.

11–12. During 1971, Schnuckendorf Markets, Inc. acquired a plot of land and constructed a warehouse on it. The total cost was $400,000. On January 1, 1972 Schnuckendorf sold the land and warehouse to Unreliable Insurance Company for $460,000 and immediately leased it back under a 20-year noncancellable lease. The lease called for rental payments at the end of each year of $40,000, which provided an interest return of 6 percent to Unreliable. The lessee will pay for insurance, maintenance, property taxes, etc. The lease provides no residual rights to Schnuckendorf Markets at the end of the 20-year period. It is expected that the warehouse will be worthless by then, but that the land will have a residual value of $40,000.

a) Record the sale and lease-back transaction on the books of Schnuckendorf Markets on January 1, 1972. Assume the transaction is recorded following APB *Opinion No. 5* and that the lease is to be capitalized.
b) Record the entry for the first year's lease payment.
c) Evaluate the rationale behind the procedure employed in parts (*a*) and (*b*).
d) What entries would Unreliable Insurance Company make to record the purchase and lease-back and to record receipt of the first lease payment?
e) Is the return to the lessor the same as the cost to the lessee? Explain.

11–13. Gimbel Brothers, Inc. showed in its annual report the following long term liability:

	As of January 31	
	1969	1968
Pensions and deferred contingent compensation (Note 6)	$10,788,551	$9,323,987

A note to the statement contains the following information:

Note 6: The Company has a non-contributory pension plan. The financial statements reflect accruals equal to the present worth of its existing pension commitments. In addition, effective February 1, 1967, the Company began amortizing past service costs of active participants over a twenty-year period. The total charge for the year ended January 31, 1969 was $1,746,000 (including $720,000 to amortize past service costs) as compared with $1,620,000 for the prior year. The Company is not making any provision for insuring or funding the plan or any benefits thereunder, but it may at its option make such arrangements in the future. The total amount which would have been necessary to fund the plan as of January 31, 1969, with respect to past services in excess of amounts accrued is estimated at $10,000,000.

a) What was the total amount *added* to the liability during the fiscal year ending January 1, 1969? Why did the balance in the liability account not increase by this amount?

b) Calculate the original amount of past service cost on February 1, 1967 if the interest rate used in determining amortization of it is 4 percent.

c) Explain the meaning of the $10 million mentioned in the last line of the footnote. How does (or will) this amount affect the financial statements?

d) What impact on expense and liability recognition does the fact that Gimbel Brothers does not make "any provision for insuring or funding the plan" have?

11–14. The 1967 annual report of Armco Steel Company showed for the first time a noncurrent asset of $114,467,000 called Unamortized Lease Rights and a noncurrent liability of $116,900,000 called Long-Term Lease Obligations. The following note explained these accounts:

> The Company has entered into lease agreements for the use of facilities that have been or are being constructed with funds provided from the proceeds ($116,900,000) of Industrial Revenue Bonds issued by municipalities. The lease agreements provide for the payment in annual amounts ($4,825,000 in 1969, $10,722,000 in 1970, $9,569,000 in 1971, $9,152,000 in 1972, $9,271,000 in 1973 and in decreasing annual amounts to approximately $7,000,000 in 1978 and thereafter to 1991) sufficient to service principal and interest (combined effective rate of approximately 4.4%) on the bonds. Amounts, which comprehend lease rights, equivalent to the aggregate lease payments generally are being amortized and charged to income on a straight-line basis over the estimated productive (guideline) lives of the facilities, which for the most part are shorter than the terms of the leases. Armco has options to purchase the facilities at any time during the term of the leases at the scheduled redemption prices of the bonds or for nominal amounts at the end of the lease periods. Unamortized lease rights as shown in the statement of consolidated financial position at December 31, 1967 include $60,079,000 of remaining proceeds held by trustees.

a) If the $116,900,000 of bonds were issued by municipalities, why does a liability appear on Armco's balance sheet?

b) Why would Armco choose to acquire the use of asset services in this indirect manner?

c) The amounts of the asset for lease rights and the liability for lease obligations are not the same. Explain why.

11–15. On January 1, 1972 Fido Fertilizer Corporation adopted a pension plan for its employees. Pension benefits were based on an employee's total length of service, including years prior to adoption of the plan. At the date of an employee's retirement, the company would purchase from a life insurance company an annuity policy which would pay the employee the monthly benefits he was entitled to.

As of January 1, 1972 the present value at 4 percent of future pension benefits related to years of service prior to January 1, 1972 (past service costs) was $200,000. The increase in present value of the future pension benefits attributable to each subsequent year (normal cost) was $60,000. During 1972 and 1973 retirement annuities were actually purchased for employees retiring in those years in the amounts of $14,000 and $18,000 respectively.

The company is considering a number of funding and expense recognition plans. These include the following:

1. Charge to expense each year only the amount paid for retirement annuities that year.
2. Fund the past service cost immediately, with a trustee, and each year's normal cost as incurred. Recognize as expense the maximum amount allowed under GAAP.
3. Fund normal cost each year and past service costs over a 20-year period. Recognize as expense the amount funded each year.
4. Fund only normal cost and interest on past service cost. Recognize as expense the minimum amount allowed under GAAP.

a) Is the first method a suitable way to measure pension expense and liability? Explain your answer.
b) Contrast the second, third, and fourth plans in terms of their impact on the financial statements. For each plan, show the pension expense that would be charged in 1972 *and* 1973 and any balance sheet accounts related to the pension plan that would appear at the end of each of the two years.
c) After reviewing your figures from part (*b*), the controller states, "This is a good example of the diversity in generally accepted accounting principles. The financial statements are made to look different depending on which principles we follow, yet the real financial position and performance of the company remain the same." Carefully evaluate his reaction.

11–16. During 1971 Sticks Bar & Barney, a midwest department store company, acquired land costing $200,000 and had constructed on it a suburban shopping center. The construction was done according to the specification of Sticks Bar & Barney and cost $6 million. On January 1, 1972 Sticks Bar & Barney sold the shopping center to Gibralter Insurance Company for $6.5 million cash. At the same time a 30-year lease agreement was signed covering the entire property, under which Sticks Bar & Barney agreed to make lease payments of $577,000 at the end of each year. The payments are designed to repay Gilbralter Insurance Company for its cash outlay and to provide an 8 percent return on its investment. All insurance, maintenance, property taxes, and operating costs are to be borne by the lessee. At the end of the lease, the property will be sold to Sticks Bar & Barney for $5,000.

a) Prepare the journal entries on the books of Sticks Bar & Barney to record the sale and the first two lease payments under the following conditions:
1. The transaction is treated not as a sale but as a borrowing arrangement.
2. The transaction is handled as a sale and lease-back under APB *Opinion No. 5,* and the lease is capitalized.
3. The transaction is handled as a sale and lease-back under APB *Opinion No. 5,* and the lease is not capitalized.

b) Rank these three alternatives in the order that you believe reflects their appropriateness for recording this transaction. Explain your reasoning.

11–17. The following notes describe the pension policies of four different companies for the year 1968.

> *Swift & Company.* The Company has pension plans covering substantially all employees. Contributions are made to irrevocable trust funds as authorized by the Board of Directors. The excess of accrued pension expense over contributions to the trusts, together with accrued deferred compensation, is shown as a noncurrent liability in the balance sheet. At October 26, 1968, all vested benefits of pensioners and present and former employes not yet retired are fully funded.
>
> Prior to adoption in 1968 of the practice of determining pension expense on an accrual basis, as recommended by the American Institute of Certified Public Accountants, it had been the Company's policy to reflect the amount of contributions under the plans as pension expense in the year of authorization. Pension expense for 1968, after giving effect to the cost of increased benefits, amounted to $14,366,641, as compared to $4,142,799 in 1967. These amounts include authorization of prior service costs under certain of the plans over periods of twenty-five years or less.
>
> *Continental Steel Corporation.* Noncontributory pension plans are in effect covering all employees of the company. The amounts of $1,358,000 and $1,361,000 charged to income in 1968 and 1967 respectively represent actuarially determined normal cost, interest on the unfunded prior service liability, and provision for vested benefits. The assets of all of the trusts together with the balance sheet accrual exceed the total vested benefits. However, in one plan, a deficiency of approximately $920,000 at December 31, 1968 became a legal liability of the company in 1968 and accordingly has been recorded as a liability with a corresponding deferred charge.

Libby, McNeill & Libby. The Company and its subsidiaries have several pension plans covering substantially all of their employees. Contributions to the pension trust, charged to earnings, for plans administered by the Company approximate current service costs, less a portion of the unrealized market appreciation on common stocks held by the trust. Payments under plans administered by unions, at contribution rates defined in the contracts, have also been charged to earnings.

Tenneco, Inc. The companies have in effect several pension plans, covering substantially all of their employees. Total pension expense was $16,700,000 and $16,100,000 for the years 1968 and 1967, respectively. The unfunded past service cost of certain plans of acquired companies is estimated to be approximately $70,900,000 at December 31, 1968, which generally is being amortized over periods ranging from 11 to 40 years. The excess of actuarially computed vested benefits over funded amounts and accruals approximates $40,700,000.

a) All notes except that of Libby, McNeill & Libby refer to vested benefits, but each of the other three notes reports different information about them. Explain what vested benefits are and discuss the significance to be attached to each of the three companies' statements about them. What significance do you attach to the fact that Libby, McNeill & Libby says nothing about vested benefits?

b) Tenneco, Inc. refers to unfunded past service costs of $70,900,000 and unfunded vested benefits of $40,700,000. How are these items different? Similar? How should the statement reader interpret them?

c) Contrast the companies' handling of past service cost. Which treatment is most liberal? Most conservative?

d) Discuss the deficiencies in the old method of pension accounting employed by Swift & Company.

e) In Libby, McNeill & Libby, pension expense and pension funding is reduced by market appreciation of common stocks. Why is this done, particularly when the appreciation is "unrealized"?

11–18. Loose Tile Manufacturing Company leased a piece of equipment. The initial period of the lease is five years, but Loose Tile has the option to renew for another five years. The lease rental is $8,000 for the first five years, payable at the end of each year, and $1,000 for the next five years if the company elects to renew the lease. Loose Tile is to pay all costs of insurance, property taxes, and maintenance during the life of the lease. The useful life of the equipment is estimated at 10 years.

a) If 10 percent is an appropriate rate of interest, what amount would you assign to the lease rights and obligations if they are to be capitalized?

b) Prepare a 10-year schedule showing the entries for the periodic lease payments.

c) Should this lease be capitalized? If so, how should the lease rights be amortized?

11–19.   Table 11–3 on page 389 shows financial statement information for a pension plan based on recognition of past service cost expense over 20 years and funding of past service costs over 30 years. Using the same pension plan, prepare a similar table assuming the company (1) recognizes past service cost in expense over 20 years, and (2) *contracts* with an insurance company to pay the past service costs in three equal installments beginning at the end of the first year. (*Note:* Because of the legal contract with the insurance company, an asset and liability would be recognized at the beginning of year 1 in the amount of $120,061.)

11–20.   Land owned by Wynn was leased to Place for eight years at an annual rental of $30,000, payable at the end of each year. At the end of five years, the location had increased in value. Shough approached Place offering to sublease the land for the remaining three years at $70,000. The offer was accepted by Place.

a) Record the lease right and related obligations under the original lease in the accounts of Place. The applicable interest rate is 6 percent.

b) What entry would Place record at the beginning of the sixth year, when the sublease is signed with Shough?

c) What difference would it make to your answer in (b) *if* the current interest rate were 8 percent?

d) Assume that instead of subleasing directly from Place, Shough agrees to assume Place's contractual lease payments of $30,000 to Wynn and to pay a lump-sum cash payment to Place for taking over the advantageous lease. What is the minimum lump sum payment that Place should accept?

CHAPTER TWELVE

ACCOUNTING FOR INCOME TAXES

CORPORATE income taxes are periodic charges levied by federal and state governments on the taxable income, as defined by law, of incorporated business entities. Such charges are accounted for in Chapter Five as a reduction in stockholders' equity (a debit to Income Taxes) and an increase in a liability (a credit to Estimated Liability for Income Taxes or Income Taxes Payable). In this accounting the amount of taxes legally owed for the period and the periodic tax expense to income were assumed to be the same. This assumption, however, may not be valid. Taxable income is a legal concept. The regulations underlying tax accounting do not necessarily coincide with the informational needs of investors and the basic concepts of financial accounting.

This chapter takes a closer look at the accounting problems encountered in the recording of certain aspects of the federal corporate income tax. We are concerned here with how properly to record the income tax charge for a period rather than how to compute a corporation's tax liability. We must thus distinguish between the nature of the income tax charge as a revenue deduction and the basis of its calculation. The principal problems in accounting for income taxes fall into three categories.

1. Interperiod tax allocation. Some accounting transactions affect the determination of financial accounting income in one year and the computation of taxable income in a different year. These timing differences cause the income tax charge legally owed for a period to differ from the amount which is related to the events reported on the income statement.

2. Carry-back and carry-forward of "net operating losses." Current tax regulations allow corporations to deduct certain operating losses incurred in one year from the taxable income of prior and subsequent years.

This provision raises the question of whether to record the tax effects of such losses in the period of loss or in the prior and subsequent periods.

3. Intrastatement tax allocation.   Extraordinary items are reported in a separate section of the income statement and sometimes in a separate statement of retained earnings. These items influence the computation of income taxes as well. How should the tax effects of these unusual items be reported in the financial statements?

DIFFERENCES BETWEEN ACCOUNTING INCOME AND TAXABLE INCOME

On the surface the differences between accounting income and taxable income may appear to be minimal. The Internal Revenue Code, in Section 446, requires that taxable income be computed in accordance with the method of accounting regularly employed by the taxpayer, if that method clearly reflects income. However, authorized throughout the Code and in the regulations interpreting the law are many modifications, exceptions, adjustments, and special provisions. Certain types of revenue and gains recognized in accounting income are excluded from taxable income. Also, deductions for financial accounting purposes may be denied or limited under the tax laws, while special tax deductions are allowed for items not recognized on the income statement.

All of these differences reflect either policy goals of Congress to be attained through the income tax law or administrative rulings to implement the law conveniently. For instance, tax regulations tend to focus more on ability to pay as measured by cash receipt or disbursement than on accrual concepts of revenue and expense measurement. In addition, other goals—regulation of corporations, special benefits to particular industries, stimulation of economic development, and redistribution of income—find reflection in income tax procedures from time to time. In other words, the complex set of rules and regulations comprising the income tax law arises from purposes other than just measurement of business income. Once these tax options are written into the law, however, companies deliberately take advantage of them to reduce current taxable income.

Financial accounting, on the other hand, is interested in properly matching costs and revenues to measure business income, not in determining taxable income. Where the two concepts of income are not the same, business firms should, and often do, maintain tax accounting records separate from their financial accounting records. But even when separate records are kept, a financial accounting problem still may be involved, because the income tax expense and income tax liability may be affected by events that are treated in one way on the books and in another on the tax return. Should income tax expense on the income statement be determined necessarily from the legal liability shown on the tax return for the period, or should it be related to the events reported on the income statement? To begin to answer this question requires distinguishing relatively permanent differences between tax accounting and financial accounting from timing differences caused by items not being taken into account at the same time for tax purposes as they are for accounting purposes.

Permanent Differences

Certain items of revenue are excluded by law from the determination of income taxes. Interest revenue from state and municipal bonds, for instance, is not taxed but is properly recognized as accounting revenue. A portion of the dividends received by a corporation from other taxable domestic corporations is treated in a basically similar manner.

Particular deductions also may be treated differently for tax and financial accounting purposes. For example, goodwill is not subject to amortization under current tax regulations, yet may be written off periodically as an expense on the financial statements. Similarly, life insurance premiums paid on insurance policies of employees are not tax-deductible if the corporation is the beneficiary under the policy, yet may be claimed as a valid expense on its income statement. Another example illustrating a tax deduction but not a financial accounting deduction is "percentage depletion." Certain producers and owners of special natural resources may be allowed to deduct as a depletion allowance a fixed percentage of "gross income" rather than a portion of the *cost* of the natural resource, as on the income statement.

The foregoing examples represent some relatively permanent differences between tax accounting and financial accounting income. Unless and until the statutory provisions of the tax laws are changed, these items will always be a cause of difference. Although they may cause the relationship between income taxes and net income before tax to be different from what one would normally expect, permanent differences seldom create financial accounting problems. Separate disclosure of any of these items which are material in amount satisfies the reporting requirements of financial accounting.

Timing Differences

Timing differences, on the other hand, do raise the important accounting questions posed earlier. Over a sufficiently long period, timing differences should disappear, and in the long run taxable income and accounting income are the same except for the permanent differences.[1]

---

[1] Even though the differences disappear in the long run, the present value of these differences is significant. It is for this reason that companies try to minimize current taxes even though this adds to future taxes.

Therefore, many accountants argue that the income tax expense applicable to any particular accounting period should be based on the amount of income (aside from adjustments for permanent differences) shown on the income statement, regardless of when the tax legally has to be paid to the government.

Let us briefly review some of the major causes of timing differences. Two basic situations can exist in any one year: net income before tax on the income statement either exceeds or is less than taxable income. However, each of these situations can arise from either revenue or expense timing differences.

1. Net income before tax exceeds taxable income:
    a) Revenue is recognized in the accounting records prior to its recognition on the tax return.
    b) Expense is recognized in the accounting records after its deduction on the tax return.
2. Net income before tax is less than taxable income:
    a) Revenue is recognized in the accounting records after its inclusion on the tax return.
    b) Expense is recognized in the accounting records prior to its deduction on the tax return.

Examples of 1(a) include the recognition of revenue on the books at the time of sale but reporting for tax purposes on the installment basis, so that revenue recognition is deferred until later periods, when the cash is actually received. A similar situation would exist if a construction company recognized revenue using percentage of completion for book purposes but reported revenue for tax purposes only when contracts were completed.

The most prevalent example of 1(b)—expenses being deducted earlier on the tax return than in the accounting records—is depreciation. Many firms use accelerated depreciation methods (double-declining-balance or sum-of-the-years'-digits) for tax purposes but prefer straight-line depreciation for measuring financial accounting income. This use of alternative procedures results in larger depreciation deductions on the tax return than on the income statement in the earlier years of an asset's life and smaller depreciation deductions in the later years. Hence, taxable income is lower than accounting income in the early years, but there is an offsetting effect in later years. Similar results occur if research and development or bond refunding expenditures are deducted in the year incurred for tax purposes but amortized over some future period for financial accounting purposes.

The situation in which net income before tax is less than taxable income does not occur as frequently as the opposite case. However, it can arise, for example, if a corporation receives prepayments or advances from customers for goods or services to be rendered over future periods. In some cases such cash receipts are taxable as revenue before the goods are delivered or the services rendered—2(*a*). However, in the accounting statements, some of these receipts are normally treated as liabilities and recognized as revenue in future periods only as the earning process occurs.

Similarly, the Internal Revenue Service does not allow a tax deduction for certain types of expenses which create estimated liability accounts or contra asset "reserves." Examples include estimated provisions for product warranties, collection costs, sales returns and discounts, etc. (Bad debts and depreciation are specific exemptions to this provision.) Under the matching concept it is proper to reflect these expenses on the books during the period when the related revenue is recognized. However, they must be reported in the tax return only on a "cash" or "incurred" basis —2(*b*).

INTERPERIOD TAX ALLOCATION

How should a firm account for the income tax charge when, because of timing differences, revenues or expenses are reported on the income statement and on the tax return in different periods? The accounting profession has wrestled with this question for more than a decade, finally resolving it in favor of what is called "interperiod tax allocation." But before investigating the procedures used to implement this concept, let us attempt an intuitive answer to this question, by reference to our conceptual framework.

Ignoring permanent differences, we know that in total the same revenues and expenses eventually are reported for both tax and financial accounting purposes. Timing differences merely result in period-to-period variations in reporting these common items. Therefore, we can say that the income taxes paid to the government are caused by the revenues and expenses reported at *some* time for financial accounting purposes. Because of this cause-and-effect relationship, it is a simple extension of our matching concept to say that we ought to record as tax expense each period the tax that sometime—this period, last period, or next period— has to be paid because of this period's revenues and expenses. Tax expense should be accrued and matched against the income that gives rise to the tax, regardless of when it has to be paid.

It is precisely this logical extension of the matching concept that interperiod tax allocation implements. The tax effects of revenues and expenses are reported in (allocated to) the same periods in which the items are recognized for book purposes. After adjustments have been made for permanent differences, the period's tax expense is recorded in an amount equal to the tax rate applied to the differences between the period's revenues and expenses. To the extent that timing differences cause *taxable* income to be lower in a particular period, this expense exceeds the amount legally owed. The difference represents an increase in a future liability, because eventually the causative timing difference cancels itself, thus increasing tax payments correspondingly. Conversely, timing differences may be such as to make this period's legal liability more than the tax expense shown in the statements. In effect, we are paying this period tax liabilities arising out of prior or future period's activities. Accordingly, the excess represents a reduction in the deferred tax liability established in prior years or an asset applicable to operations in future years.

Deferred Income Taxes Payable as a Liability

Let us take an example in which taxable income initially is lower than accounting income because sum-of-the-years'-digits depreciation is used for tax purposes while straight-line depreciation appears on the income statement. Assume that a firm purchases for $20,000 a depreciable asset with a useful life of four years. If no allowance is made for salvage value, depreciation expense will be $5,000 ($20,000 ÷ 4) each year on the income statement. On the tax return, however, the firm will deduct $8,000, $6,000, $4,000, and $2,000 respectively in each of the four years (4/10 × $20,000, 3/10 × $20,000, etc.). To focus attention specifically on the relevant tax aspects, we shall assume that the tax return and the income statement are the same with respect to all other items; furthermore, the revenues of $160,000 and other expenses of $60,000 remain the same for four years.

Under these circumstances the company's partial income statement for each of the next four years appears as follows:

```
Sales.......................               $160,000
Other expenses.............  $60,000
Depreciation expense.......    5,000         65,000
Net income before tax......               $ 95,000
```

If a 50 percent tax rate is applicable, the schedule shown in Table 12–1 summarizes the tax return calculations for the four-year period. Taxable income will be less than accounting income in the first two years and more in the remaining two years.

TABLE 12–1

(in thousands of dollars)

	Year 1	2	3	4	Total
Sales......................	160	160	160	160	640
Other expenses.............	60	60	60	60	240
Depreciation expense.......	8	6	4	2	20
Total deductions...........	68	66	64	62	260
Taxable income.............	92	94	96	98	380
Income tax (50%).........	46	47	48	49	190

Without income tax allocation the tax charge shown on each year's income statement would be the amount legally applicable to the period—from $46,000 for the first year up to $49,000 in the fourth. As a consequence, net income *after tax* each year would vary—$49,000 in the first year, $48,000 the second, $47,000 the third, and $46,000 the fourth.

Inasmuch as total taxable income and accounting income are the same over the four years, a more accurate matching occurs if the $190,000 of income tax is recognized as a periodic expense as the income is reported on the financial statements. The entries to allocate income taxes would be:

```
Year 1   Income Tax Expense (50% × $95,000).. 47,500
              Current Income Taxes Payable....          46,000
              Deferred Income Taxes Payable...           1,500

Year 2   Income Tax Expense.................. 47,500
              Current Income Taxes Payable....          47,000
              Deferred Income Taxes Payable...             500

Year 3   Income Tax Expense.................. 47,500
              Deferred Income Taxes Payable.......   500
              Current Income Taxes Payable....          48,000

Year 4   Income Tax Expense.................. 47,500
              Deferred Income Taxes Payable....... 1,500
              Current Income Taxes Payable....          49,000
```

The current tax liability is determined from the tax return. But the income tax expense is based on the information shown on the income statement. Each year it would show a constant $47,500 net income after tax.

Interperiod tax allocation views the income tax as an expense caused by the earning of accounting income. Therefore, income tax expense should be recognized on the income statement as the earned income is recorded in the accounting records. When the tax liability has to be paid is determined by the tax regulations. However, since timing differences tend to be temporary and the business entity is assumed to be a going concern, the real question is not *when* the tax is paid, but with what items of income it should be reported. A tax reduction in the current period caused by timing differences gives rise to an estimated liability—a future outlay of cash occasioned by events recognized in the current period. In subsequent periods the timing difference reverses (years three and four above). Then taxes currently payable exceed the income tax expense accrued and include tax amounts provided for in prior years.

Deferred Tax Charges as an Asset

The opposite situation can be illustrated by a firm which accrues an expense on its books that is not deductible until future years. Assume that income of $100,000 each year for three years is identical for financial accounting and tax purposes. In addition, however, the company accrues an expense of $20,000 in the first year that is deductible at the rate of $10,000 in years two and three. Normally, pretax financial accounting income would be reported as $80,000 in the first year and $100,000 in the latter two years.

However, for tax purposes the entire $100,000 must be included as income in year one. The tax effect of this, at a rate of 50 percent, is to cause a current tax liability of $50,000. Under interperiod tax allocation the income and its related income tax effect are recorded in the same accounting period. Entries to accomplish this are:

```
Year  1   Income Tax Expense................  40,000
          Deferred Tax Charges...............  10,000
               Current Income Taxes Payable...              50,000

Years 2   Income Tax Expense................  50,000
and   3        Deferred Tax Charges...........               5,000
               Current Income Taxes Payable...              45,000
```

Under this approach Deferred Tax Charges is an asset, a type of prepayment of a future tax. The firm has the right to earn income in future years without having to pay additional taxes.

Measurement Problems with Deferred Tax Liability

Most firms having timing differences combine Deferred Tax Charges and Deferred Income Taxes Payable into a single account, Deferred Income Taxes, having either a debit or a credit balance. In the former case it appears as an asset; in the latter and much more common situation, Deferred Income Taxes is presented with the liabilities. However, this treatment poses two additional measurement problems.

Change in Tax Rates. If the credit balance resulting from interperiod tax allocation is truly a liability, then a reduction in tax rates at some future time may result in an overstated liability. Conversely, if tax rates were to increase, the credit balance in the Deferred Income Tax account probably would be less than the cash payments necessary in future years. In either case an adjustment to the account and an offsetting entry to an extraordinary item on the income statement would appear necessary.

Present-Value Recording. In Chapters Ten and Eleven the concept of present value is employed rather extensively in the valuation of liabilities. Liabilities are recorded at the present value of their future cash outlays. Some accountants have suggested that this concept is equally applicable to the deferred tax liability. They argue that the same reasoning which requires discount notes to be recorded at less than maturity value requires that deferred income taxes be recorded only at the present value of the postponed amounts. In subsequent years interest is charged and the Deferred Tax Liability is credited to reflect the increase in the present value of the liability.

The major point at issue is the existence of an interest or discount rate. The more commonly accepted view is that the appropriate discount rate is zero; therefore, the present value is the same as the future value. Accountants record bonds and notes at present value, using the rate of interest which is explicitly stated or implicitly indicated by the negotiations between borrower and lender. With tax deferrals the circumstances are not the same. The government charges no explicit interest rate on its "loan," and no rate is implicit in the transaction. Using an opportunity interest rate not related to the transaction would involve sanctioning a procedure which is not used for valuing other long-term liabilities.

Deferred Charge–Deferred Credit Approach

The foregoing material illustrates one approach to interperiod allocation of income taxes. This approach treats the problem as an extension of accrual accounting, with the resulting debit or credit balance being analyzed within the conventional asset-liability framework. This approach is presented first because of its relative understandability and its theoretical merit. Nonetheless, one other method of handling the problem of timing differences should be mentioned. It is important because it carries the endorsement of the Accounting Principles Board of the AICPA.[2]

The merits of alternative approaches to interperiod tax allocation have been extensively debated in the accounting literature. After a careful consideration of the problem, including an extensive research study,[3] the Accounting Principles Board affirmed an approach slightly different from the asset-liability method. The debit and credit balances resulting from tax allocation are treated for position statement purposes as "deferred charges and deferred credits" rather than as assets and liabilities:

Interperiod tax allocation under the *deferred method* is a procedure whereby the tax effects of current timing differences are deferred currently and allocated to income tax expense of future periods when the timing differences reverse. The deferred method emphasizes the tax effects of timing differences on income of the period in which the differences originate. . . . The tax effects of transactions which reduce taxes currently payable are treated as deferred credits; the tax effects of transactions which increase taxes currently payable are treated as deferred charges.[4]

The emphasis of APB *Opinion No. 11* is almost exclusively on the income statement. Revenues and expenses seem to be viewed in two parts— the item itself and its tax effect. The two parts must be reflected in income during the same accounting period for proper income measurement. Procedures to do this are almost identical with those illustrated on page 410 in connection with the liability approach—just eliminate the word

---

[2] *Accounting for Income Taxes, Opinion of the Accounting Principles Board No. 11* (New York: AICPA, December 1967).

[3] Homer A. Black, *Interperiod Allocation of Corporate Income Taxes*, Accounting Research Study No. 9 (New York: AICPA, 1966).

[4] APB *Opinion No. 11, op. cit.*, pp. 162–63.

"payable" from the title of the deferred account and split Income Tax Expense into two parts, one representing taxes currently payable and the other the net effect of timing differences.

Unfortunately, balance sheet logic is a secondary consideration under the deferred credit approach. Throughout this book, we view the balance sheet as a statement of assets and equities. Therefore, real accounts having credit balances are classified as either liabilities, part of stockholders' equity, or contra assets. The Accounting Principles Board made it emphatically clear that Deferred Income Taxes (credit balance) is neither part of stockholders' equity nor an offset to some asset. Yet it also states, "Deferred charges and deferred credits relating to timing differences represent the cumulative recognition given to their tax effects and as such do not represent receivables or payables in the usual sense."[5]

The result is an item in limbo. It bears little resemblance to unearned revenue or advance payments, other items which are also sometimes described as "deferred credits." This failure by the APB explicitly to come to grips with the nature of this item detracts from the logic of tax allocation and reinforces a belief that "income smoothing" is of greater concern than the underlying theory.

Evaluation of Interperiod Tax Allocation

Accounting for the impact of timing differences has been one of the most controversial issues in accounting since World War II.[6] The Accounting Principles Board opinion passed just by the minimum two-thirds vote required.[7] Consequently, it seems appropriate to evaluate the pros and cons of interperiod tax allocation. The case *for* tax allocation has already been made in connection with the preceding descriptions. To summarize, proponents of tax allocation (and in particular supporters of the liability approach) view income tax as an expense that should be allocated to accounting periods in relation to the pretax accounting income

---

[5] *Ibid.*, p. 178.

[6] A third alternative, called the net-of-tax approach, also achieved considerable attention during this period. However, it was specifically deemed unacceptable by the Accounting Principles Board. Its name comes from the offsetting of the debit and credit balances resulting from timing differences against the liability or asset accounts involved in the transactions causing the timing differences. The particular asset and liability accounts are reported net-of-tax on the premise that tax deductibility (or lack of same) influences the valuation of these items. The net-of-tax approach does not face the basic issue of the relationship that should exist between book income and the annual tax charge.

[7] It appears that the Board's *Opinion No. 11* in favor of the deferred credit approach was a compromise. Adherence to either the liability approach or the net-of-tax approach as *the* method could not have captured sufficient support to overcome the votes of those opposing tax allocation. However, some of those supporting the liability and the net-of-tax approaches could unite to accept the middle ground.

included on the income statement for each period. The corporation, by earning income, has occasioned a tax charge that must be paid to the government. This charge should be part of the recording of the period causing it, not of the period in which it is paid. By postponing the time of payment the corporation receives a type of interest-free loan.

Arguments against Tax Allocation. Opponents of tax allocation focus on three points: (1) deferred debit and credit balances are not assets and liabilities; (2) tax allocation may result in a permanent or an ever-increasing deferred tax liability which never has to be paid; and (3) tax charges are not like other expenses, but are more in the nature of distributions of income to the government. Let us consider each of these more fully.

Some accountants have difficulty fitting the deferred tax accounts into the conventional asset-liability framework. The government recognizes no legal or contractual claim against the corporation for the deferred liability, and the corporation cannot demand payment from the government for any deferred asset. Payment of taxes equal to the amount shown on the income tax return effectively discharges all legal claims of the tax authorities. Moreover, even if the lack of legal recognition is ignored, the uncertainties surrounding future tax payments rule out an objective valuation of the "liability." Recognition of the Deferred Income Taxes account as a liability rests, they claim, on very tenuous assumptions about future income, stability of tax rates, and the similarity of tax regulations in future periods.

This first argument stems from a narrow, legalistic concept of liability and measurement. Such a concept is not necessarily employed with other items commonly treated as liabilities. Witness, for example, estimated liabilities for warranties, pensions, and certain leases that are capitalized. These also do not lend themselves to precise measurement, nor are they necessarily legal claims on the firm. But, like deferred taxes, they do fit the broader concept of liability suggested in Chapter Two—a future outlay of cash which can be reasonably estimated, occasioned by some event that has already occurred in a past or present period. Certainly the assumptions about the future made in order to measure the liability are not unrealistic when viewed in the light of similar assumptions necessary to estimate other liabilities, depreciate plant assets, or adjust for bad debts.

The second objection to tax allocation focuses on the question of the existence of any future tax payment. Advocates of this point of view claim that tax deferral from accelerated depreciation for many firms actually amounts to a permanent tax reduction. These firms tend to have a continual flow of new investments—replacing old assets or expanding the company. It can be demonstrated that for static or growing firms the higher tax depreciation charges (relative to book depreciation) on new assets will offset or more than offset the lower tax depreciation charges on older assets. Therefore, as long as tax provisions regarding accelerated depreciation remain the same and the firm maintains a regular policy of investing in new assets, the deferred tax account *in total* will never be reduced and, in fact, may grow larger every year. In this case the contention is that future income tax payments are permanently reduced.

The foregoing argument views the deferred tax liability account as a single amount. Really, though, the Deferred Income Tax Liability account is a control account for the deferral pattern on each individual timing difference the firm has. So, although the total balance may remain constant or even grow, tax liabilities caused by specific timing differences are being paid while other tax liabilities caused by new timing differences are being created. This is somewhat analogous to the continual turnover in other liabilities such as accounts payable. In a growing firm, total accounts payable may increase, but individual accounts do mature and are replaced by new accounts. The fact that different creditors are involved should not change the principle involved. An expense should not be ignored simply because the related liability may be replaced by another liability in the future, even if this process should go on for an indeterminable time.

The third objection to interperiod tax allocation concerns the fundamental nature of income taxes. The argument states that income tax, unlike other expenses, has no relation to accounting income. The government in each period levies a claim against the firm's assets based on a set of concepts and procedures which depart substantially from those underlying financial accounting. With the increasing divergence between accounting and taxable income, the "income tax" appears to be simply a tax on corporations based on a continually changing formula that happens to have the term "income" in it. Income taxes, under this view, represent a type of periodic, involuntary distribution of income. Hence, the period charge is best measured by the actual levy, the amount legally owed. Except for the permanent differences, this view does not hold up under close scrutiny of the tax code. Business income and taxable income basically *are* the same in the long run.

CARRY-BACK AND CARRY-FORWARD OF OPERATING LOSSES

Income taxes normally are assessed on an annual basis. A potential inequity can result between a corporation earning taxable income each year and one having larger taxable income in some years but losses in other years. For the latter firm, a strict annual accounting for taxes would impose a larger tax levy, even though the average yearly earnings of the two firms were the same.

To help alleviate such problems, Congress included in the tax regula tions a net operating loss deduction. This loss deduction allows a corporation to offset the operating loss (unused tax deductions) incurred in one particular year against the taxable income of other years. Specifically, the law allows operating losses to be carried back for three years and offset against the income of those years. If an unused loss still remains, it then can be carried forward for as many as five additional years.[8]

This provision creates a slightly different tax allocation problem from that caused by timing differences. The loss deduction creates a claim for tax refund in the case of the carry-back or a potential tax savings in the future in the case of the carry-forward. The financial accounting question is whether the tax effects of the operating loss should be recognized in the period of loss or in the periods in which income tax is actually reduced. Specifically, with a loss carry-back, should the tax refund be treated as a reduction in the current period's loss (in effect, a negative income tax charge) or as an extraordinary item reflecting a correction of prior years' taxes? Similarly, with a loss carry-forward, should the tax savings be recognized immediately as a reduction in the loss or only in future periods when taxes are actually reduced?

Carry-Back Case

The guideline developed in the preceding discussion of timing differences is that income tax effects should be reported in the same accounting period as the factors which cause them. Application of this concept to the questions posed above leads to the conclusion that the tax benefits from carry-forwards and carry-backs should be recognized in the year the causative net loss is incurred. For operating loss carry-backs, this conclusion has almost universal support. The tax loss causes an allowable, measurable claim for refund. The creation of this asset should be considered in the measurement of the net results of the current period.

For example, assume that a corporation has averaged $50,000 of taxable income in each of the three preceding years. In the current year a net loss of $120,000 is incurred. This loss can be carried back to offset the taxable income of these prior years. Since taxes for these years probably have been paid already, the corporation would enter a claim for a tax refund and make the following entry:

```
Receivable for Refund of Income Tax....... 60,000
    Refund of Income Taxes Due to Loss
    Carry-Back.........................            60,000
```

The credit account would be closed to Income Summary for the year and appear on an income statement for the current year as follows:

---

[8] Actually, the accounting loss is subject to various adjustments before it becomes a carry-back or carry-forward operating loss. However, for most corporations these adjustments are minor and specialized. Consequently, they are ignored in subsequent discussions.

```
Net loss before income tax........ $(120,000)
Less: Refund of prior years'
      income taxes due to loss
      carry-back...................    60,000
Net loss after income tax effects. $ (60,000)
```

Carry-Forward Case

Assume, however, that the loss in the current year is $220,000 instead of $120,000. In this case, $150,000 of the loss can be carried back, completely offsetting the income of the three preceding years and giving rise to a tax refund of $75,000 (50% × $150,000). The other $70,000 of the loss can be carried forward to offset taxable income for the next five years. Some accountants would recognize this unused tax deduction (future potential tax savings) as an asset also and reduce the current year's loss accordingly. The entry would be:

```
Receivable for Refund of Income Tax from
    Loss Carry-Back...................... 75,000
Future Tax Benefits from Loss Carry-
    Forward.............................. 35,000
    Reduction in Loss Due to Loss
       Carry-Overs......................            110,000
```

The Future Tax Benefits account would then serve to reduce Taxes Payable in future years (but not tax expense). Since the loss in the current year causes the reduction in taxes, the tax savings should be reported in the current loss year rather than in future years.

This treatment follows the same concept illustrated in connection with the carry-back. However, another important factor must be considered—the "realizability" of the carry-forward (the probability that the carry-forward will actually reduce future tax payments). Like any asset, the Future Tax Benefits from Loss Carry-Forward must have future value. Its future value, however, is directly related to the existence of taxable income during the next *five* years sufficient to make use of the carry-forward. The fact that the company has already experienced a loss may cast doubt on its ability to generate income in future years.

The tremendous uncertainty concerning the value of a loss carry-forward caused the Accounting Principles Board to prefer a different treatment in most circumstances. The loss in the current year should be reported without consideration of any potential tax savings. If and when taxable income does arise in the future, the tax benefits of the carry-forward should be reported as extraordinary items to the extent actually "realized." The immediate recognition of the tax benefits of loss carry-forwards should be employed only "in unusual circumstances when realization is *assured beyond any reasonable doubt* at the time the loss carry-forwards arise."[9] Assurance beyond a reasonable doubt exists, in the opinion of the APB, only if:

---

[9] APB *Opinion No. 11, op. cit.,* p. 173.

(a)   the loss results from an identifiable, isolated and nonrecurring cause and the company either has been continuously profitable over a long period or has suffered occasional losses which were more than offset by taxable income in subsequent years, and

(b)   future taxable income is virtually certain to be large enough to offset the loss carryforward and will occur soon enough to provide realization during the carryforward period.[10]

Tables 12–2 and 12–3 illustrate how certain amounts would appear in the current year and in future years under each of the treatments dis-

TABLE 12–2

Immediate Recognition of Tax Benefits from Loss Carry-Forward
(in thousands)

	Year		
	Current	1	2
Net income before taxes.............	$(220)	$40	$60
Income tax expense.................	(110)	20	30
Net income after tax*..............	(110)	20	30
Future tax benefits from carry-forward†..................	35	15	. . .
Taxes payable (refund).............	(75)	. . .	15

* The total for the three years is $60,000.
† Balance at end of year. Decrease represents yearly offset against Taxes Payable as benefits from loss carry-over are actually taken.

cussed. It is assumed that taxable income (and book income before taxes) for the next two years will be $40,000 and $60,000 respectively, and that the applicable tax rate remains 50 percent.

With hindsight the net income figures in Table 12–2 appear to be more reasonable than those in Table 12–3, because all tax effects are reported in the same year as the factors causing the tax effects. Keep in mind, however, that the ability to utilize completely the $70,000 loss carry-forward is contingent on the generation of sufficient future income, which is not so certain at the time of the loss as it is two years hence. The APB prefers the approach in Table 12–3 in most circumstances. The reader is invited to prepare similar tables assuming much smaller amounts of taxable income in future years to obtain a comparison.

Notwithstanding the importance of the "realizability" argument, the Accounting Principles Board probably is being unduly conservative. Its position of not recognizing an asset unless its value is assured beyond any reasonable doubt seems inconsistent with the treatment of other assets, which are recognized as assets on the expectation that they will have

---
[10] *Ibid.*

TABLE 12–3

Recognition of Tax Benefits from Loss Carry-Forward Only
When Realized (in thousands)

	Year		
	Current	1	2
Net income before tax..............	$(220)	$40	$60
Income tax expense................	(75)*	20	30
Extraordinary gain†................	. . .	20	15
Net income‡......................	(145)	40	45
Taxes payable (refund)............	(75)	. . .	15

* Refund from carry-back only.
† Equal to the realized tax benefits from loss carry-forward. Offsetting debit is to Taxes Payable.
‡ Total for the three years is $60,000.

future value. They are written down or off only when evidence arises negating their future value. A similar view could be taken with loss carry-forwards. The tax benefits should be recognized in the loss period unless specific doubts exist concerning their future realizability.

TAX ALLOCATION WITHIN A PERIOD

Tax allocation arising from timing differences and from carry-backs and carry-forwards involves determining the appropriate tax charge for an accounting period. A separate tax allocation question involves the proper reporting of the tax charge determined for an accounting period when extraordinary items and adjustments of prior periods exist in addition to normal operating income. Following the guidelines in APB *Opinion No. 9*, the income statement includes all items except adjustments to prior periods, which are reported on a separate statement of retained earnings. On the income statement itself, extraordinary items are segregated. However, each of these items—income before extraordinary items, extraordinary items, and adjustments of prior periods—may have an impact on the determination of the taxable income and tax charge for the period. *Intraperiod* tax allocation involves allocating the total amount of income taxes for the period among sections of the income statement or between the income statement and the statement of retained earnings.

For instance, it would be quite misleading to report a favorable adjustment of prior years' income in the statement of retained earnings but to include the increased taxes that have to be paid because of the item as part of the tax expense on the income statement. It is fairly generally agreed that if an unusual item is shown on a separate statement of retained earnings, then the tax charge or saving related to it should be shown there also. In effect, then, this procedure divides the tax charge for the period between the income statement and the retained earnings statement. The portion shown on the former would be the tax applicable to the income shown there. The additional tax (in the case of a favorable adjustment) or the estimated tax reduction (in the case of an unfavorable adjustment) is reported with the adjustment itself in the statement of retained earnings.

The same idea applies to extraordinary gains and losses reported in the separate category of the income statement. Table 12–4 illustrates this type

TABLE 12–4

BRUNSWICK CORPORATION
Partial Statement of Earnings for
the Year Ended December 31, 1968
(in thousands)

Earnings before income taxes.............	$24,206
Provision for income taxes..............	11,600
Earnings before extraordinary credits....	$12,606
Extraordinary credits:	
Reduction of reserves no longer required for possible losses on receivables and termination of foreign operations, less related income tax effect of $4,600,000......	3,900
Gain on sale of 15% of common stock of Sherwood Medical Industries, Inc., less related income taxes of $5,535,000.........................	10,250
Net Earnings for the Year...............	$26,756

of reporting. The tax effect (in this case, an increase) modifies the extraordinary credits rather than the normal income tax provision. Total tax expense for 1968 is $21,735,000 ($11,600,000 + $4,600,000 + $5,535,-000), but this amount has been allocated to three different parts of the income statement. Had Provision for Income Taxes been reported simply as $21,735,000, net income would be the same but operating income would be understated.

SUMMARY

An old saying states that nothing in this world is certain but death and taxes. In light of the discussion in this chapter, we might extend the adage to include financial accounting problems caused by taxes. Income tax authorities, admittedly a separate audience for accounting reports, nevertheless provide a source of thorny problems in the preparation of financial statements for other external users.

Three of those problems form the focal points in this chapter. The concept used in approaching all of them is that income taxes are caused by certain transactions and events of the firm. The effect of these transactions and events on the income tax charge should be reported along with the items themselves. Following this concept, we reach these conclusions:

1. Normal income tax expense should be based on the amount of income subject to eventual taxation that is shown on the income statement. Any difference between that amount and the amount legally owed should be reflected in the balance sheet as a liability or asset.
2. The tax reductions (either refunds or future savings) from net operating loss carry-backs and carry-forwards should be recognized in the year a net loss is incurred. This conclusion does not apply if extensive doubt exists that a carry-forward will ever actually result in future tax savings because of a lack of future taxable income.
3. The tax impact of events which are reported as extraordinary items or as adjustments of prior years' income should be reported with the events causing them.

In most instances these conclusions agree with the generally accepted accounting principles of the Accounting Principles Board. The reasoning leading to the conclusions and the procedures employed in implementing them are described, explained, and evaluated in the chapter.

SUGGESTIONS FOR FURTHER READING

Black, Homer A. *Interperiod Allocation of Corporate Income Taxes*, Accounting Research Study No. 9. New York: AICPA, 1966.

Davidson, Sidney. "Accelerated Depreciation and the Allocation of Income Taxes," *Accounting Review*, Vol. 33 (April 1958), pp. 173–80.

Drinkwater, David, and Edwards, James Don. "The Nature of Taxes and the Matching Principle," *Accounting Review*, Vol. 40 (July 1965), pp. 579–82.

Jaedicke, Robert K., and Nelson, Carl L. "The Allocation of Income Taxes —A Defense," *Accounting Review*, Vol. 35 (April 1960), pp. 278-81.

Keller, Thomas F. "The Annual Income Tax Accrual," *Journal of Accountancy*, Vol. 114 (October 1962), pp. 59–65.

Moonitz, Maurice. "Income Taxes in Financial Statements," *Accounting Review*, Vol. 32 (April 1957), pp. 175–83.

Perry, Raymond E. "Comprehensive Income Tax Allocation," *Journal of Accountancy*, Vol. 122 (February 1966), pp. 23–32.

Waugh, James B. "The Interperiod Allocation of Corporate Income Taxes: A Proposal," *Accounting Review*, Vol. 43 (July 1968), pp. 535–39.

Williams, Doyle Z. "Reporting Loss Carryovers in Financial Statements," *Accounting Review*, Vol. 41 (April 1966), pp. 226–34.

Winborne, Marilynn G., and Kleespie, Dee L. "Tax Allocation in Perspective," *Accounting Review*, Vol. 41 (October 1966), pp. 737-11.

QUESTIONS AND PROBLEMS

12–1. The following figures are taken from the financial accounting records and income tax return for the Payless Company for a three-year period:

Income Before Deducting Income Taxes

Year	Accounting Records	Income Tax Return
19 × 1	$180,000	$150,000
19 × 2	120,000	130,000
19 × 3	138,000	160,000

Revenues and expenses are the same on the tax return as in the financial accounting records in each of the years, with the following exceptions:

1. In 19x1 a $30,000 gain was recognized for book purposes. This gain will be recognized for tax purposes in the amount of $10,000 each year for the next three years, beginning in 19x2.
2. In 19x3 the company accrued a $12,000 expense on its books. For income tax purposes, this expense cannot be deducted until future years when the cash is actually disbursed.

a) Calculate the amount of income tax legally owed for each year, assuming a tax rate of 40 percent.

b) Prepare journal entries to record income tax expense in each of the three years under interperiod tax allocation procedures.

12–2. Neverlite Bulb Manufacturing Company began operations in 1961 and operated profitably for 10 years. In 1971 the company introduced a new photographer's "whitelite" dark room bulb. The bulb allowed film to be processed in full light. Unfortunately, this characteristic of the bulb did not have permanence, so that after a few hours of use, any film exposed under it was ruined. Consequently, the bulb was withdrawn from the market after three months.

The company suffered large losses from the disposal of inventory and settlement of claims. As a result, the income statement for 1971 showed a net loss of $120,000. The loss could be carried back to offset the taxable income of 1968, 1969, and 1970. The company is subject to a tax rate of 30 percent. Earnings since 1968 are shown below:

	Net Income	Income Tax
1968	$ 25,000	$ 7,500
1969	30,000	9,000
1970	21,000	6,300
1971	(120,000) loss	(22,800) refund

Since the tax loss carry-back exhausted only $76,000 of the loss, giving rise to the $22,800 tax refund, there is a tax loss carry-forward of $44,000 that can be offset against income for the next five years. The potential future tax savings from this carry-forward are $13,200. The president wishes to reflect the $13,200 as an asset at the end of 1971 and report only an $84,000 loss after tax. The chief accountant says that the $13,200 should be reflected as a benefit only in future years, when it is realized. He would report a loss in 1971 of $97,200 after taxes. The company's net income before tax in subsequent years was: 1972, $17,000; 1973, $21,000; and 1974, $28,000.

a)   Prepare a comparative schedule showing the amount of aftertax net income that would be shown for 1971, 1972, 1973, and 1974 under the treatment proposed by the president.

b)   Prepare journal entries in 1971, 1972, 1973, and 1974 to record tax expense and related entries under the president's procedure.

c)   Repeat part (*a*) under the treatment proposed by the chief accountant.

d)   Repeat part (*b*) under the chief accountant's procedure.

e)   Which procedure would you recommend in 1971? Explain.

12–3.   The following information is taken from the records of Unusual Enterprises, Inc. for the year 1971:

	Dr.	Cr.
Sales...		$590,000
Rent revenue...................................		33,000
Renegotiation refunds from 1968 contract..........		12,000
Gain on sale of building.........................		24,000
Cost of goods sold.............................	$350,000	
Selling and administrative expenses...............	150,000	
Fire loss......................................	38,000	
Loss on retirement of bonds.....................	4,000	
Write-off of intangibles.........................	25,000	
Income taxes..................................	38,800	
Dividends.....................................	25,000	
Increase in retained earnings....................	28,200	
	$659,000	$659,000

All items are subject to a tax rate of 50 percent except the gain on sale of building, which is taxed at a capital gains rate of 25 percent, and the renegotiation refund, which is taxed at 1968's tax rate of 40 percent. Retained earnings at the beginning of the year are $92,300.

a)   Show how the income tax figure of $38,800 was derived.

b)   Prepare in good form an income statement and a separate statement of retained earnings for 1971. Report extraordinary items separately in the income statement and adjustments of prior periods' earnings in the statement of retained earnings. Employ tax allocation between the statements and within the income statement.

12–4.   The Sperry and Hutchinson Company sells and redeems S & H Green Stamps. Its balance sheet contains the following accounts among the current assets:

	Jan. 3, 1970	Dec. 28, 1968
Future Federal tax benefits..............	$24,601,000	$22,854,000

The accompanying note explains the derivation of this account:

The Company records stamp service revenue and provides for the cost of redemptions at the time stamps are furnished to licensees. The provision for redemption consists of estimates, based upon current operating experience, of the cost of merchandise and the related redemption service expenses required to redeem 95% of the stamps issued. At January 3, 1970, the liability for stamp redemptions of $211,750,000 included $164,698,000 for the cost of merchandise and $47,052,000 for redemption service expenses representing all other direct expenses related to redemptions. This liability is classified wholly as a current liability although some portion of the stamps provided for may not be presented for redemption within one year.

Since redemption service expenses are deducted for Federal income tax purposes as actually incurred, the future tax benefit attributable to the difference between the provision for redemption service expenses and the actual expense incurred in each period has been recognized in the financial statements.

a) Reconstruct the journal entry made during the year to record income tax expense. The income tax charge on the statement of earnings was $27,109,000.

b) Were redemption service expenses deducted for tax purposes greater or less than the amount shown on the income statement? How do you know? If the tax rate was 48 percent, what was the dollar difference between the two figures?

c) How would you justify treating the taxes applicable to the difference between the provision for redemption expense and the amount deducted for tax purposes as an asset?

d) Why is it shown as a *current* asset?

12–5. At the beginning of 1971, Pawahese Corporation acquired for $240,000 some plant assets with an average economic life of three years and no estimated salvage value. Income *before* depreciation and taxes was as follows from 1971 to 1973:

> 1971.............. $200,000
> 1972.............. 200,000
> 1973.............. 150,000

The company decided to depreciate the $240,000 for financial accounting purposes by the straight-line method. However, it elected to use the sum-of-the-years'-digits method for tax accounting purposes. The tax rate from 1971 to 1973 was 60 percent.

a) Compute the annual tax liability reported by the company on its *tax return* for the three years.

b) Make journal entries for tax expense for the three years using income tax allocation procedures.

c) Prepare and post a T account for the entries in (b) to the account Deferred Tax Liability for the three years.

d) What would happen to the balance in the Deferred Tax Liability account if the company were to spend $240,000 *per year* indefinitely, beginning in 1971, for plant assets with a three-year life and no salvage value? Explain carefully or illustrate.

e) Repeat part (d) assuming the company's annual expenditures for plant assets would grow by $30,000 each year.

f) What implications (if any) do the results in parts (d) and (e) have for your interpretation of the Deferred Tax Liability account? Explain.

12-6. The partial income statement in comparative form shown below is taken from the 1969 annual report of Allis-Chalmers Manufacturing Company.

	1969	1968
Income (loss) before income taxes and extraordinary charges.............	$ 40,582,667	$(93,094,627)
Federal, state, and foreign income taxes...............	(22,160,000)	51,942,000
Income (loss) before extraordinary charges.............	$ 18,422,667	$(41,152,627)
Extraordinary charges —net of income taxes of $15,057,211......	...	(13,437,093)
Net Income (Loss) for the Year...........	$ 18,422,667	$(54,589,720)

The balance sheet as of December 31, 1969 showed among the current assets, $20,952,622 called Income Tax Refunds and Future Income Tax Benefits, and among the noncurrent assets, $21,078,149 called Estimated Future Income Tax Benefits. The following excerpts have been taken from a note to the statements:

Provisions were recorded in the last quarter of 1968 to establish special reserves for the anticipated costs and losses which would result from implementation of the Company's proposed programs for substantial changes in the organization, products and production facilities, marketing and relations with dealers and customers. Changes in these reserves during 1969 are summarized as follows:

Balances in reserves at beginning of year............	$68,754,410
Costs and losses incurred........................	31,878,574
Balances in reserves at end of year................	$36,875,836

Although the costs and losses to be charged to the reserves in the future cannot be finally determined at the present time, management believes that the remaining reserves represent a fair and reasonable determination of the amounts required.

The Company will file a consolidated federal income tax return for 1969 and no taxes will be payable. Federal taxable income, before application of tax loss carry-forwards, will be nominal because the current year's charges to the special reserves recorded in 1968 will be deducted in arriving at taxable income and because of normal book-tax timing differences.

The tax benefits expected to be realized from future charges to the special reserves and from future utilization of tax loss carry-forwards were recorded in 1968. An amount equivalent to such tax benefits realized in 1969 of $16,992,678 is included in the current year's income tax provision, together with $3,077,996 relating to normal book-tax timing differences, primarily depreciation of plants and equipment, and $2,089,326 relating principally to state and foreign taxes payable.

The realization of the remaining estimated future income tax benefits at December 31, 1969 of $40,824,530, including $19,746,381 in current assets relating to normal book-tax timing differences, is dependent upon the generation of future taxable income; in the opinion of management, the realization of such tax benefits is assured beyond any reasonable doubt.

a) What was the total tax loss carry-back and carry-forward from 1968? Why is it treated as a negative income tax?

b) Explain why the company shows a tax savings on the extraordinary loss in 1968 when, in fact, no taxes would have been paid in any case?

c) Prepare the journal entry made in 1968 to record income taxes.

d) Prepare the journal entry made in 1969 to record income taxes.

e) Do you agree with management's opinion that "the realization of such tax benefits is assured beyond any reasonable doubt?"

12–7. Leap Year Calendar Corporation undertook a major advertising program to smooth out its sales volume, which tended to be quite cyclical in nature. The campaign cost $200,000 and was deducted on the company's tax return in 1975. However, on its financial statements the firm decided to reflect the amount as an asset, amortizing it to expense over a four-year period beginning in 1976.

In 1975, the company reported taxable income of $100,000, which was taxed at a rate of 40 percent (financial accounting income was $300,000). In 1976 taxable income was $180,000 and book income was $130,00. In 1977 taxable income was $150,000 and book income was $100,000. However, in 1977 the tax rate was reduced from 40 to 30 percent.

a) Prepare journal entries to record income tax expense, current income taxes payable, and deferred income taxes in 1975 and 1976.

b) Prepare journal entries in 1977 for taxes under the "liability" approach. Explain your reasoning.

c) Prepare journal entries in 1977 for taxes under the "deferred credit" approach. How would the Accounting Principles Board justify this approach, inasmuch as tax expense does not bear a normal relation to reported net income?

12–8. Helena Rubenstein, Inc. showed the following figures in its income statement for 1968:

Revenues................................	$37,902,036
Expenses...............................	35,416,516
	$ 2,485,520
Income taxes...........................	1,041,038
Income before extraordinary items........	$ 1,444,482
Extraordinary items (Note E).............	1,474,209
Net income.............................	$ 2,918,691

Note E: Extraordinary Items. During 1968, the Company sold the lease on the New York City building containing its executive offices and salon. The sale resulted in a net gain of $1,597,609 after deducting applicable income taxes of approximately $556,000. This sale is being reported on the installment basis for Federal Income tax purposes, resulting in $204,101 of income taxes being deferred.

A major devaluation of the Brazilian cruzeiro resulted in a foreign exchange loss for the current year of $123,400.

a) How much tax was legally owed for 1968?

b) Prepare in summary form the journal entry to record all aspects of income tax for 1968.

c) Was the tax rate on the extraordinary items the same as on ordinary income?

d) What are the advantages and disadvantages of splitting the income tax for the period between ordinary and extraordinary items?

e) Explain the disposition of the $204,101 referred to in the note, both in the current and in future periods.

12 9. Headman Corporation sells a line of equipment that carries a three year warranty. The company establishes an Estimated Liability for Warranty (with a corresponding debit to Product Warranty Expense) equal to 10 percent of dollar sales. The percentage is based on past experience and generally has proven quite accurate. The costs of servicing actual warranty claims each year are then charged to this liability account. Sales, expenses, and actual warranty expenditures are given below for the years 1971 to 1974 (in thousands):

	1971	1972	1973	1974
Sales.............................	$200	$220	$130	$190
Expenses other than warranty expense and income tax.................	120	130	90	110
Actual warranty expenditures........	12	15	22	20

For tax purposes, warranty expense is not deductible until costs are actually incurred to meet claims. The company's tax rate is 52 percent.

a) Set up a ledger (T) account for Estimated Liability for Warranty and post entries to it for the four-year period. Determine the balance in the account at the end of each year.

b) Prepare a schedule showing the amount of financial accounting income before taxes and income tax expense, and the amount of taxable income and taxes legally owed for each of the four years.

c) Set up a ledger (T) account for Deferred Income Taxes and post entries to it for the four years. Determine the balance in the account at the end of each year. Where would you show this balance on the position statement? Explain.

d) Explain any relationship that exists between the balance in the estimated liability account and the deferred taxes account.

12–10. Williamson and Son, Inc. purchased a piece of equipment for $160,000. For tax purposes, the equipment will be depreciated over a four-year life using the straight-line method. However, for the financial accounting statements, the useful life is eight years. In both cases, there is no salvage value. The income tax rate is 50%.

The company's CPA, M. I. Bright, and the corporate treasurer, I. M. Smart II, disagree over how to record the tax impact of the timing difference. They both agree that there is a deferral of income taxes from the first four years to the last four years. The CPA wishes to debit the tax effect of the difference in depreciation charges as additional income tax expense and to credit Deferred Income Taxes Payable for a similar amount for the first four years. In years 5–8, the reverse entry would be made·as the liability is paid off. He says that this treatment is in accordance with generally accepted accounting principles.

The treasurer agrees with the format of the entries but disagrees with the dollar amounts. He claims that the deferred tax liability should reflect only the present value of the amounts deferred. For example, since the tax deferred in year 1 does not have to be paid until year 5, the debit to additional income tax expense and credit to Deferred Income Taxes Payable would be the present value of the deferred tax amount due in four years discounted at 8 percent, the aftertax earning rate of the company. Each year would be handled similarly, except that in subsequent years interest on any previous deferrals would also be included as part of the income tax expense. He says that this treatment is more in keeping with the way liabilities payable in the future should be valued.

a) Prepare a schedule for each of the eight years under the CPA's suggested treatment. Show the amount charged (or credited) to Income Tax Expense each year and the balance in the Deferred Taxes Payable account at the end of each year.

b) Repeat part (a) following the treatment recommended by the treasurer. Show the basis for your computations.

c) Carefully evaluate these two procedures, particularly the one suggested by the treasurer.

12–11. Cummins Engine Company, Inc. in 1968 showed on its balance sheet two accounts relating to deferred taxes. One was listed among the current assets and was labeled Prepaid Expenses and Deferred Tax Effects. The other amount was listed on the equity side in a special

"Reserves" section below long-term debt. It was called Deferred Income Taxes. The following note accompanied the statement:

Note 2: Reclassifications and Deferred Income Taxes. In accordance with an accounting pronouncement which became effective in 1968, deferred income tax effects resulting from timing differences have been reclassified in the financial statements to conform to 1968 presentation. This had no effect on net earnings. Deferred income taxes are provided on the excess of accelerated tax depreciation over straight-line book depreciation and for the Federal income taxes on the net earnings of a foreign subsidiary which are payable upon repatriation. Cummins provides for estimated costs of product warranty, inspection and related costs, and for certain other costs in advance of the period in which these costs are deductible for Federal income tax purposes. The tax effects of these costs are recognized in the periods in which the costs are charged to earnings.

a) Which timing differences relate to which of these accounts? Explain.
b) Why does Cummins not offset them and just show a single net debit or credit balance? How can one be classified as current while the other is noncurrent?
c) Comment on the use of a "Reserve" category in which to classify Deferred Income Taxes. How would you classify it?

12–12. Tandy Corporation used the following format in its 1968 income statement to show income taxes and tax loss carry-forward effects.

Partial Income Statement for the Year Ended
June 30, 1968

Income before taxes...................	$8,672,645
Income taxes:	
Provision for income taxes..........	2,339,936
Charge equivalent to reduction in	
federal income tax arising from	
utilization of Radio Shack tax	
loss carry-forward...............	1,916,222
Income before extraordinary credit....	$4,416,487
Extraordinary credit arising from uti-	
lization of Radio Shack tax loss	
carry-forward.......................	1,916,222
	$6,332,709

The following note accompanied the statements:

Federal income tax has been provided on the basis of separate returns to be filed for each of the approximately 115 corporations.

Radio Shack Corporation was merged into Tandy Corporation at June 30, 1967 at which time Radio Shack had loss carry-overs for federal income tax purposes aggregating $4,000,000 which in the opinion of the Company's tax counsel may be applied against the taxable income of the parent company. All of the carry-overs were utilized in 1968.

a) What role might the tax loss carry-forward have played in the decision to merge Radio Shack, which was a separate company almost 100 percent owned by Tandy?

b) When Tandy recorded the assets received in the merger with Radio Shack, did it record the carry-forward as an asset? How do you know? Was the carry-forward an asset?

c) How much income tax did Tandy actually legally owe for fiscal 1968?

d) Comment on the format used to present the relevant information.

12–13. Revere Copper and Brass, Inc. and Pet, Inc. both prepare combined statements of income and retained earnings. Portions of their statements for 1968 (Revere) and 1970 (Pet) are presented below.

REVERE COPPER AND BRASS, INC.
Year Ended December 31, 1968

Net income for year	$ 16,791,151
Dividends	8,351,742
Earnings for year retained	$ 8,439,409
Earnings retained balance as previously reported	96,776,599
Settlement of anti-trust litigation, less related federal income tax of $1,591,452	(1,422,661)
Earnings retained balance at end of year	$103,793,347

PET, INC.
Year Ended March 31, 1970

Earnings before extraordinary item	$ 18,408,617
Extraordinary item—costs and expenses incurred in connection with the disposition of diet food products containing cyclamates; after reduction of $2,125,000 for income taxes	(1,775,000)
Net earnings	$ 16,633,617
Earnings invested, beginning of year	143,559,527
Dividends	(8,217,831)
Earnings invested, end of year	$151,975,313

a) What basic tax reporting concept is involved in both of these presentations? Explain carefully.

b) What was the gross amount of loss in each of the cases? Why are they reported net of tax?

c) Why is the tax-adjusted item for Pet included in the net earnings figure while the tax-adjusted item for Revere is subtracted after the net income figure is computed?

12–14. Robnud Corporation is engaged in the building of condominiums and apartment houses. Most projects take from one and three years to complete. Consequently, the management of the firm decides to recognize revenue on a percentage-of-completion basis for its external reporting. However, for income tax purposes it elects to use the completed-contract method. During the first three years, the company worked on four different contracts. Information related to them is given below:

	Contract No.			
	100	101	102	103
Contract price.............	$200,000	$800,000	$500,000	$600,000
Total cost................	150,000	600,000	400,000	450,000
Year completed............	Year 1	Year 2	Year 3	In progress
Percentage of completion:				
Year 1.................	100%	40%	25%	
Year 2.................		60%	50%	20%
Year 3.................			25%	40%

General administrative expenses were $30,000, $50,000, and $60,000 in years 1, 2, and 3, respectively. Assume a tax rate of 50 percent.

a) Determine net income before taxes for each of the three years for financial accounting purposes.

b) Determine taxable income for each of the three years.

c) Prepare journal entries to record income tax expense each year under interperiod tax allocation.

d) What is the balance in the Deferred Income Tax account at the end of year 3? Prove directly that this balance is the tax effect of timing differences yet to be reversed.

12–15. The bottom half of the income statement for the calendar year 1968 of Belding Heminway Company, Inc. is presented below

```
Income before Federal income taxes and extra-
    ordinary items.............................  $3,456,000
Provision for Federal income taxes............   1,746,000
Income before extraordinary items............   $1,710,000
Extraordinary items:
  Reduction of provision for Federal income
    taxes due to utilization of net operating
    loss and investment credit carryovers.....     298,000
  Gain on sale of security--net of related
    Federal income tax effect.................      74,000
Net Income....................................  $2,082,000
```

On the balance sheet, a current liability, Reserve for Federal Income Taxes, increased from $820,000 in 1967 to $1,407,000 in 1968, and a noncurrent liability, Deferred Federal Income Taxes, increased from $271,000 to $320,000.

a) What deficiencies do you see in the company's presentation of the gain on sale of security?

b) Assuming that the gain on sale of security was taxed at a rate of

25 percent, what was the total amount of tax legally owed for 1968?

c) How much in actual cash payments was made in 1968 for income taxes?

d) Belding Heminway did not offset the tax loss carry-forward directly against the provision for income taxes. Why not? Was the net operating loss carry-forward set up as an asset? Should it have been?

12–16. The following information concerns the computation of net income and retained earnings for the year 1971 for a midwestern corporation:

	Dr.	Cr.
Sales..		$527,000
Interest on Missouri State bonds..................		18,000
Gain on sale of investments.......................		17,000
Correction of 1970 inventory error................		28,000
Cost of goods sold.............................	$314,000	
Selling expenses...............................	67,000	
Administrative expenses.........................	46,000	
Amortization of goodwill.........................	10,000	
Loss on settlement of 1968 lawsuit................	40,000	
Uninsured tornado damage.......................	5,000	
Income taxes..................................	44,090	
Dividends.....................................	30,000	
Increase in retained earnings.....................	33,910	
	$590,000	$590,000

Gain on sale of investments is taxed at a 25 percent rate. The interest on Missouri State bonds and the amortization of goodwill are permanent differences between tax accounting and financial accounting; they do not affect the computation of income taxes. All other income is taxed at the normal tax rate of 48 percent. Retained earnings at the beginning of the year are $73,980.

a) Verify the computation of the total income tax figure of $44,090.

b) Prepare in good form a combined statement of net income and retained earnings for 1971. Follow the reporting guidelines of *APB Opinion No. 9* concerning extraordinary items and prior years' adjustments, and follow income tax allocation where appropriate.

12–17. Gibson Corporation, in 1971, earned a net operating income before taxes of $800,000. The company is subject to a tax rate of 40 percent. On January 1, 1971 the company had refunded a bond issue prior to its maturity. The call premium, unamortized bond discount, and unamortized bond issue costs relating to the refunded issue totaled $500,000, which amount was deducted in determining taxable income for the year.

The chief accountant decided to write off these costs over a five-year period (the remaining life of the old bond issue) for financial statement purposes. The write-off is to be reported as an extraordinary item each year. The refunding costs (less amortization) will be shown on the balance sheet as a deferred charge.

a) Prepare a partial income statement for 1971 (beginning with net operating income) following the chief accountant's recommendation, but making any necessary *interperiod* and *intrastatement* allocations of income tax.

b) Prepare the journal entry, in summary form, necessary to record income taxes for the year. Indicate any balance sheet accounts that are directly related to this proposed accounting treatment. Indicate the title of the account, its dollar amount, and its location on the balance sheet.

c) If the results for 1972 are identical to those for 1971 except for the bond refunding, repeat parts (*a*) and (*b*) for 1972.

CHAPTER THIRTEEN

STOCKHOLDERS' EQUITY

THE ACCOUNTING emphasis in the recording of equities has been to separate them by source. This is a primary reason for our distinguishing between liabilities (claims of outside interests) and owners' equity (the source of assets from the owners). Because stockholders' equity is a major subdivision of the financial interests in a corporation, accountants segregate it even further. They report capital stock separately from retained earnings, because they are interested in knowing the amount of assets contributed directly by the owners as opposed to the amount arising from the retention of earned assets in the business. This classification by source aids in the interpretation of the historical development and current position of the firm. It also clarifies the status of any asset distributions in the form of dividends—that is, whether they are based on earnings or are simply a return of a portion of the originally invested capital. In fact, from a strict accounting viewpoint the main requirement for recording stockholders' equity is that each major source should be identified in a separate account. In our discussion so far, this simply involves a fundamental distinction between contributed or invested capital and retained income.

However, accounting does not operate in an environment free from other influences. A corporation is a separate *legal* entity endowed with certain powers through its state charter. One of these advantages is that of limited liability—the owners cannot be held personally responsible for the debts of the corporation. The creditors' claims are on the assets of the corporation and do not carry over to the assets of the individual stockholders. To offer some degree of protection to corporate creditors, most state incorporation laws require that there be a certain minimum amount of capital per share invested by the owners. This *stated* or *legal* capital cannot be reduced by voluntary action of the board of directors and serves as a buffer to protect the claims of the creditors.[1] The purpose of stated or legal capital is to prevent excessive distributions of corporate assets to stockholders.

At first glance, one might think that stated or legal capital would automatically correspond to total contributed capital, the relatively permanent investment made by the owners in exchange for shares of stock. This is not the case. Stated capital is a special legal concept, defined in varying ways in each of the different states. These legal concepts and definitions of stated capital have exerted a large influence on the recording procedures for stockholders' equity and have modified the basic accounting distinction between contributed capital and retained income.

In addition to legal considerations, the accounting for stockholders' equity reflects many financial intricacies, conventions, and policies. The use of different types of capital stock, varying security provisions and modifications, stock splits, and dividend declarations are more a matter of financial management than of accounting policy. Yet in the accounting records these matters find their final expression.

ENTRIES FOR THE ISSUANCE OF STOCK

The legal expression of the owners' investment in a corporation is the share of stock. To the individual stockholder it represents a personal asset. To the corporation, however, the shares are simply a tangible representation of an ownership interest. Its state charter authorizes a corporation to issue a certain number of shares. Authorized stock, however, has no accounting significance. Only when assets actually flow into the firm as the result of a stock issue is a record made of the increase in stockholders' equity.

Preferred Stock

Heretofore we have assumed that only one kind of ownership interest is present, that represented by capital stock. One of the minor complexities we shall be talking about arises out of the fact that there are actually two different types of capital stock, common and preferred. The former corresponds to what we have been calling capital stock. It represents the residual ownership and control of the corporation. Preferred stock

---

[1] Of course, misuse of assets in the operation of the business could completely deplete all the owners' equity. Stated capital protects the creditor against voluntary withdrawals of capital by the owners, not against dissipation of assets through poor management.

represents a special type of ownership interest with certain modifications of the basic rights inherent in common stock.[2]

The term "preferred" originates from two customary provisions of this type of stock. Preferred stock usually has preference over common stock in the payment of dividends and has a prior claim on assets (after liabilities have been paid) in the event of liquidation. The latter provision need not concern us here, since we are recording under the concept of continuity. The dividend preference modifies the risk of the preferred stock. If (and only if) dividends are declared, they must first be paid to the preferred stockholders up to the amount stated in the preferred stock contract. Usually the return is fixed, however. Once the preferred dividends are paid, any remaining dividends declared are applicable only to the common stock. Also, in most cases preferred dividends are cumulative; that is, before dividends can be paid on common stock, *all* preferred dividends, including any skipped in past years, must be paid.

Preferred stock is a hybrid security. Economically and financially, it is very similar to long-term debt. Preferred stock has less risk than common, as reflected in the prior but limited claim on earnings. It is often callable, like a bond issue. On the other hand, legally it resembles common stock. Its claim on earnings is not mandatory, as is the case with interest. Only if dividends are declared does preferred stock have a prior claim. There is no accrued liability for the payment of preferred dividends nor specific maturity date on a preferred stock issue. Logically, as a hybrid equity element, it probably should be reported in a separate category between liabilities and common stock equity. Nevertheless, on actual financial statements, preferred is practically always included in an overall category labeled "stockholders' equity."

Par Value and No-Par Value Stock

In most cases it is common practice to assign an arbitrary amount to each share of stock. This amount, called "par value," is printed on each stock certificate. Historically, the amount was usually $100. Except perhaps as a convenient way of determining how many shares to assign to various investors when the stock is first issued, par value has little accounting significance. Obviously, an arbitrary amount printed on a piece of paper does not determine what the stock will be issued for at a later date or what the value of the stock is. The latter is governed by investors' appraisal of the future earning potential of the business.

The reason for the heavy use of par value stock lies in its historical

---

[2] The reader is referred to books on business finance for detailed descriptions of various provisions pertaining to preferred stock. Our discussion is limited to some of the basic and more usual differences between preferred and common stock, particularly those which have accounting implications.

significance. Par value defined the *minimum* amount of stated capital per share a firm had to have. Creditors could presume that at least an amount equivalent to the par value of the shares outstanding was permanently invested by the stockholders. Indeed, in many states anyone buying stock directly from the corporation at less than par value could be held assessable for the difference at some later time, if the amount was necessary to pay creditors' claims.[3] Currently many corporations use low par value stock ($1, $5, $10). Low par stock practically always sells above par, so that the assessability problem is eliminated. Unfortunately, out of this assigning of par values to shares there sometimes arises the mistaken notion that par value represents the real value of the stock.

Beginning in 1912 no-par value stock was introduced in many states. A share of no-par stock simply represented a certain proportionate share of ownership in the business. Its value was a function of how individual investors analyzed the corporation. No-par stock has the advantage of avoiding the implication that par value represents the real worth of the stock. Also legal capital and invested capital become one and the same. However, many states allowing no-par stock have passed laws giving the board of directors the power (within limits) to assign a stated value to the no-par shares. These laws are designed ostensibly to protect the creditors by insisting that there be a minimum stated capital. But legal capital again becomes something distinct from invested capital; and stated value, while having the same slight significance as par value, may still convey the impression of representing the fair value of the stock.

Entries to Record Stock Issues

From an accounting and financial standpoint, the important consideration is the increase in resources arising from the issuance of capital stock. The real increase in stockholders' equity, the amount of contributed capital, is determined by the amount of assets actually invested, not by the par or stated value arbitrarily assigned to the shares. Generally, the issuance of no-par shares involves little difficulty. Cash is debited and Capital Stock is credited for the total amount received, segregated, of course, by common or preferred. Nevertheless, as a reflection of legal tradition and the concept of stated capital, par values and stated values are practically always recognized in the accounts whenever they are present.

Par or Stated Value Shares. Assume that 1,000 shares of common stock, each having a par value of $100, are issued for $150 a share. In-

---

[3] To avoid issuing stock at less than par value, companies sometimes overvalued noncurrent assets received in exchange for shares of stock by recording the assets at the par value of the stock exchanged for them. Stock issued under these circumstances, when discovered (often with somewhat disastrous consequences to creditors), was called "watered" stock, inasmuch as no real asset value ever lay behind it.

vestors contribute $150,000 in cash to the corporation, because this is the value they attach to the ownership interest represented by 1,000 shares. Assets and owners' equity increase by $150,000. The increase in stock-holders' equity is conventionally reflected in two accounts:

```
Cash....................................  150,000
     Common Stock—$100 Par..............              100,000
     Common Stock—Excess over Par.......               50,000
```

The Common Stock—Excess over Par account is an equity adjunct account. It represents a part of the total invested capital of the firm. Under no circumstances should it be considered a gain on sale of stock. A cor-poration does not profit by issuing its own shares of stock in a capital-raising transaction. Common Stock—Excess over Par simply reflects a part of the total capital invested which has been segregated for legal reasons. Other titles are frequently used in accounting practice for this account—Premium (particularly when preferred stock is sold above par), Paid-In Capital, Capital Surplus, or Paid-In Surplus. The latter two con-stitute poor terminology; the connotation of the word "surplus" as in-dicating something of an unnecessary, residual, or supplementary nature is obviously inappropriate in this case.

Issuing stock at a price below par value has been very rare in recent years. It is illegal in many states because of the impairment of stated capital (defined as par value). Even if legal, issuing stock below par may result in the undesirable state of shares being subject to assessment. If it does occur, a contra equity, Discount on Stock, is debited and deducted from the overstated par account.[4]

Stock-Issue Costs. When either common or preferred stock is issued, certain costs for legal fees, printing, registration, etc., have to be incurred. Like bond issue costs, they should be recorded as an intangible asset to be amortized over 40 years or less.[5] They represent an expenditure necessary to raise capital in a corporation, the benefit of which is received in future periods.

DETERMINING THE AMOUNT OF CAPITAL RECEIVED

Often practical problems occur in the determination of the dollar amount to be entered in the asset and equity accounts. Usually the in-crease in stockholders' equity is measured by the amount of assets received in exchange for the shares. If the asset received is cash, no problem re-

---

[4] Preferred stocks may behave somewhat like bonds. Preferred stock prices vary inversely to changes in the dividend rate demanded by the investing public. If the stated dividend rate (based on par value) on the preferred stock is only 7 percent and the market dividend rate is 8 percent, the stock would have to be issued at a discount.

[5] *Intangible Assets, Opinion of the Accounting Principles Board No. 17* (New York: AICPA, August 1970), p. 341.

sults. Whether one or more capital accounts are used to record owners' equity, the total net increase is the amount of cash received. If noncash assets are invested in exchange for shares of stock, the increase in stockholders' equity is measured by the fair market value of the asset received. For example, if a stockholder invests land having a fair market value of $25,000 in exchange for 2,000 shares of $10 par value common stock, the entry should be:

```
Land.......................................  25,000
     Common Stock—$10 Par.................           20,000
     Common Stock—Excess over Par.........            5,000
```

In many cases the accountant may encounter difficulty in establishing the fair market value of certain noncash assets. If so, he may look to the market value of the stock issued for evidence concerning the monetary measurement of the transaction. Heavy reliance is often placed on the market value of the stock when a firm issues its stock in exchange for the entire net assets of another business. The assets, including any intangible assets being acquired, should be recorded at their fair market value. Practically speaking, the fair market value may be measured by a valuation of the shares of stock given up in exchange. Further discussion of the recording complexities of mergers is contained in Chapter Fourteen.

Of course, using the market value of outstanding stock is not without its pitfalls. The market price on an organized stock exchange on any particular date may be distorted by temporary influences; thus, it may not reflect "true" market value. Nor can one extend a price per share paid for a few shares to determine accurately the fair market value of a large block of stock. Nevertheless, the practical measurement problem boils down to a question of relative accuracy and objectivity. Ideally, we should like to determine the value of the asset received and let that govern the credit to stockholders' equity. Sometimes, however, we may find more reliable and objective measurement by determining the fair market value of the equity shares and using that in making the debit to the asset. The question is not one of right or wrong but one of where the best evidence can be found. This answer varies, depending on the situation and the professional judgment of the accountant.

Stock Options

The measurement of invested capital is also difficult in the case of stock options. Assume that the president of a corporation is hired at a salary of $80,000 a year. In addition, he is granted the privilege (option) of acquiring 3,000 shares of common stock (par $10) at a price of $20 per share. He must wait a year, however, before he can exercise the option (actually buy the shares). The market price of the stock on the date the option is granted is $25 per share and stands at $27 per share at the end of the year, when he exercises the option.

Two factors seem clear. The value of the option is part of the president's compensation; at the same time, the executive is investing services in the corporation. The option agreement is a compensation plan whereby part of the total value of the president's services is paid in cash and the balance is invested in exchange for a right to receive stock. It also is an investment agreement whereby the president invests his services during the option period and cash at the end of the period. To obtain a correct picture of both the total compensation and the total investment, we need to place a dollar value on the option and the services represented thereby.

One approach would be to attempt to value the total services of the president directly and assign any difference between the total cash value of the service and the salary paid to the value of the option. Often, such an approach is difficult. An alternative is to value the option privilege and assign that amount as an addition to the value of services received (expense). For instance, the president receives the right to buy 3,000 shares at a price $5 below fair market value. If the difference between the option price and the fair market value for these shares is deemed to be the best evidence of the amount of services being invested, the following entry would be appropriate:

```
Salary Expense............................ 80,000
Compensation Expense—Stock Option........ 15,000
     Cash.................................          80,000
     Capital Received—Unexercised Options..          15,000
```

The credit of $15,000 is made to a special stockholders' equity account. Then when the option is exercised, the following entry is made:

```
Cash..................................... 60,000
Capital Received—Unexercised Options..... 15,000
     Common Stock—$10 Par.................          30,000
     Common Stock—Excess over Par.........          45,000
```

Accountants disagree over the best way to value the option. The approach illustrated is the one preferred by the AICPA.[6] However, in actual business practice often no material spread exists between the option price and current market price at the date of grant. To provide certain tax benefits for the recipient, the option price is set at or above the existing market price. Under these circumstances this approach would attach no value to the option for accounting purposes. The value of services is assumed to be only $80,000, and the capital invested is recorded only at

---

[6] Some accountants advocate using the spread between market value and option price on the date the option becomes exercisable ($27 − $20) instead. This approach, however, may postpone recognition of expense until after the periods for which the options were granted. It also implies that compensation expense (the value of services) under an agreement negotiated on one date is actually influenced by an unknown stock market price on some future date.

$60,000. Certainly, however, the option agreement does possess some value. The right to be able to acquire shares of stock at a fixed price sometime in the future in most instances has a current worth. Consequently, the value of the option and, hence, expenses and invested capital are probably understated.

Stock Purchase Warrants and Package Issues

Corporations sometimes issue securities in packages to investors for a single price. Investors buying bonds or preferred stock may also receive some shares of common stock (a package issue) or the right to acquire common stock at a later date (a stock purchase warrant). The general procedure for recording both types of issues is the same. There are really two separate sources of capital—the senior security (bond or preferred stock) and the common stock or right to acquire common stock (stock purchase warrant). Since these two elements exist independently, they should be accounted for as separate securities. The total proceeds should be allocated between the two elements for accounting purposes, usually in the ratio of their market values.

Stock Purchase Warrants. Take, for instance, the following situation. A firm wishes to issue 7 percent bonds for a par amount of $100,000. In order to attract investors the firm offers the purchaser of each $1,000 bond a warrant entitling him to acquire one share of common stock (par value $40) within the next six months at a price of $50. If the current price of the stock is above $50, the stock warrant obviously has a value at least equal to the difference between the market price and the $50 warrant price. But even if the current market price is at or slightly below $50, the warrant has value because of the possibility that the stock could rise above $50 within the next six months.

In most instances the warrants are detachable. After issuance the warrant can be bought and sold among investors separately from the bond itself. Consequently, an independent market valuation is placed on the worth of the warrant. The price paid for the warrant represents a down payment on the purchase of stock and should be accounted for as contributed or paid-in capital. If after issuance the bonds sell at 98.5 percent and the warrants at $15 each, the following entry would be appropriate:

```
Cash.....................................  100,000
Bonds Payable—Discount.................    1,500
    Bonds Payable..........................              100,000
    Common Stock Warrants Outstanding...                  1,500
```

In this case the independent values of the bond and the warrant exactly equal the total amount received by the company. It is quite possible that the total market value could be slightly different, in which case the proportional fair market values would be the basis for the allocation.

Upon exercise of the warrants, the entry would be:

```
Cash......................................  50,000
Common Stock Warrants Outstanding.........   1,500
      Common Stock—$40 Par.................            40,000
      Paid-In Capital......................            11,500
```

Should the warrants lapse without being exercised, a reclassification within stockholders' equity should be made:

```
Common Stock Warrants Outstanding............  1,500
      Paid-In Capital..........................           1,500
```

Package Issuance. Assume that a firm offers a package deal to investors. The package consists of one share of $100 par value preferred stock and two shares of $20 par value common stock. The price of the package is $150, and 1,000 such packages are sold. Again, an attempt should be made to divide the $150,000 between the amounts applicable to the preferred stock and to the common stock. This split can be made on the basis of relative market values. For example, if immediately after issue the common stock sells in the stock market at $35 per share and the preferred at $95 per share, 70/165 ($63,636) would be allocated to the common and 95/165 ($86,364) to the preferred. The entry would be:

```
Cash.....................................  150,000
Discount on Preferred Stock..............   13,636
      Preferred Stock—$100 Par Value.....            100,000
      Common Stock—$20 Par Value.........             40,000
      Common Stock—Excess over Par.......             23,636
```

When a determinable market price exists for only one of the securities, say the common stock, an incremental approach can be used. An amount equal to the measurable fair market value of the common stock is allocated to it and the remainder of the issuance price assigned to the preferred.

MODIFICATIONS IN CAPITAL ACCOUNTS

In addition to an understanding of the basic entries when stock is issued, an informed reader of financial statements should be familiar with the concepts and terminology associated with later modifications in some of the capital accounts. Two fairly common changes—stock split and stock conversion—are discussed in this section.

Stock Split

A stock split simply increases the number of shares outstanding. The corporation distributes additional shares of stock to the shareholders for which the latter invest nothing. Capital received in total does not change, nor do total assets. The entire stockholders' equity remains constant in dollar amount. However, now it is indicated by a larger number of shares, each share representing a proportionately smaller interest.

The stock split is a financial mechanism used to increase the investor appeal of the stock by reducing its market price and to broaden ownership by having more shares outstanding. If the company has 200,000 shares of stock outstanding, a two-for-one stock split involves distributing an additional 200,000 shares. Each shareholder holds two shares for each share previously owned. If the market price of the stock is $100 per share before the split, theoretically it should fall to $50 per share after the split.[7] However, since no change in resources or financial interests occurs, no accounting entry is needed. But if the capital stock has a par value, the stock split requires a reduction in par value, inasmuch as total stated value does not change.

Conversion of Stock

Often preferred stock, like some bond issues, contains a provision allowing the owners of the stock to exchange (convert) the preferred stock for common stock. If conversion takes place, the transaction simply involves swapping one kind of equity for another. Common stock equity increases by the amount that preferred stock equity decreases. Total corporate assets remain the same.

On February 1 a corporation issues 1,000 shares of convertible preferred stock at $60 a share. The stock has a par value of $50 and can be converted at any time into five shares of $5 par value common stock. By October 15 the common stock has increased in market value to $15 a share, and holders of 500 shares of preferred elect to convert them to common stock. The entries on February 1 and October 15 are:

```
Feb.  1  Cash............................... 60,000
            Preferred Stock—$50 Par.......          50,000
            Preferred Stock—Premium.......          10,000
Oct. 15  Preferred Stock—$50 Par........... 25,000
         Preferred Stock—Premium...........  5,000
            Common Stock—$5 Par...........           12,500
            Common Stock—Excess over Par..           17,500
```

Obviously, the preferred stockholders have elected to convert because the market value of the common stock has risen. However, as far as the corporate entity is concerned, no increase in equities or assets has occurred. Half of the preferred stock is canceled, and common stock equity takes its place. Total sources of capital remain constant.

---

[7] Often the market does not fall exactly this amount. If the dividend amount per share is maintained on the new shares, the stock split is a disguised way of increasing dividend payout. Or, because the price is lower, more people may be willing to buy the stock, which causes the market price to rise after the split. Neither of these increases in value can be traced directly to the split; they are the result of other factors —increased dividends or greater demand for the stock.

DECREASING STOCKHOLDERS' EQUITY:
REACQUISITION OF SHARES

When a corporation reacquires its own shares of stock, essentially the reverse of a stock-issuing transaction occurs. Corporate assets are decreased, with a corresponding reduction in stockholders' equity. How the reduction is recorded is the subject of this section. Of course, a corporation is under no obligation to buy back the shares of any particular stockholders. Sometimes, however, a firm does so because it needs shares for stock option or employee purchase plans or because it wishes to retire the ownership interest of a specific stockholder—or simply to bolster the market price of its stock.

The reacquired stock is called treasury stock. Formally defined, treasury stock is the company's own stock which has been previously issued and then reacquired but not legally retired. Economically and financially, it is similar to unissued stock. Legally, however, treasury stock is interpreted differently from unissued stock.[8] But these slight legal differences should not be allowed to overshadow the fundamental effect on assets and equities. When shares are issued, assets and stockholders' equity increase. Conversely, when shares are reacquired, assets and stockholders' equity decrease. The acquisition of treasury shares represents a contraction of capital—perhaps a partial and temporary one, but a liquidation of capital nevertheless. Similarly, when shares are issued, be they treasury shares or unissued shares, contributed capital increases.

Treasury Stock—Par Value Method

Perhaps the truth of the foregoing statements may become more evident if we first take a direct approach to recording the reacquisition of stock. Assume that on any given date the stockholders' equity appears as follows:

```
Common stock—$1 par (20,000 shares)..... $20,000
Common stock—excess over par............   5,000
Retained earnings.......................   15,000
                                         $40,000
```

A particular stockholder owns 5,000 shares of stock of the corporation. Since all common stock has the same proportionate interest regardless of what the stockholder's original investment was, he now has a one-quarter

---

[8] For example, treasury stock can be issued at any price above or below par if it was "fully paid" when issued originally. Also, it is not subject to preemptive rights. Many state incorporation laws specify that existing common stockholders have the right to acquire any new shares of stock issued by the corporation in proportion to their existing holdings. By issuing treasury stock, a corporation can avoid the preemptive rights and issue the shares to anyone. For this reason treasury shares frequently are employed in mergers and in stock option plans.

interest in each of the above accounts. The book value of his investment is $10,000 ($40,000 × 25%).

If the corporation were to buy back those shares at book value, the entry would be:

```
Treasury Stock—$1 Par.....................  5,000
Common Stock—Excess over Par..............  1,250
Retained Earnings.........................  3,750
   Cash...................................             10,000
```

Cash decreases by $10,000 and total stockholders' equity drops by a like amount, each account being reduced proportionately. To show that the shares are not permanently retired, the debit of $5,000 is made to a contra account, Treasury Stock—$1 Par, instead of directly to Common Stock. The Treasury Stock account appears as a deduction from Common Stock on the balance sheet.

If the stockholder receives more or less than book value, the adjustment normally takes place in retained earnings. The retiring stockholder is assumed to have withdrawn either more or less than his proportionate interest in retained assets. For example, assume that a fair market valuation of the 5,000 shares of stock is $12,000. Both cash and total stockholders' equity would decrease by $12,000, recorded as follows:

```
Treasury Stock—$1 Par.....................  5,000
Common Stock—Excess over Par..............  1,250
Retained Earnings.........................  5,750
   Cash...................................             12,000
```

As treasury stock the shares can be reissued at some later date. As a potential source of capital, they differ little from unissued stock. If they are reissued later for $13,000, the entry would be the same as with unissued stock. Assets and contributed capital both increase by $13,000:

```
Cash......................................  13,000
   Treasury Stock—$1 Par..................              5,000
   Common Stock—Excess over Par..........              8,000
```

This approach to the recording of treasury stock is called the par value method. In essence, it takes the position that treasury stock transactions should be no different in effect from a retirement and later issuance of new shares.

Treasury Stock—Cost Method

The foregoing method, although perhaps theoretically preferable, is not widely used in current practice. Particularly for shares that remain in the treasury only a short time before they are reissued, a simpler but potentially confusing alternative called the cost method is used. Instead of separate debits to each stockholders' equity account, a single debit is made to a general contra equity account called Treasury Stock. Under this procedure the entry to reacquire the shares of stock at a price of $12,000 would be:

```
Treasury Stock..........................  12,000
     Cash...................................           12.000
```

This method views the acquisition and subsequent reissuance of the treasury shares as a continuous transaction. The corporation serves as a temporary intermediary between the retiring stockholder and the new stockholder. The entry above is only a temporary contraction in total capital which will shortly be reinstated. Consequently, no need exists to reduce each of the stockholders' equity accounts directly. Treasury Stock is debited in lieu of each account individually. It represents an indirect way of decreasing stockholders' equity through the use of a contra account.

Unfortunately, treasury stock sometimes finds its way to the asset side of the position statement, on the ground that the shares can be resold. Such an interpretation is erroneous. Treasury shares are no more an asset than are all the unissued shares. At best, they represent possible sources of additional capital funds. But until they are issued the corporation has received no asset. A firm cannot create an asset by *returning* cash to the stockholders. Logically, treasury stock should be shown as a deduction from total common stock equity on the position statement, as an unapportioned contraction of total capital.

Reissuance of Treasury Stock. If treasury stock is not an asset, there can be no gain or loss on its reissuance. Issuing shares of stock, whether from unissued or from treasury stock, is a capital-raising transaction. On the other hand, since the acquisition of the stock is handled indirectly, the reissuance is recorded differently. Nevertheless, the substance is the same. If the treasury shares are reissued for $13,000, the entry is:

```
Cash......................................  13,000
     Treasury Stock........................           12,000
     Common Stock—Excess over Par.........            1,000
```

Cash increases by $13,000; contributed capital increases $13,000—part of it recorded as a cancellation of a contra equity and part of it as an addition to the Excess over Par or Paid-In Capital account. If the treasury stock is reissued at a price below its acquisition price, the difference could be debited to the Excess over Par account, if there is one, or to Retained Earnings.[9] The latter entry is justified on the grounds that the net result of the continuous transaction (reacquisition and reissuance) has

---

[9] If a corporation has numerous transactions involving treasury stock, some accountants recommend establishing a special source of stockholders' equity, Capital Adjustment—Treasury Stock Transactions. This account is then debited or credited with the difference between the reissuance price and acquisition cost. In most situations, however, such a procedure appears to add little to the clarity or usefulness of the position statement.

been that a part of the entity assets have been distributed as a special kind of dividend.

The acquisition of treasury stock not only reduces contributed capital but also stated or legal capital. Consequently, state laws governing corporations usually place fairly stringent, detailed limitations on when, how, and in what amount a company can repurchase its own shares. Often retained earnings must be restricted (made unavailable for dividends) in an amount equal to the cost of the treasury stock purchased. This is discussed later in the chapter.

Retiring Preferred Stock

Normally when preferred stock shares are acquired by the firm they are retired rather than held in the treasury for possible reissue. Like bonds, preferred stock issues usually are subject to call, or they can be repurchased on the stock market. Assume that we have $80,000 of par value preferred stock outstanding, which was originally issued at a discount of $5,000. By contract, the preferred stock issue can be called in for retirement at a price equal to 105 percent of par value. The following entry would be necessary to record the retirement:

```
Preferred Stock—Par.....................  80,000
Retained Earnings........................   9,000
    Preferred Stock—Discount.............            5,000
    Cash (105% × $80,000)................           84,000
```

The excess of the redemption price ($84,000) over contributed capital ($75,000) is debited to Retained Earnings to reflect the decrease in total common stock equity—a special type of dividend to the preferred stockholders. In practice, a debit to Paid-In Capital is frequently made instead. Likewise, if preferred stock were retired for less than book value, the difference would be credited to Paid-In Capital.

DECREASING STOCKHOLDERS' EQUITY: DIVIDENDS

Dividends represent a pro rata distribution of assets to the stockholders. Assets decrease and owners' equity decreases. Dividend declaration and payment, however, are primarily legal and financial matters. Legal requirements place limitations on which stockholders' equity accounts can be decreased so that dividends cannot impair the stated or legal capital of the firm. As a general rule, dividends are assumed to be distributed out of earnings. Consequently, a credit balance in Retained Earnings is normally a requisite to dividend declaration.[10] However, retained earnings is not

[10] This is only a very rough guide. Many states allow dividends to be declared legally out of capital surplus, paid-in surplus, excess over par, etc. Since these still represent part of the contributed capital, sound accounting would require that any decrease in these accounts caused by dividends be disclosed as a return of contributed capital. Therefore, our general rule that normal dividends should only reduce retained earnings is valid.

cash. The financial requirement for dividends is that there be some distributable asset, usually cash. A firm may have a large balance in the Retained Earnings account but very little cash in the bank. Assets retained in the business from profitable operations rarely remain as cash but are usually reinvested in various productive resources.

Dividend Declaration and Payment

A firm planning to pay dividends would normally follow the procedure outlined below, providing that it has sufficient retained earnings and cash to fulfill the legal and financial requirements. The board of directors makes a formal announcement, declaring the dividend. Since dividends do not accrue, no liability exists until formal declaration. On the *date of declaration* a liability is created. If a dividend of $0.50 a share is declared on common stock and 30,000 shares of common are outstanding, the entry is:

```
Common Dividends......................... 15,000
     Common Dividends Payable.............          15,000
```

All stockholders owning stock on a specified date are entitled to receive the dividend. This date is called the *date of record* and is stated in the announcement of the dividend. No accounting entry is made on the date of record. The next entry comes on the *date of payment*. At that time the dividend checks are sent out, and the following entry is made:

```
Common Dividends Payable................. 15,000
     Cash.................................          15,000
```

The same general procedure is followed with preferred stock. The dividend rate on preferred stock is usually set in the preferred stock contract. It is expressed as a fixed dollar amount per share if the stock is no-par or as a fixed percentage of par for a par value preferred stock. As pointed out earlier, there is no liability to pay preferred dividends until they are declared. The dividend preference simply states that the preferred dividends have to be paid first, before common dividends.

This fact raises a major question concerning preferred dividends in arrears. If the preferred stock is cumulative and dividends in the past have been skipped, these must be paid first, before common dividends can be declared and paid. Yet, until they are declared, even preferred dividends in arrears are not a liability. At the same time, if they exist, a very important piece of financial information to the common stockholders is not reflected in any way on the financial statements. Arrearages represent a dark shadow hanging over any future earnings. A footnote to the financial statements or some other disclosure should be included to explain this contingency.

Stock Dividends

Not infrequently, corporations declare "dividends" payable in their own shares of stock. Additional shares are issued pro rata to the stockholders without their giving or the business entity receiving anything in return. No distribution of assets is ever involved. The term "dividend," for this situation, is actually a misnomer. Stock dividends are not really dividends at all, but a type of small stock split. No change in total assets or total equities results. The shares of stock received via a stock dividend add nothing that the stockholder does not already have. The recipient ends up with more shares, each one representing a proportionately smaller interest. For example, an individual owning 1,000 shares of a corporation with total outstanding stock of 20,000 shares has a 5 percent ownership interest. If the company declares a 10 percent stock dividend, he receives an additional 100 shares. However, the total number of shares outstanding is now 22,000; his interest is still 5 percent (1,100/22,000). He has received no real income by having the extra shares.[11] Indeed, if he sells the dividend shares, he is simply liquidating a portion of his investment.

Capitalization of Retained Earnings. The factor which differentiates a stock dividend from a stock split in the accounting process is that the former is accompanied by a transfer from retained earnings to the contributed capital accounts. This phenomenon is called capitalizing retained earnings. An entry is made when the shares are issued.

```
Retained Earnings.................................. xxx
    Common Stock (and Paid-In Capital if the
        amount is greater than par value)........        xxx
```

The total financial interest of the common stockholder remains exactly the same; all that results is a transfer from one stockholders' equity account to another. The capitalization permanently removes a portion of retained earnings from being available for dividend declaration. The related assets retained in the business probably have been reinvested in the form of buildings, equipment, and other long-term assets. To reflect this relatively permanent commitment, a portion of the retained earnings is reclassified, and the stockholders are given additional shares as separate evidence of their increased investment. However, it should be clear that the stock dividend gives rise neither to a change in corporate assets nor to a stockholders' proportionate interest in them.

One additional question must be answered before the above entry can be made. How much retained earnings should be capitalized? Possible

---

[11] Like stock splits, stock dividends may actually cause stock prices on the exchange to increase temporarily (logically, they should decline), either because of disguised dividend changes or a somewhat irrational reaction on the part of the investing public. This, unfortunately, simply adds to the illusion that they are something real.

alternatives include multiplying the number of shares distributed by the par or stated value, the average contributed capital per share, the average book value per share, or the current market value. State statutes require as a minimum the capitalization of the par or stated value of the additional shares issued to maintain legal capital, and may specify more. Beyond that, there is no clear answer in logic; it is really a matter of corporate financial policy, not of accounting theory.

The AICPA has recommended the use of market value to determine the amount to be capitalized for stock dividends when new shares being issued amount to less than 20 to 25 percent of the outstanding shares. For larger stock dividends, only the legal requirement needs to be capitalized. The reasoning is that large stock dividends clearly will be interpreted for what they are—stock splits. But with small stock dividends, stockholders view the dividend shares as income equivalent to their fair market value. Therefore, this should be the amount transferred out of retained earnings.[12] Another argument for the use of market value is that the end result agrees with what the situation would have been had the corporation paid cash dividends and the stockholders turned around and reinvested the cash in the newly issued shares.

RESTRICTIONS OF RETAINED EARNINGS AND RESERVES

Generally the balance in the Retained Earnings account represents the amount that is legally available for dividend declaration, if the firm has the cash. Sometimes, however, management may wish to restrict a portion of retained earnings to inform the reader of the statement that this portion is not available for dividends. Permanent removal can be accomplished by a capitalization of retained earnings via a stock dividend. Temporary segregation can be accomplished through the establishment of special retained earnings accounts. These should then be shown in stockholders' equity as separate subdivisions of retained earnings. Unfortunately, these accounts are often called retained earnings reserves (or,

---

[12] It is somewhat ironic that in the AICPA bulletin this particular justification follows a very strong, learned, and sound argument that a stock dividend is not income. The result is an inconsistency—an admonishment that stock dividends do not constitute income to the recipient, followed by a recommendation that they be treated in the accounting records in a particular way because stockholders may think they are income. See American Institute of Certified Public Accountants, *Restatement and Revisions of Accounting Research Bulletins, Accounting Research Bulletin No. 43* (New York, 1953), chapter vii (b), for a complete discussion of the reasoning of the Committee on Accounting Procedure relating to both stock dividends and stock splits. Some authors have suggested that the requirement for capitalization of market value rather than par value was instituted more as a penalty provision than as an accounting principle. It was designed to discourage companies with low earnings from declaring numerous stock dividends, which might mislead investors.

worse yet, surplus reserves). Such terminology is poor, because it implies that assets have actually been set aside. Such is not the case. A better general title would be Earnings Restricted.

Legal Restrictions on Retained Earnings

A certain amount of retained earnings may be unavailable for dividend declaration because of legal restrictions. Many bond issues, for example, require that dividends in future years be declared only out of future years' earnings. In essence, all or practically all of the retained earnings at the time the bonds are issued become frozen. If management wishes to call attention to this restriction by formally recognizing it in the accounts, the following entry could be made:

```
Retained Earnings.............................. xxx
      Earnings Restricted by Bond Contract.......        xxx
```

Retained earnings is now recorded in two accounts. Both accounts should be reported under the headings of retained earnings on the position statement. When the bond issue is eventually retired the restriction ceases, and the special account is transferred back to the main Retained Earnings account. Indeed, the only correct disposition of an account appropriated out of retained earnings is to return it to retained earnings.

Restrictions Due to Treasury Stock. When treasury stock is acquired by a firm, assets are distributed to the stockholders. To avoid the impairment of legal capital which results, many state laws require that retained earnings must be restricted for the cost of the treasury stock. This action limits potential dividend distributions by the amount that is distributed through a reacquisition of shares. Freezing this portion of retained earnings maintains a total amount of owners' equity at least equal to the original legal capital. If management wishes to reflect this restriction, the entry is:

```
Retained Earnings.............................. xxx
      Earnings Restricted—Treasury Stock........        xxx
```

This is an additional transaction, separate from the one for the actual acquisition of the stock. The amount restricted is the cost of the treasury stock. When the treasury stock is reissued, stated capital is restored. The reverse entry would then be appropriate:

```
Earnings Restricted—Treasury Stock............ xxx
      Retained Earnings...........................        xxx
```

Management Segregation of Retained Earnings

In addition to legal restrictions on the amount of retained earnings, management often uses similar accounts as a means of communicating information to the readers of the statement about possible events in the future. Examples in practice include such accounts as Reserve for Future Price Declines, Reserve for Possible Losses on Foreign Investments, and Reserve for Contingencies. Each of these accounts usually arises from a debit to Retained Earnings. No change in assets or in total equities results, only a reclassification of retained earnings in a number of different accounts. Ostensibly, the purpose of these appropriations of retained earnings is to call the reader's attention to the fact that in management's opinion these portions of retained earnings are not available for dividend declaration because of some possible unfavorable event in the future.

The entry establishing the retained earnings "reserve" does not make the firm any stronger. The only possible impact that the entry might have is that dividends *might* actually be reduced because of this segregation of retained earnings. Usually, however, this is not the case; the amount restricted is often small in relation to total retained earnings. Moreover, management can cut back on dividends without making any entry. Unfortunately, sometimes in business practice these reserve accounts are misused to absorb future losses that do arise. The loss is debited to the reserve account and buried there. Rather than disclosing information, this procedure conceals it, screening it from the income statement.

Evaluation of Retained Earnings Reserves

Restrictions of retained earnings must be evaluated only on their value as a means of communication. We have already seen that such restrictions (reserves) add neither to total assets nor to equities. Unfortunately, their use may tend more often to hinder than to enhance the clear communication of information. First, the account title "reserve" may mislead some readers into believing that the firm is stronger because of the reserve or that assets have been segregated for the purpose indicated by the reserve. Second, if a number of retained earnings accounts exist, the reader might infer that the unappropriated retained earnings *are* available for dividends or that surplus assets equivalent in amount exist unused in the business. Added to the preceding two points, the concealment of information that results when reserve accounts are misused raises serious doubts concerning the wisdom of using them at all.

What we may end up with is an apparent dispersion of retained earnings over a number of different accounts, with possible confusion and misunderstanding the result. Although reserve accounts are not theoretically incorrect when they are used properly, a better procedure might be to eliminate them entirely. Any significant information regarding legal restrictions or contingencies can then be disclosed in footnotes to the financial statements just as easily and certainly more clearly. Nevertheless, an understanding of their nature and use is important, for they often appear on financial statements.

Other Types of Reserve Accounts

To complicate this situation further, the term "reserve" is actually used in accounting practice to describe three different types of accounts. One type is the segregation of retained earnings which we have been discussing above. Additionally, contra assets and estimated liabilities often are described by the term "reserve." Examples of the former include the Reserve for Depreciation (Accumulated Depreciation) and the Reserve for Bad Debts (Allowance for Bad Debts). Liability reserves encompass the Reserve for Pensions (Liability for Employee Pensions), the Reserve for Income Taxes (Estimated Income Taxes Payable), and the Reserve for Product Warranties (Estimated Liability under Product Warranties).

It would be better if the term "reserve" were entirely stricken from accounting terminology. Its use is not limited to any particular type of account, and the term carries with it misleading and confusing connotations. The reader should analyze very carefully items classified as reserves to determine their true nature. Each so-called reserve account should bear a label which clearly reveals its exact classification and should be placed where it belongs—either as a liability, as a deduction from specific assets, or as a segregated portion of retained earnings.

SUMMARY

We have discussed a number of problem areas concerning stockholders' equity. Each of them has some direct impact on the concepts, accounts, or terminology of the financial statements. Yet only the surface has been scratched. Space does not permit a discussion of all the possible ways certain entries are recorded in practice. Moreover, variations in terminology are numerous; only a brief sample of commonly used titles has appeared here. The terms "surplus" and "reserve," in particular, are often used as catch-alls for a number of relatively dissimilar items.

Most of the problems in stockholders' equity involve questions of classification rather than valuation or measurement. Usually, the total change in owners' equity is determined by measurable changes in other assets and liabilities. The primary accounting problem becomes how to classify or divide up this total change among the various accounts comprising stockholders' equity. The fundamental division in stockholders' equity is between invested capital and retained earnings, even though this distinction becomes blurred in the case of stock dividends. It would seem that other desirable, albeit secondary, objectives in classifying stockholders' equity would be to distinguish between par or stated value and total contributed capital and to separate equities representing interests of different classes of investor, such as preferred stockholders and common stockholders. Usually these objectives can be met without undue complexity. But in some special circumstances, such as conversions, retirements, and treasury stock transactions, the classification objectives conflict, and the recording problems become more difficult. Perhaps what is needed is a threefold classification of stockholders' equity—contributed capital (by type of stockholder and reflecting legal distinctions), retained earnings, and other sources and adjustments.

Certainly, little doubt exists that major changes in all stockholders' equity accounts should be disclosed and explained. In fact, in *Opinion No. 12* the Accounting Principles Board requires that changes in the individual accounts comprising stockholders' equity and in the number of shares of stock be disclosed either in footnotes to the statements or in separate schedules. Before changes can be classified, however, the intricacies of some of the common events affecting owners' equity must be understood. From this chapter the reader should acquire a basic ability to analyze stockholders' equity transactions. This will often necessitate looking behind the facade of legal and financial convention, for many entries are indicated more by these factors than by accounting theory.

The diversity in terminology and procedures that characterizes the area of owners' equity extends to the presentation of stockholders' equity on the position statement. Many formats are employed; some stress legal considerations more than others. Table 13–1 shows one possible arrangement, incorporating most of the preferred views discussed earlier.

TABLE 13–1

SAMPLE CORPORATION
Stockholders' Equity
December 31, 19—
(in thousands)

Preferred stock equity:		
8% cumulative preferred stock (authorized and outstanding, 500,000 shares of $10 par value—Note 1)	$ 5,000	
Premium on preferred stock	5,322	$10,322
Common stock equity:		
Common stock—$10 par value, (authorized, 1,000,000 shares; issued, 500,000, of which 480,000 are outstanding)	$ 5,000	
Excess over par value	1,390	
	$ 6,390	
Additional paid-in capital and capital adjustments	183	
Retained earnings (Note 2)	18,632	
	$25,205	
Less: Treasury stock at cost (20,000 shares)	1,389	23,816
		$34,138

Note 1: The preferred stock can be redeemed by call at a price of $20 per share beginning in 19—and has an aggregate claim in liquidation of $10 million. [This information and information concerning preferred dividend arrearages are required disclosures under APB *Opinion No. 10.* Normally the par or stated value of preferred stock represents its claim in liquidation, but occasionally firms issue no-par preferred stock or preferred stock which has a liquidation claim or call price much greater than par or stated value.]

Note 2: Under the terms of the bond agreements, approximately $10 million of earnings retained on December 31, 19—, is unavailable for dividend declaration, and $1.389 million of retained earnings, equal to the cost of the treasury stock, is restricted by state law.

SUGGESTIONS FOR FURTHER READING

Birnberg, Jacob G. "An Information Oriented Approach to the Presentation of Common Stockholders' Equity," *Accounting Review*, Vol. 39 (October 1964), pp. 963–71.

Bomeli, Edwin C. "Stock Option Plans—Full Disclosure," *Accounting Review*, Vol. 37 (October 1962), pp. 741–45.

Burke, John T. "Stock Dividends—Suggestions for Clarification," *Accounting Review*, Vol. 37 (April 1962), pp. 283–88.

Buttimer, Harry. "The Evolution of Stated Capital," *Accounting Review*, Vol. 37 (October 1962), pp. 746–52.

Lowe, Howard D. "The Classification of Corporate Stock Equities," *Accounting Review*, Vol. 36 (July 1961), pp. 425–33.

Paton, W. A. "Postscript on 'Treasury' Shares," *Accounting Review*, Vol. 44 (April 1969), pp. 276–83.

Raby, William L. "Accounting for Employee Stock Options," *Accounting Review*, Vol. 37 (January 1962), pp. 28–38.

Ray, J. C. "Accounting for Treasury Stock," *Accounting Review*, Vol. 37 (October 1962), pp. 753–57.

QUESTIONS AND PROBLEMS

13–1. Prepare journal entries to record the following selected transactions involving stockholders' equity of the Ivory Tower Corporation. You may assume the company operated profitably.

1. Issued 2,000 shares of $10 par value common stock for $12 cash per share.
2. On the next day, gave 100 shares of common stock to the corporation's attorneys for legal services rendered in connection with securing the charter and getting the corporation in operation.
3. Issued 500 shares of common stock in exchange for a plant site. The board of directors placed a value of $6,500 on the site.
4. Declared a cash dividend of $2 per share.
5. Paid the cash dividend declared in item 4.
6. Declared and issued a 10 percent stock dividend. The current market price of the stock was $18 per share.
7. Repurchased 500 shares of stock from one of the original stockholders at a price of $25 per share. The stock was to be held in the treasury.
8. Sold 200 shares of the stock purchased in item 7 for $20 cash per share.

13–2. The president of the Lost Cause Company makes the following announcement in his letter to stockholders:

> In years past the company has paid a cash dividend of 5 percent and purchased new assets with the remaining cash retained out of net income. These reinvestment policies are now beginning to reap additional benefits in the form of increased profits. As a consequence, your board of directors has decided

to expand the dividend payout of the firm. Beginning this year, a 5 percent stock dividend will be added to the 5 percent cash dividend. In this way the firm can continue to expand as in the past. Yet the stockholders will have additional shares that they can convert into cash if necessary. In a sense, by selling dividend shares, an individual stockholder can increase his cash dividends from 5 percent to 10 percent:

a) Prepare journal entries to record the declaration and "payment" of the cash dividend and the stock dividends. Assume the firm has 100,000 shares of $100 par value common stock outstanding. The current market price of the stock is $130.

b) Evaluate the president's statement. Comment on all the misunderstandings and inaccuracies contained therein.

c) One of your close friends has recently purchased 1,000 shares of Lost Cause stock at $120 a share. He says that with the cash dividend of $5,000 ($5 per share × 1,000 shares) plus the stock dividend worth $6,500 (50 shares @ $130), he will already have earned over 9.5 percent ($11,500/$120,000) on his investment. Is his calculation correct? Why, or why not? Explain.

13–3. On January 1, 1971 the Unger Corporation entered into a contract with Stanley Cup to obtain Cup's services as its chief executive officer for the next two years. The contract specified that Cup will receive a salary of $100,000 in cash per year and granted him a stock option to acquire 1,000 shares of stock each year at a cash price of $20 per share. The market price of the stock was $25 per share at the time the agreement was reached.

During 1971, Stanley Cup exercised his option to acquire 1,000 shares. The market price of the stock was $30 at the date he acquired it. Because of a decline in the fortunes of the company and in the stock market, the price of the shares declined to $18 in 1972. Consequently, Cup did not exercise his option for the 1,000 shares in 1972, and the option expired.

a) Prepare any journal entries necessary to record the granting, exercise, and lapsing of the stock option.

b) How would your entries be modified if the option price had been set at the market price of $25 per share? Why might it be claimed that the conventional treatment in this case understates compensation expense?

c) A member of the board of directors of Unger Corporation was heard to say, "Stock options are a wonderful device. They can be used to compensate a highly valued employee, yet they cost the company nothing." Comment.

13–4. PPG Industries, Inc. shows a separate category of items called "accumulated provisions" on the equity side of its balance sheet. The accumulated provisions are presented between deferred credits and stockholders' equity. The accounts and amounts listed there are given below as of Dec. 31, 1967, 1968, and 1969 (in thousands of dollars):

	1969	1968	1967
Accumulated provisions for:			
Maintenance and repairs.....	$10,086	$6,623	$5,517
Insurance and unfunded and uninsured pensions........	3,355	3,733	3,476
Foreign operations.........	843	543	543

Carefully evaluate these items. Indicate how you would classify each one, and the kinds of entries that probably were and will be made to each of them.

13–5. The stockholders' equity of Wobbly Machine Parts, Inc., appeared as follows:

Stockholders' Equity
As of December 31, 1971

Capital stock—$50 par (1,000 shares authorized and outstanding).............	$ 50,000
Paid-in capital...........................	14,000
Retained earnings........................	40,000
	$104,000

On April 1, 1972, the corporation reacquired 100 shares at $95 per share. On October 15, 1972, it reissued 50 of the shares at a cost of $110 per share.

  a) Make the necessary journal entries on April 1 and on October 15, using the cost method of recording treasury stock.
  b) Prepare the stockholders' equity as of April 1 and as of October 15 (ignore income earned during the year).
  c) How much income did the corporation make on buying and selling its own stock? Explain.
  d) Repeat parts (*a*) and (*b*) using the par value method of recording treasury stock.
  e) Why might a corporation wish to reacquire and later reissue its own stock?

13–6. On January 1 the stockholders' equity of Grabgrass, Inc., was made up of the following items (in thousands):

Convertible preferred stock—$100 par......	$ 100
Discount on preferred stock................	(3)
Common stock—no par (stated value $10)....	1,000
Paid-in capital—common...................	800
Retained earnings........................	1,500
	$3,397

During the year the following transactions took place with respect to stockholders' equity:

Mar. 15   Cash dividends were declared on preferred stock, $1.50 per share, and on common stock, $1 per share, payable on April 10.

Apr. 10 Paid the dividends declared on March 15.
     11 Half of the preferred stock was converted into common at the rate of five shares of common for each share of preferred.
May 1 Purchased 2,000 shares of its own common stock for cash, $18 per share, to be held as treasury stock.
Jun. 15 Cash dividends were declared on preferred stock, $1.50 per share, and on common stock, $1 per share, payable on July 10.
Jul. 10 Paid the dividends declared on June 15.
    18 The board of directors authorized an appropriation of retained earnings in the amount of $300,000 for future losses on plant modernization programs.
Aug. 9 Issued the 2,000 shares of treasury stock in exchange for patent rights held by another company. The market value of the stock was $13 per share.
Nov. 2 In order to raise the market price of the stock, the board of directors approved a "reverse" stock split. Each stockholder received one share of new no-par common stock with a stated value of $20 per share for every two existing shares held.
    30 A 10 percent stock dividend was declared and distributed. The current market price of the stock to be used in capitalizing retained earnings was $25 per share.
Dec. 15 Declared a dividend of only $1 per share on the preferred stock, due to a cash shortage. Date of payment was January 10. The remaining $2 per share dividends on the preferred stock were in arrears.

a) Prepare journal entries to record the above transactions.
b) Prepare the stockholders' equity section of the position statement as of December 31 in good form. Assume that the net income before any dividends for the year was $130,000.

13–7. In February, 1972 Bowman Trading Company issued 3,000 shares of 8 percent preferred stock with a par value of $100. Each share of preferred carries with it two detachable rights to purchase two shares of common stock at a price of $16 any time within three months. The average market price of the common stock during February was $18 per share. The preferred stock was sold at a price of $110 per share. Both the preferred stock and the rights were traded on the stock market separately. Immediately after issue, the preferred stock was quoted at a price of $108, and the right to purchase one share of common was quoted at $4. During March and April, 5,000 rights were exercised and 5,000 shares of common stock were issued upon receipt of $80,000 in cash. The other 1,000 rights were never exercised and therefore lapsed after three months.

a) Prepare journal entries to record the issuance of the preferred, the exercise of the 5,000 rights, and the lapsing of the 1,000 rights.

b) If the rights were not detachable, and therefore would not have been traded separately from the preferred stock itself, how would you have made the above entries?

13–8. The ownership interest in a corporation is customarily reported in the balance sheet as stockholders' equity.*

a) List the principal transactions or items that reduce the amount of retained earnings. (Do not include appropriations of retained earnings.)

b) In the stockholders' equity section of the balance sheet, a distinction is made between contributed capital and earned capital. Why is this distinction made? Discuss.

c) There is frequently a difference between the purchase price and sale price of treasury stock, but accounting authorities agree that the purchase or sale of its own stock by a corporation cannot result in a profit or loss to the corporation. Why isn't the difference recognized as a profit or loss to the corporation? Discuss.

13–9. You are called in to audit the books of N. A. Rominded, Inc. The firm has been in operation for three years. You discover that the company has been using a single owners' equity account called "Capital." This account is reproduced below:

Capital

12–31–70 (d)	30,000	1–1–70 (a)	500,000
		1–1–70 (b)	180,000
7–31–71 (h)	5,000	12–31–70 (c)	53,000
9–30–71 (i)	50,000		
9–30–71 (j)	10,000	2–26–71 (e)	25,000
		7–1–71 (f)	200,000
1–1–72 (l)	97,500	7–1–71 (g)	10,000
3–31–72 (n)	30,000	12–31–71 (k)	37,000
12–31–72 (p)	8,000		
12–31–72 (r)	112,500	2–1–72 (m)	45,000
		4–10–72 (o)	13,000
		12–31–72 (q)	48,000
		12–31–72 (s)	40,000

Upon further analysis of the entries, you uncover these explanations:

a) Issued 10,000 shares of no-par common stock, stated value $50 per share.

b) Excess of paid-in amount over stated value of no-par common.

c) Balance transferred from Income Summary account.

d) Cash dividends declared and paid.

e) Current market value of a plant site donated by the city fathers to encourage expansion.

f) Issued 2,000 shares of preferred stock, par value $100. Dividend rate is 5 percent.

---

* Adapted from AICPA November 1964 examination.

g) Premium received on issuance of preferred stock.
h) Write-off of uncollectible note from a customer who went bankrupt.
i) Stated value of 1,000 shares of common stock, to be held as treasury stock.
j) Excess of amount paid over stated value of reacquired common stock.
k) Balance transferred from Income Summary account.
l) Total amount paid to retire half of the preferred stock at a cost of $95 per share plus dividends in arrears.
m) Stated value of common shares issued in exchange for patents. Current market price of the stock was $55 per share.
n) Transferred to reserve for future price declines in inventory.
o) Reissuance of 300 treasury shares.
p) Discount on $100,000 par value of 4 percent bonds issued.
q) Reissuance of 600 treasury shares.
r) Total amount paid to retire rest of the preferred stock at a cost of $105 per share plus dividends in arrears.
s) Balance transferred from Income Summary account.

Indicate how each of the above items should be reclassified to obtain a more accurate and detailed presentation of stockholders' equity. Set up whatever new ledger accounts are appropriate, and transfer the amounts entered in the Capital account to them. Where necessary, indicate your reasoning.

Prepare the stockholders' equity section of the position statement as of December 31, 1972.

13–10. On the equity side of the position statement of the Blooper Company appear the following account titles in a special section called "reserves," located between long-term liabilities and owners' equity:

Reserve for Pensions
Reserve for Replacement of Inventories
Reserve for Contingencies
Reserve for Depletion
Reserve for Risks Not Covered by Insurance Policies
Reserve for Restoration of Leased Property
Reserve for Employee Bonus
Reserve for Uncollectible Notes and Accounts
Reserve for Product Guarantees
Reserve for Bond Retirement Fund

a) Criticize the existing presentation used by the company.
b) For each of these accounts, indicate (1) where you would report it on the position statement, (2) any change in account title that seems appropriate, (3) the account that was debited when the reserve was set up, and (4) the account that should be credited when the reserve is reduced.

13-11. The business year for Sperry Rand Corporation ends on March 31. The stockholders' equity section of its balance sheet as of March 31, 1968 is presented below:

```
Stockholders' Equity:
  Capital stock:
    Preferred stock, $4.50 cumulative, $25
    par value (entitled to $100 per share
    on redemption, dissolution or liquida-
    tion); authorized—250,000 shares,
    issued—102,267 shares.................  $  2,556,675
    Common stock, $0.50 par value; authorized
    —50,000,000 shares, outstanding—
    33,908,835............................     16,954,418
  Capital surplus..........................    213,259,520
  Retained earnings........................    363,504,708
                                              $596,275,321
  Less 4,790 shares of preferred stock in
    treasury, at cost......................        368,399
                                              $595,906,922
```

In a note to the statement, the company indicated that all outstanding shares of preferred stock had been called for redemption on July 1, 1968 at the redemption price of $100.

a) Comment on the firm's presentation of its preferred stock. What deficiencies do you see? Does Sperry Rand present owners' equity by source?

b) What does the capital surplus account represent, and why is it so large relative to the preferred and common stock account?

c) Prepare the journal entry that the company should make on July 1, 1968 when the shares are actually redeemed. Explain your reasoning.

d) Why would Sperry Rand wish to redeem its preferred stock?

13-12. Belding Heminway Company presented the following stockholders' equity section in the comparative balance sheet contained in its 1968 annual report (in thousands):

	December 31	
	1968	1967
Stockholders' Equity:		
Common stock—par value $1 per share; authorized—1,500,000 shares, issued—1,028,000 and 815,000 shares, respectively.....	$ 1,028	$ 815
To be issued....................	430	12
Capital surplus..................	6,358	6,066
Retained earnings................	13,937	13,137
	$21,753	$20,030
Less: Treasury stock—226,000 and 36,000 shares, respectively, of common stock—at cost.........	864	602
	$20,889	$19,428

Additional information contained in notes to the statements indicate the following transactions:

1. Issued 2,000 shares in connection with the exercise of stock options. The option price was $27,000.
2. Issued 31,000 shares via a 4 percent stock dividend. The market value was $707,000.
3. Purchased for its treasury 4,000 shares of its common stock at a price of $96,000.
4. Declared a 3 for 2 stock split; 430,000 shares are to be issued, including 20,000 shares issuable on shares held in the treasury at date of declaration. The par amount was charged to Capital Surplus.
5. Issued 13,000 of common stock, representing the final installment of the purchase price for a company acquired in 1965. These included the 12,000 shares shown in 1967 as "to be issued."
6. Acquired the assets of H. Brothers & Sons, Inc., whose capital stock is owned by officers and directors of the company. The assets consisted of $22,000 cash and 166,000 shares of the company's common stock. In exchange, the company issued 167,000 shares of its common stock.

a) Reconstruct the journal entries that were probably made to record the above events.

b) Post your entries to ledger (T) accounts for Common Stock, Capital Surplus, and Treasury Stock to see that you properly account for the change in dollar balances.

c) Compare the stock dividend with the stock split as to each one's basis of valuation, accounts involved, and impact on total stockholders' equity. Why does their recording differ?

d) Compare the price at which the options were exercised with the market price of the stock during 1968. Where is this increased value reflected on the financial statements? Explain.

e) Were the amounts in the transaction with H. Brothers & Son based on arm's-length (objective) valuation? How do you know? Comment on the possible reasons for this unusual transaction.

13–13. City Stores presents a separate group of accounts under a heading of "reserves" on the equity side of its balance sheet. The reserve section is presented between liabilities and stockholders' equity. The accounts and amounts listed there are given below for 1968, 1969 and 1970.

	1-31-70	2-1-69	2-3-68
Other reserves:			
Deferred compensation...............	$1,788,713	$1,668,689	$ 998,784
Real estate dispositions..............	1,370,995	1,370,995	1,110,615
Termination of store operations.........	214,046	314,145	301,062
Pensions............	1,760,915	892,626	.....
Other...............	179,590	179,590	302,476
	$5,314,259	$4,426,045	$2,712,937

In interpreting the balance sheet, where would you classify each of these reserves? Explain carefully, including your assumptions as to the nature of the entries that are made to each of them.

13–14. The Luck Corporation was organized on July 1, 1971. In its charter, it was authorized to issue 10,000 shares of 4 percent preferred stock having a par value of $100 per share, and 100,000 shares of common stock with a par value of $10 per share. Each share of preferred stock was convertible into 10 shares of common stock and callable at 105. The following are selected transactions of the corporation:

1971:

July 2 Issued 5,000 shares of preferred stock at $104 per share.

2 Issued 7,000 shares of common; 6,500 were issued for $65,-000 in cash, and the other 500 shares were issued to the lawyers and other groups in lieu of services rendered and expenses incurred in organizing and promoting the corporation.

July 3 To induce the corporation to locate there, the city of Washout Gully donated a plant site. The fair market value of the land was estimated to be $15,000.

Sept. 21 Issued 8,000 shares of common stock to various individuals in Washout Gully at a price of $11 per share.

22 Issued 10,000 shares of common stock in exchange for some equipment.

Dec. 31 Declared and paid preferred dividends for six months.

1972:

Mar. 2 Repurchased 2,000 shares of its common stock at $12 per share. In addition a formal entry was made to restrict retained earnings by the amount of the cost of the treasury stock.

July 1 Called in the preferred stock for retirement at 105 plus accumulated dividends. Preferred stockholders owning half of the shares elected to convert their preferred stock into common; the rest of the preferred stock was retired by the corporation. The price of the common stock on this date is $10.75.

Aug. 15 Issued 4,000 shares of common stock at a price of $15 per share. Half of these represented the shares acquired on March 2; the rest were previously unissued shares.

Sept. 1 A 2 for 1 stock split is declared on the common stock. Present shareholders of common stock receive an additional share of common stock for each share currently held. The par value is formally reduced to $5 per share.

Dec. 31 Dividends of $3 per share were declared on each share of common stock outstanding.

a) Make journal entries to record the above transactions.

b) What is your opinion of issuing the 500 shares on July 2?

c) Justify your method of valuation in recording the conversion of preferred shares on July 1.

13–15. On December 14, 1969 the board of directors of the Needleman Company authorized a grant of nontransferable (restricted) stock options to company executives for the purchase of 10,000 shares of common stock at 52½ any time during 1972 if the executives were still employed by the company.* The closing price of Needleman common stock was 55 on December 14, 1969; 57 on January 2, 1972; and 59 on December 31, 1972. Half of the options were exercised on January 2, 1972 and the other half on December 31, 1972.

a) Compute the amount of compensation cost which you would attribute to the option of Needleman Company.

b) What alternative valuations could be employed? Discuss their merits and deficiencies compared to the method you chose.

c) Assume that the market price of Needleman stock dropped to 52 during 1972 and that none of the options were exercised. Did the company incur a cost for executive compensation? Discuss how you would handle this possibility in the accounting records.

13–16. The Unknown Corporation purchased $144,000 of equipment in 1965 for $90,000 cash and a promise to deliver an indeterminate number of treasury shares of its $5 par common stock, with a market value of $15,000, on January 1 of each year for the next four years.† Hence $60,000 in "market value" of treasury shares will be required to discharge the $54,000 balance due on the equipment.

The corporation then acquired 5,000 shares of its own stock for $45,000 in the expectation that the market value of the stock would increase substantially before the delivery dates. A total of 4,000 of those shares were subsequently issued in settlement of the remaining balance on the equipment contract.

a) Discuss the propriety of recording the equipment at:
   1. $90,000 (the cash payment).
   2. $144,000 (the cash price of the equipment).
   3. $150,000 (the $90,000 cash payment plus the $60,000 market value of treasury stock that must be transferred to the vendor in order to settle the obligation according to the terms of the agreement).
   4. $126,000 (the $90,000 cash payment plus the $36,000 cost of treasury stock issued in payment for equipment).

b) Discuss the arguments for treating the balance due as:
   1. A liability.
   2. Capital stock to be issued (a separate segment of stockholders' equity).

c) Assuming that legal requirements do not affect the decision, discuss the arguments for treating the corporation's treasury shares as:

---

* Adapted from AICPA November 1967 examination.
† Adapted from AICPA May 1966 examination.

1. An asset awaiting ultimate disposition.
2. A capital element awaiting ultimate disposition.

13–17. The 1966 annual report of United States Steel Corporation showed the following long-term equities as of December 31, 1965 and 1966:

	1966	1965
Reserves (see separate schedule)................	$ 141,939,635	$ 143,142,245
Ownership:		
Preferred stock, 7% cumulative par value $100....................	......	360,281,000
Common stock, par value, $30 per share..........	$1,624,144,110	
Income reinvested in the business................	1,553,862,182	
	$3,178,006,292	$3,264,581,527

A separate schedule of the reserves was contained in the report. It is presented below.

		Reserves for:			
	Insurance	Contin-gencies	Accident, Hospital	Investment Credit	Total
Balance 12/31/65......	$50.0	$58.4	$ 9.4	$25.3	$143.1
Additions............	4.2	...	24.3	20.8	49.3
Deductions...........	4.2	17.8*	24.3	4.2	50.5
Balance 12/31/66......	$50.0	$40.6	$ 9.4	$41.9	$141.9

* See notes to financial statements.

In addition the following note described other capital changes occurring in 1966:

On January 1, 1966, United States Steel Corporation, a New Jersey Corporation, was merged into a wholly-owned Delaware subsidiary, retaining the same name. In the merger, each outstanding share of $100 par value 7% cumulative preferred stock of the Corporation was exchangeable for $175 principal amount of 4⅝% Subordinated Debentures due January 1, 1996, a total of $630.5 million. As the debentures were issuable only in denominations of $100 and multiples thereof, stockholders entitled to fractional interests received cash in lieu thereof. Also, holders of five shares or less were given the opportunity to exchange their shares for cash. As a result, $7.7 million was paid in cash and debentures are outstanding for the balance of $622.8 million.

The par value of the preferred stock exchanged was $270.2 million less than the principal amount of debentures to be issued. Of this amount, $234.5 million represents the excess of the December 31, 1965 market value of the preferred stock exchanged over its par value and has been charged to Income Reinvested in Business; the balance of $35.7 million has been charged to Costs Applicable to Future Periods and is being amortized over the life of the debentures.

The merger also involved an increase in the par value of the out-standing common stock from $16⅔ per share to $30 per share for a total increase of $721.9 million. Of this amount, $704.1 million was transferred from Income Reinvested in Business and the remainder, $17.8 million, from Capital Surplus (included with the Reserve for Contingencies at December 31, 1965 in the financial statements).

The changes for the year 1966 in Income Reinvested in Business were as follows:

```
                                                  (in millions)
Balance at December 31, 1965...................   $2,362.3
Less—effect of January 1, 1966 merger: excess
  of market value over par value of preferred
  stock exchanged for subordinated deben-
  tures........................................      234.5
  Increase in par value of common stock........      704.1
Balance as adjusted January 1, 1966............   $1,423.7
Income reinvested in 1966......................      130.1
Balance at December 31, 1966...................   $1,553.8
```

a) Evaluate the accounting for reserves for contingencies, accident and hospital, and insurance. Develop the probable journal entries that would be made in these reserves. How would you classify them on the balance sheet?

b) Reconstruct in general journal form the entries made in connection with the preferred and common stock.

c) Why would a firm wish to replace preferred stock with subordinated debentures? Do you agree with the charging of $35.7 million to an intangible asset? Explain.

d) Why would the company decide to increase the par value of its common stock? What impact does this have on stockholders' equity?

13–18. On May 23, 1972 Bangup Steel Corporation made a package issue of securities. Each package consisted of a $100 five-year debenture bond bearing interest at 6 percent per year; one share of 7 percent, $50 par value preferred stock; and three shares of $10 par value common stock. The total price of the package was $200, and $200,000 was received from the issuance of 1,000 such packages.

The debenture bonds and preferred stock were new securities and were not sufficiently traded after issuance to establish any independent market price. It was estimated that the current market rate of interest for the type of bond being issued was 8 percent. Over 200,000 shares of common stock were outstanding prior to this issuance, and the common stock was widely traded. The closing stock price on May 22 was $30 per share.

Make entries to record the issuance of these securities. Comment on the procedure you used to allocate the total amount received among the three types of securities.

13–19. W. T. Grant Company's statement of financial position as of January 31, 1969 and 1968 is given below:

	1969	1968
Current liabilities	$372,493,085	$290,118,371
Long-term debt	35,402,000	43,251,000
Deferred federal income taxes..	8,286,401	7,940,968
Reserves:		
For self-insured risks and repainting stores	3,300,000	3,300,000
For deferred contingent compensation	2,399,242	2,219,454
Total Reserves	$ 5,699,242	$ 5,519,454
Capital:		
Capital stock:		
Cumulative preferred—$100 par value: authorized, 250,000 shares; issued, 114,500 and 132,500 shares, respectively of 3¾% series	11,450,000	13,250,000
Common—$1.25 par value: authorized, 22,500,000 shares; issued, 14,306,-640 and 13,854,220 shares, respectively	17,883,300	17,317,775
Capital in excess of par value of shares issued	70,224,570	58,661,960
Amounts paid by employees under purchase contracts for unissued common stock	1,330,474	1,283,958
Earnings retained for use in the business	211,679,286	188,606,659
	$312,567,630	$280,120,352
Less 432,764 shares of treasury of common stock, at cost	21,879,131	
Total Capital	$290,688,499	$280,120,352
	$712,569,227	$626,950,145

In addition, listed among the assets was:

	1969	1968
Common stock of W. T. Grant Company, at cost, held for Deferred Contingent Compensation Plan (145,400 and 140,500 shares, respectively)	$2,381,044	$2,158,108

A separate statement summarizes the changes in the Capital in Excess of Par Value account during the year ended January 31, 1970:

Balance at the beginning of the year	$58,661,960
Excess of proceeds over par value of 232,415 and 263,430 shares respectively, of common stock issued under the Employee's Stock Purchase Plan	4,988,060
Excess of the conversion price over par value of 220,005 and 638,177 shares respectively, of common stock issued for 4% convertible debentures	5,811,527
Excess of par value over the cost of 18,000 and 15,000 shares respectively, of 3¾% cumulative preferred stock purchased and canceled	763,023
Balance at the end of the year	$70,224,570

a) Reconstruct in general journal form the entries affecting the Capital in Excess of Par Value account.

b) Comment on the nature of the items classified under reserves. How would you classify them and why?

c) Explain the nature of the account "amounts paid by employees under purchase contracts for unissued common stock." What types of entries are made to this account? Do you agree with its classification as part of "capital"? Explain.

d) Why is the amount of the company's own shares shown in two places (as an asset and as a contra-equity)? Do you agree with this treatment? Explain.

SECTION IV

INTERPRETATION OF FINANCIAL STATEMENTS

CHAPTER FOURTEEN

INTERCOMPANY
INVESTMENTS AND
CONSOLIDATIONS

It is common for one corporation to own substantial holdings of stock of other corporations. In some cases the stockholder company acquires shares of stock solely as an intermediate or long-term investment with the objective of earning a profitable return directly in the form of dividends. In other cases the purpose is control.

Two basic methods exist for one company to acquire control of another company. Company A may buy the assets of Company B outright, or it may purchase the outstanding stock of Company B from Company B's stockholders. If Company A owns all of the stock of Company B, it may liquidate Company B and transfer all the assets to Company A. Such a combination is called a *merger*. If Company A owns a controlling interest in the stock, it may choose not to liquidate Company B but rather to operate it as a separate corporation in harmony with the overall objectives of Company A. In this case the controlling company is called the *parent*, and the company controlled is called the *subsidiary*.

Whatever its reasons for investing in shares of stock of another company, the parent company may exchange for those shares a number of different considerations. The obvious one is cash. Others include shares of common stock of the parent (either unissued or treasury stock), bonds, and preferred stock. In many cases the parent may exchange combinations of cash and securities to acquire the stock of other companies. The acquisition and merger trend of the last two decades has fostered more alternatives than could possibly be described here.

The initial result of an acquisition is the recording by the parent com-

471

pany of an asset, Investment in Stock of Subsidiary. The investment account remains as an asset, or, if the subsidiary company is legally merged, disappears. This chapter explores three aspects of the accounting for these intercorporate relationships. The first is the proper accounting for intercompany investments when the parent company and the subsidiaries are treated as separate accounting entities. Two different methods—cost and equity—are used. The second aspect is the preparation of consolidated financial statements which treat the parent and subsidiary companies as if they were a single company. The concluding section considers the valuation and recording problems involved when businesses merge or combine as a result of an exchange of shares. The alternative procedures, called purchase and pooling of interests, constitute the focal point in that section.

INVESTMENT IN UNCONSOLIDATED SUBSIDIARIES

In accounting for its intercompany stock investments, the parent may employ the cost method, the equity method, or perhaps both. These two methods differ in how the investment in and subsequent earnings of the subsidiaries are recorded by the parent company. Under the *cost* method the parent company's investment is recorded at cost, as is any other asset investment. The investment account remains at cost[1] despite any future increases or decreases in the underlying net assets of the subsidiary as a result of its periodic operations. Likewise, no income is recognized by the parent company unless and until the subsidiary declares and pays a dividend.

Under the *equity* method the Investment in Subsidiary account reflects changes in the underlying investment as a result of subsidiary operations, and income or loss also appears on the books of the parent company in the period it is earned by the subsidiary. If the subsidiary operates profitably, the investment account is debited and income credited for the parent company's share of the net income of the subsidiary. The reverse procedure is followed if the subsidiary operates at a loss. The effect of the equity method is to carry the investment account at cost plus a proportionate share of the subsidiary's undistributed retained earnings since acquisition.

Comparative Example

To illustrate the effect of the two different methods on the amount and timing of income, the following example gives a series of events and the journal entries to record them under the cost and equity methods.

---

[1] If there is a serious, permanent impairment of the investment, the cost basis is often modified to record a decrease in the investment account. If, for example, half of the subsidiary's assets were destroyed, the investment account would be written down.

1. The parent company acquires 40,000 shares of the common stock of the subsidiary at $5 per share on January 1, 1971. The purchase represents an 80 percent interest in the subsidiary.

```
Cost Method:
    Investment in Subsidiary............. 200,000
        Cash.............................             200,000
Equity Method:
    Investment in Subsidiary............. 200,000
        Cash.............................             200,000
```

2. During 1971 the subsidiary earns a net income of $30,000 and pays a dividend of $10,000.

```
Cost Method:
    Cash.................................   8,000
        Dividend Revenue.................               8,000
Equity Method:
    Investment in Subsidiary.............  24,000
        Equity in Earnings of Subsidiary².               24,000
    Cash.................................   8,000
        Investment in Subsidiary.........               8,000
```

3. During 1972 the subsidiary operates at a loss of $5,000 and pays no dividends.

```
Cost Method:
    No entry.
Equity Method:
    Equity in Loss of Subsidiary.........   4,000
        Investment in Subsidiary.........               4,000
```

4. During 1973 the subsidiary earns a net income of $15,000 and pays dividends of $20,000.

```
Cost Method:
    Cash.................................  16,000
        Dividend Revenue.................              16,000
Equity Method:
    Investment in Subsidiary.............  12,000
        Equity in Earnings of Subsidiary.             12,000
    Cash.................................  16,000
        Investment in Subsidiary.........              16,000
```

Analysis of Cost Method

This method views the parent and the subsidiary as separate legal corporations. It assumes that the parent as partial owner of the subsidiary exercises little or no control over it. Revenue derived from the investment is recognized only in the periods when assets are actually distributed to the parent in the form of dividends and only to the extent of the dividend amount. Consequently, total revenue of only $24,000 ($8,000 + $16,000) is recorded by the parent, representing the amount received in dividends

---

² Sometimes under the equity method the revenue is split into two categories—Dividend Revenue of $8,000 and Equity in Undistributed Earnings of Subsidiary of $16,000.

over the period. In 1972, when no dividends are paid, the cost method shows no loss, even though the subsidiary operates at a loss in that year. Then in 1973 revenue of $16,000 (80% × $20,000) is recorded under the cost method, when one might argue that the subsidiary has only earned $12,000 applicable to the parent company's interest.

Under the cost basis the Investment in Subsidiary account remains at $200,000, the amount initially invested. Even though the subsidiary operates profitably over the years, increasing its total net assets, no reflection of this increase is recorded in the parent company's accounts.

Analysis of the Equity Method

The equity method recognizes total net earnings of $32,000 ($24,000 − $4,000 + $12,000) over the three-year period. The parent recognizes as income its share of the net income of the subsidiary in the period the income is earned by the subsidiary. The parent's share is determined by the percentage of the total outstanding shares held by the parent. Dividends received from the subsidiary are credited to the investment account. Since they reduce the net assets of the subsidiary, this fact is reflected through a reduction in the parent's investment account.

The difference of $8,000 between the income figures recognized under the equity method ($32,000) and under the cost method ($24,000) is the parent's interest in subsidiary earnings which have not been distributed to the parent as dividends. This same amount, of course, is reflected as a net increase in the Investment in Subsidiary account, which reflects the entries shown above:

Investment in Subsidiary

1971 cost	200,000	8,000	1971 dividends
1971 income	24,000	4,000	1972 loss
1973 income	12,000	16,000	1973 dividends
		√208,000	Balance 12–31–73
	236,000	236,000	
Bal. 12–31–73	√208,000		

A separate position statement of the subsidiary would show a retained earnings balance $10,000 larger than on January 1, 1971. Since the net assets of the subsidiary have increased $10,000 and the parent has an 80 percent interest, the investment account properly reflects the $8,000 increase in the parent's interest.

Two major arguments are advanced in support of the equity method. First, the results shown by the parent company bear a direct relationship to the periodic operations of the subsidiary. While still maintaining the existence of the parent and subsidiary as separate companies, the equity method recognizes that they may be very closely related. The parent's financial statements, if based on the equity method, give a more useful picture of this relationship, since they reflect the underlying changes in net assets occurring in the subsidiary.

Second, often the parent company can control the dividend policy of the subsidiary. The cost method, under which income is recorded only when dividends are received, allows the management of the parent company to determine how much income it wishes to recognize and when it will be recognized. By taking the subsidiary's earnings onto the parent company's books as earned and treating dividends simply as a reduction in the amount invested, the equity method avoids this possible pitfall and thus may provide a more objective measure of income.

The substance of both of these arguments is that dividends poorly measure, in both timing and amount, the periodic benefit from many stock holdings. The equity method simply extends the concepts of accrual accounting and revenue recognition to substantial intercompany investments. Recognition by the subsidiary of net income measured according to generally accepted accounting principles is deemed to meet satisfactorily the earning criterion for revenue recognition by the parent. Likewise, changes in the underlying net assets of the subsidiary constitute sufficient objectivity and certainty in measurement. A specific exchange of assets (dividend payment) adds little more to the fulfillment of the revenue recognition criteria.

APB Opinion. For the above reasons, the Accounting Principles Board requires the equity method for investments where the investor influences to some degree the operating or financial decisions of the investee. The control is arbitrarily assumed to exist with a 20 percent or more interest in the voting stock. The cost method is to be used for other stock holdings. Full disclosure of methods used, dividends received, equity in net assets of the investee, etc. is also required.

CONSOLIDATED FINANCIAL STATEMENTS

The equity method attempts to show some interrelationship between the parent and the subsidiary by adjusting the parent's investment account for changes that take place in the subsidiary's net assets. It fails to disclose, however, the complete interrelationship, particularly where the companies closely coordinate their operations and financial positions. A more complete picture results when the actual accounts of the subsidiary are meshed with those of the parent on a single set of statements, called consolidated financial statements, which indicate the results that would have transpired if all transactions had been recorded in a single set of accounts.

The purpose of the consolidated statement is to provide the management and stockholders of the parent company with an overall view of the activities of their company and its related subsidiaries considered as one unit. This picture typically is more meaningful than separate statements, since the legal entities often act in concert to achieve an overall goal for the parent company and its stockholders rather than autonomously to attain individual company objectives. In consolidated statements the investor in the parent company can see the results of his investment at work —directly, and also indirectly through the parent's investments in other companies. The user of consolidated financial statements can often obtain a better picture of the financial and operating activities of the complex of companies. He gets a better idea of the total asset investment subject to common control, the sales volume of the entire group of companies, indirect financial arrangements using subsidiary companies which borrow heavily (primarily on the credit of the parent company), etc.

Consolidation Policy

In consolidated statements the business entity becomes a group of affiliated companies. Therefore, the consolidated statements are concerned only with the transactions and relationships between the affiliates viewed as one and parties outside the family circle. The mere existence of intercompany holdings of securities, however, does not automatically lead to the preparation of consolidated statements. Presentation of the activities and relationships of a number of companies as if they were one can be justified only when there is reason to believe that it would provide more useful information than would separate statements of the parent and the individual subsidiaries. The parent company, therefore, should adopt a reasonable and consistent consolidation policy governing which subsidiaries are consolidated and which remain as investments. The consolidation policy being followed should be clearly disclosed, usually in a footnote to the consolidated statements, so that the reader can make proper interpretations.

A number of criteria may influence the choice of consolidation policy, but the two most important are control and relatedness of activities. In order for a group of firms to function as a single company one of the group must have sufficient control over the others to influence their activities. This would suggest that consolidation of statements is applicable when there is clearly only one parent company and the parent company owns a substantial controlling interest in the subsidiaries. In practically no case is consolidation suggested when the parent owns less than a majority of the voting stock, and many companies consolidate only 80 to 100 percent owned subsidiaries. Sometimes foreign subsidiaries are not consolidated because of restrictions on the parent's control over the subsidiary's operations or on the withdrawal of earnings by the parent in the form of dividends.

Even when the criterion of clearly defined control is met, consolidation may offer no advantages if the companies involved are not operationally related; in fact it may conceal meaningful differences. Consolidated statements for a manufacturing firm and a bank would probably provide little additional information not contained in individual reports of each company. On the other hand, the mere fact that the subsidiary is in a different line from the parent is insufficient reason not to consolidate. This seems particularly true currently, with the emphasis on diversification. Careful judgment is required to ascertain whether a particular subsidiary is an organic part of the consolidated entity. Consideration must be given to the objectives of the parent in acquiring the subsidiary, the sameness of their general business activity, the extent of intercorporate transactions, and the degree of similarity in the structure of their financial statements.

Consolidated Position Statement

When consolidated statements are needed, the accountant works from the individual statements of the companies being consolidated. He then eliminates the items that would not appear if the separate companies had been one company. Let us examine a few simplified illustrations to see what eliminations are called for in various typical situations.

Complete Ownership at Book Value. For the first example, assume that the parent company acquires 100 percent of the common stock of the subsidiary for $10,000 on December 31, 1971; consolidated statements are desired as of that date. Table 14–1 presents the major accounts of each company. Note that the $10,000 amount shown as an asset on the parent company books as Investment in Subsidiary equals the owners' equity (capital stock plus retained earnings) of the subsidiary, because the parent has paid book value for its 100 percent ownership interest in the subsidiary.

In this simple case the only items to eliminate are the Investment in Subsidiary account on the parent's books and the Capital Stock and Retained Earnings accounts on the subsidiary's books. The investment ac-

TABLE 14–1

Account Titles	Parent	Subsidiary	Eliminations Dr.	Eliminations Cr.	Consolidation
Cash......................	$10,000	$ 5,000			$15,000
Accounts receivable.........	5,000	2,000			7,000
Other assets...............	25,000	8,000			33,000
Investment in subsidiary.....	10,000	...		(a) $10,000	
	$50,000	$15,000			$55,000
Accounts payable..........	$20,000	$ 5,000			$25,000
Capital stock..............	20,000	7,000	(a) $ 7,000		20,000
Retained earnings..........	10,000	3,000	(a) 3,000		10,000
	$50,000	$15,000	$10,000	$10,000	$55,000

count as an asset represents an interest in the net assets of the subsidiary. Since the subsidiary's net assets will be counted as part of the consolidated assets, it would be double counting to consider the investment also as a separate asset. Consolidation in essence substitutes the individual net assets of the subsidiary ($5,000 cash + $2,000 accounts receivable + $8,000 other assets − $5,000 accounts payable) for the single $10,000 balance in the investment account.

Similarly, the stockholders' equity of the subsidiary should not be counted as equity of the consolidated companies, because it is already reflected on the parent company's books. The subsidiary's capital stock plus retained earnings represent a financial interest in the net assets of the subsidiary. But the parent company's owners' equity reflects a financial interest in the investment in subsidiary's shares, which in turn represents an interest in those same subsidiary assets. Consequently, the double counting of equities is avoided by elimination of the owners' equity of the subsidiary, inasmuch as it does not represent a relationship with those outside the family.

Minority Interest at Book Value. Assume now that the parent company purchases only 80 percent of the capital stock of the subsidiary, paying $8,000 for it. (The Cash account will be larger by $2,000 than in the first example.) The other 20 percent, owned by someone else, is called the minority interest. The parent company has the majority or controlling interest, so consolidation is deemed desirable. The analysis appears in Table 14–2.

The eliminations are basically the same, except that only 80 percent of the capital stock and retained earnings of the subsidiary is eliminated. This is the only portion represented by intercompany holdings of stock. The

TABLE 14–2

Account Titles	Parent	Subsidiary	Eliminations Dr.	Eliminations Cr.	Consolidation
Cash..................	$12,000	$ 5,000			$17,000
Accounts receivable.....	5,000	2,000			7,000
Other assets...........	25,000	8,000			33,000
Investment in S........	8,000	. . .		(a) $ 8,000	. . .
	$50,000	$15,000			$57,000
Accounts payable.......	$20,000	$ 5,000			$25,000
Capital stock—P.......	20,000				20,000
Capital stock—S.......		7,000	(a) $ 5,600 (b) 1,400		
Retained earnings—P...	10,000				10,000
Retained earnings—S...		3,000	(a) 2,400 (b) 600		
Minority interest.......	. . .	. . .		(b) 2,000	2,000
	$50,000	$15,000	$10,000	$10,000	$57,000

remaining 20 percent represents the interest of a separate group outside of the family. Since we wish to include all assets under common control in the consolidation, the financial interest of the minority stockholders in those assets rightfully belongs in the consolidated statement. Elimination (*b*) segregates this equity interest in a single figure. For the consolidated entity, minority interest is a special portion of owners' equity apart from that of the parent stockholders. Often, it is placed as a separate category between the total liabilities and the consolidated stockholders' equity of the parent company stockholders.

Investment at More or Less than Book Value. It is not necessary that the subsidiary's stock sell at book value; in fact, it usually does not. How does the consolidated balance sheet appear if the parent company pays $9,000 for 80 percent of the stock in the subsidiary? The parent's investment account has a debit balance of $9,000; however, the subsidiary's books remain unchanged. Following the entity concept, the subsidiary does not record subsequent resales of its stock between investors. What the parent company has to pay at some later date to purchase the shares from the original investors is not recorded in the subsidiary's accounts.

To eliminate the investment account a credit of $9,000 must be made, but debits of only $5,600 and $2,400 are required to eliminate 80 percent of the subsidiary's owners' equity. The difference of $1,000 is an additional asset. If the parent company is willing to pay $9,000 for the stock it acquires, there is reason to believe that it is acquiring an interest in assets worth $9,000. In other words, an additional $1,000 of tangible or intangible asset value presumably is present in the transaction. When this excess cost of the stock investment to the parent company over its book value is recognized as a consolidated asset, the elimination entry will balance, as shown in Table 14–3.

The excess cost over book value commonly appears in the consolidated position statement among the intangible assets, with the caption "Consolidated Goodwill." This description may be accurate in some cases, but probably is an oversimplification. The excess may represent undervalued tangible assets of the subsidiary—e.g., Lifo inventory, fully depreciated buildings, or appreciated land values recorded at original cost—as well as an intangible asset, "goodwill."[3] Another possibility is that the $1,000 represents payment for benefits expected to arise in the future out of the closer coordination of the two firms—the synergistic advantages springing from the affiliation itself, not ones associated with the subsidiary as a separate entity.

If the parent company pays less than book value, a credit to Excess

---

[3] When the excess is attributable to understated subsidiary assets, the possibility exists of also revaluing the minority interest. If 80 percent of the subsidiary is worth $9,000, then 100 percent should be worth $11,250. Logic would suggest adding another $250 to the excess account and a credit of $250 to the minority interest.

TABLE 14–3

Account Titles	Parent	Subsidiary	Eliminations Dr.	Eliminations Cr.	Consolidation
Cash..................	$11,000	$ 5,000			$16,000
Accounts receivable......	5,000	2,000			7,000
Other assets............	25,000	8,000			33,000
Investment in S.........	9,000			(a) $ 9,000	. . .
Excess cost over book value...........	. . .	. . .	(a) $ 1,000		1,000
	$50,000	$15,000			$57,000
Accounts payable........	$20,000	$ 5,000			$25,000
Capital stock—P........	20,000				20,000
Capital stock—S........		7,000	(a) 5,600 (b) 1,400		
Retained earnings—P...	10,000				10,000
Retained earnings—S...		3,000	(a) 2,400 (b) 600		
Minority Interest	. . .	. . .		(b) 2,000	2,000
	$50,000	$15,000	$11,000	$11,000	$57,000

Book Value over Investment Cost would be required. This item recognizes an overstatement in the subsidiary assets, as measured by what the parent is willing to pay to acquire an interest in them. Unless the specific overvalued assets can be identified, this amount should be treated as a general contra to the consolidated assets on the position statement.

Consolidation in Subsequent Periods. Now let us consider the problems introduced when a consolidated position statement is prepared after the date of acquisition. The parent and subsidiary may operate as related units, but they maintain separate accounting records as individual entities. For our example let us assume that as a result of operations during 1972 the parent company earns $10,000 and the subsidiary earns $4,000, and that there are concomitant changes in assets and liabilities in each case. Now, at the end of 1972, another consolidated position statement is desired. Table 14–4 illustrates the procedures for this situation as well as for some other intercompany relationships discussed in the next section.

The eliminations remain the same as in the previous example except for the amount added to the subsidiary's retained earnings since acquisition. It must be treated differently in consolidation from the retained earnings existing on the date of acquisition. The latter are reflected in the investment account on the parent company's books and thus in the parent's equity accounts. They are eliminated as part of the normal consolidating process in eliminations (a) and (b). But retained earnings since acquisition are not reflected anywhere in the parent's accounts,[4] because they are

---

[4] This is not the case if the parent employs the equity method in accounting for its investment prior to consolidation. In that case its share of the subsidiary's retained earnings since acquisition is already recorded in the parent's retained earnings.

TABLE 14-4

Account Titles	Parent	Subsidiary	Eliminations Dr.	Eliminations Cr.	Consolidation
Cash.....................	$16,000	$ 6,000			$22,000
Accounts receivable.........	6,000	3,000		(d) $ 1,500	7,500
Other assets...............	27,000	9,000		(e) 900	35,100
Investment in S...........	9,000	. . .		(a) 9,000	. . .
Excess cost over book value..	. . .	. . .	(a) $ 1,000		1,000
	$58,000	$18,000			$65,000
Accounts payable...........	$18,000	$ 4,000	(d) 1,500		$20,500
Capital stock—P...........	20,000				20,000
Capital stock—S..........		7,000	(a) 5,600		
			(b) 1,400		
Retained earnings—P.......	20,000		(e) 900	(c) 3,200	22,300
Retained earnings—S......		7,000	(a) 2,400		
			(b) 600		
			(c) 4,000		
Minority interest..........	. . .	. . .		(b) 2,000	2,800
				(c) 800	
	$58,000	$18,000	$17,400	$17,400	$65,600

subsequent to the investment being made and consequently should appear on the consolidated position statement—divided, of course, between majority (parent company) and minority interests. Eighty percent of the subsidiary's earnings since acquisition inures to the ultimate benefit of the parent company. The remaining 20 percent represents the portion of earnings applicable to the minority stockholders. Elimination (c) apportions the $4,000 increase in retained earnings since acquisition to the respective ownership interests. Consolidated retained earnings represent the retained earnings of the parent plus the parent's share of the subsidiary's retained earnings since acquisition.[5]

Other Intercompany Relationships. Two other common eliminations are illustrated in Table 14-4. One involves intercompany receivables and payables. The second concerns the intercompany sale of assets which have not been resold to outsiders. Let us consider the first situation. Whenever one company owes another company, either on a short- or long-term basis, and the two are to be consolidated, the resulting overlapping asset and liability should be eliminated. The receivable does not represent an asset to the consolidated entity; it is not an amount owed by an outsider. Neither does the payable represent an amount owed to an outside group. In our example we assume that as a result of intercompany transactions

[5] The amount initially recognized as excess cost over book value also must be amortized as an expense in the consolidation process according to the APB's *Opinion No. 17* on intangibles. The amortization entry causes a reduction in the excess and in consolidated retained earnings.

the subsidiary owes the parent company $1,500 on open account. Elimination (d) reduces the receivables and payables of the consolidated entity accordingly.

The second situation, that of intercompany sales of assets, is not quite so simple. If the assets are sold at cost, no problem arises. Similarly, if the assets are sold from one company to another and then resold to outsiders, no position statement problems arise since the assets no longer appear in the accounts of any member of the consolidation. The problem occurs only when assets are sold by the parent to the subsidiary, or vice versa, at a gain or loss, and the assets are not resold to outsiders.

If by consolidating we are to treat the two companies as if they were one, then no gain or loss should be recorded on the intercompany transfer of assets that are not resold to outsiders. For example, assume that the parent sells to the subsidiary for $5,000 land which cost the parent $4,100. From the parent's point of view as a separate entity, a profit of $900 is realized. Also, from the subsidiary company's perspective, an asset is purchased which cost $5,000. However, from the viewpoint of the consolidated entity the asset has simply gone from one member of the family to another. Consequently, elimination (e) is necessary to subtract $900 from other assets. The cost of the land to the consolidated entity is only $4,100 and will be overstated unless the elimination is made. The corresponding elimination is from the parent's retained earnings, where the gain or profit on the sale has been reflected. Consolidated companies can realize gains or losses only upon sales to outsiders.

Consolidated Income Statement

A consolidated position statement reports only the consolidated assets and equities, eliminating any which represent existing relationships between the individual companies. In like manner, the income statement should report only revenues and expenses arising out of transactions with outsiders during the period. If there are no intercompany transactions—sales, dividend payments, interest payments—the consolidated procedure is a simple combination of the individual income statements.

Intercompany Revenues and Expenses. The difficulties arise when there are intercompany transactions to be eliminated. The most frequent of these is the intercompany sale. Take the case of a wholly owned subsidiary which sells 100 percent of its product to the parent company. The parent resells to outsiders all that it buys from the subsidiary (none is left in ending inventory) and makes no sales other than what it buys from the subsidiary and resells. Also assume that the parent rents a warehouse from the subsidiary for $5,000 a year. The individual income statements, the necessary eliminations, and the resultant consolidated income statement are presented in Table 14–5. Notice that the net income figures have been in-

TABLE 14–5

Account Titles	Parent	Subsidiary	Eliminations Dr.	Cr.	Consolidation
Sales...............	$100,000	$80,000	(a) $80,000		$100,000
Other revenue..........	...	5,000	(b) 5,000		...
	$100,000	$85,000			$100,000
Cost of sales...........	$ 80,000	$50,000		(a) $80,000	$ 50,000
Other expenses.........	10,000	20,000		(b) 5,000	25,000
Net income............	10,000	15,000			25,000
	$100,000	$85,000	$85,000	$85,000	$100,000

cluded along with the expenses to enable us to take advantage of the self-balancing mechanism of the work sheet.

The subsidiary sells goods costing $50,000 to the parent for $80,000. The parent, in turn, resells them to outside parties for $100,000. The subsidiary has a gross margin of $30,000 on the goods, and the parent a gross margin of $20,000. If the two companies are one, sales to outsiders are only the $100,000 revenue recorded by the parent, cost of sales is only the $50,000 incurred by the subsidiary, and the consolidated gross margin is $50,000. In other words, in this case the income figures are stated correctly; only the revenues and expenses are misstated from the viewpoint of the consolidated entity. Elimination (a) removes the double-counting effect of the intercompany purchase and sale. From a consolidated viewpoint, these are merely interfirm transfers, not revenue and expense items. No elimination is necessary in profits. Since all goods were eventually resold to outsiders, all profits have been realized.

Elimination (b) corrects for the overstatement of rent revenue and rent expense from a consolidated standpoint. Revenues and expenses cannot arise from dealing with oneself. Again, no adjustment is necessary in consolidated net income. The increase in parent income caused by elimination of $5,000 of its rent expense is offset by a decrease in subsidiary net income caused by elimination of its rent revenue of like amount.

Partial Intercompany Sales and Incomplete Reselling. A more complicated case arises when we assume that the parent company does not resell all it buys from the subsidiary and that the latter also makes some sales directly to outsiders. In addition, let us relax our assumptions that the parent has no additional sales of its own and that the subsidiary is wholly owned. Suppose that the subsidiary, which is only 90 percent owned by the parent, sells only 50 percent of its products to the parent and the other 50 percent directly to outsiders. The parent resells 80 percent of what it purchased from the subsidiary, as well as some merchandise purchased

TABLE 14–6

Account Titles	Parent	Subsidiary	Eliminations Dr.	Eliminations Cr.	Consolidated
Sales..........................	$200,000	$80,000	(a) $40,000		$240,000
Other revenue................	...	5,000	(b) 5,000		...
	$200,000	$85,000			$240,000
Cost of sales.................	$150,000	$50,000	(c) 3,000	(a) $40,000	$163,000
Other expenses..............	30,000	20,000		(b) 5,000	45,000
Net income..................	20,000	15,000		(d) 700	
				(c) 3,000	31,300
Minority interest in net income..	...	...	(d) 700		700
	$200,000	$85,000	$48,700	$48,700	$240,000

from other sources. The resultant income statements for this example and the consolidation procedures are summarized in Table 14–6.

The total consolidated revenues are only $240,000 ($200,000 sold to outsiders by the parent and $40,000 sold to outside parties directly by the subsidiary). Similarly, from the viewpoint of the consolidated entity, cost of sales is $163,000, consisting of three elements: (1) $118,000 cost of goods purchased by the parent from outsiders and sold to outsiders (the parent company's reported cost of sales of $150,000 includes $32,000 which is bought from the subsidiary and resold); (2) $25,000 cost of goods purchased by the subsidiary and sold directly to outside parties; and (3) $20,000 cost of goods purchased by the subsidiary, transferred to the parent, and sold by it (80 percent of the other $25,000 cost of sales reported by the subsidiary; the rest resides in the parent company's ending inventory).

The eliminations in Table 14–6 achieve the desired results. Item (a) eliminates 50 percent of the subsidiary's sales ($40,000) because they are not made to outsiders. This same $40,000 was included among the parent company's purchases and thus increased its cost of sales (beginning inventory + purchases − ending inventory = cost of goods sold), although the purchases were not made from persons outside the consolidated family. Elimination (b) is the same as in the previous example; it corrects the overlapping revenue and expense associated with rental of the warehouse.

Item (c) eliminates the impact on income of the ending inventory of the parent which was acquired from the subsidiary. Twenty percent, or $8,000, of the parent's purchases from the subsidiary is on its books in the form of ending inventory. This inventory actually represents a consolidated cost of only $5,000 (the subsidiary's gross margin percentage is 37.5 percent). Likewise, $3,000 ($8,000 × 37.5%) of the subsidiary's gross margin is unrealized, because the merchandise on which it was earned has not been resold to outsiders. This unrealized subsidiary profit is eliminated by part of (c).[6] The other part reflects the impact of the overstated ending inventory on cost of sales. Because the ending inventory is overstated by the $3,000 profit element, cost of sales is correspondingly understated.

Notice that the only information needed to make the eliminations so far is the subsidiary sales made to the parent and the goods purchased from the subsidiary left in the parent's inventory at the year-end. The percentage of ownership of the subsidiary by the parent does not influence the elimination entries.[7] However, the existence of a minority interest does have an impact on the distribution or division of the consolidated income. The income of the subsidiary adjusted for unrealized income arising from intercompany transactions is $7,000 ($15,000 − $5,000 rent revenue − $3,000 intercompany gain on unsold inventory). Elimination (d) merely segregates 10 percent of that as being applicable to the minority interest.[8]

The figures in the last column of Table 14–6, when rearranged in proper form, make up the consolidated income statement. Both the net income of the consolidated entity and the net income applicable to the stockholders of the parent company are shown; the minority's interest is treated as a distribution of income. Sometimes in published financial statements the minority's interest is buried among the expenses. In theory,

TABLE 14–7

PARENT COMPANY
Consolidated Income Statement
For the Year 19__

Sales........................		$240,000
Less expenses:		
Cost of sales.............	$163,000	
Other expenses............	45,000	208,000
Consolidated net income.......		$ 32,000
Less minority interest......		700
Net Income.................		$ 31,300

[6] The reader may recall that a corresponding elimination is made on the consolidated position statement, crediting Inventory for $3,000 for the overstatement of its true cost from the consolidated viewpoint and debiting the subsidiary's Retained Earnings account for the unrealized intercompany profit. Of course, balances in the Retained Earnings account on the position statement come from figures on income statements. Elimination (c) is simply the same one made to retained earnings on the position statement being made to profits on the income statement.

[7] Some authors advocate eliminating only the majority interest in the unrealized earnings of the subsidiary, arguing that from the viewpoint of the minority stockholders all profits are realized whether earned on sales to outsiders or to the parent company. True as this may be, the consolidated statements are prepared for the parent company stockholders, not the minority stockholders. For consistency with the switch in entity from individual companies to a single combined company, the total unrealized earnings of the subsidiary must be eliminated.

[8] Notice again that the $700 is the minority's interest in the income of the consolidated entity, not its interest in the income of the subsidiary as a separate legal entity. Only the latter figure is of interest to the minority shareholders.

though, it is the income of the consolidated entity, including the interests of all stockholders, which best measures overall results of operations and which should be related to total assets in the calculation of a return on investment. The formal statement appears in Table 14–7.

RECORDING BUSINESS COMBINATIONS

As discussed earlier, a business combination occurs when two or more businesses come together as a single entity to carry on the activities previously conducted by the separate entities. Usually one company acquires the outstanding stock of another company, giving up cash or issuing various types of securities. If the two companies are merged, the acquired company ceases to exist as a separate legal entity, although it often operates intact as a division of the combined company.

When the acquisition is made for cash, the situation is analogous to a lump-sum purchase of assets (discussed in Chapter Seven). The cost assigned to the acquired shares is the amount of cash paid out. This amount in turn is allocated to the individual net assets—tangible and intangible—when the acquired company's shares are retired and its net assets are combined with those of the acquirer. For example, Company A buys all the outstanding stock of Company B for $125,000 with the intent to merge the two companies. Company B has tangible assets with a book value of $115,000 and a fair market value of $145,000; its liabilities are $40,000. The entries are:

```
Investment in Company B Stock........... 125,000
     Cash................................           125,000
     To record purchase of stock.
Tangible Assets (recorded in detail at
     their fair market value).............. 145,000
Goodwill................................  20,000
     Liabilities........................            40,000
     Investment in Company B Stock.......           125,000
     To record the retirement of Company B
     stock and the merging of its assets
     and liabilities into A.
```

In brief, the only valuation problem is one of allocating the total cash consideration among the net assets acquired.

In the last decade or so, most business combinations have been accomplished through an exchange of shares rather than by an outright purchase for cash. The acquiring company offers to issue a certain number of its shares in exchange for the shares of the acquired company. Under most state laws, if a required percentage of each firm's stockholders agrees to the proposal, the exchange is binding and the firms are legally merged.

Two methods of accounting for business combinations effected through an exchange of shares are used in accounting practice. They are called *purchase* and *pooling of interests*. Both are strongly supported by different groups of accountants and businessmen. The choice between these two accounting procedures may significantly affect the financial statements, since they value the net assets acquired and record the increase in stockholders' equity very differently.

Illustrative Data

Let us use for our basic data the following two companies. Jeckle, Inc., has worked out an arrangement for merging with Hyde Company. Jeckle, Inc., issues 15,000 shares of its common stock to the owners of Hyde Company in exchange for the 10,000 outstanding shares of that company. Jeckle promptly retires the Hyde shares, thereby liquidating and dissolving it as a separate corporation and formally consummating the merger.

Position statements for each of the corporations immediately prior to the merger are given in Table 14–8. The Hyde Company's inventory of

TABLE 14–8
(in thousands)

	Jeckle, Inc.	Hyde Co.
Cash..	$ 200	$ 10
Accounts receivable....................	1,400	75
Inventory..............................	2,830	90
Land..................................	550	150
Buildings and equipment (net)........	6,020	350
Total Assets....................	$11,000	$675
Accounts payable......................	$ 2,800	$145
Capital stock—$10 par...............	2,000	100
Paid-in capital......................	1,700	70
Retained earnings....................	4,500	360
Total Equities..................	$11,000	$675
Shares outstanding (thousands).......	200	10
Market value per share (not in thousands)...............	$ 50	Not available

$90,000 is on a Lifo basis; its current replacement cost is approximately $130,000. A recent appraisal for insurance purposes of its buildings and equipment indicates a current value of about $440,000. The Hyde Company possesses a very fine market reputation. Its brand names are well known, and the company is noted for turning out a quality product. In fact, one of the reasons that Jeckle, Inc., wishes to acquire Hyde Company is to obtain the benefits from this reputation.

Purchase

Although we frequently describe this type of transaction as a "purchase with stock," the transaction actually involves the receipt of a whole group of noncash assets and the issuance of shares of stock. The assets are recorded at their fair market value (their current acquisition cost), including any intangible assets being acquired, and the contributed capital accounts of the acquiring company are credited. The final effect of the entries made by Jeckle is summarized as follows:[9]

```
Cash.....................................    10,000
Accounts Receivable.....................    75,000
Inventory...............................   130,000
Land....................................   150,000
Buildings and Equipment.................   440,000
Goodwill................................    90,000
    Accounts Payable....................              145,000
    Capital Stock—$10 Par...............              150,000
    Paid-In Capital.....................              600,000
```

It is reasonable to assume that the negotiations between the two companies are based on an equal exchange of values—the value of the net assets received by Jeckle and the value of the stock issued by it. The fair market value can be measured either by an appraisal of the individual assets or by a valuation of the shares of stock given up in exchange, whichever can be more objectively determined. Because of the likely existence of an intangible asset, goodwill, in the above entry, the market value of the shares being issued is assumed to provide a close approximation to the real substance of the transaction. Jeckle, Inc., has issued shares with a market value of $750,000 (15,000 shares at $50) and therefore values the net assets received at $750,000. Each individual asset is stated at its fair market value, and the excess of $90,000 is assigned to Goodwill. The $750,000 increase in contributed capital is recorded in two accounts: the par value of the shares (15,000 × $10) in the Capital Stock account and the excess over par value in a separate Paid-In Capital account.

Evaluation of Purchase. The purchase approach views a business combination, however consummated, as primarily an acquisition of one company's assets by another company. The acquiring entity is the dominant party. From its perspective the acquisition of assets is the result of a bargained exchange. Consequently, the valuation of the assets should not differ from that under a cash purchase merely because shares of stock are the consideration exchanged. Similarly, the effect on stockholders' equity should not vary simply because noncash assets rather than cash are received upon issuance of the stock.

The objections to accounting for business combinations as purchases center on two aspects of the valuation problem. First, some opponents contend that the determination of the values being exchanged is not as clearly evident as the above example might imply. It is difficult to ascertain the fair market value of a group of assets in a going concern, and reliance on the market value of stock places undue emphasis on the vagaries of the

---

[9] We have skipped the intermediate steps of recording the investment in shares and then formally retiring them.

stock market. Second, even if values are reasonably determinable the purchase method merges unlike asset values. The tangible assets of the acquiring corporation are not revalued to current cost. The goodwill of the acquired company is recognized, but any excess value of the acquiring corporation as a going concern goes unrecorded.

Pooling of Interests

An alternative method widely used in handling mergers involves a simple combining of assets and equities. Under pooling of interests the assets of the acquired firm are carried over to the acquiring firm at their book values. Likewise, the stockholders' equity amounts of the two firms are combined, including the respective retained earnings. The entry to record the combination under pooling of interests is:

Cash.................................	10,000	
Accounts Receivable...................	75,000	
Inventory.............................	90,000	
Land.................................	150,000	
Buildings and Equipment...............	350,000	
Accounts Payable...................		145,000
Capital Stock—$10 Par.............		150,000
Paid-In Capital...................		20,000
Retained Earnings.................		360,000

Pooling of interests assumes a fusion or marriage of the two companies instead of an acquisition. The merged company is seen to be little different from the sum of the two companies prior to the merger. Total assets and stockholders' equity after the merger are the sums of the assets and stockholders' equity of each of the companies prior to the merger. And the shareholders are the same, as the acquired company shareholders are now shareholders in the acquiring company. Notice that the only adjustment made is to reflect the par value of the shares issued by the acquiring firm. Since the additional contributed capital is now represented by 15,000 shares of Jeckle, Inc., stock with a total par value of $150,000, instead of 10,000 shares of Hyde Company stock with a total par value of $100,000, $50,000 of the $70,000 in the Paid-In Capital account of Hyde has to be reclassified to make legal capital conform to the number of shares issued.[10]

Evaluation of Pooling. The major justification for the pooling of interests approach is the contention that nothing of substance has occurred in the combination necessitating a new basis of accountability for the assets. The combined entity is nothing more than a combination of the two businesses formerly conducted separately. The assets and stockholders' interests remain the same with the exception that they are now together instead of separate. Useful comparisons with past periods can be

---

[10] If there were insufficient paid-in capital, then retained earnings would be reduced also. But outside of this minor legal adjustment, pooling basically involves a simple combining of owners' equity accounts.

made, then, if the accounting for the merged company is only a continuation of the accounts of the two companies combined.[11]

The conceptual arguments against pooling tend to be the same as those in favor of the purchase approach. First, the underlying rationale of pooling—i.e., that two groups of stockholders owning businesses are coming together to operate henceforth as equal partners—just does not apply to most business combinations. There is almost always a clearly identifiable acquiring company which is taking over the business of another company. One party to the merger is a continuing entity which exercises dominant control after the merger. Acquisition of another company is simply an alternative means of growth, and the accounting should be consistent with that resulting from internal expansion. Second, something of substance does occur in most combinations. Two independent parties bargain at arm's length to reach agreement on an exchange of values. To record the transfer of assets at book value seems to fly in the face of the real substance of the transaction and agreement between the parties.

Impact on the Financial Statements

The purchase-pooling controversy is an extremely important one because of the impact that the alternative accounting procedures have on the financial statements. The initial effect can be seen in our example. Position statements after the merger under the two approaches are presented in Table 14–9. In most instances pooling of interests gives an understated balance sheet relative to the purchase approach.

TABLE 14–9

(in thousands)

	Purchase	Pooling
Cash..........................	$ 210	$ 210
Accounts receivable...........	1,475	1,475
Inventory.....................	2,960	2,920
Land..........................	700	700
Buildings and equipment.......	6,460	6,370
Goodwill......................	90	. . .
Total Assets.............	$11,895	$11,675
Accounts payable..............	$ 2,945	$ 2,945
Capital stock—$10 par.........	2,150	2,150
Paid-in capital...............	2,300	1,720
Retained earnings.............	4,500	4,860
Total Equities...........	$11,895	$11,675
Shares outstanding (thousands)..	215	215

[11] Pooling also draws practical support from the fact that most exchanges of stock in conjunction with a merger are treated as tax-free exchanges under the income tax law. Consequently, for tax purposes the old asset values must be carried over.

Perhaps even more important is the impact on measurement of future income. Under the purchase approach, with plant assets recorded at their actual current market values instead of book values, subsequent depreciation charges are higher. Assume for the sake of illustration that the Hyde Company plant assets have a remaining useful life of 10 years. Straight-line depreciation expense will be $44,000 ($440,000/10 years) if the combination is accounted for as a purchase, but only $35,000 ($350,000/10 years) if it is accounted for as a pooling. Moreover, in accordance with APB *Opinion No. 17* the acquiring company must also amortize the goodwill recognized in the purchase, thus further reducing post-merger earnings.[12] So pooling of interests gives greater income and lower assets, a double infusion to return on investment. Theoretical reasons aside, one can understand why acquisition-minded companies favor pooling.

Purchase-Pooling Controversy and the Entity Concept

Clearly the nature of the accounting entity lies at the heart of this controversy. Purchase accounting presumes that the relevant entity is the acquiring company and that all recording should be viewed from its perspective. Pooling of interests asserts that the combination creates no new entity, merely a continuation of two old entities. Once the entity-identification issue is resolved, many of the other arguments fall into perspective.

For instance, if the relevant entity is the acquiring company, then the transfer of assets from one corporate entity to another should serve as the basis for a new accountability for the assets. The problems mentioned earlier concerning the revaluation of assets and the recognition of goodwill of the acquired company become only problems of conventional financial accounting and not ones unique to business combinations. In any acquisition of new assets—cash purchase or otherwise—the new assets are recorded on the entity's books at the current acquisition costs, even though other assets are valued at past purchase prices. Purchased goodwill is a fact, and its cost is part of the transaction entered into by the entity. Internally developed goodwill goes unrecognized in acquisitions for cash as well. Under the entity concept, transactions between the entity and outside parties give rise to recordable events that appear on the financial statements.

When viewed from the perspective of the acquiring entity, a merger under pooling of interests with an unrelated entity implies that a firm can generate retained earnings simply by acquiring another business. One firm can buy another's assets and can assume its liabilities, but it cannot generate retained earnings in a capital-raising transaction. Retained earnings bear

---

[12] If the merger were a tax-free exchange, neither the amortization of goodwill nor the depreciation on amounts in excess of book values would be deductible for tax purposes. The burden on after-tax earnings would therefore be almost double.

significance only to the entity which produced the income. Thus, if we accept the entity interpretation of the purchase approach, the combination of owners' equity accounts under poolings of interest is nonsensical.

Pooling applies in concept only when there is truly a mutual exchange of risks and control by relatively equal parties with the intention of conducting *together* a combined business. Similarity in size, continuity of former ownership interests, and continuation of existing operations have all been suggested in the past as evidence of a pooling of interests. But the real issue centers on who exercises control over the acquired assets and the policies that govern their use. Except in rare instances, a single identifiable company has acquired this control over the assets of another firm through an arm's-length bargain and exchange of values. Hence, purchase accounting comes closer to reflecting the nature of most business combinations.

Accounting Principles Board Opinions

The accounting profession long has wrestled with the purchase-pooling controversy. Authoritative pronouncements, beginning in 1950, attempted to suggest criteria for distinguishing between purchases and poolings of interests. The criteria emphasized as requisite for pooling were continuity of ownership interest and operations as well as other factors that would tend to imply continuity—relative size, proportional voting rights, continuity of management, etc.; and pooling was applicable only to exchanges of common stock.

The decades of the 1950s and 1960s saw these criteria gradually erode, however. The individual criteria were to be interpreted as guidelines and not necessarily as determinative standards. Often they were vague and loosely construed. As a result businesses could usually find one or more criteria which would justify handling the combination as a pooling. At the same time exchanges that once were common stock for common stock now involved preferred stock, bonds, notes, cash, stock warrants, contingent issues of stock, and various other exotic combinations. The net result was that a business could account for a combination in almost any manner it wished. Some evidence exists to suggest that one prevalent criterion used in making the choice was the relationship of book values and market values. When book values were less than market values, pooling was used; when book values exceeded market values (not a common occurrence), purchase was used.

In the late 1960s the Accounting Principles Board set forth to remedy the "abuses" of pooling of interests.[13] Two research studies were prepared

---

[13] The "abuses" fell into three categories: (1) the use of pooling where its rationale was obviously lacking so as to allow low asset values to be recorded and future earnings to be boosted as much as possible; (2) the creation of "instant earnings" by issuance of stock valued significantly higher than the book value of the acquired

dealing with business combinations and the related subject of goodwill.[14] Both essentially recommended the abolition of pooling of interests accounting. That conclusion was strongly opposed by many elements of the financial and business community. The APB then issued a compromise opinion. Both purchase and pooling are allowed, but not as alternatives. Business combinations meeting rather specific criteria can be accounted for as poolings of interest; all other combinations are to be handled as purchases.[15] Among the criteria are the following: (1) the combination has to result from a single transaction completed within one year between companies that have been independent for at least two years, (2) only voting common stock can be issued in exchange for substantially all (90 percent) of the voting common stock of the acquired company, (3) there can be no major realignment of voting interests, and (4) there can be no retirement of voting stock or disposition of assets after the combination (except to eliminate duplicate assets).

SUMMARY

We talk about three aspects of intercorporate relationships in this chapter. They all concern the accounting problems when one firm acquires a substantial stock holding in another company. If a subsidiary company is to be dissolved and merged, then whether to record the acquisition as a purchase or a pooling of interests is the relevant accounting question. If the subsidiary remains as a separate legal entity, the decision must be made whether to prepare a consolidated statement or to report it as an investment in unconsolidated subsidiaries. The procedures are founded on one underlying objective   to present the situation as if the companies were a single company. Finally, if the subsidiary remains unconsolidated, should it be accounted for by the cost or equity method?

To keep the discussion manageable, we treat these aspects independently. They may, however, exist together. For example, a company may use the equity method for handling the investment in a subsidiary and yet still include it in a consolidated statement. Such a practice would require some modification of the eliminations but would not change the underlying concepts or procedures of consolidated statements.

---

assets, suppression of this increased value by recording under a pooling, sale of some of the acquired assets at their current values after the merger, and inclusion of the profit in income; and (3) retroactive poolings in which companies combined current figures and restated past figures to reflect the merger, even if it occurred after the end of the accounting period.

[14] Arthur R. Wyatt, *A Critical Study of Accounting for Business Combinations*, Accounting Research Study No. 5 (New York: AICPA, 1963); and George R. Catlett and Norman O. Olson, *Accounting for Goodwill*, Accounting Research Study No. 10 (New York: AICPA, 1968).

[15] *Business Combinations, Opinion of the Accounting Principles Board No. 16* (New York: AICPA, August 1970), pp. 295–304.

Similarly, we imply that purchase versus pooling concerns legally merged subsidiaries. This is not always the case. Sometimes a firm will record the acquisition of another company as a pooling of interests but not actually liquidate it. Instead, it will include it as a consolidated subsidiary. The valuation of assets and the entries to stockholders' equity are the same, however, as for a merger. The investment is recorded at the book value of the net assets of the acquired company, and credits are made to both the contributed capital and the retained earnings accounts. In the consolidation process the investment is eliminated, and the net assets of the subsidiary are counted instead. The consolidated effect is the same as under a pooling with a legally merged subsidiary.

All of these problems and complexities involve the entity concept. The direct consequences of the entity concept are clear—i.e., we treat the entity as separate and distinct from groups associated with it. However, the antecedent problems of defining *what* the accounting entity should be, deciding when it starts and ceases, and identifying the relevant entity in given situations are still present.

SUGGESTIONS FOR FURTHER READING

American Institute of Certified Public Accountants. *Accounting Principles*, Vol. 2: "Consolidated Financial Statements," *Accounting Research Bulletin No. 51*, pp. 6091–96. Chicago: Commerce Clearing House, Inc., 1968.

Briloff, Abraham. "Dirty Pooling," *Accounting Review*, Vol. 42 (July 1967), pp. 489–96.

Catlett, George R., and Olson, Norman O. "Accounting for Goodwill," *Accounting Research Study No. 10*. New York: AICPA, 1968.

Hendrickson, H. S. "Some Comments on 'Dirty Pooling'," *Accounting Review*, Vol. 43 (April 1968), pp. 363–66.

Jaenicke, Henry R. "Management's Choice to Purchase or Pool," *Accounting Review*, Vol. 37 (October 1962), pp. 758–65.

Lauver, R. C. "The Case for Poolings," *Accounting Review*, Vol. 41 (January 1966), pp. 65–74.

Sapienza, S. R. "The Divided House of Consolidations," *Accounting Review*, Vol. 35 (July 1960), pp. 503–10.

Wyatt, Arthur R. "A Critical Study of Accounting for Business Combinations," *Accounting Research Study No. 5*. New York: AICPA, 1963.

QUESTIONS AND PROBLEMS

14-1.   On January 1, 1970, the DuPant Corporation acquired 50 percent of the outstanding stock of General Matters, a newly organized corporation, for a cost of $2 million.

On January 1, 1972, DuPant invested another $1.3 million for an additional 30 percent of the outstanding stock of General Matters. The following table gives the results of General Matters' operations in the years 1970–73:

	Net Income Reported	Dividends Declared and Paid
1970	$150,000	$100,000
1971	80,000	100,000
1972	30,000	20,000
1973	100,000	30,000

a) Prepare journal entries to record the original investment and subsequent events, assuming that the cost method of accounting for unconsolidated subsidiaries is to be used.

b) Repeat part (*a*), assuming that equity method is used.

c) On December 31, 1971 DuPant describes its Investment account under part (*b*) as being recorded at the underlying book value or equity in the subsidiary's assets. Show that this is true. Is the same description appropriate on December 31, 1973? Explain.

14–2. The following represent the ledger account balances of the Washington Company and its subsidiary, the Missouri Company, as of December 31, 1971 (in thousands):

	Washington	Missouri
Cash	$ 40	$ 6
Accounts receivable	58	13
Inventories	70	50
Investment in Missouri stock	100	...
Land	45	22
Plant	150	50
Accumulated depreciation	(40)	(8)
	$423	$133
Accounts payable	$ 82	$ 24
Capital stock	250	90
Retained earnings	91	19
	$423	$133

The Washington Company acquired 90 percent of the stock of the Missouri Company on January 1, 1971, for $100,000 cash. The owners' equity accounts of Missouri on that date were: capital stock, $90,000; retained earnings, $12,000.

During the year the Missouri Company sold merchandise costing $6,000 to the Washington Company for $7,500. The merchandise was still in the latter's inventory on December 31, 1971. The Washington Company still owed the Missouri Company $1,000 in connection with this purchase.

Also, during the year, the Washington Company sold to the Missouri Company a piece of land for $5,000 cash which had been carried on the books of Washington at $9,000.

a) Prepare a consolidated position statement in good form for the two companies.

b) If Washington Company had used the equity method of accounting for its investment in Missouri, rather than the cost method, how would the consolidated process and the consolidated balance sheet differ? Explain.

14–3. On September 30, 1970 Mississippi Corporation exchanged 8,000 shares of its $5 par common stock for all of the outstanding stock (50,000 shares, par value $2) of Missouri, Inc. At that time, Mississippi stock was selling at a market price of $50 per share. Missouri Corporation's stock was not widely traded; the last sale of its shares in September, 1970 was at a price of $7 per share. After the exchange of shares, Missouri was formally merged into Mississippi and became an operating division. Balance sheets drawn up for the two corporations before the merger showed the following:

	Mississippi	Missouri
Assets...................................	$1,300,000	$290,000
Equities:		
Liabilities......................	$ 300,000	$ 40,000
Common stock—par................	200,000	100,000
Common stock—excess over par....	300,000	70,000
Retained earnings................	500,000	80,000
	$1,300,000	$290,000

Earnings for the two companies separately for 1970 were:

	Mississippi	Missouri
January 1–September 30..............	$140,000	$30,000
October 1–December 31..............	30,000	5,000
	$170,000	$35,000

The market value of Missouri's noncurrent assets are $60,000 above book value. These noncurrent assets have a remaining life of 5 years as of the date of the merger. Any goodwill recognized should be amortized over 15 years.

Fill in the blanks in the following table. Show calculations where necessary.

	If Acquisitions Were Recorded As:	
	Purchase	*Pooling of Interest*
Total assets, September 30..............		
Goodwill, September 30................		
Retained earnings, September 30.........		
Common stock—par, September 30......		
Common stock—excess over par.........		
Net income for all of 1970..............		
Total assets, December 31*.............		
Goodwill, December 31..............		
Retained earnings, December 31.........		

* Assume no change in liabilities.

14–4. On January 1, 1972 the Able Company acquired 80 percent of the common stock of the Baker Company for $150,000. The stockholders' equity of Baker on that date showed:

Common stock—par............	$100,000
Common stock—excess.........	50,000
Retained earnings.............	37,500
	$187,500

During the year, the Baker Company earned $25,000 of net income and paid cash dividends of $15,000. The Able Company reported net income of $80,000 (including dividend income) and paid dividends of $42,000. The unconsolidated stockholders' equity of the Able Company on December 31, 1972, was:

Common stock—par..................	$300,000
Common stock—excess over par.........	180,000
Retained earnings.....................	320,000
	$800,000

a) Determine the consolidated net income and dividends of the Able Company and the subsidiary.

b) Prepare the consolidated stockholders' equity section of the position statement as of December 31, 1972.

14–5. The Signal Companies, Inc. owns substantial interests in a number of subsidiaries. Most of them are included in the consolidated statements, but a few are shown separately under an asset category called "Investments and long-term receivables." These interests are (in thousands):

Occidental Petroleum Corporation (at cost).......	76,500
Equity in wholly owned unconsolidated subsidiaries:	
Mack Financial Corporation....................	26,566
Signal Equities Company......................	15,097
Golden West Broadcasters (at cost plus equity in earnings since acquisition)....................	25,513
American President Lines, Ltd. (at cost)........	11,699
Other investments (principally at cost) and long-term receivables.........................	46,110
Total investments and long-term receivables......	$201,485

Note 3 to the statements describes the investments in greater detail:

The investment in Occidental Petroleum Corporation represents 500,000 shares of $4.00 cumulative convertible preferred stock (convertible into approximately 1,471,800 shares of common stock) and $30,000,000 of 6½% promissory notes received on the sale of the European marketing and refining operations. An additional $10,000,000 of such notes are included in current assets. In 1968, Signal received income of approximately $4,476,000 from this investment, which amount is included in dividends and interest in the statement of consolidated income.

Income concerning other significant investments as of December 31, 1968 and for the year then ended is as follows (dollar amounts in thousands):

a) How much income related to these investments was included in the 1968 consolidated statement of income?

	Approximate Ownership	Equity in Net Assets	Equity in Net income	Dividends Received
Mack Financial Corp. (1)...............	100%	$26,566.0	$1,969 (4)	...
Signal Equities Co. (1)...............	100	15,097.7	945 (4)	$ 37
Golden West Broadcasters (2).........;	50	6,549.0	600 (3,4)	954
American President Lines, Ltd. (at cost).........	48	44,500.0	3,417	

(1) Investment is carried at equity in net assets of the subsidiaries.
(2) Investment is carried at cost plus Signal's equity in the increase in net assets since the date of acqui-
    sition in July 1968. The excess of cost over equity in net assets, $18,964,000, is considered by manage-
    ment to have a continuing value (station licenses, etc.) and accordingly is not being amortized.
(3) Represents equity in income since date of acquisition in 1968.
(4) Included in equity in income of unconsolidated subsidiaries in the consolidated statement of income.

  b) Why are two wholly owned subsidiaries not included in the consolidated statement?

  c) Why is the investment in Mack Financial Corporation and Signal Equities Company described as being "at equity in net assets" while the investment in Golden West Broadcasters is described as "at cost plus equity in earnings since acquisition"? Are two different accounting methods being employed here? Explain.

  d) The equity method is sometimes described as a "one-line consolidation." Explain the basis for this statement. How would assets and income differ in total amount and in classification if a subsidiary is reported as an investment under the equity method rather than being consolidated?

  e) Why do you think the company uses the cost method for its investment in Occidental Petroleum Corporation and in American President Lines, Ltd.?

14–6. The consolidation policies of five companies are given below. Each statement has been taken from the firm's 1969 or 1970 annual report.

> Borg-Warner Corporation: The accompanying financial statements include all subsidiaries except South American subsidiaries, the investments in which are carried at cost, and B-W Acceptance Corporation, the investment in which is carried at the amount of the underlying net assets.

> W. T. Grant Company: The financial statements include the accounts of two wholly owned subsidiaries, W. T. Grant Financial Corporation and Jones & Presnell Studios, Inc. The Company carries its investment in Zeller's Limited (a 50.3% owned Canadian Subsidiary, cost $8,457,144) at equity and has included in net earnings its share of the increase in the undistributed equity of that company.

> Greyhound Corporation: Consolidated financial statements include all subsidiaries in which company owns 51% or greater equity. . . . Accounts of Greyhound Leasing and Financial Corporation and Consultants and Designers, Inc. are not included in the balance sheet but investment in the consolidated statements is carried at underlying equity.

> Pan American World Airways: The consolidated financial statements include two wholly-owned companies organized in 1968, one for overseas financing purposes and the other for overseas insurance purposes. International Hotels Corporation, an unconsolidated subsidiary, has 16 subsidiaries or branches operating outside the continental limits of the United States.

> Westinghouse Electric Corporation: The consolidated financial statements include all wholly owned subsidiaries except Westinghouse Credit Corporation. Majority owned subsidiaries

are not consolidated. Equity in the income of majority owned subsidiaries and Westinghouse Credit Corporation is included in the consolidated statements.

a) Comment on the consolidation policies of each of these companies. What criteria does each seem to be using in determining which subsidiaries to consolidate?

b) Do you see any differences among the companies? What factors might account for these differences?

14–7.   The following balances appeared in the ledger accounts of Rotton Lumber Company and Warped Wood, Inc. on December 31, 1972:

	Rotten Lumber	Warped Wood
Current assets......................	$ 65,000	$ 45,000
Investment in subsidiary...............	60,000	.....
Loans to subsidiary..................	8,000	.....
Land..............................	5,000	3,000
Plant assets (net)...................	137,000	105,000
	$275,000	$153,000
Current liabilities...................	$ 47,000	$ 28,000
Bonds payable......................	.....	12,000
Advances from parent................	.....	8,000
Capital stock—par..................	100,000	75,000
Capital stock—excess................	50,000	.....
Retained earnings...................	78,000	30,000
	$275,000	$153,000

You uncover the following facts:

1. Rotton Lumber acquired 80 percent of the capital stock of Warped Wood on January 1, 1972 for $60,000 cash. At this time the stockholders' equity of Warped Wood consisted of capital stock of $75,000 and retained earnings of $15,000.

2. Warped Wood issued its bonds at par during the year. On December 31, 1972, Rotton Lumber acquired $5,000 par value of these bonds on the open market at a cost of $6,000. Rotton Lumber shows the bonds under marketable securities in its current assets.

3. On December 31, 1972, Rotton Lumber sold equipment to Warped Wood for $8,000. This equipment had been carried in the accounts of Rotton Lumber at a cost of $15,000 less accumulated depreciation of $9,000.

a) Prepare a consolidated position statement for Rotton Lumber Company and subsidiary as of December 31, 1972.

b) What complications in preparing consolidated balance sheets and income statements will arise in future periods because of the transactions described above? Be explicit in describing the impact of each transaction on future consolidated statements.

14-8.   At the end of 1971, Alpha Company began negotiations to acquire the net assets and business of Beta Corporation. Condensed balance sheets of the two companies as of December 31, 1971 appear below:

	Alpha	Beta
Assets....................	$522,000	$212,000
Equities:		
Liabilities...............	$142,000	$107,000
Common stock—$10 par....	100,000	
Common stock—$1 par.....		15,000
Paid-in capital..........	177,000	60,000
Retained earnings........	103,000	30,000
	$522,000	$212,000

On January 1, 1972 Alpha issued 3,000 of previously unissued stock to stockholders of Beta in exchange for the 15,000 shares of Beta. The market price of Alpha Company shares was $40 per share. Beta became a wholly owned operating subsidiary. Income statements for the year 1972 for each of the corporations appear below:

	Alpha	Beta
Sales...........................	$200,000	$ 86,000
Cost of goods sold..............	(87,000)	(42,000)
Selling and general expense......	(44,000)	(19,000)
Net Income before Tax...........	$ 69,000	$ 25,000

a) Prepare the journal entry Alpha would make to record its investment, on the assumption that the acquisition is to be treated: (1) as a purchase; (2) as a pooling of interests.

b) Prepare a consolidated balance sheet as of January 1, 1972, on the assumption that the acquisition is treated: (1) as a purchase; (2) as a pooling of interests.

c) Prepare a consolidated income statement for 1972 under the assumption that the acquisition is treated: (1) as a purchase; (2) as a pooling of interests. There were no intercompany transactions during the year. Assume a tax rate of 40 percent. Any consolidated goodwill recognized should be amortized over 10 years.

14-9.   Brunswick Corporation listed the following account under the heading of "other assets" on its comparative position statement:

	12-31-68	12-31-67
Investment in fifty percent owned foreign affiliate, at cost plus equity in undistributed earnings (Note 1)......................	$2,002,000	$1,220,000

Its comparative income statement shows an income item of $782,000 in 1968 ($442,000 in 1967) labeled "equity in undistributed net earnings of fifty percent owned foreign affiliate (Note 1)." A condensed statement of Consolidated Retained Earnings presented the following information (in thousands):

	1968	1967
Balance at beginning of year, as previously reported..............	$ 77,086	$70,962
Equity in undistributed net earnings of fifty percent owned foreign affiliate (Note 1)...............	1,206	764
Balance at beginning of year, as restated........................	$ 78,292	$71,726
Net earnings for the year..........	26,756	6,566
Balance at end of year............	$105,048	$78,292

Note 1—PRINCIPLES OF CONSOLIDATION: The consolidated financial statements include the accounts of the Company and all its domestic and foreign subsidiaries.

Prior to 1968, the investment in a fifty percent owned foreign affiliate was carried at cost, and consolidated net earnings included only cash dividends received. In 1968, Brunswick adopted the equity method of accounting for this investment and included in consolidated net earnings its equity in the undistributed net earnings of this affiliate, in addition to the cash dividends received of $464,000 in 1968 and $222,000 in 1967. The accompanying consolidated financial statements for 1967 have been restated to reflect this change. As a result of this change, net earnings for the years 1968 and 1967 were increased by $782,000 and $442,000, respectively, and the balance of retained earnings as of January 1, 1967, was increased by $764,000 (representing accumulated undistributed net earnings of the affiliate since inception).

a) Evaluate the decision to change the accounting method for this affiliate. What factors may have influenced the decision?

b) Reconstruct the entries that were made during 1968 by Brunswick in connection with this investment. How much was Brunswick's *total* share of affiliate income in 1968? Where is this amount reflected on the income statement?

c) At what figure would the Investment account appear if the cost method were still being used? Show your derivation. What amount of income would Brunswick show if the cost method were still being used?

14–10. The following trial balances were prepared after completion of the examination of the December 31, 1964 financial statements of Adam Corporation and its subsidiaries, Seth Corporation and Cain Corporation.* The subsidiary investments are accounted for by the cost method.

The audit working papers provide the following additional information:

1. The Seth Corporation was formed by the Adam Corporation on January 1, 1964. To secure additional capital, 25 percent of the

* Problem adapted from AICPA May 1965 examination.

capital stock was sold at par value in the securities market. Adam purchased the remaining capital stock at par value for cash.

ADAM CORPORATION AND SUBSIDIARIES

Consolidated Statements Working Paper
Trial Balances at December 31, 1964
(in thousands)

	Adam	Seth	Cain
Debits:			
Cash	$ 82	$ 11	$ 27
Accounts receivable	104	41	143
Inventories	241	70	78
Investment in Seth Corporation	150	. . .	. . .
Investment in Cain Corporation	175	. . .	. . .
Investment, other	185	. . .	. . .
Fixed assets	375	58	99
Accumulated depreciation	(96)	(7)	(21)
Cost of sales	820	300	350
Operating expenses	60	35	40
Total	$2,096	$508	$716
Credits:			
Accounts payable	$ 46	$ 33	$ 24
Sales	960	275	570
Gain on sales of assets	9	. . .	. . .
Dividend income	18	. . .	. . .
Capital stock, $20 par value:			
Adam	500	. . .	. . .
Seth	. . .	200	. . .
Cain	. . .	. . .	100
Retained earnings:			
Adam	563	. . .	. . .
Cain			12
Appropriation for contingency	. . .	. . .	10
Total	$2,096	$508	$716

2. On July 1, 1964 Adam acquired from stockholders 4,000 shares of Cain Corporation capital stock for $175,000. A condensed trial balance for Cain Corporation at July 1, 1964 follows (in thousands):

	Debit	Credit
Current assets	$165	
Fixed assets (net)	60	
Current liabilities		$ 45
Capital stock, par value $20		100
Retained earnings		36
Sales		200
Cost of sales	140	
Operating expenses	16	
Total	$381	$381

3. The following intercompany sales of certain products were made in 1964 (dollars in thousands):

	Sales	Gross Profit on Sales	Included in Purchaser's Inventory, 12–31–64
Adam to Cain..........	$ 40	20%	$15
Seth to Cain............	30	10%	10
Cain to Adam..........	60	30%	20
Total................	$130		$45

4. On January 2, 1964 Adam Corporation sold a punch press to Seth Corporation. The machine was purchased on January 1, 1962 and was being depreciated by the straight-line method over a 10-year life. Seth Corporation computed depreciation by the same method, based on the remaining useful life. Details of the sale are as follows:

Cost of punch press................	$25,000
Accumulated depreciation............	5,000
Net book value....................	$20,000
Sales price.......................	24,000
Gain on sale......................	$ 4,000

5. Cash dividends were paid on the following dates in 1964:

	Adam	Cain
June 30......................	$22,000	$ 6,000
December 31.................	26,000	14,000
Total......................	$48,000	$20,000

6. Adam Corporation billed $6,000 to each subsidiary at year-end for executive services in 1964. The billing was treated as an operating expense to the subsidiaries and a reduction of operating expenses to Adam Corp. The invoices were paid in January 1965.

7. At year-end Cain Corporation appropriated $10,000 for a contingent loss in connection with a law suit that had been pending since 1962.

Prepare consolidated financial statements for Adam Corporation and its subsidiaries for the year ended December 31, 1964. The sales, costs, and expenses of the subsidiaries are to be included in the consolidation as though the subsidiaries had been acquired at the beginning of the year. You plan to deduct the current year's preacquisition earnings of Cain Corporation at the bottom of the consolidated income statement.

14–11. Kemo Corporation and Sabe Company had been considering the possibility of a merger of their business. As of May 1, 1972 the condensed balance sheets of the two firms were as follows:

	Kemo	Sabe
Assets...........................	$500,000	$320,000
Equities:		
Liabilities......................	$ 80,000	$100,000
Common stock, $10 par............	100,000	50,000
Excess over par.................	200,000	100,000
Retained earnings...............	120,000	70,000
	$500,000	$320,000

Both stocks sell in a very close range around $50 per share. An appraisal of the tangible assets of each company indicates that the fair market value of the tangible assets is $550,000 for Kemo and $340,000 for Sabe.

Two plans are under consideration. One calls for Kemo Corporation to issue 5,000 shares of its stock on a one for one basis in exchange for the 5,000 outstanding shares of Sabe Company. Sabe Company would be liquidated as a separate entity and formally merged into Kemo Corporation. The transaction would be treated as a purchase. The other plan calls for a new company called Kemosabe Corporation to be chartered. Its authorized capital would consist of 50,000 shares of $20 par value common stock. The new corporation would issue its shares on a one for one basis to the stockholders of the two existing companies in exchange for their stock. The two existing companies would be dissolved and their assets and liabilities transferred to the new corporation. The transaction is to be handled as a pooling of interests.

a) Prepare a position statement for Kemo Corporation after the merger under the first plan. Comment on the advantages and disadvantages of this approach.

b) Prepare a position statement for the new Kemosabe Corporation after the merger under the second plan. Comment on the advantages and disadvantages of this approach.

c) An accounting professor at a nearby university has suggested that if the second plan is followed, a "fair-value pooling" should be employed. Under his approach, the assets of both entities would be revalued and Kemosabe Corporation would start off afresh as a new economic entity. Prepare a position statement under this approach and evaluate the merits of his suggestion.

14–12. The following note was taken from the annual report of Kimberly-Clark Corporation for the year ended April 30, 1968:

The consolidated financial statements include the accounts of significant domestic and foreign subsidiaries more than 50% owned and controlled by Kimberly–Clark Corporation ("the Corporation") —such subsidiaries are referred to in these Notes as "consolidated subsidiaries." In addition, the Corporation uses the equity method of accounting with respect to foreign and domestic companies which are not consolidated but which are approximately 50% owned—such companies are referred to in these Notes as "equity companies." The consolidated financial statements include in consolidated net income the Corporation's share of the net income of equity companies, and the Corporation's investments in such companies are stated on the equity basis. . . . The Corporation's investments in companies which are neither consolidated subsidiaries nor equity companies are stated at cost and income from these companies is included in consolidated net income only as dividends are received. The basis of consolidation represents a change from prior years' practice when only those companies which were 66⅔% or more owned were included in consolidated statements, while investments in companies less than 66⅔% owned were stated at cost and consolidated net income included only dividends received from these companies.

For comparative purposes, the financial statements for the year ended April 30, 1967, have been restated to give effect to the new basis of consolidation. Following, in summary form, is the effect of the change on net income:

| | (thousands of dollars) | |
	1968	1967
Equity in net income of equity companies...	$1,705	$2,193
Less: Dividends received from these companies...	940	1,550
	765	643
Earnings, net of dividends, of consolidated subsidiaries not previously consolidated...	1,373	657
Increase in net income...	$2,138	$1,300
Per share...	$ 0.21	$ 0.13

Retained earnings as of April 30, 1966, as previously reported, were also adjusted by $13,891,000, to reflect the results of the change in the basis of consolidation.

a) Comment on the company's change in policy. Why did the company change its accounting methods? Do you agree with the change?

b) Why was an adjustment of $13,891,000 made to retained earnings? What other accounts were changed to counterbalance the increase in retained earnings? Explain carefully.

14–13. The Big Company owned 80 percent of the stock of the Little Company. During the year, 75 percent of the sales of the subsidiary were made to the parent. The year-end inventories of the Big Company still included 10 percent of the goods it purchased during the year from the Little Company. In addition, the Big Company provided managerial advisory services for the Little Company, for which it received $10,000. Little Company paid $1,000 of interest on a note owed to Big Company. Income statements, in summary form, for the two companies are given below (in thousands). Prepare a consolidated income statement in good form.

	Big	Little
Sales	$600	$180
Interest revenue	10	2
Other revenue	15	
	$625	$182
Cost of goods sold	$370	$110
Other expenses	185	30
Interest charges	8	3
	$563	$143
Net Income	$ 62	$ 39

`4–14. In their consolidated balance sheets for 1968 each of the following companies displays a credit balance account on the equity side described as follows.

1. Ex-Cell-O Corporation:

   Deferred Credit:
   Unamortized excess of equity (at book value)
   in subsidiaries at date of acquisition
   over cost of the investment..................... $387,000

   This amount is being taken into earnings ratably over the estimated lives of depreciable properties acquired in purchases; such properties continue to be depreciated by the subsidiaries on the basis of book value.

2. United States Smelting Refining and Mining Co.:

   Deferred Credit................................. $2,177,553

   This amount represents the excess of book value over cost of the net assets of Mueller Brass Co. acquired in 1965. It is being amortized over a seven-year period.

3. United States Shoe Corporation:

   Deferred Credits and Other Provisions:
   Excess of book value of net assets acquired
   over cost of investment in subsidiary,
   net of amortization........................... $1,507,026

   The company also showed an asset of $6,993,167 for excess of cost over book value. This account arose out of the purchase of two subsidiaries in 1966 and 1968. The amount is not being amortized. The amount listed under Deferred Credits arose in connection with a purchase in 1961 and is being amortized to earnings at the annual rate of approximately $120,000.

a) Explain carefully how each of these credit balance accounts arise in the consolidation process.

b) For each account, evaluate the company's amortization policy and classification of the item in the balance sheet.

c) What inconsistencies do you see in the policy of U.S. Shoe? Should the asset and deferred credit be combined into a single account? Explain.

14–15. The following note was taken from the annual report of Pet, Incorporated for the year ended March 31, 1970.

PRINCIPLES OF CONSOLIDATION AND NEW INVESTMENTS:

The consolidated financial statements include the accounts of Pet Incorporated and all subsidiaries. . . .

Starting in Fiscal 1970, the Company adopted the policy of consolidating its wholly-owned financing subsidiary, Hussmann Acceptance Co., and, accordingly, the accompanying financial statements for Fiscal 1969 have been restated. This restatement did not change the amounts previously reported as consolidated net earnings or earnings invested in the business, since the Company's investment was previously stated at equity in its net assets and the annual increase in equity was included in net earnings.

During the year the Company acquired, in exchange for 169,058 shares of its $1.00 cumulative convertible second preferred stock and 281,762 shares of its common stock, all of the common stock of Merchants Refrigerating Company. This transaction has been accounted for as a pooling of interests. The consolidated financial statements shown on pages 22 through 25 have been restated for Fiscal 1969 to include the accounts and operations of Merchants Refrigerating Company.

In addition, the Company acquired for 75,000 shares of $1.00 cumulative convertible second preferred stock, 120,055 shares of common stock, and $1,734,000, the net assets and business of the following companies. . . . These acquisitions were accounted for as purchases and, accordingly, the operations of these companies are included in the accompanying financial statements from their respective dates of acquisition.

A schedule of stockholders' equity accounts has been prepared from information contained in the 1969 and 1970 annual reports:

	3-31-69 As Reported	3-31-69 As Restated	3-31-70
$0.80 cumulative convertible preference stock..........	$ 8,289,446	$ 8,289,446	$ 7,825,832
$1 cumulative convertible second preferred stock...........	9,475,208	9,934,667	11,877,270
Common stock.......	33,793,904	35,323,446	40,750,625
Earnings reinvested...........	133,615,503	143,559,527	151,975,313
Common stock in treasury, at cost.............	(840,774)	(840,774)	(2,206,311)
	$184,333,287	$196,266,312	$210,222,729

Proceeds from the sale of capital stock under stock option plans was $1,103,770 during fiscal 1970. Assume that all of these were common shares.

Expenditures to acquire treasury stock during fiscal 1970 were $2,638,352.

The decrease in the $0.80 cumulative convertible preference stock was caused solely by conversion into common stock.

Net earnings for 1970 were $16,633,617, and dividends (of all types) were $8,217,831.

The asset account Excess of Purchase Price of Companies Acquired over Net Assets at Date of Acquisition increased $4,314,209 during fiscal 1970.

a) Comment on the change in consolidation policy to include Hussman Acceptance Company. What reasons might have prompted the decision? Why does the company state that the change had no effect on reported net earnings? What effect in general would it have on the balance sheet?

b) Prepare the journal entry in summary form (i.e., a single debit to Net Assets) that the company probably made in recording the acquisition of Merchants Refrigerating Company as a pooling of interests.

c) Prepare the summary journal entry that the company probably made in recording the acquisitions which were accounted for as purchases. Explain your computations.

d) The financial statements have been restated to include the accounts of the pooled companies for 1969 and 1970. However, acquisitions recorded as purchases are included only from their dates of acquisition. Explain this difference in treatment, consistent with the theories underlying poolings and purchases.

14-16. Condensed financial information for Parenco and Subsico is given below:

Balance Sheet, December 31, 1972

	Parenco	Subsico
Current assets..........................	$ 70,000	$ 50,000
Investment in Subsico, at cost.............	164,000	.....
Other assets...........................	417,000	174,000
Total.............................	$651,000	$224,000
Liabilities.............................	$122,000	$ 29,000
Common stock........................	350,000	150,000
Retained earnings.....................	179,000	45,000
	$651,000	$224,000

Income Statement for 1972

Sales.................................	$550,000	$195,000
Dividend revenue......................	10,000	.....
Total.............................	$560,000	$195,000
Cost of goods sold.....................	$307,500	$127,500
Other expenses........................	201,500	43,500
Total.............................	$509,000	$171,000
Net income...........................	$ 51,000	$ 24,000
Dividends.............................	(25,000)	(12,500)
Increase in Retained Earnings.............	$ 26,000	$ 11,500

Parenco had acquired an 80 percent interest in Subsico on January 1, *1971.* At that time, Subsico had common stock of $150,000 and retained earnings of $20,000. The excess of cost over book value is attributable to limited-life intangible assets. Management authorized amortization of these costs over a period of seven years on the consolidated statements.

During 1972, Parenco sold products costing $20,000 to Subsico for $30,000. Half of these were resold during 1972 by Subsico to its customers; the rest is in Subsico's inventory as of December 31, 1972.

a) Prepare a consolidated balance sheet as of December 31, 1972.
b) Prepare a consolidated income statement for the year 1972.
c) How would the statements in (a) and (b) be modified if the inventory of Subsico on December 31, *1971* included inventory bought from Parenco during 1971. This merchandise cost Parenco $7,000 and was sold to Subsico for $10,000. Subsico in turn sold it during 1972.

14–17.   On January 1, 1966 Lincoln Corporation exchanged 10,000 shares of its own $20 par value common stock for 90 percent of the capital stock of the Juilliard Company.*

a) The principal limitation of consolidated financial statements is their lack of separate information about the assets, liabilities, revenues, and expenses of the individual companies included in the consolidation. List the problems which the reader of consolidated financial statements encounters as a result of the limitation.

* Adapted from AICPA November 1966 examination.

b) Depending upon the examination of the accompanying circumstances, the combination of Lincoln Corporation and Juilliard Company may be accounted for as a purchase or as a pooling of interests. Discuss the differences between (1) a consolidated balance sheet prepared for a purchase and (2) a consolidated balance sheet prepared for a pooling of interests.

c) The minority interest in Juilliard Company can be presented several ways on the consolidated balance sheet. Discuss the propriety of reporting the minority interest on the consolidated balance sheet: (1) as a liability; (2) as a part of stockholders' equity; (3) in a separate classification between liabilities and the equity of the Lincoln Corporation.

14–18. The following table represents the position statements of the Mammoth Corporation and its two subsidiaries, Little and Tiny, as of December 31, 1972. Prepare a consolidated position statement in good form.

	Mammoth	Tiny	Little
Current assets............	$150,000	$ 60,000	$30,000
Investment in Tiny.........	20,000		
Investment in Little........	9,000		
Other assets..............	221,000	40,000	20,000
	$400,000	$100,000	$50,000
Current liabilities..........	$100,000	$ 76,000	$40,200
Capital stock.............	200,000	20,000	9,000
Retained earnings..........	100,000	4,000	800
	$400,000	$100,000	$50,000

Mammoth owns 100 percent of the stock in Tiny and 90 percent of the stock in Little. Retained earnings of Tiny and Little at the date of acquisition are $2,000 and $1,000, respectively.

During the year, the Tiny Company sells land costing $10,000 to the Mammoth Company for $10,500. On December 31, Tiny owes Little $5,000 from an advance.

14–19. On August 1, 1971 Busybody Book Company and Chuck Record Sales agree on a plan for Busybody Book Company to acquire Chuck Record Sales. Busybody Book plans to issue 1,630 shares of its $50 par value common stock for all 1,500 of Chuck Record Sales' outstanding $100 par value common shares.

The parties to the negotiation agreed that the ownership interest in Chuck Record Sales is overvalued by $55,000. This overstatement is attributable primarily to the lack of any substantive value to the intangible asset, "brand names, trademarks, etc." Also the marketable securities of Chuck Record Sales have a market value $5,000 less than their book value. Balance sheets for the separate companies on July 31, 1971 appeared as follows (in thousands):

Assets	Busybody	Chuck
Cash..	$ 70	$ 10
Marketable securities.........................	...	15
Receivables and inventory.....................	173	100
Fixed assets, net.............................	225	120
Brand names, trademarks, etc..................	...	50
	$468	$295

Equities		
Accounts payable..............................	$ 70	$ 30
Long-term debt................................	100	50
Capital stock.................................	175	150
Paid-in capital...............................	45	...
Retained earnings.............................	78	65
	$468	$295

a) Prepare the journal entry on the books of Busybody Book Company to record the merger with Chuck Record Sales, assuming that the combination is treated as a purchase. Prepare the balance sheet for the combined entity as of August 1, 1971.

b) Prepare the journal entry and balance sheet as in part (a) but assume that the combination is treated as a pooling of interests.

c) From a practical standpoint, which would the management of Busybody Book Company prefer to use in this case? Explain.

CHAPTER FIFTEEN

FUNDS STATEMENTS

THE POSITION STATEMENT and the income statement stand at the center of the reporting function in financial accounting. However, many users see a need for an additional formal statement to summarize the major transactions affecting the *financing* of the entity during the period. The income statement and comparative balance sheet, of course, provide some information about financial activities, but only in a limited manner. The income statement deals solely with operations, and comparative balance sheets show only *net* changes in assets and equities for all activities between the balance sheet dates. Since an important responsibility of management is adequately to finance the short- and long-run activities of the firm, a special report relating particularly to financing activities seems a desirable addition to the reporting package. Such a statement is the funds statement.

ALTERNATIVE CONCEPTS OF FUNDS

The term "funds" is not precisely defined in either accounting theory or practice, partly because different users with varying needs wish to employ alternative concepts of funds. Consequently, four common definitions have gained some measure of acceptance: (1) cash, (2) net monetary assets, (3) net working capital, and (4) all financial resources.

Cash probably comes closest to the everyday interpretation of funds. For short-term financial planning, funds frequently are defined narrowly as cash. In this case the funds statement becomes a statement of cash receipts and disbursements. For longer term planning purposes and for many analyses by external audiences, however, a cash funds statement

513

probably involves too much detail. Numerous purchases and sales of marketable securities or borrowings and repayments of short-term bank loans may be important in cash forecasting by management but not in an overall analysis of major sources and uses of financial resources. Also, cash is subject to short-term fluctuations. A delay in paying an account payable, for example, would decrease the uses of funds (defined as cash) but not really affect the general financial condition of the firm from the perspective of an external analyst.

A somewhat broader definition of funds is *net monetary assets*, consisting of monetary assets (cash, marketable securities, and accounts receivable) less current liabilities. The concept is thus broadened to include all current means of payment. Sales and purchases for cash are viewed as having the same financial impact as sales and purchases for short-term credit. Because it is a broader measure, net monetary assets has greater stability than does cash. Therefore, it may be particularly useful in analyzing intermediate financing decisions.

The definition of funds which is most widely accepted for external use by stockholders and creditors is *net working capital* (current assets less current liabilities). This concept does not get bogged down in the detailed fluctuations in individual items. It focuses on the overall impact of events on the current financial position of the firm and ignores the numerous offsetting transactions within the current asset–current liability area (e.g., the payment of a current liability or the collection of a receivable).

A working capital concept of funds, although not entirely free from disadvantages, represents a middle ground. Changes in net working capital reflect normal accrual accounting procedures. Hence, a funds statement based on this concept articulates well with the other statements. At the same time, net working capital also is a measure of the short-term liquidity of a firm. Changes in the balance of current assets less current liabilities during a period of time provide information about the fluidity of capital, which is relevant for many short-term decisions of stockholders, creditors, and management.

Despite its wide usage, the net working capital concept, according to some accountants, conceals too much. An inventory build-up financed by short-term bank borrowings would not appear on the funds statement under the net working capital concept. Neither would an increase in land received in exchange for the issuance of shares of stock. In both these cases net working capital (current assets less current liabilities) does not change.

To overcome these deficiencies, a fourth concept of funds—*all financial resources*—has received increased attention and support from the Accounting Principles Board. This concept defines funds very broadly, as all financial resources arising from transactions with parties external to the business enterprise. Exactly what the term "financial resources" means in this context is not entirely clear. The intent seems to be to show the "financial aspects of all significant transactions,"[1] including such events as the conversion of bonds into stock, the acquisition of property through the issuance of long-term bonds and capital stock, and the exchange of noncurrent assets.

The additional disclosure desired under the concept of all financial resources often can be achieved through a broadening of the interpretation of the concept of net working capital and by the provision of a supplementary schedule of changes in individual current assets and current liabilities. For this reason, and because of its common use in external reporting, net working capital is the definition used in most of this chapter. We review the major sources and uses of working capital, discuss the interpretation and uses that can be made of a funds statement, and explore the problems involved in preparing it. The last section then takes a look at the preparation of a cash funds statement.

SOURCES AND USES OF FUNDS

With funds initially defined as net working capital, our purpose is to determine and classify those transactions that cause the balance of net working capital to change from the beginning to the end of the period. To achieve this objective, we must analyze the transactions of the period to see if they affect any of the current asset or liability accounts. We should realize at the outset that many transactions are of no interest to us in this quest. Many of the transactions in the period affect only current accounts—e.g., a cash payment of an outstanding account payable. While these transactions affect the composition of net working capital, they do not change the total amount or balance. Similarly, some transactions affect only noncurrent accounts—e.g., a stock dividend. These nonfund transactions cause no change in any element of net working capital.

Generally then, the events in which we are interested must affect both a fund account (current asset or current liability) and a nonfund account (noncurrent asset or equity). Specifically, transactions that cause an increase in total current assets or a decrease in total current liabilities cause the difference between the two to increase; they are *sources*. Transactions that result in either a decrease in total current assets or an increase in total current liabilities represent *uses* of net working capital.

Sources

Those events which result in a net increase in funds can be divided into three broad categories—revenues, sale of noncurrent assets, and financing.

---

[1] *The Statement of Source and Application of Funds, Opinion of the Accounting Principles Board No. 3* (New York: AICPA, October 1963), p. 16.

Revenues of a business measure the inflow of assets from operations. Specifically, the asset received is usually cash or a short-term receivable. The corresponding credit is to an owners' equity account (revenue). Since they result in an increase in current assets and hence in net working capital, revenue transactions are one major source of funds.

On occasion a firm sells one or more of its noncurrent assets. If the sale is made for cash or a receivable, a current asset increases. This transaction is a source of funds. Whether the noncurrent asset is sold at a gain or at a loss is not relevant to the flow of funds. For instance, assume that a company sells for $8,000 in cash some excess land which originally cost $10,000. The journal entry to record this sale would be

```
Cash.......................................  8,000
Loss on Sale of Land.......................  2,000
     Land..................................          10,000
```

The loss indicates the decrease in owners' equity because total assets decrease (land decreases more than cash increases). However, the funds viewpoint is concerned with changes in net current assets. This transaction, although reducing total assets, increases current assets. Therefore, it should appear on the funds statement as a source of funds of $8,000.

Long-term financing is the third major source. If a company engages in long-term borrowing or issues additional common or preferred stock, current assets (in most cases, cash) may increase. For example, if a company issues for $101,000 bonds with a face value of $100,000, then cash and thus net working capital increase $101,000. The offsetting credits are to noncurrent liability accounts, Bonds Payable and Premium on Bonds Payable. This event is a source of funds. The issuance of preferred stock or common stock could be analyzed in a similar manner. The amount of change in the par or face value of the security is not governing. The important aspect is the increase in current assets resulting from the transaction.

Uses

Many events affecting a business also cause a decrease in net working capital, either because current assets decrease or because current liabilities increase. Certain expense transactions have this effect. In addition, recurring payments to investors, retirement of noncurrent equities, and the acquisition of noncurrent assets may decrease net working capital.

Expenses record decreases in owners' equity as assets are used up in the production of revenues. However, only those expenses arising from a decrease in current assets (or an increase in current liabilities) are uses of funds. Cost of goods sold (decreases Merchandise), labor expense (decreases Cash or increases Wages Payable), income taxes (decreases Cash or increases Taxes Payable), and rent expense (decreases Cash or Prepaid Rent) are some common examples of fund expenses. Depreciation expense, amortization of patents, and depletion expense represent transactions that decrease owners' equity and decrease a noncurrent asset. Although these expenses represent uses of assets, they do not involve a current outlay or decrease in net working capital. Therefore, they are called nonfund expenses, and care must be taken to see that they are properly interpreted as such.

Similar to the fund expenses are recurring payments to investors—interest charges and dividends. In most cases the transactions giving rise to these items involve a debit to an owners' equity account (Interest Charges, Preferred Dividends, Common Dividends) and a credit to either Cash or a current liability such as Interest Payable or Dividends Payable. Therefore, recurring payments to investors represent another use of funds.

If current assets, usually cash, are used to retire bonds or preferred stock or to acquire treasury stock, the opposite situation from financing occurs. In this case funds are being used to reduce long-term equities. Again, the face value or par amount retired is not significant from a funds viewpoint. Only the amount of the decrease in current assets is relevant.

The fourth major type of transaction which should appear as a use of funds is the acquisition of noncurrent assets, such as land, plant assets, intangibles, etc. These noncurrent assets can be acquired in a number of ways (purchase, investment, donation). The funds statement includes only those acquisitions which have a concomitant decrease in current assets or increase in current liabilities.

Statement Form

Of the three major sources of funds and four major uses of funds named above, the first source (revenues) and the first use (expenses that use funds) both relate to the operations of the business. In preparing the funds statement, it is common practice to offset the revenues and fund expenses to obtain a net source, funds from operations. If this is done, the funds statement can be divided into six major sections—three sources of funds and three uses of funds. The form in Table 15–1 is a convenient and useful way to present the major changes in net working capital, although this format is only one of many that could be used. Appropriate details would, of course, be listed under each of the major subheads. The important objective is that the funds statement should summarize the major changes that take place during a period of time and present and classify them in some reasonable manner.

TABLE 15–1

SAMPLE COMPANY
Statement of Sources and Uses of Funds
for the Year 1971

```
Sources:
  Funds from operations.......................... $xxx
  Sale of noncurrent assets......................  xxx
  Financing......................................  xxx
      Total sources..............................        $xxx
Uses:
  Recurring payments to investors................ $xxx
  Return of invested capital.....................  xxx
  Acquisition of noncurrent assets...............  xxx
      Total uses.................................        $xxx
Increase (Decrease) in Net Working Capital........        $xxx
```

INTERPRETATION AND USE OF THE FUNDS STATEMENT

An adequate supply of current resources or funds is essential to insure proper functioning of the business and to maintain its financial soundness. The funds statement explains the basic causes of changes in net current resources. In doing so, moreover, it reflects the major financial events and policy decisions made during the period with respect to financing and asset expansion. Together with the schedule of changes in individual current assets and current liabilities, it presents a fairly complete picture of the current area of the business. In general, the most important use of the funds statement is to disclose information which would not be available or readily apparent from an analysis of other financial statements, information about how activities are financed, how financial resources are used or accumulated during a period, and how the liquidity position of the firm is affected.

A funds statement may be used by external audiences to appraise the firm's financing policies. It may help answer questions similar to the following: How much reliance has been placed on external versus internal sources of funds? Is the present fund-generating capability of the firm adequate? How was the firm able to pay large dividends in a period of low earnings or operating losses? How did the firm manage to expand its plant and equipment without borrowing or while at the same time retiring debt? How were additions to plant and equipment financed?

In addition, stockholders and creditors may use a funds statement to appraise management's channeling of financial resources into alternative uses, particularly expansion. By showing how funds are applied, the funds statement sheds some illumination on a number of pertinent questions: What happened to profits? Why did dividends not increase with the increased net income? How were the proceeds from a stock or bond issue used? How did the firm use the money it received from selling the plant assets of a particular division? Why did the firm have to borrow money when it made a large income? Is management using its fund inflow for any single purpose?

The outside investor also may wish to focus on the net result of the inflows and outflows of funds. The maintenance of a satisfactory current position is essential to financial health. Moreover, funds flow information may provide a measure of future growth potential. What factors caused the increase in working capital? Why did working capital go up even though net income declined, or vice versa? Is management depleting net working capital in order to finance needed expansion or to meet required debt payments?

A funds statement can not only highlight historical answers to questions like those posed above; it can also be projected into the future. Indeed, management's primary use of the funds statement is as a planning tool. Using a forecasted (pro forma) funds statement, management can see what financial plans must be made to insure that the desired future level of operations, dividends, expansion, etc., is achieved. Some creditors also use forecasted funds statements in estimating the firm's ability to pay its debts, and investors undoubtedly project funds flows using prior periods' funds statements.

PREPARATION OF THE FUNDS STATEMENT

Equipped with a definition of funds as current assets less current liabilities, and a general understanding of the major sources and uses of funds, let us turn our attention to the techniques of preparing a funds statement.

Illustrative Data

In Tables 15–2 and 15–3 are the financial statements of the Cardinal Company. Included are a comparative position statement as of the beginning and end of 1971 and an income statement for 1971. These normally would be the basic information sources available to an external user.

Schedule of Changes in Net Working Capital

The difference between net working capital at the beginning and end of the period is the change we are attempting to explain. For Cardinal Company, the change is an increase of $76,100—from net working capital of $38,800 at December 31, 1970 to net working capital of $114,900 at December 31, 1971.

To provide additional information, we may want to prepare a schedule

TABLE 15–2

CARDINAL COMPANY
Comparative Position Statement as of December 31

	1971	1970
Cash...............................	$ 78,300	$ 80,000
Marketable securities...........	10,000	20,000
Accounts receivable.............	44,600	33,800
Inventories......................	100,000	63,000
Total Current Assets..........	$232,900	$196,800
Land.............................	155,000	150,000
Equipment*.......................	332,000	310,000
Accumulated depreciation........	(81,000)	(72,000)
Investments.....................	30,000	50,000
Patents..........................	13,000	15,000
Goodwill.........................	0	6,000
Total Assets...............	$681,900	$655,800
Accounts payable (for merchandise).............	$ 85,000	$132,000
Taxes payable....................	8,000	5,000
Wages and salaries payable......	4,000	3,000
Interest payable................	3,000	2,000
Bank loans payable..............	14,000	11,000
Other current liabilities.......	4,000	5,000
Total Current Liabilities.....	$118,000	$158,000
Bonds payable—par..............	200,000	200,000
Bonds payable—premium..........	28,000	30,000
Preferred stock.................	76,000	25,000
Common stock....................	240,000	225,000
Retained earnings...............	19,900	17,800
Total Equities.............	$681,900	$655,800

*New equipment purchases totaled $27,000.

of changes in net working capital which would detail the change in each current account making up the overall change. Table 15–4 on page 522 shows that the increase in funds of $76,100 is represented primarily by a build-up of inventory and liquidation of accounts payable.

Funds from Operations

Since the income statement summarizes the operations of a firm, we look to it for the information necessary to calculate funds from operations. Extraordinary gains and losses do not relate to normal operations. Moreover, they frequently require special analysis to determine their full impact on funds. Consequently, we focus our attention on the items comprising net income before extraordinary items.

Funds from operations represent the difference between the revenues which provide funds and those expenses that use funds. Cardinal Company's net sales of $294,400 represent the inflows of funds from operations. From this amount should be subtracted the fund expenses, those representing decreases in current assets or increases in current liabilities.

TABLE 15-3

CARDINAL COMPANY
Income Statement for the Year 1971

Revenues:		
Net sales......................		$294,400
Expenses:		
Cost of goods sold..............	$178,000	
Wage and salary expense.........	24,000	
Advertising expense.............	1,000	
Insurance expense...............	1,500	
Depreciation expense............	12,000	
Patent amortization.............	2,000	
Other operating expenses........	16,000	
Interest expense................	15,000	249,500
Net income before taxes...........		$ 44,900
Income taxes....................		18,100
Net income before extraordinary		
items...........................		$ 26,800
Extraordinary gains and losses:		
Gains on sale of equipment......	$ 400	
Loss from write-off of		
goodwill......................	6,000	5,600
Net income to stockholders........		$ 21,200
Retained earnings, January 1......		17,800
Dividends:		
Preferred dividends.............	$ 3,000	
Common dividends................	1,100	
Market value of common shares		
issued as stock dividend......	15,000	19,100
Retained Earnings, December 31....		$ 19,900

Depreciation expense and patent amortization expense are nonfund deductions. They represent decreases in noncurrent assets and hence reduce net income, but they do not reduce net working capital. Subtracting only those expenses that use funds ($238,600) from sales gives $55,800 as funds

Cost of goods sold.....................	$178,000
Wage and salary expense................	24,000
Advertising expense....................	1,000
Insurance expense......................	1,500
Other operating expenses...............	16,000
Income taxes...........................	18,100
Total expenses that use funds...........	$238,600

from operations. Interest expense also has been excluded from the expenses using funds, since it is to be reported as a separate use under recurring payments to investors.[2]

An alternative method of computing funds from operations is frequently employed. This method begins with a net income figure and *adds*

---

[2] This classification is a matter of personal preference. Many funds statements include interest as an operating expense and hence as a deduction in arriving at funds from operations. The important point is that it does represent a use of funds, but should be deducted only once.

TABLE 15–4

CARDINAL COMPANY
Schedule of Changes in Net Working Capital

	1971	1970	Increase
Cash......................	$ 78,300	$ 80,000	$ (1,700)
Marketable securities......	10,000	20,000	(10,000)
Accounts receivable........	44,600	33,800	10,800
Inventories................	100,000	63,000	37,000
Total Current Assets.....	$232,900	$196,800	$ 36,100
Accounts payable...........	$ 85,000	$132,000	$(47,000)
Taxes payable..............	8,000	5,000	3,000
Wages and salaries payable.................	4,000	3,000	1,000
Interest payable...........	3,000	2,000	1,000
Bank loans payable.........	14,000	11,000	3,000
Other current liabilities..............	4,000	5,000	(1,000)
Total Current Liabilities............	$118,000	$158,000	$(40,000)
Net Working Capital........	$114,900	$ 38,800	$ 76,100

back those items not related to funds or reported elsewhere in the funds statements.

Net income before extraordinary items.............	$26,800
Add deductions not using funds:	
Depreciation expense.........................	12,000
Amortization expense........................	2,000
Add interest expense reported separately..........	15,000
Funds from operations........................	$55,800

The advantage of this procedure lies in the fact that it ties the income statement and the funds statement together. The first item appearing on the funds statement is a subtotal taken from the income statement. Then the net income is converted to funds from operations by the addition of certain expenses which are subtracted in calculating net income but not in obtaining funds from operations.

The primary disadvantage of this method is possible confusion and misinterpretation. Depreciation and amortization expenses are *not* sources of funds. They are added back because the initial starting figure, net income, is understated from a funds standpoint. Net income arises after all expenses are deducted—including depreciation and amortization, which do not use funds. If the desired goal is funds from operations, these expenses should not be deducted. But if we begin with net income, they have to be added back. Unfortunately, all too frequently these items, particularly depreciation, are looked upon as generating funds simply because they appear to be an addition to net income. The direct method, beginning with sales and deducting only those expenses which use funds, avoids the possibility of misinterpreting the impact of depreciation on funds from operations. One solution to this problem might be to simply show a single figure as funds from operations in the funds statement. Its detailed calculation could be provided in a footnote.

Sale of Noncurrent Assets

To determine whether funds have been generated through the sale of noncurrent assets, we have to investigate three areas. First, look at the comparative position statement to see if any noncurrent assets have decreased during the period. Look also at the income statement for any gains or losses indicating that noncurrent assets have been sold. Finally, take into consideration other information relating to asset retirements that accompanies the financial statements.

The comparative position statement of Cardinal Company reveals that three noncurrent assets—investments, patents, and goodwill—have decreased. The decreases in patents and goodwill are explained in total by charges appearing on the income statement. Amortization and the loss from write-off reduce noncurrent assets and owners' equity, but they have no funds effect. Based on the information available concerning the investments, a reasonable conclusion is that $20,000 of them must have been sold, since this account typically decreases by sale. Since no gain or loss is reported, we presume that the sale is at book value. Thus, sale of investments of $20,000 is one source of funds appearing in this section.

The Gain on Sale of Equipment account on the income statement indicates that a sale of equipment has occurred even though this account increased in total during the period. However, as mentioned earlier, it is the net proceeds, not the gain, that is the funds effect. We should go behind the transaction to determine the proceeds from the sale. The gain discloses only that total assets increased as a result of the transaction; funds statement preparation is concerned with the increase in current assets. To find the source of funds we must reconstruct the journal entry that was probably made when the equipment was sold. The entry probably involved the following accounts:

```
Cash.................................................. xxx
Accumulated Depreciation......................... xxx
     Equipment...................................       xxx
     Gain on Sale...............................         xxx
```

The funds statement is concerned with the amount of the debit to Cash. If the other amounts can be found, the debit to Cash can be calculated. The gain on sale is found on the income statement. The debit to Accumulated Depreciation and credit to the Equipment account can be determined through reconstruction of these ledger accounts:

Accumulated Depreciation		Equipment	
72,000	Beginning balance	Beginning balance	310,000
12,000	Depreciation expense added during the year—see income statement	New equipment purchases	27,000

If no other events had affected Accumulated Depreciation and Equipment during the year, then the ending balances in those accounts should be $84,000 and $337,000 respectively. The position statement as of December 31, 1971, reveals balances of only $81,000 and $332,000 in these accounts. Therefore, Accumulated Depreciation must have been debited for $3,000 and the Equipment account credited for $5,000 when the equipment was sold.

Combining the information into the original journal entry, we can infer that Cash was debited for $2,400, the source of net working capital from the sale of equipment:

```
Cash........................................  2,400
Accumulated Depreciation....................  3,000
    Equipment...............................           5,000
    Gain on Sale............................             400
```

Financing

The increase in funds from financing transactions is usually relatively easy to find. Look at the comparative position statement to see if any long-term liabilities or capital stock accounts have increased. Check to see if the increase, in total or in part, might be explained in another way, such as a conversion of bonds into stock or a conversion of retained earnings into stock (stock dividend). If the change cannot be explained in some other manner, then the total change probably represents a source of funds.

For the Cardinal Company, long-term debt has actually decreased; only preferred stock and common stock have increased. The increase of $15,000 in common stock, however, represents a stock dividend, according to the income statement. Retained earnings have decreased and common stock has increased. Since no current asset or liability is involved, the stock dividend is a nonfund transaction. Therefore the only source of funds from financing must be $51,000 from the sale of preferred stock, the only other unexplained increase in noncurrent equity accounts.

Recurring Payments to Investors

Turning now to the uses of funds, let us first consider periodic distributions to investors. The declaring of cash dividends and the accruing of interest usually represent decreases in net working capital. The amounts of these items can be found on the income statement. For example, the Cardinal Company used $15,000 of funds to pay interest, $3,000 for preferred stock dividends, and $1,100 for cash dividends to the common stockholders.

Return of Invested Capital

This use of funds is the counterpart of providing funds through financing transactions. It refers to those transactions, such as retiring bonds or preferred stock or acquiring treasury stock, involving decreases in net working capital to reduce long-term equities. The procedure to find the information is similar to that described for financing. Look at the comparative position statement to see if long-term liability or capital stock accounts have decreased. If the decrease cannot be explained in another way, then it probably represents a use of funds.

As we have noticed earlier, the only long-term equity of the Cardinal Company to decrease is bonds payable, and even here it is the adjunct account, Bonds Payable—Premium, which actually decreased. If we remember the journal entries for interest when bonds are issued at a premium, this decrease appears to be a logical use of funds. When bonds are issued at a premium, the effective interest charge for using money is less than the actual cash disbursed. Part of the periodic "interest" payment really represents a return of a portion of the bondholders' original investment, a use of funds to reduce long-term capital. The entry for the Cardinal Company for the year must have been

```
Interest Charges.........................  15,000
Bonds Payable—Premium....................   2,000
    Cash (or Interest Payable)...........           17,000
```

The credit to Cash or Interest Payable represents the use of funds. Part of it, $15,000, has already been recorded under recurring payments to investors. The $2,000 reduction in Bonds Payable—Premium also reflects a use of funds and is most appropriately classified under return of invested capital.

Acquisition of Noncurrent Assets

An analysis of changes in the noncurrent assets during the period as revealed by a comparative position statement is the starting point for this third major category of funds application. However, the net change in a noncurrent asset may not reveal the full amount of funds applied. Consideration must be given to the effect of retirements in a computation of the gross additions to noncurrent assets. This may require reconstructing the ledger accounts for certain noncurrent assets. Having determined the gross addition to each noncurrent asset account, we see if it can be explained in some other way, such as through stockholder investment or donation. Otherwise, the gross increase in noncurrent assets probably represents a use of funds.

In the Cardinal Company example, the gross equipment purchases are given as an additional piece of direct information. Keep in mind, however, that in some cases this figure would become available only through a reconstruction of the entries made in the Equipment account, similar to that involved earlier in the determination of the equipment retirements. In addition to the $27,000 purchase of equipment, the Land account has increased $5,000. Inasmuch as this increase cannot be accounted for by some other type of transaction, we can assume that it represents a use of funds to purchase land.

Statement of Sources and Uses of Funds

When we put together all the information uncovered in our analysis of these six areas, the result is the statement in Table 15–5. The increase agrees with the change shown on the schedule in Table 15–4.

TABLE 15–5

CARDINAL COMPANY
Statement of Sources and Uses of Funds
for the Year 1971

Sources:			
Funds from operations:			
Sales...................	$294,400		
Less: Expenses using funds...............	238,600	$55,800	
Sale of noncurrent assets:			
Equipment...............	$ 2,400		
Investments.............	20,000	22,400	
Financing:			
Issuance of preferred stock.................		51,000	
Total sources..........			$129,200
Uses:			
Recurring payments to investors:			
Interest.................	$ 15,000		
Preferred dividends......	3,000		
Common dividends........	1,100	$19,100	
Return of invested capital:			
Return of bond premium................		2,000	
Acquisition of noncurrent assets:			
Land....................	$ 5,000		
Equipment...............	27,000	32,000	
Total uses............			53,100
Increase in Net Working Capital...................			$ 76,100

Problem Areas: Nonfund Transactions

Perhaps the most difficult problems encountered in the preparation of funds statements lie in the adjustments and eliminations required because of nonfund transactions. These transactions do not affect current assets or current liabilities and therefore should not affect the funds statement. They do, however, influence items on the income and position statements. Since these are the major sources of information for the funds statement, we must be careful to evaluate the impact of nonfund transactions in moving from the income and position statements to the funds statement. In the previous example, depreciation, amortization, stock dividends, and write-off of goodwill all fall into this category. In addition to those nonfund transactions, some other fairly common transactions require special attention—bond discount, deferred taxes, investment of noncurrent assets, and conversion of bonds into stock.

When bonds are issued at a discount, the current market rate of interest is greater than the coupon rate. The investor receives a portion of his interest at maturity date when he receives the face value of the bond. In each period the true interest charge exceeds the amount actually credited to Cash or Interest Payable. The remaining credit is made to Bonds Payable—Discount, a contra liability account. For example, let us analyze the following entry made for interest when bonds have been issued at a discount:

```
Interest Charges........................... 2,300
     Cash (Interest Payable)................          2,000
     Bonds Payable—Discount................           300
```

Owners' equity is decreased by $2,300, the amount of the charge for using money. The decrease in owners' equity is offset by a $2,000 decrease in net working capital and a $300 increase in a long-term liability (actually recorded as a decrease in a contra liability account). From a funds viewpoint the only use of funds is $2,000. Therefore, in reporting the use of funds "recurring payments to investors," care must be taken to adjust the interest charge shown on the income statement for the decrease in Bonds Payable—Discount. Only a portion of the interest charge results in an actual decrease in net working capital. If, alternatively, interest is included as part of funds from operations, then the amortization of the bond discount would have to be added back as a nonfund expense similar to depreciation or amortization.

You may recall from our discussion in Chapter Twelve that under interperiod tax allocation, income tax expense for the period may be more or less than the amount legally payable for that period. For instance, assume that income tax expense, based on the revenues and expenses shown on the income statement, is $20,000. Because of timing differences, the amount of tax owed, based on the tax return, is only $15,000. The entry is

```
Income Tax Expense....................... 20,000
    Income Taxes Payable (or Cash)........        15,000
    Deferred Income Taxes................         5,000
```

Deferred income tax is a nonfund item. The use of net working capital is only $15,000. The increase in the long-term liability Deferred Income Taxes would have to be subtracted from tax expense (or added back to net income as a nonfund expense) in the calculation of funds from operations.

In the introductory discussion on alternative concepts of funds, the problem of major financial events not affecting net working capital was mentioned. One such event involves the acquisition of noncurrent assets through some means other than purchase. If land is acquired through a stockholder investment, the entry is

```
Land...............................................  xxx
    Capital Stock..............................        xxx
```

Since no current asset or current liability is involved, the entry represents a nonfund transaction. Technically, this increase in land should not appear as a use of net working capital, nor should the increase in capital stock appear as a source. On the other hand, this event may reflect an important financing step and a major asset expansion. The communication function dictates that some sort of disclosure be given to this transaction on the funds statement. One possibility is to stretch the funds concept to assume that funds are received from issuance of capital stock and then instantaneously applied to the acquisition of the relevant noncurrent asset.

Another example is the conversion of bonds to stock, technically a nonfund transaction. Some have suggested here too that the conversion be viewed as a simultaneous source of funds from financing and use of funds for return of invested capital.[3] The conversion may reflect changes in financial policy and for this reason at least ought to be disclosed.

Not all transactions fit neatly into one of the three sources or three uses of funds outlined earlier. For example, a fire loss on inventory represents a use of funds, since inventory is a current asset. This use, however, is not covered by the categories discussed, unless the concept of expenses that use funds is broadened sufficiently to include this kind of loss. Nevertheless, for most situations the direct approach illustrated in this chapter leads to a correct funds statement. Never lose sight of the original transaction. Whenever doubt arises, a reconstruction of the journal entry reveals the effect on funds. Indeed, preparation of an accurate, useful funds statement always entails the reconstruction of some transactions and the analysis of some ledger accounts. However, if we keep in mind the definition of funds as current assets less current liabilities and know exactly where to begin looking for each category on the funds statement,

---

[3] Another means of depicting changes arising out of transactions solely involving noncurrent assets and equities would be to change the definition of funds from net working capital to all financial resources.

the preparation is not difficult. Moreover, the schedule of changes in net working capital serves as a check on the result shown by the funds statement.

CASH FUNDS STATEMENT

A net working capital concept of funds ignores movements among the individual current assets and liabilities. Treating increases in inventories and cash receipts as similar and viewing decreases in prepayments and cash disbursements in the same light may conceal short-term financial movements that have significance—definitely to internal users and perhaps to external users. The working capital funds statement may reveal a favorable situation, and yet the firm may be unable to pay its bills. A statement of cash flows is necessary to provide the more detailed information.

This last section illustrates how a cash funds statement can also be constructed from a basic set of financial statements. Let us take the Cardinal Company data in Tables 15–2 and 15–3 and try to present in an orderly fashion the major financial events responsible for the decrease in cash of $1,700 during 1971. We can use the framework of three sources and three uses to present the sources and uses of cash also.

Cash from Operations

Many of the transactions reported on the working capital funds statement were presumed to involve cash receipts or disbursements—e.g., issuance of preferred stock, sale of equipment, etc. These also appear on a cash funds statement. The major area where the two types of funds statements differ is the flow from operations. Funds from operations under a net working capital concept still reflect accrual accounting procedures; for example, sales are a source of funds, and cost of goods sold is a use of funds. However, under a cash concept of funds we are concerned with a cash basis of accounting; collections from customers and payments to suppliers for purchased inventory are the source and use of cash corresponding to sales and cost of goods sold.

To compute cash from operations we must convert net working capital from operations from an accrual to a cash basis. This means adjusting each operating item for the effect of changes in other current assets or liabilities operationally related to it. Some common adjustments are outlined in Table 15–6, and other items usually can be handled in a similar manner.

Let us see what adjustments are necessary in the Cardinal Company example. Net sales were $294,400. However, accounts receivable increased $10,800. This means that collections from customers (credits to Accounts Receivable) were less than the sales (debits to Accounts Receivable).

TABLE 15–6

Net Working Capital Item	±	Adjustments	=	Cash Item
1. Sales	− +	Increase in accounts receivable Decrease in accounts receivable		Cash collections from customers
2. Cost of goods sold	+ −	Increase in inventory Decrease in inventory		
	=	Purchases		
	− +	Increase in accounts payable Decrease in accounts payable		Cash payments for purchases
3. Insurance expense	+ −	Increase in prepaid insurance Decrease in prepaid insurance		Cash expenditures on insurance
4. Income tax expense	− +	Increase in taxes payable Decrease in taxes payable		Cash outlays for taxes

Consequently, the source of cash from customer collections is only $283,600 ($294,400 − $10,800).

With merchandise, we note that inventories increased $37,000 and accounts payable related to inventory purchases decreased $47,000. These facts indicate that merchandise purchases exceed goods sold, and cash payments exceed the amount of purchases. The use of cash can be calculated as follows:

Cost of goods sold	$178,000
Add: Increase in inventory	37,000
Merchandise purchases	$215,000
Add: Decrease in accounts payable	47,000
Cash payments for purchases	$262,000

Because Wages and Salaries Payable increased $1,000, we can infer that cash payments to employees were only $23,000, $1,000 less than the expense. Similarly, the increase in Taxes Payable of $3,000 means that cash disbursements for taxes were only $15,100 ($18,100 − $3,000). Assume that "other current liabilities" applied to the various accruals related to advertising, insurance, and other operating expenses. Since this liability declined $1,000 during the period, cash expenditures for these items must have exceeded the total of the expenses by that amount. The use of cash is $19,500.

The following schedule summarizes the cash flow from operations:

Cash collections from customers		$283,600
Cash payments:		
For merchandise purchases	$262,000	
For wages and salaries	23,000	
For taxes	15,100	
For other operating expenses	19,500	319,600
Cash outflow from operations		$ 36,000

This figure is derived from a restatement of individual revenues and expenses on a cash basis. Notice that it shows a net *outflow* of cash, even though net working capital increased as a result of operations.

Practically, it may be difficult to relate specific current assets and current liabilities to particular revenues and expenses on the income statement. The one-to-one correspondence, although helpful in understanding the derivation of the cash funds statement, is not really necessary if we only wish to focus on the single figure of cash from operations. If we can identify those current assets and current liabilities related to operations, an adjustment can be made to the total only, as shown in Table 15–7.

TABLE 15–7

Net working capital from operations*.........		$55,800
Adjustments to convert to cash basis:		
Add:		
Increase in taxes payable..............	$ 3,000	
Increase in wages and salaries payable......	1,000	4,000
Deduct:		
Increase in accounts receivable............	$10,800	
Decrease in accounts payable.	47,000	
Increase in inventories..................	37,000	
Decrease in other current liabilities.......	1,000	95,800
Cash outflow............................		$36,000

* We could start with net income before extraordinary items and then adjust for non-fund items as well as for changes in other current items.

Complete Statement

The complete cash funds statement is presented in Table 15–8. The analysis of cash events in other major areas is straightforward for the most part. New or different items appearing on the cash funds statement are summarized below:

1. The $10,000 liquidation of marketable securities during the year is a source of cash. Presumably, they were sold at book value.
2. During 1971 Cardinal Company borrowed additional cash from the bank on a short-term basis. This $3,000 is a source of cash from financing.
3. Since interest payable increased $1,000 during 1971, the cash payments for interest are only $14,000 rather than the $15,000 shown as interest expense.

The Concept of "Cash Flow"

One of the currently popular concepts related to funds is that of "cash flow." This term is sometimes used by businesses in reporting on the results of their operations and by security analysts in their evaluations and recommendations concerning the common stock of various com-

TABLE 15–8

CARDINAL COMPANY
Statement of Sources and Uses of Cash
for the Year 1971

```
Sources:
  Sale of assets:
    Equipment...................  $ 2,400
    Investments................    20,000
    Marketable securities......    10,000      $32,400
  Financing:
    Issuance of preferred
      stock....................  $51,000
    Increase in bank loans.....    3,000        54,000
      Total sources...........                              $86,400
Uses:
  Cash outflow from
    operations................                 $36,000
  Recurring payments
    to investors:
    Interest...................  $14,000
    Preferred dividends........    3,000
    Common dividends..........     1,100        18,100
  Return of invested capital:
    Return of bond premium.....                  2,000
  Acquisition of assets:
    Land......................   $ 5,000
    Equipment..................    27,000        32,000
      Total uses..............                               88,100
Decrease in Cash..............                             $ 1,700
```

panies as investments. As used in these situations, "cash flow" is commonly defined as net income plus depreciation (and other expenses not using funds).

"Cash flow" is a misnomer for the concept of net income plus depreciation. What really is meant is funds from operations, with funds defined more broadly than cash. As we have just seen, net income computed on an accrual basis does not represent a net cash inflow. Adding back depreciation does not adjust for the other accrual items reflected in net income. All that net income plus depreciation shows is the increase in net working capital, *not cash*, arising from the operations of the business.

The "cash flow" concept may be misleading if not used with care. First, it is incomplete, since it ignores other sources and uses of funds. Funds from operations represent only one source of current working capital and logically should be presented as a part of an overall funds statement. The use of funds from operations or "cash flow" by itself may lead to inaccurate judgments concerning dividend, debt reduction, and asset replacement and expansion policies. Moreover, adding back depreciation carries with it the implication that depreciation is a source of cash.

Unfortunately, some users of this concept suggest that cash flow is a substitute for net income, the implication being that depreciation is somehow not a valid expense. Such an implication is false. Any asset, the services of which expire during the period in generating revenue, is an expense of the period and hence a determinant of net income. That the resource may have been paid for in a prior period is irrelevant. Net income measures the effect of operations on assets and owners' equity. Only such a figure can be meaningfully related to investment in the determination of how well resources have been managed.

"Cash flow" earnings are a misuse of both the concept of cash and the concept of earnings. To the extent that funds from operations are a meaningful and helpful supplementary measure, cash flow would be also. However, when clothed in a false title, presented in a misleading manner apart from the rest of the funds statement, and used where it does not belong, the result may be confusing rather than enlightening.

SUGGESTIONS FOR FURTHER READING

Bierman, Harold, Jr. "Measuring Financial Liquidity," *Accounting Review,* Vol. 35 (October 1960), pp. 628–32.

Corbin, Donald A., and Taussig, Russell. "The AICPA Funds Statement Study," *Journal of Accountancy,* Vol. 114 (July 1962), pp. 57–62.

Mason, Perry. *Cash Flow Analysis and the Funds Statement,* Accounting Research Study No. 2. New York: AICPA, 1961.

Paton, William A. "The 'Cash Flow' Illusion," *Accounting Review,* Vol. 38 (April 1963), pp. 243–51.

Rosen, L. S., and DeCoster, Don T. " 'Funds' Statement: A Historical Perspective," *Accounting Review,* Vol. 44 (January 1969), pp. 124–36.

Staubus, George, Jr. "Alternative Asset Flow Concepts," *Accounting Review,* Vol. 41 (July 1966), pp. 397–12.

QUESTIONS AND PROBLEMS

15–1.   The following list contains some selected accounting events. For each of these items, indicate whether it would result in an increase, a decrease, or no change in funds under four alternative definitions: (*a*) cash, (*b*) net monetary assets, (*c*) net working capital, and (*d*) all financial resources:

1. Sale of marketable securities for cash at more than their original cost.
2. Payment of accounts payable.
3. Issuance of common stock in exchange for shares of preferred stock presented to the company for conversion.
4. Recording of depletion cost.
5. Issuance of a "stock dividend."
6. Collections of accounts receivable.

7. Purchase of inventories on account.
8. Issuing shares of stock in exchange for a patent.
9. Sale of securities held for three years for cash at less than their original cost.
10. Declaration of a cash dividend on common stock on December 15, payable on January 10.
11. Write-off of a specific uncollectible account.
12. Recording of cost of goods sold under Fifo.
13. Sale of merchandise on account.
14. Sale of partially depreciated equipment for cash at less than its book value.
15. Flood damage to merchandise.

15–2. From the following condensed financial data of the Barter Company, prepare (a) a statement of sources and uses of funds, defined as working capital, for the year 1972; and (b) a schedule for changes in net working capital.

BARTER COMPANY

Comparative Position Statement Data as of
December 31, 1971 and 1972

	1972	1971
Cash.................................	$ 84,800	$ 18,400
Receivables, net.................	118,400	104,000
Inventories......................	92,500	61,900
Investments......................	90,000	100,000
Plant assets*....................	240,000	220,000
Accumulated depreciation.........	(60,000)	(50,000)
	$565,700	$454,300
Accounts payable.................	$100,000	$ 67,300
Mortgage payable.................	50,000	73,500
Deferred income taxes............	5,200	5,000
Common stock.....................	175,000	125,000
Retained earnings................	235,500	183,500
	$565,700	$454,300

*New plant assets costing $80,000 were purchased during the year.

BARTER COMPANY

Income Statement for the Year Ended December 31, 1972

Sales....................................	$300,000	
Interest and other revenue.........	10,000	$310,000
Less:		
Cost of goods sold...............	$151,000	
Selling and general expenses.....	10,000	
Depreciation....................	22,000	
Interest charges................	3,000	
Income taxes....................	54,000	240,000
Net income before extraordinary items...........................		$ 70,000
Loss on sale of plant assets.......		8,000
Net income........................		$ 62,000
Dividends..........................		10,000
Income retained in business........		$ 52,000

15-3. Condensed financial data for the Main Corporation are given below:

THE MAIN CORPORATION
Comparative Position Statement Data as of December 31

	1971	1972
Cash..............................	$ 5,000	$ 18,200
Accounts receivable..............	7,000	5,000
Inventories.......................	13,000	30,000
Land..............................	100,000	110,000
Machinery and equipment...........	100,000	55,000
Investments......................	150,000	170,000
Patents...........................	50,000	40,000
Bonds payable—discount...........	1,000	800
	$426,000	$429,000
Accounts payable..................	$ 4,000	$ 5,000
Accrued liabilities...............	3,000	—
Taxes payable.....................	2,000	3,000
Allowance for uncollectibles.......	500	1,000
Accumulated depreciation..........	10,000	7,000
Bonds payable.....................	50,000	50,000
Preferred stock, $100 par.........	40,000	32,000
Premium on preferred stock........	10,000	8,000
Common stock, no par.............	250,000	270,000
Retained earnings................	56,500	53,000
	$426,000	$429,000

THE MAIN CORPORATION
Income Statement for the Year Ended December 31, 1972

Sales revenue.....................		$211,600
Less:		
Returns........................	$ 10,000	
Uncollectibles.................	2,700	12,700
Net sales.........................		$198,900
Less:		
Cost of goods sold.............	$120,000	
Operating expenses.............	44,000	
Taxes..........................	6,000	
Interest charges...............	2,600	
Amortization of patent.........	10,000	182,600
Net income before extraordinary gains.........................		$ 16,300
Gain on sale of equipment.........	$ 500	
Gain on retirement of preferred stock........................	1,200	1,700
Net income.......................		$ 18,000
Preferred dividends...............	$ 5,500	
Common dividends.................	16,000	21,500
Reduction in Retained Earnings....		$ (3,500)

Additional Information: (1) Equipment costing $60,000 was sold. The book value of the equipment on the date of sale was $53,000. (2) Specific uncollectible accounts amounting to $2,200 were charged off to the allowance account.

      a)   Prepare a statement of sources and uses of working capital for the year 1972.

      b)   Prepare a cash funds statement.

15–4.   The following statement of source and application of funds was prepared by the controller of the Clovis Company.* The controller indicated that this statement was prepared under the "all financial resources" concept of funds, which is the broadest concept of funds and includes all transactions providing or requiring funds.

CLOVIS COMPANY

Statement of Source and Application of Funds
December 31, 1968

Funds were provided by:
Contribution of plant site by the City of Camden (Note 1)..............................	$115,000
Net income after extraordinary items per income statement (Note 2)............................	75,000
Issuance of note payable—due 1972..............	60,000
Depreciation and amortization..................	50,000
Deferred income taxes relating to accelerated depreciation...................................	10,000
Sale of equipment—book value (Note 3).........	5,000
Total funds provided........................	$315,000

Funds were applied to:
Acquisition of future plant site (Note 1)......	$250,000
Increase in working capital....................	30,000
Cash dividends declared but not paid...........	20,000
Acquisition of equipment.......................	15,000
Total funds applied........................	$315,000

Notes to Statement of Source and Application of Funds:

    1.   The City of Camden donated a plant site to Clovis Company valued by the board of directors at $115,000. The Company purchased adjoining property for $135,000.

    2.   Research and development expenditures of $25,000 incurred in 1968 were expensed. These expenses are considered abnormal.

    3.   Equipment with a book value of $5,000 was sold for $8,000. The gain was included as an extroardinary item on the income statement.

      a)   Why is it considered desirable to present a statement of source and application of funds in financial reports?

      b)   Identify and discuss the weakness in presentation and disclosure in this statement for Clovis Company. Your discussion should explain why you consider them to be weaknesses and what you consider the proper treatment of the items to be. Do not prepare a revised statement.

15–5.   Phillip Morris Incorporated presented the following statement of source and application of funds in its 1968 annual report.

---

* Adapted from the AICPA May 1969 examination.

```
Source:
  Net earnings...............................  $ 48,866,000
  Add (deduct), items not requiring outlay
    of funds:
    Depreciation............................    12,139,000
    Amortization............................       765,000
    Deferred income taxes and investment
      credit................................     4,676,000
    Equity in net earnings of unconsolidated
      foreign subsidiaries..................    (3,323,000)
    Dividends received from unconsolidated
      foreign subsidiaries..................       864,000
      Funds from operations.................  $ 63,987,000

Financing:
  New long-term debt........................  $115,250,000
  Less: Prepayments and retirement of
    long-term debt..........................    86,350,000
    Net additional long-term debt..........  $ 28,900,000
  Shares issued under stock options.........     5,156,000
    Funds from financing...................  $ 34,056,000
      Total funds available................  $ 98,043,000

Application:
  Dividends.................................  $ 19,677,000
  Expansion and modernization of property,
    plant, and equipment:
    Additions.............. $26,373,000
    Disposals..............     867,000
    Net cost of expansion and moderniza-
      tion.................................    25,506,000
  Investments in and advances to uncon-
    solidated foreign subsidiaries........    41,146,000
  Cost of domestic business acquired.......     5,415,000
  Other, net...............................        65,000
  Increase in working capital..............     6,234,000
    Total funds applied....................  $ 98,043,000
```

a) Why do sources of funds exactly equal applications?

b) Explain why the "equity in net earnings of unconsolidated foreign subsidiaries" is deducted from net earnings in deriving funds from operations? How would you normally expect that account to be handled in a funds statement? Is it correct to include dividends from unconsolidated foreign subsidiaries as a source of funds when the company uses the equity method?

c) Comment on the classification and disclosure of items on the statement.

15–6. The L. E. Nor Typewriter Company presented the following financial statements and supplementary information for the year 1972. Prepare a statement of sources and uses of funds. Define funds as net working capital.

Comparative Position Statement

Assets	December 31	
	1971	1972
Current:		
Cash..........................	$ 40,000	$ 74,000
Accounts receivable............	179,000	206,000
Allowance for doubtful accounts....................	(4,000)	(6,000)
Inventory (Fifo cost)..........	230,000	249,000
Total Current Assets..........	$445,000	$523,000
Noncurrent:		
Securities held for plant modernization...............	$ 25,000	....
Land...........................	22,000	$ 22,000
Buildings and machinery.........	200,000	225,000
Accumulated depreciation........	(40,000)	(50,000)
Goodwill.......................	5,000	....
Patents........................	....	7,000
Total Noncurrent Assets.......	$212,000	$204,000
Total Assets...............	$657,000	$727,000
Equities		
Current liabilities:		
Accounts payable...............	$ 70,000	$ 77,000
Accrued liabilities............	47,000	49,000
Total Current Liabilities.....	$117,000	$126,000
Bonds payable (5%):		
Face value....................	$120,000	$120,000
Premium.......................	2,000	1,500
Total Bonds Payable..........	$122,000	$121,500
Reserve for contingencies........	$ 60,000	$ 25,000
Common stockholders' equity:		
Common stock, $100 par value....	$200,000	$225,000
Premium on common stock.........	50,000	62,500
Retained earnings..............	108,000	167,000
Total Common Stockholders' Equity....................	$358,000	$454,500
Total Equities..............	$657,000	$727,000

Additional information: (1) Depreciation expense included in the above expenses amounts to $18,000. (2) Expenditures on plant assets for new equipment and other modernization programs amounted to $44,000. Of this amount, $4,000 was charged to the Accumulated Depreciation account; the rest was charged directly to the buildings and machinery account. (3) Patents were acquired during 1972 at a cost of $8,000.

Statement of Income and Retained Earnings, 1972

Sales revenue:

Gross sales.....................	$1,350,000	
Less: Returns, allowances, and provision for doubtful accounts.................	(50,000)	
Net sales revenue............		$1,300,000

Expenses:

Cost of goods sold.............	$ 980,000	
Selling........................	146,000	
Administrative.................	85,500	
Interest.......................	5,500	
Federal income tax.............	38,000	
Total expenses..............		1,255,000
Net income before extraordinary items........................		$ 45,000

Extraordinary gains (losses):

Gain on sale of securities held for plant modernization.....	$ 15,000	
Loss on disposal of machinery..	(1,000)	
Write-off of goodwill..........	(5,000)	9,000
Net income.....................		$ 54,000
Retained earnings, January 1, 1972.......................		108,000
		$ 162,000
Add reserve for contingencies no longer needed...............		35,000
Deduct cash dividends...........		(30,000)
Retained Earnings, December 31, 1972.......................		$ 167,000

15–7.   The Kingfish Corporation just completed its second full year of operations. During the first year, the company operated at a very slight profit. The president is very concerned, however, over the results of operations for the second year. The firm seems to have been in a continuous cash bind all year long. In fact, just recently, the bank had notified the firm that its bank balance had fallen below the $10,000 level required under a long-term loan agreement.

After preparing the financial statements for the second year, the controller proudly announced that the firm had earned net income of $40,000. When pressed by the president as to how the firm could be operating profitably and yet be in financial difficulties, the controller turned to you for help. The balance sheets at the end of years 1 and 2 are given below:

	End of Year	
	1	2
Cash	$ 19,000	$ 8,000
Accounts receivable	24,000	61,000
Inventories	13,000	42,500
Prepayments	2,500	4,500
Machinery	45,000	45,000
Furniture and fixtures	10,000	28,000
Accumulated depreciation	(9,000)	(22,000)
Total Assets	$104,500	$167,000
Accounts payable	$ 9,000	$ 12,000
Wages payable	3,000	5,000
Taxes payable	2,000	4,500
Five year bank loan	40,000	35,000
Capital stock	30,000	50,000
Retained earnings	20,500	60,500
Total Equities	$104,500	$167,000

Prepare a report for the controller and president which will explain what has happened. Include some type of funds statement as part of your explanation.

15–8. The condensed financial statements of the Howburne Corporation for 1972 were as follows:*

THE HOWBURNE CORPORATION

Statement of Income for the Year Ended December 31, 1967

Income:
Gross operating income......... $2,410,655
Nonoperating income, including
    dividends and interest.....   21,708
    $2,432,363

Deductions:
Operating charges:
  Materials and supplies
      used.................... $870,531
  Wages and salaries........... 906,387
  Provision for depreciation... 114,079
  Taxes (other than federal
      income tax)............. 26,221
  Other operating charges...... 33,762
  Interest charges............. 1,297
  Loss on investments.......... 6,016
  Estimated federal income tax... 284,442   2,242,735
Net Income...................... $ 189,628

---

* Problem adapted from AICPA examination.

THE HOWBURNE CORPORATION

Balance Sheets, December 31, 1966 and 1967

	1967	1966	Change
Current Assets:			
Cash...............................	$ 215,221	$ 225,351	−$ 10,130
Marketable securities, at cost....	180,767	251,388	− 70,621
Trade receivables, less estimated uncollectibles....	266,559	195,991	+ 70,568
Inventories at cost...............	322,438	359,175	− 36,737
Prepaid operating expenses........	15,209	17,894	− 2,685
Total Current Assets......	$1,000,194	$1,049,799	−$ 49,605
Less: Current Liabilities:			
Accounts and notes payable (trade)...	$ 108,623	$ 254,181	−$145,558
Wages and salaries payable.........	12,602	11,495	+ 1,107
Estimated Federal income taxes payable...	295,580	299,466	− 3,886
Dividends payable..................	23,726	25,591	− 1,865
Interest payable...................	750	296	+ 454
Other accrued operating expenses payable...	12,622	14,942	− 2,320
Total Current Liabilities......	$ 453,903	$ 605,971	−$152,068
Working Capital.......................	$ 546,291	$ 443,828	+$102,463
Property, plant, and equipment (less cumulative depreciation to date)......	1,356,132	1,200,816	+ 155,316
	$1,902,423	$1,644,644	+$257,779
Less: Long-term bank loans........	50,000		+ 50,000
Net Assets.....................	$1,852,423	$1,644,644	+$207,779
Stockholders' Equity:			
Preferred stock, 6% cumulative, $100 par...	$ 260,200	$ 265,200	−$ 5,000
Common stock, $100 par.............	1,272,400	1,092,300	+ 180,100
Paid-in surplus....................	61,524	42,043	+ 19,481
Retained earnings..................	258,299	245,101	+ 13,198
Total Equity...............	$1,852,423	$1,644,644	+$207,779

The board of directors recognizes that readers of the corporation's annual report to stockholders may be puzzled by the fact that despite a substantial net income after taxes, the cash balance of the company decreased and the corporation resorted to some long-term borrowing. Accordingly, the directors have requested a statement that will reveal clearly the flow of cash into and out of the Howburne Corporation during the past fiscal year.

Prepare the cash-flow statement of the corporation for the year. Prepare a supporting schedule showing the statement of income, adjusted to a cash basis.

The following additional information is available: (1) During the year, marketable securities were purchased at a cost of $24,692. (2) The estimated uncollectible receivables increased $11,448, despite the write-off of $2,605 of bad accounts. During the year, an account receivable of $2,000, written off in a prior year, was collected; the credit was made to Recovery of Bad Debts, which was netted against other operating charges in the statement of income. (3) During the year, 50 shares of preferred stock were reacquired by purchase at a premium of 9 percent over par. These shares were canceled, at which time the excess of the purchase price over the average amount originally contributed for these shares ($105 per share) was debited to Retained Earnings. (4) The only entries in the Retained Earnings account for the year were for net income, dividend declarations, and the cancellation of preferred stock. (5) There were no sales or retirements of fixed assets during the year.

15–9. The following condensed information is taken from the records of the Nonesuch Company for the year 1972.

	December 31	
	1972	1971
Current assets..............................	$42,600	$45,000
Investments...............................	8,500	5,000
Land......................................	3,500	3,000
Buildings and machinery...................	35,000	27,000
Accumulated depreciation..................	(8,700)	(8,000)
Patents (less amortization)................	4,200	5,400
	$85,100	$77,400
Current liabilities.........................	$14,500	$ 8,200
8% debenture bonds payable...............	....	14,500
6% debenture bonds payable...............	13,000	....
Common stock, par value..................	16,000	15,000
Common stock, excess over par...........	16,500	15,000
Reserve for future losses on investments...	1,200	2,000
Retained earnings.........................	23,900	22,700
	$85,100	$77,400

Additional information: (1) A reconciliation of the balances in retained earnings is as follows:

Balance, January 1, 1972	$22,700
Net income for 1972	1,000
Award received from settlement of 1968 patent infringement case	5,200
Dividends	(5,000)
Balance, December 31, 1972	$23,900

(2) Included in net income was a loss of $1,600 on the sale of the Missouri plant, sold for $3,000 cash at the beginning of the year. Accumulated depreciation was $2,000. The Missouri plant site (land) originally cost $300. (3) Investments were sold during the year at a loss. The loss was charged to the Reserve for Future Losses on Investments and did not appear on the income statement. (4) During 1972, the 8% debenture bonds were called for redemption. Most of them were refunded through the issuance of new 6% debenture bonds, and the rest were retired for cash. (5) The shares of common stock were issued in exchange for some land and machinery. The rest of the buildings and machinery were purchased for cash.

a)   Prepare a statement of sources and uses of working capital for the year 1972. Show how you arrived at the figures in the statement.

b)   Discuss carefully the treatment of the bond refunding and the issuance of stock in exchange for land and machinery. What problems do these transactions cause? How did you solve it?

15–10.   Bristol-Myers Company presented the following funds statement for the year ended December 31, 1969 in its annual report.

```
Source of funds:
  Net earnings.............................. $ 67,605,836
  Depreciation..............................   13,362,087
  Proceeds from stock issued under stock
    option plans............................    6,578,823
  Capitalization of Doan's operations prior
    to the acquisition of Foster-Milburn
    Company.................................      234,066
  Increase in current and other
    liabilities.............................   14,383,249
  Disposition of Doan's operations as part
    of the Foster-Millburn Company
    acquisition.............................    4,200,000
  Conversion of debentures and preferred
    stock...................................      938,782
                                             $107,302,843

Application of funds:
  Additions to property, plant, and equip-
    ment, net of disposals................. $ 32,842,715
  Increase in receivables...................   30,800,797
  Increase in inventories...................   19,561,338
  Increase in prepaid expenses and prepaid
    taxes...................................    2,272,786
  Change in other assets....................    1,028,229
  Excess of cost over net tangible assets
    received in business acquisitions.....     1,398,037
  Decrease in long-term debt...............     2,388,098
  Merger costs.............................       639,508
  Dividends on preferred and common stock...   37,151,444
                                             $128,082,952

Net Change in Cash and Securities.......... $(20,780,109)
```

a) What definition of funds is the company using? What advantages and uses does this concept have compared to others?

b) Explain how each of the sources and uses listed relates to that concept of funds.

c) Comment on the presentation of information on the statement.

15–11. Stu Pidity, the president of Planned Obsolescence, Inc., calls you on the telephone. Quite irately he says, "The better we do, the worse off we get. Net income was over $17,000, but working capital went down by almost $3,000 and cash decreased even more, over $8,000. And we didn't even buy any plant assets this year. Can't anyone in the accounting area explain to me what's going on?"

Financial information for the year is summarized below:

Income Statement

Sales (less adjustment for doubtful accounts of $3,000)		$ 90,500
Equity in earnings of subsidiary		17,000
		$107,500
Expenses:		
Cost of goods sold	$51,700	
Depreciation	2,100	
Other	37,200	91,000
Net income before extraordinary gain		$ 16,500
Gain on sale of equipment (net of income tax of $200)		400
Net Income		$ 16,900

Retained Earnings

Beginning balance	$ 8,800
Net income	16,900
Dividends	(16,700)
Ending balance	$ 9,000

Position Statement Data

	Beginning	End of Year
Cash	$14,400	$ 6,100
Accounts receivable	6,000	10,500
Inventory	7,700	11,000
Prepayments	600	700
Investment in subsidiary	6,000	8,900
Land	5,000	6,000
Plant assets	22,000	20,900
	$61,700	$64,100
Allowance for doubtful accounts	$ 500	$ 700
Accumulated depreciation	8,400	9,800
Accounts payable	3,400	6,100
Other accrued liabilities	800	300
Dividends payable	1,100	1,200
Long-term notes payable	6,000	3,900
Capital stock	20,000	20,200
Paid in capital	12,700	12,900
Retained earnings	8,800	9,000
	$61,700	$64,100

a) Prepare a funds statement for the year which will explain the decrease in working capital.

b) Prepare a funds statement for the year which will explain the decrease in the cash balance.

c) Write a brief memo to the president summarizing your major conclusions and explanations for "what's going on."

15–12. Crown Cork & Seal Company, Inc., presented the following statement of source and application of cash for the year ended December 31, 1969 in its annual report.

```
Cash obtained from:
  Net income...........................  $23,005,000
  Depreciation.........................   13,909,000
  Income appropriated for future years'
    taxes..............................      365,000
  Minority shareholders' equity in
    retained profits of subsidiaries.....    634,000
  Total derived from operations..........  $37,913,000
  Accounts payable and accrued
    liabilities—increase................   14,485,000
  Plant and equipment sold less
    accumulated depreciation............    6,708,000
  Inventories—decrease..................    2,530,000
  Other.................................      361,000
                                                        $61,997,000
Cash applied to:
  Purchase of preferred stock...........  $     327,000
  Investments in and advances to new
    subsidiaries........................    5,888,000
  Purchase of debentures for sinking
    fund................................    3,164,000
  Plant and equipment expenditures.......  32,730,000
  Repayment of bank and other loans......  10,456,000
  Preferred dividends...................      134,000
  Accounts receivable and other
    current assets—increase.............    9,777,000
                                                         62,476,000
Decrease in cash resources..............                $  (479,000)
```

a) Is $37,913,000 really the *cash* derived from operations? Explain. Estimate the cash-from-operations figure more accurately.

b) Why are depreciation, income appropriated for future years' taxes, and minority interest in profits shown as sources in deriving cash from operations?

c) The $6,708,000 shown as a source of cash is the book value of the plant and equipment sold. What assumption underlies this treatment? What probably has taken place?

d) Comment on the usefulness of the information on the statement and the manner in which it is presented.

15–13. The president of Tuttle Specialties Company requests that you prepare a statement of source and application of funds for the benefit of the stockholders.* Comparative balance sheets for the Company are presented below

---

* Adapted from the AICPA May 1967 examination.

TUTTLE SPECIALTIES COMPANY

General Ledger Post-Closing Trial Balances For the
Years Ended December 31, 1966 and 1965

Debits	1966	1965	Increase (Decrease)
Cash...	$ 157,700	$ 100,400	$ 57,300
Certificates of deposit due March 31, 1967......	175,000		175,000
Marketable securities.........................	100,000	262,100	(162,000)
Customers' notes and accounts receivable........	390,000	327,300	62,700
Inventories.................................	155,400	181,200	(25,800)
Investment in wholly owned subsidiary at equity in net assets............................	140,000	190,400	(50,400)
Bond sinking fund...........................		62,200	(62,200)
Advance to suppliers.........................	137,500		137,500
Plant and equipment.........................	2,138,600	1,952,600	186,000
Goodwill....................................	. . . .	150,000	(150,000)
Discount on bonds payable....................	. . . .	10,200	(10,200)
Total debits...........................	$3,394,300	$3,236,400	$ 157,900

Credits

	1966	1965	Increase (Decrease)
Notes receivable discounted....................	$ 100,000		$ 100,000
Accounts payable............................	192,400	$ 147,600	44,800
Bank loans, current..........................		70,000	(70,000)
Allowance for depreciation....................	510,000	359,700	150,300
Accrued payables............................	47,100	72,300	(25,200)
Income and other taxes payable................	128,700	25,500	103,200
Deferred income taxes.......................	58,500	65,000	(6,500)
5% mortgage bonds due 1974.................	. . . .	320,000	(320,000)
4% serial bonds.............................	100,000	. . . .	100,000
Capital stock, $10 par value..................	1,110,000	900,000	210,000
Premium on capital stock.....................	152,100	. . . .	152,100
Retained earnings appropriated for the retirement of 5% mortgage bonds......................	. . . .	62,200	(62,200)
Retained earnings unappropriated..............	995,500	1,214,100	(218,600)
Total credits...........................	$3,394,300	$3,236,400	$ 157,900

Additional information:

1. An analysis of the Retained Earnings Unappropriated account follows:

Retained earnings unappropriated, Dec. 31, 1965.....		$1,214,100
Add: Net income for the year.....................		112,200
Transfer from appropriation for retirement of 5% mortgage bonds........................		62,200
Total		$1,388,500
Deduct: Write-off of good will....................	$150,000	
Cash dividends.......................	90,000	
10% stock dividend.....................	153,000	393,000
Retained earnings unappropriated, Dec. 31, 1966.....		$ 995,500

2. On January 2, 1966 marketable securities costing $162,000 were sold for $165,800. The proceeds from the sale of the securities, the

funds in the bond sinking fund, and the amount received from the sale of the 4% serial bonds were used to retire the 5% mortgage bonds at 102½.

3. The company paid a stock dividend of 10% on stock outstanding at February 1, 1966. The market value per share at that date was $17.

4. The company advanced $137,500 to a supplier on August 15 for the purchase of special machinery which is to be delivered in June 1967.

5. Accounts receivable of $15,000 and $12,500 were considered uncollectible and written off against income in 1966 and 1965 respectively.

6. The stockholders approved a stock option plan on September 1, 1966. Under the plan 100,000 shares of capital stock were reserved for issuance to key employees at prices not less than market value at the dates of grant. The options would become exercisable in three equal installments starting one year after the date of grant and would expire five years after the date of grant. At December 31, 1966 options were granted for 20,000 shares at $16 per share. The options were carried on a memo basis and were not recorded in the accounts.

7. Extraordinary repairs of $12,500 to the equipment were charged to the Allowance for Depreciation account during the year. No assets were retired during 1966.

8. The wholly owned subsidiary reported a loss for the year of $50,400. The loss was booked by the parent.

a) Prepare the statement requested by the president. Define funds as net working capital. Show funds from operations as a single figure on the statement, but provide supporting schedules wherever necessary.

b) How would an advocate of the all financial resources concept of funds treat the retirement of bonds?

15–14. Presented below are the financial statements of Sykes Corporation for 1972, and certain other information.

SYKES CORPORATION

Comparative Position Statement, December 31, 1971 and 1972

Assets	1971	1972
Current:		
Cash............................	$ 30,500	$ 39,000
Marketable securities...........	10,000	11,000
Accounts receivable.............	60,000	100,000
Allowance for bad debts.........	(2,000)	(4,000)
Inventories.....................	130,000	150,000
Total Current Assets.........	$228,500	$296,000
Noncurrent:		
Buildings and equipment.........	$100,000	$155,000
Accumulated depreciation........	(20,000)	(10,000)
Patents, net of amortization....	15,000	20,000
Total Noncurrent Assets.......	$ 95,000	$165,000
Total Assets...............	$323,500	$461,000

Equities		
Current Liabilities:		
Accounts payable................	$ 90,000	$182,000
Salaries payable................	15,000	30,400
Taxes payable...................	20,000	24,000
Total Current Liabilities.....	$125,000	$236,400
Noncurrent Liabilities:		
Bonds payable, par..............	$ 20,000	$ 20,000
Bonds payable, discount.........	(500)	(400)
Deferred income taxes...........	11,000	18,000
Total Noncurrent Liabilities..	$ 30,500	$ 37,600
Stockholders' Equity:		
Preferred stock.................	$ 50,000	$ 60,000
Common stock, no par value......	90,000	110,000
Retained earnings...............	28,000	35,000
Cost of treasury stock..........	0	(18,000)
Total Stockholders' Equity....	$168,000	$187,000
Total Equities..............	$323,500	$461,000

SYKES CORPORATION

Income Statement for the Year Ending December 31, 1972

```
Sales............................                    $413,000
Less:
  Returns and allowances..........  $  4,000
  Provision for bad debts.........     8,000           12,000
Net sales.........................                   $401,000
Less:
  Cost of goods sold..............  $230,000
  Selling and general expense.....    80,000
  Depreciation expense............     6,000
  Patent amortization expense.....     5,000
  Interest expense................       900          321,900
Net income before tax.............                   $ 79,100
Income taxes......................                     39,000
Net income before extraordinary
  items...........................                   $ 40,100
  Gain on sale of equipment*......  $ 10,000
  Loss on sale of marketable
    securities....................   (15,600)         (5,600)
Net Income........................                   $ 34,500
Preferred dividends...............                      2,500
Earnings of common stockholders...                   $ 32,000
  Common dividends—cash...........  $  5,000
  Common dividends—stock..........    20,000           25,000
Earnings retained in the
  business........................                   $  7,000
```

* The original cost of the equipment sold in 1972 was $30,000.

a) Prepare a statement of sources and uses of funds for 1972, de-fining funds as net working capital. Compute funds from opera-tions, starting with sales.

b) Compute funds from operations, starting with net income.

c) Prepare a schedule showing *cash* from operations.

15–15. The Warren Company's financial statements for fiscal 1973 showed the following (all figures are in thousands of dollars):

Consolidated Position Statements

Assets	June 30	
	1973	1972
Current Assets:		
Cash................................	$ 921	$ 922
Accounts receivable, net...........	1,413	1,110
Claim for income tax refund........	17	...
Inventories........................	1,811	819
Total Current Assets..............	$4,162	$2,851
Noncurrent Assets:		
Investment in subsidiaries.........	496	319
Land...............................	181	122
Buildings and equipment............	1,800	1,850
Less: Accumulated depreciation......	(470)	(200)
Excess of cost over book value......	100	120
Total Assets....................	$6,269	$5,062

| | June 30 | |
Equities	1973	1972
Current Liabilities:		
Accounts payable.....................	$ 180	$ 178
Wages payable.......................	100	110
Interest payable....................	40	...
Total Current Liabilities.........	$ 320	$ 288
Long-Term Liabilities:		
Bonds payable.......................	1,000	...
Discount on bonds payable...........	(54)	...
Reserves:		
Reserve for deferred income taxes...	170	210
Reserve for contingencies...........	60	80
Total Liabilities and		
Reserves........................	$1,496	$ 578
Minority interest....................	130	118
Stockholders' Equity:		
Common stock, par...................	1,320	1,300
Paid-in capital.....................	1,794	1,600
Retained earnings...................	1,745	1,850
Less: Treasury stock................	(216)	(384)
Total equities...................	$6,269	$5,062

Consolidated Income Statement
for the Year Ended June 30, 1973

Sales...................................		$2,520
Equity in income of unconsolidated		
subsidiaries........................		291
		$2,811
Deductions:		
Cost of goods sold..................	$2,374	
Selling and administrative..........	281	
Other...............................	125	
Interest............................	46	
Minority interest in earnings.......	12	2,838
Net loss before taxes...............		$ (27)
Tax refund from loss carry-back.......		10
Net loss before extraordinary loss....		$ (17)
Loss on sale of equipment, net of tax		
savings of $7,000...................		(15)
Net Loss.............................		$ (32)

Consolidated Statement of Retained Earnings
for the Year Ended June 30, 1973

Retained earnings, July 1, 1972....................	$1,850
Add: Excess reserve no longer needed..............	20
	$1,870
Deduct:	
Net loss..	(32)
Cash dividends on common stock....................	(40)
Market value of common shares issued as a stock	
dividend..	(53)
Retained Earnings, June 30, 1973..................	$1,745

Other information: (1) Depreciation of $494 thousand is included among the various expense accounts. (2) Buildings and equipment purchased during the year cost $376,000. (3) Treasury stock was issued during the year for land and for cash. (4) The bonds were issued on January 1, 1973. The stated interest rate on the bond is 8 percent.

The president of the company would like to know how it was possible to increase total assets over 20 percent and working capital almost 50 percent when the company operated at a loss.

a)   Prepare a statement of sources and uses of funds for the year. Define funds as net working capital.

b)   Repeat part (*a*), defining funds as cash. Is this a more useful statement in this case? Explain.

c)   Write a brief one-paragraph report to the president summarizing and integrating your funds statements.

CHAPTER SIXTEEN

ANALYSIS OF
FINANCIAL
STATEMENTS

IN THE PRECEDING chapters we have been developing a system of collecting and reporting financial information about the performance and position of the business entity. We have had one major goal in mind—the preparation of reports primarily for external groups interested in the activities of the business. Nearly all decisions made by management ultimately are reflected on the financial statements. Hence, the statements provide major assistance to stockholders or creditors making judgments concerning the firm.

This chapter studies the financial statements from the viewpoint of their use by an analyst. Our purpose is to develop some procedures to make the statement figures more meaningful. The development of such procedures includes not only a knowledge of particular techniques, but also an understanding of the concepts and methods employed in the preparation of the statements and an appreciation of the context in which statement analysis is carried out.

OBJECTIVES OF STATEMENT ANALYSIS

The analysis of financial statements serves a number of different objectives—appraisal of past performance, evaluation of present condition, prediction of future potential, or possibly all three. Being basically historical, financial statements are better suited for the first two purposes. Yet the majority of statement readers are concerned with the future—the capacity of the firm to grow and prosper and the ability of the firm to adapt to varying conditions. Wisely used, financial statement analysis also can provide a base from which to project the future and can supply insights as to how the firm may respond to future economic developments.

Whatever their time perspectives, analysts generally desire information about the financial soundness, profitability, and efficiency of the business under study. Within these three areas though, different statement users will employ different analytical procedures and emphasize different information, depending on their individual purposes. Creditors, for example, may be primarily interested in financial safety. Yet they cannot entirely ignore profitability, for in the long run a firm that continually operates unprofitably will inevitably encounter difficulty in acquiring financial capital to remain solvent. Stockholders, on the other hand, presumably are more concerned with the profitability of the firm. Nonetheless, they are also interested in keeping the business financially sound. Managers are interested in all three areas in making internal operating decisions.

Because of this overlap in interests, it is extremely difficult to talk about statement analysis from the viewpoint of any individual user group. This chapter follows an approach of presenting statement analysis in a general framework organized around the major areas of financial strength, profitability, and efficiency. These areas can be analyzed historically to yield answers to questions such as: How has the financial condition of the firm changed over time? In what areas has the firm exhibited superiority or inferiority? Do the financial statements support management's opinion of the condition of the business? How well has management performed its function as a steward of invested resources? In addition, these same areas can be viewed prospectively to shed light on questions like: How will management's plans for the future affect the financial statements? Do the statements indicate an inability or difficulty in reaching future goals? How will the firm be affected by a contraction or expansion of economic activity? Do any areas show a deteriorating condition that is likely to become critical in the future?

PRESENTATION OF THE FINANCIAL STATEMENTS

Before turning his attention to specific methods of statement analysis, an analyst first must consider the nature and quality of his "raw material." The depth of analysis possible and the reliability and meaning of the results are directly related to the accuracy and soundness of the statements themselves. Any limitations of the financial statements carry over to the analysis.

Some of these limitations are inherent in the basic nature of financial accounting. For instance, most resources on the position statement are listed at amortized cost. Current market values may be more appropriate for the intended purpose, yet they may diverge greatly from the book values shown. Moreover, the position statement represents only one moment in time. Any ratio taken from position statement data represents a relationship that has existed on that one date. It may not be a normal relationship if the position statement date represents an unusual point in time or has been influenced by a major event that has just recently occurred. Similarly, the income statement may contain extraordinary items which could distort the analysis.

Still other limitations may be introduced into the analysis through inadequate or misunderstood accounting policies or the lack of full and fair disclosure in reporting. One way to avoid errors and to become cognizant of these kinds of limitations is for the analyst to begin his investigation with an overview of the statements in order to understand and interpret the firm's accounting practices. Some guidelines are suggested in this section under the headings of accounting principles, disclosure and terminology, and the auditor's report.

Accounting Principles

Most financial statements are prepared in accordance with generally accepted accounting principles. However, we have seen numerous examples of alternative procedures that are considered equally acceptable and instances of the failure of GAAP to come to grips with economic realities. Consequently, anyone who analyzes statement relationships or makes interfirm comparisons without comprehending the accounting principles employed runs a grave risk of error and misinterpretation. An analyst may be unable to change the statements to a different set of principles, but at least he should be able to understand the general effects of alternative procedures on the statements.

A few examples illustrate the importance of this point. Statement analysis involves the study of relationships—between revenues and expenses, assets and liabilities, income and investment, etc.—and the comparison of these relationships between companies or over several times periods. The basic amounts shown for these items, and hence any relationships derived from them, may be significantly altered through the use of different accounting procedures. Lifo inventory results in a higher cost of goods sold and a lower inventory than Fifo. A company that leases significant amounts of fixed assets without capitalizing the leases shows fewer assets and smaller liabilities than a firm that borrows money explicitly to purchase assets. A merger recorded as a pooling affects asset investment and income measurement differently from one recorded as a purchase.

In brief, sound interpretations and meaningful comparisons require a knowledge of what accounting principles are applied in the preparation of the financial statements. Present-day standards of disclosure require that the policies followed in most of the areas where alternatives exist be indicated to the reader of the statement. It behooves the analyst to review these disclosures, to assess their impact on the financial statements and his analysis, and perhaps even to make adjustments to the statements, where practicable, to achieve meaningful relationships and comparisons.

Disclosure and Terminology

Ample disclosure and clarity of presentation are also essential to an intelligent use of the financial statements. The analyst must understand the terminology and classifications shown on the statements and be alert to the importance of additional interpretive information found in the notes to the statements. Previous chapters contain guidelines for full and fair disclosure, proper terminology, and reasonable classification of accounts. Some general comments may be helpful, however.

Notes contain not only descriptions of accounting policies but other types of supplementary information as well. Explanations of extraordinary items, prior period adjustments, or major changes in accounting methods and their financial impact can be found there. Financial commitments, lease agreements, backlogs of sales orders, preferred dividends in arrears, and descriptions of contingencies are other examples of footnote information. Notes also call attention to material facts occurring after the date of the statements. The statements may be accurate as of the end of the year. However, they may be published two or three months later. If major changes in such items as capital stock, indebtedness, dividends, and plant assets have occurred, a note should accompany the statements indicating these. The reader is then able to interpret the statements in the light of existing conditions which are *materially* different from those reflected in the statements.

The best accounting system fails in its communication task if the captions used on the report are foreign to the analyst. Fortunately, recent years have seen the increasing use of more descriptive terms on the financial statements. Nevertheless, the analyst is still going to be faced with items that require careful study in order to be classified properly. Three particular areas that cause trouble are "deferred charges," "deferred credits or income," and "reserves." In most cases, the items classified as deferred charges are long-term prepayments and other intangible assets. However, the term does serve as a catch-all for items that could be classified separately. Deferred credits or income usually means current or long-term liabilities, often for goods and services to be given up in the future. And as noted in Chapter Thirteen, reserves can encompass contra-assets, liabilities, or restrictions on retained earnings. Before working with the figures themselves, the analyst should review the statements for understanding and make any reclassifications which he feels are necessary.

The Auditor's Report

Accompanying the financial statements for many companies is an auditor's report (sometimes called an opinion or certificate), in which the company's independent certified public accountant expresses his judgment concerning the financial statements. Most reports contain opinions similar to the one presented below, which provides positive assurance that there is a sound basis for the representations shown on the financial statements.

We have examined the statement of financial position of the X Company as of December 31, 19___, and the related statement of income for the year then ended. Our examination was made in accordance with *generally accepted auditing standards,* and such other auditing procedures *as we considered necessary* in the circumstances.

In our opinion, the accompanying statements of financial position and statement of income present *fairly* the financial position of the X Company at December 31, 19___, and the result of operations for the year then ended, in conformity with *generally accepted accounting principles* applied on a basis *consistent with that of the preceding year.* [Italics added.]

In the first paragraph, commonly called the scope paragraph, the auditor states that his examination of the statements and records was conducted properly. Notice that the auditor, not management, has determined the nature and extent of the audit work performed. The second, or opinion, paragraph attests to three conclusions of considerable importance to the analyst. Italics have been supplied to highlight the key words in these conclusions. The first affirms that the statements represent what they purport to represent, undistorted by the value judgments of the persons preparing them. Secondly, the particular statements involved conform to generally accepted accounting principles. Thirdly, the accounting and reporting principles have been applied consistently from one period to the next.

If the CPA cannot attest to all of these factors or if the scope of his examination has been limited for some reason, he issues a "qualified" opinion. He may say, for example, that "subject to the settlement of the patent infringement suit" or "except for the change in the valuation of inventories" the statements present fairly, etc. When the qualification involves a material item, the auditor, in rare circumstances, may decline to express an opinion at all (issue a disclaimer of opinion).

The standards followed in the preparation of an audit report require that the CPA make sure that the reason for the qualification (or disclaimer) is fully disclosed either in notes to the financial statements or in his opinion. For example, if accounting principles have not been applied consistently, full disclosure must be given to the nature of the change, including the quantitative impact. If the firm follows an accounting principle at variance with an opinion of the Accounting Principles Board, this fact must be indicated.

INTRODUCTION TO STATEMENT ANALYSIS

The preceding section suggests three preliminary steps to be undertaken: (1) ascertain the accounting principles employed; (2) review statement terminology, classification, and footnote disclosure; and (3) read the auditor's report. From this overview of the financial information, the analyst then proceeds to select particular items from the statements for detailed study. But statement analysis cannot be made in a vacuum. Implicit in our earlier discussions have been the companion ideas of relationships and comparison.

Comparison—The Key Point

Statement analysis requires a basis for comparison. Accounting figures have little meaning by themselves. They take on meaning only when compared to something. The only way to determine whether an amount is adequate, improving or deteriorating, in or out of proportion, is by relating it to other items. For example, a firm reports net operating income of $500,000. Is this satisfactory? If last year the company reported only $400,000 of net operating income, then $500,000 looks good. But if industry profits have expanded an estimated 50 percent during the year, 20 percent does not look so good. On the other hand, if the firm generated the $500,000 of income with an asset investment of only $1.5 million, a 33⅓ percent return on investment, even before tax, appears very reasonable. Its reasonableness may diminish however, if we discover that a major competitor was able to earn $300,000 net operating income on an asset investment of $700,000—a before-tax return of almost 43 percent.

The major point is that some comparison is essential to put the analysis into proper perspective. Different bases of comparison are used in different circumstances, and they do not all necessarily lead to the same judgments. Obviously, the starting point is to relate specific statement items to each other. The study of specific statement relationships is called ratio analysis and comprises the major part of our subsequent discussion. Nevertheless, this is only the starting point. The ratios, themselves, also must be evaluated by comparison with similar ratios. Three common bases of comparison are discussed below.

Comparison with Prior Periods. One customary approach involves comparing a firm over time. Here, the company's own past performance serves as the basis for comparison. By looking at changes from year to year, we can spot trends and tendencies as well as appraise current periods in the light of historical relationships. We must be careful, however, to see that we are dealing with comparable data. Accounting methods may have changed; business entities may have been modified; or the measuring unit, the dollar, may have been drastically altered in size because of changing price levels.

Comparison with Predetermined Goals. A second basis of comparison is some type of standard set in advance. Frequently employed by internal management, this type of analysis compares the actual results reflected in the financial statements with what the results should be or were predicted to be. Actual income is related to budgeted income; actual rate of return on investment is compared to a target percentage. If predetermined goals are carefully formulated, this type of comparison is valuable, particularly when followed up by a detailed study to determine why the actual results turned out differently from expectations. External analysts sometimes use preestablished "rules of thumb" as guides in their analysis—e.g., the ratio of current assets to current liabilities should be at least 2:1. However, in many instances such external guidelines are too general, failing to take into consideration changes in the operating, legal, or economic environment that might invalidate the comparison.

Comparison with Other Companies. An alternative comparison, often made by investors, employs intercompany contrasts. Standards of comparison include ratios calculated from the financial statements of competing companies or average ratios for the industry. A number of organizations publish financial statistics for individual firms and industry groups. Dun & Bradstreet, Inc., for instance, reports 14 different ratios for 125 industry groups. Other sources include Robert Morris Associates, investment advisory services such as Moody's Investors Services and Standard & Poor's Corporation, brokerage firms, and numerous trade associations.

Although this type of comparison is valuable, the analyst must be cautious in using the results. The problems of noncomparable data become magnified. Differences in accounting procedures may mask real differences or significant similarities among firms. And mergers and diversification may make tenuous at best the classification of a firm in a particular industry or the identification of its major competitors.

Reporting Problems of Diversified Companies

Comparisons of diversified companies with industry trends or competing companies are especially perplexing. The last 20 years have witnessed an accelerating trend toward diversification, either through internal expansion or by means of the acquisition of other companies. In some instances the outcome of these combinations has been the creation of huge conglomerate corporations which operate a number of unrelated businesses. The individual components function, often quite autonomously, in widely diverse industries and are linked only by top management control and overall stock ownership.

The existence and growth of these large diversified firms raises important questions about the disclosure necessary in financial statements to enable investors to make intelligent judgments. The reporting of only a single income statement and balance sheet combining all the unrelated businesses causes three potential difficulties for the investor. First, the evaluation of management is made complex because profitable and unprofitable lines may offset each other. One of the risks in management's decision to diversify is the possibility of expanding into unprofitable lines. Yet a combined statement allows management to "bury its mistakes" and avoid external assessment of the costs and benefits from its diversification policy. Second, industry lines are blurred or disappear with conglomerate companies. Industry analysis is an essential element in evaluating past performance and even more crucial in predicting the future. Some industries are declining; others are growing. Different industries may be developing at different rates. A highly diversified company does not operate in a single industry, and combination reporting makes it extremely difficult to obtain information for each of its industry lines. The third difficulty concerns the inability to make meaningful comparisons on an individual company or competitor basis. A conglomerate may compete with one firm in one line of business but with an entirely different firm in another of its lines. To what (if anything) does the analyst compare the overall financial statements?

Numerous analysts and accountants have suggested as a solution that diversified companies be required to report separate income statements for each of their major lines of business. Indeed, some would extend the requirement to include complete financial statements. The Securities and Exchange Commission already requires that companies indicate the relative importance of all segments that contribute 15 percent or more to the *revenues* of the firm. The Accounting Principles Board has recommended that diversified firms experiment with the voluntary disclosure of revenue and income figures for major separable segments of the business and complete financial statements for segments that operate autonomously and employ distinctly different financial structures.[1]

Numerous difficulties are involved in any attempt to provide financial data by business segments, and many businesses strongly oppose disclosure of this information on these grounds. One obvious problem is identification of the segments on which to report. If firms were to report according to their own organizational structure (geographic area, cus-

---

[1] *Disclosure of Supplemental Financial Information by Diversified Companies, Statement of the Accounting Principles Board No. 2* (New York: AICPA, September 1967).

tomer class, product line) comparability between firms would not necessarily be improved. A second, peculiarly accounting difficulty involves the measurement of income by segment. Some expenses are joint to a number of segments—the president's salary, interest costs, home office administrative expenses, etc. Assignment of these common costs to individual lines of business can be accomplished only through the use of arbitrary bases of allocation. (The assignment of assets and liabilities may be even more difficult.) The result may simply confuse investors and provide them with very unreliable data for predicting the future. An alternative is the reporting of a "defined" income subtotal, such as "contribution to earnings before general corporate expenses." Only revenues and expenses directly assignable to segments would be included. This solution might aid in predictability of the future, but resultant figures would, of course, not be comparable to those of other firms operating as separate entities.

Percentage Comparisons of the Financial Statements

Most analysts begin their quantitative study of the financial statements with an examination of the general percentage relationships and changes shown on the comparative financial statements for a number of years. The two techniques used are called vertical and horizontal analysis, and they focus attention on the entire income statement or position statement.

Vertical Analysis. Vertical analysis abstracts from the absolute amounts on the statements to look at the relative magnitude of figures expressed as percentages of some base item. On the income statement all the revenue deductions and the net income are usually converted to a percentage of net sales. On the position statement total assets (total equities) serve as the base, and all individual assets and equities are translated into their relative percentage of the total. The result is a set of financial statements, called *common-size statements,* all expressed in percentages rather than dollar amounts. They provide a means by which the analyst can determine important figures at which to take a closer look; for example, "selling expense was 20 percent of net sales last year but is 25 percent of net sales this year." Similarly, current liabilities may have increased from 10 to 30 percent of total equities, indicating a much heavier reliance on short-term sources of assets. Common-size statements tend to highlight relationships that could be masked by changing absolute dollar amounts.

Horizontal Analysis. Horizontal analysis employs percentages to show how individual items change from *year to year*. A percentage increase or decrease from the prior year is calculated for each component on the current income and position statements. For example, horizontal analysis might reveal that accounts receivable have increased 50 percent over last year, while net sales have increased only 35 percent. Abstracting in this way from the absolute dollar changes may add insight to trends that are developing. But it must be used carefully; the base chosen may cause an unusually large or small percentage change which can be misinterpreted.

Ratio Analysis

Ratio analysis is the study of specific relationships and forms the heart of statement analysis. Ratios link different parts of the financial statements in an attempt to provide clues about the status of particular aspects of the business. Specifically, the three major areas where ratio analysis is helpful are financial strength or solvency (both long-term and short-term), efficiency (both investment efficiency and operating efficiency), and profitability.

It is easy to get carried away with ratios. Wise use of statement analysis involves knowing the objective of each calculation—the area the analysis is attempting to provide information about. Each ratio that we discuss has a definite purpose. Although our coverage is broad, it is not exhaustive of all the possible ratios that are computed or of the numerous ways the relationships are defined and expressed. Nevertheless, these matters of convention and individual preference are far less important than one's understanding of the purpose of each ratio.

Keep in mind also that ratios are merely one aid in the evaluation of a business. It is impossible for the financial statements from which ratios are taken to present all the relevant information about the operations, management, and environment of an enterprise. Ratios represent past data and, therefore, can only hint at the future. Moreover, there are probably no ratios that get better and better indefinitely as they move in one direction. When closely analyzed, ratios are "satisfactory" in a middle range and become "unsatisfactory" out of this range in either direction. Therefore, the best that we can hope for from an analysis of accounting reports is to spot exceptions and variations—relationships which seem out of line or trends which, if continued, might cause trouble. Ratios do not make decisions, for they neither pinpoint precise problems nor indicate causes. They may, however, *aid* in decision making by highlighting areas that may be problems or may require further investigation.

Company Statements

The financial statements of Lockett Company, a hypothetical concern, are presented in Tables 16–1 and 16–2. Our discussion of specific ratios draws upon these statements for illustration.

TABLE 16–1

LOCKETT COMPANY

Position Statement as of December 31

Assets	1972	1971
Current Assets:		
Cash..................................	$ 34,600	$ 32,300
Accounts receivable...................	57,100	39,800
Inventory.............................	88,700	85,900
Prepaid expenses......................	5,700	5,300
Total Current Assets...............	$186,100	$163,300
Land..................................	31,000	31,000
Buildings and equipment...............	162,900	159,100
Less: Accumulated depreciation........	(88,100)	(79,400)
Intangibles...........................	18,000	20,000
Total Assets......................	$309,900	$294,000

Equities		
Current Liabilities:		
Accounts payable......................	$ 34,800	$ 31,600
Taxes payable.........................	22,200	17,300
Other accrued liabilities.............	12,000	11,600
Total Current Liabilities..........	$ 69,000	$ 60,500
Long-Term Liabilities:		
Bond payable—6%.......................	46,000	50,000
Total Liabilities..................	$115,000	$110,500
Stockholders' Equity:		
7% Preferred stock—$100 par..........	$ 20,000	$ 20,000
Common stock—$10 par.................	50,000	50,000
Paid-in capital......................	70,000	70,000
Retained earnings....................	54,900	43,500
Total Stockholders' Equity.........	$194,900	$183,500
Total Equities....................	$309,900	$294,000

TABLE 16–2

LOCKETT COMPANY

Income Statement

For the Year Ending December 31, 1972

Sales.............................		$402,500
Expenses:		
Cost of goods sold..............	$227,400	
Selling expenses................	87,700	
Administrative expenses.........	46,500	
Interest........................	2,900	
Income taxes....................	15,200	379,700
Net income.......................		$ 22,800
Dividends on preferred stock....	$ 1,400	
Dividends on common stock.......	10,000	11,400
Earnings Retained in Business.....		$ 11,400

FINANCIAL STRENGTH

One group of ratios deals with the financial soundness of the business. Financial strength can be analyzed in terms of financial strength in the near future or in terms of financial solvency in the long run.

Short-Term Financial Strength

To obtain an indication of a firm's capacity to meet its short-term obligations as they mature, we calculate the two ratios shown below for 1972:

$$\text{Current ratio} = \frac{\text{Current assets}}{\text{Current liabilities}} = \frac{\$186,100}{\$69,000} = 2.7 \text{ to } 1$$

$$\text{Quick (acid-test) ratio} = \frac{\text{Monetary assets}}{\text{Current liabilities}} = \frac{\$91,700}{\$69,000} = 1.3 \text{ to } 1$$

On the ground that in the short run a firm must look to its current assets and particularly to its monetary assets—cash, marketable securities, and accounts receivable—for debt-paying ability, these relationships are among the most widely used measures of current financial solvency. Low or declining current and quick ratios may indicate an insufficient margin of safety between the assets that presumably are or will become available to liquidate claims and the amount of obligations to be paid. On the other hand, an extremely high ratio may indicate the presence of excessive or unproductive assets.

Turnover of Receivables and Inventory. How well the current and quick ratios indicate short-term debt-paying ability depends on how rapidly inventory and receivables can be converted into cash. Consequently, two supplementary ratios are computed to measure the movement of these current assets.

Inventory turnover is a calculation of how fast inventory on hand normally is sold and converted into accounts receivable. The formula is:

$$\frac{\text{Cost of goods sold}}{\text{Average inventory}} = \frac{\$227,400}{(\$88,700 + \$85,900)/2} = 2.6 \text{ times}$$

Many analysts divide the inventory turnover into 365 days to obtain the average length of time units are in inventory—140 days in our example.[2]

The turnover of receivables provides information on the liquidity of the receivables. How fast are the accounts collected? It is computed as follows:

$$\frac{\text{Credit sales}}{\text{Average accounts receivable}} = \frac{\$402,500}{(\$57,100 + \$39,800)/2} = 8.3 \text{ times}$$

The higher the turnover of receivables, the shorter the time between sale and cash collection. Division of the turnover into 365 days yields an estimate of the average collection period. For Lockett Company the estimate is 44 days (365 ÷ 8.3). By adding the inventory turnover period and col-

---

[2] For a manufacturing company an analyst might calculate three separate inventory turnovers—one for raw materials, one for work in process, and one for finished goods. In all cases the numerator represents the inventory flow—cost of raw materials used, cost of goods manufactured, and cost of goods sold—and the denominator indicates the average inventory available.

lection period, the analyst gains an idea of the average total elapsed time before an inventory item finally winds up as cash. The longer this time period is, the weaker the current ratio becomes as an indicator of debt-paying ability.

Long-Term Financial Strength

Equity Ratios.   The relationship between borrowed capital and owners' equity is one common measure of long-term financial solvency. Two common ways of expressing this relationship are shown below:[3]

$$Stock\text{-}Equity\ Ratio$$
$$\frac{\text{Common stock equity}}{\text{Total equities}} = \frac{\$174,900}{\$309,900} = 56.4\%$$

$$Debt\text{-}Equity\ Ratio$$
$$\frac{\text{Long-term debt}}{\text{Total equities}} = \frac{\$46,000}{\$309,900} = 14.9\%$$

The stock-equity ratio tells what portion of the assets has been contributed by common stockholders. A higher ratio generally indicates greater long-term financial safety, because less reliance is placed on debt and preferred capital, which have definite maturity dates and mandatory periodic payments. A common stockholder might calculate this ratio to judge the firm's ability to acquire additional funds in the future. A high ratio would indicate room for capital expansion via additional bond borrowing or preferred stock issuance; a low ratio might indicate a firm that is already "borrowed up." A bond holder might use the alternative version, the debt-equity ratio, to obtain some idea of how much the corporation could lose in assets without endangering the creditor's capital.

However, regardless of how it is expressed, the general purpose of an equity ratio is still the same—to yield some information about long-term financial strength. What a proper equity ratio should be, of course, must be judged considering the type and size of the business, the stability of the firm's revenues and earnings, and its susceptibility to general economic fluctuations.

Coverage Ratios.   Perhaps a more direct measure of a firm's capacity to employ large amounts of financial capital from senior securities is its ability to pay the recurring fixed charges imposed. This ability is indicated by coverage ratios (times-fixed-charges-earned ratios)—relationships between what is normally available from periodic operations and the interest charges and preferred dividend requirements.

---

[3] An alternative denominator which is frequently used includes only the long-term capital or *capitalization*. In this case the stock equity ratio would be 72.6 percent ($174,900/$240,900) and the debt ratio 19.1 percent ($46,000/$240,900).

$$\text{Interest coverage} = \frac{\text{Net income before interest and taxes}}{\text{Interest charges}}$$
$$= \frac{\$22,800 + \$2,900 + \$15,200}{\$2,900}$$
$$= 14.1 \text{ times}$$

The number of times interest is protected (covered) by earnings gives an idea of the firm's ability to handle interest-bearing liabilities in the normal course of events. Since interest is an allowable deduction for income tax purposes, an income figure before income taxes is used in the numerator. Income before interest and taxes of Lockett Company could shrink to one 14th of its present amount, and the firm would still be earning an amount equivalent to the interest charge.

When a firm has both debt and preferred stock outstanding, many analysts calculate a total fixed charge coverage ratio. Failure to pay preferred dividends, while not legally harmful, is viewed as a serious weakness in the financial community. Before-tax earnings of Lockett Company could decline to almost one eighth of the 1972 level and still be sufficient to cover its fixed financial charges.[4]

$$\frac{\text{Net income before interest and taxes}}{\text{Interest charges} + \text{pretax pfd. div. requirement}}$$
$$= \frac{\$22,800 + \$2,900 + \$15,200}{\$2,900 + (\$1,400/0.6)}$$
$$= \frac{\$40,900}{\$2,900 + \$2,334}$$
$$= 7.8 \text{ times}$$

EFFICIENCY

There are two aspects of efficiency in which an analyst may be interested—investment efficiency and operating efficiency. Investment efficiency relates the size of various asset investments to the volume of activity. Operating efficiency measures how efficiently assets are consumed in generating revenues.

---

[4] Since preferred dividends, unlike interest charges, are not deductible for tax purposes, the income before tax needed to cover preferred dividends is necessarily higher because there is no tax "shield." Dividing the amount of preferred dividends by $(1 - \text{tax rate})$ gives the before-tax burden of preferred dividends. Note that $2,334 of Net Income before Taxes, less income taxes of 40 percent, leaves the $1,400 needed for preferred stock dividends. Many analysts ignore this tax adjustment unless the coverage is low. In fact, for a rough guide, some analysts calculate all times-charges-earned ratios on an after-tax basis, although this result is not as logical or interpretable as those presented above.

Investment Efficiency

Turnover of Receivables and Inventory. These two turnovers are introduced on page 564 as supplementary measures of short-term financial strength. They also serve as primary indicators of efficiency in two particular investment areas. For example, comparison of the average collection period with the selling terms may signify poor credit selection or collecting effort. A series of years in which the turnover of receivables declines may disclose a situation which is getting out of control. With no change in selling terms, a growing investment in receivables relative to sales volume indicates either sales to more marginal customers or insufficient effort being devoted to collection.

In a similar manner a study of inventory turnovers may reveal an over- or underinvestment in inventory. A steadily decreasing turnover of inventories may denote overstocking, with its unnecessary carrying costs, or obsolescence and its attendant risks and losses. An unusually high inventory turnover may evidence an inventory investment inadequate to meet the current volume of sales. It may foretell a future loss of sales and customer goodwill because the firm might not be able to deliver promptly, or the need for additional funds to rebuild the inventory level.

Turnover of Total Assets. A measure of overall investment efficiency is the turnover of total assets, computed as follows:

$$\frac{\text{Sales}}{\text{Average total assets}} = \frac{\$402,500}{(\$309,900 + \$294,000)/2} = 1.33 \text{ times}$$

This relationship is an attempt to show how many dollars of recurring revenue are generated by each dollar of assets. If a firm's turnover is low compared to that of similar firms or if the trend is downward over a number of years, the analyst may suspect that there are unnecessary assets (such as idle cash balances) or inefficiently used assets (such as obsolete equipment) present. On the other hand, a sudden jump in the turnover should not always be interpreted as a favorable sign. It may actually result from a sharp increase in sales volume and a temporary underinvestment in assets. In fact, if the increased volume of sales is to be maintained, additional investment in plant and inventories may be necessary.

Operating Efficiency

In this area we are interested in income statement relationships. Most of them are usually expressed as a percentage of sales.

Operating Ratio. One useful relationship is that between recurring operating expenses and operating revenues (commonly only sales):

$$\frac{\text{Operating expenses}}{\text{Operating revenues}} = \frac{\$227,400 + \$87,700 + \$46,500}{\$402,500} = 89.8\%$$

This ratio measures the proportion of sales revenue consumed in normal operating activities—manufacturing, marketing, administration, research, etc. Definitions of the revenue and expense activities which constitute normal operations vary among analysts. For Lockett Company, we are excluding interest expense and income taxes from operating expenses; other analysts, however, might include one or both of them. Despite its definitional pitfalls, when applied consistently within industry lines the operating ratio can provide a rough index of operating efficiency.

Income or Profit Margins. Another approach to operating efficiency is to look at what remains after various expenses have been deducted. A number of margin figures can be computed according to the general formula, *income/revenue.* Each attempts to measure what portion of the revenue dollar ends up as income. However, revenue can be defined as sales only or can include all recurring revenues. Even greater diversity exists among possible numerators—gross income (sales less cost of goods sold), net operating income (the complement to the operating ratio), net income before interest and after taxes (the reward to the various suppliers of investor capital), and net income to common stockholders. Some of these reflect varying interpretations of operations; some reflect alternative uses or viewpoints; and others simply reflect the personal preferences of individual analysts.

Operating Leverage. An important aspect of statement analysis is the attempt to shed light on the future, particularly future earnings. The prediction of earnings encompasses more than a simple extension of past trends, important as these may be. Of equal significance is the prediction of environmental changes, particularly industry conditions, and the firm's reaction to these changes. The concept of operating leverage can be helpful in this area as well as in the explanation of historical changes in the operating ratio or in the profit margins. Operating leverage refers to the impact on operating profits caused by changes in volume of activity. A more than proportional change in net operating income may result from a change in sales volume because of the existence of fixed costs among the business' operating expenses.

Broadly speaking, the operating expenses of a business tend to be fixed or variable in relation to number of units sold (i.e., volume). Fixed expenses are incurred in approximately the same amount regardless of the level or volume of operations in the period. Salaries, rent, and most depreciation charges are examples of fixed expenses. Variable expenses change in total more or less proportionately with changes in the volume of operations in the period; raw materials, hourly wages, and sales commissions are usually variable expenses.

The rate at which income changes with volume depends upon the expense structure. If all expenses are variable and price remains unchanged, income will change at the same rate as volume. There is no operating leverage. It some expenses are fixed, however, income will change at a rate greater than volume, because not all the expenses rise or fall as volume increases or decreases. The difference in rates of change between income and volume is magnified as fixed expenses become more significant.

Operating leverage, then, deals with the volatility of earnings with changes in volume. An external analyst may be unable to measure the precise impact of operating leverage, because under current reporting practices the breakdown of expenses between fixed and variable is not provided in the annual report. Nevertheless, he may make rough guesses based on his knowledge of the firm and perhaps a comparison of expense figures from one year to the next. But even a general understanding of the expense structure and the concept of operating leverage may improve the accuracy of his projections.

PROFITABILITY

Perhaps the most important overall ratios are those which reflect the earning power of the enterprise. The ultimate test of the success of a firm is its ability to earn a return on the resources invested in it. Thus the central measure of profitability is the relationship between income and investment. This relationship is expressed as a percentage rate of return on investment (*income/average investment*). The precise definition of income and investment to be used varies with the viewpoint and purpose of the analyst. Some of the more commonly used rates of return are discussed below.

Rate of Return on Total Capital

In using the concept of return on investment to evaluate overall performance, we usually begin by computing a rate of return on total capital —the rate of earnings available to all capital suppliers. This percentage is useful in the evaluation of operating management, for it measures how productively the total resources of the business have been employed, irrespective of how they are financed. Consequently, it facilitates comparisons between firms with different capital structures and comparisons over time for the same firm when its capital structure has changed.

Two commonly used formulas are illustrated below for the Lockett Company. The first defines investment as average total assets (equities);[5]

---

[5] In this and other ratios we use a simple average of the beginning and ending balances. In many instances this is all the information available to the external analyst. Where there is reason to believe that such a simple average might not indicate the average amount available during the period, the analyst should make appropriate adjustments—e.g., new assets invested on December 31 obviously were not available for use during the year and should be eliminated entirely in calculating average total

the second excludes the impact of current liabilities and views average investment as the relatively permanent capital supplied by stockholders and long-term creditors. The reasoning behind the latter approach is that current liabilities usually are a fairly stable, somewhat automatic source of capital arising out of normal accruals and trade credit. Consequently, most managerial decisions concern the employment of assets from long-term sources.

Rate of return on total assets
$$= \frac{\text{Tax-adjusted net income before interest}}{\text{Average total assets}}$$
$$= \frac{\$24,540}{(\$309,900 + \$294,000)/2} = 8.1\%$$

Rate of return on total investment
$$= \frac{\text{Tax-adjusted net income before interest}}{\text{Average capitalization}}$$
$$= \frac{\$24,540}{[(\$309,900 - \$69,000) + (\$294,000 - \$60,500)]/2} = 10.35\%$$

A few words of explanation about the numerator is in order. The income component should be consistent with the investment component. Therefore, if we are concerned with total assets or total long-term investment, the return should eliminate the effect of alternative financing arrangements. That is, the return calculation should be unaffected by how management has chosen to finance the total assets. Seemingly, this figure would simply be net income before the deduction of interest expense. However, if interest expense were eliminated, tax expense would increase by an amount equal to the tax rate times the interest charge. So instead of adding back the entire interest charge, we add a tax-adjusted interest expense ($\$2,900 \times 0.6 = \$1,740$)—the after-tax burden of the interest charge—to net income ($\$22,800 + \$1,740 = \$24,540$). Alternatively, we could apply the effective tax rate (40 percent in our example) to the net income before interest and taxes of $40,900 to calculate an adjusted tax charge of $16,360, to arrive at the $24,540 tax-adjusted net income before interest. Either way, the resultant figure is the amount that would have been generated if all assets (or long-term capital) had been supplied by the common stockholders.[6]

---

assets. Many analysts ignore the theoretical refinement of averages and simply use investment figures as of the beginning or end of the period.

[6] Many analysts do not worry about tax adjustments or internal consistency. Consequently, the reader will often see the numerator in the rate of return calculation defined as net income before interest ($25,700), net income ($22,800), or net income before interest and taxes ($40,900). All of these are theoretically incorrect for measuring a return on total capital; but, employed consistently, they still can provide meaningful information in many instances.

In analyzing differences among firms or changes in the return on investment from one year to the next for the same firm, we may find it helpful to visualize the rate of return as the product of two component parts —a profit margin and a turnover of investment. We thus emphasize the fact that overall profitability is dependent upon both operating efficiency and investment efficiency.

$$\text{Return on investment} = \text{Margin} \times \text{Turnover}$$

$$\frac{\text{Income}}{\text{Average total assets}} = \frac{\text{Income}}{\text{Revenue}} \times \frac{\text{Revenue}}{\text{Average total assets}}$$

$$\frac{\$24,540}{\$301,950} = \frac{\$24,540}{\$402,500} \times \frac{\$402,500}{\$301,950}$$

$$8.1\% = 6.1\% \times 1.33 \text{ times}$$

By studying the margin and turnover figures separately, we often can glean additional information about the basic causes of differences or changes in the total return on investment.

Rate of Return on Common Stock Equity

Another application of the general concept of return on investment takes the viewpoint of the owner of the business. Not only is he interested in how well management uses the total assets available, he also is interested in the profitability of his particular equity interest in the firm. How well has management used the assets *and* modified the capital structure to the benefit of the common stockholders of the business?

$$\frac{\text{Net income to common stock equity}}{\text{Average common stock equity}} = \frac{\$21,400}{\$169,200} = 12.65\%$$

Income in this case is defined as the amount of net income from recurring sources which remains after provision has been made for rewarding sources of capital other than common stockholders. Hence, it consists of net income after taxes, interest, and *preferred* stock dividends, but before common stock dividends. The investment denominator includes all portions of common stock equity—par or stated value of the outstanding common stock, the excess over par or stated value, and retained earnings.

Financial Leverage

Notice in the preceding calculations that the various rates of return on investment differ.

Rate of return on total assets .... 8.1 %
Rate of return on total investment................. 10.35
Rate of return on common stock equity....... .... 12.65

The differences result from "financial leverage." Financial leverage is the process by which the rate of return on common stockholders' equity is modified from what it otherwise would be by the use of debt or preferred stock capital to finance the acquisition of part of the assets.

Management employs capital supplied by creditors and preferred stockholders in lieu of common stockholders' equity in the expectation that the business will earn more on the noncommon capital than the fixed charges (interest and preferred dividends) associated with this capital. If so, the excess inures to the common stockholders, thereby increasing the rate of return on their investment, and the firm experiences favorable financial leverage. On the other hand, the firm may earn at an overall rate that is less than the cost of this capital to the business. Since the return to the bondholders and preferred stockholders is fixed, the deficiency reduces the earnings applicable to the common stockholders' equity. As a result, the rate of return on common is less than the overall earning rate because of negative financial leverage.

The effect of favorable financial leverage upon the rate of return on common equity for Lockett Company can be illustrated as follows. Lockett earned an average return of 8.1 percent on total assets. Some of these assets are financed by current liabilities (an average of $64,750 for the year) for which no explicit interest charge is made. Hence, the earnings available to the long-term suppliers of capital are greater than if no current liabilities existed. Favorable financial leverage from current liabilities causes the rate of return on total investment to increase to 10.35 percent.

There is also favorable financial leverage from the bonds and preferred stock. The average amounts of capital supplied by the bondholders and preferred stockholders are $48,000 and $20,000, respectively. The overall earning power of this capital is $7,038 ($68,000 × 10.35%). However, these suppliers of debt and preferred stock contractually are entitled to no more than interest and preferred stock dividends. The *after-tax* interest charge is $1,740 (see calculation on page 570) and the preferred dividends are $1,400—a total of only $3,140. The remaining $3,898 ($7,038 − $3,140) added 2.3 percent ($3,898/$169,200) to what otherwise would have been only a 10.35 percent return on common equity.

The extent to which a firm employs financial leverage is a function of the amount of fixed-charge securities in its capital structure. How favorable the financial leverage effect is, though, depends upon the differential between the earning rate on total assets (or investment) and the fixed-charge-cost of debt and preferred stock.

Earnings per Share

In the financial press, we almost never see a calculation of return on investment. Instead, the most popular measure of earning power is earnings per share (EPS). Earnings per share is computed by dividing the net income available to common stock by the weighted average number of shares outstanding during the period. For Lockett Company, the calculation is

$$\frac{\text{Net income} - \text{Preferred dividends}}{\text{Average number of shares}} = \frac{\$22,800 - \$1,400}{5,000 \text{ shares}} = \$4.28/\text{share}$$

Since shares of stock are what an investor holds or buys and sells, earnings per share relates the income stream of the corporation directly to the element involved in the stockholders' investment decision. A stockholder can see the impact of earnings on his interest in the firm. Changes in EPS can be used to evaluate past managerial performance or to project the future growth and potential of the firm. Quite commonly, EPS is related to the current market price as an indicator of "inherent" value. If the market price of Lockett Company stock, for example is $48.50, we say that the *price-earnings ratio* is 11 times ($48.50/$4.28) or that the stock market values (capitalizes) Lockett earnings at almost 9 percent ($4.28/$48.50).

APB Opinions. Because of the importance attached to earnings per share figures, the Accounting Principles Board has issued two opinions dealing with the subject.[7] *Opinion No. 9* requires that earnings per share be reported on the face of the income statement and, hence, be subject to audit by the certified public accountant. It is to be calculated both before and after extraordinary items. *Opinion No. 15* provides fairly elaborate rules and procedures for the calculation.

For simple capital structures, such as that of Lockett Company, the calculation of EPS is straightforward. However, numerous complexities are involved when a firm has convertible securities, stock options, warrants, etc. To handle the reporting problem in these circumstances, the APB requires that two earnings per share figures—primary earnings per share and fully diluted earnings per share—be disclosed with equal prominence.

Primary Earnings per Share. This figure is net income available to common stock divided by the number of common shares outstanding plus the number of *common stock equivalent* shares. Many securities that a firm might have outstanding—stock options, fully participating preferred, certain convertible securities—have some of the characteristics of common stock, yet in name they are not common stock. With the concept of common stock equivalent, the APB looks through this difference in name, saying that securities with many of the characteristics of common stock should be treated as common stock for purposes of calculat-

---

[7] *Reporting the Results of Operations, Opinion of the Accounting Principles Board No. 9* (New York: AICPA, December 1966); and *Earnings per Share, Opinion of the Accounting Principles Board No. 15* (New York: AICPA, May 1969).

ing EPS. This is done by converting these securities to an equivalent number of common shares and adding this amount to the shares of common outstanding. Primary earnings per share is a pro forma calculation based on the assumption that if other securities have the characteristics of common stock, the usefulness of the EPS figure for predicting the future is increased when they are counted as common stock.

Fully Diluted Earnings per Share.   This per-share figure measures the maximum dilution in earnings per share that could take place if all contingent issues of common stock that could reduce earnings per share actually do take place. Here, to determine the number of shares used in the denominator, one assumes *full* conversion of bonds and preferred stock, exercise of warrants, etc., and so includes all shares that might have a future claim on earnings. It obviously is another prospective calculation, showing what would occur under the most unfavorable circumstances.

Of course, the income figure in the numerator must be consistent with the number of shares in the denominator. For example, if a convertible bond issue is treated as if it were converted, then the income figure would have to be modified for the interest expense (and related tax effects). Likewise, if stock options are treated as if they were exercised, then some assumption must be made as to the use of the proceeds received upon exercise. APB *Opinion No. 15* contains the procedures for making these adjustments as well as the criteria for classifying securities as common stock equivalents.[8] Both are extremely complex and beyond the scope of the discussion in this book. Hopefully, when complex capital structures necessitate this dual presentation, a note or schedule will accompany the financial statements explaining the basis for the calculations.

Dividends per Share and the Payout Ratio

Dividends per share supplements the earnings-per-share figure. It measures the *amount* of earnings actually distributed per share in the form of cash dividends to the common stockholders and is reported in most statements as an historical fact. The only adjustments necessary are when dividends per share are presented in comparative form over time and the number of shares has been affected by stock dividends or stock splits. Then past years' dividends should be restated in terms of the current equivalent number of shares.

The payout ratio measures the *proportion* of earnings distributed as cash dividends. It is calculated as follows for the Lockett Company:

$$\frac{\text{Cash dividends to common}}{\text{Net income to common}} = \frac{\$10,000}{\$21,400} = 46.7\%$$

[8] APB *Opinion No. 15, op. cit.,* pp. 227–35.

The usefulness of both of these ratios in the evaluation of a firm's dividend policies is apparent. As with EPS, dividends per share are commonly related to the current market price to show a dividend yield rate.

SUMMARY

The analysis of financial statements is a paradoxical subject. On the one hand, it is, in a sense, the ultimate reason for preparing accounting reports and certainly a logical capstone to a study of financial accounting. At the same time the area is fraught with difficulties and potential traps. The first half of this chapter points out some of the important "qualitative" considerations the analyst should be cognizant of—the impact of alternative accounting principles and procedures, differences in account classification and terminology, the influence of diversification on interfirm comparisons, the major problems associated with comparisons in general, and the limitations of the underlying accounting data.

The "quantitative" aspect of statement analysis is presented in the second half of the chapter. Here again the analyst is faced with a variety of ratios and alternative definitions. Each user is obliged to select the relevant information and analytical procedures for his particular purposes. The techniques discussed provide a start in this direction. However, in the computation of ratios keep four points in mind: (1) ratios are only a clue to areas needing further investigation; they rarely supply answers and cannot make decisions; (2) ratios are only as valid as the statements themselves; (3) ratio analysis requires a basis for comparison; and (4) ratio analysis is meaningful only if there is a clear understanding of the purpose of each relationship.

SUGGESTIONS FOR FURTHER READING

Backer, Norton, and McFarland, Walter B. *External Reporting for Segments of a Business.* New York: National Association of Accountants, 1968.

Harrigan, James O. "A Short History of Financial Ratio Analysis," *Accounting Review*, Vol. 43 (April 1968), pp. 284–94.

Kemp, Patrick S. "Controversies on the Construction of Financial Statements," *Accounting Review*, Vol. 38 (January 1963), pp. 126–32.

Mautz, R. K. *Financial Reporting by Conglomerate Companies.* New York: Financial Executives Institute, 1968.

Rappaport, Alfred; Firmin, Peter A.; and Zeff, Stephen A. (eds.). *Public Reporting by Conglomerates: The Issues, the Problems, and Some Possible Solutions.* Englewood Cliffs, N.J.: Prentice-Hall, 1968.

Simmons, John K. "A Concept of Comparability In Financial Reporting," *Accounting Review*, Vol. 42 (October 1967), pp. 680–92.

QUESTIONS AND PROBLEMS

16–1. The condensed financial data for the Canocorn Company appear below (in thousands):

Position Statement Data

Debits:		Credits:	
Cash....................	$ 19	Accounts payable...........	$ 26
Marketable securities.......	5	Accrued liabilities..........	14
Receivables..............	17	5% mortgage bonds........	20
Inventories..............	38	Preferred stock-7.5%.......	20
Cash reserved for plant		Common stock............	40
expansion..............	5	Retained earnings..........	24
Plant assets (net)..........	65	Reserve for contingencies....	5
	$149		$149

Income Statement Data

Net sales...........................		$250,000
Cost of goods sold.................	$170,000	
Operating expenses.................	50,000	220,000
		$ 30,000
Other income.....................	$ 2,000	
Other expenses....................	1,000	1,000
		$ 31,000
Interest charges...................		1,000
Net income.......................		$ 30,000
Preferred dividends.................	$ 1,500	
Common dividends.................	6,000	7,500
Increase in retained earnings.........		$ 22,500

From this information, calculate and explain the meaning and use of:

a) Current ratio.

b) Ratio of common stock equity to total investment.

c) Times interest earned.

d) Average number of days' sales uncollected as of the end of the year.

e) Ratio of plant assets to mortgage bonds.

f) Acid-test ratio.

g) Turnover of merchandise using year-end inventories. (What limitations do you see in using year-end rather than average inventories?)

h) Return on total year-end assets.

i) Margin and investment turnover figures consistent with part (h).

j) Return on common stockholders' equity (Why is this figure higher than part (h)?)

16–2. The following financial statement was prepared by employees of the Melhus Corporation.*

---

* Adapted from AICPA November 1967 examination.

MELHUS CORPORATION
Statement of Income and Retained Earnings
Years Ended December 31, 1966 and 1965

	1966	1965
Revenues:		
Gross sales, including sales taxes......................	$876,900	$782,500
Less returns, allowances, and cash discounts................	18,800	16,200
Net sales..........................	$858,100	$766,300
Dividends, interest, and purchases discounts......................	30,250	18,300
Recoveries of accounts written off in prior years..................	11,800	3,000
Gains on sale of treasury stock....	2,050	
Total revenues..................	$902,200	$787,600
Costs and expenses:		
Cost of goods sold, including sales taxes..........................	$415,900	$332,200
Salaries and related payroll expenses........................	60,500	62,100
Rent...............................	19,100	19,100
Freight-in and freight-out.........	3,400	2,900
Bad debt expense...................	24,000	26,000
Addition to reserve for possible inventory losses................	3,800	2,000
Total costs and expenses........	$526,700	$444,300
Income before extraordinary items....	$375,500	$343,300
Extraordinary items:		
Loss on discontinued styles (note 1)........................	$ 24,000	$ 4,800
Loss on sale of marketable securities (note 2)..............	52,050	...
Loss on sale of warehouse (note 3)........................	86,350	...
Retroactive settlement of federal income taxes for 1965 and 1964 (note 4)........................	31,600	...
Total extraordinary items........	$194,000	$ 4,800
Net income...........................	$181,500	$338,500
Retained earnings at beginning of year...............................	310,700	163,100
Total..........................	$492,200	$501,600
Less: Federal income taxes..........	$120,000	$170,000
Cash dividends on common stock.....	21,900	20,900
Total..........................	$141,900	$190,900
Retained earnings at end of year.....	$350,300	$310,700
Net income per share of common stock..............................	$1.81	$3.38

Notes to the Statement of Income and Retained Earnings:

1. New styles and rapidly changing consumer preferences resulted in a $24,000 loss on the disposal of discontinued styles and related accessories.
2. The Corporation sold an investment in marketable securities at a loss of $52,050 with no income tax effect.
3. The Corporation sold one of its warehouses at an $86,350 loss.

4. The Corporation was charged $31,600 retroactively for additional income taxes resulting from a settlement in 1966. Of this amount $14,000 was applicable to 1965 and the balance was applicable to 1964.

Identify and discuss the weaknesses in classification and disclosure in the above statement. Your discussion should explain why you consider these treatments to be weaknesses and what you consider to be the proper treatment of the items. Do not prepare a revised statement.

16–3. The Fastbuck Finance Company is attempting to evaluate an applicant for a short-term loan. The following information has been taken from the company's records:

		December 31	
	1970	1971	1972
Cash.........................		$ 4,000	$ 2,000
Marketable securities............		12,000	4,500
Receivables.....................	$19,000	33,000	27,000
Inventories.....................	32,000	40,000	30,000
Prepayments...................		10,000	4,500
Current liabilities...............		53,000	29,000
		1971	1972
Sales.........................		$97,000	$105,000
Cost of goods sold..............		73,000	80,000

a) Compute for 1971 and 1972 the following ratios: current ratio, quick ratio, inventory turnover, and receivable turnover.
b) Based on the results, what recommendations would you make to management?
c) What limitations do you see in your analysis?
d) Why might an analyst desire quarterly data in this type of situation?

16–4. The following tables have been condensed from information presented in the 1969 annual reports of two diversified companies. In the original reports, comparative statements for 1968 and 1969 were presented.

Westinghouse Electric Corporation
(in thousands)

	Sales	Income after Taxes
Power systems....................	$1,038,831	$ 50,624
Consumer products...............	647,495	9,449
Industry........................	1,087,255	58,234
Defense.........................	495,880	6,420
Broadcasting, learning, and leisure time...........................	173,324	23,124
Other...........................	66,368	2,037
	$3,509,153	$149,888

American Brands, Inc.
(in millions)

	Net Sales	Operating Income*
Tobacco products:		
Domestic.....................	$1,066.9	$172.8
International.................	1,069.0	50.7
Distilled beverages..............	136.4	19.0
Food products.................	354.6	16.7
Other.........................	50.3	5.7
Intercompany sales.............	(15.7)	....
	$2,661.5	$264.9

* Earnings before interest, other income and expense items, taxes and minority interest.

a) Contrast the two presentations in terms of the income concepts employed. What are the advantages and disadvantages of each of these concepts?

b) How would an investor use this type of information? What other similar information would be useful to an investor?

16–5. Near the close of your audit, the treasurer of Ezy Corporation, your client, informs you that the company is considering the acquisition of the ATU Corporation and requests that you analyze the following statements of ATU Corporation.*

* Problem adapted from AICPA November 1966 examination.

ATU CORPORATION

Balance Sheet, December 31, 1965 and 1964
(in thousands)

	1965	1964
Assets		
Current Assets:		
Cash...............................	$ 1,610	$ 1,387
Marketable securities, at cost (market value $550,000)............	510	
Accounts receivable, less allowance for bad debts: 1965, $125,000; 1964, $110,000....................	4,075	3,669
Inventories, at lower of cost or market...........................	7,250	7,050
Prepaid expenses....................	125	218
Total Current Assets..............	$13,570	$12,324
Plant and Equipment, at Cost:		
Land and buildings..................	$13,500	$13,500
Machinery and equipment.............	9,250	8,250
Total plant and equipment..........	$22,750	$22,020
Less allowances for depreciation.....	13,470	12,549
Total Plant and Equipment, Net.....	$ 9,280	$ 9,471
Long-term receivables.................	$ 250	$ 250
Deferred charges......................	25	75
Total Assets.....................	$23,125	$22,120
Liabilities and Shareholders' Equity		
Current Liabilities:		
Accounts payable....................	$ 2,950	$ 3,426
Accrued expenses....................	1,575	1,644
Federal taxes payable...............	875	750
Current maturities on long-term debt............................	500	500
Total Current Liabilities.........	$ 5,900	$ 6,320
Other Liabilities:		
5% sinking fund debentures, due Jan. 1, 1976 ($500,000 redeemable annually)...........................	$ 5,000	$ 5,500
Deferred taxes on income, related to depreciation.......................	350	210
Total Other Liabilities...........	$ 5,350	$ 5,710
Shareholders' Equity:		
Preferred stock, $1 cumulative, $20 par, preference on liquidation $100 per share (authorized, 100,-000 shares; issued and outstanding, 50,000 shares)....................	$ 1,000	$ 1,000
Common stock, $1 par (authorized, 900,000 shares; issued and outstanding: 1965, 550,000 shares; 1964, 500,000 shares).............	550	500
Capital in excess of par value of common stock.....................	3,075	625
Retained earnings...................	7,250	7,965
Total Shareholders' Equity........	$11,875	$10,090
Total Liabilities and Shareholders' Equity...............	$23,125	$22,120

ATU CORPORATION
Statement of Income and Retained Earnings
For the Years Ended December 31, 1965 and 1964
(in thousands)

	1965	1964
Income:		
Net sales..........................	$48,400	$41,700
Royalties..........................	70	25
Interest...........................	30	...
Total............................	$48,500	$41,725
Costs and expenses:		
Cost of sales......................	$31,460	$29,190
Selling, general, and administrative..............................	12,090	8,785
Interest on 5% sinking fund debentures.......................	275	300
Provision for federal income taxes...	2,315	1,695
Total............................	$46,140	$39,970
Net income.........................	$ 2,360	$ 1,755
Retained earnings, beginning of year...	7,965	6,760
Total............................	$10,325	$ 8,515
Dividends paid:		
Preferred stock, $1 per share (cash)............................	$ 50	$ 50
Common stock:		
Cash—$1 per share................	525	500
Stock—(10%) 50,000 shares at market value of $50 per share....	2,500	
Total............................	$ 3,075	$ 550
Retained Earnings, End of Year........	$ 7,250	$ 7,965

Additional information: (1) The inventory at January 1, 1964 was $6,850,000. (2) The market prices of the common stock at December 31, 1965 and 1964 were $73.50 and $47.75 respectively. (3) The cash dividends for both preferred and common stock were declared and paid in June and December of each year. The stock dividend on common stock was declared and distributed in August 1965. (4) Plant and equipment sales and retirements during 1965 and 1964 were $375,000 and $425,000 respectively. The related depreciation allowances were $215,000 in 1965 and $335,000 in 1964. At December 31, 1963 the plant and equipment asset balance was $21,470,000 and the related depreciation allowances were $11,650,000.

a) Prepare a schedule computing the following selected statistics for 1965 and 1964:
1. Book value per common share.
2. Earnings per common share.
3. Inventory turnover.
4. Price earnings ratio for common stock.
5. Times interest earned.
6. Times total fixed charges (interest and preferred dividends) earned.
7. Gross capital expenditures.

b) Calculate any other ratios you consider to be important in this situation.

16–6. The vice president of finance has directed you to prepare the earnings per share figures to be included in the annual report for 1972. He would also like to release them to the financial services, but wants to make sure that they conform to generally accepted accounting principles. The following information is available to you.

Net income to all stockholders was $100,200 in 1971 (includes gain on sale of land of $13,200) and $76,800 in 1972 (includes loss on sale of investments of $25,800).

On January 1, 1971 the company had outstanding 20,000 shares of $10 par common stock and 5,000 shares of 7% convertible preferred stock with a par value of $50 per share. The preferred stock is currently convertible into one share of common stock any time within the next five years. However, since the market prices of the common stock and preferred stock are $36 a share and $48 a share respectively at the end of 1972, no immediate conversion is anticipated. Preferred dividends were declared and paid in both 1971 and 1972.

On March 31, 1972, the company issued 2,000 shares of common stock for cash.

On June 30, the company issued a two-for-one stock split. (Prior to then, the convertible preferred had been convertible into only one-half share of common stock).

a) Prepare a comparative schedule of earnings per share for 1971 and 1972. It should include primary and fully diluted earnings per share and give explicit recognition to the extraordinary items.

b) Discuss the uses that stockholders might make of the EPS data you have prepared.

16–7. Condensed financial statements for Flush Plumbing Company for the last three years are presented below.

FLUSH PLUMBING COMPANY

Income Statements, Years Ended December 31

	1970	1971	1972
Sales.........................	$45,000	$40,000	$50,000
Cost of goods sold..............	$30,000	$26,000	$32,000
Selling expenses................	3,000	2,600	4,000
Administrative expenses.........	6,000	5,900	7,000
Total expenses...............	$39,000	$34,500	$43,000
Net income before tax...........	$ 6,000	$ 5,500	$ 7,000
Income taxes..................	3,000	2,700	3,500
Net Income after Tax............	$ 3,000	$ 2,800	$ 3,500

FLUSH PLUMBING COMPANY

Balance Sheets, December 31

	1970	1971	1972
Cash............................	$ 1,300	$ 3,000	$ 2,700
Accounts receivable.............	4,100	7,000	7,500
Inventory.......................	5,000	6,200	6,500
Plant and equipment.............	10,100	10,600	10,100
	$20,500	$26,800	$26,800
Current liabilities.............	$ 2,700	$ 6,300	$ 2,800
Bonds payable...................	5,000	5,000	5,000
Common stock....................	10,000	10,000	10,000
Retained earnings...............	2,800	5,500	9,000
	$20,500	$26,800	$26,800

a) Express the income statements and balance sheets in common-sized percentages. Comment on any significant fluctuations.

b) Calculate the following ratios for all three years and comment on your findings: (1) current ratio; (2) quick or acid-test ratio.

c) Calculate the following ratios for 1971 and 1972 only and comment on your findings: (1) rate of return on stockholders' equity; (2) turnover of total assets; (3) turnover of inventories; (4) turnover of receivables.

16–8. The United Electric Company sold 20-year bonds at par. The funds derived from this issue were to be used over the next three years to pay for a new atomic generating plant. The company invested the funds in U.S. Treasury notes which matured throughout the three-year period in amounts approximately equal to the payments which it would be required to make to the plant contractor as his work progressed. Immediately after these two transactions occurred but before any construction work was started, the fiscal year ended, and the company was preparing its financial statements. Three alternative suggestions were made concerning the proper place to show the Treasury notes in the position statement:

1. Since Treasury notes are readily marketable, they should be shown as current assets.

2. Since 20 percent of the notes would mature in the next fiscal year, only this amount should be shown among the current assets; the

other 80 percent should be carried in the "investment" classification.

3. Since they were being held to finance the new plant expansion, the entire amount should be shown as an item in the "plant and equipment" classification.

a) You, as the chief accounting officer, are asked to state the treatment you would prefer, whether one of these or a different procedure. Explain why your treatment is preferable to the ones you discard.

b) Indicate what influence your decision, compared to the alternatives, would have on the following ratios: (1) current ratio, (2) ratio of long-term debt, (3) rate of return on total assets.

16–9. The information below is taken from the records of two companies in the same industry:

	Alphonse Co.	Gaston Co.
Cash	$ 14,000	$ 32,000
Receivables—net	22,000	63,000
Inventories	82,000	95,000
Plant—net	113,000	240,000
	$231,000	$430,000
Current liabilities	$ 67,000	$105,000
Bonds payable	38,000	50,000
Common stock	110,000	225,000
Retained earnings	16,000	50,000
	$231,000	$430,000
Sales	$280,000	$410,000
Cost of goods sold	$210,000	$340,000
Other expenses	54,000	43,000
Interest expense	2,000	3,000
Income taxes	7,000	12,000
Dividends	5,000	8,000

Answer each of the following questions by making a comparison of one or more relevant ratios:

a) Which company is using the stockholders' investment most profitably?

b) Which company is better able to meet its current debts?

c) If you were going to buy the bonds of one company, which one would you choose? (Assume you would buy them at the same yield.)

d) Which company collects its receivables faster?

e) Which company is earning the higher rate of return on its total asset investment?

f) Explain the general reasons for the results in part (e) in terms of investment efficiency and operating efficiency.

g) How long does it take each company to convert an investment in inventory to cash?

h) Which company retains the larger proportion of income in the business?

16–10. Stokely-Van Camp, Inc. presented the following schedule of earnings per share in its annual report for the year ended May 31, 1970.

```
Earnings per common share (Note 9):
  Primary:
    Earnings before extraordinary charge.... $1.26    $1.46
    Extraordinary charge, net of income
      taxes................................     .20
    Net earnings...........................  $1.06    $1.46

  Pro forma, assuming full dilution:
    Earnings before extraordinary charge.... $1.23    $1.41
    Extraordinary charge, net of income
      taxes................................     .19
    Net earnings...........................  $1.04    $1.41
```

Note 9. Earnings per share: Primary earnings per share is based on average common shares outstanding plus shares issuable for options and warrants as common stock equivalents, after deducting from net earnings the dividend requirements on preferred stock. Pro forma (fully diluted) earnings per share gives effect to assumed conversion of outstanding debentures and elimination of related interest expense net of the effect on income tax and profit-sharing plan expense.

a) Describe in your own words the difference between primary earnings per share and fully diluted earnings per share in this case. Discuss the reasons for the adjustments made in each case.

b) Do you agree with the company's labeling of the fully diluted EPS as "pro forma"? Why? In what sense are the primary EPS also pro forma?

c) How would an investor use these EPS figures?

16–11. Derr Sales Corporation's management is concerned over the corporation's current financial position and return on investment.* They request your assistance in analyzing their financial statements and furnish the following statements:

---

* Problem adapted from AICPA May 1969 examination.

DERR SALES CORPORATION
Statement of Working Capital Deficit
December 31, 1968

```
Current liabilities...................                    $223,050
Less: Current assets:
  Cash................................  $  5,973
  Accounts receivable, net...........     70,952
  Inventory...........................    113,125           190,050
  Working capital deficit............                     $ 33,000
```

DERR SALES CORPORATION
Income Statement for the Year Ended December 31, 1968

```
Sales (90,500 units)..............................  $760,200
Cost of goods sold................................   452,500
Gross profit......................................  $307,700
Selling and general expenses, including $22,980
  depreciation....................................   155,660
Income before taxes...............................  $152,040
Income taxes......................................    76,020
Net income........................................  $ 76,020
```

Additional data: Assets other than current assets consist of land, building, and equipment with a book value of $352,950 on December 31, 1968.

a) Assuming Derr Sales Corporation operates 300 days per year, compute the following (show your computations):
1. Number of days' sales uncollected.
2. Inventory turnover.
3. Number of days' operations to cover the working capital deficit.
4. Return on total assets as a product of asset turnover and the net income ratio (sometimes called profit margin).

b) Sales of 100,000 units are forecasted for 1969. Within this relevant range of activity costs are estimated as follows (excluding income taxes):

	Fixed Costs	Variable Costs per Unit
Cost of goods sold........................	....	$4.90
Selling and general expenses, including		
$15,450 depreciation...................	$129,720	1.10
Totals................................	$129,720	$6.00

The income tax rate is expected to be 50 percent. Past experience indicates that current assets vary in direct proportion to sales. Management feels that in 1969 the market will support a sales price of $8.30 at a sales volume of 100,000 units. Compute the rate of return on book value of total assets after income taxes assuming management's expectations are realized.

16–12.   Assume you have just completed a ratio analysis of a company. The notes to the financial statements disclose the following material facts happening after the date of the statements. The company sold its main office building to an insurance company. The proceeds from the sale were used to pay off mortgage bonds secured by the building. The company then entered into a long-term lease with the insurance company.

a)   Predict the impact of these events on your calculation of the following ratios, assuming the lease is not capitalized: (1) current ratio, (2) rate of return on assets, (3) interest coverage, (4) stock-equity ratio.

b)   Discuss the comparability of your projected ratios with the historical ones.

c)   Repeat part (a) assuming the lease is capitalized.

16–13.   You are the new small-loan officer at Mark Time State Bank. Two companies have submitted requests for six-month unsecured loans of $20,000. Because of lending limits imposed by bank policies on this type of loan, only one of the loans will probably be granted. Condensed financial information appears below:

Assets	Company B	Company L
Cash..........................	$ 10,200	$ 18,100
Accounts receivable..............	19,500	24,200
Inventories.....................	53,500	42,500
Noncurrent.....................	52,500	62,000
	$135,700	$146,800

Equities		
Accounts payable................	$ 23,000	$ 38,100
Mortgage payable................	45,000	50,500
Stockholders' equity.............	67,700	58,200
	$135,700	$146,800

Income Statements		
Sales.........................	$155,800	$121,500
Cost of goods sold..............	(109,700)	(75,800)
Operating expenses..............	(37,600)	(33,900)
Interest expense................	(4,000)	(5,000)
Net income before taxes..........	$ 4,500	$ 6,800
Income taxes...................	1,800	2,700
Net Income....................	$ 2,700	$ 4,100

a)   Discuss the general areas of a financial nature which you would want to look at.

b)   Calculate some ratios that would be helpful to you in each of those areas.

c)   Calculate the time it takes each company to convert an investment in inventory to cash.

d)   Your assistant says that your calculation in (c) is an overstatement of the operating cycle (the time it takes to go from cash to inventory to cash) because it ignores the financing supplied by current trade creditors.

1. Assuming that accounts payable arise entirely from inventory purchase transactions, can you devise a measure of the extent of supplier financing? (Hint: What would be helpful is the average number of days before the firms have to remit cash to their suppliers.)

2. Which operating cycle calculation (yours or your assistant's) is most useful? For what purpose?

16–14. Standard Oil of Ohio presented the following earnings per share data in its 1969 annual report.

	For the Year Ended December 31, 1969
Net Income	$51,922,000
Net income per share of common stock	$2.86

Based on weighted average number of common shares outstanding and assuming the special stock (see Note E) had attained dividend rights equal to common stock and assuming exercise or conversion of all dilutive securities, the latter having no material effect. (1969—17,940,000 shares; 1968—17,832,000 shares).

The above per share calculation, which does not recognize the differences between the dividend rights of the common and special stock, complies with the Company's understanding of the present interpretation of Accounting Principles Board Opinion No. 15 "Earnings Per Share." Presently the special stock has not attained dividend rights (see Note E). Based on projections of operations of the Prudhoe Bay properties, it is management's opinion that net income per share of common stock will not be diluted at such time as the special stock becomes entitled to dividends. The more appropriate net income per share, in management's opinion, based on weighted average number of dividend-paying common shares outstanding (1969—13,172,000 shares; 1968—13,082,000 shares), was $3.87

Cash dividends per share on outstanding common stock, excluding equivalents of special stock, were.. $2.70

Note E—Capital Stock at December 31, 1969:

	Shares	
	Authorized	Issued
Preferred—cumulative $100 par value (issuable in series)	424,251	
Series A, 3¾%		144,426
Series B, 4% convertible		95,885
Special—without par value (Note B)	1,000	
Common—$5 par value	40,000,000	13,416,752

Shares issued include 8,878 Series A preferred and 165,811 common shares held in treasury.

Provisions of the preferred stock require annual retirement of 2% of the aggregate number of shares of Series A theretofore issued and, starting in 1979, 5% of the aggregate number of shares of Series B theretofore issued. The Company may redeem Series A at a price of $100 per share. Series B may be redeemed at a price of $150 per share through January 15, 1971, at $104 per share through January 15, 1972, such price decreasing annually thereafter to a minimum of $100. Series B is convertible into common stock at a conversion price of $67.087 per share, and 142,926 shares of common stock are reserved for conversion.

Each share of special stock has rights equivalent to those of a holder of 4,466 shares of common stock, except that until January 1, 1975, or such earlier date as the rate of sustainable net production of crude oil from the Prudhoe Bay properties in Alaska equals or exceeds 200,000 barrels per day, such special stock is not entitled to dividends. After the earlier of such dates, if a dividend is declared on the common stock, a dividend must also be declared on the special stock in an amount commensurate with the number of shares of common stock to which the special stock is then equivalent. The number of shares of common stock to which each share of special stock is equivalent is based on the achievement of sustainable net production from the Prudhoe Bay properties, at any time prior to January 1, 1978, as set forth in the table below:

Rate of Sustainable Net Production (Barrels Per Day)	Number of Shares of Common Stock to Which Each Share of Special Stock Is Equivalent
200,000	6,903
250,000	7,870
300,000	8,933
350,000	10,109
400,000	11,415
450,000	13,947
500,000	14,517
550,000	15,111
600,000	15,730

a) Comment on the nature of the disagreement between management and the opinion of the Accounting Principles Board. Which figure do you think is more useful to the investor? Explain.

b) What is meant by the statement, " . . . and assuming exercise or conversion of all *dilutive securities,* the latter having no *material effect,*" with particular reference to the italicized words?

16–15. One of your college friends, Will Thie, recently inherited a large sum of money. He plans to invest quite extensively in the common stock of either Rubble Corporation or Confusion, Inc. He has asked you to assist him in selecting relevant quantitative factors on which to base his decision.

Using the condensed financial statements shown below, comment on some comparative features of the two companies at which Will should look. Support your comment with appropriate calculations.

Balance Sheets as of December 31 (in thousands of dollars)

	Rubble Corporation			*Confusion Sales*		
	1972	*1971*	*1970*	*1972*	*1971*	*1970*
Current assets..........	525	350	300	210	100	80
Property and plant.......	1,475	1,830	1,830	1,580	1,200	1,180
Accumulated depreciation.	(800)	(900)	(860)	(400)	(350)	(330)
	1,200	1,280	1,270	1,390	950	930
Current liabilities........	275	290	240	90	50	40
Bonds payable, 10%......	200	300	300	500	200	200
Common stock, $10 par...	200	200	200	200	200	200
Retained earnings........	525	490	530	600	500	490
	1,200	1,280	1,270	1,390	950	930

Income Statements for Year Ended, December 31 (in thousands of dollars)

	Rubble Corporation			*Confusion, Inc.*		
	1972	*1971*	*1970*	*1972*	*1971*	*1970*
Sales.................	1,080	1,240	1,140	975	650	700
Costs and expenses.....	820	1,010	930	695	490	515
Interest...............	30	30	30	35	20	20
Income taxes	90	80	70	100	95	55
Net income............	140	120	110	145	45	110
Dividends.............	105	160	100	45	35	35
Increase in retained earnings.............	35	(40)	10	100	10	75

16–16. Ratio analysis is often applied to test the reasonableness of the relationships among current financial data against those of prior financial data.* Given prior financial relationships and few key amounts, a CPA could prepare estimates of current financial data to test the reasonableness of data furnished by his client.

---

* Problem adapted from AICPA May 1969 examination.

Argo Sales Corporation has in recent prior years maintained the following relationships among the data on its financial statements:

Gross profit rate on net sales.....................	40%
Net profit rate on net sales.......................	10%
Rate of selling expenses to net sales..............	20%
Accounts receivable turnover....................	8 per year
Inventory turnover...........................	6 per year
Acid-test ratio...............................	2 to 1
Current ratio.................................	3 to 1
Quick-asset composition: 8% cash, 32% marketable securities, 60% accounts receivable	
Asset turnover...............................	2 per year
Ratio of total assets to intangible assets............	20 to 1
Ratio of accumulated depreciation to cost of fixed assets................................	1 to 3
Ratio of accounts receivable to accounts payable......	1.5 to 1
Ratio of working capital to stockholders' equity.....	1 to 1.6
Ratio of total debt to stockholders' equity..........	1 to 2

The corporation had a net income of $120,000 for 1968, which resulted in earnings of $5.20 per share of common stock. Additional information includes the following:

Capital stock authorized, issued (all in 1960), and outstanding: common, $10 per share par value, issued at 10% premium; preferred, 6% nonparticipating, $100 per share par value, issued at a 10% premium. Market value per share of common at December 31, 1968 was $78. Preferred dividends paid in 1968 were $3,000.

The times interest earned ratio in 1968 was 33. The amounts of the following were the same at December 31, 1968 as at January 1, 1968: inventory; accounts receivable; 5% bonds payable, due 1970; and total stockholders' equity. All purchases and sales were "on account."

a) Prepare in good form the condensed balance sheet and income statement for the year ending December 31, 1968, presenting the amounts you would expect to appear on Argo's financial statements (ignoring income taxes). Major captions appearing on Argo's balance sheet are: Current Assets, Fixed Assets, Intangible Assets, Current Liabilities, Long-Term Liabilities, and Stockholders' Equity. In addition to the accounts divulged in the problem, you should include accounts for Prepaid Expenses, Accrued Expenses, and Administrative Expenses. Supporting computations should be in good form.

b) Compute the following for 1968:
   1. Rate of return on stockholders' equity.
   2. Price-earnings ratio for common stock.
   3. Dividends paid per share of common stock.
   4. Dividends paid per share of preferred stock.
   5. Yield on common stock.

16–17. The following statistics for 1969 have been taken from *Moody's In-dustrial Manual* for the three largest brewing companies in the United States (all figures are in thousands):

	Anheuser Busch	Pabst	Joseph Schlitz
Sales...........................	$666,609	$341,356	$418,786
Interest........................	7,401	375	1,341
Net income before extraordinary items........................	45,311	26,749	24,874
Average total assets...............	538,287	195,029	262,726
Average stockholders' equity........	299,719	149,806	190,652

a) Compute a rate of return on average total assets as a product of margin and turnover for each of the companies. Assume a 50% tax rate in adjusting for the interest add-back.

b) Compute a rate of return on average stockholders' equity.

c) Comment on the differences in parts (*a*) and (*b*). What potential pitfalls do you have to be aware of in making such comparisons?

d) Upon further investigation of the actual financial statements, you discover that included in Anheuser Busch's net income in 1969 is $1,020,000 income from investment in the St. Louis Cardinal Baseball Club, and the average total assets include $5,797,000 labeled investment and advances to St. Louis Cardinal Baseball Club. How does this factor affect the calculation and interpretation of your results?

16–18. Avco Corporation presents a fairly detailed Business Line analysis of consolidated revenues and net earnings in its annual reports. The following analysis appeared in its 1969 report (all figures are thousands of dollars):

	Revenues or Sales		Net Earnings	
	1969	1968	1969	1968
Financial Services:				
Insurance:				
Life and accident and health insurance, variable annuity and mutual fund operations (including capital gains: $7,069,000 in 1969 and $10,893,000 in 1968)....	120,326	118,808	16,235	20,392
Finance:				
Consumer finance:				
Finance operations......	211,946	88,988	13,554	3,792
Equity in insurance earnings (including capital gains: $1,208,000 in 1969 and $2,139,000 in 1968)...	....	....	5,557	3,553
	211,946	88,988	19,111	7,345
Credit card operations....	20,405	10,107	455	394
Savings and loan operations...................	4,141	7,189	525	397
	236,492	106,284	20,091	8,136
Interest on Avco debentures issued for Seabord Finance			(4,537)	
Allocation of Avco's corporate expenses not charged to business lines*....................	....	....	(4,213)	(2,601)
	356,818	225,092	27,576	25,927
Recreation and Land Development:				
Motion pictures and broadcasting..................	57,968	72,049	7,459	12,163
Land development...........	23,209	1,369	269	(284)
Gain on sale of Meredith-Avco, Inc................	....	....	2,057	....
Allocation of Avco's corporate expenses not charged to business lines*....................	....	....	(528)	(356)
	81,177	73,418	9,257	11,523
Products and Research:				
Commercial:				
Aircraft products.........	94,786	81,273	6,936	5,635
Other....................	166,860	171,763	1,847	4,483
	261,646	253,036	8,783	10,118
Government:				
Aircraft products.........	385,668	382,435	5,965	8,188
Other....................	169,593	230,682	4,534	4,799
	555,261	613,117	10,499	12,987
Allocation of Avco's corporate expenses not charged to business lines*....................	....	....	(4,668)	(3,533)
	816,907	866,153	14,614	19,572
	898,084	939,571	51,447	57,022

* Interest and corporate expenses have been allocated as appropriate to the business lines and the three groups shown above.

    a) Explain Avco's use of the terms "business lines" and "groups."

    b) How has Avco treated administrative costs, interest, and taxes? What additional information would you like as an analyst?

    c) Why is the interest on Avco debentures issued for Seaboard Finance treated separately from other interest? Do you agree?

    d) What use would an analyst make of this type of information?

16–19. The following ratios have been calculated from the financial statements of three actual companies. One of the companies is a utility, one is a manufacturer of consumer durables, and the third is a retailer. From the differences in the ratios, attempt to identify each company. Explain what industry conditions would cause each ratio to differ from one company to another.

	Company		
	A	*B*	*C*
Current ratio....................	1.5	2.3	0.5
Stock equity ratio (common stock equity ÷ total equities..........	48%	67%	28%
Turnover of average total assets.....	2.95 times	1.7 times	0.24 times
Margin (net income before interest but after tax ÷ sales)..........	3.6%	7.1%	20.6%
Rate of return on average total assets.......................	10.6%	12.1%	4.9%

CHAPTER SEVENTEEN

ALTERNATIVE
CONCEPTS OF
INCOME

THE DISCIPLINE of economics long has theorized about the nature of and relationship between wealth and income. Wealth (or capital, as some economists use the term) represents the totality of economic values accessible to a person, business, or nation at a point in time. It is a *stock* concept. Income represents the change in wealth between two points of time; it is a *flow* concept, the amount of value coming in (or going out). Income not consumed increases the wealth of the owner. Applied to a business then, income can be viewed as either the increase in business wealth during the period, exclusive of transactions with stockholders, or the amount that the company could distribute to investors during the period and still leave a stock of wealth at the end of the period equivalent to that at the beginning.

In financial accounting, we find the concepts of wealth and income reflected respectively in the position statement and the income statement. Wealth is commonly measured by the amount of net assets (stockholders' equity) apart from additional capital investments and dividends. In addition to theorizing about these concepts, however, the accountant has the responsibility to accumulate and report financial measurements of them. Because the concepts of wealth and income are common to both economics and accounting, one might expect to find accountants using as a guide the measurement ideas suggested by economists. This is not the case.

In this chapter we pursue some of the reasons for this disparity in approach between economics and accounting. A discussion of alternative valuation (measurement) concepts points up the illusiveness and tentativeness of any income measurement process. It also lays the groundwork for a discussion of two suggested procedures for implementing some of the suggestions found in economics—the adjustment of accounts for general price-level changes and the recording of current cost valuations in the accounts.

Before we begin this discussion, one admonition is in order. Just as income and wealth conceptually are closely intertwined, so also are the processes of income measurement and asset-liability valuation. This interrelationship can be seen readily in the simple case of a single income-producing asset. Assume the business owns a $10,000 bond bearing interest at 6 percent and maturing in two years. Also assume bonds having similar risk characteristics normally carry a 10 percent interest rate. Economic theory (and accounting practice in this case) would establish the initial worth of the bond at the present value of expected future receipts—that is, the present value of the two interest payments of $600 plus the present value of the $10,000 principal repayment.

$$P_{\overline{2}|.10} \qquad 600 = \$ \quad 600 \times 1.736 = \$1,042$$
$$p_{\overline{2}|.10} \quad 10,000 = \$10,000 \times 0.826 = \underline{\quad 8,260}$$
$$\$9,302$$

Initial wealth (asset value) is $9,302. Cash receipts will be $600 at the end of Year 1 and $10,600 at the end of Year 2. Table 17–1 reflects the asset position at the end of each year.

TABLE 17–1

	Asset Position—End of Year		
	0	1	2
Cash....................................	. . .	$ 600	$11,200
Bond investment.......................	$9,302	9,635	. . .
Total wealth..........................	$9,302	$10,235	$11,200
Change in wealth (income).............	. . .	933	965

The revenue (income) flows for Years 1 and 2 are revealed in the following journal entries (amounts are subject to minor rounding):

```
                              Year 1            Year 2
Cash.........................  600               600
Investment in Bond...........  333               365
    Interest Revenue.........         933               965
```

One can look at comparative position statements (statements of wealth) to measure the periodic changes and define income to be that change. Or one can look to the income statement flows directly and achieve the same result. This same type of connection between asset valuation and income measurement can be seen in many areas analyzed in previous chapters. For instance, the valuation of equipment at historical cost means that depreciation expense is also based on historical cost.

So it is evident that we really have but a single approach to income measurement, originating from two different but closely related points of view. Although users of financial reports may display more interest, at times, in the components of income as reflected on the income statement, that statement's measures have no validity apart from the valuations presented on the balance sheet. In economic theory, how income is measured (i.e., discounting expected future net receipts) determines how assets are valued. In accounting, the tendency more commonly has been the other way around—how assets are valued determines how income is measured. Nevertheless, although emphasis may vary between the two points of view, their interrelationship remains. The income statement cannot be divorced from the position statement if there is to be a consistent set of concepts underlying financial accounting.

ALTERNATIVE VALUATION CONCEPTS

Because of the close association between asset valuation and income measurement, discussion of one automatically has implications for the other. For convenience in discussing economic wealth and income, the attention in this section centers initially on asset valuation.

Direct Valuation of Business

In the case of the bond investment, we see that the economic value of an asset is the present value of its expected net cash receipts. Theoretically, this same idea could be applied to the entire business. We could calculate the economic value of the entire business (its wealth) by discounting the excess of its expected total cash receipts over total cash disbursements for each future period at the appropriate rate of interest and summing the results. If the excess were expected to be the same each period, wealth or the total value of assets (including going-concern value or goodwill) would be represented by the present value of an annuity. The usual approach in economics is to value the entire business as if it were a single asset. Alternatively, we could value each individual asset, tangible and intangible, by discounting its particular future net cash receipts. The sum of the individual asset values would be, in theory, the value of the business.

In this valuation process, one other point is relevant. Although the measurement of wealth is expressed in monetary units (dollars), the meaning of wealth is in terms of real goods and services. Economic income exists only if the change in wealth between two points in time represents an increase in expected command over goods and services. This change can be measured in dollars only if the size (purchasing power) of the measuring unit does not vary.

Under direct valuation, then, income is the change in value; value is the discounted amount of expected future net receipts. Two elements of measurement are inherent in the implementation of a direct valuation theory for a particular business. Future net receipts must be predicted and an appropriate rate of interest chosen to reduce these receipts to their present value. In fact, if these two elements are known with certainty, income measurement reduces to a simple matter of accruing interest at the discount rate times the balance at the beginning of the period. What income will be in future periods is already known now.

However, in a real situation, uncertainty prevails. Future net receipts have to be estimated on the basis of the expectations of either the owners or the managers of the firm. To the extent that actual net receipts during a period differ from those estimated originally, net income is correspondingly modified. More importantly, actual cash receipts could cause the estimators to revise their predictions of future cash receipts. The present value of these *changes* in the amount of estimated receipts would be part of wealth at the end of the period and, therefore, income for the period. Further, changes in expectations may affect not only predicted cash receipts but also the discount (interest) rate. The interest rate used to derive present value supposedly reflects risk and uncertainty. If risk conditions change from one period to the next, a different discount rate becomes appropriate. A change in rate will change the present-value calculation of wealth. The effects of this change, therefore, would also be included in the income measurement for the period of change.

The problems of using direct valuation in financial accounting are apparent from the above discussion. Income and wealth under economic theory are extremely subjective, being based solely on the individual manager's expectations. For reporting to external audiences, the degree of possible error and disagreement is too great. Nevertheless, economic income represents a theoretical model toward which some accountants believe conventional accounting should move. Various alternatives have been suggested to narrow the gap and still maintain a tolerable standard of reliability and objectivity.

Use of Selling Market Prices (Output Values)

One suggested alternative relies on market prices, the price at which a firm can sell an asset, as a proxy for direct valuations. This concept hypothesizes that the price of an asset established in a relatively competitive market reflects the judgments of many individuals concerning the present value of its future cash receipts. Therefore, market values of assets (after adjustment for any effect that quantities offered would have on price) presumably provide a more objective measure of discounted value because of their reliance on the expectations of others outside of the firm. Such a value probably understates the *subjective* economic value; otherwise, the firm would not continue to hold the asset. Of course, valuation through the use of market selling prices does not determine the *total* economic value of the firm, because it is impossible to measure the value of goodwill (going-concern value); no market exists for this economic quantity. However, output values may come close to the economic model of valuation with respect to individual assets.

There are a few instances of using market values in conventional accounting. The idea of recording inventory at net realizable value, discussed in Chapter Eight, is an example of indirect valuation by means of market selling prices. Of course, net realizable value is only used when it is below cost, and not always then. Hence, the practice is not truly consistent with the economic theory behind the use of net realizable values as *the* basis for asset valuation, since this involves using market when it is above cost also. The other major practical example is the initial valuation of certain monetary assets (and liabilities). Prices in the bond market are presumed to represent the present value of the receipts (or disbursements) under the contract. However, after the initial recording, no subsequent changes are made in the valuation to reflect market changes in interest rates.

No true selling market exists for most noncurrent assets, such as plant and equipment. Any output market values for them probably represent liquidation figures rather than serious attempts to estimate and discount the net future cash receipts resulting from the use of the asset's services. Even with inventory, establishing net realizable value may require very uncertain estimates of the costs necessary to complete the product, the costs of selling, the length of time before sale, and the quantity that can be sold at the existing market prices. The further removed the asset is from normal sale, the more numerous and uncertain these estimates become.

Use of Acquisition Market Prices (Input Values)

Accountants for the most part have questioned the use of output market prices on the grounds of both the impracticality of measurement and the recognition of anticipated income. Rather, they have preferred to value assets in terms of acquisition market prices—that is, the amount the asset costs to purchase, not what it can be sold for. This approach focuses more on a conventional matching or transaction approach to income measurement than on a valuation-of-asset approach. Under it, the accountant traces inputs through the firm as they are combined into salable products or services. When the product or service is sold, the sacrifice made by the firm for the inputs is compared to the sales price. Income exists only if the price exceeds the firm's sacrifice made for inputs.

This approach rejects an income concept under which asset services are valued at their sales value prior to the time of sale or earning. Accordingly, valuation based on output values is inconsistent with this matching concept; instead, some input value is called for. Three input values receive prominent attention: (1) historical costs measured in monetary terms, (2) historical costs measured in real terms (purchasing power), and (3) current acquisition costs.

Historic Acquisition Cost.   The concept of income conventionally used employs historic, dollar acquisition costs as the entry value. It derives from three of the fundamental assumptions—matching, monetary, and revenue recognition. First, we record assets at their acquisition cost because this is a monetary expression of the effort the firm has expended in acquiring productive resources. The periodic matching of these costs against revenues presumably provides a meaningful, historic measure of business performance. Second, the monetary postulate influences asset valuation and income measurement by providing the dollar as a unit of measurement assumed to be stable. Therefore, amounts of and changes in monetary values supposedly reflect real values and changes as well, even over a substantial time horizon. Finally, the revenue postulate sets forth standards for the recognition of new values in the business. Increases in the valuation of total assets are not recorded until they have been earned and can be measured with a reasonable degree of objectivity and certainty. In most instances, this generally means that no change in asset values is recognized until the point of sale.

As a consequence, conventional financial accounting income is solely a monetary concept. No attention is given to changes in the general price level or to changes in the prices of individual assets. Income under this concept implicitly defines recovery of capital in terms of monetary units only; a firm has maintained its capital if it recovers from revenue the same number of dollars it originally expended on the assets consumed.

Purchasing Power Approach.   A basic criticism of the use of historical cost as *the* input value is directed against the monetary postulate and arises when the general level of prices changes. When prices on the average have increased, then each dollar can command fewer goods and services than before, i.e., the general purchasing power of the dollar has declined. This means that the measuring unit used by the accountant also has changed. Under these circumstances, a number of accountants, including many who accept the matching concept, question whether these changes in the size of the monetary unit can be ignored, as the monetary postulate assumes. They suggest that in the process of matching costs against revenues, both must be stated in the same common denominator— that is, in terms of the same price level. Otherwise, the number of dollars originally expended for an asset is not a realistic representation of cost (effort) in light of the current purchasing power of the revenue stream (accomplishment).

The purchasing power approach would substitute, as input values, original acquisition costs adjusted by means of a general price index to their equivalent in current purchasing power units. Valuation still is at historic acquisition cost, but this cost is restated in terms of an equivalent number of monetary units having a common amount of purchasing power. Capital is assumed to be recovered only when a firm receives an equivalent amount of general purchasing power represented by the initial acquisition cost of the asset consumed. When an expenditure is made, part of the firm's pool of general purchasing power has been committed. Alternative purchase opportunities have been forgone. The firm is as well off as it was only if it recovers the same general ability to command goods and services as that represented by the original investment.

Procedures to implement the purchasing power approach are called common-dollar accounting. They are discussed more deeply later in this chapter.

Current Cost Approach. A second criticism leveled against the use of historic acquisition cost denies the relevance of historic acquisition costs as a measure of input effort altogether. When changing conditions of supply and demand cause the current acquisition cost (replacement cost) of a particular productive resource to increase or decrease, the original cost has lost its economic significance as a measure of the effort involved in the asset's use. A more accurate measure of effort is what it would cost currently to acquire or replace the asset *services* being consumed in the production of revenue. Recovery of capital is viewed in terms of the firm's ability to command the particular good or service being consumed.

The current cost approach significantly modifies the conventional interpretation of the matching concept. Net operating income is best measured, under this approach, by matching the current cost of assets consumed against revenues recognized. The difference between the original acquisition cost and the current acquisition cost represents a revaluation of the assets. The corresponding equity change is a *holding gain or loss*— i.e., a change in equity resulting from changes in the acquisition cost of inputs while they are being held for future use in operations. To the extent that holding gains and losses would be reflected in income, this approach entails some modifications in the revenue recognition concept as well.

The current cost approach is illustrated in the last section of this chapter.

BACKGROUND DISCUSSION:
THE PROBLEM OF CHANGING PRICES

The preceding discussion of alternative valuation methods highlights two major differences among the methods. One difference is found in the recording of anticipations of future inflows and outflows. The second difference lies in the timing and means of recognizing changing prices. Changes in prices, either of all items in general or of only specific items, have plagued the accountant's measurement process even within a framework that limits the impact of expectations. Consequently, accountants have addressed themselves to this problem more than to the first.

The Nature of Price Changes

In reality, two types of price changes—general and specific—are of concern to accountants. That they often cannot be separated precisely should not mask the fact that they reflect quite different economic changes and cause quite different theoretical problems.

Prices are quoted in monetary units—the dollar in the case of the United States. The monetary unit in an economic system has three basic functions; it acts as a medium of exchange, a standard of value, and a store of value. To serve effectively as a medium of exchange, the monetary unit must be readily acceptable in exchange for goods and services at a particular time. On the other hand, in its capacity as a standard and store of value, the monetary unit must provide a measuring stick for the highly diverse goods and services the values of which are continually being compared and contrasted. In all three functions the dollar serves only as a common denominator in which the real quantities of goods and services can be expressed.

Specific Price Changes. Specific price changes involve the monetary unit in its functions as medium of exchange and standard of value. In economic terms the price of any one item is its exchange value in relation to other goods and services. A specific price, then, becomes the number of dollars of general exchange value required to acquire a particular good or service. The decision to sell a specific item can be viewed as one of electing to exchange the specific item for all other goods and services. The dollar simply serves as a proxy for the exchange values of all other items. A specific price measures the exchange value of the particular item relative to all other items. Likewise, a specific price change refers to a change in the relative value of an item. More or fewer dollars, which represent a general claim over other goods and services, must be exchanged for it. Specific price or value changes are caused by changes over time in the interaction of demand and supply for the particular good or service.

General Price Changes. The monetary unit serves to measure relative exchange values not only at a point in time but also through time. Moreover, dollars can be accumulated as a store of generalized purchasing power, allowing persons and firms to make a conscious choice between present exchange and future exchange. These functions, of standard of value and store of value over time, are made complicated if the monetary unit itself changes in value. Just as the price of a good depends on the items that can be exchanged for it, the price or value of the dollar rests on the real quantities of goods and services that can be exchanged for it. When people exchange less goods in general each year for a dollar, as has been the case in the United States for about 30 years, the purchasing power of the dollar declines.

To serve effectively as a stable measuring unit for other economic commodities, the dollar should maintain its own exchange value. The quantity of things in general which the monetary unit can command should not vary; otherwise, the size of the economic yardstick changes. Such shifts in the exchange value of money as do in fact occur constitute general price-level changes. General price changes reflect a host of factors associated with general inflation and deflation having reference to no particular goods or services. General price-level changes connote that prices in general throughout the economy have changed. If the price of everything increased 20 percent, relative values would not have changed. However, the exchange or purchasing-power value of the dollar, and hence the size of the accountant's measuring unit, would have changed.

It is obvious that both types of price changes probably occur at the same time. The price change for any particular good or service may reflect a change in its real value relative to all other goods and a general change in the price level. Often, this mixed price change is interpreted to be a specific price change. Such an interpretation is in error, however, because it fails to allow for the effect of a lack of comparability in the size of the measuring unit. For example, assume that price quotations for fork-lift trucks were $1,500 and $1,610 in years one and two, respectively. During the period, prices of all goods and services increased 5 percent on the average. The price increase of $110 really is a combination of two factors: (1) a *fictional* increase of $75, resulting from inflation between the two years having made the original price quotation of $1,500 not comparable in terms of general purchasing power to year two dollars, ($1,500 × 5%), and (2) a *real* increase of $35 ($1,610 − $1,575) in the value of fork-lift trucks relative to other goods and services.

Authoritative Pronouncements on Price Changes

Any discussion of the accounting problems caused by changing prices would be incomplete without some mention of the formal accounting literature on the subject. Space limitations prohibit an exhaustive review of all significant contributions. Consequently, only those pronouncements directly or indirectly associated with the American Accounting Association and the American Institute of Certified Public Accountants are highlighted.

Prior to World War II, little formal attention was paid to the problems of changing prices. To be sure, upward asset adjustments were not uncommon. These appraisal write-ups supposedly reflected "current values," although, like beauty, the value was sometimes only in the eye of the beholder—management. The write-ups were more than offset by the subsequent write-downs in the early 1930s. The downward adjustments usually were as spotty and subjective as the preceding write-ups.

Out of these contortions seemed to grow a firmer adherence to historic acquisition cost. The American Accounting Association issued the first in its series of periodic statements of accounting principles in 1936. The six-page document strongly urged historical cost for asset valuation and expense determination. The price change controversy was temporarily buried.[1]

American Accounting Association Publications.   The inflation in the 1940s during and following the war rekindled the interest of accountants in the problems caused by the continual shrinking in the purchasing power of the dollar and by the disparity in the prices of specific assets before and after the war. Statements of principles issued in 1941 and 1948 both reiterated unswerving support for the use of original acquisition cost, except for a footnote reference to fluctuations in the purchasing power of the dollar. The AAA's major efforts to deal directly with price change problems began in 1951 and are briefly outlined below.[2] (Except where otherwise noted, materials listed were published by the AAA at Columbus, Ohio.)

1. *Supplementary Statement No. 2* (1951).[3]   This statement was one of eight supplements to the 1948 statement of principles. It recommended presentation of primary financial statements reflecting historical costs and

[1] Three notable exceptions deserve mention: (1) John B. Canning in *The Economics of Accountancy* (New York: Ronald Press Co., 1929) discussed the use of direct and indirect valuations of assets; (2) Henry W. Sweeney in *Stabilized Accounting* (New York: Harper & Bros., 1936) presented theoretical discussions and ledger-account illustrations for both general and specific price changes; and (3) Kenneth MacNeal in *Truth in Accounting* (Philadelphia: University of Pennsylvania Press, 1939) pleaded for the use of "economic values" (market values) in the accounts.

[2] Although not listed separately, the influence of Professor William A. Paton pervaded most of the publications of the AAA. It would not be an overstatement to say that he has been one of the foremost advocates of price-level adjustments. His numerous books, articles, speeches, testimony, etc., provided a wealth of analysis and illustrations upon which later writers frequently built their own work.

[3] *Accounting and Reporting Standards for Corporate Financial Statements and Preceding Statements and Supplements* (1957), pp. 23–29.

a full set of supplementary financial statements adjusted for general price-level changes.

2. *Case Studies of Four Companies* (1955).   This book by Professor Ralph C. Jones of Yale attempted to determine empirically how financial statements adjusted for general price-level changes would differ from conventionally prepared statements.

3. *Basic Concepts and Methods* (1956).[4]   This small monograph outlines and illustrates a procedure for comprehensive adjustment of financial statements for price-level changes.

4. *Effects of Price Level Changes on Business Income, Capital, and Taxes* (1956).   Professor Jones' second book is a classic in the literature. It summarizes the theory and discusses the meaning and uses of price-level adjusted financial data.

5. *Accounting and Reporting Standards* (1957).[5]   Reflecting a two-year effort to revise the 1948 statement, the AAA committee again recommended that primary statements should adhere to cost, and supplementary statements should be presented showing the effect of price changes. In a significant departure from past publications, the committee recommended adjustment for either specific price changes, general price-level changes, or both. No preference was expressed.

6. *Subsequent AAA Committee Reports.*   Committee reports designed to supplement the 1957 statement were more forceful. The committee on noncurrent assets[6] advocated that noncurrent assets be valued whenever possible at *current cost*. Holding gains and losses, whether real or due solely to changes in the size of the measuring unit, were to be included in income. The majority of the committee on inventory[7] similarly favored valuation at replacement cost and split on the issue of recognizing holding gains and losses in income. The committee on realization[8] also advocated the recognition of specific holding gains; the majority preferred to include only realized holding gains in income.

7. *A Statement of Basic Accounting Theory* (Evanston, Ill., 1966). This attempt to draft an integrated statement of theory recommended a dual presentation of financial statements—one set based on original cost and the other based on current cost valuations but with explicit recognition given to changes in general price levels. Holding gains and losses were to be included on the income statement.

---

[4] Perry Mason, *Price-Level Changes and Financial Statements: Basic Concepts and Methods.*

[5] *Accounting and Reporting Standards for Corporate Financial Statements and Preceding Statements and Supplements,* pp. 1–12.

[6] "Accounting for Land, Buildings, and Equipment, Supplementary Statement No. 1," *Accounting Review*, July 1964, pp. 693–99.

[7] "A Discussion of Various Approaches to Inventory Measurement, Supplementary Statement No. 2," *Accounting Review*, July 1964, pp. 700–14.

[8] "The Realization Concept," *Accounting Review*, April 1965, pp. 312–22.

AICPA Publications. The American Institute of Certified Public Accountants historically has acted as the quasi-official spokesman for the accounting profession. Its official publications, for the most part, have discouraged departures from historical cost. At the same time, unofficially it has recognized the growing problem and has sponsored significant research in the area. A brief listing of its contributions to the literature appears below. (Except as otherwise noted, materials were published by the AICPA at New York.)

1. *Accounting Research Bulletin No. 5* (1940). This bulletin advocated original cost recording. However, it recommended that if assets were written up, depreciation should be based on the higher valuations.

2. *Accounting Research Bulletin No. 33* (1947). Again, the AICPA recommended continuation of historic acquisition cost. In the 1940s some firms based depreciation charges on current asset values or made additional charge-offs of historical cost, supposedly to compensate for excessive costs caused by increased price levels. This bulletin was issued to check the extension of these "undesirable" practices. Restrictions of retained earnings were suggested as an acceptable way of dealing with the problem. Little distinction was made between specific price changes and general price-level changes. The viewpoint expressed in *Bulletin No. 33* was reaffirmed in 1948 in a letter to the AICPA membership. However, the letter did give "full support to the use of supplementary financial schedules."

3. *Accounting Research Bulletin No. 43* (1953).[9] This bulletin constituted a restatement and revision of the preceding 42 bulletins. It repeated the old *Bulletin No. 33* and the 1948 letter.[10]

4. *Study Group on Business Income* (1947–52). Out of this interdisciplinary group, jointly sponsored by the AICPA and the Rockefeller Foundation, came four background publications[11] and a final report.[12] The latter acknowledged the necessity of retaining conventional income statements but recommended that selected items on the income statement—cost of goods sold and depreciation expense—be measured and reported in terms of their purchasing-power equivalents. A clearly secondary

---

[9] *Restatement and Revision of Accounting Research Bulletins.*

[10] In October 1965, the APB issued *Status of Accounting Research Bulletins, Opinion of the Accounting Principles Board No. 6.* It left this portion of *Bulletin No. 43* in full force. It also stated that noncurrent assets should not be written up to reflect values which are above cost.

[11] These publications were: Arthur H. Dean, *An Inquiry into the Nature of Business Income under Present Price Levels* (1949); George O. May, *Business Income and Price Levels: An Accounting Study* (1949); Sidney S. Alexander *et al.*, *Five Monographs on Business Income* (1950); and Howard C. Greer and Edward B. Wilcox, "The Case Against Price-Level Adjustments in Income Determination," *Journal of Accountancy*, December 1950.

[12] *Changing Concepts of Business Income* (New York: Macmillan Co., 1952).

objective was the eventual development of a fully integrated set of price-level adjusted financial statements.

5. *Accounting Research Study No. 3* (1962).[13] This study was one of the first monographs prepared under the AICPA's research program and recommended the use of direct valuation for monetary assets, net realizable values for inventories, and periodic revaluations to current cost for most noncurrent assets. Although dealing primarily with specific price changes, the study made clear that measurement with a stable dollar was essential. Because of the controversy engendered by *ARS No. 3*, the Accounting Principles Board issued a statement that the study contained "inferences and recommendations in part of a speculative and tentative nature" and that its conclusions were "too radically different from present generally accepted accounting principles for acceptance at this time."[14]

6. *Accounting Research Study No. 6* (1963).[15] This study concerned general price-level changes only. It recommended the supplementary presentation of the entire financial statements expressed in units of uniform purchasing power.

7. *APB Statement No. 3* (1969).[16] After reviewing *ARS No. 6* and field-testing its procedures on 18 companies for 1966 and 1967, the Accounting Principles Board formally commented in June 1969. It recommended the methodology contained in *ARS No. 6* for presenting general price-level financial statements. The Board confined its recommendations primarily to methodology and did not specifically require the reporting of price-level information.

That the accounting profession has wrestled with the problem of changing prices for a long time is evident from even this incomplete cataloguing of published works.[17] Various ideas have been advanced, modified, discarded, and then readvanced. Out of this evolution has come two major procedures to recognize price changes on a continuing basis. These methods—common-dollar accounting and current cost recording—

---

[13] Robert T. Sprouse and Maurice Moonitz, *A Tentative Set of Broad Accounting Principles for Business Enterprise*.

[14] *Statement by the Accounting Principles Board No. 1* (1962).

[15] Staff of the Accounting Research Division, *Reporting the Financial Effects of Price-Level Changes*.

[16] *Financial Statements Restated for General Price-Level Changes*.

[17] One additional work must be cited—Edgar O. Edwards and Philip W. Bell, *The Theory and Measurement of Business Income* (Berkeley. University of California Press, 1961). Although not a publication affiliated with one of the two major accounting organizations, this work sets forth a theory and procedure for incorporating current acquisition costs into accounting records. The term "holding gain (loss)" was coined by the authors. Much as Professor Paton's work laid the foundation for a purchasing-power approach in accounting, Professors Edwards and Bell provide the framework used by many of the recent writers advocating a current cost approach.

encompass a comprehensive set of internally consistent procedures. They are described and illustrated in the next two sections.

COMMON-DOLLAR ACCOUNTING

Common-dollar accounting deals with general price-level changes only. It adjusts only for changes in the size of the measuring unit used in accounting. In conventional financial statements asset and equity items and changes are measured in terms of dollars of the period in which the transactions arise. These dollars represent varying amounts of purchasing power when general inflation or deflation occurs. On the other hand, financial statements restated for general price-level changes reflect these items and changes in terms of dollars representing a uniform purchasing power because the dollar at a specified date, typically that at the end of the current period, is selected as the measuring unit.

Therefore, common-dollar accounting differs from conventional financial accounting only with respect to the unit of measure employed. All other assumptions, conventions, principles, and procedures basically remain the same. In this sense, it is not a departure from traditional accounting but rather a *restatement* of original transactions in terms of dollars of uniform general purchasing power.

Restatement of Accounts

Changes in the general price level typically are measured by some index of general prices. As the prices of items in general increase, the purchasing power of the dollar decreases. Since it is impractical to measure the price increases of all items, a price index of a general sample of items is used.[18] The index expresses the relationship between an average of all prices at a point in time and those same prices in some base year. The changes in a general price index—or, more precisely, the reciprocal of the index—over time provide a reasonably accurate indication of movements in the value of the dollar.

By means of general price indices, dollar amounts recorded at any particular point in time can be restated in dollars as of any other point in time. For example, if land were purchased for $5,000 in year one, when the general price-level index was 80, the equivalent amount of purchasing power invested expressed in year five dollars, when the index is 120, is $7,500 ($5,000 × 120/80). Since prices have increased 50 percent, the $5,000 originally invested is equivalent to $7,500 of year five purchasing

---

[18] The most comprehensive general price index in the United States is the Gross National Product Deflator. Its use is recommended by the Accounting Principles Board. Two other, perhaps more widely known, indices of general prices are the Consumers Price Index and the Wholesale Price Index of the Department of Labor.

power. No increase in *value* results from this adjustment; the original cost is merely being restated in terms of a different-sized measuring unit. The index of general prices measures the size of the accountant's yardstick.

Under common-dollar accounting, we normally wish to express the financial statements in terms of the measuring unit existing at the end of the current accounting period. We can do so by multiplying each unadjusted accounting item by a fraction, the numerator of which is the price index at the current time and the denominator the index of the price level when the item was originally recorded. Thus, the restatement for machinery and equipment involves aging the book costs by year of acquisition. Then the balance of each year's costs remaining on the books is expressed in year-end dollars by means of the index appropriate for each year. In a similar manner, the capital stock account is subdivided according to the year of origin of the various contributions. Each subdivision is then converted to year-end dollars and added to the others. Other examples of the restatement process can be found in the comprehensive illustration presented later.

Monetary Assets and Liabilities

The preceding restatement procedures apply to nonmonetary items—that is, items whose real value may change. Since these items conventionally are recorded at cost, to recognize the effect of price-level changes we merely restate their acquisition costs (or financial interest therein, in the case of owners' equity) in terms of the purchasing power of the year-end dollar. The situation is somewhat different for monetary assets and liabilities. These items represent cash or claims to cash. Their value is established at a specified number of dollars; the number cannot change with changing economic conditions. Take, for instance, an account receivable. This is a contractual right to receive a fixed number of dollar units. It does not require the customer to remit a certain amount of general purchasing power. Thus, the realistic figure at which to record the current balance of receivables at all times is the number of dollar units originally transacted. Current payables, being merely the opposite side of the coin, can be analyzed similarly. Monetary claims, in essence, require no restatement. By their very nature they are always expressed in terms of dollars of current purchasing power.

On the other hand, the *value* of the stock of dollars on hand, receivable, or payable depends on what the number of monetary units will purchase. Therefore, a business in fact can gain or lose purchasing power as a result of inflation or deflation. Assume that a firm has $1,000 in cash in the bank at the beginning of the year and holds it until the end of the year. In the interim, a general price index moves from 100 to 110. In terms of the year-end dollar, it takes $1,100 ($1,000 \times 110/100$) to equal the same amount of purchasing power originally represented by $1,000 one year ago. Yet, at the end of the year the firm has only 1,000 dollar-units. As a result of holding cash (or claims to cash) during inflation, the business has suffered a loss of $100 in purchasing power.

Conversely, assume that the same business is liable throughout the year for an account payable of $500. In terms of the year-end dollar, the initial $500 liability is actually equivalent to $550 of purchasing power ($500 × 110/100). Yet, at year-end the business contractually owes only 500 dollar-units and, therefore, has gained $50 of general purchasing power at the expense of the creditor.

The above example illustrates that when we comprehensively apply common-dollar accounting, gains and losses on monetary accounts can occur. Statements prepared under the monetary postulate fail to measure such changes. Consequently, there is no precedent for how the monetary gain or loss is to be reported. The prevailing opinion is to report the net gain or loss on all monetary items as a separately identifiable item of net income, although some other alternatives are possible. The Accounting Principles Board recommended this one on the grounds that the gain or loss arises from the *holding* of the monetary item during a period of inflation or deflation rather than from the original purpose or ultimate disposition of the claim.[19]

Comprehensive Illustration

The Neverchange Corporation presents the financial information shown in Tables 17–2 and 17–3, prepared under customary accounting practices. In addition, it presents the following supplementary data:

TABLE 17–2

NEVERCHANGE CORP.

Comparative Balance Sheet as of December 31

	19x0	19x1
Cash..........................	$ 90,000	$ 60,000
Receivables...................	75,000	90,000
Inventory.....................	150,000	180,000
Land..........................	30,000	30,000
Plant and equipment...........	180,000	180,000
Accumulated depreciation......	(38,000)	(56,000)
	$487,000	$484,000
Current payables..............	$100,000	$ 75,000
Bonds payable.................	50,000	50,000
Capital stock.................	200,000	200,000
Retained earnings.............	137,000	159,000
	$487,000	$484,000

---

[19] APB, *Financial Statements Restated for General Price-Level Changes, op. cit.*, p. 17.

TABLE 17–3

NEVERCHANGE CORP.

Income Statement for the Year Ended December 31, 19x1

Sales..............................		$800,000
Expenses:		
Cost of goods sold..............	$580,000	
Selling and administrative......	126,000	
Depreciation....................	18,000	
Taxes...........................	30,000	
Interest........................	4,000	758,000
Net income........................		$ 42,000
Dividends.........................		20,000
Increase in Retained Earnings.....		$ 22,000

1. The general price index stood at 100 and 110 at the end of 19x0 and 19x1, respectively. The average index for 19x1 was 105.
2. The business was started four years ago, when the general price index was 80. All of the capital stock was issued then. The land and $100,000 of the plant and equipment also were acquired at that time. The rest of the plant and equipment was acquired two years ago, when the general price index was 90. All plant and equipment has a 10-year useful life.
3. The bonds were issued at the end of 19x0.
4. Sales, selling and administrative expense, taxes, and interest occur evenly throughout the year; dividends are accrued or paid in year-end dollars.
5. The company uses Fifo inventory flow. The inventory on hand at the end of 19x0 was acquired when the general price index was 100. Purchases during 19x1 were $390,000 when the index was 105 and $220,-000 when the index was 110.

Restatement of this information in terms of a common dollar as of December 31, 19x1, results in the financial statements shown in Tables 17–4, 17–5, and 17–6. The calculation of the net loss of purchasing power from holding monetary items during the period of inflation is calculated in Table 17–7.

The 19x0 balance sheet has been restated in terms of December 31, 19x1 dollars in two stages. The general procedures described in the preceding paragraphs have been used to restate the nonmonetary items to equivalent amounts of purchasing power expressed in dollars as of December 31, 19x0. The monetary items as of that date are automatically expressed in dollars as of the end of 19x0. Retained earnings has been entered as a balancing figure rather than restated separately. To restate it would require the restating of all prior years' income statements, including a calculation of gains and losses on monetary items for each year. Such a procedure is impractical and unnecessary, since the difference between the total restated assets and the sum of restated liabilities and capital stock

TABLE 17-4

NEVERCHANGE CORP.

Balance Sheet as of December 31,19x0

	Transaction Amount	Conversion Factor	Restated to 12/31/x0 $	Conversion Factor	Restated to 12/31/x1 $
Cash.............	$ 90,000	...	$ 90,000	110/100	$ 99,000
Receivables.......	75,000	...	75,000	110/100	82,500
Inventory.........	150,000	100/100	150,000	110/100	165,000
Land.............	30,000	100/80	37,500	110/100	41,250
Plant and equipment.......	{ 100,000 / 80,000	100/80 / 100/90	125,000 } / 88,889 }	110/100	235,278
Accumulated depreciation....	{ (30,000) / (8,000)	100/80 / 100/90	(37,500) } / (8,889) }	110/100	(51,028)
	$487,000		$520,000		$572,000
Current payables..	$100,000	...	$100,000	110/100	$110,000
Bonds payable.....	50,000	...	50,000	110/100	55,000
Capital stock.....	200,000	100/80	250,000	110/100	275,000
Retained earnings.	137,000		120,000	110/100	132,000
	$487,000		$520,000		$572,000

TABLE 17-5

NEVERCHANGE CORP.

Balance Sheet as of December 31, 19x1

	Transaction Amount	Conversion Factor	Restated to 12/31/x1 $
Cash.....................	$ 60,000	...	$ 60,000
Receivables..............	90,000	...	90,000
Inventory................	180,000	110/110	180,000
Land....................	30,000	110/80	41,250
Plant and equipment......	{ 100,000 / 80,000	110/80 } / 110/90 }	235,278
Accumulated depreciation..........	{ (40,000) / (16,000)	110/80 } / 110/90 }	(74,556)
	$484,000		$531,972
Current payables.........	$ 75,000	...	$ 75,000
Bonds payable............	50,000	...	50,000
Capital stock............	200,000	110/80	275,000
Retained earnings........	159,000		131,972
	$484,000		$531,972

gives a completely restated retained earnings.

Once the balance sheet has been recast in 19x0 dollars, it can be "rolled forward" to 19x1 dollars by a 10 percent increase in every item. This updating records the exact same assets and equities as before, except that they are now expressed in a different monetary unit—the dollar of December

31, 19x1—which has less purchasing power than before. It probably goes without saying that only the final column of figures restated to December 31, 19x1 dollars is comparable to the figures on Table 17–5 for the balance sheet as of December 31, 19x1. In fact, one of the reasons for the roll-forward procedure is that it enables us to prepare comparative balance sheets.

TABLE 17–6

NEVERCHANGE CORP.

Income Statement for 19x1

	Transaction Amount	Conversion Factor	Restated to 12/31/x1 $
Sales................	$800,000	110/105	$838,095
Expenses:			
Cost of goods sold..............	⎧$150,000 ⎨ 390,000 ⎩ 40,000	110/100 ⎫ 110/105 ⎬ 110/110 ⎭	$613,571
Selling and administrative.....	126,000	110/105	132,000
Depreciation........	⎧10,000 ⎨ 8,000	110/80 ⎫ 110/90 ⎬	23,528
Taxes...............	30,000	110/105	31,429
Interest............	4,000	110/105	4,190
Total expense......	$758,000		$804,718
Net operating income..............	$ 42,000		$ 33,377
General price-level loss................	...		(13,405)
Net income...........	$ 42,000		$ 19,972
Retained earnings, 12/31/x0.............	137,000		132,000
	$179,000		$151,972
Less dividends.......	20,000	110/110	20,000
Retained earnings, 12/31/x1.............	$159,000		$131,972

Table 17–6 presents the adjustments for the income statement. The conventional net income calculation of $42,000 does not represent the net gain in purchasing power from operations during the year. This is because the dollars in the individual revenue and expense accounts are not comparable. The sales were transacted when the general price index stood at 105. Some expenses being matched against these revenues were also transacted then. But other expenses, such as cost of goods sold and depreciation, measure the expiration of costs incurred when the price index was 80, 90, and 100. The proper relating of revenue inflows and expense outflows requires a restatement to a common unit of measure.

The restatement of net income reconciles with the restatement of re-

TABLE 17–7

NEVERCHANGE CORP.
Schedule of General Price Level Loss
on Net Monetary Items in 19x1

	Transaction Amount	Conversion Factor	Restated to 12/31/x1 $
Net monetary items, 12/31/x0................	$ 15,000	110/100	$ 16,500
Additions:			
Sales revenue...........	800,000	110/105	838,095
Deductions:			
Selling and administrative........	$126,000	110/105	$132,000
Taxes..................	30,000	110/105	31,429
Interest...............	4,000	110/105	4,190
Purchase of merchandise...........	390,000	110/105	408,571
Purchase of merchandise...........	220,000	110/110	220,000
Dividends..............	20,000	110/110	20,000
Total deductions......	$790,000		$816,190
Restated net monetary items 12/31/x1..........			$ 38,405
Actual net monetary items 12/31/x1..........	$ 25,000		25,000
General price-level loss..................			$ 13,405

tained earnings from the two comparative balance sheets, after the general price-level loss of $13,405 has been considered. The detailed calculation of this loss is presented in Table 17–7. Here, the individual increases and decreases in monetary assets or liabilities are analyzed and expressed in common dollars. The resulting net balance shows the amount of purchasing power that *should be* contained in the net monetary assets on December 31, 19x1. Subtracting the actual net balance, since monetary items are self-adjusting, provides the amount of gain or loss (the latter in our example).

Advantages and Uses of Common-Dollar Accounting

The user of common-dollar accounting statements must be careful not to interpret them as reflecting current values or costs. Common-dollar accounting makes no attempt to measure what it would cost currently to replace the assets or what the business is worth. It seeks only to restore comparability in terms of general purchasing power among the dollars originally recorded in the accounts. It converts original transaction prices to equivalent numbers of dollars of purchasing power as of a particular date. The assets on the position statement show the amount of current purchasing power committed to them. The equities show the amounts of current purchasing power owed to creditors and the amount of general purchasing power represented by the stockholders' investment, which presumably is to be preserved and enhanced. And finally, the income statement represents a measurement in current dollars of the company's gain in general purchasing power during the year.

Perhaps the greatest contribution of procedures that adjust for general price-level changes is the introduction of comparability of measurement. It is inherently logical that any measurement system should have a unit that does not change between measurements. By standardizing the accountant's measuring unit, common-dollar accounting should provide more meaningful summations of data within the generally accepted framework. To the extent that this framework is useful for evaluating management and predicting future income, common-dollar accounting logically should make it better.

Little is known about how the actual decision making of external audiences would be affected by the availability of restated financial reports. Nevertheless, ample evidence exists that the magnitude of the differences between financial statement amounts before and after restatement is significant. Although only relatively modest inflation has occurred each year in the United States, the cumulative effect on such items as depreciation, asset restatements, and long-term monetary items over a period of years can cause major changes in many financial accounting variables. Moreover, the investor cannot hope to judge the magnitude or even direction of the changes. Different firms are affected in different ways, depending upon capital intensity, financing policies, inventory turnover, etc.

For these reasons, many advocates of common-dollar accounting claim that the use of financial statements restated for general price changes are a necessity for sound investor evaluation of managerial policies. Financial policies with respect to a firm's use of borrowed capital and the relationship between its monetary assets and liabilities can be appraised better if data are available which reveal the losses or gains from holding or owing monetary items. Current dividend policy could be evaluated in relation to the increases in purchasing power represented by net income and retained earnings. Distributions of capital being made in the guise of dividends, as in our example (see Table 17–6, where dividends exceeded net income in real terms), would be disclosed.

Interpretations of trends in financial accounting information over time also are facilitated and clarified when that information is in dollars of common general purchasing power. For example, trends depicting growth in sales, net income, plant, retained earnings, net working capital, and the like will already be adjusted for their inevitable upward biases during inflationary periods if they are developed from common-dollar accounting information. Certainly, comparative statements or statistics encompassing periods of substantial general price changes (e.g., 5- or 10-

year summaries included in annual reports) should be restated so as to reveal the real economic changes that occurred.

Ratios calculated from historic accounting data likewise can be distorted by changes in general price levels. Rate of return on investment is one example. Conventional net operating income (the numerator) is usually overstated in terms of general purchasing power, and the average investment (the denominator) is understated when expressed in historic dollars. Working together, they commonly result in an overstated rate of return. The use of restated data to calculate rates of return and other ratios insures against distortions of this kind, because the dollars contained in the numerators and denominators are comparable in terms of general purchasing power.

Objections to and Limitations of Common-Dollar Accounting

Over the many years that price-level restatements have been debated, the primary points of opposition have appeared to center on four items:

1. No legal or tax recognition is accorded to common-dollar accounting.
2. It is not the purpose of financial accounting to deal with other than monetary values.
3. Common-dollar accounting reports would cause confusion among users.
4. Procedures to restate accounting data for price-level changes are too difficult to implement.

Neither the Internal Revenue Service nor the Securities and Exchange Commission, nor most other legal agencies, use accounting data restated for price-level changes. Although this fact may be regrettable, it offers little real opposition to common-dollar accounting. Financial accounting's main job is to report economic data to stockholders and creditors. This reporting, particularly if done through supplementary statements, is not hampered by legal or tax considerations to any great extent. Besides, if recognition of these restatements is desirable in the legal and tax systems, then accountants should be at the forefront in pressing for improvements, not waiting for others to take the lead.

The second objection accepts the goal of financial accounting but argues that common-dollar accounting statements are not necessary to achieve it. Accounting only for dollars of cost and dollars of revenue seems to do an acceptable job in providing information about stockholder *investments.* Common-dollar accounting is premised on the idea that real values rather than money values should be reported to investors. However, real values have significance only to the ultimate users of money for *consumption* purposes. Since the investors in a firm are a heterogeneous group, each will have his own measure of real value (purchasing power). But in the preparation of financial statements for the separate business entity, adjustment of dollar values to real values is unnecessary. What financial accounting should do is report money values and then let each individual stockholder make purchasing power adjustments consistent with his own particular situation.

Third, many have claimed that restated accounting data would cause confusion among the readers of these statements. The conventional reports embodying historic acquisition costs are well understood. Reports adjusted for price-level changes, on the other hand, are complicated and require expert interpretation. People are used to thinking in terms of dollars, not in terms of units of purchasing power. If some firms prepare supplementary data and others do not, comparability of financial statements will suffer, and misunderstanding and misinterpretation will increase. These arguments posit the existence of a rather unsophisticated user of financial information. Certainly, those who understand the limitations of present accounting data would not be confused. And it would appear that, with full disclosure and explanation, stockholders familiar with the fluctuating dollar would be able to understand changes in the "corporate cost of living" as well as they comprehend changes in the consumers' cost of living. Perhaps with this objection in mind, the Accounting Principles Board laid down some careful guidelines concerning the disclosure and explanation that should accompany the presentation of any general price-level information.[20]

Finally, there are those who agree with the theory of price-level restatement but who oppose its implementation because of the difficulties involved in selecting an index and the complexities associated with applying the restatement procedures. Some are concerned that index numbers are not sufficiently accurate. In reply, we merely observe that this search for perfection seems somewhat curious in the light of other accounting estimates and choices. Field tests conducted under the auspices of the Accounting Principles Board cast some doubt on the contention that comprehensive restatement is too complex to be feasible. Certainly, once the basic information has been gathered for the first restatement, the procedures thereafter to roll forward prior years and to restate the current year appear relatively straightforward.

RECORDING CURRENT COSTS

The following discussion concerns the incorporation of changes in specific prices of assets in the statements of income and financial position. This approach divides period income into two categories—current operating income and holding income. The latter category includes changes

---

[20] *Ibid.*, pp. 20–21.

in the prices of specific goods and services between the time they are acquired and the time they are used or sold. The basis for the representation of assets on the position statement becomes the current acquisition cost of asset inputs.

Normally, the entire difference between revenue and the historic acquisition cost of expired assets is recognized as income in the period of sale. And except for specifically designated extraordinary gains and losses, the impression is given that the entire difference reflects operations. In fact, a significant portion of this difference may be attributable to the *holding* of asset inputs during a time of specific price change. Moreover, some of these holding or price gains may occur prior to the period in which the asset is consumed.

To correct these perceived defects in conventional accounting, many theorists have argued for a procedure which would separate holding activities from operating activities. Operating activities comprise the production activities in a broad sense, the conversion of asset inputs to outputs. Income from operating activities is measured by the difference between revenue and current cost. It represents the difference between the value of goods and services provided by the firm, as reflected in the marketplace, and the value of goods and services used by the firm, as determined by the current marketplace. Operating income is recognized as it occurs.

The procedure also recognizes that income can arise from the firm's buying resources when they are low priced and holding them while they increase in value. These holding gains may result from shrewd buying or conscious speculation on the part of the firm or simply from fortuitous circumstances. But in any case, the gain or loss results from decisions concerning the timing of acquisition rather than decisions concerning effective use in operations.

Illustration

To illustrate how an accounting system could measure management's success in both holding and operating activities, the following simple but fairly complete example is given. The following transactions are made by the Willing-to-Change Company during the year.

1. January 1:
    a) The company issues capital stock in exchange for $50,000 cash.
    b) A delivery truck costing $5,000 is purchased for cash. The truck has an expected useful life of five years.
    c) Four units of merchandise, each costing $10,000, are purchased for cash.

2. June 30:
    a) Two units are sold for cash at a price of $15,000 each.
    b) The company pays sales commissions of $3,000 on these sales.
    c) Three more units of merchandise, each costing $9,000, are pur-
        chased on open account.
3. December 31:
    a) Three units, including the two remaining units purchased on
        January 1, are sold for cash. The selling price is $16,000 each.
    b) Sales commissions amounting to $4,000 on these sales are paid in
        cash.
4. Relevant current price information:

	Merchandise (per Unit)	Delivery Truck
January 1	$10,000	$5,000
June 30	9,000	
Average for 1975		5,500
December 31	11,000	6,000

Entries. Each of the transactions during the year is recorded in conventional journal form with two modifications. First, asset expirations
are measured in terms of current costs; second, the differences between
acquisition and current costs at the time of use or at the end of the period
are isolated as holding gains or losses.

```
Jan.  1  Cash................................. 50,000
            Common Stock....................            50,000

         Delivery Truck.....................  5,000
         Merchandise........................ 10,000
            Cash...........................            45,000
June 30  Cash............................... 30,000
            Sales Revenue..................            30,000

         Selling Expense....................  3,000
            Cash...........................             3,000

         Holding Gain—Merchandise..........  2,000
            Merchandise....................             2,000
            To record holding loss on two
            units for difference between
            acquisition cost of $20,000 and
            current cost when sold
            at $18,000.

         Cost of Goods Sold................. 18,000
            Merchandise....................            18,000
            To record expense equal to cur-
            rent cost of asset consumed.

         Merchandise........................ 27,000
            Accounts Payable...............            27,000
Dec. 31  Cash............................... 48,000
            Sales Revenue..................            48,000

         Selling Expense....................  4,000
            Cash...........................             4,000
```

```
Merchandise.......................   8,000
    Holding Gain—Merchandise......              8,000
    To record holding gain on units
    sold ($33,000-$29,000) and those
    still on hand at end of year
    ($22,000-$18,000).

Cost of Goods Sold................  33,000
    Merchandise...................             33,000
    To record expense equal to cur-
    rent cost of three units sold.

Delivery Truck....................   1,000
    Accumulated Depreciation.......                100
    Holding Gain—Truck............                  900
    To record holding gain on truck
    as follows: portion used during
    year ($5,500 — $5,000) × 1/5;
    portion held all year
    ($6,000 — $5,000) × 4/5.

Depreciation Expense..............   1,100
    Accumulated Depreciation.......              1,100
    To record depreciation based on
    current cost at the time the
    truck was used, which is
    measured by the average value
    during the year.
```

Income Statement. Notice that the income statement (Table 17–8) reports the operating and the holding results separately.

TABLE 17–8

```
             WILLING—TO—CHANGE COMPANY
           Statement of Income for the Year 19_
Current operating income:
  Sales revenue................          $78,000
  Expenses:
    Cost of goods sold.........  $51,000
    Selling expense...........     7,000
    Depreciation expense.......     1,100   59,100      $18,900
Holding gains:
  Merchandise................            $ 6,000
  Delivery truck.............                900        6,900
Net Income....................                        $25,800
```

Balance Sheet. The balance sheet (Table 17–9) reports assets at their current input values as of the end of the year.[21]

Measurement of Current Costs

In the foregoing example, current cost is determined for each specific asset at the time it is used. It would probably be more practical to deter-

---

[21] In this example, the entire amount of holding gain has been included as part of Retained Earnings. One logically could argue that, since these are *real* value changes, this income will eventually be subject to taxation. If the holding gains are to be recognized on the books before they are recognized for tax purposes, a provision for Deferred Income Taxes should be established (see Chapter Twelve).

TABLE 17-9

WILLING-TO-CHANGE COMPANY

Balance Sheet as of December 31, 19_

Assets

Current Assets:
Cash......................................	$76,000	
Merchandise.............................	22,000	$ 98,000

Noncurrent Assets:
Delivery truck...........................	$ 6,000	
Less: Accumulated depreciation.........	1,200	4,800
Total Assets......................		$102,800

Equities

Current Liabilities:
Accounts payable........................		$ 27,000

Stockholders' Equity:
Common stock............................	$50,000	
Retained earnings.......................	25,800	75,800
Total Equities....................		$102,800

mine the current cost as of the end of the period and apply it to all transactions during the period. This procedure would tend to overstate holding gains and understate operating income in a period of increasing prices. However, unless material increases in specific asset values occur during the period or unless prices fluctuate drastically within the period, the overstatement probably would be slight.

A more difficult measurement problem than *when* to measure current cost is *how* to measure it. Current input costs should be the cost of the same or equivalent asset services. These specific prices can be noted from three sources: (1) an established market price for the particular good or service, (2) purchase prices of assets providing equivalent service potentials, and (3) an adjustment of acquisition cost by means of a price index restricted to assets of like kind. Each of these is not without its shortcomings.

Realization of Holding Gains

In our example, holding gains on the merchandise and the delivery truck are included in the determination of total net income. This treatment derives from the idea that value increases from holding activities are a part of income and should therefore be reported in the period in which the holding activity occurs. Many advocates of current cost reporting, however, would sharply disagree. To them, holding gains should not enter income until the inputs to which the gains attach are sold—i.e., when they enter operating activity. This is when the business puts the end result of the input—a product or service—to its ultimate test in the marketplace. It is viewed as the relevant point of income recognition for all activities, operating and holding. Under this view only the holding gains on the merchandise *sold* during the year ($2,000) and the delivery truck *used* during the year ($100) would be included in income. To this author, though, the first view is more consistent with the objectives behind current cost recording. Holding gains and losses occur due to holding activity. If they are objectively measurable during the holding period, they should enter income then.

Advantages and Disadvantages of Current Cost Recording

The total dollar income of a business is not modified under current cost recording. Its difference from income under historical dollar cost accounting lies in its timing and sources. Through the valuation of assets at current input cost, significant changes in asset values are not deferred until sale or consumption takes place. These value increases and decreases are reported in the period in which they occur. As a result the balance sheet reports costs at current input values, the income statement reports expenses at the current values of the resources consumed, and holding gains are reported separately from operating income.

This separation of operating income from holding income constitutes one of the major advantages claimed for current cost accounting. It is argued that because different kinds of decisions give rise to these two types of income, the decision-making framework can be improved if we distinguish between success or failure in production on the one hand and gains or losses from speculation or holding resources on the other. Ostensibly, one of the purposes of financial information is to predict future earnings. The operating income figure based on current costs provides a better measure of future earning power for two reasons: (1) it excludes gains and losses that might not occur again, and (2) the margin between revenues and expenses reflects current, and hopefully future, operating conditions.

However, current operating income, by itself, is not satisfactory for another purported use of accounting information, the complete evaluation of managerial performance. Here is where the holding income becomes important, because it gives credit for the favorable acquisition of resources when prices are low. The procedures outlined above provide separately disclosed information useful for evaluating both operating and holding aspects of management's activity.

The arguments opposing the recognition of current costs appear to fall into two groups. One group asserts that current cost recording violates the fundamentals of the historical cost concept, the realization principle, and the stewardship of financial resources. This class of objection states the obvious. It is clear that current cost recording *is* premised on different concepts of cost, value recognition, and stewardship. The major point should be to determine which theoretical structure provides more useful information to the external audience of financial accounting.

The second type of objection, having more substance, concerns measurability. Some accountants feel that there is insufficient objective, verifiable information concerning current values of assets, particularly special-purpose assets such as technical machinery, complex assets such as buildings and manufactured inventory, and unreproducible assets such as land. In the minds of some, these measurement problems are too staggering to overcome, and piecemeal application—i.e., revaluation of some assets but not others—would be inconsistent and confusing.

Specific and General Price Levels Combined

In our example we concentrate solely on specific price changes, assuming that the general price index remains constant during the period. What happens if we relax this assumption and attempt to incorporate both specific and general price-level changes? How can current cost recording and common-dollar accounting be combined?

The answer is not as complicated as one might expect. The major differences are in the stockholders' equity section of the position statement and in the income statement. Assets stated at current cost at the end of the year are already stated in dollars of year-end purchasing power. Holding gains and losses would have to be recalculated in terms of year-end dollars. Depending on the degree of general price-level increase, the amount of *real* holding gain generally would be reduced. Of course, gain or loss in purchasing power on the holding of monetary items would appear in the income statement, and items of revenue and expense would be restated in terms of year-end dollars. The reader may wish to experiment with the example of the Willing-to-Change Company by assuming a general price-level change during the period and preparing financial statements encompassing both general and specific price changes.

SUMMARY

The discussion in this chapter ranges over a number of topics. The economic model of direct valuation through the discounting of expected future net receipts is explored. It is rejected as a general framework because of a lack of reliable measurements and because of the incorporation of expectations and changes in expectations into the income calculation. Indirect valuation based on current output values is rejected for much the same reasons.

However, from the study of the theoretical model come two ideas that could be incorporated into the theories and procedures of financial accounting—(1) the measurement of dollar values in *real* terms, in terms of the command over goods and services, and (2) the recognition of changes in the current input values of the firm's resources. Attempts to deal with these ideas are discussed under the headings of common-dollar accounting and current cost reporting, respectively. The first reexamines the validity of the monetary postulate; the second modifies the matching and recognition (realization) concepts. Stated in another way, common-dollar accounting modifies the dollar amounts of income reported but not their timing. Current cost reporting, on the other hand, changes the timing of recognition but not the total amounts.

None of the approaches discussed in this chapter are recognized under generally accepted accounting principles. Even common-dollar accounting is only mildly recommended, not required; and if used, it must be a supplement to, not a substitute for, historical cost. Yet, the suggestions for modification in the theoretical structure of financial accounting are not new. Why little recognition of these alternative theories in GAAP and little experimentation with them in accounting practice can be found must be explained in terms of more fundamental considerations.

Financial accounting lacks any clear-cut objectives or criteria for a theory of income. For example, how much do we really know about the informational needs of the audiences of financial accounting reports? Have we adequately identified the primary audience and its purposes, analytical abilities, preferences, etc.? The fundamental judgment that must be made concerns which theory provides the most meaningful information to the user. Related to this point is a second consideration—measurability. What criteria should be used in evaluating measurements under each of these theories? If the measurements are to be "reliable" and "objective," precisely what do these concepts imply? Since each is a relative concept, what minimum standards must be met? To what extent are accountants, or more accurately the ultimate users of financial statements, willing to sacrifice reliability and objectivity to achieve greater usefulness?

Until questions like these can be answered, the controversies probably will continue. Nonetheless, the time is ripe for experimentation with alternative concepts to begin to find the answers. Supplementary statements, recommended by so many and employed by so few, are a very satisfactory vehicle. Accounting systems are becoming sufficiently sophisticated and data processing equipment sufficiently powerful to enable firms to minimize the recording and processing efforts. The methodologies have been perfected at least to a satisfactory level. What remains now is the need for a commitment by the accounting profession to broaden its horizons and explore alternative possibilities. Until such a commitment is made, readers of financial statements may experience a gnawing feeling that what they need is not being reported to them, and what is being reported to them they do not need.

SUGGESTIONS FOR FURTHER READING

Any of the authoritative pronouncements or historical works mentioned on pages 604–7.

Gynther, Reg S. "Capital Maintenance, Price Changes, and Profit Determination," *Accounting Review*, Vol. 45 (October 1970), pp. 712–30.

Hannum, William H., and Wasserman, W. "General Adjustments and Price Level Measurement," *Accounting Review*, Vol. 43 (April 1968), pp. 295–302.

Hendriksen, Eldon S. "Purchasing Power and Replacement Cost Concepts—Are They Related?" *Accounting Review*, Vol. 38 (July 1963), pp. 483–91.

Kohler, Eric L. "Why Not Retain Historical Cost?" *Journal of Accountancy*, Vol. 116 (October 1963), pp. 35–41.

Mathews, R. L. "Income, Price Changes and the Valuation Controversy in Accounting," *Accounting Review*, Vol. 43 (July 1968), pp. 509–16.

Rosenfield, Paul. "Accounting for Inflation," *Journal of Accountancy*, Vol. 127 (June 1969), pp. 45–50.

Spencer, Charles H., and Barnhisel, Thomas S. "A Decade of Price-Level Changes—The Effect on the Financial Statements of Cummins Engine Company," *Accounting Review*, Vol. 40 (January 1965), pp. 144–53.

Tierney, Cecilia. "Price-Level Adjustments—Problem in Perspective," *Journal of Accountancy*, Vol. 116 (November 1963), pp. 56–60.

Tracy, John A. "A Dissent to the General Price-Level Adjustment Proposal," *Accounting Review*, Vol. 40 (January 1965), pp. 163–75.

Zeff, Stephen A. "Replacement Cost: Member of the Family, Welcome Guest, or Intruder?" *Accounting Review*, Vol. 37 (October 1962), pp. 611–25.

QUESTIONS AND PROBLEMS

17–1. A common objective of accountants is to prepare meaningful financial statements. To attain this objective many accountants maintain that the financial statements must be adjusted for changes in price level. Other accountants believe that financial statements should continue to be prepared on the basis of unadjusted historical cost.*

    a) List arguments for adjusting financial statements for changes in price level.

    b) List the arguments for preparing financial statements on only the basis of unadjusted historical cost.

    c) In their discussions about accounting for changes in price levels and the methods of measuring them, uninformed individuals have

---

* Adapted from the AICPA November 1964 examination.

frequently failed to distinguish between adjustments for changes in the price levels of specific goods and services and adjustments for changes in the general purchasing power of the dollar. What is the distinction? Which are "price-level adjustments"? Discuss.

17-2.   Indiana Telephone Corporation since 1954 has presented two sets of financial statements. One set shows the results under conventional historical cost accounting; the other presents figures adjusted for changes in the purchasing power of the dollar. Excerpts from the 1968 annual report are given below.

Income Statement
(in thousands of dollars)

	Column A Historical Cost		Column B Restated for Changes in Purchasing Power	
	1968	1967	1968	1967
Operating revenues........	$8,172	$6,777	$8,172	$6,777
Operating expenses:				
Depreciation provision:				
To recover historic cost..............	$1,319	$1,148	$1,319	$1,148
To recover cost of inflation............	...	...	227	199
Total..............	$1,319	$1,148	$1,546	$1,347
Other operating expenses...............	5,300	4,438	5,300	4,438
Total operating expenses...............	$6,619	$5,586	$6,846	$5,785
Operating income.........	$1,553	$1,191	$1,326	$ 992
Income deduction.........	515	459	515	459
Net income...............	$1,038	$ 732	$ 811	$ 533
Preferred dividends.......	99	68	99	68
Earnings applicable to common stock..............	$ 939	$ 664	$ 712	$ 465
Earnings per common share..................	$ 3.97	$ 2.89	$ 3.00	$ 2.02
Book value per share......	$27.63	$25.10	$40.15	$35.67

Statement of Telephone Plant Assets*
December 31, 1968
(in thousands)

	Column A Historical Cost	Column B Restated
In service....................	$26,343	$31,144
Less: Accumulated depreciation....................	7,295	9,131
	$19,048	$22,013
Plant under construction......	743	743
	$19,791	$22,756

*All other assets were the same in columns A and B.

Statement of Common Shareholders' Interest**
December 31, 1968
(in thousands)

	Column A Historical Cost	Column B Restated
Common stock, net of treasury shares and discount.........	$2,289	$2,289
Capital set aside from retained earnings..................	1,490	1,490
Retained earnings............	2,766	547

Capital maintained through
  recognition of price-level
  depreciation...............
	...	2,219

Effect of price-level changes
  on unrecovered plant in-
  vestment..................
	...	2,965

Total.......................	$6,545	$9,510

** All other equities were the same in columns A and B.

Note 1 to Financial Statements: In the accompanying financial statements, costs measured by the dollars disbursed at the time of the expenditure are shown in column A—Historical Cost. In column B —Historical Cost Restated for Change in Purchasing Power of Dollar —these dollars of cost have been restated in terms of the price level at December 31, 1967 and 1968, as measured by the Gross National Product Implicit Price Deflator, to recognize the inflation experienced to the date of these statements. The effect of inflation on these dollars of cost has been redetermined each year since 1954 in order to recognize the constantly changing price levels.

Since 1954, the Corporation has presented such supplemental financial statements recognizing the effect of the change in the purchasing power of the dollar on the cost of telephone plant and on depreciation expense in the annual report to shareholders in the same basic manner. This accounting has the approval of Arthur Andersen & Co., the Corporation's independent public accountants, as set forth in their report included herewith.

Dollars are a means of expressing purchasing power at the time of their use. *Conversion or restatement of dollars of differing purchasing power to the purchasing power of the dollar at the date of conversion results in all the dollars being treated as mathematical likes for the purpose of significant data.* The resulting financial statements recognize the change in price levels between the periods of expenditure of funds and the periods of use of property. *Accordingly, the earnings, results of operations, assets and other data available for use by management and other readers of financial statements provide important information and comparisons not otherwise available.*

No one would attempt to add, subtract, multiply, or divide marks, dollars, and pounds. The failure to change the title of the monetary unit may be partially responsible for this violation of mathematical principle. This is important, for it conceals the fact that mathematical unlikes are being used and therefore unfortunate results are produced by generally accepted accounting methods. *This should help explain why we are talking about income and expenses in terms of current dollars.*

Portion of Note 2 to the financial statements: Since the present Internal Revenue Code does not recognize the increase in depreciation cost measured in current dollars, it is not deductible for computing Federal income tax payments, *and the Corporation in fact pays taxes on alleged earnings which economically do not exist.* Therefore, Federal income taxes for 1968 and 1967 are stated in column B in the same amounts as in column A. If the depreciation provisions to recover the cost of inflation were deductible, as they should be, reductions in Federal income taxes of $120,089 in 1968 and of 95,688 in 1967 would result.

Portion of auditor's opinion: In our opinion, however, the accompanying financial statements shown under column B more fairly present the financial position of the Corporation and the results of its operations since appropriate recognition has been given to variations in the purchasing power of the dollar, as explained in Notes 1 and 2 to the financial statements.

a) What income concept is the company attempting to implement? Comment on its methodology. What deficiencies do you see in the reporting procedures?

b) Explain the meaning and derivation of the two additional accounts in column B of the Statement of Common Shareholders' Interest.

c) Why is book value per share higher, but earnings per share lower, in the adjusted figures?

d) Compare the rate of return on common shareholders' equity on an unadjusted and on an adjusted basis.

e) Explain the meaning of the emphasized words in the portion of Note 2.

f) Do you agree with the auditors that the figures in column B "more fairly present" the company's financial situation? Explain.

17–3. A company owns a warehouse and rents space in it to various customers. Gross rentals are expected to be $30,000 per year for the next 10 years. Cash operating expenses will be $8,000 each year. Assume that 10 percent is the proper discount factor and that all cash flows occur at the end of the year.

a) Determine the value of the warehouse now and a year from now, using direct valuation. How much income was applicable to year 1?

b) At the end of year 2, you anticipate that cash operating expenses will be $9,000 each year in the future. What is the value of the warehouse at the end of year 2 and the income attributable to year 2? What factors influenced the income in year 2?

c) The warehouse originally cost $100,000; its current market value is $130,000. What asset value is most relevant and useful to an investor in the company?

17–4. Nonuttin Button Company reports a net income of $135,000 in 19x9. Dividends declared and paid amounted to $120,000. Depreciation expense of $117,000 is included among the deductions from revenue. The depreciation was calculated from the following schedule.

Cost of Noncurrent Asset	Year of Acquisition	Useful Life	Depreciation Charge $(S - L)$
$450,000...............	19 × 0	10	$ 45,000
160,000...............	19 × 3	8	20,000
170,000...............	19 × 7	10	17,000
175,000...............	19 × 8	5	35,000
			$117,000

An index of the general price level is 180 in 19x9. It was 175 in 19x8, 170 in 19x7, 150 in 19x3, and 120 in 19x0.

a) Restate the depreciation expense in terms of dollars of 19x9 purchasing power. Determine the restated net income figure.

b) Comment on the company's dividend policy in light of the restated net income from part (*a*).

c) Assume that in addition to the net book value of the noncurrent assets, there are $100,000 of current assets. Calculate and compare the rate of return on total assets in unadjusted dollars and in restated dollars of 19x9 purchasing power.

17–5. In this chapter, entries and statements for the Willing-to-Change Company (pp. 617–620) are presented under a system of current cost recording. However, that illustration assumed that the general price index remains constant during the year.

Assume instead that the general price level index stood at 100 on January 1, 110 on June 30, and 120 on December 31. Prepare a statement of income and a balance sheet incorporating both specific and general price-level changes. Express all amounts in terms of December 31 dollars.

17–6. The Melgar Company purchased a tract of land as an investment in 1963 for $100,000; late in that year the company decided to construct a shopping center on the site.* Construction began in 1964 and was completed in 1966; one third of the construction was completed each year. Melgar originally estimated the costs of the project would be $1,200,000 for materials, $750,000 for labor, $150,000 for variable overhead, and $600,000 for depreciation. Actual costs (excluding depreciation) incurred for construction were:

	1964	1965	1966
Materials................	$418,950	$434,560	$462,000
Labor...................	236,250	274,400	282,000
Variable overhead.........	47,250	54,208	61,200

---

* Problem adapted from the AICPA November 1967 examination.

Shortly after construction began, Melgar sold the shopping center for $3 million with payment to be made in full on completion in December 1966. $150,000 of the sales price was allocated for the land.

The transaction was completed as scheduled and now a controversy has developed between the two major stockholders of the company. One feels that the company should have invested in land, because a high rate of return was earned on the land. The other feels that the original decision was sound and that changes in the price level which were not anticipated affected the original cost estimates.

You were engaged to furnish guidance to these stockholders in resolving their controversy. As an aid, you obtained the following information: (1) using 1963 as the base year, price-level indices for relevant years are: 1960 = 90, 1961 = 93, 1962 = 96, 1963 = 100, 1964 = 105, 1965 = 112, and 1966 = 120; (2) the company allocated $200,000 per year for depreciation of fixed assets allocated to this construction project. Of that amount $25,000 was for a building purchased in 1960 and $175,000 was for equipment purchased in 1962.

a) Prepare a schedule to restate in base-year (1963) costs the actual costs, including depreciation, incurred each year. Disregard income taxes and assume that each price-level index was valid for the entire year.

b) Prepare a schedule comparing the originally estimated costs of the project with the total actual costs for each element of cost (materials, labor, variable overhead, and depreciation) adjusted to the 1963 price level. Is the contention correct that changes in the price level were responsible for the unfavorable costs compared to the original estimate?

c) Prepare a schedule to restate the amount received on the sale in terms of base year (1963) purchasing power. The gain or loss should be determined separately for the land and the building in terms of base-year purchasing power and should exclude depreciation.

17–7.   A comparative balance sheet as of December 31, 1971 and 1972 and an income statement for 1972 for Boondoggle, Inc. are presented below:

BOONDOGGLE, INC.

Balance Sheet as of December 31

Assets	1972	1971
Cash.............................	$ 150,000	$ 155,000
Accounts receivable..............	294,000	227,500
Inventory, at Lifo cost..........	178,000	160,000
Land.............................	90,000	90,000
Buildings........................	300,000	300,000
Less: Accumulated deprecia- tion.........................	(75,000)	(60,000)
Equipment........................	450,000	450,000
Less: Accumulated deprecia- tion.........................	(200,000)	(150,000)
Total Assets.................	$1,187,000	$1,172,500

Equities

```
Current liabilities..............  $  174,000   $  195,000
Capital stock...................      600,000      600,000
Retained earnings...............      413,000      377,500
      Total Equities............  $1,187,000   $1,172,500
```

Income Statement for the year 1972

```
Sales (76,000 @ $7)..............                 $  532,000
Cost of goods sold:
  Beginning inventory (40,000 @
    $4)...........................  $  160,000
  Purchases (80,000 @ $4.50).....      360,000
                                    $  520,000
  Ending inventory (40,000 @ $4;
    4,000 @ $4.50)...............     (178,000)      342,000
Gross margin.....................                 $  190,000
  Depreciation on building.......  $   15,000
  Depreciation on equipment......       50,000
  Other expenses.................       89,500      154,500
Net income.......................                 $   35,500
```

Other information:

1. The replacement cost of the inventory was $4.20 on December 31, 1971 and $4.80 on December 31, 1972. Of the unit sales, 70,000 occurred when the replacement cost was $4.50 and the rest when it was $4.80.

2. The land had an appraised value of $100,000 and $105,000 on December 31, 1971 and December 31, 1972, respectively.

3. An index of nonresidential construction costs was 120 when the building was acquired. It stood at 150 on December 31 of both 1971 and 1972.

4. The replacement cost of similar new equipment on December 31, 1971 was $480,000 and was $500,000 during and at the end of 1972.

Prepare a comparative balance sheet and an income statement for Boondoggle, Inc., using a current cost system of reporting. On the income statement, separate operating activities from holding activities. Prepare a separate schedule showing the calculation of holding gains and losses.

17-8. A speculator purchased land for $100,000 on January 1, 19x1, when an index of the general price level was 80. At the end of 19x1, the cost of similar land was $150,000, and the general price index stood at 100. During 19x2, he sells the land. At that time the general price index is 110.

a) If the speculator pays taxes at a rate of 30 percent of conventional accounting income, how much would he have to sell the land for in order to recover his original purchasing power after taxes?

b) If he sells the land for $140,000, has he made a profit in 19x2? Discuss carefully. How would his activities be reported under a current cost recording system?

17–9. An investor purchases an asset for $60,820, the value of the net cash receipts expected to be derived from it, discounted at 6 percent. The schedule of anticipated net receipts is $10,000 at the end of year 1, $20,000 at the end of year 2, and $40,000 at the end of year 3.

    a) Verify the initial asset value. What will be the value of the asset at the end of year 1 and at the end of year 2, assuming no change in expectations? How much income will be recognized each year under direction valuation? (Note: the amount should be equal to the cash received plus the change in the value of the asset.)

    b) During year 1, actual net cash receipts are $12,000, but future expectations are not changed. How much income will be recognized under direct valuation in year 1? Identify two separate causes of it.

    c) During year 1, actual net cash receipts are $12,000, and expectations are that future net cash receipts in years 2 and 3 will also be twenty percent higher. How much income will be recognized under direct valuation in year 1? Identify three separate causes of it.

    d) Under direct valuation, the value of the asset is influenced by the subjective expectations. The suggestion is made that a more objective substitute would be to measure income by the amount of cash received plus the change in market value of the asset, the latter presumably measuring objectively the present value of expected future net cash receipts. What weaknesses or limitations do you see in this approach?

17–10. The president of Exaggeration, Inc. presented the following comparative statistics at the annual stockholders' meeting in 19x9.

	19x0	19x9
Sales......................	$100,000	$200,000
Net working capital:		
Cash.....................	$ 20,000	$ 63,000
Receivables...............	40,000	70,000
Inventories...............	80,000	104,000
Prepayments..............	5,000	6,000
Current payables...........	(30,000)	(42,000)
	$115,000	$201,000

A portion of the president's remarks were: "Your management is to be congratulated on the growth your company has made over the past 10 years since it was founded in 19x0. Not only has our sales volume doubled, but our net working capital has also increased from $115,000 to $201,000—an increase of 75 percent."

    a) As an enlightened stockholder, prepare information similar to that presented by the president but restated into common dollars as of 19x9. Assume the pertinent general price-level index stood at 90 in 19x0 and 120 in 19x9. Further, assume that the company uses Lifo inventory valuation during this period. Of the $24,000 increase in inventory, $20,000 was acquired when the price index was 100 and the other $4,000 was added in 19x9. Half of the prepayments existing in 19x9 were acquired when the index was 110.

b) Carefully interpret your results. Exactly what do they mean?

17–11. Ayrshire Collieries Corporation since 1948 has made a provision for price-level depreciation. The company uses the relationship between the Consumer Price Index at the end of the year and the average Consumer Price Index in the year the asset was acquired to adjust the historical cost depreciation figures.

The income statement for the year ended June 30, 1967 is given below in summarized form (amounts in thousands):

Revenues..	$63,838
Expenses (including depreciation and depletion on a historical cost basis of $3,545,058)..........	59,816
Net income (conventional net income)..............	$ 4,022
Provision for price-level depreciation (Note 1)...	353
Net Income after Deducting Provision for Price-Level Depreciation.............................	$ 3,669

On the balance sheet, among the shareholder's equity items, was a special item labeled:

	June 30	
	1967	1966
Capital maintained by recognition of price-level depreciation (Note 1)...............	4,243	3,890

This item is viewed as a permanent part of stockholders' equity, and it is not affected by plant retirements.

Note (1): The provision for price-level depreciation represents the excess of depreciation expense measured by the current purchasing power of the dollar over depreciation expense measured by the purchasing power of the dollar at the dates of acquisition or construction of the Companies' depreciable property, as measured by general price-level indices. The Companies believe the provision for price-level depreciation should be deducted before arriving at the net income, but are informed that such treatment would not be in conformity with "generally accepted accounting principles." Reference is made to the opinion of Arthur Andersen & Co.

Portion of auditor's opinion: Generally accepted principles of accounting for cost of property consumed in operations are based on historical costs and do not recognize the effect of changes in the purchasing power of the dollar since dates of acquisition or construction of the Companies' depreciable property. In our opinion, therefore, the consolidated net income for the year is more fairly presented after deducting the provision for price-level depreciation because such provision does recognize the effect of changes in the purchasing power of the dollar.

a) Why is the treatment preferred by the company not in conformity with generally accepted accounting principles?

b) Explain carefully the effect on assets, stockholders' equity, and income of the entry the company made in connection with the price-level depreciation. In what sense does the entry "maintain capital"? Do you agree with the company's concept of the Capital Maintained account?

c) Do you agree with the auditors that "net income for the year is more fairly presented after deducting the provision for price-level depreciation"?

d) In what ways is the company's presentation misleading or incomplete?

17–12. Lee V. Plant purchased a tract of land with standing timber on it at a cost of $800,000. The residual value of the land is negligible. The timber was estimated to contain one million board feet. The following statistics relate to operations during his first three years:

Board Feet

Year	Beginning of Year	Yearly Growth	Amount Cut
1...	1,000,000	40,000	100,000
2...	940,000	30,000	120,000
3...	850,000	25,000	150,000

Financial Data

Sales of Cut Timber	Cash Operating Expenses	Value per Board Feet of Standing Timber
$150,000...	$40,000	$0.80
$192,000...	$50,000	0.90
$255,000...	$60,000	1.00

Lee has suggested measuring income in two segments:

Income from Cutting: Sales of Cut Timber − (Cash Operating Expenses + Current Value of the Standing Timber Cut)

Income from Growth and Appreciation: Current Value of Standing Timber at End of Year + Current Value of Standing Timber Cut − Current Value of Standing Timber at the Beginning of the Year

a) Prepare an income statement for each of the three years under his proposed system.

   b) Comment on the usefulness of this system of income measurement. What are its strengths and weaknesses?

   c) Does this system employ input or output values? Explain.

17–13.   Balance sheet and income data for Flexibility, Incorporated appear below:

Balance Sheet

	Jan. 1	Dec. 31
Cash and receivables................	$ 20,000	$ 40,000
Inventory...........................	30,000	40,000
Land................................	10,000	10,000
Buildings and equipment.............	80,000	80,000
Accumulated depreciation............	(24,000)	(30,000)
	$116,000	$140,000
Accounts payable....................	$ 10,000	$ 18,000
Bonds payable.......................	15,000	15,000
Capital stock.......................	50,000	60,000
Retained earnings...................	41,000	47,000
	$116,000	$140,000

	Income Statement for Year	
Sales.....................................		$90,000
Expenses:		
Cost of goods sold....................	$60,000	
Salaries and wages....................	10,000	
Depreciation..........................	6,000	
Miscellaneous.........................	2,000	
Interest..............................	600	
Taxes.................................	5,400	84,000
Net Income...............................		$ 6,000

Relevant Price Information

	General Price Index
January 1..	100
December 31......................................	120
Average for year.................................	110
Acquisition of noncurrent assets.................	60
Bonds issued	60
Capital stock issued	60 & 100
Acquisition of January 1 inventory...............	90
Acquisition of December 31 inventory.............	115

Assume that all revenues and expenses occurred evenly throughout the year and that the cost of goods sold is accounted for by exhaustion of the initial inventory plus purchases when the price index averaged 110.

   a) Prepare a *comparative* balance sheet in which all amounts are stated in dollars of uniform purchasing power as of the end of the year.

b) Prepare an income statement in which all amounts are stated in dollars of uniform purchasing power as of the end of the year. Include a showing of purchasing power gain or loss on holding of net monetary items. Be sure the income statement reconciles with the comparative balance sheet prepared in part (*a*).

c) Prepare a schedule showing the calculation of purchasing power gain or loss on holding net monetary items.

17–14. A. M. Ritual has always said "It is better to have people owe you money than for you to owe other people money." As a result of this belief, he has always minimized the amount of borrowing he does and has sold on very liberal credit terms. Recently, however, he has read that creditors lose and debtors gain during inflation. Knowing that for the last two years there has been inflation and not wishing to lose, he has come to you for advice. He presents the following schedule of his monetary assets and liabilities (in thousands):

	Jan. 1 19x1	Dec. 31 19x1	Dec. 31 19x2
Cash............................	$ 40	$ 50	$ 50
Accounts receivable..............	120	150	200
Monetary assets...............	$160	$200	$250
Accounts payable.................	$ 50	$ 60	$ 80
Wages payable...................	20	20	30
Mortgage on building.............	100	80	60
Monetary liabilities.............	$170	$160	$170

You determine that an index of the general price level stood at 80 on January 1, 19x1; 100 on December 31, 19x1; and 120 on December 31, 19x2.

a) Explain to Ritual how creditors lose and debtors gain during inflation.

b) Calculate the net gain or loss in purchasing power experienced by Ritual over the two years. Assume that changes in the price level occur evenly throughout the year and that changes in any of the account balances also occur evenly throughout the year.

17–15. The Cwagmire Realty Company speculates on land prices. It buys parcels of undeveloped land and holds them for a number of years. Then, when the "time is ripe," it develops them by putting in streets and clearing some trees, and sells them to subdivision builders.

In 19x1 the company buys a piece of land for $100,000. In 19x9, it spends $30,000 on developing the land and sells it for $198,000. Cwagmire calculates its profit on this deal as follows:

Revenue...............................		$198,000
Expenses:		
Cost of land........................	$100,000	
Development costs...................	30,000	130,000
Profit from land development..........		$ 68,000

Additional data: the general price-level index in 19x1 was 120, in 19x9 150; the value of the undeveloped land in 19x9 was $150,000.

a) Prepare a revised income statement, taking into account changes in the general price level. Convert to a common dollar of 19x9 purchasing power.

b) Of the profit you calculate in part (a), how much is attributable to actual development work? What does the remainder represent?

17–16. The income statement for Termite Furniture Company in 19x7, prepared in accordance with the monetary concept, was as follows:

Sales....................................		$100,000
Expenses:		
Cost of goods sold...................	$60,000	
Wages................................	10,000	
Depreciation.........................	20,000	
Insurance............................	2,000	92,000
Net Income...........................		$ 8,000

Investigation reveals that sales and wages were transacted, on the average, in the middle of 19x7. Depreciation consists of $15,000 on a building bought in mid-19x4 and $5,000 on delivery equipment acquired in mid-19x5. The insurance policy was purchased in mid-19x6. Cost of goods sold consists of $20,000 purchased in mid-19x6, $20,000 purchased at the beginning of 19x7, and $20,000 purchased in the middle of 19x7. An index of general prices behaved as follows during the recent past:

Year	Index
Mid-19x4...............	90
Mid-19x5...............	100
Mid-19x6...............	120
19x7:	
Beginning.............	132
Middle...............	126
End.................	120

a) Prepare a revised income statement for 19x7 using common dollar accounting. Restate amounts in terms of the dollar as of the end of 19x7.

b) Explain carefully how the meaning of net income as calculated under common dollar accounting differs from net income as determined by conventional procedures.

17–17. The balance sheet of Clandestine Sales Company as of December 31, 1972, and operating information for the year 1973 are presented below.

CLANDESTINE SALES COMPANY

Balance Sheet, December 31, 1972

Assets

Cash...	$ 33,000
Inventory (2,100 units @ 19.00).................	39,900
Land..	41,000
Buildings...	175,000
Less: Accumulated depreciation...............	(50,000)
Equipment..	50,000
Less: Accumulated Depreciation...............	(20,000)
Total Assets..............................	$268,900

Equities

Accounts payable.................................	$ 25,000
Accrued liabilities...............................	5,000
Capital stock.....................................	150,000
Retained earnings................................	88,900
Total Equities............................	$268,900

Transactions during 1973:

		Jan.–Jun.	Jul.–Dec.
(1)	Cash sales.......................	1,100 @ $50 = $55,000	1,300 @ $60 = $78,000
(2)	Inventory purchases on account......	1,500 @ $26 = $39,000	1,700 @ $30 = $51,000
(3)	Other accrued expenses............	10,750	9,400
(4)	Cash payments on:		
	Accounts payable...............	35,000	40,000
	Accrued liabilities..............	10,000	11,000
(5)	Straight-line depreciation:		
	Buildings (25-year life)...........	3,500	3,500
	Equipment (10-year life).........	2,500	2,500

Replacement cost data:

(1)	Replacement cost of inventory:		
		January 1, 1973..............................	$ 25
		June 30, 1973.................................	30*
		December 31, 1973...........................	40*
(2)	Appraisal value of land:		
		January 1, 1973..............................	45,000
		December 31, 1973...........................	48,000
(3)	Building construction cost index:		
		Acquisition date of building....................	80
		January 1, 1973..............................	100
		June 30, 1973.................................	120†
		December 31, 1973............................	120
(4)	Replacement cost of equipment (new):		
		January 1, 1973..............................	60,000
		June 30, 1973.................................	65,000‡
		December 31, 1973...........................	70,000‡

* Assume these are applicable during the preceding six-month period also.
† The change occurred uniformly during the first six months.
‡ The change in cost occurred uniformly during each six-month period.

a) Prepare a journal entry that will restate the December 31, 1972 asset balances in terms of replacement cost as of that date.

b) Prepare journal entries to record the transactions during 1972 in a manner such that holding gains and losses are properly isolated and expenses are measured in terms of current cost.

c) Prepare a *comparative* balance sheet as of December 31, 1972 and 1973, and an income statement for 1973 under current cost recording procedures.

17-18.   To obtain a more realistic appraisal of his investment, Martin Arnett, your client, has asked you to adjust certain financial data of the Glo-Bright Company for price-level changes.* On January 1, 1964 he invested $50,000 in the Glo-Bright Company in return for 10,000 shares of common stock. Immediately after his investment the trial balance appeared as follows:

	Debit	Credit
Cash and receivables....................	$ 65,200	
Merchandise inventory..................	4,000	
Building..............................	50,000	
Accumulated depreciation, building........		$ 8,000
Equipment............................	36,000	
Accumulated depreciation, equipment......		7,200
Land.................................	10,000	
Current liabilities......................		50,000
Capital stock, $5 par...................		100,000
	$165,200	$165,200

Balances in certain accounts as of December 31 of each of the next three years were as follows:

	1964	1965	1966
Sales..................	$39,650	$39,000	$42,350
Inventory..............	4,500	5,600	5,347
Purchases..............	14,475	16,350	18,150
Operating expenses.......	10,050	9,050	9,075

Assume the 1964 price level as the base year, and that all changes in the price level take place at the beginning of each year. Further assume that the 1965 price level is 10 percent above the 1964 price level and that the 1966 price level is 10 percent above the 1965 level.

The building was constructed in 1960 at a cost of $50,000, with an estimated life of 25 years. The price level at that time was 80 percent of the 1964 level.

The equipment was purchased in 1962 at a cost of $36,000, with an estimated life of 10 years. The price level at that time was 90 percent of the 1964 level.

* Problem adapted from AICPA November 1962 examination.

The Lifo method of inventory valuation is used. The original inventory was acquired in the same year that the building was constructed, and was maintained at a constant $4,000 until 1964. In 1964 a gradual build-up of the inventory was begun in anticipation of an increase in the volume of business.

a) Prepare the 1966 income statement in terms of 1964 dollars. Compute the 1966 earnings per share in terms of 1964 dollars and in terms of mixed dollars (conventional accounting practice).

b) Restate the 1966 income statement in 1966 dollars. Explain carefully how the statement differs from the results in part (a). Recompute the earnings per share in terms of 1966 dollars.

c) Compute the return on investment (earnings per share ÷ original investment per share) for 1966 in terms of 1964 dollars and in terms of mixed dollars. Would this rate of return have been different if expressed in 1966 dollars? Explain.

17–19. Assume that a machine is purchased at a cost of $10,000 when an index of the general price level and an index of machinery replacement cost both stand at 100. The machine has a useful life of five years, with zero salvage value. During the next three years the indices are as follows (assume that the price changes occur at the beginning of each year and apply throughout that year):

	General Price Index	Replacement Cost Index
19x0	100	100
19x1	100	120
19x2	130	160

a) Prepare entries to record depreciation for 19x0.

b) Prepare entries in 19x1 to adjust the accounts and record depreciation, assuming that changes in replacement cost are to be recognized (credit Holding Gain).

c) Prepare entries in 19x2 to adjust the accounts and record depreciation, assuming that *only* general price-level changes are to be recognized (credit Capital Adjustment—Purchasing Power Restatement).

d) Prepare entries in 19x2 to adjust the accounts and record depreciation, assuming that both general price-level changes and replacement cost changes are to be recognized. Assume that entry (b) had been made in 19x1.

17–20. Catapult Construction Company purchased a machine for $10,000 at the beginning of 1970. The machine has a useful life of five years and no salvage value. The straight-line method of depreciation is applied to the machine.

In each year from 1970 to 1973, the company earned net income before depreciation of $3,000. Prices behaved as follows in this period (assume that price changes occur at the beginning of the year and apply throughout the year):

Year	General Price Index	Machine— Replacement Cost, New
1970	110	$10,000
1971	110	$12,000
1972	120	$14,000
1973	130	$18,000

For 1971, 1972, and 1973, determine (1) net income after depreciation (including identifiable holding gains if applicable), and (2) the machine's net book value, under each of the following costing methods: (a) unadjusted historical cost, (b) historical cost adjusted for changes in the general price level, (c) replacement cost, and (d) replacement cost adjusted for changes in the general price level.

17–21. Presented below are the comparative balance sheets of VLR Corporation as of December 31, 19x0 and 19x1, and the income statement for 19x1. These statements are prepared using conventional accounting procedures.

VLR CORPORATION
Comparative Balance Sheets, December 31

	12–31–x0	12–31–x1
Assets		
Current:		
Cash	$100,000	$121,000
Net accounts receivable	.. ...	15,000
Inventory, Fifo	40,000	90,000
Total Current Assets	$140,000	$226,000
Noncurrent:		
Plant and equipment, at cost	$150,000	$150,000
Less: Allowance for depreciation	.. ...	(25,000)
Total Noncurrent Assets	$150,000	$125,000
Total Assets	$290,000	$351,000
Equities		
Liabilities:		
Current:		
Accounts payable	$ 40,000	$ 60,000
Noncurrent:		
4% bonds payable	100,000	100,000
Total Liabilities	$140,000	$160,000
Stockholders' Equity:		
Common stock	$150,000	$150,000
Retained earnings	.. ...	41,000
Total Stockholders' Equity	$150,000	$191,000
Total Equities	$290,000	$351,000

VLR CORPORATION

Income Statement, 19x1

```
Sales (30,000 units x $5)............          $150,000
Operating expenses:
  Cost of sales:
    Beginning inventory (20,000
      units x $2)...................  $ 40,000
    Purchases (40,000 units x $3)....  120,000
    Ending inventory (30,000
      units x $3)...................   (90,000)  $ 70,000
    Depreciation ($150,000/6 years)....           25,000
    Selling, general, administrative...           10,000
    Interest...........................            4,000
                                                 $109,000
Net Income.............................          $ 41,000
```

All of the asset and equity accounts on the balance sheet at December 31, 19x0, were transacted on December 31, 19x0. Sales; purchases; selling, general, and administrative expenses; and interest occurred uniformly throughout 19x1. There were no dividends declared or taxes payable in 19x1. The following table summarizes price behavior in 19x1.

	12–31–x0, 1–1–x1	19x1 Average	12–31–x1
General price index, base = 100......	100%	105%	110%
Current replacement cost:			
Plant asset index, base = 100.......	120%	140%	150%
Merchandise market quotations......	$2	$3	$3.50

a) Restate the comparative balance sheets and the income statement in common dollars as of December 31, 19x1.

b) Restate the same statements by using current costs for valuation purposes and including changes in value from holding in income as they occur.

c) Convert the statements in (b) to real terms, using the value of the dollar as of December 31, 19x1.

d) Assume the market rate of interest on long-term debt comparable to the company's 20-year bond rises to 5 percent on December 31, 19x1. What impact would this have on your statements in part (b)?

SECTION V

ACCOUNTING CONTROL

CHAPTER EIGHTEEN

ACCOUNTING
SYSTEMS AND
CONTROL

UP TO THIS point we have studied financial accounting primarily from a conceptual viewpoint. Our interest has been in understanding and using the end product—the financial statements. In addition, however, accounting can be viewed as a data processing system and as a control system.

A system consists of a group of interrelated components designed to accomplish an objective. A large system is usually composed of a number of subsystems which contribute to its overall functioning. The human body, for example, is a system including the nervous, circulatory, respiratory, and digestive subsystems. Likewise, accounting can be studied as a system—an assemblage of parts functioning together. We already have been exposed to some of these parts—journals, ledgers, reports—in a manual accounting system. But we focused on their use as analytical tools and not on their role in overall data processing or in one of the accounting subsystems (e.g., sales, cash collection, purchases, cash disbursements, manufacturing costs).

The purpose of the accounting system is the collection, processing, and reporting of financial information. These objectives point to three major components in the system: $input \rightarrow processing \rightarrow output$. It is not enough, however, that some procedure exist. An effective accounting system must have these components designed and coordinated in such a way that accurate information is available promptly and at a reasonable cost. Moreover, the system should aid in preventing the misappropriation or misuse of the firm's assets and the falsification of its records and reports.

This chapter presents an overview of the operation and control of an accounting data processing system. Specifically, we investigate four areas: (1) general principles of internal control, (2) electronic data processing (EDP), (3) internal control in an EDP system, and (4) the relationship of accounting systems and information systems.

INTERNAL CONTROL

Internal control includes the procedures and techniques used to safeguard assets, to promote operational efficiency and compliance with prescribed policy, and to achieve accurate reporting of information. In this sense, internal control is a management function, much broader than just accounting. We are primarily concerned, however, with the contribution that a well-designed accounting system can make to the overall internal control function.

The role of the accounting system is to prevent fraud by making it extremely difficult to misappropriate assets without discovery, to provide assurance that errors and irregularities are detected, and to otherwise check the integrity of the accounting records. The accomplishment of these tasks requires that the accounting system be operated according to a number of commonsense principles. Some of these are discussed in the sections below.

Systematic Organization and Procedures

Perhaps the primary prerequisite for achieving internal control is that there *be* a system to follow. The organizational structure of the firm must be planned with clear lines of authority and responsibility. It should be clear, for example, who has the authority for extending credit to customers, for acquiring new plant and equipment, for signing checks, etc. Throughout the entire firm as well as in the accounting area per se, each person should understand the extent of his own duties and accountabilities as well as those of the persons with whom he interacts.

This principle implies that there must be adequate personnel, in terms of both quantity and quality, to carry out the functions of the system. Furthermore, they should be carefully selected, trained, and instructed on the importance of compliance with procedures.

Within the established lines of authority, a set of procedures for authorization and approval of business transactions should be understood and followed. A few brief examples illustrate this concept. When supplies are requisitioned from a storeroom, the authorized recipient should evidence receipt by signing for the supplies. Foremen should be required to review and initial the time records of all employees in their departments. No plant assets should be retired and sold without formal approval of the plant manager or other designated individuals. The factory repair shop should do repair work for another department only upon the receipt of an authorization signed by the department supervisor.

Voucher System. Perhaps the best example is the formalized, uniform procedure called the voucher system for the authorization of cash disbursements and the issuance of checks. Its purpose is to control cash expenditures, detect errors, and block unauthorized disbursements.

The key to the operation of a voucher system is the regulation that no check may be issued except in payment of a valid, approved voucher. A voucher consists of a set of documents which support the authorization for a disbursement of funds. A voucher may consist of a supplier's invoice (and supporting data), a check request from some division of the company, a weekly payroll summary, a travel expense report, etc. In each case the voucher should show the reason for the disbursement and must be signed by the person authorized to make that particular kind of disbursement. Often the documents making up the voucher are enclosed in a cover known as a voucher jacket or voucher cover. The various individuals who have accumulated the underlying documents, compared them, and reviewed them, initial the voucher cover. Also the numbers or names of the accounts to be debited in the journal entry are listed on the voucher jacket.

Many firms formally modify the recording mechanism to incorporate the voucher system. Standard prenumbered voucher forms are used, with the voucher numbers often corresponding to identical check numbers. Under a formal voucher system all purchases and other transactions which involve an eventual cash outlay are recorded in a special journal called the voucher register.

Assume that a company orders raw materials from a supplier. When the purchase order is sent to the supplier, a copy also goes to the accounting department. When the material is delivered by the supplier, a receiving report is filled out, a copy of which goes to the accounting department. Then, when the supplier's invoice or bill is received, a voucher cover is prepared and circulated. Someone in the accounting office compares the invoice with the purchase order and receiving report to insure that the company is being billed for what it actually ordered and received. After the three documents are checked for numerical accuracy, the voucher is filed systematically to await the date of payment. The bookkeeper journalizes it in the voucher register, debiting Raw Materials and crediting Vouchers Payable. The subsidiary ledger for Vouchers Payable consists of the individual unpaid vouchers.

On the payment date the voucher is taken from the file and a check is prepared, perhaps in the cashier's office. The voucher and check are forwarded to the treasurer for final review and signing of the check, which is separated from the voucher and mailed. The voucher is stamped or marked in some manner so it cannot be presented again for payment. The cash disbursements book becomes a simple check register with only two money columns—a debit column for vouchers payable and a credit column for cash in bank. The check number and voucher number are entered in the check register, and the date and check number are entered in the appropriate columns of the voucher register for cross-reference.

Segregation of Duties

In the design of systematic procedures, no single individual should be responsible for all aspects of an area or transaction. This concept is known as segregation of duties and has two aspects—separation of the major functions of authorization, custodianship, and accounting; and division of duties within and between departments.

Persons having access to physical possession of assets should not also maintain the accounting records of those assets. Those who possess operating control over the assets—i.e., can authorize their use or disposition— should have neither custodial nor record-keeping responsibilities. When these functions are combined, the opportunities for misappropriation of assets and manipulation of the accounting records to cover theft increases materially. For instance, if the raw materials inventory clerk had access to the inventory, he might abscond with some material and simply fail to enter incoming purchases. Similarly, the storeroom manager might take supplies for his own personal use and authorize an entry charging Factory Overhead if the two functions were not kept separate.

Within a particular area or department there should also be a division of duties wherever possible. For example, in the control of accounts receivable, separate groups should have the responsibility for approving credit, authorizing shipment of the goods, preparing bills, mailing statements to the customer, collecting the cash remittances, maintaining the detailed subsidiary records, and making entries in the general ledger control account. Similarly, the duties of time-keeping, payroll preparation, distribution of payroll checks, and recording labor cost distributions should be separated. The assignment of definite responsibilities to various individuals for portions of an area makes it extremely difficult for fraud to occur without collusion. Often a policy of periodic rotation of personnel among departments, where feasible, aids in preventing a single individual from extending his command over an entire area.

This principle of segregation of duties is particularly important in the area of cash. The people who actually receive and count cash obviously should not make journal or ledger entries. Similarly, the same person should not be responsible for both cash receipts and cash disbursements. Rather, all receipts should be deposited intact in a bank, and all disbursements should be made in another department. No current disbursements should be made from the daily receipts. As soon as the two functions of receiving and disbursing cash become intermixed, effective control begins to break down.

The procedures followed for cash receipts usually provide many examples of the division of duties principle. The person opening the mail from customers makes a daily list of checks received by customer name. One copy of the list goes to the auditing or accounting department. Another copy, perhaps along with a portion of the bill returned by the customer, goes to the accounts receivable department for posting to individual accounts. The checks themselves are turned over to someone else, who prepares the bank deposit. A duplicate deposit slip is sent to the accounting department for comparison with the remittance list. Then general journal entries are authorized and made. For cash sales, cash registers are employed. Each salesclerk has his own cash drawer. At the end of the day the cash is turned over to a separate person for deposit, and the sales tape from the register is the underlying document for general journal entries. The sales tape is normally not accessible either to the person making the cash deposit or to the salesclerk. The accounting or auditing group has the responsibility of comparing the sales tape with the bank deposit and with the general journal entries.

Imprest Fund System. The procedure for processing a voucher and preparing a check is time-consuming and costly. Occasions arise when expenditures have to be made immediately or when the cost of operating the formal cash disbursement procedure is too large relative to the amount of the expenditure. To introduce a measure of flexibility into the system, some procedure is necessary to bypass the formal routine but still maintain some degree of control. Such a procedure is the imprest fund system. Perhaps the most common illustration of an imprest system is the petty cash fund used for minor or emergency expenditures in an office. Keep in mind, however, that the imprest fund principles may also be applied to large amounts of money, as in the case of branch offices.

The establishment of a petty cash fund requires the issuance of a check for a set amount to a person selected to have control over and responsibility for the fund. Assume that a petty cash fund in the amount of $500 is to be set up. A voucher and check for that amount are processed, and an entry is made:

```
Petty Cash...................................... 500
    Cash in Bank...................................    500
```

After cashing the check, the custodian has currency and coin amounting to $500 under his control. Since only one individual has access to the currency and coin in the fund, responsibility is limited and pinpointed.

Not only is the fund under the control of one person, but also it must be operated under a specified set of procedures for particular purposes only. No money is to be released from the fund except in exchange for authorized withdrawal slips (petty cash vouchers). Each one indicates the amount disbursed, the purpose of the withdrawal, and the signatures of the person receiving the funds and the person authorizing the expenditure.

For every expenditure out of the fund, the custodian (petty cashier) should receive an authorized withdrawal slip for an equivalent amount. Consequently, at all times the amount of currency and coin plus the petty cash vouchers in the fund should equal the basic amount of $500. A means of control over the imprest fund exists through periodic surprise comparisons to see that the currency, coin, and withdrawal slips equal the amount of the fund, and that the slips comply with procedures.

When the currency and coin in the fund nears exhaustion, a reimbursement check is drawn to replenish the fund. The withdrawal slips are presented as evidence of valid disbursements having been made from the fund. A check payable to the custodian is issued to bring the currency in the fund back to its original amount. If the fund has been operated correctly and accurately, the amount of the check should equal exactly the amount of the withdrawal slips.

Assume that during the period the petty cashier makes disbursements totaling $478.61 from the fund. The petty cash vouchers are summarized as follows:

Miscellaneous office expenses	$101.91
Freight charges on incoming merchandise	36.90
Travel advances to the president	290.00
Refunds to customers for returned goods	49.80
	$478.61

To record the reimbursement the following entry is made, debiting the various accounts indicated by the petty cash vouchers and crediting Cash in Bank:

Miscellaneous Office Expense	101.91	
Freight-In	36.90	
Executive Travel Expense	290.00	
Sales Returns	49.80	
Cash in Bank		478.61

Reimbursement can occur any time that more currency is needed. Many firms, as a matter of policy, always issue a reimbursement check on the last day of the period to ensure that all disbursements get recorded.

The withdrawal slips should be canceled or perforated so that they cannot be used again. Minor discrepancies between the total amount of the withdrawal slips and the amount necessary to replenish the fund are debited or credited to a miscellaneous loss or gain account called Cash Over and Short. Theoretically, no difference should exist, but occasionally mistakes are made in counting change, etc.

Notice that under the imprest system, no formal journal entries are made when the cash outlays are actually made from the fund. The formal recording is deferred until the reimbursement check is issued. Likewise, the Petty Cash account is not debited when the fund is replenished. The debit entries are made to the individual accounts for which currency is disbursed. No debit is made to Petty Cash except when the fund is set up or increased in size. Petty Cash is credited only to reduce the size of the fund or to eliminate it.

Verification and Comparison

To aid in the detection of errors, checks and balances should be built into the standard operating procedures of the accounting system wherever possible. In the normal course of performing his duties, one employee should be able to verify or review the work of another. We have already had a good illustration of this concept with the general-subsidiary ledger relationships. The subsidiary ledger clerk maintaining the individual accounts receivable or accounts payable provides a check on the accuracy of the entries made by the general ledger bookkeeper in the respective control accounts, and vice versa.

Other examples are prevalent. The manager of the receiving department fills out a report on the types and quantities of goods passing through his department. Similarly, the warehouse manager maintains a record of incoming goods, often on perpetual inventory cards. A comparison of these should indicate whether the merchandise received by the firm actually ends up in the company's warehouse. Mention has been made of the comparisons of invoices, receiving reports, and purchase orders when checks are issued and the comparison of remittance lists and sales tapes with bank deposits. The formal bank reconciliation is another example in the cash area. It involves a systematic comparison of the bank's record of deposits and charges against the Cash in Bank account with the accounting records for cash receipts and disbursements.

Prompt and Systematic Recording

Another procedure which materially aids in internal control is the maintenance of prompt, accurate, and systematic records. The origination of accounting transactions and the flow of documents and reports should follow a well-defined, orderly, preestablished pattern. Written policies governing accounting procedures should be available. The chart of accounts and the accounting manual relating to it are good examples. One of the important factors in error detection is the ability to follow a transaction through the accounting system by means of a series of underlying documents, reports, entries, etc. This is referred to as the "audit trail." If record keeping and records control are careless and slow, the chances of undetected fraud or error increase.

One of the advantages of the perpetual inventory system is that entries are made immediately upon use of the asset rather than at the end of the period. Often recording can be made more prompt and systematic through the use of various mechanical devices and forms. Cash registers, check-writing machines, punched-card apparatus, and other electronic equipment provide a rapid, accurate, and fairly automatic recording procedure. Also useful are prenumbered forms—checks, sales slips, invoices, receipts, and various other documents. By requiring that all prenumbered documents be accounted for, management can exert very tight control over their use.

ELECTRONIC DATA PROCESSING

Previously we defined an accounting system as an assemblage of inter-related parts designed to gather, process, and report financial information. Processing consists of converting various data inputs into meaningful information outputs. In this section we describe the role that electronic computers play in the input → processing → output cycle.

Electronic data processing (EDP) does not change the basic functions of recording, classifying, summarizing, etc., nor does it reduce the need for an effective system of internal control. But the introduction of electronic computers requires quite radical changes in the format of many of the accounting records, in the nature and sequence of procedures, and in the implementation of the general principles of internal control described in the preceding section. Major changes and developments have arisen in all of these areas from the use of EDP.

Electronic computers and related equipment allow information to be collected and disseminated more rapidly and economically than was possible in manual accounting systems. Computer facilities handle thousands of pieces of data in a few seconds. Moreover, a single piece of basic data can be reprocessed to produce different sets of information without the need to reenter the basic data. Hence, EDP systems can deal effectively with complex informational needs and problems.

A computer system has five distinct features which contribute materially to its usefulness.

1. *Data Inputs.* Most computer systems can process data captured in a variety of forms—punched cards, paper tape, magnetic tape.
2. *Memory.* A significant feature of computer systems is their ability to electronically store data in an internal magnetic form.
3. *Programmed Direction.* A complex set of instructions for processing the data can be stored and then executed in the indicated order with-

out further operator involvement. The instructions to the computer are called a program.[1]

4. *Manipulative Speed.* Computer systems are able to process numeric and alphabetic data with the speed of electricity.

5. *Logical Decisions.* An electronic computer can select from among alternative processing procedures, depending on the decision obtained from simple yes-no comparisons such as, "Is A larger than B?"

Elements of a Computer Processing System

The diagram in Figure 18–1 shows schematically the elements of a computer system. The solid lines indicate actual data flows, and the broken lines signify flows of instructions.

FIGURE 18–1

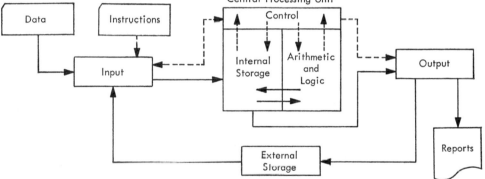

Input. This function in the EDP system translates instructions and data to be processed into electronic codes which the computer is capable of understanding. The input of data to a system usually consists of punched cards or magnetic tape. Business data are recorded on cards and paper tape by means of punched holes, with different combinations indicating numbers and letters. Source data may also be recorded as magnetized spots on a tape. Magnetic tapes are more convenient to handle, less bulky to store, and faster to process than punched cards. Often a firm has auxiliary "off-line" equipment to convert punched cards to tape before processing the data.

More recent data recording developments include point-of-origin recording, wherein data are captured in a computer processible form as a

---

[1] The whole collection of programs and routines associated with a computer system are referred to as the "software"; the equipment itself is called the "hardware."

by-product of some other necessary function. For instance, electric cash registers and typewriters may include a punching attachment with which information is automatically punched into a tape as amounts are entered in the register or are typed on invoices. In some cases the underlying documents may be processed directly by input units through the use of magnetic ink character recognition (MICR) or optical character recognition (OCR). In the first instance (MICR) information is inscribed on the document in magnetic ink which can be read by special input equipment. Banks make extensive use of MICR in processing checks. In the second instance (OCR), the information is recorded on the basic document in graphic characters that can be detected directly by special reading devices. Oil companies use optical scanning techniques to process charge slips from retail customers.

The central processing unit (CPU) consists of three components—arithmetic-logic, internal storage, and control. The arithmetic-logic unit, which need not concern us here, actually carries out the numerical manipulations, makes comparisons, and performs other processing operations.

Memory and Storage.   One of the distinguishing features of computer systems is their capacity to store information internally. By means of magnetic cores, discs, or drums, data is retained in individual memory locations or addresses. Each memory location contains magnetic bits which, in various combinations, indicate different numerical or alphabetical characters or various symbols. Internal storage capacity is used, during the actual processing of data, as a temporary depository for partially processed data. The arithmetic unit draws the information it needs for a particular computation from storage and returns the computed results to storage. While some permanent information may be stored on discs accessible to the system, long-term storage, such as of account balances, is usually done on tapes outside of the processing system itself. Then this information can be reintroduced as input data. The processing capability of an electronic computer system is a direct function of its storage facilities, including capacity and access time (the time required for getting information in and out of storage).

Control.   The control unit enables the computer to guide itself through the actual data processing operations. It receives detailed instructions, in the form of a program, concerning the exact sequence of steps to be followed in processing a given set of data. The control unit then interprets these instructions and directs the other components as to when, where, and how to execute them. The control unit transmits data to and from memory and the arithmetic unit and activates the output units when necessary. With internal direction from the program, data processing on a computer most often is automatic, with an uninterrupted flow from input to output. On occasion, however, the operator may wish to enter a special piece of information or check for errors along the way. This communication with the computer can be accomplished through the control console.

Output. This component of the EDP system translates the results of processing from machine code into various output media. It may produce a reel of tape, a deck of punched cards, a printed document, etc. Some output is intended for reuse, as in the case of a subsidiary ledger for accounts receivable which consists of a reel of magnetic tape that is periodically processed and updated. Among the types of output equipment are high-speed printers that produce reports, documents (invoices), or other forms (payroll checks) with exceptional speed and cathode ray tubes (CRT), similar to a television screen, on which the output may be displayed visually. The type and form of output are major considerations in the design of the system and the writing of programs.

Data Processing Example

The foregoing discussion of electronic data processing and computers is only a brief introduction to the subject. Each system has different characteristics, equipment, and capabilities, of course. The selection of the proper equipment, the arrangement of the processing units, the type of input and output, and the actual internal workings of the machines are subjects of interest to those planning to enter the data processing and systems area of accounting. Our purpose is only to gain an appreciation of the numerous uses of electronic systems. Payroll, inventory, cash receipts, cash disbursements, sales, billing, and many other areas which involve masses of data can be processed rapidly and efficiently through the use of computers.

Let us look at one brief example to see how an EDP system might operate in the billing function of an electric or gas utility. One possible system is shown in Figure 18-2.

Meter readers record current readings on special forms. These could well be preprinted forms already containing the customer's name, address, meter number (if such is used), and rate classification. The cards might be in punched-card form. If not, the information is transferred to punched cards either through manual card punching or in some cases by input machines capable of reading mark senses made on the meter card. The punched cards are then converted into tape input for faster processing.

Two other tapes also comprise part of the input. Probably stored on a master tape is the subsidiary ledger account for each customer. This tape contains, in addition to routine information (name, address, etc.), the current dollar balance, the last meter reading, and cumulative quantities used to date. Another permanent tape contains the various rates to be charged for electricity or gas, depending on customer class and quantity

FIGURE 18–2

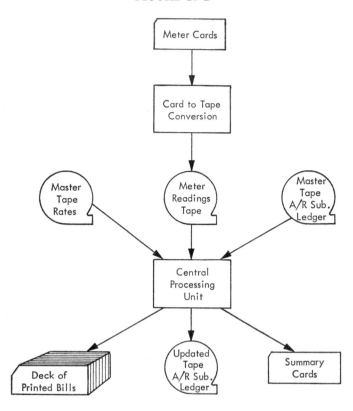

used. The three input tapes are processed together according to the computer program.

The output consists of an updated subsidiary accounts receivable tape, printed bills in punched-card form ready for direct mailing to the customers, and perhaps summary cards for the total amounts billed, for later use in general ledger entries. The punched-card bill is probably in sections, one of which is to be returned with the customer's payment, to facilitate processing and recording of cash collections. If the firm's general ledger is stored internally, then summary cards are unnecessary. As part of the processing routine, the general ledger can be updated by direct entries to Accounts Receivable and Sales. Nevertheless, some printout of the general ledger entries probably would be desirable.

This particular illustration involves *batch processing*. Periodically, probably daily for a large utility, the meter cards are run and the bills are prepared for a particular group (batch) of customers. The records of the transactions affecting the accounts receivable master file are accumulated over a period of time. Then they are processed as a group or lot.

Integrated Data Processing

The above example involves only the single function of billing. With many computer systems, more than one processing function can be handled in a single program. The system is then termed an integrated data processing (IDP) system. The coordination of a number of related processes improves efficiency by eliminating duplicate input data, records, and processing operations.

One way to design an IDP system is to make the subsystems compatible. Ideally, such systems make multiple use of the same input data. Records for different subsystems using similar data are combined into a single record file. One source document updates all records associated with the particular item. For example, an integrated program can be formulated to include not only the sales—accounts receivable—billing function but also the maintenance of the perpetual inventory records, the computation of cost of goods sold, a test of inventory for needed replenishment, and the printing out of purchase orders for replenishment and shipping orders to the customer. The customer's sales order is the initiating input to this integrated system.

Obviously, data processing systems may exhibit varying degrees of integration. Most perform more than a single function, yet none is completely integrated in the sense that all processing subfunctions are performed at once. Nevertheless, EDP systems appear to be moving more and more toward what is called a *single information flow* or single data base system. Indeed, some systems analysts claim that future integrated data processing systems should be designed as a single system around a common data base rather than as the integration of separate subsystems. Under this concept, fundamental items of data are converted to machine-readable form at their point of entry into the system. They are stored in a central location accessible for all subsequent uses. Then, all desired reports would be prepared from a single recording of transactions.

On-Line, Real-Time Systems. Systems employing the single information flow concept employ on-line, real-time processing. This entails practically simultaneous processing of data with their generation and immediate feedback of information from the system at any time. Technically, on-line equipment is those units in direct communication with and under the control of the central processing unit. An on-line, real-time system has many input units and storage files directly connected to the CPU.

Input units may be console terminals from which users can feed in information or ask the computer for information. Certain recording devices, such as a cash register, may be hooked directly into the processing unit, so that any amount entered is immediately processed. Or the input may consist of electronic transmission of data over wires from other computers, as when branch offices process data on their own computers, which communicate the output to the company's central processing unit as well. (The science fiction fantasy of "computers talking to computers" has become a reality.) The common data base is stored in *direct access* files. The files are indexed in such a way that all storage locations are readily accessible. Direct access storage allows the computer to retrieve desired information rapidly without having to review all items sequentially.

Direct access computer systems, of course, require large storage facilities and specialized equipment. Careful attention must be paid to the design of the data base and to the analysis of input/output sources. All these add significantly to the cost. Nevertheless, real-time processing may offer great advantages where an updated master file must be readily available at all times. Airline reservation systems employ real-time, direct access concepts. Each transaction is processed as it occurs, without intervening sorting or batching. Some banks also use real-time processing in recording savings account transactions, and some firms use it in the maintenance of their perpetual inventories. Nevertheless, most accounting data are still processed in the batch mode, with varying degrees of integration.

INTERNAL CONTROL IN EDP SYSTEMS

We have only sketched the barest outline of the electronic data processing field. The details must be left for other courses. Nevertheless, the impact of EDP on accounting procedures is obvious, and this impact extends to the internal control of EDP systems. Much less opportunity exists in EDP systems than in manual systems for division of duties. Activities that serve as checks in a manual system may be combined in a computer system, especially once the processing begins. It normally proceeds without human intervention. Traditional audit trails may be modified or completely eliminated (as in the case of some on-line, direct access systems) as records, files, and transactions appear in machine-readable form rather than in conventional journals and ledgers.

Nevertheless, the four principles of internal control—systematic organization and procedures, segregation of duties, verification and comparison, and prompt and systematic recording—apply to EDP systems also. Their implementation varies, however, as we will see subsequently. Moreover, computerized systems possess certain characteristics that strengthen internal control. The speed of the computer allows more checking of detail to be done by the computer and facilitates more timely reporting. For example, a cash disbursements routine can compare invoices, receiving reports, and purchase orders in detail for hundreds of bills in a few minutes. In addition, the computer achieves a much higher uniformity in its execution of procedures and accuracy in its processing than is possible in manual systems. Like transactions are handled identically, and numerical computations are carried out precisely. This is not to say that computers never make mistakes. But they are far superior to human data processors in terms of speed, accuracy, and reliability. In fact, of the few computer "errors" that do arise most are traceable to human error somewhere along the way.

Internal control in EDP must be oriented toward the entire system rather than toward the control of individuals. New controls must substitute for the human review and division of duties consolidated in the computer program. Inasmuch as the major system components are input, processing, and output, it is not surprising to find that the internal control procedures can be organized around these elements.

Control over Input

Because of the automatic nature of electronic data processing, control over input becomes a key consideration. An oft-repeated apothegm in systems work is GIGO—"garbage in, garbage out." No amount of speed, accuracy, or reliability in processing can overcome inaccurate or invalid input into the system. Management must exercise control over input to verify the conversion of data into machine-readable form and to determine that data are not distorted or lost in transmission into the central processing unit.

The attention given to point-of-origin input (optical scanning, original source documents in punched-card form, etc.) reflects a desire to minimize errors in copying and transcribing input. When data must be entered in punched cards, firms often employ a keypunch verifier, a machine that checks the accuracy of keypunching by rekeying the data and comparing it to the original results. Check digits are often associated with numbers as a way of verifying accurate numerical transcription.

Control over data entering the CPU is achieved in many ways. Many card and tape readers have duplicate reading units. Also various validity checks are programmed into the input routine to test the accuracy, completeness, and propriety of the input transactions. For example, the computer can test the input data for valid codes (e.g., particular account numbers), characters (e.g., that no alphabetical characters are incorrectly included where only numeric characters should be), data field size, authorization, sequence of records, etc.

With direct access systems, authorized usage of input units is critical. Only certain people may have access to the input units, or the CPU may accept only certain types of input data from particular units. A record should be maintained of all input entered into the system. A log locked into each input unit is available for review and detection of any unauthorized entry to the system.

To detect loss of data in transmission or processing, firms employ serially numbered forms and *batch totals*. A group of sales invoices to be processed together may be prelisted and totaled on an adding-machine tape. The control total can be compared with the dollar total processed by the computer. Sometimes the control totals consist of documents or record counts or simply numbers of items processed. The latter are called *hash* totals. Their objective is to assure that all input data that are supposed to be processed are in fact processed.

Control over Processing

Because of the complexity of the processing function, control is exerted on a number of levels. We discuss three control areas in this section —organization, procedures, and equipment checks.

Organizational Division of Duties. The principle of division of duties applies with equal validity to the organization of the systems and data processing functions. Failure to segregate the major duties in the computer system may lead to alterations or manipulations that are not in the best interests of the firm. The data processing department should be subdivided into at least three separate areas—systems design and programming, operations, and control. Of particular importance is the separation of the program development activities from the day-to-day operation of the equipment.

The first group has the responsibility for designing the system and developing programs. Personnel in systems design and programming also analyze the system on an ongoing basis. They are responsible for modifications in the system and for making and testing changes in the program. The crucial point is that they do not operate the machines in normal processing. In fact, they should have no access to the equipment during normal operations or the library of program tapes actually used to process data.

A separate group has the responsibility for actual computer operations. This group acquires the data to be processed, converts it into machine-readable form, and physically operates the equipment. But the operations group does not write computer programs or maintain custody of the processing tapes. Consequently, there should be no modifications or interruptions in the computer program by operating personnel. Any communications (instructions or additional input) between the operator and the computer system are recorded on the computer console log. The log also records the processing time, which can be reviewed for deviations from the normal pattern.

The control group performs only review and custodial functions. It maintains and protects the tape and program library and supervises the flow of data in and out of the department. For example, control personnel log in all input data and control information (batch totals, etc.). They review all output for reasonableness, making comparisons with the control totals, reconciling errors, and noting unprocessed data. The control group has the responsibility for review of the console logs and various error messages from the central processing unit. Finally, it supervises the distribution of output and handles inquiries and criticisms from recipients of the processed information.

Sound Procedures.   The second area of processing control is the employment of standard operating procedures within the division of duties outlined above. Sound procedures are needed to guard against the misuse of files and programs and to prevent and detect operator or machine error. Two of the most important of these procedures are authorization and documentation.

An up-to-date documentation for each computer run or routine is a prerequisite to proper control over programs. The documentation should contain systems and program flow charts, operator instructions, input-output formats, the detailed program instructions, and an approval and change sheet. On the latter is indicated the initial approval of the program for operating use. Moreover, any modifications in the program must be entered there. These must be properly authorized and approved by responsible officials.

Various means are employed by the control group to ensure physical control and protection of the programs and other tapes. The master files and tapes are checked out of the library only to authorized individuals and are returned at the end of processing. Tape identification labels are affixed externally to file holders and also recorded internally at the beginning and end of the magnetic tapes. Most programs then contain a program label check subroutine to ensure that the right tapes are being used for the right processing runs. In addition, the possibility of inadvertent use of the wrong tape is minimized through the use of plastic or metal file protection rings attached to the reel of tape. If the ring is attached, new data can be written on the tape; if the ring is removed, data can be read off of the tape but nothing can be entered on it. Finally, firms develop record security procedures for reconstructing records in case of damage or error. In magnetic tape systems, three generations of tape files—appropriately called grandfather, father, and son—are maintained. In direct access systems, record recovery procedures involve periodic copying of all storage files so as to allow reconstruction of the records if necessary.

An operator's manual and run schedule set forth the procedures for the actual machine operations. They indicate how the equipment is to be operated for each routine and when each routine should be run. Periodic rotation of personnel in the operations area among the processing runs adds to the internal control. The console log serves as a monitor on the operating procedures. It indicates what processing was done, when it was done, how long it took, and what type of communication existed between the operators and the control unit of the computer. In addition, most computer programs have subroutines that print out error messages concerning rejected (unprocessed) input items or other malfunctions in the system. It is extremely important that procedures exist for the review and control of these error messages and unprocessed items in order for the control group to detect functional failures of the data processing system and to ensure the eventual completeness of all processing.

Equipment Checks.   A third aspect of processing control is the checks built into most computer equipment. They help detect loss of data through hardware malfunction. The dual reading units mentioned in our discussion of input are one example. Others include *echo* checks and *parity* checks. In the former, information received by one unit is relayed back to its source and compared with the original data. It is used to check data transmitted between input-output units and the control unit. Parity checks guard against errors in the movement of data. All stored data are converted to either odd or even parity through the addition of an extra bit (binary digit) where needed. Then departures from parity can be detected in subsequent processing. Their exact working need not concern us here. They do, however, enhance the internal control over the actual data processing.

Control over Output

Output is the third component in the data processing system. Most computer output results from specific programmed instructions from the control unit of the CPU to write out on tape, punch out on cards, or print out certain items of processed information. Before printed output is distributed to the intended recipients, it should be carefully reviewed for completeness and reasonableness.

Prenumbered output forms should be used where appropriate, and all forms should be accounted for. For example, invoices in the billing routine and payroll checks in the payroll routine should be serially numbered for output control. Pages of reports should be numbered and a review made to see that all pages are intact. Data on tapes frequently are stored in groups called blocks or records. Output routines should include record or block counts to make sure everything on the tape gets written or printed out (similar routines are used as an input control). Reasonableness tests include visual scanning for quality (e.g., Does the last page have totals?), consistency reviews (e.g., Do the totals crossfoot if they are supposed to?), comparison with source data or control totals if appropriate, and a general review for creditability (i.e., Do the figures seem to make sense?).

The control group within the data processing department should maintain a report distribution log or schedule. This indicates what reports are to be prepared and when. It also specifies the number of copies to be made and who is to receive them. The schedule serves as a check on whether all reports were prepared and where they were distributed.

MANAGEMENT INFORMATION SYSTEMS

In the preceding sections we have focused our attention primarily on the processing of accounting data. But accounting is only one part of the communication system. It does not and cannot supply all the needed information for management decisions. Computers have made possible the collection and dissemination of more information more quickly and economically than ever before. As a result, concurrent with the development of electronic data processing has been an increasing emphasis on management information systems (MIS). The focus of attention has broadened from just financial accounting information to all kinds of information relevant to the conduct of the management function.

The management information system is the formal communications link between the business and its environment and among the individuals within the business. Its components include data collection (input), data manipulation and storage (processing), and data selection and reporting (output). Although the components are similar to what we have been discussing, the data base is more extensive. It encompasses all types of data and information necessary for management to plan and control decision making within the firm. In addition to accounting transactions, MIS include environmental information of an economic, social, or political nature; planning information (budgets and goals); and internal feedback (both financial and physical data and perhaps even nonquantitative data). The accounting data processing system as we have described it becomes only a major subsystem of MIS.

Management information systems require a high degree of integration, particularly between financial data and operating data. Such systems tend to cross traditional functions to focus on decisions and their implementation. Consequently, the design of an MIS is inextricably linked to organizational structure, for information flows have to be related to managerial needs and objectives. A great deal of attention must be given to specifying what information is required (desired) for making decisions and how best to report it—in addition to the problems of capturing and processing the information which we have been discussing in the more restricted setting of accounting systems.

The concepts of organization theory, communication theory, and behavioral theory that underlie a sound management information system, as well as the advanced data processing techniques required, are all beyond the scope of this book. Suffice it to say that in constructing such systems the designer must do the following:

1. Classify the types of decisions made.
2. Analyze the information requirements for each decision in terms of the type and characteristics of the data needed.
3. Plan a man-machine configuration that will sense and capture the required data.
4. Determine the most effective and efficient manner in which to process and store the information.
5. Formulate a means for transmitting, with a minimum risk of misinterpretation by the receiver, the right information messages at the right time to the right people.
6. Provide for effective internal control over the system.

Each of these steps has ramifications that extend far beyond accounting. Hopefully, our brief introduction to accounting data processing and internal control will provide some assistance in understanding the developments in management information systems that are yet to come.

SUGGESTIONS FOR FURTHER READING

Bower, James B., and Schlosser, Robert E. "Internal Control—Its True Nature," *Accounting Review*, Vol. 40 (April 1965), pp. 338–44.

Kaufman, Felix. "Effects of EDP on Internal Control," *Journal of Accountancy*, Vol. 111 (June 1961), pp. 47–59.

May, Phillip T. "System Control: Computers the Weak Link?" *Accounting Review*, Vol. 44 (July 1969), pp. 583–92.

Porter, W. Thomas, Jr., and Mulvihill, Dennis E. "Organization for Effective Information Flow," *Management Services*, Vol. 2 (November–December 1965), pp. 13–20.

Schlosser, Robert E., and Bruegman, Donald C. "The Effect of EDP on Internal Control," *Management Services*, Vol. 1 (March–April 1964), pp. 44–51.

QUESTIONS AND PROBLEMS

18–1. Discuss briefly what you regard as the more important deficiencies in the system of internal control in the following situation; and in addition, include what you consider to be a proper remedy for each deficiency.*

The cashier of the Easy Company intercepted customer A's check payable to the company in the amount of $500 and deposited

_____

* Adapted from AICPA May 1958 examination.

it in a bank account which was part of the company petty cash fund, of which he was custodian. He then drew a $500 check on the petty cash fund bank account payable to himself, signed it, and cashed it. At the end of the month, while processing the monthly statements to customers, he was able to change the statement to customer A to show that A had received credit for the $500 check that had been intercepted. Ten days later, he made an entry in the cash receipts book which purported to record receipt of a remittance of $500 from customer A, thus restoring A's account to its proper balance but overstating cash in bank. He covered the overstatement by omitting from the list of outstanding checks in the bank reconcilement two checks, the aggregate amount of which was $500.

18–2. On March 1, the Lorenzo Surplus Sales Company installed an imprest fund system for minor expenditures at its branch office. The fund was to be the responsibility of the junior assistant branch manager. However, because the branch received large amounts of cash, the policy was established that all cash receipts were to be remitted directly to the home office by the cashier. Under no circumstances were any cash receipts to be given to the junior assistant branch manager to replenish the fund; it was to be used for disbursements only.

On March 1, a check for $500 was written to the junior assistant branch manager to set up the fund. On March 12 the fund was reimbursed. Vouchers for the following expenditures were turned in:

Miscellaneous labor services	$ 40
Travel	125
Entertainment expense	75
Sales returns	120

Also in the fund were an IOU from the branch manager for $40 and currency and coins amounting to $93. On March 23, it was decided to increase the size of the fund to $800.

Make journal entries to record the transactions on March 1, March 12, and March 23.

18–3. May T. Phillip is the owner and operator of a computer service bureau. After preliminary discussions, Phillip agrees to do keypunching, computer processing, and report preparation for a new client. The client, understandably, expresses a great deal of concern about how control over input and output will be exercised.

a) What should the service bureau require from the client to aid in controlling *input?*

b) What should the client be able to check in the *output* to verify that the output was processed correctly?

c) What should the service bureau provide to the client to give evidence that the input was properly controlled and processed and that the output is accurate?

18–4. It was possible for the following unrelated incidents to occur or to remain undetected because of internal control weaknesses. The questions below each incident may appear on an internal control questionnaire. In each case there is one question that, if answered "no" by the CPA after his investigation, would have been most likely to disclose the internal control weakness that permitted the incident to occur or to remain undetected. Select the best answer choice for each of the following items.*

1. Payroll checks are completely prepared on a typewriter. A discharged employee increased the amount of his termination paycheck and cashed it before he left town.

   a) Are payroll accounts reconciled by someone other than the persons doing the timekeeping, payroll preparation, and payroll distribution?

   b) Are amounts on checks protected against alteration by means of a protective writing device such as a check protector?

   c) Are employees added to or removed from the payroll only upon written authorizations from responsible persons outside the payroll department?

   d) Are payrolls subject to formal approval by a responsible person outside the payroll department?

2. Unclaimed salary checks are left with the custodian of the petty cash fund until claimed. The custodian cashed an unclaimed salary check (and took the proceeds) by forging the payee's endorsement and depositing the check along with salary checks that he had cashed for employees by the use of petty cash funds.

   a) Are unclaimed wages deposited in a separate bank account and recorded as a liability?

   b) Are paid checks examined for amount, date, payee, authorized signatures, and endorsements as a part of the bank reconciliation process?

   c) Are employee separations reported immediately to the payroll department?

   d) Is the payroll paid through a separate bank account?

3. A manufacturing company received a substantial sales return in the last month of the year, but the credit memorandum for the return was not prepared until after the auditors had completed their field work. The returned merchandise was included in the physical inventory.

   a) Are aging schedules of accounts receivable prepared periodically?

   b) Are credit memoranda prenumbered and all numbers accounted for?

* Problem adapted from AICPA November 1964 examination.

c) Is a reconciliation of the trial balance of customers' ledgers with the general ledger control prepared periodically?

d) Are receiving reports prepared for all materials received and such reports numerically controlled?

4. The sales manager credited a salesman, Jack Smith, with sales that were actually "house account" sales. Later Smith divided his excess sales commissions with the sales manager.

   a) Are the summary sales entries checked periodically by persons independent of sales functions?

   b) Are sales orders reviewed and approved by persons independent of the sales department?

   c) Does the internal auditor compare the sales commission statements with the cash disbursements record?

   d) Are sales orders prenumbered and all numbers accounted for?

5. Over a three-month period the person in charge of the mail room took a substantial number of postage stamps and sold them to a stamp dealer.

   a) Are all petty cash and stamp funds in the custody of one person?

   b) Are all petty cash funds on an imprest basis?

   c) Are periodic expense reports to management compared with reports of prior periods and with budgets?

   d) Are surprise counts of petty cash funds made by responsible officials?

6. A sales invoice for $5,200 was computed correctly but, in error, was posted as $2,500 to the sales journal and to the accounts receivable ledger. The customer remitted only $2,500, the amount on his monthly statement.

   a) Are prelistings and predetermined totals used to control posting routines?

   b) Are sales invoice serial numbers, prices, discounts, extensions and footings independently checked?

   c) Are the customers' monthly statements verified and mailed by a responsible person other than the bookkeeper who prepared them?

   d) Are unauthorized remittance deductions made by customers or other matters in dispute investigated promptly by a person independent of the accounts receivable function?

7. The purchasing agent of Company A used a regular written purchase order to order building materials for the company. Later he instructed the building material supply company by telephone to deliver the materials to his home and to charge the account of Company A.

   a) Are purchases made on behalf of employees?

   b) Is a receiving report an essential part of each voucher?

   c) Are purchase orders and changes therein subject to approval, before commitments are made, by a responsible official?

    d) Are purchase orders prenumbered and all numbers accounted for?

8. Long Company purchased some bearer bonds as a temporary investment. The bonds were kept in the company's safe-deposit box at the local bank. The treasurer of Long Company removed the bonds from the safe-deposit box and used them as collateral for a personal loan.

    a) Are registered securities made out in the name of the company or so endorsed?

    b) Does the accounting department keep a list of all securities in the safe-deposit box?

    c) Are all persons who have access to securities covered by a fidelity bond?

    d) Is the presence of two or more responsible persons required for access to the safe-deposit box?

9. A factory foreman discharged an hourly worker but did not notify the payroll department. The foreman then forged the worker's signature on time cards and work tickets and, when giving out the checks, diverted to his own use the payroll check drawn for the worker.

    a) Are written authorizations required for all employees added to or taken off the payroll?

    b) Is distribution of payroll checks made by a paymaster who has no other payroll responsibility?

    c) Is custody of unclaimed wages vested in someone other than persons who prepare or distribute the payroll?

    d) Are persons distributing the payroll rotated from time to time?

10. A vendor was paid twice for the same shipment. One payment was made upon receipt of the invoice. The second payment was made upon receipt of monthly statement, which showed the amount of the open invoice but not the remittance. No stop-payment order was issued for either check and the vendor deposited both checks without comment.

    a) Does the person signing the check examine supporting data at the time of signing?

    b) Are vouchers, invoices, and supporting papers canceled upon payment?

    c) Is a cash disbursement record maintained which lists in numerical sequence each check issued?

    d) Are all payments made on predetermined days?

11. The cashier diverted cash received over the counter from a customer to his own use and wrote off the receivable as a bad debt.

    a) Are aging schedules of accounts receivable prepared periodically and reviewed by a responsible official?

b) Are journal entries approved by a responsible official?

c) Are receipts given directly to the cashier by the person who opens the mail?

d) Are remittance advices, letters, or envelopes which accompany receipts separated and given directly to the accounting department?

18–5. The advent of EDP has increased the need for a combination of strong traditional internal controls and specific data processing controls. Analyze the following problem from the standpoint of both types of control.

The CPU Company has recently acquired a small computer and is in the process of converting several accounting functions which were previously handled manually. The company has decided that the procedures for handling customer billing and cash receipts should be as follows:

1. Customer invoices are prepared and mailed by a secretary in the accounting department.

2. The accountant opens the customer mail and removes the checks. The checks are deposited in total every Monday.

3. After receiving the checks, the accountant prepares a customer remittance form showing customer name, address, and amount paid.

4. The remittance form is then assigned a customer account number and this number is entered on the form.

5. The remittance form is sent to the data processing department for keypunching and is converted into punched cards.

6. The punched cards are then sent to the computer room, where they are processed daily to update customer accounts receivable.

7. The cards are then thrown away. A listing of the updated balances is sent to the accounting department, and a new summary card is punched which contains the updated customer balance. The summary cards are used to process the remittance detail of the next day.

a) Evaluate the above steps from the standpoint of sound accounting internal control. Specify how fraud could occur if these steps are followed.

b) How would you strengthen the weaknesses in internal control uncovered in part (a)?

c) What controls would you include in the procedures in part (b) to assure (1) accuracy in punching and control over the input cards, and (2) assurance that the cards were accurately processed?

18–6. One standard feature of good data processing control relates to the measures taken for protecting files from loss due to accidental or intentional destruction. One technique used with magnetic tape files is referred to as the "grandfather-father-son" principle. Study the following diagram and explain:

a) How it illustrates the "grandfather-father-son" principle.
b) How this principle protects the files from complete destruction.

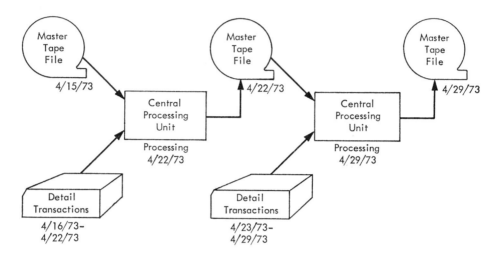

18–7. A primary feature of sound internal control calls for the segregation of duties, especially where the handling of cash is involved. In the case of small firms with few employees, this is a difficult principle to employ. Suppose the Tie-Knee Company has only three office employees; (1) the office manager, (2) a secretary, and (3) a bookkeeper.

The following duties, among others, must be performed. Indicate how you would assign these duties to obtain the maximum degree of internal control. Explain your reasoning.

a) Handle and deposit cash receipts.
b) Maintain the petty cash fund.
c) Maintain the general ledger accounts.
d) Prepare checks for signing.
e) Maintain the cash disbursements journal.
f) Maintain the cash receipts journal.
g) Prepare and send customer invoices.
h) Maintain the accounts payable subledger.
i) Sign checks.
j) Maintain the accounts receivable subledger.

18–8. The accounting and internal control procedures relating to purchases of materials by the Branden Company, a medium-sized concern manufacturing special machinery to order, have been described by your junior accountant in the following terms:*

---
* Adapted from the AICPA May 1963 examination.

After approval by manufacturing department foremen, material purchase requisitions are forwarded to the purchasing department supervisor, who distributes such requisitions to the several employees under his control. The latter employees prepare prenumbered purchase orders in triplicate, account for all numbers, and send the original purchase order to the vendor. One copy of the purchase order is sent to the receiving department where it is used as a receiving report. The other copy is filed in the purchasing department.

When the materials are received, they are moved directly to the storeroom and issued to the foremen on informal requests. The receiving department sends a receiving report (with its copy of the purchase order attached) to the purchasing department and sends copies of the receiving report to the storeroom and to the accounting department.

Vendors' invoices for material purchases, received in duplicate in the mail room, are sent to the purchasing department and directed to the employee who placed the related order. The employee then compares the invoice with the copy of the purchase order on file in the purchasing department for price and terms and compares the invoice quantity with the quantity received as reported by the shipping and receiving department on its copy of the purchase order. The purchasing department employee also checks discounts, footings, and extensions, and initials the invoice to indicate approval for payment. The invoice is then sent to the voucher section of the accounting department, where it is coded for account distribution, assigned a voucher number, entered in the voucher register, and filed according to payment due date.

On payment dates prenumbered checks are requisitioned by the voucher section from the cashier and prepared except for signature. After the checks are prepared they are returned to the cashier, who puts them through a check-signing machine, accounts for the sequence of numbers, and passes them to the cash disbursement bookkeeper for entry in the cash disbursements book. The cash disbursements bookkeeper then returns the checks to the voucher section, which then notes payment dates in the voucher register, places the checks in envelopes, and sends them to the mail room. The vouchers are then filed in numerical sequence. At the end of each month one of the voucher clerks prepares an adding machine tape of unpaid items in the voucher register and compares the total thereof with the general ledger balance and investigates any difference disclosed by such comparison.

Discuss the weaknesses, if any, in the internal control of Branden's purchasing and subsequent procedures and suggest supplementary or revised procedures for remedying each weakness with regard to:

a) Requisition of materials.

b) Receipt and storage of materials.

c) Functions of the purchasing department.

d) Functions of the accounting department.

18–9. The Granada Drug Store established an imprest fund procedure for paying small bills. The operations of the fund during the month of November are shown below.

Nov. 1 A check for $2,000 was written to establish the fund.

10 A petty cashier submitted authorized withdrawal slips totaling $1,730 in support of a request for reimbursement. At that time the cash balance in the fund was $280. A detailed breakdown of the withdrawal slips shows:

Part-time labor	$1,080
Delivery charges on merchandise received	170
Postage	32
Supplies	220
Travel advances	228
	$1,730

15 Because of the heavy use of the fund, a check for $1,000 was written and cashed to increase the size of the fund.

30 The internal auditing staff of the firm checked the fund on November 30 and found the items listed below:

Cash	$1,136
Withdrawal slips:	
Part-time labor	890
Delivery charges	49
Travel advances	437
Miscellaneous administrative expenses	18
Other items:	
Employees' payroll checks	470
	$3,000

A check was written for $1,864 to replenish the fund.

a) Prepare general journal entries to record these transactions.

b) Assume that a replenishing check had not been issued on November 30, but that the company's accounting period ended then. What entry would have been necessary on November 30? Why?

18–10. Assume your firm is planning to use the computer for processing payroll. Punched cards are to be used for input. Each week cards are to be prepunched for each employee who was on the payroll in the prior week. The prepunched cards will contain the employee's name and clock number and will be used for timekeeping purposes. Employees will use the cards to record the times they punch in and out each day. At the end of each week, the cards are to be sent to the data processing center for keypunching the total hours worked and processing of the payroll.

a) List the types of errors which can occur in the input stage (i.e., keypunching and entering to the computer for processing). What would you prescribe to control or prevent these errors?

b) What types and form of processing controls and output controls need to be included to catch errors related to:

1. Paying an employee an excessive amount?
2. Paying for work not performed?
3. Paying an employee after he has terminated his employment?
4. Paying fictitious employees?

18–11. Flash Camera and Film Company has established a number of "island" outlets around the city. The outlets consist of small booths manned usually by a single individual. The "islands" are often located in the parking lots of large stores or shopping centers. Customers can drive up in their cars and purchase film and camera supplies very conveniently. Also, they can leave film to be processed and return another day to pick it up.

Describe the system that you would establish to obtain satisfactory internal control over cash receipts and inventory.

18–12. Refer to the example shown in Figure 18–2. List five possible errors which could occur during the input, processing, and output phases of the billing function. What five steps would you prescribe to detect or prevent these errors?

18–13. The Mississippi Sand and Gravel Company provided sand and gravel in truckload lots to builders, road construction firms, and individuals desiring the use of such materials for patios, driveways, etc.

The normal procedure followed in selling and delivering the product was as follows:

1. Upon receipt of an order (usually over the phone), the delivery agent would prepare a delivery ticket in triplicate, indicating the customer's name and address, type and quantity of material desired, date to be delivered, and price.

2. When delivery time came (which was often the same day), the delivery agent authorized a truck to be loaded. The truck driver was given a weight check-out ticket by the weighing station. The driver gave the weight check-out ticket to the delivery agent, who compared it with the delivery ticket. If they agreed, the driver was given two copies of the delivery ticket and sent on his way to deliver the material. The delivery agent retained the weight check out ticket and the original copy of the delivery ticket.

3. Most deliveries were made c.o.d. The driver would collect the amount shown on the delivery ticket in cash from the customer. The driver would leave one copy of the delivery ticket with the customer and return the other copy, signed by the customer (usually with the pencil the driver carried), and the cash col-

lected to the delivery agent. The tickets and collections were checked with the original delivery tickets by the delivery agent. If correct, everything (cash, delivery tickets, weight check-out tickets, etc.) was turned over to the bookkeeper for preparation of journal entries.

4. If customers did not accept delivery or no one was available to pay for the delivery, the driver returned the material to the yard and the delivery tickets to the delivery agent. The agent would mark "void" on the original delivery tickets. This voiding of tickets was not an uncommon event, particularly with individual customers.

The company made very little net income, although its volume of activity was quite large. After five years on the job, and at the tender age of 32, the delivery agent suddenly quit and "retired" to Mexico. Then, it was discovered that he had been stealing in two ways: (1) He would mark "void" on delivery tickets for delivered merchandise, erase from them the customers' signatures, and pocket the cash turned in by the driver. (2) He often changed figures on the delivery and weight check-out tickets to understate the amount of delivery and cash received; he then stole the difference.

a) How could this system be modified (without undue cost) to prevent thefts such as that described above? Be as specific as possible.

b) Do you see any other potential "leaks" in this system? How would you prevent them?

18–14. In January 1971 the Central Savings and Loan Association installed an on-line real-time computer system.* Each teller in the association's main office and seven branch offices has an on-line input-output terminal. Customers' mortgage payments and savings account deposits and withdrawals are recorded in the accounts, by the computer, from data input by the teller at the time of the transaction. The teller keys the proper account by account number and enters the information in the terminal keyboard to record the transaction. The accounting department at the main office has both punched and typewriter input-output devices. The computer is housed at the main office.

You would expect the association to have certain internal controls in effect because an on-line real-time computer system is employed. List the internal controls which should be in effect *solely* because this system is employed, classifying them as:

a) Those controls pertaining to input of information.

b) All other types of computer controls.

18–15. The following descriptions of procedures for handling mail receipts, cash receipts, and cash payments give evidence of reasonably good

---

* Problem adapted from the AICPA May 1968 examination.

internal control. For each description, indicate why the internal control is good and discuss what possible problems are being avoided.

a) Mail receipts:
   1. Two employees are present when the mail receipts are opened.
   2. One individual records the amount of each check received and forwards this record directly to the accounting department.
   3. The second employee endorses all checks with a company stamp, prepares the deposit slip, makes a daily deposit of checks, and has a duplicate copy of the deposit slip sent directly to the accounting department by the bank.

b) Cash receipts:
   1. All cash receipts are placed in a cash register having the following characteristics:
      a) Each sales person has his own drawer and drawer key.
      b) A tape which shows all sales is locked in the register and is not accessible to the sales clerks. All sales and openings of the register are automatically recorded on the tape.
   2. Each sales clerk begins the day with a certain amount of change in his cash drawer. This amount of cash is signed for by the clerk when picking up his drawer.
   3. When a clerk rings up a sale, he identifies his sale by pressing a designated key identifying himself.
   4. At the end of the day, the clerk takes his drawer and total cash amount (beginning change plus cash sales) to be counted by a member of the treasurer's office. The clerk receives a receipt for the total cash returned.
   5. The count of total cash and beginning change amount is forwarded to the accounting office.
   6. A supervisor removes the locked tape from the cash register daily and sends it to the accounting office.
   7. The accounting function reconciles the cash amount reported with the cash sales shown on the register tape.

c) Cash payments:
   1. Invoices from suppliers are sent to the accounting department.
   2. Invoices are matched with company purchase orders and reports of materials received from suppliers by the accounting department.
   3. When invoices, purchases orders, and receiving reports match, they are sent to the treasurer's office to support the preparation of a check.
   4. Checks and the supporting documents are sent to the company president for signature.

5. All checks are countersigned by the treasurer and the president. When the check is prepared, it is signed by the treasurer and the supporting documents are canceled by perforating them with the word "paid" and the current date.
6. The president then receives the check and perforated documents prior to his signature.
7. The president mails the check, after signing, and returns the canceled documents to the accounting office.

CHAPTER NINETEEN

FACTORY OVERHEAD

Our discussion in Chapter Seven explores the conceptual framework of accounting for manufacturing companies. Raw material, direct labor, and factory overhead represent the factors of production, which are combined and converted in the manufacturing process into the end product. The costs of these assets are attached to the units being produced in work in process. When units are completed, the total manufacturing cost assigned to them is transferred to finished goods inventory. From there, the cost flows to the expense account, Cost of Goods Sold, when the units are sold.

INTRODUCTION TO COST ACCOUNTING

The specialized branch of accounting which deals with the complexities of this flow of costs is called cost accounting. Specifically it consists of the systems and procedures used to measure and control the cost of particular products, departments, or functions. Most of the procedures exist because they contribute to one or both of the dual purposes of cost systems—cost measurement and cost control.

Cost measurement is the process of collecting information about the particular cost of doing something. For example, one of our major concerns is product cost measurement. This entails tracing costs to determine the manufactured cost of the units sold; the material, labor, and overhead attached to the completed but unsold units in finished goods inventory; and the costs assigned to the partially completed goods remaining at the end of the period in work in process. Such information is needed in total for income measurement and inventory costing, and in detail for product pricing.

Cost measurement extends beyond product costs, however. Management needs to know the cost of operating particular processes and departments, of performing particular activities, or of carrying out particular programs. These figures often are required for special analyses and decisions. For example, a company which generates its own electric power internally may be considering whether to acquire its power from the local electric company instead. Certainly, one of the relevant factors is the cost of continuing to operate its own power department. Detailed cost knowledge may also be helpful to management in making long- and short-range planning decisions.

Cost control is the process of collecting information about how individual managers have exercised their responsibilities over the cost of resources used. Control entails the assignment of responsibility for cost incurrence and extensive cost comparisons for each stage in the productive process and for each organizational unit within the firm. Costs for the current period are compared with those of past periods or with various bench marks representing what the costs are expected to be or should be. In addition, cost control includes the analysis of reasons for costs being out of line and the taking of corrective action.

In both of these major areas, various cost concepts and information may be employed. The product costs relevant to a long-run pricing decision may not be the same ones used in the pricing of a special order. The costs that are controllable by the foreman of the power department may not be identical with those that would be eliminated if the department were closed and power were purchased from the outside. In other words, cost information must be prepared in terms of specific purposes. The cost accounting system should supply the basic building blocks. Management must then analyze these basic cost figures, select those it needs, and rearrange them, in light of its particular objectives. No single cost figure is useful for all purposes. Different costs are needed for different purposes.

In this chapter and the next we take a brief look at cost accounting systems. Our purpose is to help form a bridge from financial to managerial accounting. Our interest centers on certain basic procedures of cost accumulation both for product cost measurement and for control. The detailed selection and arrangement of costs for particular management decisions is left to other courses. This chapter focuses on the measurement and control of factory overhead; Chapter Twenty looks at the Work in Process account.

INTRODUCTION TO FACTORY OVERHEAD

In Chapter Seven factory overhead (burden) is defined as including all elements of manufacturing cost except direct labor and raw material.

Items falling under the heading of factory overhead are assets used up to produce other assets and should be charged as part of the cost of the manufactured product. However, the diversity of items comprising factory overhead and their indirect association with specific units of product make the procedures for putting overhead into Work in Process more complex and less precise than those applicable to direct labor and raw material. Many elements of factory overhead can be assigned only indirectly to Work in Process. Some items, such as heat, light, and janitorial service are costs of maintaining the environment in which production takes place and cannot be specifically related to the product. Other costs, like supervision and indirect materials, although related to the making of the product, still cannot be assigned to specific units of product.

In addition to difficulty in assigning the overhead costs to work in process, businesses may experience trouble in controlling them. Factory overhead includes labor services, allocations of current expenditures (e.g., utility costs), and allocations of past expenditures (e.g., depreciation). As a consequence, nearly every available means of cost control has its place in factory overhead; no universal system of control will suffice for all the diverse burden elements. Moreover, these costs may be incurred in a number of different places by a number of different people.

Recognizing the impossibility of designing a system which will solve all the problems of factory overhead, let us turn our attention to some general procedures applicable to this area. Our eventual goals are a reasonable allocation of overhead to Work in Process and the exercise of some control over its individual elements.

CONTROL OF FACTORY OVERHEAD

The heart of factory overhead cost control lies in the assignment of managerial responsibility for the individual overhead costs and the provision of guidelines as to what those costs should be. These guidelines, in the form of budgets, are most frequently established for the various organizational units in which the manufacturing activity takes place. A necessary first step in narrowing responsibility is to determine where particular costs are incurred. In this section we look at these two aspects— the departmental distribution of costs and the departmental overhead budgets.

Departmental Distribution of Overhead

For both cost measurement and cost control, the accountant has to gather cost information by departments. It is not sufficient for him to know only the *kind* of cost being incurred—e.g., wages, supplies, material, etc. He must ascertain the *purpose* or functional classification of the cost as well. To do this necessitates the establishment of accounts for each department or function.

Cost Centers. Through study of the manufacturing process, the cost accountant identifies areas where manufacturing overhead costs are incurred. The term "cost center" is usually used to describe these areas. Typically, the cost centers correspond to actual factory departments in the firm. These become the focal points around which the manufacturing costs are collected. In designing the cost system the accountant establishes for each cost center one or more accounts in which to record applicable manufacturing costs. We use departmental cost accounts in gathering factory overhead costs in this chapter and in collecting Work in Process costs by production department in Chapter Twenty.

Responsibility Accounting. An important elaboration of the cost center concept, employed particularly to aid in cost control, is responsibility accounting. Costs are gathered and reported on the basis of the people responsible for their control. A number of responsibility centers are established. These are organizational units headed by single individuals who control the activities of each unit and the costs incurred therein. In this manner, cost collection and reporting are directly tied to the organizational structure. The person in charge of the responsibility center is held accountable only for those costs he can control. He is charged with those which he can significantly affect through his own action or which he has ultimate authority over because he can influence the people directly responsible. Responsibility accounting provides a means of appraising the performance of the individual manager in terms of the costs which he has the authority to do something about.

On this latter point rests the difference between cost centers and responsibility centers. To the former are charged all costs applicable to a particular department, whether or not the head of the department can control them. For instance, the depreciation on factory equipment in the painting department is charged to that cost center, although the foreman may exercise little influence on the type or amount of equipment purchased for use in his department. Under responsibility accounting he would not be held accountable for this depreciation charge. Practically, if departmental lines are finely enough drawn, responsibility accounting is a natural outgrowth of the cost center concept. If each department is headed by one individual and performs only a few related functions, the advantages of responsibility accounting can be gained simply by the *reporting* of the departmental costs in two categories—controllable and noncontrollable by the person responsible for the operations of that department.

Factory overhead costs then are commonly accumulated and recorded in various departmental accounts or cost centers. Pinpointing the particular areas where costs are incurred and utilized can bolster effective control. Two major types of departments exist—producing and service departments. The former are the departments which actually make the product. The latter contribute to production only indirectly, by supplying needed services to the producing departments. Examples of service departments are the power department, the factory clerical office, the maintenance department, the scheduling department, the factory cafeteria, etc.

The arrangement of the departmental overhead accounts may vary from one firm to another, but their function is the same. In many businesses the general ledger contains only one factory overhead account which is supported by a subsidiary ledger consisting of the departmental accounts. Each departmental overhead account would then have its own additional subsidiary ledger for classification of departmental costs by type. The detailed overhead costs are easily maintained in subsidiary ledgers concurrently with the recording of the overhead in summary form in the control account. For ease in illustrating entries, however, we assume that the departmental overhead accounts are in the general ledger.

Example. Assume that the Select Products Company has two producing departments—the framing shop and the machine shop—and one service department, called factory administration. During the year the following actual overhead costs are incurred:

Indirect labor	$ 16,575
Supplies	6,950
Electricity	14,600
Repairs	2,500
Supervision	18,000
Equipment depreciation	22,000
Equipment insurance	2,000
Building depreciation	24,000
	$106,625

Each overhead cost, as it is incurred during the year, is analyzed and distributed to one or more of the departmental cost centers. Some costs, called *direct costs*, can be traced directly to the proper department. For example, an analysis of labor time slips or of requisitions for supplies from the storeroom would indicate the specific department to be charged. Assume that in our example indirect labor, supervision, supplies, electricity, repairs, and equipment depreciation are all direct costs.

Other overhead costs cannot be directly traced to cost centers and have to be indirectly assigned to the departments. Examples are insurance and building depreciation. Each of these costs is distributed according to some base that represents a logical relationship between the cost and each of the various departments. For example, management of Select Products Company decides to assign building depreciation to departments on the basis of floor space and insurance according to the dollar amount of departmental investment.

In the distribution of this type of cost by department, we should employ reasonable and logical bases. This will enhance the accuracy of our functional cost analysis and eventual cost measurement of the product. However, we must bear in mind that for control purposes these arbitrary allocations should be isolated on departmental reports. In most cases, departmental supervisors can exercise little direct control over such items as depreciation and insurance.

To minimize the need for numerous general journal entries and to facilitate reporting of overhead cost information, many companies employ an overhead cost distribution sheet. One copy goes to the general accounting office to serve as the source document for one combined general journal entry to record the actual overhead costs. Other copies of the cost sheet go to various levels of management as a periodic report on actual overhead costs. The overhead cost distribution sheet for the Select Products Company is shown in Table 19–1. Although this one covers the

TABLE 19–1

Actual Overhead Cost Distribution Sheet for the Year 197—

Overhead Cost	Basis of Distribution	Total	Factory Administration	Framing Shop	Machine Shop
Indirect labor..........	Direct, from time slips	$ 16,575	$ 6,800	$ 5,750	$ 4,025
Supplies..............	Direct, from requisitions	6,950	2,200	2,950	1,800
Electricity............	Direct, meter reading	14,600	2,850	3,470	8,280
Repairs..............	Direct, from invoices	2,500	. . .	1,600	900
Supervision...........	Direct, personnel records	18,000	9,600	4,200	4,200
Equipment depreciation..	Direct, from plant ledger	22,000	. . .	8,000	14,000
Equipment insurance....	Dollars of investment	2,000	. . .	1,100	900
Building depreciation....	Floor space	24,000	3,000	12,000	9,000
		$106,625	$24,450	$39,070	$4

whole year, normally the cost distribution sheet would be prepared each month.

The summary journal entry to record and distribute both the direct and indirect costs to departmental overhead accounts would be:[1]

---

[1] For information purposes sometimes each overhead cost is debited first to a separate account. For example, the cost of factory supplies used could be recorded initially as:

```
Factory Supplies Used.....................  6,950
     Supplies Inventory....................          6,950
```

However, to be assigned to product and to be controlled, supplies usage would then have to be analyzed and the cost distributed to the various overhead cost accounts of the departments incurring it.

```
Framing  Shop—Overhead...................  39,070
Machine  Shop—Overhead...................  43,105
Factory Administration Department........  24,450
     Wages Payable........................          16,575
     Salaries Payable.....................          18,000
     Supplies Inventory...................           6,950
     Accumulated Depreciation—
        Equipment.........................          22,000
     Accounts Payable (electricity and
        repairs)..........................          17,100
     Prepaid Insurance....................           2,000
     Accumulated Depreciation—
        Building..........................          24,000
```

With this entry, the actual overhead costs are distributed among the three departments as a first step in cost control (and in cost measurement as well). There undoubtedly would be a subsidiary ledger for each department containing a record of the detailed costs by type.

Allocation of Service Department Costs. Many firms go through an additional step of redistributing to the producing departments the overhead costs recorded in the service departments. Inasmuch as the service departments provide service, the argument is made that each producing department should be charged a portion of the cost of the service department based on the amount of service received. For each service department it is necessary to select some reasonable base for allocation, reflecting the activity in the service department in its relationship to the producing departments. Some commonly used bases are floor space for a maintenance department, number of machines for a repair department, number of employees for a factory cafeteria or a factory personnel office, power used for a power department, etc.

In most instances cost control is not enhanced appreciably through the redistribution of service department costs. The persons responsible for activity in the producing departments usually have no command over costs incurred in another department. Holding producing department supervisors accountable for service department costs violates the basic tenets of cost control and responsibility accounting.[2]

It is true that for product cost measurement, service department costs should be charged to Work in Process. But, as we shall see shortly, this is accomplished through the use of predetermined overhead rates. Consequently, an after-the-fact allocation of *actual* service department costs to producing departments is usually unnecessary for either cost measurement or cost control. Some firms simply allocate a predetermined *budgeted* amount to make supervisors of producing departments aware of the total "cost" of their area. However, these allocations should be clearly

---

[2] There may be some unusual situations in which the producing department does in fact influence the costs incurred in another department, so that allocation of service department costs may aid in cost control as well as cost measurement. For example, the producing departments influence power department costs to the extent that they determine the *quantity* of power needed.

labeled noncontrollable (except in rare instances) and should not enter into the evaluation of the performance of the producing department.

Departmental Overhead Budgets

The collection of actual overhead costs by organizational units cannot stand alone and still provide assistance in cost control. Some basis of comparison is needed to judge whether actual spending is in control. In effective cost control systems the basis of comparison is the departmental budget. The budget is the numerical expression of the plan of factory operations for the coming period. Costs have to be budgeted for each individual department in line with its planned activities. Consideration must be given to past periods' cost relationships, cost trends, anticipated changes in costs and volume of activity, etc. The budget establishes in advance what the costs should be.

Table 19–2 presents the results of this budgetary process for the fram-

TABLE 19–2

Overhead Budget for Framing Shop for 197—
(planned activity: 25,000 direct labor hours)

	Budget Allowance for DLH of:			
Overhead Costs	17,500	20,000	22,500	25,000
Controllable costs:				
Variable:				
Indirect labor...............	$ 1,750	$ 2,000	$ 2,250	$ 2,500
Supplies...................	2,100	2,400	2,700	3,000
Electricity..................	2,625	3,000	3,375	3,750
Repairs....................	525	600	675	750
Total....................	$ 7,000	$ 8,000	$ 9,000	$10,000
Fixed:				
Indirect labor...............	3,000	3,000	3,000	3,000
Total controllable........	$10,000	$11,000	$12,000	$13,000
Noncontrollable costs (all fixed):				
Supervision....................	4,000	4,000	4,000	4,000
Equipment depreciation.........	8,000	8,000	8,000	8,000
Equipment insurance...........	1,000	1,000	1,000	1,000
Building depreciation...........	12,000	12,000	12,000	12,000
Total budgeted costs.............	$35,000	$36,000	$37,000	$38,000

ing shop for the year. Established at the beginning of the year, the departmental budget reflects the planned costs for the year. Achievement of the company's production goals requires that an estimated 25,000 direct labor hours be worked in the framing shop this year. The budgeted costs listed at the far right are those that should be incurred to do that level of work. Similar budgets would be prepared for the other departments.

Notice that the overhead costs are divided between those that are controllable at the departmental level and those that are not. In an actual business situation one would expect to find a more detailed budget. Our illustration lists only a sample of the overhead items that would have to be considered, but it does portray the major ideas.

Fixed and Variable Costs. One other distinction should be noted on the overhead budget. The costs have been separated into fixed and variable categories. As mentioned in Chapter Sixteen, the fixed-variable division relates to how costs behave with changes in the volume of productive activity.

Variable costs are those which increase and decrease as the volume of activity increases or decreases. The *total* dollar amount of the cost varies directly with fluctuations in volume. For example, we have assumed that electricity is variable in the framing shop. For a level of activity of 25,000 direct labor hours, electricity is budgeted at $3,750 (15 cents per hour). If this cost is variable, a 20 percent decrease in volume, to 20,000 direct labor hours, should cause approximately a 20 percent reduction in electricity cost, to $3,000. Variable costs are constant *per unit* of activity but fluctuate in total dollar amount as activity changes. The total cost equation for electricity is: $TC = \$0.15(DLH)$.

Fixed costs, on the other hand, remain unchanged irrespective of the level of productive activity. For example, depreciation, insurance, and supervision costs are not expected to change if we work more or fewer hours in the framing shop. The *total* dollar amount of the cost remains constant. The fixed cost *per unit* of activity, of course, will become progressively smaller as the volume of activity increases. This is why businesses are concerned with operating at or as close as possible to full capacity. The fixed costs will be incurred regardless of the level at which capacity is used. The larger the volume of activity, the smaller will be the per unit cost, because the same total dollar amount is spread over more volume.

The distribution between fixed and variable costs, as in Table 19–2, should be made on the basis of a detailed study of the behavior of each individual cost. In actual situations many costs are neither all variable or all fixed but are combinations thereof. Indirect labor, for instance, is a mixed or semivariable cost. Its total cost equation is: $TC = \$3,000 + 0.10(DLH)$. Often statistical correlations are made to help determine the cost-volume relationship.

Flexible Budget for Spending Control. Dividing our budgeted costs between fixed and variable allows us to adjust the initial planning budget to any desired level of activity. Management can be provided with a schedule that indicates what each cost should be at any level of activity. The type of budget shown in Table 19–2 is called a flexible budget and is used in evaluating control over spending. We can have a cost budget for each responsibility center for any level of operations.

A supervisor or foreman should only be held responsible for the amount of controllable spending budgeted for the level of activity actually worked. It would make little sense to compare the actual spending at one level of activity, say 20,000 direct labor hours, with the original budgeted amount for controllable items of $13,000 for a different level, namely 25,000 direct labor hours, and conclude that the supervisor or foreman has done a good job of controlling his costs. What is needed is a comparison between actual spending at 20,000 and what should have been spent at 20,000 hours. The flexible budget provides this meaningful control figure.

APPLICATION OF OVERHEAD TO WORK IN PROCESS

The other important step, in addition to controlling overhead costs, is assigning or allocating the overhead costs from the producing department overhead accounts to Work in Process as work is done in the producing departments. At first glance this would seem to be a relatively simple task of making a journal entry. However, there are some problems in assigning the factory overhead costs to Work in Process.

Overhead Allocation Problems

One of the primary problems is a timing dilemma. At one extreme, we cannot wait until the end of the year to assign overhead to product. Cost figures are necessary for pricing purposes during the year and for financial statements prepared at times other than the end of the year. On the other hand, it is not reasonable to assign the actual overhead costs of a short period of time to the production of that period. First, such a procedure may lead to widely fluctuating unit costs, depending on the volume of activity in the producing department. The existence of fixed overhead costs would cause the per unit product costs to be high in a month of low activity and low in a month of high-volume production. The vacillating unit costs might lead to misleading pricing decisions or exaggerated notions of efficiency and inefficiency in production operations. Second, the seasonal incurrence of certain overhead costs would make the resulting product costs unrealistic. For instance, many companies schedule their maintenance and repair work during slack production periods. It would be unreasonable to charge the major portion of the year's maintenance and repair costs that is incurred in one particular month to the small number of units produced that month. Rather, these maintenance and repair costs benefit the production activities of the whole year and should be prorated in some way to all the units produced during the year.

In addition to the timing dilemma, a second difficulty arises. Excessive or unproductive overhead costs should not be charged to Work in Process at all but should be treated as a loss. Only those overhead costs that are necessary for and contribute to production should be charged as a necessary cost of the product. Overhead costs representing waste and inefficiency should be isolated for control purposes. However, when actual overhead costs are allocated to Work in Process, no distinction is made between the productive and the unproductive elements of factory burden. Waste and inefficiency remain hidden as part of the Work in Process cost.

Use of Predetermined Overhead Rates

A solution to both of these problems is to apply overhead for the whole year to production for the whole year by means of a predetermined overhead rate. The overhead rate established for each producing department at the beginning of the year is a function of the budgeted overhead costs (including an allowance for service departments) and the budgeted level of production activity. The rate itself is expressed as so many dollars per unit of production activity.

If we are to apply overhead to Work in Process as work is done during the year in the producing departments, we need some measure of work activity in each department to serve as a base for applying the overhead. The most appropriate measure is that with which the use of overhead services in the particular department is most closely associated. At first thought, we might be tempted to use units of production as the base. Usually, however, this base is not used. Units of varying products or jobs may not be the same or represent the same amount of productive activity. Also, many overhead items are more closely related to productive input than to units of output.

Consequently, other bases (measures of work) are more common. Many firms use direct labor hours or machine hours, depending on which best reflects the relative usage of overhead and the activity in a particular department. Direct labor cost is also widely used, because the information is easily obtainable; but the results may be misleading if wage differentials or fluctuations do not in fact reflect basic differences in the utilization of overhead costs. Different bases can and in many cases should be used for different departments.

The predetermined overhead application rate is calculated by dividing budgeted overhead costs for the year by budgeted activity for the year. Accountants use the rate *during* the year to put overhead into Work in Process instead of having to wait until the total actual overhead costs are known. They also do not have to fear month-to-month fluctuations and possible distortions in product costs caused by changing volumes of production or irregular incurrence of particular overhead costs. The overhead rate is based on the total expected overhead costs for the year, and each unit of work activity throughout the year is charged at the same overhead rate.

In addition to providing an answer to the timing dilemma, the use of predetermined overhead rates also helps to isolate excessive or unproductive overhead costs. If the expected overhead costs are established after careful analysis and study of what the overhead costs should be, the rate used to apply overhead to Work in Process reflects, to a large extent, efficient use of resources. Additional overhead costs due to waste and inefficiency will not creep into Work in Process, inasmuch as they are not reflected in the application rate used during the year.

Setting the Overhead Rate

The establishment of the predetermined overhead rates begins with the detailed budgets that have been prepared for each department. However, for the purpose of cost measurement we make two modifications. First, we must include in the overhead rate the anticipated costs of both producing *and* service departments. We accomplish this by allocating the *budgeted* service department costs to the producing departments. We must also select a *single* level of activity at which to set the overhead rate. Some firms use expected sales volume or average sales volume as the budgeted activity level; others use a production-oriented concept called practical capacity.

The setting of the predetermined overhead rate for the framing shop is shown in Table 19–3.

TABLE 19–3

Overhead Planning Budget for Framing Shop for 197—

Total budgeted costs at planned level of activity (see Table 19–2)	$38,000
Allocation of budgeted costs of factory administration....	12,000
Total budgeted costs	$50,000
Budgeted activity	25,000 DLH
Predetermined overhead rate	$2 per DLH

We have assumed that the departmental budget for factory administration totals $24,000 and that it services the two producing departments—framing shop and machine shop—equally. Also we have assumed that budgeted activity, for purposes of determining the overhead rate, is set at relatively full capacity of 25,000 DLH. The rate can be separated into a variable overhead rate of $0.40 per DLH ($10,000 variable costs from Table 19–2 per 25,000 hrs.) and a fixed overhead rate of $1.60 per DLH ($40,000 per 25,000 hrs.). Similar procedures would be followed in the machine shop.[3]

---

[3] Some firms use a plantwide overhead rate instead of separate departmental rates. The resulting product cost figures may be quite unreasonable, however, particularly if the amount of overhead cost varies significantly from one department to another and products do not spend the same amount of time in the various departments.

Overhead Application

With the predetermined overhead rates for each department computed at the beginning of the year, management can charge overhead to Work in Process during the year at the same time actual overhead costs are being gathered. Assume that during 197_ the framing shop actually works 22,500 direct labor hours. The entry to apply overhead in *summary* form for the year would be:

```
Work in Process......................... 45,000
     Framing Shop—Overhead (22,500 × $2)...          45,000
```

Actually, entries would be made throughout the year, at least monthly. However, the end result of a series of overhead applications would be the same as the summary entry shown above.

After the applied overhead is posted, the producing department overhead account would appear as follows:

Framing Shop—Overhead

39,070	45,000
12,000	6,070 √
51,070	51,070
√ 6,070	

The *actual* overhead costs of $39,070 (see Table 19–1 and the journal entry to record actual costs) are recorded as debits. Also included as a debit is an allocation from the Factory Administration service department. In this case the amount is the one originally budgeted. The *applied* overhead costs are credits. The balance of $6,070 in the producing department overhead account represents the overhead variance.[4]

OVERHEAD VARIANCES

The predetermined overhead rate is designed to charge all necessary overhead, both of the producing departments and of the service departments, to Work in Process, *provided* the estimates of activity and of budgeted spending are accurate. If actual overhead cost turns out to be the same as that shown in the budget and actual activity is the same as planned activity, applied overhead will equal actual overhead. No overhead variance arises. Such a situation, even with accurate budgeting and forecasting, is rare. Usually some difference exists between the actual and the applied overhead.

---

[4] A separate departmental account called Factory Overhead Applied, rather than Factory Overhead itself, is sometimes credited during the year as overhead is applied. Then, at the end of the year, Factory Overhead Applied and Factory Overhead are closed to each other or to a variance account. In the above example the use of only one account for both the actual and the applied overhead in each department is assumed.

If a department works fewer hours than budgeted, or if actual spending (cost incurrence) is greater than budgeted spending, the overhead account has a debit balance. Actual overhead cost exceeds applied overhead; we have *underapplied* or *underabsorbed* overhead. Conversely, a department working more hours than planned or incurring fewer actual overhead costs than budgeted has a credit variance in its overhead account. Overhead has been overapplied; we have put into Work in Process more overhead than has actually been incurred.

It can be seen from the foregoing discussion that part of the total overhead variance is caused by differences in volume of activity, and part stems from over- or underspending or usage of overhead costs. Thus the overhead variance of $6,070 can be divided into two variances:

1. *Overhead Spending Variance:* Excess overhead cost not applied to Work in Process because of cost incurrence above the adjusted budget (adjusted for changes in the volume of activity).
2. *Overhead Volume Variance:* The portion of the nonvariable overhead costs not applied to product because of productive activity below the budgeted level.

Spending Variance

For this variance to have significance, the effect of the volume of activity must be taken into consideration. We would expect that actual cost incurrence would differ from that originally budgeted if the actual volume of activity differed. In our example, planned activity was 25,000 DLH for the framing shop. However, we only worked 22,500 DLH— 90 percent of capacity. Unless all overhead costs are fixed, spending at 90 percent of capacity should be lower than originally planned. As pointed out earlier, what management needs for assessing over- or underspending is a comparison between the actual spending of 22,500 hours and budgeted spending at 22,500 hours.

Making this comparison requires adjusting the original budget for 25,000 hours to one for 22,500 hours. In this context flexible budgeting becomes important as a control device. The adjusted or flexible budget allowance indicates how much should have been spent at the actual level of 22,500 hours and represents a consistent base against which the actual spending can be compared. According to Table 19–4, the $2,070 difference ($51,070 actual less $49,000 adjusted budget) measures the degree of overspending in the framing shop. These flexible budget allowances came primarily from Table 19–2.

The spending variance is often called the burden budget variance. It is perhaps more subject to immediate control at the departmental level than the volume variance. Notice that the spending variance report not only

TABLE 19-4

Comparison of Actual and Budgeted Spending for 197—
Framing Shop

Overhead Cost	Actual Costs	Flexible Budget Allowance	Spending Variance
Controllable:			
Indirect labor	$ 5,750	$ 5,250	$ 500
Supplies	2,950	2,700	250
Electricity	3,470	3,375	95
Repairs	1,600	675	925
	$13,770	$12,000	$1,770
Noncontrollable:			
Supervision	$ 4,200	$ 4,000	$ 200
Equipment depreciation	8,000	8,000	. . .
Equipment insurance	1,100	1,000	100
Building depreciation	12,000	12,000	. . .
Allocation of factory administration costs	12,000	12,000	. . .
	$37,300	$37,000	$ 300
Total	$51,070	$49,000	$2,070

shows the total amount of overspending but also isolates it by individual type of cost and by locus of responsibility. All but $300 of the $2,070 spending variance is deemed controllable at the departmental level. Indirect labor and, particularly, repairs appear to be the major items out of line.

Volume Variance

The $2,070 spending variance, however, does not account for the total amount which has not been applied to Work in Process. Even if overspending had not occurred, there would still have been a $4,000 difference between the applied overhead of $45,000 and the adjusted budget of $49,000. This difference arises because the rate used in applying overhead presumed a higher than actual level of activity. Thus, some of the nonvariable costs incurred have not been charged to Work in Process.

A simple comparative schedule shows that this is, in fact, what the volume variance represents. We are comparing the budgeted costs incurred with the cost applied to Work in Process. Any spending over the budgeted costs already has been isolated in the spending variance:

Budgeted Costs Incurred (Adjusted Budget)		Costs Applied to Work in Process	
Fixed	$40,000	$36,000	(22,500 × $1.60)
Variable	9,000	9,000	(22,500 × 0.40)
	$49,000	$45,000	(22,500 × 2.00)

Notice that the budgeted variable costs have been put into production. Whereas the lower volume of activity has resulted in less applied overhead than originally planned, the variable costs incurred have declined as well. However, with the fixed costs, the decline in volume of activity has caused only $36,000 to be applied, even though the amount incurred is still $40,000. Consequently, fixed costs have been underapplied by $4,000 because of the lower volume of activity; hence the term "volume variance."

Another way of expressing the same idea is to look upon the fixed overhead rate (FOR) of $1.60 per hour as the amount of fixed overhead per hour worked, provided that the 25,000-hour capacity is fully utilized. Since a comparison of actual hours (AH) to budgeted hours (BH) shows we have had idle hours, the fixed cost of these hours of unused capacity should not be treated as a cost of production; no units were produced during those hours. A formula for the overhead volume variance which expresses this idea is:

$$OVV = (BH - AH) \times FOR$$
$$\$4,000 = (25,000 - 22,500) \times \$1.60$$

The volume variance highlights the costs that are not being recovered because of failure to utilize capacity. The responsibility usually rests outside the production area. Either a lack of sales orders or excess capacity caused by too rapid expansion might be the cause. Although it is true that fixed costs do not increase because of idle capacity, the resources they represent are not being used to their fullest potential. The volume variance serves as a reminder to management of this fact.

Disposition of Overhead Variance

Three logical possibilities exist for the disposition of the overhead variance in the accounts. Monthly variances due to seasonal conditions should be left as balances in the overhead accounts. Because the overhead rate is in fact designed to even out seasonal fluctuations over the year, we should expect this type of variance to be canceled by the end of the year.

Overhead variances could also result from inaccurate budgeting of either costs or activity. Conditions may have changed during the year that are not reflected in the budget or in the overhead rate. In this situation the variances seem to be adjustments to an inaccurate estimate. Therefore, they should be allocated among the accounts affected by the overhead rate—namely, Work in Process, Finished Goods, and Cost of Goods Sold.[5]

---

[5] Many companies charge the total variance to Cost of Goods Sold. No great distortion arises from this procedure if the amount of the ending inventories of work in process and finished goods is small in comparison with cost of goods sold. However, logic would suggest that if the variances are interpreted as adjustments to Cost of Goods Sold, they are adjustments to inventories as well.

Thirdly, if the budget has been carefully established, representing what overhead and production activity should be under efficient operations, the variances may depict losses due to waste and idle time. Therefore, they should be closed to Income Summary. In any given situation, any of the three alternatives might explain portions of the variance. The need for a careful analysis of the overhead variance by type, department, and cause is obvious.

VARIABLE (DIRECT) COSTING

The preceding discussions about the assignment of overhead costs to units of product are founded on a concept known as *absorption costing*. All manufacturing overhead costs, with the possible exception of the spending and volume variances, are assumed to be inventoriable—that is, included in the cost of the product being manufactured. The theory behind absorption costing is that manufacturing costs, including both fixed and variable overhead, "attach" to units of product. They are product costs rather than period expenses, such as most selling and administrative costs. Therefore, they are matched against revenue when the product is sold, not when it is manufactured. The benefit received from the use of production facilities during a period initially is manufactured units, not revenue. Production facilities help produce "form utility," and the cost of producing this extra "value" is stored in inventory until released by sale.

Definition of Variable Costing

An alternative view which has attracted many supporters in the last decade or so is that of *variable costing*.[6] It is a method of recording and reporting in which only variable manufacturing costs are treated as product costs; fixed manufacturing costs are written off as period expenses as they are incurred. Variable manufacturing costs follow the flow of costs to Work in Process, then to Finished Goods, and finally to Cost of Goods Sold. But fixed manufacturing costs are shown on the income statement for the period in which they are incurred, completely unrelated to the cost of the product.

Advocates of variable costing argue that fixed manufacturing costs are costs of standing ready to produce, not costs of actually producing. Because they do not increase or decrease with production, the fixed costs are

---

[6] Historically, this concept was called *direct* costing and is still so named in much of the accounting literature. However, direct costing is a misnomer, because "direct" implies traceability, which is not necessarily the same as variability with volume. Hence, the term "variable costing" more accurately describes the concept and seems to be increasing in popularity.

deemed unrelated to actual production and hence are period costs, not product costs. Variable costs, on the other hand, are caused directly by the use of production facilities. They vary with the amount of productive activity; therefore, they are chargeable to the units produced.

Comparative Example

Let us use a simple example to contrast variable and absorption costing. Assume that the cost of a unit of product, which sells at a price of $2 per unit, is as given below.

Material........................	$0.50
Labor..........................	0.25
Variable overhead...............	0.25
Fixed overhead..................	0.50
	$1.50

The $0.50 fixed cost per unit is based on a total fixed cost per period of $1,500 and a practical capacity production of 3,000 units. The other manufacturing costs are assumed to be variable, and selling and adminis-trative costs are ignored.

The following examples present comparative income statements under absorption costing (any volume variances are written off each period against revenues) and under variable costing for each of three sets of conditions.

Produce 2,500, Sell 2,500. The company makes and sells 2,500 units during the period. The comparative income statements in Table 19–5

TABLE 19–5

	Absorp- tion Costing		Variable Costing	
Sales............	$ 5,000		$ 5,000	
Cost of goods sold...........	−3,750	(1.50 × 2,500)	−2,500	(1 × 2,500)
	$ 1,250		$ 2,500	
Fixed costs......	...		−1,500	
Volume variance..	− 250		...	
Net Income.......	$ 1,000		$ 1,000	

show the same net income for each alternative, although the format of the statements differs. The volume variance under absorption costing arises because the firm produced at less than the planned capacity of 3,000 units. Since fixed overhead was being absorbed in product at the predetermined rate of $0.50 per unit, only $1,250 (2,500 × $0.50) of the $1,500 fixed overhead is charged to goods produced and, hence, to Cost of Goods Sold. Variable costing, of course, excludes all fixed overhead from cost of goods sold but instead records it as a period expense.

Produce 3,000, Sell 2,500. In the second period, production volume exceeds sales volume. The resulting income statements and inventory position are shown in Table 19–6. No volume variance exists under ab-

TABLE 19–6

	Absorp- tion Costing		Variable Costing	
Sales...........	$ 5,000		$ 5,000	
Cost of goods sold..........	−3,750	(1.50 × 2,500)	−2,500	(1 × 2,500)
	$ 1,250		$ 2,500	
Fixed costs......	...		−1,500	
Volume variance..	...		...	
Net Income.......	$ 1,250		$ 1,000	
Ending inventory (500 units)....	$ 750	(1.50 × 500)	$ 500	(1 × 500)

sorption costing in this case, because the firm produced at full capacity. All $1,500 of fixed cost is charged to product—$1,250 to the 2,500 units sold and $250 to the ending inventory. The variable costing income statement is the same as in the first period, and the inventory is stated at variable cost only, a lower figure than under absorption costing.

Produce 2,500, Sell 3,000. In this period we assume that the firm

TABLE 19–7

	Absorp- tion Costing		Variable Costing	
Sales...........	$ 6,000		$ 6,000	
Cost of goods sold..........	−4,500	(1.50 × 3,000)	−3,000	(1 × 3,000)
	$ 1,500		$ 3,000	
Fixed costs......	...		−1,500	
Volume variance..	− 250		...	
Net Income.......	$ 1,250		$ 1,500	

depletes the 500 unit inventory built up in the preceding example by selling 500 more units than it produces. The cost of goods sold figure in Table 19–7 is the beginning inventory plus the cost of goods manufactured during the period ($750 + $3,750 for absorption costing; $500 + $2,500 for variable costing). There is a volume variance again under absorption costing, since $250 of *this* period's fixed costs were not applied to product because of the company's producing at a level of only 2,500 units.

Summary of Results. When sales volume and production volume are equal, the income under the two approaches is the same. This is true whether the firm produces and sells at capacity or less than capacity. If sales volume is less than production volume, absorption costing gives a higher net income than variable costing. Some of the fixed costs are deferred in inventory, not to be treated as an expense until the units are sold in later periods. Under variable costing, all fixed costs of the period show up as expenses that period. When sales volume exceeds production volume, variable costing shows the higher income, because under absorption costing sales are charged with all the fixed costs of this period plus some fixed costs incurred in a prior period and stored in inventory.

Evaluation of Variable Costing

Little argument exists as to the usefulness of variable costing concepts in managerial accounting. The division of costs into fixed and variable is helpful in planning, in control, and in decision making by management. The major controversy concerns its appropriateness for income measurement and inventory valuation in financial accounting.

Proponents of variable costing point out that it eliminates the "unreasonable" results that occur under absorption costing when production and sales differ. In our example, absorption costing shows an increase in net income from the first to the second period even though sales remain the same. Likewise, from period two to period three net income remains the same under absorption costing even though sales volume increases. Under variable costing income varies solely with sales volume (if there is no change in cost efficiency). When sales volume goes up, so does net income. Conversely, when sales volume declines, net income does also. Net income is not influenced by the volume of production. Therefore variable costing reports presumably are easier to interpret and more helpful to the analyst. Moreover, under variable costing management cannot manipulate periodic income by building up inventories through heavy production.

The theoretical rationale for variable costing argues that fixed costs do not benefit future periods. If there is idle capacity in the future, production for inventory now decreases only future variable costs, but future fixed costs will be incurred anyway. Therefore, only variable costs are properly deferrable to future years.

The proponents of absorption costing counter that although its results may be difficult to understand, they are not unreasonable. Both productive capacity utilization and sales generation influence reported profits. They argue that it is equally "unreasonable" for a firm to show the same net income, as is the case with variable costing, regardless of how efficiently the fixed resources are used. In our example, variable costing would show $1,500 net income whenever 3,000 units are sold, even though in one period the plant may produce at capacity and in the next period operate with idle capacity.

The theoretical rationale for absorption costing is that the firm pays for fixed capacity in order to produce goods. Therefore, the cost of the capacity used is a product cost. If management is acting as a prudent steward, presumably inventories will not be built up unless there is a valid reason (future economic benefit).

Variable costing as a practical concept of income measurement may give rise to some peculiar situations. For example, labor costs of workers paid on an hourly basis are variable and hence a product cost. Change the compensation to a salary basis or install a guaranteed annual wage plan, and the labor costs become fixed and, according to variable costing, a period cost. Is it reasonable to conclude that hourly employees create future value but salaried employees (or machines that perform the same functions) do not?

Unfortunately, existing pronouncements of generally accepted accounting principles do not resolve the controversy. The only applicable statement of the APB is that "the exclusion of all overheads from inventory costs does not constitute an accepted accounting procedure."[7] The issue is more fundamental. What precisely is an asset and how should accountants measure net income? Until these issues are resolved, the controversy will continue. Nevertheless, most companies employ some type of absorption costing system.

SUMMARY

Because cost accounting is more highly developed in the manufacturing area, we focus our discussion there. Of course, there is a need for cost measurement and cost control information in the distributive and administrative functions of the firm as well. Although manufacturing serves as our example, the field of cost accounting should not be confined to a single area. Many of the techniques we have discussed—departmental collection of costs, responsibility accounting, flexible budgets—can be applied to other areas as well.

The major portion of this chapter deals with factory overhead. For purposes of cost measurement, we want to achieve a reasonable allocation of the overhead costs to the various products as they are made. In addition we wish to establish some general procedures for controlling the overhead costs. The procedures designed to achieve these goals are

---

[7] *Accounting Research and Terminology Bulletin* (New York: AICPA, 1961), p. 29.

1. Preparing detailed overhead budgets at the beginning of the year for each factory department.
2. Determining overhead application rates for each producing department by dividing the total budgeted overhead cost for the year in each producing department by the total planned activity in that department.
3. Recording the actual factory overhead costs and distributing them to the departments in which they are incurred or utilized.
4. Applying overhead to Work in Process during the year from the producing department overhead accounts, using the predetermined overhead rates.
5. Analyzing the differences between actual and applied overhead costs into spending and volume variances.

In the last section we analyze a concept of product costing alternative to the conventional concepts employed earlier. Under variable or direct costing only the variable manufacturing costs are processed through the flow of costs in manufacturing; fixed costs are treated as period expenses. Variable costing results in lower inventory valuations and in different amounts of net income when sales and production volumes are unequal.

SUGGESTIONS FOR FURTHER READING

Ferrara, William L. "Overhead Costs and Income Measurement," *Accounting Review*, Vol. 36 (January 1961), pp. 63–70.

Ferrara, William L. "Responsibility Accounting—A Basic Control Concept," *NAA Bulletin*, Vol. 46 (September 1964), pp. 11–19.

Fess, Philip E. "The Relevant Costing Concept for Income Measurement—Can It Be Defended?" *Accounting Review*, Vol. 38 (October 1963), pp. 723–32.

Fremgen, James M. "The Direct Costing Controversy—An Identification of Issues," *Accounting Review*, Vol. 39 (January 1964), pp. 43–51.

Gordon, Myron J. "Cost Allocations and the Design of Accounting Systems for Control," *Accounting Review*, Vol. 26 (April 1951), pp. 209–20.

Lentilhon, Robert W. "Direct Costing—Either . . . Or?" *Accounting Review*, Vol. 39 (October 1964), pp. 880–83.

Sorter, George H., and Horngren, Charles T. "Asset Recognition and Economic Attributes—The Relevant Costing Approach" *Accounting Review*, Vol. 37 (July 1962), pp. 391–99.

QUESTIONS AND PROBLEMS

19-1. From the following list of overhead costs indicate those that would be considered to be fixed and those that would be variable. In addition, indicate whether the cost would be controllable or noncontrollable by the head of the department indicated. Make clear any assumptions inherent in your classifications.

1. Small tools used in a framing department.
2. Repairs on equipment in the milling department.
3. Labor costs in a material-mixing department.
4. Foreman's salary in the painting department.
5. Power costs in the machine shop, assigned on the basis of individual departmental meters.
6. The cost of the brooms used by the janitor in the factory building.
7. Lubricants used in the machine tooling department.
8. Factory rent allocated to framing department on the basis of floor space.
9. Salary of clerk in materials storeroom.
10. Fire insurance premium cost assigned to milling department on the basis of dollar value of equipment located there.
11. Supplies costs requisitioned by painting department.
12. Clean-up labor in the cutting department.
13. Salary of production manager assigned to the finishing department. Allocation is made equally to all departments.
14. Costs of blueprints and patterns used by engineering design department.
15. Glue used in basic construction department of a furniture manufacturer.

19–2. Each of the unrelated cases below presents a different set of figures relating to the flow of costs in manufacturing. Compute the missing figures.

	Case No. 1	Case No. 2	Case No. 3	Case No. 4
Raw materials used..........	$ 200	$ 670	$?	$ 4,200
Direct labor................	1,200	?	2,000	4,000
Actual overhead............	2,000	1,600	?	?
Work in process—beginning..	800	210	590	?
Finished goods—beginning....	700	?	530	1,020
Applied overhead ($1.50 per $1 of direct labor)........	?	?	?	?
Work in process—ending	650	320	550	2,870
Finished goods—ending.......	930	410	600	1,100
Cost of goods sold..........	?	3,300	6,000	14,000
Overhead variance..........	?	100 Dr.	350 Dr.	90 Cr.

19–3. Scratchubacki Manufacturing Company makes radios. The average unit costs are as follows:

Raw materials................................ $ 5.00
Direct labor................................ 6.00
Variable manufacturing overhead............. 3.50
Fixed manufacturing overhead................ 7.00
                                             $21.50

The fixed manufacturing overhead of $7 is based on normal production of 40,000 units a year and total fixed costs of $280,000. The units sell for $30 each. The only other costs are a 10 percent sales commission on each unit sold and $50,000 of fixed administrative costs a year. Production and sales data for 1971 and 1972 are given below:

	Number of Units
Inventory, January 1, 1971...............	3,000
Production in 1971......................	40,000
Sales in 1971..........................	30,000
Production in 1972......................	35,000
Sales in 1972..........................	44,000

a) Assume that actual costs in both years are average. Prepare income statements for 1971 and 1972 assuming that the company employs conventional absorption costing.

b) Prepare income statements for 1971 and 1972 assuming that the company employs the variable costing method.

19–4. The following overhead information has been gathered for the three producing departments of the Rapid Manufacturing Company:

	Department		
	A	B	C
Budgeted fixed costs..............	$36,000	$10,000	$ 6,000
Budgeted variable costs...........	$12,000	$10,000	$10,000
Budgeted machine-hours...........	16,000	....	....
Budgeted direct labor hours........	....	10,000	4,000
Actual fixed costs................	$36,000	$10,200	$ 6,000
Actual variable costs.............	$17,800	$ 9,900	$10,400
Actual machine-hours.............	15,000	....	....
Actual direct labor hours..........	....	9,500	4,000

a) Calculate the predetermined overhead rate for each department using machine-hours in A and direct labor hours in B and C as activity bases.

b) Determine the amount of overhead applied to work in process.

c) Has overhead been over- or underapplied in each of the three departments? By how much? Subdivide each departmental overhead variance into a spending variance and a volume variance.

d) Discuss how you would dispose of the overhead variances in each department.

19–5. Component X-561 is manufactured in department Z of Plusorminus Adding Machine Co. The following overhead costs are included in the departmental budget set at 50,000 direct labor hours.

Variable overhead:	
Indirect labor..........................	$ 30,000
Payroll taxes...........................	3,000
Supplies...............................	15,000
Maintenance...........................	6,000
Power.................................	4,000
Lubrication............................	1,000
Fixed overhead:	
Supervision............................	20,000
Indirect labor.........................	10,000
Telephone.............................	2,000
Insurance..............................	2,000
Depreciation...........................	9,000
Allocation of heat and light..............	6,000
	$108,000

The manager of department Z is held responsible for all variable costs plus the fixed indirect labor and telephone costs.

a) Assume that 50,000 direct labor hours is capacity. Prepare a flexible budget at 70, 80, 90, and 100 percent of capacity. The budget will be used primarily for control purposes.

b) Assume that during the period, department Z operated at a level of 42,500 direct labor hours and incurred the following actual costs:

Indirect labor (V)........	$27,000	Supervision..............	$20,000
Payroll..................	2,700	Indirect labor (F).........	10,500
Supplies.................	13,500	Telephone...............	1,800
Maintenance.............	4,500	Insurance................	2,100
Power...................	3,300	Depreciation.............	9,000
Lubrication..............	700	Allocation of heat and light..	6,300

Prepare a report comparing actual and budgeted spending that can be used to evaluate the performance of the departmental manager.

19–6. The Skullduggery Manufacturing Company operates two producing departments. The following table gives some information relevant to the question of how to set the overhead rate:

	Machining	Assembling	Total
Budgeted direct costs..............	$50,000	$20,000	$ 70,000
Budgeted allocation from service departments:			
Power.......................	15,000	5,000	20,000
Others......................	5,000	5,000	10,000
Total budgeted costs..............	$70,000	$30,000	$100,000
Budgeted activity:			
Direct labor hours..............	20,000	20,000	40,000
Machine-hours.................	10,000	....	10,000

a) Compute one overhead rate for the company as a whole using direct labor hours as a base.

b) Compute separate overhead rates for the two operating departments, using direct labor hours as a base in assembling and machine-hours in machining.

c) Assume that a particular job consisting of 30 units is worked on for 20 DLH (15MH) in machining and five DLH in assembling. Compute the *applied overhead cost per unit,* assuming the use of the rate in part (*a*), and assuming the use of the rates in part (*b*). Which do you prefer? Why?

d) How can the use of individual departmental rates aid in cost control?

19-7. D. C. Electric Motor Corporation manufactures electric motors. Although differing from each other in some ways, each motor takes approximately the same time to make. Data concerning production, sales, and fixed manufacturing costs for a five-year period are given below:

	1970	1971	1972	1973	1974
Units sold..............	7,000	9,000	12,000	12,000	10,000
Units manufactured......	8,000	10,000	15,000	12,000	8,000
Fixed overhead costs.....	$50,000	$50,000	$50,000	$50,000	$50,000

For each of the five years, determine whether the net income under variable costing would be higher or lower than the net income under absorption costing and by how much. Under absorption costing, fixed costs are charged to product assuming a normal volume of 10,000 units, and the volume variance is written off each year as an expense.

19-8. The overhead costs of Mass Production Company are applied to work in process using predetermined overhead rates. The company has three departments—factory administration, machining, and polishing. The latter two are producing departments. The predetermined overhead rates were based on the following departmental budgets:

Overhead Cost	Basis of Allocation	Machining	Polishing
Fixed costs:			
Supervision............	Direct	$10,000	$10,000
Indirect labor.........	Direct	10,000	10,000
Engineering services....	Past usage	2,000	500
Depreciation—equip....	Direct	11,000	4,000
Depreciation—bldg.....	Floor space	3,000	2,000
		$36,000	$26,500
Variable costs:			
Supplies..............	Direct	$ 4,000	$16,500
Power................	Direct	14,000	4,000
Maintenance..........	Direct	2,000	500
		$20,000	$21,000
Allocation of budgeted costs of factory administration...............		$25,000	$12,500
Total budgeted costs....................		$81,000	$60,000
Budgeted activity........................		120,000 MH	80,000 DLH
Predetermined overhead rate..............		$ 0.675/MH	$ 0. 75/DLH

Departmental foremen in the producing departments have direct control over all variable costs and over the cost of engineering services.

During the year the actual overhead costs for 100,000 machine hours in machining and for 80,000 direct labor hours in polishing amounted to $144,800, broken down as follows:

Type of Cost	Total	Factory Administration	Machining	Polishing
Supervision..............	$ 40,000	$20,000	$10,000	$10,000
Indirect labor............	25,500	5,500	9,000	11,000
Supplies.................	31,000	9,000	3,000	19,000
Engineering services.......	4,000	....	3,000	1,000
Depreciation—equip.......	18,000	3,000	11,000	4,000
Depreciation—bldg........	6,000	1,000	3,000	2,000
Power...................	17,800	....	13,000	4,800
Maintenance.............	2,500	500	1,000	1,000
	$144,800			

Based on a detailed study of the activities of the department, factory administration costs are allocated two thirds to machining and one third to polishing.

a) If a particular job requires seven hours of work in the machining department and five hours of work in the polishing department, how much overhead in total will be charged to it?

b) Compute a spending and a volume variance for each producing department.

c) Prepare a report for each department that will show a detailed breakdown of the spending variance by type of cost. The report should contain three money columns—one for actual spending, one for the flexible budget, and one for the variance. Arrange the report so that it makes clear what portion of the spending variance is the responsibility of the departmental foreman.

d) What limitation do you see in the procedure of allocating *actual* factory administration costs to the producing departments? Why are the budgeted costs of the factory administration department included in the budgets of the producing departments?

e) Referring to part (*a*), how much overhead cost would have been assigned to the job if the firm employed variable costing procedures? Why is there no volume variance under variable costing procedures?

19–9. The Marvin Corporation has two service departments and three production departments. Overhead costs are applied to work in process by the use of a predetermined rate set for each production department. The rate is compiled at the beginning of each year on the basis of budgeted activity and overhead costs. The budgeted data for a given year are as follows:

	Overhead	Activity
Service departments:		
A	$ 16,000	....
B	18,600	....
Production departments:		
1	24,000	20,000 DLH
2	25,300	20,000 DLH
3	18,700	10,000 DLH
	$102,600	

Actual overhead costs and activity are:

	Department				
	A	B	1	2	3
Actual activity	...	...	20,000DLH	20,000DLH	9,000MH
Indirect labor	$14,000	$12,000	$15,000	$18,200	$10,000
Supplies	2,000	4,000	3,000	4,600	4,000
Depreciation	...	...	4,000	3,000	1,000
Other	...	2,600	2,000	500	3,000

Service from department *A* (both budgeted and actual) is used by the production departments in the proportion 25–50–25. Department *B* services (both budgeted and actual) apply equally to all departments.

a) Compute the predetermined overhead rate for each of the production departments, being sure to include the budgeted costs of the service departments.

b) Prepare general journal entries to record (1) the actual costs incurred during the period, (2) the allocation of service department costs to the production departments, (3) the application of overhead from the production departments to work in process, and (4) the transfer of any unapplied overhead to a Factory Overhead Variance account.

c) In general terms, what factors accounted for the overhead variance in each of the production department accounts? Explain.

19–10. The Dingaling Bell Corporation manufactures bells for fire and burglar alarm systems. Its operating characteristics in 1971 and 1972 were as follows:

1. Unit production cost:

Raw material.............................	$1.00
Direct labor.............................	1.30
Variable overhead........................	0.40
Fixed overhead ($96,000 ÷ 120,000 units at normal volume)........................	0.80
Total.................................	$3.50

2. Unit selling price: $4.50.
3. Selling and administrative costs: $48,000 fixed plus 0.20 per sales dollar.
4. Production and sales data:

	1971	1972
Beginning inventory.........	....	30,000
Production.................	130,000	100,000
Sales.....................	100,000	120,000
Ending inventory...........	30,000	10,000

a) Prepare income statements for the two years under variable costing and under absorption costing. Assume any overhead not assigned to units of product is treated as an adjustment to Cost of Goods Sold.

b) Explain why the net income figures differ in each year under the two methods of costing. Illustrate with calculations where appropriate.

c) Which method do you think better reflects net income and asset values? Briefly explain why.

d) "The heart of the variable-absorption costing controversy for financial accounting lies in the definition of an asset as it applies to fixed manufacturing costs." Explain the meaning of this sentence.

19–11. The plant manager of the DMB Corporation is dissatisfied with the control reports generated by the accounting department. A condensed example for the welding department for the month of June is given below:

	Budget	Actual	Variance
Indirect labor............	$20,000	$17,300	$2,700 F
Supplies................	10,000	8,100	1,900 F
Rework time.............	4,000	3,000	1,000 F
Electricity..............	16,000	14,800	1,200 F
Foreman salaries.........	5,000	5,000	...
Depreciation............	3,000	3,000	...
Other indirect costs.......	17,000	17,200	200 U
	$75,000	$68,400	$6,600 F

The budget figure is the planning budget for the forecasted volume of activity of 50,000 direct labor hours. The actual costs were incurred at 42,500 direct labor hours of activity. The foreman is pleased with the results, but the plant manager feels that such reports do not help him evaluate the performance of his foreman.

a) Explain the source of the plant manager's dissatisfaction. Why does this report fail to present useful information for the evaluation of the foreman's performance?

b) Prepare a flexible budget at 30,000, 40,000, and 50,000 direct labor hours of activity. All costs are variable with hours worked except foreman salaries, depreciation, and other indirect costs.

c) Express the information in the flexible budgets in a formula that can be used to predict total welding department costs at any level of activity.

d) Prepare a performance report that would be more meaningful to the plant manager in this case. Has the foreman's performance been favorable?

e) The plant manager states, "Since only variable costs change with levels of production, we should report only the variable costs on our performance reports." Evaluate his suggestion.

CHAPTER TWENTY

COST ACCOUNTING
SYSTEMS IN
MANUFACTURING

COST ACCOUNTING in part consists of the procedures and systems used to keep track of the flow of costs from raw materials, direct labor, and factory overhead into Work in Process; from Work in Process into Finished Goods; and finally from Finished Goods into the expense account, Cost of Goods Sold. In this chapter the discussion relates to the detailed methods of collecting the work in process costs.

Basically, there are two kinds of systems for accumulating these costs during production. These methods are job order costing (job lot costing) and process costing. Their names imply their nature. Under job order costing the material, labor, and overhead costs are collected by job. Under process cost accounting systems, production costs are collected by individual processes or production departments. Also to be discussed in this chapter are the concept of standard cost and standard cost accounting systems, which can be used with either job order costing or process costing.

JOB ORDER COSTING

The distinguishing feature of job order costing is that the production operations are oriented around individual jobs to be done. Each of these jobs is kept physically separate in the manufacturing operations, and each job has its own identifiable costs. The material, labor, and overhead costs applicable to each job in process are entered in a separate subsidiary ledger.

Job order costing is used most where there is no standardized production system, where every job presents a different manufacturing problem involving different manufacturing operations. In specialty production, for instance, each job or product made is different from any previous one. Construction companies are excellent examples. Job order costing can also be used where a large variety of individual products are being produced in batches.

Job Cost Sheet

The job cost sheet is the central feature in this cost accounting system. On the job cost sheet are accumulated the material, labor, and applied overhead cost applicable to each particular job. As each new job is started, a job cost sheet, similar to the one in Table 20–1, is begun. There

TABLE 20–1

Job Cost Sheet

ARTICLE: QUANTITY:			DATE STARTED: DATE COMPLETED:			JOB ORDER No.___			
Raw Material			Direct Labor			Overhead Applied			
Date	Requisition No.	Amount	Date	Reference	Amount	Date	Labor-Hours	Rate	Amount
				(Can be used for employee numbers, work order numbers, department names, etc.)					
						Summary			
						Material			
						Labor			
						Overhead			
						Total			

is a separate form for each job in process. A job number identifies the particular job to which the costs entered on that form relate. Since all material, labor, and overhead costs put into Work in Process are related to some job, these costs are recorded on *some* job cost sheet. Thus the job cost sheets together form the subsidiary ledger to Work in Process. They show the detailed information (detailed by type of cost and by job) which is entered in summary form in the general ledger account.

The procedures for charging materials, labor, and overhead to Work in Process and to the job cost sheets are fairly easy to follow. As raw materials are taken from the storeroom for use in manufacturing operations, a material requisition form is filled out and signed by the person receiving the raw materials. The material requisition slip indicates not only the quantity and cost of materials being withdrawn but also the particular job on which the raw materials are going to be used. In this way, all materials taken from the storeroom must be assigned to a particular job. Periodically, these material requisition slips are summarized. Assume that they total $30,000 for the period. A general journal entry is made for the total raw material used during the particular period (day or week).

```
Work in Process.......................... 30,000
    Raw materials........................        30,000
```

Also, the individual material requisition slips are sorted by job number, and entries are made on the job sheets for the amount of materials used on each.

A similar procedure is followed for direct labor charges and factory overhead. Each direct laborer keeps a time card, on which he records the amount of time he spends on each job. These time slips are summarized and serve as the basis for the payroll. The total direct labor costs for the period (assume they amount to $60,000) are debited to Work in Process.

```
Work in Process.......................... 60,000
    Wages Payable........................        60,000
    To record total direct labor costs
    (20,000 hours @ $3).
```

If overhead is being applied on the basis of direct labor hours, entries are made for factory overhead at the same time that the entry is made for direct labor. If the predetermined overhead rate is $3.50 per hour, the amount debited to Work in Process and credited to Factory Overhead is $70,000.

```
Work in Process.......................... 70,000
    Factory Overhead.....................        70,000
    To apply overhead (20,000 × $3.50).
```

The time slips must then be sorted by job and entries made on the job cost sheets for the labor and overhead costs applicable to each. The $60,000 of direct labor cost is split according to the amount of labor time spent on each individual job. Likewise, each job is assigned overhead according to the predetermined overhead rate and the number of hours worked on that particular job. In a more complicated job order manufacturing situation, some departmentalization of labor and overhead may exist. Consequently, more than one labor rate and overhead rate would be employed. For control purposes we would probably also wish to segregate, or at least to identify, the departments involved in special reference columns on each job cost sheet.

If the accounting entries are up to date, the total of the costs entered on the job cost sheets should always equal the balance in the Work in Process control account. When the job is physically completed, we total the job cost sheet to determine the amount of cost to transfer to Finished Goods. Frequently the job cost sheet has a special column for summarizing the total costs. Assume that the sorting of material requisitions and time slips reveals that $8,000 of material and 2,000 hours of direct labor are used in completing Job No. 35. Individual entries are made in the appropriate columns on the cost sheet for Job No. 35. When it is completed, the summary section is prepared as follows:

```
                    Summary
          Material.....................  $ 8,000
          Labor.......................     6,000
          Overhead....................     7,000
                                         $21,000
```

The completed cost sheet serves as the underlying document for the general journal entry:

```
Finished Goods..........................  21,000
     Work in Process....................           21,000
     To record completion of Job No. 35.
```

The job cost sheet itself, after totaling, is moved to the finished goods file and becomes the subsidiary ledger for the Finished Goods Inventory account.

Summary of Job Order Costing

Under the job order method of collecting work in process costs, the specific costs of each job are known. Each job has a different cost, and job order costing picks up these differences. This specific cost may be helpful wherever it is necessary or desirable to keep track of separate batches or jobs—for price determination, for instance. Certainly, job order costing facilitates inventory valuation and the determination of cost of goods sold.

On the other hand, cost control under job order costing is sometimes difficult. Knowledge of the specific cost of a particular job can be helpful for control purposes only if there is some basis of comparison. Similar jobs, the cost of which could be compared from time to time, would provide one means of telling whether the costs for a particular job are excessive. As noted earlier, however, job order costing often has to be used where, in fact, the jobs are dissimilar, as in custom production. To foster control in some of these cases, a cost budget or estimate, perhaps one developed in contract bidding, could be established for each job and serve as a basis for comparison. Even here, it still may be difficult to assign responsibility for costs that are out of line, since the focal point of actual cost collection is the job, not departments or responsibility centers. Furthermore, the control information, coming after the job has been completed, may have only limited usefulness in the prevention of excessive costs on future, dissimilar jobs.

PROCESS COST ACCOUNTING

Unlike job order costing, no attempt is made under process cost accounting to assign raw material, direct labor, and overhead costs initially to individual units of product. Rather, these costs are collected by the process or production department in which they are incurred. Each production department or process, rather than a job, becomes a cost center to which are charged the material, labor and applied overhead costs incurred in that *particular department* for a *particular period of time*. Instead of one Work in Process account, under process costing there is a series of accounts, one for each process in which productive activity takes place.[1]

Process cost accounting is used by firms making a single product or a few standardized products in a continuous, assembly-line type of production activity. Both the units of product and the processing within each department are uniform. The manufacture of chemicals, steel, and cement are good examples. The manufacturing operations are divided into various departments—grinding, mixing, finishing, packaging, etc. For purposes of cost measurement, the total unit cost of the product is the sum of the average unit costs for each process.

Rather than noting the jobs on which raw materials are used or direct labor employed, the accountant using process costing needs only to note the department in which the manufacturing costs are incurred. Similarly, overhead is applied from the departmental overhead accounts to the departmental work in process accounts. Gathering costs initially by process is frequently helpful also in cost control.

Recording Costs into Process

For an example, let us take a two-process production operation. In this example, raw materials, direct labor, and applied overhead are charged to Work in Process accounts for two production departments, milling and grinding. Units completed in the milling process are transferred to the grinding process. After the goods are completed in the grinding process, they are transferred to finished goods. This is an illustration of sequential process cost accounting—the product must pass through a series of pro-

---

[1] Like so much of cost accounting, these production department Work in Process accounts may sometimes be found in the subsidiary ledger. In this case, there will be one Work in Process account serving as a control, and the detail will be broken down by departments in the subsidiary ledger.

cesses before ending up in Finished Goods. There are, of course, many
variations to the process cost accounting system, depending upon the
number of productive departments in a particular manufacturing operation and the physical flow of the products through these departments.
This simple case is sufficient to illustrate the concepts and basic entries.

Assume that during a particular month $15,000 of raw materials are
charged out from the storeroom. The material requisition forms indicate
that $10,000 of these raw materials are used in the grinding process and
$5,000 in the milling department. The journal entry to record the use of
raw materials is:

```
Work in Process—Milling.................  5,000
Work in Process—Grinding...............  10,000
    Raw Materials........................           15,000
```

The total direct labor payroll for the month is $20,000. An analysis of
the time slips of the direct laborers indicates that $10,000 of this cost is
incurred in each of the production departments. The entries to record
direct labor costs are

```
Direct Labor............................ 20,000
    Wages Payable (Cash).................           20,000
Work in Process—Milling................. 10,000
Work in Process—Grinding................ 10,000
    Direct Labor.........................           20,000
```

As labor hours are worked in the grinding and milling departments,
overhead is applied on the basis of the predetermined overhead rate set for
each department multiplied by the number of hours worked in each. Let
us assume a total applied overhead of $12,000 in the grinding department
and $7,000 in the milling department. The entries to record the application
of overhead for the month are

```
Work in Process—Milling.................  7,000
Work in Process—Grinding................ 12,000
    Overhead—Milling.....................            7,000
    Overhead—Grinding....................           12,000
```

After all the entries above have been posted, the Work in Process accounts appear as follows:

Work in Process—Milling	Work in Process—Grinding
5,000	√ 5,730
10,000	10,000
7,000	10,000
	12,000

It has been assumed that in the milling department there is no beginning
inventory but that in the grinding process there is a beginning inventory
of 2,000 units (one-quarter completed) with a total cost to date of $5,730.
The $5,730 represents the balance in the grinding account as of the end of

last month. It consists of $3,900 of costs transferred in from milling and $1,830 of costs incurred in grinding last month. The costs to complete these in-process units are included in the current period's costs.

Transferring Cost Out of the Process Accounts

Assume that the production records of physical units show that during the month 12,000 units are started in the milling process. Of these, 8,000 are completed during the month and transferred to the grinding process. The remaining 4,000 units are in the ending inventory of the milling process and are approximately three-quarters completed. The beginning inventory of the grinding process, noted earlier, is 2,000 units, approximately one-quarter completed. During the month 7,000 units are completed in the grinding process and transferred to finished goods. The ending inventory of the grinding process amounts to 3,000 units, which are approximately one-half completed.

The problem we encounter now is to obtain the *dollar amount* transferred from one process to another and from the grinding process to Finished Goods. A corollary problem is to establish the cost of the ending inventories in the Work in Process accounts. Although we know, by physical count and production records, the number of *units* that have been transferred and the number of units in the ending inventories, we have not yet established the cost to be assigned to these units. Under job order costing this task is relatively easily accomplished; we could determine the cost of the units directly by consulting the job cost sheet. Such is not the case, however, under process cost accounting. The costs have been gathered not by specific units but rather only by processes during a period of time.

The assignment of costs to units transferred and to units in the ending inventories requires the calculation of unit processing costs and an inventory cost flow assumption. The most common assumption used in process costing is average costing. We find the average unit cost by dividing the production costs for the process by the number of units of manufacturing work accomplished. The debit side of each of the Work in Process accounts summarizes the costs of doing work in that department. We now need some measure of the production work done. This measure is called *equivalent units of production* (EUP).

Calculation of EUP. In determining the amount of work done, we cannot simply use the number of units finished and transferred out. Some of the work done is not completed by the end of the period; the amount of work represented by units in the ending inventories must also be included in the calculation of work to which the costs apply. However, the amount of work (cost) represented by a partially completed unit in the ending inventory is not the same as that represented by a finished unit.

We use the EUP measure to express all of these in terms of their equivalent in fully completed units.

In the milling process there is no beginning inventory. The work done is represented by the 8,000 units completed and transferred and the 4,000 units remaining in the ending inventory. Since the latter units are only approximately three-quarters completed, the amount of work done is equivalent to that done on 3,000 fully completed units. Total equivalent production is 11,000 units (8,000 + 3,000).[2]

In the grinding process equivalent units of work include the 7,000 units transferred, for they are completely finished. The 3,000 units represented by the ending inventory are only half done. They amount to the equivalent of only 1,500 units fully completed. Total equivalent full production, then, for the grinding department work is 8,500 units.

  Costs of Units Transferred. Having determined the amount of work done, our next step is to divide the cost of doing the work by the equivalent units of production to get the *per-unit cost of goods manufactured* in each of the production departments. We can then use that figure to obtain the cost of goods transferred and to cost the ending inventory.

For example, in the milling process the total material, labor, and overhead costs incurred during the month are $22,000. In the above calculation we have determined that the amount of work done, expressed in equivalent fully completed units, is 11,000 units. Dividing the total cost by the EUP gives us a per-unit milling cost of $2. Production records indicate that 8,000 units were transferred to the grinding process during the month. Therefore, the dollar amount to be debited to Work in Process—Grinding and credited to Work in Process—Milling should be $16,000 (8,000 × $2). After the posting of this entry, the balance in the Work in Process—Milling account is $6,000, the cost of the ending inventory (4,000 × ¾ × $2).

The grinding process transfer to finished goods is a little more complicated because of the existence of a beginning inventory and the costs transferred in from the milling department. Nevertheless, the first step is to obtain a per-unit cost of grinding. The total raw material, labor, and applied overhead costs in the grinding process for the month are $33,830 ($32,000 incurred this month and $1,830 from last month residing in the beginning inventory). The EUP calculated above is 8,500 units; the result is a per-unit grinding cost of $3.98.

In addition to attaching $3.98 of costs to each of the 7,000 units that were transferred from the grinding process to finished goods, we must

---

  [2] It is possible to have equivalent units of production for materials different from those for labor and overhead. The above calculation assumes that materials are added throughout the process. In many cases the raw material cost is entered at the beginning of the process; therefore, ending inventories are fully completed as to material costs but may only be partially completed as to labor and overhead costs.

also attach their portion of the milling costs. Total milling costs transferred into the grinding process are $19,900 ($16,000 this month and $3,900 from last month residing in the beginning inventory). These costs are applicable to 10,000 units, both the 7,000 transferred and the 3,000 in the ending inventory, for the latter are complete with respect to milling department work. Consequently the milling department costs to be attached to each unit of finished product is $1.99 ($19,900 ÷ 10,000 units). The total cost of completed product is $41,790 (7,000 × $5.97 [$3.98 + $1.99]).[3]

After the entry debiting Finished Goods and crediting Work in Process —Grinding for $41,790 is posted, the grinding process account appears as:

Working in Process—Grinding

√	5,730	(2)	41,790
	10,000		
	10,000		
	12,000		
(1)	16,000		

The balance of the account is $11,940 which should be the cost of the ending inventory. This can be demonstrated by the following calculation:

Milling costs of 3,000 units in the grinding process ending inventory (3,000 × $1.99)	$ 5,970
Grinding work partially completed (3,000 × 1/2 × $3.98)	5,970
Total cost of 3,000 units in ending inventory	$11,940

Summary of Process Costing

In process costing the technique of equivalent units of production makes it possible to determine a cost per unit of work done, which is useful for both cost control and cost measurement. With this per-unit cost we can obtain the cost of units transferred from one process to another, the cost of completed units transferred to finished goods, and the cost of the ending inventories in each of the departmental work in process accounts.

Of even greater consequence, however, is the additional information that is helpful in cost control. The production process is a standardized function, and the cost per unit of work done can be compared from period to period for control purposes. Moreover, if predetermined cost estimates

---

[3] The above calculations assume that an average cost inventory flow is appropriate. The calculations of equivalent units of production, per-unit costs, and cost of goods transferred would be slightly different if other inventory methods were used. For example, under a first-in, first-out inventory flow, the beginning inventory is assumed to be transferred out first and is costed as a separate batch. Per-unit costs and equivalent units of production concern only the work done *during the current period* and are not averaged with work done in prior periods.

exist, such as standard costs, the cost per unit can be compared to that predetermined standard for an indication of whether the costs are out of line. By breaking the cost per equivalent unit into material, labor, and overhead elements, we can determine exactly *which* elements are responsible for the excessive costs. And, since the costs have been gathered by individual departments, we can more easily pinpoint *where* costs are not in control.

STANDARD COST SYSTEMS

Although comparisons of the cost of a job or process with the cost of similar jobs or processes in the past is helpful in control, the question still remains whether the costs in past periods represent efficient operations. Using the actual costs of previous periods as a basis of comparison may simply embody past inefficiencies in the yardstick used to evaluate current operating performance. A more meaningful base for comparison would be a determination of what the product, process, or function *should* cost according to a detailed study of the operations. Such a cost base is called a standard cost and serves as the salient feature in many cost accounting systems.

A *standard cost* for a product or department is a predetermined yardstick which indicates what costs should be under efficient operating conditions. In a standard cost system, work in process, finished goods, and cost of goods sold are carried at standard. The differences between the actual cost and standard cost are recognized as cost variances. Since standard costs represent what the cost should have been, the variances serve as a measure of efficiency and a means by which management can appraise performance. These variances normally are recorded formally in the accounts.

Setting Standards

Standards should be set as a result of a careful analysis of the production operations to determine what the materials, labor, and overhead ought to cost. The job of setting standards usually does not fall within the accounting function; the actual setting of standards is a function of the industrial engineering, product design, personnel, and purchasing departments. Nevertheless, the accountant should have a thorough knowledge of the problems involved in establishing them.

To obtain a standard cost we have to set a per-unit standard for two factors—quantity and price. A standard material cost, for example, consists of the quantity standard (how much raw material should be used, allowing for normal spoilage) multiplied by the price standard (what the price per unit of raw material should be in the coming period, taking into consideration efficient buying, quantity discounts, quality requirements, freight charges, etc.). A standard bill of materials is prepared containing the physical quantity of each type of raw material that should be used to manufacture a unit of product. These standard quantities are combined with standard prices set for the coming period to determine the total raw material cost per unit, which appears on the standard cost card.

The same elements are involved in the determination of standard labor cost. Management must decide how many labor hours (quantity of time standard) are necessary to produce the product efficiently, considering normal downtime, speed of equipment, training of employees, etc. For the list of operating procedures involved in making the product, a standard time is set on the basis of time and motion studies, past performance, or test runs. The labor price or wage rate standard reflects job descriptions, union contracts, etc. and indicates what the labor cost per hour should be for the coming period. The quantity standards, expressed in hours per unit, are multiplied by the standard wage rates to yield the total standard labor cost per unit of product. The standard cost of factory overhead is determined by multiplication of the predetermined overhead rate (established by a budget of cost and activity for the coming year, as described in Chapter Nineteen) by the standard labor time allowed for the particular product or function.

The process of setting standards is not simple. Companies devote much time and effort to analyzing operations to determine what the *necessary* costs of production should be. Often the standards are tested over a number of periods before being introduced into the accounts. Moreover, they should continually be checked and updated, if necessary, so that they reflect attainable goals of efficiency.

Advantages of Using Standard Cost Systems

The primary uses and advantage of a good standard cost system lie in the control area. Standards provide a carefully determined measure of efficiency that management can use as a basis for evaluating actual performance. Differences between the actual and the standard for each cost element, when isolated in a special variance account, focus managerial attention on those costs that are out of line. The variance accounts signal to management areas where actual performance may not be in accordance with preestablished objectives as reflected in the standard. Thus they call management's attention to areas needing further investigation. Focusing on those items that appear abnormal is known as the *principle of exceptions*.

Standards can also serve as a communication and motivation device. The existence of a standard for each cost element at each stage of the productive process conveys to those responsible for implementing the production plans exactly what is expected of them. Moreover, if the standard cost system is carefully developed and properly administered, it may motivate employees toward good performance. If employees feel that standards are attainable, they may sense the importance of meeting them. The standard then becomes a personal as well as a company goal. The chances of this happening are greater when employees participate in the establishment of the standard.

In addition to its use in cost control, a properly established standard cost system aids in cost measurement. If standards are set at what the costs should be, then any excess costs are not really necessary costs of production but rather an unnecessary usage of assets—a loss. Under a standard cost system the product is charged only with the truly necessary costs of production, and the variations from standard are reported separately. The general ledger accounts carried at standard do not include the costs of inefficiencies and waste. As a result, standard cost systems are sometimes easier and cheaper to operate than actual cost systems, because transfers and inventory balances are costed at the predetermined standards.

Illustration

Let us organize the rest of our discussion around a specific example. Assume the following facts. The company manufactures one product in a single production department. The following standard cost card is developed from a detailed study of the operations:

STANDARD COST PER WIDGET

Material: 2 pounds @ $3.50.................	$ 7
Labor: 5 hours @ $3.......................	15
Overhead:	
Variable: 5 hours @ $2....................	10
Fixed: 5 hours @ $1.....................	5
	$37

Total *fixed* overhead is budgeted at $20,000; budgeted activity is 20,000 hours or 4,000 units (20,000 hours divided by five standard hours per unit).

Events during the period are:

1. Raw material purchases: 10,000 pounds at $3.60.
2. Raw material used: 9,000 pounds.
3. Direct labor cost incurred: 15,500 hours at $3.25.
4. Actual overhead costs: $52,300.
5. Beginning inventory: none.
6. Units transferred to finished goods: 2,000 units.

7. Ending inventory: 2,000 units, complete as to material, half complete as to labor and overhead.

Entries. The following journal entries record the basic transactions, including isolation of the standard cost variances in separate accounts:

1. Raw Materials.......................... 35,000
   Material Price Variance............... 1,000
     Accounts Payable..................   36,000
     To record purchase of 10,000 pounds
     of raw material at an actual price
     of $3.60 per pound. Inventory re-
     corded at standard cost of $3.50
     per pound. Variance of $0.10 per
     pound.

2. Work in Process....................... 28,000
   Material Quantity Variance............ 3,500
     Raw Materials.....................   31,500
     To record the standard cost of raw
     materials used in production (4,000
     EUP × $7) and to isolate cost
     of excess quantity used (1,000 lbs.
     × $3.50).

3. Direct Labor.......................... 50,375
     Wages Payable.....................   50,375
     To record the direct labor payroll
     (15,500 hours × $3.25).

4. Work in Process....................... 45,000
   Labor Wage Variance................... 3,875
   Labor Quantity Variance............... 1,500
     Direct Labor......................   50,375
     To charge the standard labor cost
     used in production (3,000 EUP ×
     $15) and to isolate the excess
     labor cost caused by above standard
     wage rates (15,500 × $0.25) and by
     inefficient use of labor hours (500
     × $3).

5. Factory Overhead...................... 52,300
     Credits to Various Accounts.......   52,300
     To record in summary form the in-
     currence of actual overhead costs.

6. Work in Process....................... 45,000
   Factory Overhead Variance............. 7,300
     Factory Overhead..................   52,300
     To apply the standard overhead cost
     (3,000 EUP × $15) to produc-
     tion for the period and to isolate
     the total overhead variance.

7. Finished Goods........................ 74,000
     Work in Process...................   74,000
     To transfer the standard cost of the
     units completed to finished goods
     (2,000 × $37).

After these entries have been posted to the Work in Process account, it shows a balance of $44,000. This represents the standard cost of the 2,000 partially completed units in the ending inventory.

Material: 2,000 @ $7...................... $14,000
Labor: 2,000 × 1/2 @ $15................. 15,000
Overhead: 2,000 × 1/2 @ $15.............. 15,000
                                          $44,000

In the above entries the variances are isolated generally when costs are put into production. Work in Process is debited and credited at standard cost.[4] Any differences between actual and standard costs are screened out before they get to Work in Process. The next section offers more detailed discussion of these variances, including a subdivision of the total factory overhead variance.

Analysis of Variances

Formulas for the calculation of material, labor, and overhead variances follow quite easily from an understanding of their meanings. They are presented in this section, in both words and symbols, along with a brief discussion of possible causes of the variances.

Material Price Variance. This variance measures the additional cost incurred because too high a price has been paid for raw materials.

MPV = Actual price per unit of raw material (AP) less standard price per unit (SP) gives the excess price per unit. This excess price times the number of actual units of raw material (AQ) gives the total price variance

= $(AP - SP) \times AQ$

= $(\$3.60 - \$3.50) \times 10,000 = \$1,000$

Notice that we have isolated the price variance at the time the raw material is purchased. Raw Material is debited at standard rather than actual prices. An alternative procedure is to compute the price variance on the actual quantity of raw material *used*. Theoretical, managerial, and practical advantages result from the former practice, and most companies using standard cost systems follow this alternative. Conceptually, the price variance is a function of purchasing rather than of use, so if the price standard is accurate, then the excessive price paid is a loss at the time of purchase, much like a lost discount. From a managerial viewpoint, the sooner a variance is known the faster management can take corrective

---

[4] The particular standard cost system illustrated is only one of a number of alternative systems that can be found in practice. Usually these systems differ in the point at which the accounts change from actual costs to standard costs. For example, Work in Process may be debited with actual costs and credited at standard costs. The full standard costs enter the ledger accounts when completed units are transferred to finished goods. Another common alternative is to debit Work in Process at *standard prices* times *actual quantities*. However, we need not be concerned with the detailed entries in these systems, since their general purposes and procedures are the same.

action if necessary. Use of the alternative method may delay the reporting of the variance until a subsequent period. Finally, the simplification introduced through the use of this procedure represents a strong case for its adoption solely on practical grounds. With inventories at standard prices, all subsidiary records for individual raw materials can be kept in terms of quantities only. Costing the inflow and outflow of raw materials is thereby greatly facilitated. Through the use of standard prices, clerical calculations are simplified, and the possibility of error is reduced. Moreover, assumptions as to inventory flow are unnecessary, inasmuch as any unit used in work in process is charged at the standard price.

The material price variance may be caused by fluctuations in the market price (seasonal or permanent), special handling or freight charges arising from purchasing in uneconomical order quantities or on rush orders, or excessive prices paid because of poor selection of suppliers or acquisition of the wrong grade of raw material. Assigning responsibility and taking any corrective action depend to a large extent on a more detailed analysis of cause.

Material Quantity Variance.   The formula is given below for calculating the additional cost because more raw material has been used than the standard allows for:

MQV = Actual quantity of raw material used (AQ) less standard quantity (SQ) gives the total excess quantity. This excess multiplied by the *standard price* (SP) determines the total dollar amount of the quantity variance

= $(AQ - SQ) \times SP$

= $(9,000 - 8,000) \times \$3.50 = \$3,500$

The quantity variance is converted to dollar amounts through multiplication by the standard price. Usually the production departments, which shoulder major responsibility for the usage of raw material, do not influence the price paid. Consequently, a better measure of their performance for control purposes is attained if no fluctuations in price influence the quantity variance.

A number of possible reasons may exist for the overusage of raw material. Included among the possible causes might be excessive spoilage due to defective raw materials, inefficient processing, or poor inspection; loss or destruction of raw materials because of unskilled workers, lack of proper tools and equipment, improper specifications, etc.; or carelessness in handling scrap. Insofar as possible, management should determine which of these many factors is at fault. Sometimes the causes may be indicated on a control report, but in most cases determining why the material quantity variance has arisen involves a careful study of the entire process or department.

Labor Wage (Rate) Variance.   Formulas similar to those for raw material are applicable to labor also. The labor wage or rate variance measures the additional cost caused by an excess wage paid for particular labor operations:

LWV = Actual wage rate paid per hour (AW) less standard wage rate per hour (SW) gives the excess wage per hour. This multiplied by the actual hours (AH) worked gives the total wage rate variance

$$= (AW - SW) \times AH$$
$$= (\$3.25 - \$3) \times 15,500 = \$3,875$$

The wage variance may result from unplanned wage increases or from overtime premiums not originally anticipated. Another common cause of labor wage variances is the use of higher or lower grades of labor than those specifically considered when the standard was established.

Labor Quantity Variance. This variance often is called by other names, such as labor time, labor efficiency, or labor usage variance. It measures the additional cost of the excess labor hours used.

LQV = Actual hours of labor time (AH) less standard hours allowed for the work done (SH) gives the excess labor time. Multiplying by the standard wage rate (SW) results in the total dollar amount of the quantity variance

$$= (AH - SH) \times SW$$
$$= (15,500 - 15,000) \times \$3 = \$1,500$$

Standard hours (SH) is an after-the-fact calculation indicating the amount of time that should have been employed in relation to the amount of work accomplished.[5] It is computed by multiplication of the predetermined per-unit standard by the equivalent units of production, which measures the work done. In this example the 3,000 equivalent units of production times five hours per unit gives the 15,000 standard hours allowed.

Excessive usage of labor time relative to the standard may be caused by a number of different factors. Some of the more common reasons may be indicated on the labor time summary sheets used in preparing the payroll. These reasons might include extra time spent on partially spoiled units from this or other departments (rework time) or time spent on nonstandard operations. Delay and idle time caused by poor scheduling, machine breakdown, or long setup periods would also show up as part of the labor quantity variance. Or poor performance by the employees themselves might be at the root of the problem. Below-standard performance, in turn, may be caused by a number of factors—inadequate training due to high labor turnover, lack of qualified foremen to supervise, etc. In each of these possibilities the persons responsible and the corrective action necessary may be very different. If the labor time variance is material, operating management must ferret out the specific cause.

---

[5] Standard hours are also referred to as "allowed" or "earned" hours.

Overhead Variance Analysis. The total overhead variance of $7,300 can be subdivided into a spending, a volume, and an efficiency variance. The first two have been discussed in Chapter Nineteen. The adoption of a complete standard cost system introduces the third factor of efficiency.

Recall that the spending variance measures the excess overhead costs caused by more costs being incurred than were budgeted for the actual number of hours worked (15,500). It arises out of a comparison of actual costs with the flexible budget for the actual hours. For our example it would be $1,300:

Actual cost..................................		$52,300
Less: Flexible budget for 15,500 hours:		
Fixed..................................	$20,000	
Variable (15,500 @ $2)....................	31,000	51,000
		$ 1,300

Of course the detailed departmental budgets would indicate those individual items on which overspending has occurred.

One modification needs to be made to the overhead volume variance (*OVV*) formula presented in Chapter Nineteen. There we saw that because actual activity did not reach the budgeted level used in establishing the predetermined overhead rate, some fixed overhead was not absorbed into product cost. Under a full standard cost system, overhead is applied to product on the basis of standard hours (*SH*) rather than actual hours. Consequently, if productive activity as measured by standard activity (the hours it *should have taken* for the amount of work done) is not at the same level as that originally budgeted (budgeted hours, *BH*), the fixed overhead costs incurred will exceed the fixed overhead costs assigned to units of product. In our example the fixed overhead rate (*FOR*) of $1 per hour is premised on the assumption that activity will be 20,000 direct labor hours or 4,000 units. Since the 3,000 EUP should have taken only 15,000 standard hours, fixed overhead of $5,000 applicable to 5,000 hours (20,000 − 15,000) remains as a volume variance. The formula given in the last chapter becomes:[6]

$$OVV = (BH - SH) \times FOR$$

The overhead efficiency variance reflects the efficiency with which actual hours worked are converted into units of product. The actual hours (*AH*) represent the input; standard hours allowed for work done

---

[6] There are actually two reasons for the unabsorbed fixed costs. First, the company did not put in the number of hours originally budgeted (20,000 BH − 15,500 AH), and second, some of the hours actually worked did not result in effective production (15,500 AH − 15,000 SH). Some analysts separate these two aspects. More common, however, is the treatment here, combining them into a single variance concerned with unabsorbed nonvariable costs. The fixed costs, of course, have not increased as a result of idle hours or wasted hours. They simply have not been absorbed as product costs.

measure output. The difference between input and output multiplied by the variable overhead rate (*VOR*) gives the additional dollar cost associated with time inefficiently spent. The overhead efficiency variance measures the excess *burden* cost incurred because it takes more time to make the product than the standard allows for. The formula is similar to that for the labor quantity variance, except that the variable overhead rate is used to convert to dollar amounts:[7]

$$
\begin{aligned}
OEV &= (AH - SH) \times VOR \\
&= (15{,}500 - 15{,}000) \times \$2 \\
&= 500 \text{ inefficient hours} \times \$2 \\
&= \$1{,}000
\end{aligned}
$$

The causes of the burden efficiency variance generally are the same as those listed for the labor quantity variance. The efficiency here refers to labor use. Had labor been used more efficiently, variable overhead costs could have been saved. The efficiency variance shows additional costs incurred for which no productive benefit has been received. Sometimes the overhead efficiency variance is combined with the spending variance in the evaluation of supervisors' performance.

The ultimate disposition in the accounts of any variances from standard costs theoretically should depend on the results of the detailed analysis. Generally, the same comments contained in Chapter Nineteen concerning over- or underapplied overhead befit all variances. The important point is that different variances can be handled in different ways, depending on the validity of the standard and the reasons for their incurrence. If the variance reflects seasonal conditions, it should be deferred. Such might be the case with a material price variance or part of the overhead spending variance.

If the standards are not accurate or are used only as rough estimates, the variances could be viewed as adjustments to inaccurate estimates. The logical treatment then would be to allocate the variances to the accounts affected by the inaccurate standards—Work in Process, Finished Goods, and Cost of Goods Sold. Material price standards, for example, may represent only a general estimate used for convenience and as a base for measuring price trends.

If, on the other hand, the standards are carefully set and frequently revised, the variances should be charged directly to Income Summary. Under these circumstances the standard is viewed as the "true" cost, and variances are looked upon as losses caused by waste, inefficiency, or idle time. Quantity variances often fall in this category.

---

[7] An alternative way to calculate the overhead efficiency variance is to compare the flexible overhead budget for the actual hours worked (input) with the flexible overhead budget for the equivalent units produced (output).

SUMMARY

This chapter focuses on a very important stage in the flow of costs, the Work in Process account. We are concerned with recording the material, labor, and applied overhead costs applicable to production in a manner that would aid both product cost measurement and cost control.

The two primary cost systems are job order and process. Often the differences between them show up only in the manner in which the detailed information is kept in the subsidiary ledgers. The former views work in process as a series of individual jobs on which work is being done. Consequently, the cost accounting system is job-centered. The detailed information is kept in a subsidiary ledger containing the individual job costs sheets. Process costing, on the other hand, views work in process as a series of production operations or departments. Hence, these become the focal point for cost collection and the detailed information is recorded in departmental Work in Process accounts.

Standard cost systems represent a further elaboration to aid in cost control. They help to highlight the areas that need attention. Through a systematic comparison of actual costs of work done with predetermined standard costs of what the work done should cost, the standard cost system isolates the differences in variance accounts. These differences, if significant, can be analyzed further by cause and responsibility. The seven common standard cost variances—material price variance, material quantity variance, labor rate variance, labor quantity variance, overhead spending variance, overhead efficiency variance, and overhead volume variance—provide a starting point.

Admittedly, we have only scratched the surface of cost accounting. It is for other courses in managerial and cost accounting to explore in detail the systems of collecting specialized managerial information, the procedures for establishing standards, the impact of control systems on behavior, and alternative methods of computing and interpreting variances. A knowledge of the topics in Chapters Nineteen and Twenty should equip the student with some of the basic concepts, tools, and terms he will run across. A bridge from financial to managerial accounting has been constructed.

SUGGESTIONS FOR FURTHER READING

Copeland, Ben R. "Analyzing Burden Variance for Profit Planning and Control," *Management Services*, Vol. 2 (January–February 1965), pp. 34–41.

Solomons, David. "Standard Costing Needs Better Variances," *NAA Bulletin*, Vol. 43 (December 1961), pp. 29–39.

Zannetos, Zenon S. "On the Mathematics of Variance Analysis," *Accounting Review*, Vol. 38 (July 1963), pp. 528–33.

QUESTIONS AND PROBLEMS

20–1. The Incredible Gadget Corporation manufactured a single product.* Its operations were a continuing process carried on in two departments, the machining department and the assembly department. Materials were added to the product in each department without increasing the number of units produced.

In the month of May 1972, the records showed that 75,000 units were put in production in the machining department. Of these units, 60,000 were completed and transferred to assembly and finishing, and 15,000 were left in process, with all materials applied but with only one third of the required labor and overhead.

In the assembly department, 50,000 units were completed and transferred to the finished-stock room during the month. On May 31, 9,000 units were in process, 1,000 units having been destroyed in production with no scrap value. All required materials had been applied to the 9,000 units and two thirds of the labor and overhead, but only one half of the prescribed material and labor and overhead had been applied to the 1,000 units lost in process.

There was no work in process in either department at the first of the month. Lost units should be treated as an abnormal loss. Cost records showed the following charges during the month:

	Materials	Labor	Overhead
Machining department........	$120,000	$ 87,100	$39,000
Assembly department.........	41,650	101,700	56,810

a) What is the machining cost per unit of finished product?
b) What is the assembling cost per unit of finished product?
c) What was the amount debited to the Loss on Spoilage account?
d) Make the journal entries to record the transfer of goods from the machining department to the assembling department, and from the assembling department to finished goods.

20–2. The Flawful Foundry uses a job-order cost system. The following data pertain to the month of January, 1972:

Total overhead costs for the month are $2,000, distributed as follows: production department X, $1,020; production department Y, $680; and service department Z, $300 ($150 of material and $150 of labor).

Service department Z costs are allocated as follows: two thirds to production department X and one third to production department Y.

Overhead is to be applied to job orders using the following annual predetermined application rates: production department X, $1.20 per direct labor hour; production department Y, $1.50 per direct labor hour. Balances in the overhead accounts of the producing depart-

---

* Problem adapted from the AICPA November 1956 examination.

ments, after the application of overhead, are closed to an expense account, Net Overhead Variance.

Jobs No. 1207 and No. 1208 are in process as of January 1. During the month the following costs are incurred:

Job No.	Direct Material		Direct Labor Cost		Direct Labor Hours	
	X	Y	X	Y	X	Y
1207..........	$ 125	$ 75	$ 100	$ 50	50	30
1208..........	200	100	300	150	150	80
101..........	250	150	400	200	200	100
102..........	300	200	500	300	250	160
103..........	400	200	600	300	300	160
	$1,275	$725	$1,900	$1,000	950	530

Records show that jobs No. 1207, No. 101, and No. 102 are completed in January. Jobs No. 1207 and No. 102 are delivered to customers in January, and job No. 101 is still on hand.

a) Copy and complete the job-order production record (a summarization of the individual job cost sheets):

Job No.	Jobs in Process, 1-1-72	Direct Material	Direct Labor	Applied Overhead	Total Cost of Completed Jobs	Jobs in Process, 1-31-72
1207.......	525					
1208.......	400					
101.......						
102.......						
103.......						

b) Make journal entries to record in summary form the transactions during January. Use only the following accounts:

Direct Material Inventory (assume that purchases have been recorded)
Work in Process
Finished Goods
Cost of Goods Sold
Wages Payable

Overhead—Department X
Overhead—Department Y
Overhead—Department Z
Net Overhead Variance
Miscellaneous Credits

c) What modifications can you suggest in the job-order production record (and job cost sheets) to make them more useful for control?

20–3. The Buckaneer Company manufactures machinery. The standard cost card for a small machine is as follows:

Materials: 200 pounds @ $1................... $200
Direct labor: 40 direct labor @ $4.............. 160
Overhead: 75% of direct labor cost............ 120
$480

The overhead rate for the period was established based on the following estimates:

Fixed costs................. $ 40,000
Variable costs............... 80,000
Total..................... $120,000

Direct labor cost............ $160,000

Data applicable to the period include:

Materials used........................ 162,000 pounds
Material price......................... $0.95 per pound
Labor hours worked................... 33,000 hours
Labor wage rate...................... $4.10 per hour
Actual variable overhead............... $65,600
Actual fixed overhead................. $40,300
Machines produced.................... 800

a) Calculate price and quantity variances for material and labor.

b) Determine the total overhead variance and analyze it into a spending, efficiency, and a volume variance.

c) What potential defects do you see in your analysis in part (*b*) stemming from the choice of activity base for setting the predetermined overhead rate?

20–4. The Linbar Company operates a two-process factory. The first process is cutting, and the second is assembling. On January 1, the balances of these two accounts are as follows:

Cutting Process	Assembling Process
5,000	10,500

The cutting process balance represents 1,000 units (half completed as to all cost elements). The $5,000 cost consists of $4,000 material and $1,000 labor and overhead. The company uses average cost in costing transfers from this department.

The Assembling Process account represents 1,000 units (completed as to material cost, half completed as to labor and overhead). The $10,500 opening balance consists of $10,000 of costs transferred in from the Cutting Process account and $500 of labor and overhead. The company uses the Fifo inventory method in getting transfers out from this department. During the month of January the following transactions took place:

1. Raw materials are used in the cutting department in the amount of $8,000. No separate raw materials are used in the assembly process. (Assume the company had raw materials on hand.)
2. Direct labor costs for the month:

	Department	
	Cutting	*Assembling*
Hours.................	150	100
Cost.................	$700	$500

(Assume labor cost has already been recorded in a direct labor account)

3. Factory Overhead is applied from Cutting—Overhead to Work in Process at the rate of $8 per direct labor hour and from Assembling—Overhead to Work in Process at a rate of $7 per direct labor hour. (Assume that the actual overhead has already been recorded and allocated to the producing departments.)
4. During January 1,000 units were started in the cutting process; 1,500 units were completed and transferred to assembling process. There are 500 units left in the Cutting Process (one fifth completed).
5. Two thousand units were completed in assembling process and transferred to finished goods. There are 300 units left in the assembling process (completed as to material cost, two fifths completed as to labor and overhead.) Two hundred units were completed but failed to pass inspection. These are treated as an abnormal loss.

Prepare general *ledger* entries to record the incurrence of costs during the period and the transfer of goods between departments and out of the assembling process. Show supporting calculations.

20–5. The I.M. Adope Company uses a process cost system with standard costs in keeping records of the manufacture of its product. The following is the standard cost card for the product:

Material: 3 pounds @ $1.................	$3.00	
Labor: 2 hours @ $2.....................	4.00	
Overhead:		
Variable: 2 hours @ $0.30..............	0.60	
Fixed: 2 hours @ $0.20................	0.40	
	$8.00	

The budgeted overhead is $10,000 ($6,000 variable and $4,000 fixed) at a budgeted activity level of 20,000 hours. Data for the month of April include:

1. Purchases of raw materials, 32,000 pounds @ $1.10.
2. Raw materials used, 28,500 pounds.
3. Actual labor incurred, 19,950 hours @ $2.20.
4. Actual overhead costs, $10,380.
5. Unit production summary:

```
Beginning inventory...............................    0
Units started and completed........................ 9,600
Units in ending inventory (complete
    as to material; one third com-
    plete as to labor and overhead)................  600
```

6. Sales, 6,000 units @ $10 per unit.
7. Selling and general expenses, $20,000.

    a) Set up the following ledger (T) accounts:

Raw Materials	Accounts Payable and Other Credits
Work in Process	Accrued Payroll
Overhead	Cost of Goods Sold
Finished Goods	Accounts Receivable
Material Variance	Sales
Labor Variance	Selling and General Expense
Overhead Variance	

    b) Using key letters to identify transactions, record the entries for the month in the ledger accounts. Assume that the company keeps its Raw Material Inventory at actual cost and debits Work in Process at standard costs.

    c) Prepare an income statement for the month of April. Assume the variances are to be closed out each month.

    d) Prepare a supplementary report to management in which the variances are analyzed further by major causal factors (price, quantity, volume, etc.).

20–6. On January 1, 1972 the general ledger trial balance of the Maximillian Press Company stood as follows:

	Dr.	Cr.
Cash in bank...................	$304,000	
Accounts receivable............	23,000	
Materials and supplies..........	38,000	
Prepaid insurance..............	3,000	
Building......................	200,000	
Factory equipment..............	100,000	
Accumulated depreciation.......		$118,000
Accounts payable...............		64,000
Wages payable.................		8,000
Capital stock..................		400,000
Retained earnings..............		78,000
	$668,000	$668,000

During the year the following transactions, given in summary form below, occurred:

1. Purchases of materials and supplies, on account, $160,000.

2. Wages earned: direct labor, $200,000; indirect labor, $50,000. The direct labor costs, as indicated by time slips, were incurred as follows:

Job No.	Dept.1	Dept. 2
30...................	.....	$ 25,000
31...................	$25,000	20,000
32...................	42,000	35,000
33................	23,000	30,000
	$90,000	$110,000

3. Wage payments in cash, $228,000.
4. Materials used, $150,000. An analysis of material requisitions indicated the following breakdown by job:

Job No.	Materials Used
30................	$ 42,000
31...............	34,000
32...............	48,000
33...............	26,000
	$150,000

5. Supplies used, $18,000.
6. Insurance expired, $2,000; property taxes accrued, $5,000; building depreciation, $4,000. All of these costs were assignable 60 percent to manufacturing, 10 percent to selling, and 20 percent to general administration.
7. The factory equipment depreciation rate was 10 percent per year.
8. Factory equipment repairs, paid in cash, $1,800.
9. The factory overhead costs recorded in Factory Overhead were transferred to the two departmental overhead accounts on the following bases:

	Dept.1	Dept. 2
Indirect labor.............................	$25,200	$24,800
Supplies.....................................	$10,200	$ 7,800
Insurance, taxes, and depreciation..............	50%	50%
Repairs......................................	$ 600	$ 1,200

10. Factory overhead was applied to Work in Process using a predetermined rate based on direct labor costs. The budgeted overhead costs of departments 1 and 2 for 1972 were $45,000 and $33,000, respectively. The budgeted direct labor costs were $100,000 in department 1 and $110,000 in department 2.
11. Salaries, paid in cash, during 1972 were: selling $16,000; general administration, $26,000.
12. During the year, jobs No. 30, No. 31, and No. 32 were finished.

Jobs No. 30 and No. 31 were sold to customers, on account, for $190,000.

a) Open general ledger (T) accounts for the items listed in the trial balance plus the following:

Work in Process	Sales
Finished Goods	Cost of Goods Sold
Factory Overhead	Selling Expenses
Department 1 Overhead	Administrative Expenses
Department 2 Overhead	Taxes Payable

b) Set up separate job cost sheets for jobs No. 30, No. 31, No. 32, and No. 33 to record the charges to individual jobs. Use the following headings for the job cost sheet: Material Cost, Department 1 Labor Cost, Department 2 Labor Cost, Department 1 Overhead Cost, Department 2 Overhead Cost, Total.

c) Record the summary transactions of the problem, including entries on the job cost sheets. (You may assume that subsidiary ledgers for each department were also being kept by someone else to record the detailed information concerning factory overhead.)

20–7. The following variances are isolated at the end of April:

1. A favorable overhead volume variance.
2. An unfavorable material price variance caused by excessive freight charges on a rush order for raw material which the production department had forgotten to request.
3. An unfavorable material quantity variance caused by substituting a lower quality (and cheaper) raw material.
4. An unfavorable labor quantity variance because of a scheduling delay in a preceding department.
5. A favorable labor wage rate variance caused by using lower rated operators on certain tasks in the department.
6. An unfavorable labor quantity variance because of time spent re-working some units that had not been correctly or completely done in a preceding department.
7. A favorable overhead spending variance due to very loose budgeting procedures.

Asume that all of these variances are material in amount. Explain the managerial implications of each—what action should be taken, on whom the responsibility for the variance rests, etc. Also, indicate how you would dispose of the variance in the accounting records.

20–8. The accounting department of Luslerun Corporation prepared the following report concerning the operations of the Finishing Department. A copy of the report was sent to the foreman of the Finishing Department and to the Production Superintendent for their use in controlling operations and evaluating performance.

Finishing Production Cost Report for the Month of March, 1972

	Budgeted Cost	Actual Cost	Over or (Under)
Raw materials.................	$10,000	$ 9,800	$(200)
Direct labor....................	20,000	18,000	(2,000)
Variable overhead:			
Supplies......................	1,000	900	(100)
Power.......................	1,800	1,500	(300)
Lubrication..................	200	200	....
Fixed overhead:			
Indirect labor...............	4,000	4,300	300
Depreciation.................	1,000	1,000	....
	$38,000	$35,700	$(2,300)

Actual hours worked: 4,500
Units produced: 18,000

You discover that the budgeted cost figures used in the report were based on a plan to produce 20,000 units, which normally should take 5,000 hours of labor time. Overhead is applied to Work in Process on the basis of labor time.

a) Explain the deficiencies in this report for control and evaluation purposes. No calculations are necessary. Simply discuss *why* this report would fall short of providing useful information for these purposes. Be sure to consider it from all relevant standpoints of control.

b) You discover the following additional information: each unit of product requires one pound of raw material at a standard cost of $0.50 per lb. During March, 17,500 lbs. were used at a cost of $0.56 per lb. What material variance would *you* hold the foreman responsible for? Why?

c) Calculate the Overhead Spending, Overhead Efficiency, and Overhead Volume variances. Indicate for each one whether you would use it in judging the performance of the foreman, and why.

20–9. The Kwala Corporation manufactures one line of product. During the month of October the plant operates 10,000 hours and produces 5,100 units of product. Actual manufacturing burden costs for the month total $9,630, broken down as follows:

Indirect labor..................	$2,600
Fringe benefit costs.............	310
Supplies......................	540
Repairs......................	480
Power.......................	760
Supervision...................	1,900
Depreciation..................	1,450
Insurance and taxes.............	630
Allocated services	960

A normal monthly budget of manufacturing burden appears below. The standard overhead rate of $0.87 per direct labor hour is based on this budget. The standard labor time per unit is two hours.

Budgeted Burden Costs
(12,000 direct labor hours)

Variable costs:		
Indirect labor......................	$3,000	
Fringe benefit costs................	660	
Supplies...........................	600	
Repairs and maintenance............	480	
Power..............................	900	$5,640 ($0.47/hr.)
Fixed costs:		
Supervision........................	$1,800	
Depreciation.......................	1,500	
Insurance and taxes................	600	
Allocated services.................	900	4,800 ($0.40/hr.)
		$10,440 ($0.87/hr.)

a) Compute the total burden variance.

b) Analyze the total variance into a spending variance, an efficiency variance, and a volume variance.

c) Analyze the spending variance in detail, by each overhead cost element, by preparing a detailed flexible budget.

20–10. The Mantis Manufacturing Company manufactures a single product that passes through two departments: extruding and finishing-packing.* The product is shipped at the end of the day in which it is packed. The production in the extruding and finishing-packing departments does not increase the number of units started. The cost and production data for the month of January are as follows:

---

* Problem adapted from AICPA May 1964 examination.

Cost Data	Extruding Department	Finishing-Packing Department
Work in process, January 1:		
Cost from preceding department.................	....	$60,200
Material....................................	$ 5,900	....
Labor......................................	1,900	1,500
Overhead...................................	1,400	2,000
Costs added during January:		
Material....................................	20,100	4,400
Labor......................................	10,700	7,720
Overhead...................................	8,680	11,830
Percentage of completion of work in process:		
January 1:		
Material.................................	70%	0%
Labor...................................	50	30
Overhead................................	50	30
January 31:		
Material.................................	50	0
Labor...................................	40	35
Overhead................................	40	35
January production statistics:		
Units in process, January 1....................	10,000	29,000
Units in process, January 31...................	8,000	6,000
Units started or received from preceding		
department..............................	20,000	22,000
Units completed and transferred or shipped........	22,000	44,000

In the extruding department, materials are added at various phases of the process. All lost units occur at the end of the process when the inspection operation takes place.

In the finishing-packing department, the materials added consist only of packing supplies. These materials are added at the midpoint of the process when the packing operation begins. Cost studies have disclosed that one half of the labor and overhead costs apply to the finishing operation and one half to the packing operation. All lost units occur at the end of the finishing operation, when the product is inspected. All of the work in process in this department at January 1 and 31 was in the finishing operation phase of the manufacturing process. The company uses the average costing method in its accounting system.

a) Compute the units lost, if any, for each department during January.

b) Compute the output divisor (equivalent production) for the calculation of unit costs for each department for January.

c) Prepare a cost of production report for both departments for January. The report should disclose the departmental total cost and cost per unit (for material, labor, and overhead) of the units (1) transferred to the finishing-packing department and (2) shipped. Assume that January production and costs were normal. (Submit all supporting computations in good form.)

20–11.   The following is the standard cost per unit card for a Squeezit:

Material: 2 pounds @ $1.................	$2.00
Labor: 2 hours @ $2.25..................	4.50
Overhead: 2 hours @ $1.25...............	2.50
	$9.00

The firm debits Work in Process at actual costs except for overhead, which is applied at actual hours times the predetermined overhead rate. Work in Process is credited at standard costs for transfers-out. The following transactions take place in April:

1.   Twelve thousand pounds of raw material are purchased on account at $1.08 per pound.
2.   Eleven thousand pounds of raw material are used during the month.
3.   Direct laborers work 12,500 hours in April, earning an average wage of $2.30 per hour.
4.   Actual overhead costs are $20,200 (credit Miscellaneous Accounts).
5.   Overhead is applied using the predetermined overhead rate of $1.25 per direct labor hour.
6.   During April, 5,400 units are completed and transferred to finished goods. There is no beginning inventory of work in process. Ending inventory consists of 800 units in process, 50 percent complete as to material and 75 percent complete as to labor and overhead.
7.   Five thousand units are sold to customers on account for $63,000.
8.   Variances from standard cost are transferred from the Factory Overhead and from the Work in Process accounts to Total Material Variance, Total Labor Variance, and Total Overhead Variance accounts.

   a)   Prepare journal entries to record these transactions.
   b)   Subdivide the Total Material Variance and the Total Labor Variance accounts into a price and quantity variance.
   c)   Assume the overhead rate of $1.25 per hour is derived from variable costs of $0.50 per hour and a fixed cost rate of $0.75 per hour (budgeted fixed cost of $11,250 divided by budgeted activity of 15,000 direct labor hours). Compute the overhead spending, efficiency, and volume variances.

20–12.   The Wormywood Furniture Company, in its table department, applies overhead to product through the use of a predetermined overhead rate established by reference to the overhead budget shown below:

Budgeted Overhead Costs
(1,200 tables—24,000 DLH)

Fixed costs..................................	$36,000
Variable costs................................	48,000
	$84,000
Overhead cost per hour........................	$3.50
Overhead cost per table (20 direct-labor hours @	
$3.50)....................................	$70.00

During the period, 21,000 hours of direct labor work were performed, and 900 tables were produced. Actual overhead costs were $79,000. Norman Nodoz, the cost clerk, prepared the following report about overhead cost variations for management:

Actual overhead..............................			$79,000
Standard overhead (900 tables @ $70)............			63,000
Total overhead variance.......................			$16,000
Budget (spending) variance:			
Budgeted overhead costs..........	$84,000		
Actual overhead costs............	79,000	($ 5,000)	
Volume variance:			
Budgeted output............	1200 tables		
Actual output..............	− 900 tables		
	300		
	×$ 70	21,000	
Total overhead variance........................		$16,000	

a) Compute the budget (spending), efficiency, and volume variances in a manner consistent with the presentation in the text.
b) Explain in terms of the *managerial meaning* of each of these variances *why* Nodoz's analysis is incorrect.
c) Explain *how* you would analyze the *budget* variance you calculated in part (*a*) in order to take corrective action. What additional information would you want?
d) Some accountants combine the spending variance and the efficiency variance you calculated in part (*a*) into a single "controllable variance." Why is the word "controllable" used to describe this variance? What limitation do you see in this approach?

20–13. The following is the standard cost per unit for product *Q*:

Materials: 3 pounds @ $0.50.....................	$ 1.50
Labor. 2 hours @ $3............................	6.00
Variable overhead: 2 hours @ $0.75..............	1.50
Fixed overhead: 2 hours @ $1....................	2.00
Total standard cost............................	$11.00

Data for January:

1. Budgeted activity: 40,000 hours.
2. Purchases of raw materials: 60,000 pounds @ $0.60, $36,000.
3. Raw materials used: 58,000 pounds.
4. Actual labor incurred: 39,100 hours @ $3, $117,300.
5. Actual overhead:

Fixed.................... $41,300
Variable................. 30,000
$71,300

6. Units completed: 19,000 (there was neither a beginning nor an ending work in process inventory).

a) Compute the materials price variance.
b) Compute the materials quantity variance.
c) Compute the labor rate variance.
d) Compute the labor quantity (time, efficiency) variance.
e) Compute the overhead spending (budget) variance.
f) Compute the overhead efficiency variance.
g) Compute the overhead volume (capacity) variance.
h) Does the labor efficiency (quantity) variance account fully to a firm for the cost of labor inefficiency? Explain.

20-14. The Modern Antique Lamp Company manufactures table lamps of standard size and shape. The labor operations are identical for all lamps, and a single type of shade is used. Modern Antique Lamp has three production departments—A, B, and C—which manufacture lamp bases, make lamp shades, and assemble the two parts, respectively. Below are the data relating to production orders for the month of June:

| | Production Order | | | |
	No. 97* 200 Units	No. 98* 700 Units	No. 99† 400 Units	Total
Department A—bases:				
Material....................	$450	$1,500	$1,400	$3,350
Labor.......................	$225	$ 760	$ 320	$1,305
Overhead ($1/hr.)............	225 hr.	720 hr.	310 hr.	1,255 hr.
Department B—shades:				
Material....................	$175	$ 600	$ 340	$1,115
Labor.......................	$250	$ 800	$ 250	$1,300
Overhead ($0.40/hr.).........	220 hr.	720 hr.	220 hr.	1,160 hr.
Department C—assembly:				
Labor.......................	$ 35	$ 120	. . .	$ 155
Overhead ($0.40/hr.).........	60 hr.	190 hr.	. . .	250 hr.

* Completed and sold at standard selling prices.
† All material drawn; half completed as to labor and overhead.

Actual overhead incurred, by departments, is:

$$
\begin{array}{lr}
A & \$1,600 \\
B & 500 \\
C & 125 \\
\hline
& \$2,225 \\
\end{array}
$$

Selling and general expense is $1,000.

a) Assume that the company uses a job-order cost system, and give the following information: (1) unit product cost of completed production; (2) closing work in process amount; (3) Departmental Overhead and Work in Process T accounts, showing entries made in them (charge overhead into Work in Process at the predetermined rates)—use three overhead accounts (A, B, and C) and one Work in Process account; (4) income statement (selling price, $9 each)—treat overhead variance as a charge against income.

b) Assume that the company uses a process cost system, and give the same information as in part (a). Use three work in process accounts—one for each department. Units completed in departments A and B are transferred to department C for assembling.

20–15. The Snafu Corporation manufactures a single product in five production departments. Technology for the manufacture of this product, as well as requisite labor skills, change rapidly. The company has generally kept abreast of these changes in order to remain competitive.

Mr. I Neverchange, the controller of the company, consistently has resisted all attempts to change or modify a system he has developed with respect to unit direct labor cost for the product. In 1968 the controller and the company engineer made a detailed study of the manufacture of this product and determined that the standard unit direct labor cost for it was $50. The concept followed in setting this standard was "theoretically ideal under perfect production conditions."

At the end of each year the controller calculates the unit direct labor cost for the year's production and expresses this as a percentage of the 1968 standard of $50. This gives him a trend in unit labor costs, from which he then makes control investigations and decisions. The report of these trends, as prepared at the end of 1972 is as follows:

Year	Direct Labor Cost	Units Produced	Unit Labor Cost	Percent of 1968 Standard
Standard..............	....	......	$50	100%
1968..................	$5,300,000	100,000	53	106
1969..................	6,840,000	120,000	57	114
1970..................	7,245,000	115,000	63	126
1971..................	7,375,000	125,000	59	118
1972..................	8,060,000	130,000	62	124

On the basis of your understanding of the control aspects of standard costing, evaluate from all relevant standpoints this system of the controller. Be as specific as possible.

20–16. Kaerwer Corporation operates a machine shop and employs an estimated cost system.* In March 1968 Kaerwer was low bidder on a contract to deliver 600 kartz by May 15 at a contract price of $200 each. Kaerwer's estimate of the costs to manufacture each kartz was:

40 pounds of materials at $1.50 per pound...........	$ 60
20 hours of direct labor at $2 per hour...............	40
Manufacturing overhead (40% variable).............	30
Total cost..	$130

Inventories on hand at April 1 included 30 completed kartz which had not been transferred to finished goods inventory, 70 kartz 60 percent processed, and 2,000 pounds of materials at a cost of $3,000. Production during March was at estimated costs. During April 500 kartz were started in production, 450 kartz were completed, and 480 kartz were transferred to finished goods. The work-in-process inventory at April 30 was 10 percent processed. All material was added when a kartz was started in production. The materials inventory is priced under the Fifo method at actual cost.

Accounts employed by Kaerwer included Material-in-Process, Labor-in-Process, Overhead-in-Process, Work-in-Process Inventory, Finished Goods Inventory, and Materials Inventory. The first three accounts are debited for actual costs incurred. Amounts are transferred from these accounts to Work in Process Inventory at estimated costs. Perpetual inventory systems are maintained for materials and finished goods inventories.

The following information is available for the month of April:

1. Materials purchased:

Pounds	Amount
8,000.....................	$12,000
8,000.....................	12,800
4,000.....................	5,600

---

* Adapted from AICPA May 1968 examination.

2. Materials requisitioned and put into production totaled 21,000 pounds.
3. The direct labor payroll amounted to $18,648 for 8,880 hours.
4. Actual manufacturing overhead incurred, including indirect labor, totaled $13,140 and was charged to the Overhead-in-Process account.

   a) Prepare in good form:
      1. A quantity of production report which accounts for both actual units in production and equivalent unit production for materials and for labor and overhead for April.
      2. A schedule presenting the computation of the balances (before closing) of the following accounts: Materials Inventory, Materials-in-Process, Labor-in-Process, Overhead-in-Process, Work-in-Process Inventory, and Finished Goods Inventory.
   b) Kaerwer Corporation would like to install a standard cost system and requests that you prepare a schedule presenting a computation of an analysis of the material, labor, and overhead variances they could expect from such a system for production during April. Assume that the standard cost of a kartz would have been the same as the estimated cost of a kartz. Overhead variances should be divided into spending, efficiency, and volume components, assuming a standard normal capacity of 400 kartz per month.

INDEX

INDEX

This book has been set in 10 and 9 point Janson, leaded 2 points. Section numbers and titles are in 12 point Engravers Roman. Chapter numbers are in 10 point Engravers Roman and chapter titles are in 14 point B Engravers Bold. The size of the type page is 27 by 45½ picas.